LANDMARK CASES IN THE LAW OF RESTITUTION

It is now well established that the law of unjust enrichment forms an important and distinctive part of the English law of obligations. Restitutionary awards for unjust enrichment and for wrongdoing are clearly recognised for what they are. But these are recent developments. Before the last decade of the twentieth century the very existence of a separate law of unjust enrichment was controversial, its scope and content matters of dispute. In this collection of essays, a group of leading scholars looks back and reappraises some of the landmark cases in the law of restitution. They range from the early seventeenth century to the mid-twentieth century, and shed new light on some classic decisions. Some argue that the importance of their case has been overstated; others, that it has been overlooked, or misconceived. All persuasively invite the reader to think again about some well-known authorities. The book is an essential resource for anyone, scholar, student or practitioner, with an interest in this fascinating area of the law.

Landmark Cases in the Law of Restitution

Edited by

CHARLES MITCHELL
School of Law, King's College London

and

PAUL MITCHELL
School of Law, King's College London

·HART·
PUBLISHING

OXFORD AND PORTLAND, OREGON
2006

Published in North America (US and Canada) by
Hart Publishing
c/o International Specialized Book Services
920 NE 58th Avenue, Suite 300
Portland, OR 97213-3786
USA
Tel: +1 503 287 3093 or toll-free: (1) 800 944 6190
Fax: +1 503 280 8832
E-mail: orders@isbs.com
Web Site: www.isbs.com

Hart Publishing, Salter's Boatyard, Folly Bridge, Abingdon Rd, Oxford, OX1 4LB
Telephone: +44 (0)1865 245533 Fax: +44 (0) 1865 794882
email: mail@hartpub.co.uk
WEBSITE: http//:www.hartpub.co.uk

British Library Cataloguing in Publication Data
Data Available

ISBN-13: 978-1-84113-588-5 (hardback)
ISBN-10: 1-84113-588-7 (hardback)

Typeset by Compuscript, Shannon
Printed and bound in Great Britain by
TJ International, Padstow, Cornwall

To the Memory of Peter Birks

Preface and Acknowledgements

In April 2005 we held a symposium on Landmark Cases in the Law of Restitution at the School of Law, King's College London. Our broad objective was to discuss cases of particular significance in the historical development of the law of restitution, but we left it to the contributors to decide whether to examine their cases within the framework of their contemporary settings, or to take a longer view and consider their impact on the thinking of subsequent generations. The papers provoked some fresh and lively discussion, for which we are grateful to all the seminar participants. We would also like to thank the King's College Law School for underwriting the event.

Nine of the chapters in this book were written as papers for the symposium, and they are published here for the first time. Three further chapters have previously appeared elsewhere, but we have included them here in the belief that they fit well with the other pieces in the collection. We are grateful to the authors for allowing us to reprint their work, and to their publishers for granting us permission to do so. Chapter 3, by Lionel Smith, originally appeared as 'The Stockbroker and the Solicitor General: The Story Behind *Taylor v Plumer*' (1994) 15 *Journal of Legal History* 1, published by Taylor & Francis Ltd, http://www.tandf.co.uk; he has added a postscript at the end of the chapter. Chapter 7 is a lightly revised version of William Swadling's essay 'The Myth of *Phillips v Homfray*' which was first published in William Swadling and Gareth Jones (eds), *The Search for Principle: Essays in Honour of Lord Goff of Chieveley* (Oxford, Oxford University Press, 1999). Chapter 9, by Eoin O'Dell, first appeared as 'The Case that Fell to Earth. *Sinclair v Brougham*' in Eoin O'Dell (ed), *Leading Cases of the Twentieth Century* (2001), published by Thomson Round Hall, Dublin.

For permission to publish manuscript material in Chapter 4 we also thank the Harry Ransom Humanities Research Centre, University of Texas at Austin.

We have dedicated this collection of essays to the memory of Peter Birks. Peter's interest in the law of restitution scarcely needs to be rehearsed here: by his encouragement and example, he inspired a generation of scholars to turn their attention to this area of law, and his own writings on the subject are renowned for their originality, scholarship and analytical power. We hope that he would have enjoyed this book.

Charles Mitchell
Paul Mitchell

Contents

Notes on Contributors

Tim Akkouh is a barrister at New Square Chambers, 12 New Square, Lincoln's Inn.

James Edelman is a Fellow and Tutor in Law at Keble College, Oxford, and an Adjunct Professor of Law at the University of Western Australia.

David Ibbetson is Regius Professor of Civil Law at Cambridge University.

Michael Lobban is Professor of Legal History at Queen Mary, University of London.

Catharine MacMillan is a Lecturer in Law at Queen Mary, University of London.

Charles Mitchell is a Professor of Law at King's College London.

Charlotte Mitchell is a Lecturer in English Literature at University College London.

Paul Mitchell is a Senior Lecturer in Law at King's College London.

Eoin O'Dell is a Fellow of Trinity College, Dublin.

Charlotte Smith is a Lecturer in Law at Reading University.

Lionel Smith is James McGill Professor of Law at McGill University, Montreal.

William Swadling is a Fellow and Tutor in Law at Brasenose College, Oxford.

Warren Swain is a Lecturer in Law at the University of Durham.

Sarah Worthington is a Professor of Law and Deputy Director of Research and External Relations at the London School of Economics, and also a barrister at 3/4 South Square, Gray's Inn.

Table of Cases

NEW ZEALAND

UNITED KINGDOM

UNITED STATES OF AMERICA

Table of Legislation

1

Lamplugh v Brathwaite (1615)

DAVID IBBETSON*

L AMPLUGH V BRATHWAITE, or *Lampleigh v Brathwait* as it has come to be known through Hobart's printed report of the case, does not at first sight belong in a collection of leading cases on the law of restitution. To begin with, it is hardly a case on restitution. At the core of the case was the quintessentially contractual question of whether the defendant should be liable on an express agreement to pay money to the plaintiff in exchange for the performance of some service. More precisely, the decision in the case, and the proposition for which it stood as authority in the leading books of the nineteenth century and for which it still stands in the books today,[1] was that a promise to pay was enforceable when it was grounded upon past consideration which had been performed at the request of the promisee. If we believe that there is a boundary between contract and restitution, even a blurred one, *Lamplugh v Brathwaite* looks to fall on the contract side of the line. Moreover, it is not clear that it should count as a leading case at all, since the proposition for which the case stands as authority had been more or less clear law for at least forty years. On the other hand, it came to have a place in *Smith's Leading Cases*[2] (even though we might guess that one important reason for its appearance there is nothing to do with the actual decision in the case at all, but rather Hobart CJ's usefully citable remarks on the rules for the pleading of consideration in the action of assumpsit[3]), and there can be no better qualification for the title

---

* I am grateful to Dr Christopher Tilmouth for assistance in tracing material about Richard Brathwaite.

[1] J Chitty, *A Practical Treatise on the Law of Contracts not under Seal* (London, S Sweet, 1826) 15 (2nd edn: London, S Sweet, 1834, 53); CG Addison, *A Treatise on the Law of Contracts and Rights and Liabilities ex Contractu* (London, W Benning, 1847) 30; J Beatson, *Anson's Law of Contract* (28th edn, Oxford, OUP, 2002) 94; GH Treitel, *The Law of Contract* (11th edn, London, Sweet & Maxwell, 2003) 78. It is still relied on in court: eg *Pau On v Lau Yiu Long* [1980] AC 614.

[2] JW Smith, *A Selection of Leading Cases on Various Branches of the Law: with notes* (London, A Maxwell, 1837) 67.

[3] Hob 105, 106.

Leading Case in the Common Law than its recognition as such by John William Smith. From this base the 'so-called rule in *Lampleigh v Braithwaite*'[4] has maintained its canonical status. The only change since the seventeenth century has been the introduction of a requirement that the consideration must have been performed with the intention that it should be paid for: the performance of some service as an act of generosity, albeit at the request of another person, cannot constitute consideration for a later promise to pay.[5] Nonetheless, the story behind the case is a good one, well worth the telling; and, as frequently happens, when the historian scratches the surface things turn out to be not quite as simple as they appeared at first sight.

Appearances first. The case is known to us through three printed reports and three independent manuscripts.[6] All are in agreement as to the salient facts, arguments, and result. The details are laid out in the pleadings. In July 1611 Thomas Brathwaite[7] had killed one Patrick Manning.[8] In September of that year he requested Anthony Lamplugh to labour and use his endeavours to obtain a pardon for him. Pursuant to that request Lamplugh had laboured and used his endeavours to get the pardon, first by riding to Royston[9] and back to London to find the King, and then to Newmarket and back again. Afterwards, in September 1612, in consideration of this Brathwaite promised Lamplugh that he would pay him £100. Lamplugh asked for payment in November 1613 but nothing was forthcoming, and in Michaelmas term 1615 he brought an action of assumpsit in the Court of Common Pleas. The defendant pleaded non assumpsit; the case came up for trial before Hobart CJ, and the jury found a verdict for Lamplugh.

In arrest of judgment Serjeant Thomas Harris put forward two arguments. First was that the consideration was past, ie that the promise to pay the £100 had been made after the journeys to Royston and Newmarket. That past consideration was insufficient to ground an action of assumpsit was not questioned, but on the other side Serjeant Charles Chibborne argued that where the past service had been performed at the request of the defendant the rule did not apply. The antecedent request was sufficient to link the promise and consideration reciprocally together. This had been held

---

[4] HG Beale (gen ed), *Chitty on Contracts* (29th edn, London, Sweet & Maxwell, 2004) para 29-071 n 386 (G Virgo).

[5] *Re Casey's Patents* [1892] 1 Ch 104, 115–16; *Pau On v Lau Yiu Long* [1980] AC 614.

[6] Hob 105; Moo 866 pl 1197; 1 Br & Golds 7; Harvard Law School MS 112b p 257; Cambridge University Library MS Gg 2.5 f 357v; Bodleian MS Rawl C 643 f 29. The record of the case is Public Record Office CP40/1963 m712 (printed in a slightly abbreviated English translation in AKR Kiralfy, *A Source Book of English Law* (London, Stevens, 1957) 201).

[7] Both parties' names are spelled in several different ways. For ease I adopt Brathwaite and Lamplugh.

[8] More accurately, the blow causing the death occurred in July, the death in August: below 11.

[9] The report in HLS 112b erroneously refers to Greenwich rather than Royston.

in *Hunt v Bate* in 1572, a case printed in Dyer's Reports, and in *Onely v Earl of Kent* in 1577, also printed in Dyer. If those were not enough, the point had been approved in two substantial cases at that time reported only in manuscript, *Sidenham v Worlington* in 1585 and *Dogget v Dowell* in 1602.[10] As a form of pleading it was very common, and had counsel chosen to quarry more deeply into manuscript reports they would have found a good number of other cases to the same effect as *Hunt v Bate*. It is true that some doubts had been raised in the conservative Court of Common Pleas around 1600, and so Harris's objection was not wholly without basis. But there was no life left in the point by this time, and all the judges of the court agreed that the objection was ill-founded. So much for the proposition for which *Lamplugh v Brathwaite* has come to stand as a leading authority.

Harris's second point was less flimsy. All that was alleged by Lamplugh was that he had ridden to Royston and to Newmarket, without saying that when he was there he had presented a petition to the King or done anything else to try to get a pardon for Brathwaite, still less that he had succeeded. The point troubled Warburton J. If the request had been specifically to obtain the pardon, then the promise to pay the money in consideration of the endeavours that had been made to obtain it would not have been sufficient. The consideration that had been performed would not, strictly speaking, have been that which had been requested, and Lamplugh's action would have fallen foul of the past consideration rule. Admitting that, though, according to the pleadings all that had been requested was that Lamplugh should use his endeavours, and this was exactly what he was said to have done, the jury by their verdict had found that request and promise had been made in this form, and in an argument in arrest of judgment it was impossible to go behind this jury verdict. More technically, Warburton J argued that, as a point of pleading, it was necessary to show precisely what endeavours had been made and not merely to allege generally that he had made endeavours. This would have been the case if the consideration had been purely executory: if, for example, there had been a promise to pay £100 in consideration that the plaintiff *would* use his endeavours; here the performance of the consideration would have been a condition for the liability to arise and as such it would have to have been alleged with precision. But, as was argued by Nicholls J and the other judges of the court, where the promise had been made subsequently to the performance of the consideration the rule did not apply. The fact that the defendant had promised to

---

[10] *Hunt v Bate* (1572) Dyer 272; *Onely v Earl of Kent* (1577) Dyer 355; *Sidenham v Worlington* (1585) 2 Leon 224, Godb 32, Cro El 42; *Dogget v Dowell* (1602) Owen 144, Moo 643 pl 886, Cro El 885. See DJ Ibbetson, 'Consideration and the Theory of Contract' in J Barton (ed), *Towards a General Law of Contract* (Berlin, Duncker & Humblot, 1990) 67, 88–94.

pay—and the jury had found that he had done so—was sufficient to prove that the consideration that had been performed had conformed to the request. The defendant's acceptance of it meant that there was no need for it to be pleaded in such a way that the court could be satisfied of it from examination of the written record.

Warburton J may not have been convinced, but he was alone in his doubts. In Trinity term 1616 judgment was entered for Lamplugh in the sum of £102 13s 4d assessed by the jury—£100 as damages (the amount it was said had been promised) and a standard 53s 4d as costs—together with an additional £10 6s 8d added as costs by the court.

So much for the case itself. There is nothing about it that should cause even the slightest raising of an eyebrow, let alone a place in history: a point of principle about the relationship between consideration and promise which had been reiterated time and time again in the previous few decades, and a technical point of pleading in the action of assumpsit which was well in line with earlier case law.

Behind this formal law lies a rather different story, one which is not always easy to square with the facts as found. No legal historian would be so much of a fool as to take the allegations made in Common Law pleadings as representing anything like the truth, but even by the decidedly low standards of the genre evidence from outside the case itself makes Lamplugh's claim as stated look like a farrago of lies. Alternatively, more carefully (and more accurately, given the nature of Common Law pleading at the time), we might say that Lamplugh was forced to frame his claim in apparently inappropriate language if he was to be able to bring it at all.

To understand the case in its context, we should first identify the *dramatis personae*. On the one hand were the Brathwaites, an old Westmoreland family by now widespread across northern England. The branch of the family in which we are interested revolved around Ambleside, a few miles from Kendal at Burneshead, and near Appleby at Warcop, where they had bought an estate sometime around 1590. Central to the events is Thomas Brathwaite, the defendant in our case; but we should begin with his father, also Thomas, a barrister of Gray's Inn, Recorder of Kendal in 1575, and seemingly a candidate for the position of Solicitor General in 1593.[11] This Thomas died in 1610, leaving a widow Dorothy (née Bindlose) and seven children, five daughters and two sons.[12] At the age of 27 Thomas, our

[11] J Foster, *Register of Admissions to Gray's Inn, 1521–1889* (London, Hansard, 1889) 28; BL MS Lansd 78 f 126 (letter of 1593 thanking Lord Burghley for help in pressing his claim).
[12] For biographical details, unless otherwise stated I rely on the following: J Nicolson and R Burn, *The History and Antiquities of the Counties of Westmorland and Cumberland* (London, W Strahan and T Cadell, 1777) vol 1, 126; the introduction by Joseph Haslewood to Richard Brathwaite, *Barnabae Itinerarium, or Barnabee's Journal* (London, Reeves & Turner, 1876); and MW Black, *Richard Brathwait: An Account of His Life and Works* (Philadelphia, University of Pennsylvania Press, 1928).

defendant, was the elder son.[13] Richard, the younger, had matriculated at Oriel College Oxford in 1604 aged 16, subsequently moving on to Gray's Inn, so he would have been in his early twenties on his father's death.[14] He was to gain some fame as a poet, writing in both English and Latin, earning him an entry in the *Dictionary of National Biography*.[15] Less merited is the attribution to him of one of the more surprising burlesque works of civil law published in the period: a small book on the law of social drinking, full of learned references to the Roman texts, published under the pseudonym Multibibus Blasius, which Brathwaite translated into English and published alongside his *The Smoking Age: or the Life and Death of Tobacco* in 1617.[16]

Like the Brathwaites, the Lamplughs were an established northern family.[17] The village of Lamplugh lies a few miles inland from Whitehaven; and Lamplugh Hall, the principal seat of the family, was built there in 1595, though it no longer stands in anything like its sixteenth-century form.[18] The family was well-connected at court, though the only member to attain public eminence in the seventeenth century was one Thomas, who became Archbishop of York in 1688.[19] The branch of the family with which we are concerned was settled at Dovenby, between Workington and Cockermouth.[20] Francis Lamplugh, High Sheriff of Cumberland in 1580, had died in 1602.

---

[13] 27 is the age given in the inquisition post mortem of Thomas senior (PRO C142/332/168), but he may have been a year older: one Thomas, son of Thomas, was baptised in Kendal on 15 July 1581: H Brierley (ed), *Registers of Kendal, Westmorland* (Kendal, Cumberland and Westmorland Antiquarian and Archaeological Society, 1921).

[14] A Wood, *Athenae Oxonienses* (3rd edn, London, Rivington, 1817) vol 3, 986; CL Shadwell, *Registrum Orielense* (London, 1893) vol 1, 109; *Gray's Inn Admissions Register* 121 (adm May 1609). According to Wood he had also spent a period at Cambridge, though he is not known to have matriculated.

[15] As well as the works of Haslewood and Black cited in n 12, see J Sanders, 'Brathwaite, Richard (1587/8–1673)', *Oxford Dictionary of National Biography* (Oxford, OUP, 2004), and F Waage, 'Richard Brathwait' in CD Lein (ed), *British Prose Writers of the Early Seventeenth Century* (*Dictionary of Literary Biography* vol 151) (Detroit, Gale Research, 1995) 46–54.

[16] [Multibibus Blasius,] *Disputatio inauguralis theoreticopractica jus potandi* (1616); *A solemne ioviall disputation, theoreticke and practicke; briefely shadowing the law of drinking together*, with *The Smoking Age: or the Life and Death of Tobacco* (1617). There is a recent edition of the German text of the *Jus Potandi* with an afterword by Michael Stolleis: *Jus Potandi oder Zechrecht* (Frankfurt, Alfred Metzner Verlag, 1982); the genre is briefly discussed by Stolleis (3)–(4). For a convincing rejection of the attribution to Brathwaite, see Black (n 12) 101–5. It is in any event unthinkable that he should have had the depth of knowledge of the texts of Roman law as is evidenced in this work.

[17] S Taylor, 'The Lamplugh Family of Cumberland' (1938) 38 *Transactions of the Cumberland and Westmoreland Antiquarian and Archaeological Society* (NS) 71 and (1939) 39 *Transactions of the Cumberland and Westmoreland Antiquarian and Archaeological Society* (NS) 71.

[18] B Marshall and A Lister (eds), *The Parish of Lamplugh* (Workington, Lamplugh Parish Council, 1993) 52–6.

[19] S Handley, 'Lamplugh, Thomas (bap 1615, d 1691)' *Oxford Dictionary of National Biography* (Oxford, OUP, 2004).

[20] Taylor 1939 (n 17) 71–82.

His eldest son, Thomas, married Agnes Brathwaite, eldest sister of Thomas and Richard. Anthony, the plaintiff in our case, was his sixth son; at the time the events began to unfold he was in the household of Robert Cecil, Earl of Salisbury, in London.

Of the Brathwaite brothers we know more about Richard's character than Thomas's. In his later writings he gives some impression of waywardness in his own childhood and youth. 'I held nothing so likely to make mee knowne in the world, or admired in it, as to be debauch't, and to purchase a Parasites praise by my riot.'[21] He resolved to reform, but repeatedly failed. 'How strong were my promises; how weak my performance?'[22] He looks to have been estranged from his family for a while, a stranger in his father's house, wasting away such allowance as his father afforded him. His studies at Gray's Inn he described as 'disrelishing',[23] and his biographers suggest that he gained a better knowledge of the low drinking-dives of Jacobean London than of the niceties of the Common Law.[24] Unsurprisingly, perhaps, his father's will specified that his widow should give him a reasonable allowance so long as he was obedient to her, ruled and advised by her, and of good demeanour and behaviour.[25] Thomas too seems to have been something of a ne'er-do-well. If we can judge by the successive settlements of the family estates in the first decade of the seventeenth century he was probably even worse than Richard, for Thomas senior repeatedly went out of his way to give all the lands to his widow Dorothy for life and then provide that after her death they should go to Richard and his issue ahead of Thomas and his, despite the fact that Thomas was the elder son.[26] We should not attribute this to a misplaced favouritism for the younger son over the elder: in December 1609 Thomas was granted a pardon for stealing a plate from his own father.[27]

Things did not go well in the Brathwaite family after the death of Thomas the father in 1610. It may be that there was a quarrel over the distribution of the family's land, with possible legal proceedings,[28] though it may simply have been that the two brothers had incompatibly quarrelsome

[21] *A Spiritual Spicerie* (1638) 374.

[22] *Ibid*.

[23] *Ibid*, 429.

[24] Black (n 12) 21; Waage (n 15) 52: 'an impecunious and perhaps irresponsible urban lifestyle among academic and nonacademic wits ... and much experience with theaters, alehouses, and brothels.'

[25] Haslewood (n 12) 8. This condition had first occurred in a settlement of July 1606: C142/332/168.

[26] The settlements are reproduced *in extenso* in Thomas senior's inquisition post mortem, C142/332/168. There is a more easily digestible summary of them in W Farrer, *Records of Kendale* (Kendal, Titus Wilson, 1929) vol 1, 272–3.

[27] *Calendar of State Papers, Domestic, 1611–1618* 69; PRO C66/1807/25.

[28] This is the admittedly tentative suggestion of Black (n 12) 27–8, based on some semi-autobiographical references in 'The Life of Polymorphus Simianus', found in *The Honest Ghost* (1658) and the Epistle Dedicatorie of *The Golden Fleece* to Robert Bindlose (29 below). Since almost all Thomas senior's land was vested in his widow Dorothy for her life (Thomas junior

temperaments; in any event, the dispute was ended by 1611. In the 'Epistle Dedicatorie' to *The Golden Fleece*, Richard's first published volume of poetry, addressed to his maternal uncle Robert Bindlose, he alludes to 'the troubled course of our estates, and the favourable regard you had of our attonement, which is now so happily confirmed'.[29] The work was registered with the Stationers' Company on 9 August 1611,[30] giving us a *terminus ante quem* for the breaking out of peace in the family.

The Golden Fleece, though, forms a curious volume. Printed with *The Golden Fleece* itself is a set of *Sonnets or Madrigals* addressed to his brother Thomas. Though the two works are continuously signed, from which we may fairly be confident that they were printed as a single composite book,[31] the *Sonnets or Madrigals* has a separate title page and dedication, this time to Thomas; and while the printing of both pieces was formally the work of Christopher Purset the title page of *The Golden Fleece* shows that the task was farmed out to WS (presumably the printer William Stansby), whereas that of the *Sonnets or Madrigals* suggests that it was printed by Purset himself. And, unlike *The Golden Fleece*, the *Sonnets or Madrigals* was not registered with the Stationers' Company. It is of course possible that the work which had been registered with the Stationers was the composite volume, but such a hypothesis makes it difficult to account for the clear separateness of the two works. It is more likely that the *Sonnets or Madrigals* represents an addition brought in after the registration in August 1611, printed as a separate work perhaps in order to ensure that the effective copyright protection for *The Golden Fleece* flowing from the deposit of a copy of the manuscript with the Stationers would not be lost.

The point is curious, but not wholly academic. Like that to Bindlose in *The Golden Fleece*, the 'Epistle Dedicatorie' to the *Sonnets or Madrigals* addressed to Thomas alludes to the recent disagreements, or 'civil warres', between them. Now the faction between them was ended, they could sit down together and build on their new-found friendship:[32]

> We, ... having tried the rought chasticement of discord, and exiled as it were, the borders of peace and amitie, and now enioying the content of mindes union, may

had the profits of the manors of Emilton and Withburne, Richard had nothing other than the allowance of £50 for which he was dependent on his mother), if there was a dispute between the brothers it would inevitably have involved the mother too. The series of settlements was sufficiently complex that it is easy to believe that they would have given opportunity for litigation.

[29] *The Golden Fleece* (1611) sig A3v.

[30] E Arber (ed), *A Transcript of the Register of the Company of Stationers of London, 1554–1640* (London, privately printed, 1875–94) vol 3, 463.

[31] The signatures indicated the order in which the printed sheets were to be bound: W Savage, *A Dictionary of the Art of Printing* (London, Longman, 1841; republished London, Gregg Press, 1969) *sub verb* signature.

[32] *Sonnets and Madrigals* in *The Golden Fleece* (n 29) sig E4 ii.

say, we had never beene this happy, if we had not bene unhappie, for the fruition
of happinesse hath the best taste in his palate, who hath once tasted the bitter
relish of unhappinesse.

All this is thoroughly positive. The reconciliation between the two brothers
was, no doubt, a great comfort to them and a relief to their mother. But by
its end the 'Epistle Dedicatorie' has a rather more melancholic tone.
Richard wishes Thomas 'as much comfort as earth may afford in this life',
appending two stanzas 'To his disconsolate brother':[33]

> Let not mishap deprive you of that hope,
> Which yeelds some relish to your discontent,
> Ayme your affections at heavens glorious scope,
> Which showres downe comfort when all comfort's spent.
> Then rest secure, that power which you adore,
> Will make your ioyes more full then ere before.
>
> Let not the Sunne now shadowed with a cloud,
> Make you suspect the Sunne will never shine,
> That ill, which now seemes ill, may once prove good,
> Time betters that, which was depravde by time.
> Thus let my prayers, your teares concord in one,
> To reape heav'ns comforts, when earth's comforts gone.

We are not told here what it was that had so affected Thomas's life, but
clearly it was something other than a now-past family disagreement which
was overshadowing it. If we are right to suppose that the *Sonnets and
Madrigals* is a slightly later addendum to *The Golden Fleece*, the explanation is not hard to find. In September of 1611 Thomas had been arrested
for the death of Patrick Manning and was now languishing in Carlisle gaol.
    What happened next can be reconstructed with some confidence from
proceedings initiated in Chancery in 1613 by Dorothy and Richard
Brathwaite against Anthony Lamplugh. The suit itself will concern us later,
but the Brathwaites' petition and Lamplugh's answer contain a good deal
of useful background material.[34] Allegations in Chancery petitions and
answers carry, of course, no more guarantee of truth than do allegations
made in Common Law pleadings, though there was less necessity for them
to have recourse to fictions. However, there is sufficient agreement in the
stories told by the Brathwaites and Lamplugh that we need not be too suspicious of them.

---

[33] *Ibid*, sig E4 v.
[34] PRO C3/257/50. See too J Robertson, 'Civil War in the Brathwait Family' (1938) 38
Transactions of the Cumberland and Westmoreland Antiquarian and Archaeological Society
(NS) 138, 144ff.

On Thomas's being led off to gaol, it seems, there was a council of those members of the family who were still in the north. Richard probably took no part in this. The Chancery proceedings make no reference to him at this time, and there is every reason to believe that he was still in London. The initiative looks to have been taken by Thomas Lamplugh, husband of Agnes, the eldest daughter of the family. Via Alan Aiscough, husband of the youngest daughter, Anne, he sent a letter to his brother Anthony, who was at that time a retainer of Robert Cecil, Earl of Salisbury. The letter requested that Anthony should use his or his friends' and patrons' influence to obtain a pardon for Thomas from the King.[35] By this time, it was said, the King had already made a promise to the Earl of Montgomery, Cecil's son-in-law, that he should have Thomas's lands should they be forfeit as a result of his being convicted of Manning's murder, and so Lamplugh's first recourse was to him. According to his own story, Lamplugh had been told by Aiscough that they were authorised to offer up to £1,000 for the pardon; this is probably true, for Dorothy Brathwaite claimed that she had given a bond for £1,000 to Lamplugh conditional upon his procuring a pardon by the end of January 1612. He offered this £1,000 to the Earl, but the offer was rejected. The Earl had heard that it was likely that Thomas would be found guilty of murder rather than manslaughter, and the King would not grant pardons in such cases. Lamplugh might have given up at this point— he said he was concerned that Salisbury, his then master, would not be happy with his continuing to try to intervene in the matter—but he was urged to continue pressing. He turned his attentions away from the Earl of Montgomery to the King's favourite, Robert Carr, recently created Viscount Rochester; this was half-successful, Rochester persuading the King to agree to grant Thomas a pardon for manslaughter.[36]

It was not clear that this would be enough, though. According to Dorothy, she had been led by Lamplugh to believe that Thomas might have had some sort of defence:[37]

> the said Manninge was not maliciously killed but by a misfortunate stroke upon his arme onely whereof he dyed not by the space of a fortnight after but was in good health and by his owne badd governement and distemper and openinge of the wounde died by bleadinge longe after the stroke ...

On the other hand, she had also heard from Lamplugh that there were others who were keen that he should be found guilty of murder. Nor need we

[35] Detail taken from Lamplugh's answer; Brathwaite's petition says simply that he heard of the situation.

[36] No such pardon is enrolled on the patent rolls, though. It may be that the King's agreement, which we hear about only from Lamplugh's answer in the Chancery suit, was not in fact put into execution.

[37] C3/257/50 no 1. The facts as found by the coroner's jury (below 11) were fairly close to this, though without reference to Manning's failure to take care of himself.

suspect that this was mere bias on their part. Already in August 1611, some weeks before Thomas's arrest, the Earl of Cumberland had written to the Earl of Salisbury reporting that he had killed his servant 'in so foul a manner that it must be found wilful murder'.[38] The position was wholly unclear, and the decision was taken that Lamplugh should continue his efforts to try to obtain a pardon for murder. We should note in passing that here there might have been a leading case in the making. The effect of a victim's self-neglect on the criminal liability of the person responsible for his wound was not to be settled until the end of the twentieth century;[39] and there was nothing in criminal doctrine in the Common Law of the early seventeenth century which would cast light on this problem. But the reporting of criminal cases at this time was barely in its infancy, and there was no way that something happening at the Assizes in Carlisle would have found its way into the wider legal consciousness even if the point had come up for argument there.

Things were becoming very pressing. A special commission of gaol delivery had issued to the Earl of Cumberland,[40] and Thomas's trial might occur at any time. Lamplugh therefore redoubled his efforts to get a pardon for murder through Rochester's influence. A bill for a pardon was drawn up, and Rochester promised to put it before the King for approval; but, as Lamplugh puts it, because of the Lord Treasurer's 'lameness in the arm' the pardon could not be signed speedily enough to be ready for the trial.[41] Pressure was therefore put on the Earl of Cumberland to delay the gaol delivery, successfully, providing a little more time in which the pardon could be obtained.

By this time January 1612 had passed, and the bond of £1,000 given to Lamplugh by Dorothy Brathwaite had lapsed. Moreover, the price of the pardon had increased to £1,200. Rochester had let it be known that it was his wish that this should go to one David Ramsay, gentleman of the bedchamber to Henry, Prince of Wales, a Scottish courtier of notoriously poor judgement who was later to stand trial for treason and be described as a 'pest' by King Charles I.[42] Ramsay asked for some security for the payment of the £1,200, and Lamplugh entered into a bond with him to pay this amount shortly after the pardon should have been obtained. In order to protect himself, Lamplugh returned to Carlisle to get security for himself from the Brathwaites. This time the security was given not by Dorothy

---

[38] *CSPD, 1611–1618*, 69.

[39] *R v Blaue* [1975] 1 WLR 1411.

[40] Special commissions for gaol delivery in the northern counties were common since the northern assize circuit only reached beyond Lancaster and York in the summer: JS Cockburn, *A History of English Assizes, 1558–1714* (Cambridge, Cambridge University Press, 1972) 39.

[41] C3/257/50 no 2. See BL MS Add 34218 ff 125–7 for Cecil's last illness.

[42] S Wright, 'Ramsay, David (d 1642)', *Oxford Dictionary of National Biography* (Oxford, OUP, 2004).

herself, but by Dorothy and Richard jointly. On 3 July 1612 they gave to him three bonds, payable at different dates, conditioned upon Lamplugh's procuring a pardon and giving them notice of it. In addition—either at this time or shortly beforehand—Dorothy advanced to him £120, part of the promised £1,200, presumably to cover his expenses. Lamplugh returned to London, continuing to labour to procure the pardon. At last he was successful. On 20 February 1613 a pardon under the privy seal issued to Thomas Brathwaite.[43]

But all was not well. At the Summer Assizes at Carlisle in August 1612 Thomas Brathwaite had been tried before Barons Altham and Bromley for the death of Manning.[44] He had been indicted for murder—the coroner's jury had found that he had plunged his rapier into Manning's arm from which Manning had died two and a half weeks later—but in the event he was found guilty of manslaughter, presumably on the basis that the killing had taken place in the course of a fight and was therefore chance-medley.[45] He was admitted to his clergy, duly read the neck verse, and was released from gaol. The Brathwaites asked for their bonds back, but Lamplugh refused. It is not difficult to see why he should do so. He was himself bound to the tune of £1,200 to David Ramsey in the event of a pardon being procured, and were he to release the Brathwaites from their bonds he would find himself having to bear the loss himself. We do not know whether he did in fact have to pay Ramsey once the pardon was granted, though the likelihood is that he did not do so.[46] In any event, some time after February 1613 he initiated suit at Common Law to enforce the first of bonds the Brathwaites had given to him. The action was brought in the King's Bench, leading to the arrest of Dorothy Brathwaite on a writ of latitat.

At that point the Brathwaites began the counter-attack. In June 1613 they petitioned the Chancery for an injunction to prevent the suit on the bond at Common Law and for the repayment of the £120 that had earlier been advanced by Dorothy.[47] Although the procurement of the pardon satisfied the letter of the condition, they said, it was not a performance within its spirit since it had not been obtained in due time. A few days later Lamplugh put in his reply. Painting the Brathwaites in rather black colours, he portrayed them as trying to escape from their obligations notwithstanding the labours to which he had been put, riding (according to his own estimate) in excess of four thousand miles and neglecting his own business for a year or more.

---

[43] PRO C66/1948 no 5.

[44] PRO KB9/736 m188.

[45] For chance-medley see E Coke, *Third Institute* 55. Such cases were uncomfortably on the border between murder and manslaughter at this time: J Horder, *Provocation and Responsibility* (Oxford, Clarendon Press, 1992) 15–19.

[46] There is no statement to this effect in his answer in the Chancery suit, and it would surely have been material as a matter of equity had he done so.

[47] C3/257/50.

The Chancery suit was dealt with relatively speedily. A commission to take evidence issued to the Brathwaites, though since they dragged their feet in putting it into execution a duplicate was given to Lamplugh's counsel in November 1613.[48] By 1 June 1614 a settlement was in the offing. It was decreed that Lamplugh should give up the bonds if the Brathwaites agreed to pay him the sum of 500 marks (ie £333 6s 8d).[49] They were given until the first day of the next term to make their election whether or not to accept this. On 29 June the case came up again.[50] Lamplugh's counsel, George Shurley,[51] informed the court that no election had been made. Christopher Brooke, counsel for the Brathwaites, said that his clients would be willing to pay £250, but this was not accepted. As a result the suit was dismissed and Lamplugh left to continue his action at law. It is perhaps unfortunate that nothing in the event came of the Chancery suit. It raised two difficult issues, either one of which—if it had fallen for decision—might have elevated it to a leading case.

First was the restitutionary claim: the Brathwaites were asking for the return of the money advanced to Lamplugh towards his expenses in obtaining the pardon. On the assumption that the purpose was to obtain the pardon before trial and not after it (otherwise there could be no claim since the condition would have been satisfied), the question would be whether the money could be recovered when the end for which it was paid had not eventuated but the recipient had spent the money in pursuit of that end. It seems to have been clear practice in Chancery that in the simple case, where money had been handed over for some purpose which had totally failed, an action would lie to recover the money back from the recipient.[52] *Brathwaite and Brathwaite v Lamplugh* would have constituted a significant variation on this theme; and the facts that Lamplugh had put in considerable labour and that the money had been paid in recognition of this might well have been sufficient to have moved the court in the opposite direction. But of course we cannot know.

Second was the question whether the Chancery should give relief against a bond where a condition had been performed to the letter but not according to the intent of the parties. It is well known that Chancery might by this time give relief against the enforcement of penal bonds where the condition had been technically broken but performed in substance, though the practice under Lord Ellesmere at the beginning of the seventeenth century may

---

[48] C33/125 f 241v (24 November 1613).
[49] *Ibid*, f 825.
[50] *Ibid*, f 953.
[51] Or perhaps Sergeant John Shurley.
[52] DJ Ibbetson, 'Unjust Enrichment in England before 1600' in EJH Schrage (ed), *Unjust Enrichment: The Comparative Legal History of Unjust Enrichment* (Berlin, Duncker & Humblot, 1995) 121, 132, with the references at n 61.

have been tougher than under his predecessors and successors;[53] again, *Brathwaite and Brathwaite v Lamplugh* would have been a variation on this theme, for the issue was not whether there had been a technical breach of a defeasant condition but substantial performance, but rather whether relief should be given where a positive condition had been performed to the letter but not in accordance with its spirit.

Neither of these issues, in the event, fell to be decided. They were probably not even considered as the court strove to bring the parties to some sort of settlement. Such is the way of potentially leading cases.

The Chancery litigation did not bring an end to the litigation between Anthony Lamplugh and Dorothy and Richard Brathwaite. Quite the contrary: the dismissal of the bill for an injunction in June 1614 allowed the Common Law action on the bond to proceed. We cannot be sure exactly what happened to this—I have not succeeded in tracing the record of the King's Bench proceedings—but it is possible to make an educated guess. In his next published book of poems, *A Strappado for the Divell* (1615), Richard includes one addressed to his godfather, Sergeant Richard Hutton, described to have 'proceeded from the restraint of the Author'.[54] Brathwaite's biographer interprets this as indicating that he had been imprisoned for debt,[55] but the poem reads more as if he had gone to ground to avoid arrest:

> Not in a durance suite remaine I here,
> Yet in a suite like durance hemm'd with feare
> Retir'd I am: confinement makes me thrall
> Unto my selfe, which grieves me most of all.
> If I but see the shadow of a man,
> Or th'tinkling of a Braziers copper pan,
> I feare a Sergeant, shadow saies its he,
> And th'Brazier saies, such like his buttons be.

Afraid of falling into the hands of a sergeant, he throws himself into the hands of Sergeant Hutton. The cause of his distress is made abundantly clear:

> Pray Sir (at least) if'th Courtier needes will crave it,
> Let him pursue such, where' has hope to have it:

---

[53] G Spence, *The Equitable Jurisdiction of the Court of Chancery* (London, Stevens, 1846) vol 1, 628–32; DEC Yale, *Lord Nottingham's Chancery Cases*, ii (Selden Society, vol 79) 8–30; E Henderson, 'Relief from Bonds in the English Chancery: Mid-Sixteenth Century' (1974) 18 *American Journal of Legal History* 298.

[54] 'The Catch', in *A Strappado for the Divell*, 54–8.

[55] Black (n 12) 33–4. I am heavily indebted to Black for the elucidation of imprisonment references in Brathwaite's works.

> For me theres none: but this his wit God wot
> To sue his bond, where nothing to be got.

Two years later things seem to have still been dragging on. A dedication in *The Smoaking Age* (1617) to Alexander Rigby, probably one of several members of Gray's Inn of that name, begins by making a play on the theme of assumpsit and debt and ends with an overt reference to litigation:[56]

> For th'court where now my suit depending is
> Hath forced me write in forma pauperis.

By 1619 things had perhaps run their course. In 'Bound yet free; Speaking of the Benefit of Imprisonment', a poem included in his collection entitled *A New Spring*,[57] Brathwaite writes of the advantages that flow from being imprisoned:

> Thou whom we call lifes death, Captivity,
> Yet canst contemplate in the darkest Cell
> Of things above the reach of Vanitie
> Dost in my iudgement Liberty excell;
> In that thou teachest man to mortifie
> His indisposed passions; and canst well
> Direct him how to manage his estate,
> Confin'd to th'narrow prospect of thy Grate.

Brathwaite contrasts the imprisoned state, with its opportunity for contemplation and the re-ordering of life, with the freedom of the unfortunate men outside. Amongst these, with an autobiographical bitterness, is the self-seeking pursuer of wealth:

> For these make ancient houses ruinous,
> And Charitie from out the Realme expels,
> Reducing th'Orphans teare and Widdowes curse
> To th'damn'd Elixie of their well-cramm'd purse.

The repeated references to imprisonment in his works about this time, especially when coupled with references to actions on bonds and avaricious courtiers, strongly suggest that Richard Brathwaite was indeed imprisoned for debt. Some 25 years later, in a reflection on the death of Sergeant

---

[56] *The Smoaking Age* sig G3–G3v. See too sig G1v, where errata in the volume are attributed to the author's absence.

[57] 'Bound yet free; Speaking of the Benefit of Imprisonment', in *A New Spring* (1619) sig C1v. The engraving on the title page of the volume looks very much like a prison stockade, with drink being passed over the fence.

Richard Hutton, we find a strong hint that it was Hutton who was responsible for his release. Perhaps his appeal of 1615 had been successful. Contemplating St Dunstan's in the West, where Hutton was buried, he casts his mental eye around to the nearby Fleet prison:

> For near this Holy ground of thine possest,
> A grimmer hagge than Death did me arrest
> Till thy just-judging Eye did rightly scan
> My cause, and freed me fromth' Leviathan:
> For ne're was man surprised with more deceite,
> Nor with more Grace retrieved from a Grate.[58]

Whether Lamplugh ever got his money we cannot tell for certain, though if it required Hutton's influence rather than actual payment to effect the release we can readily suppose that he did not, or at least that he did not get all that he had been claiming.

In the light of all of this we should return to the case of *Lamplugh v Brathwaite,* with which we started. The case as pleaded involved a request made by Thomas Brathwaite to Anthony Lamplugh on 10 September 1611 in the parish of St Mary le Bow in Cheapside, a year of riding around by Lamplugh, and a promise made by Brathwaite on 4 September 1612 to pay Lamplugh £100 in consideration of all of this. The jury, by their verdict, found that the request and promise had indeed been made as pleaded, an assumption central to the arguments in the case.[59] Significantly, though, there appears to have been no genuine trial of the issue. When the case arose for trial at the Guildhall before Hobart CJ, Brathwaite failed to enter an appearance and the verdict went against him by default.[60] We cannot therefore place any reliance on the apparent findings of the jury as evidence of the truth of the matter, and can look at it afresh.

We should begin with the request, supposedly made in Cheapside on 10 September 1611. This is possible, but highly improbable. In September 1611 Thomas Brathwaite was arrested in the north and imprisoned in the gaol at Carlisle. He might, of course, have rushed to London first to see Lamplugh, but it does seem unlikely. We do know, though, that at exactly this time Lamplugh had been asked by his brother, through Alan Aiscough, to intervene on behalf of Dorothy Brathwaite.[61] It does not demand a great deal of imagination to see one and the same event here, described in different ways to reflect the exigencies of different pieces of litigation. The promise, said to have been made on 4 September 1612, is less improbable, since by September 1612 Thomas had been found guilty of manslaughter and

[58] *Astraea's Teares* (1641) sig D7v.
[59] See for example Hob 105, 106.
[60] CP40/1963 m712, postea (omitted from Kiralfy's text).
[61] Above 9.

released from gaol; it is not impossible, therefore, that he had gone up to London and there seen Lamplugh. Even if this were so, whether there had been any deliberate, genuine promise to pay £100 or simply an expression of gratitude cannot be known. It is, however, significant that it was not until November 1613 that Lamplugh is said to have made a request that Thomas pay him according to the alleged promise. It was at precisely this time that Dorothy and Richard were dragging their feet in the Chancery suit,[62] and Lamplugh could not have failed to recognise the risk that he would have to restore the £120 he had already received as well as deliver up the bonds which represented his security against liability at the suit of David Ramsey. In any event, the money he had received from the Brathwaites had been expressed to be a part of the £1,200, rather than additional to it; even if he were to be successful in the Chancery action, to retain the £120, and to be able to enforce the bonds for £1,080 against the Brathwaites, he would still risk being out of pocket for the expenses he had incurred in seeking the pardon during 1611 and 1612. It is at least a possibility that the action against Thomas represented a claim for his expenses.

Nineteenth-century Common lawyers were familiar with claims in assumpsit where both request and promise were fictitious, or more accurately where neither had to be proved.[63] To our modern eyes—more concerned with substantive causes of action than the technicalities of forms of action, pleading and proof—these claims are generally re-categorised as restitutionary or as based on unjust enrichment rather than contract, and over the last half-century we have been taught that it is misguided to think of them as contractual at all. Seventeenth-century lawyers were certainly familiar with the action of assumpsit based on an implied promise—this is what *Slade's Case* at the start of the century had been all about—but that was only if there had been a genuine underlying contract. *Slade's Case* concerned the use of the action of assumpsit in place of the action of debt; it was not about allowing claims to be brought in assumpsit where there was no underlying cause of action of all.[64] More sophisticated lawyers recognised that proof of a promise was not quite as black and white as it seemed, and that in an action by a tradesman against a customer who had allegedly promised to pay what the work was worth, the classical *quantum meruit* count, it would require very little evidence for the jury to infer that such a promise had in fact been made.[65] After all, it could hardly be supposed that the tradesman had done the work for nothing. But even in that case there would have been a request by the customer that the tradesman do the work,

---

[62] Above 12.

[63] See most clearly Addison, *Contracts*, 213.

[64] JH Baker, 'The Use of Assumpsit for Restitutionary Money Claims' in Schrage (n 52) 31, 33–5.

[65] See especially the remarks of Coke CJ in *Vaux v Newman* (*The Six Carpenters' Case*) (1610) 8 Co Rep 146, 147; Baker (n 64) 37–8.

and even the most hard-line modern proponent of the rigid distinction between contract and unjust enrichment would have no qualms about treating such a claim as straightforwardly contractual.

Lamplugh v Brathwaite, if we interpret its facts correctly, looks to be just the other side of the line. If there had indeed been no genuine request by Thomas, as we strongly suspect, then even if it was absolutely true that the promise had been made in fact a purely contractual assumpsit claim against him should have failed on the basis that the consideration was past. The claim, to modern eyes, would have to be characterised as a non-contractual claim, conventionally dependent on some idea of unjust enrichment. It would still have been a difficult case, for although Lamplugh had laboured long and hard in Thomas's interests he had in fact gained no benefit from it: by the time the pardon had been obtained it was of no value to him since he had already been convicted of manslaughter. While it is very hard to find what Professor Baker describes as a chink in the camouflage of fictions,[66] an analogy might be drawn with the law relating to infants' contracts: at Common Law the infant would be liable to pay for necessary goods or services, which would presumptively be to his or her benefit, or where the benefit of a contract had irreversibly been conferred.[67] Alternatively there might have been an analogy with the liability of religious houses on contracts made by monks, where the religious house would be liable only to the extent to which it had benefited.[68] But infants' and monks' contracts constituted very particular cases with their own well-established rules, and there is no evidence of any moves to generalise from them in the early seventeenth century. It was not, in fact, until well into the eighteenth century that there were any hints that lawyers might have been beginning to think of any general principle.

But lawyers of the seventeenth century did not think in this way; they had not yet developed the technique of implying both request and promise which are found in the nineteenth century. Even if Thomas had been present at the Guildhall and the verdict had not gone against him by default, and whatever the factual matrix, *Lamplugh v Brathwaite* could never have become a leading case on the law of restitution. So long as lawyers were concerned with pleading and proof rather than substantive legal categories, something which did not really occur until the second half of the eighteenth century, the very most it could have been is a leading case on the necessity of proving request or promise in the action of assumpsit.

It would be a pity to leave the litigation between the Lamplughs and the Brathwaites without any mention of the future fate of the principal participants. Dorothy Brathwaite, the mother, continued at Burneshead into the

---

[66] Baker (n 64) 34.
[67] Ibbetson (n 52) 142; cf Baker (n 64) 39–40.
[68] Ibbetson (n 52) 142–3.

1620s; in 1623 she assigned the wardship of her grandson to Thomas's widow, Elizabeth.[69] Richard Brathwaite lived for more than half a century, dying in 1673. He continued to write, though with an increasing concentration on rather dull, spiritually inspired works which bear little comparison with the racier pieces of his early manhood. Thomas, the ostensible villain of the piece, was knighted in June 1616, at almost exactly the same time as judgment was given against him in *Lamplugh v Brathwaite*.[70] We do not know why he was knighted, though James I needed little excuse. In the event it did him no good. He went mad in 1620, and died just after Christmas 1623.[71] Thomas Lamplugh, husband of Agnes Brathwaite, was knighted in 1615 on his appointment as High Sheriff of Cumberland.[72] He died childless in 1632, though his will was not discovered until 1634; his widow survived him for another thirty years, a redoubtable dowager who clung to control over the Lamplughs' seat at Dovenby Hall until her death in 1665. Meanwhile the hapless Anthony, who was to die in 1638, had taken out letters of administration on the presumed intestacy, ensuring that the last years of his life were spent undoing things that had been done before the will was found.

[69] Cumbria Record Office, Carlisle, D LONS/L1/1/6.
[70] WC Metcalfe, *A Book of Knights* (London, Mitchell & Hughes, 1885) 167.
[71] PRO C142/388/55 (inquisition of lunacy); C142/401/127 (inquisition post mortem).
[72] Taylor 1939 (n 17) 74; Metcalfe (n 70) 165.

2

Moses v Macferlan (1760)

WARREN SWAIN

A. INTRODUCTION

MOSES V MACFERLAN[1] was one of the authorities to feature in Sir William Evans's *A General View of the Decisions of Lord Mansfield in Civil Causes,* published in 1803.[2] In his last book, *Unjust Enrichment,* published in 2005, Peter Birks referred to *Moses v Macferlan* more than almost any other decision.[3] It crops up in the literature many times in the intervening two hundred years.[4] Lord Mansfield's judgment is used to support the argument of those writers and judges who insist that there is a legal category called 'unjust enrichment' and by those who favour a remedy rooted in equity. Given the dangers inherent in using

---

[1] (1760) 2 Burr 1005, 97 ER 676; 1 Wm Bla 219.
[2] (Liverpool, 1803) 2.200.
[3] (Oxford, OUP, 2005) 5, 13–15, 40–41, 118, 208, 233, 257–8, 270, 275, 289–90.
[4] W Holdsworth, *A History of English Law* (London, Methuen, 1926) vol 9, 97; CHS Fifoot, *Lord Mansfield* (Oxford, OUP, 1936) 141; RM Jackson, *The History of Quasi-Contract in English Law* (Cambridge, CUP, 1936) 117–19; P Winfield, *The Province of the Law of Tort* (Cambridge, CUP, 1931) 127; JP Dawson, *Unjust Enrichment A Comparative Analysis* (Boston, MA, Little, Brown and Co, 1951) 11–15; P Winfield, *The Law of Quasi-Contract* (London, Sweet & Maxwell, 1952) 9; JH Baker, *An Introduction to English Legal History* (4th edn, London, Butterworths, 2002) 375–6; JH Baker, 'The Use of Assumpsit for Restitutionary Money Claims 1600–1800' in EJH Schrage (ed), *Unjust Enrichment. The Comparative Legal History of the Law of Restitution* (Berlin, Duncker & Humblot, 1995) 31, reproduced in JH Baker, *The Common Law Tradition Lawyers, Books and the Law* (London, Hambledon, 2000) 287 and W Cornish *et al* (eds) *Restitution Past, Present and Future. Essays in Honour of Gareth Jones* (Oxford, Hart, 1998) 38; P Birks, 'English and Roman Learning in *Moses v Macferlan*' (1984) 37 *CLP* 1; P Birks and G McLeod, 'The Implied Contract Theory of Quasi-Contract: Civilian Opinion Current in the Century Before Blackstone' (1986) *OJLS* 46, 55–7; D Ibbetson, *An Historical Introduction to the Law of Obligations* (Oxford, OUP, 1999) 272; J Oldham, *The Mansfield Manuscripts and the Growth of English Law in the Eighteenth Century* (Chapel Hill, NC, University of North Carolina Press, 1992) vol 1, 226–227; J Oldham, *English Common Law in the Age of Mansfield* (Chapel Hill, NC, University of North Carolina Press, 2004) 87–93; S Waddams, *Dimensions of Private Law Categories and Concepts in Anglo-American Legal Reasoning* (Cambridge, CUP, 2003) 162.

a two hundred year old decision concerning a long abolished form of action in order to support a 21st century legal analysis,[5] it is hardly surprising that legal historians have played an unusually prominent role in revealing the existence and character of the modern remedy.[6]

B. THE ACTION FOR MONEY HAD AND RECEIVED AND THE NON-CONTRACTUAL ASSUMPSITS

Before the mid-nineteenth century, English Common law was built around the forms of action.[7] They are best understood as the procedural shell into which the plaintiff slotted his claim.[8] Money had and received belonged to a group of actions known collectively as indebitatus assumpsits—so called because the declaration set out the cause of the defendant's indebtedness.[9] These actions emerged in the period after *Slade's Case*.[10] From the mid-seventeenth century, a standard form, known as a common count, was usually adopted.[11] Money had and received was one of the common counts. The other family of assumpsit actions was known as special assumpsits. A declaration in special assumpsit set out the details of the actual contract.[12] The *quantum valebant* for goods sold and delivered[13] and the *quantum meruit* for work and labour were two varieties of special assumpsit.[14] They differed from the usual form of special assumpsit because rather than the price of the contract a reasonable sum was alleged.

---

[5] On these dangers see J Gordley, 'The Common Law in the Twentieth Century: Some Unfinished Business' (2000) 88 *California Law Review* 1815, 1870–1.

[6] On the importance of legal historians in this area see D Ibbetson, 'Unjust Enrichment in English Law' in EJH Schrage (ed), *Unjust Enrichment and the Law of Contract* (The Hague, Kluwer Law International, 2001) 33, 47.

[7] The forms of action were abolished in 1852. The Common Law Procedure Act implemented the *1st Report of Her Majesty's Commissioners for Inquiring into the Process, Practice, and System of Pleading in the Superior Courts of Common Law* (1851) [1389] Parliamentary Papers vol xxii, 8. The reforms were intended to ensure that the forms of action would henceforth exist in name only.

[8] Holdsworth (n 4) vol 9, 251–2; FW Maitland, *The Forms of Action at Common Law*, AH Chaytor and WJ Whittaker (eds) (Cambridge, CUP, 1948) 7–8; Baker 'The Use of Assumpsit' (n 4) 67–9.

[9] E Lawes, *A Practical Treatise on Pleading in Assumpsit* (London, W Reed, 1810) 430.

[10] (1602) 4 Co Rep 92, 76 ER 1074. On the background and implications of this important case: JH Baker, 'New Light on Slade's Case' [1971] *CLJ* 51 and 213, reproduced in JH Baker, *The Legal Profession and the Common Law* (London, Hambledon Press, 1986) 393; DJ Ibbetson, 'Assumpsit and Debt in the Early Sixteenth Century: The Origins of the Indebitatus Count' [1982] *CLJ* 142; DJ Ibbetson, 'Slade's Case in Context' (1984) 4 *OJLS* 295.

[11] Ibbetson (n 4) 148; Baker *Introduction* (n 4) 348; HK Lücke, 'The Origins of the Common Counts' (1965) 81 *LQR* 422 and 540, and (1966) 82 *LQR* 81.

[12] J Wentworth, *A Complete System of Pleading Comprehending the Most Approved Precedents and Forms of Practice* (London, 1797) vol 2.

[13] *Ibid* vol 3, 54–5.

[14] *Ibid* vol 3, 55.

Indebitatus and special assumpsit were appropriate remedies when the parties were in a contractual relationship. Equally, both forms of pleading could be adapted for non-contractual claims. From the 1730s there is some evidence that judges were willing to entertain non-contractual *quantum meruits*.[15] The indebitatus assumpsit for money laid out began to be used for non-contractual actions around the same time. In *Morrice v Redwyn*[16] Lord Raymond allowed a plaintiff, who had paid out on a security following an action by the creditor, to recover the sum as money laid out against the principle debtor.[17] Over the course of the next forty years money laid out continued to embrace non-contractual claims. Seventeenth century judges hinted that a father might be liable in money laid out for the cost of burying his child[18] and, in *Jenkins v Tucker*,[19] Lord Loughborough upheld an action for money laid out against a husband when a father paid for his daughter's burial. He also suggested that the action could be used when a plaintiff paid out in order to secure the return of property taken as distraint for the defendant's debt[20]—a view confirmed a decade later in *Exall v Partridge*.[21]

The allegation that money had been laid out at the defendant's request[22] in the count for money laid out was sometimes a fiction. Given that a contractually agreed sum was no bar to recovery in *quantum meruit*,[23] the reasonable sum in the declaration was not confined to a genuine contractual implication. Both counts retained a contractual façade. It was impossible to

---

[15] *Hayes v Warren* (1733) W Kelynge 117; 2 Stra 933, 93 ER 950; 2 Barn KB 55, 71, 140, 94 ER 353, 363, 407; LI MS Hill 39 f 92; HLS MS 4055 f 6; *Barton v Hodgkinson* (1739) LI MS Misc 133 f 33; LI MS Hill 25 f 1; LI MS Hill 29 f 225. These authorities are discussed by J Barton, 'Contract and Quantum Meruit: The Antecedents of *Cutter v Powell*' (1987) 8 *JLH* 48, 58–9. On the non-contractual use of *quantum meruit* see Baker 'The Use of Assumpsit' (n 4) 39–41.

[16] (1731) 2 Barn KB 26, 94 ER 333.

[17] The ruling was later confirmed in *Decker v Pope* (1757) LI MS Misc 129 (unfol). Between these two decisions there were some doubts about the correct rule to apply: *Woffington v Sparks* (1754) 2 Ves Sen 569, 570; 28 ER 363, 363–4.

[18] *Church v Church* unreported, 1656, cited in *Hunt v Wotton* (1679) T Raym 260, 83 ER 133 'where in assumpsit the plaintiff declared that whereas the plaintiff had at his own charges buried the defendant's child, the defendant promised to pay him his charges, though no request was laid', and by Serjeant Strange in *Hayes v Warren* (1733) W Kelynge 117, 119. *Church v Church* was doubted by Lee CJ in *Barton v Hodgkinson* (1739) LI MS Misc 133 f 33, but was still cited as valid authority as late as the 1794 edition of *Dyer's Reports* edited by Vaillant at 272 (b). No authority on this particular point was cited either in argument or in the judgments in *Jenkins v Tucker*.

[19] (1788) 1 H Bla 90, 126 ER 55.

[20] *Ibid*, 93 (126 ER 57).

[21] (1799) 8 TR 308, 101 ER 1405.

[22] J Chitty, *A Treatise on the Parties to Actions, the Forms of Action and on Pleading* (3rd edn, London, Butterworths, 1817) 2.36; Lawes (n 9) 435.

[23] An early example is the unreported *Mr Keck's Case* (1744) discussed in F Buller, *An Introduction to the Law Relative to Trials at Nisi Prius* (London, W Strahan and M Woodfall, 1767) 129.

tell on the face of the count whether or not the claim rested on a contract. The indebitatus count for money had and received to the plaintiff's use was different. There was no shading around the edges. Although, for classification purposes, money had and received was a form of indebitatus assumpsit,[24] unlike money laid out, it did not grow out of a contractual core. The declaration simply alleged that the defendant was indebted 'for [so much money] had and received by the defendant to the use of the plaintiff'.[25] It could be used for non-contractual claims without resorting to fiction.

C. THE THEORETICAL BACKGROUND TO *MOSES V MACFERLAN*

Various attempts have been made to classify non-contractual but non-wrong based obligations. Justinian's *Institutes* used a four-fold division of obligations: 'for they arise *ex contractu* or *quasi ex contractu, ex maleficio* or *quasi ex maleficio*'.[26] The principle of unjust enrichment appeared in Justinian's *Digest* in two texts attributed to Pomponius[27] but it was not perceived as a distinct legal remedy.[28] Despite the efforts of Martinus Gosia, the early glossator, to turn the principle into a general unjust enrichment remedy,[29] by the sixteenth century the European Civilians were equating 'quasi ex contractu' with implied contract.[30]

Natural lawyers followed a different path. Drawing on the work of Thomas Aquinas[31] rather than the Civilians, in *Inleidinge tot de Hollandsche rechtsgeleerdheid*,[32] Hugo Grotius made a distinction between contract and quasi-contract, said to be analogous to[33] or 'as if' there were a contract.[34] Grotius also made some progress in turning Pomponius's

---

[24] For example C Viner, *A General Abridgement of Law and Equity* (Aldershot, printed for the author, 1741–56).

[25] Wentworth (n 12) vol 3, 55–6.

[26] T Sandars (tr), *The Institutes of Justinian* (London, Longman, 1948) 3.12.2.

[27] A Watson (tr), *The Digest of Justinian* (Philadelphia, University of Pennsylvania Press, 1985) 12.6.14: 'For this is by nature fair, that no body should be enriched to the loss of another'; 50.17.206: 'By the law of nature it is fair that nobody should be enriched to the loss of and by wrong to another.'

[28] F Schulz, *Classical Roman Law* (Oxford, OUP, 1951) 610 described the Digest texts as 'a general idea or principle, not a legal rule'. Other writers take a broadly similar line: Ibbetson (n 4) 10; R Feenstra, 'Grotius' Doctrine of Unjust Enrichment as a Source of Obligation: Its Origin and its Influence in Roman-Dutch Law' in Schrage (n 6) 197, 198; J Hallebeek, *The Concept of Unjust Enrichment in Late Scholasticism* (Nijmegen, Gerard Noodt Instituut, 1996) 1. R Zimmermann, *The Law of Obligations Roman Foundations of the Civilian Tradition* (Oxford, OUP, 1996) 852, 873 puts greater weight on these passages.

[29] Hallebeek (n 28) 4, 41.

[30] Birks and MacLeod (n 4) 68–77.

[31] Hallebeek (n 28) 88.

[32] RW Lee (tr), *Introduction to the Jurisprudence of Holland* (Oxford, OUP, 1926).

[33] Grotius in Lee, *ibid*, 3.26.2.

[34] *Ibid*, 3.26.3.

principle into a concrete remedy.[35] But the impact of this breakthrough was muted. In his later and better known *De iure belli ac pacis*,[36] quasi-contract was simply described as '*ex lege*',[37] and unjust enrichment was only discussed in the context of the institution of property.[38] Grotius's earlier analysis was also ignored by Samuel Pufendorf, whose *De iure naturae et gentium*[39] provided little more than a reheated version of Roman law.[40]

English legal writers had fewer theoretical ambitions.[41] Charles Viner's *A General Abridgement of Law and Equity*[42] was typical of legal literature in England in the first half of the eighteenth century.[43] But attitudes were changing. Robert Eden, who was heavily influenced by Heineccius,[44] used the implied contract analysis favoured by the European Civilians.[45] Another Civilian, Thomas Wood, in his *A New Institute of the Imperial or Civil Law*,[46] went beyond the implied contract theory. In a chapter headed 'Of obligations from Improper or Quasi Contracts created by Law without Agreement or Consent', he wrote:[47]

> There are some Obligations which arise amongst Mankind without any previous Consent or Agreement; and they are call'd Improper or Quasi Contracts; yet they have as firm a foundation in Justice as those which are made directly and by consent . . . An Improper or Quasi Contract is as binding to those who are unwilling or ignorant of it, as strongly as those Contracts which are enter'd into by Agreement.

Wood's description of quasi-contract was closer to Roman law than it was to the Civilians.[48] When, in a later book, he set out to describe the law in England rather than Rome,[49] he was much less confident on the nature of

---

[35] *Ibid*, 3.30.3.

[36] F Kelsey (tr), H Grotius, *The Rights of War and Peace* (1646 edn) (Oxford, OUP, 1925). The work was first translated into English in 1654.

[37] Grotius, *ibid*, 2.1.2.1.

[38] *Ibid*, 2.10.2.1

[39] CH and WA Oldfather (trs), S Pufendorf, *Of the Law of Nature and Nations* (1688 edn) (Oxford, OUP, 1934). The work was first translated into English by Basil Kennet in 1703.

[40] Pufendorf, *ibid*, 4.13.5.

[41] Sir Mathew Hale and Sir Edward Coke were the outstanding exceptions.

[42] Published between 1741 and 1756 with an index added posthumously in 1758.

[43] Other leading abridgments of the period include M Bacon, *A New Abridgment* (London, E & R Nutt, 1736) and J Comyns, *A Digest of the Laws of England* (London, T Longman and R Horsfield, 1762–76) 5 vols.

[44] H Jolowicz, 'Some English Civilians' (1949) 2 *CLP* 139, 151.

[45] R Eden, *Jurisprudentia Philologica sive Elementa juris civilis secundum Methodum et seriem Institutionum Justiniani* (Oxford, 1744).

[46] 2nd edn, London, 1712.

[47] *Ibid*, 255.

[48] Wood's category was broader than Justinian's. He included accident at 260–3 and fraud at 262–3. These were the only examples of quasi-contracts where Wood did not refer to the *Digest* or *Institutes*.

[49] T Wood, *An Institute of the Laws of England in their Natural Order, According to Common Use* (London, 1720).

the distinction between contract and quasi-contract, preferring to assert that some contracts were implied in law and omitting accident and fraud, which had appeared in the earlier work.[50] The implied contract theory was not confined to Civilian writers. It was also used by Sir Jeffrey Gilbert in the first, but unpublished, English treatise on contract,[51] where he made the observation that when obligations arise quasi ex contractu then the law implies a contract.[52]

D. THE DECISION IN *MOSES V MACFERLAN*

Moses v Macferlan[53] arose from a dispute about promissory notes—by then an important feature of the Common law landscape. Jacob made out four promissory notes in the name of Moses. Macferlan, wishing to recover in his own name against Jacob, asked Moses to indorse the notes. By indorsing the notes, Moses as well as Jacob was potentially liable to Macferlan.[54] Macferlan entered into a written agreement with Moses not to sue on the indorsement. In spite of the agreement, Macferlan brought an action in a Court of Conscience,[55] which refused to receive the agreement in evidence and ordered Moses to pay. At nisi prius,[56] Lord Mansfield ruled that on the merits of the case, Moses should be allowed to recover.[57] A verdict was given for the plaintiff, subject to the opinion of the court in banc as to whether money had and received was an appropriate form of action.

The defendant raised three objections. The first, that indebitatus assumpsit would not lie because there would be no action of debt on these facts, was easily disposed of.[58] The third objection, that the plaintiff was using money had and received in order to re-open a matter which had already been settled, was a more serious one.[59] Lord Mansfield stressed that the

---

[50] *Ibid*, 929.

[51] BL MS Hargrave 265, 266; M Macnair, 'Sir Jeffrey Gilbert and his Treatises' (1994) 15 *JLH* 252.

[52] BL MS Hargrave 265 f 202.

[53] (1760) 2 Burr 1005, 97 ER 676; 1 Wm Bla 219.

[54] On the importance of indorsement and transferability see J Rogers, *The Early History of the Law of Bills and Notes* (Cambridge, CUP, 1995) ch 8.

[55] The court of conscience was a small debts court: W Blackstone, *Commentaries on the Laws of England* (Oxford, Clarendon Press, 1768) vol 3, 81–3; M Finn, *The Character of Credit in English Culture 1740–1914* (Cambridge, CUP, 2003) 197–235.

[56] For counsel's argument at nisi prius see Oldham, *Mansfield Manuscripts* (n 4) vol 1, 258–9.

[57] 2 Burr 1005, 1006; 97 ER 676, 677.

[58] *Ibid*, 1008 (97 ER 678). In a note at 2 Burr 1009 note (c) Sir James Burrow, the law reporter, was particularly dismissive of this argument. In *Hard's Case* (1702) 1 Salk 23, 91 ER 22 it was said that indebitatus assumpsit would lie only where an action of debt could be brought but the two were not co-extensive, not least because indebitatus assumpsit would not lie on a specialty and could be brought for an installment.

[59] 2 Burr 1005, 1009 (97 ER 678).

plaintiff was not alleging that the Court of Conscience had ruled incorrectly but that there was no mechanism for him to raise the defendant's unjust retention of the money.[60] This part of his judgment continued to be controversial,[61] and Lord Kenyon later warned that '*Moses v Macferlan* had gone far enough'.[62] The King's Bench in *Marriott v Hampton* held that money had and received was not appropriate for money recovered under legal process,[63] prompting Sir William Evans to claim that the decision went 'a great way to destroying' *Moses v Macferlan*.[64]

Lord Mansfield's dismissal of counsel's remaining objection that 'no assumpsit lies, except upon an express or implied contract: but here it is impossible to presume any contract to refund money, which the defendant recovered by an adverse suit',[65] is the decision's most important legacy.[66] His Lordship held that:[67]

> If the defendant be under an obligation, from the ties of natural justice to refund; the law implies a debt, and gives this action, founded in the equity of the plaintiff's case, as it were upon a contract ('quasi ex contractu' as the Roman law expresses it.)

> This species of assumpsit ('for money had and received to the plaintiff's use') lies in numberless instances, for money the defendant has received from a third person; which he claims title to, in opposition to the plaintiff's right; and which he had, by law, authority to receive from such third person.

In a later passage, Lord Mansfield expanded on the basis of money had and received:[68]

> This kind of equitable action, to recover back money, which ought not in justice to be kept, is very beneficial, and therefore much encouraged. It lies only for money which ex æquo et bono, the defendant ought to refund: it does not lie for money paid by the plaintiff, which is claimed of him as payable in point of honour and honesty, although it could not have been recovered from him by any course of law.

---

[60] Lord Mansfield's sleight of hand is even more apparent given that in *Silk v Rennett* (1764) 3 Burr 1583, 97 ER 993, he later explained that the 'Court of Conscience has a mixed jurisdiction, as well equitable as legal: they proceed *secundum æquum et bonum*'.

[61] *Phillips v Hunter* (1795) 2 H Bla 402, 416; 126 ER 618, 625; *Brisbane v Dacres* (1813) 5 Taunt 143, 160; 128 ER 641, 648.

[62] *Marriott v Hampton* (1797) 2 Esp 546, 548; 170 ER 450, 450.

[63] (1797) TR 269, 101 ER 969.

[64] WD Evans, *Essays: On the Action for Money Had and Received, on the Law of Insurances, and on the Law of Bills of Exchange and Promissory Notes* (Liverpool, 1802) 91–102 was particularly critical of this aspect of the decision. The essay is reproduced in [1998] *RLR* 1.

[65] 2 Burr 1005, 1008; 97 ER 676, 678.

[66] Jackson (n 4) 117–19, 121; Winfield, *Province of the Law of Tort* (n 4) 128–41; Winfield, *Quasi-Contract* (n 4) 9–23; HG Hanbury, 'The Recovery of Money' (1924) 40 *LQR* 31, 35–6.

[67] 2 Burr 1008–9, 97 ER 678.

[68] 2 Burr 1012, 97 ER 680.

Jackson argued that Lord Mansfield was embracing rather than rejecting the implied contract theory; he was simply describing those situations when a contract would be implied.[69] On this view, Lord Mansfield was not suggesting anything inconsistent with the views of contemporary legal writers. His judgment was also consistent with earlier judges who had justified the action for money had and received on the basis of an implied contract.[70] The implied contract analysis is also easy to reconcile with the formal pleading status of the action given that it is grouped with the contractual assumpsits.

Other writers have argued that Lord Mansfield was more ambitious and was attempting to break free from the shackles imposed by the implied contract analysis.[71] Birks has suggested that Lord Mansfield's references to 'quasi ex contractu' allowed him to demonstrate that money had and received was not derived from an implied contract.[72] Lord Mansfield's understanding of the scope of money had and received may also have been influenced by the Roman *obligatio naturalis* (natural obligation), which prevented recovery of payment under a *condictio indebiti*.[73] Sir William Evans, writing just 40 years later, had no doubt that Lord Mansfield's views were referable to Roman law and set about making his case with examples.[74] Ibbetson has pointed out that there are good grounds to suppose that Wilmot J, the other judge in the case,[75] had a deeper understanding of Roman law.[76] After all, it was Wilmot J who explicitly likened money had and received to the *condictio indebiti*.[77] He was also a judge very much in the habit of utilising principles gleaned from Roman law.[78]

MacQueen and Sellar have put forward the alternative hypothesis that, given Lord Mansfield's friendship with Lord Kames, he may have been influenced by *Principles of Equity*,[79] published in the same year as *Moses v*

---

[69] Jackson (n 4) 119.

[70] *Jacob v Allen* (1703) 1 Salk 27, 91 ER 26; *Harris v Collins* (1725) LI MS Misc 6; *Cock v Vivian* (1743) W Kel 203, 205; 25 ER 569, 570.

[71] Winfield, *Province of the Law of Tort* (n 4) 128–9; Winfield, *Quasi-Contract* (n 4) 10; Ibbetson (n 4) 272; K Teevan, *A History of the Anglo-American Common Law of Contract* (New York, Greenwood Press, 1990) 124, 241.

[72] Birks, 'English and Roman Learning' (n 4) 3.

[73] *Ibid*, 16–18. Dawson (n 4) 12 rejects the view that Lord Mansfield was consciously importing some Roman law doctrine. On natural obligations in Roman law see WW Buckland, *A Textbook of Roman Law From Augustus to Justinian*, P Stein (ed) (3rd edn, Cambridge, CUP, 1963) 552–4. On natural obligations in English law see D Sheehan, 'Natural Obligations in English Law' [2004] *LMCLQ* 171.

[74] WD Evans (tr), R Pothier, *A Treatise on the Law of Obligations or Contracts* (1806) vol 2, 378–81. See too P Birks, 'Comparative Unjust Enrichment' in P Birks and A Pretto (eds), *Themes in Comparative Law* (Oxford, OUP, 2002) 137, 139.

[75] Wilmot J's opinion appears only in 1 Wm Bla 219.

[76] Ibbetson (n 4) 272.

[77] 1 Wm Bla 219, 220.

[78] *Pillans v Van Mierop* (1765) 3 Burr 1663, 1670; 97 ER 1035.

[79] Henry Home, Lord Kames, *Principles of Equity* (Edinburgh, A Kincaid, 1760).

Macferlan.[80] Lord Kame's discussion of quasi-contract blended Roman law, Common law and Equity. Having likened Roman quasi-contract with the situation where 'some relief is given that would be given upon an express covenant',[81] he described a *negotiorum gestio* where 'Equity interposes and makes liable, as the Common law would do had I given a mandate or commission',[82] and *condictio indebiti* which had a 'good foundation in equity'.[83] Although Lord Kames made an explicit link with Equity, his analysis perhaps falls short of the type of generalised liability envisaged by Lord Mansfield.[84]

E. THE ACTION FOR MONEY HAD AND RECEIVED AND THE COURT OF CHANCERY

The twin influences of Roman law and Lord Kames' *Principles of Equity* on Lord Mansfield should not be dismissed lightly. A third source of inspiration was closer to home. At the beginning of his career Mansfield had a large Chancery practice.[85] He drew on this experience when it came to developing the non-contractual assumpsits.[86] Three years before *Moses v Macferlan* was decided, in an action for money paid against a surety, he commented:[87]

> . . . as to the objection that the Court of Chancery is the proper court for a surety to be relieved in, there are many cases in which a court of equity may be necessary to come at the facts yet if a court of law is once possessed of facts I know of no case where it may not give relief by an action on the case.

The action for money laid out against a surety had an equivalent in Chancery in the bill for contribution.[88] Although the similarity between the two continued to be acknowledged,[89] by the 1790s Equitable terminology

---

[80] H MacQueen and WD Sellar, 'Unjust Enrichment in Scots Law' in Schrage (n 4) 289, 314–6; Ibbetson (n 4) 272 n 50.

[81] Kames (n 79) 35.

[82] *Ibid*.

[83] *Ibid*, 92.

[84] For the contrary view that Lord Kames was attempting to generate a general theory see M Lobban, 'The Ambition of Lord Kames' Equity' in ADE Lewis and M Lobban (eds), *Law and History* (Oxford, OUP, 2003) 97, 112–15.

[85] Oldham, *English Common Law* (n 4) 6; Oldham, *Mansfield Manuscripts* (n 4) vol 1, 15.

[86] W Holdsworth, *A History of English Law* (London, Methuen & Co, 1938) vol 12, 589–90 agues that Lord Mansfield was in favour of a policy of fusion or partial fusion which probably exaggerates his position. He was certainly keen on borrowing from Equity.

[87] *Decker v Pope* (1757) LI MS Misc 129 (unfol).

[88] G Jones, 'The Role of Equity in the English Law of Restitution' in Schrage (n 4) 149, 165.

[89] *Toussaint v Martinnant* (1787) 2 TR 100, 105; 100 ER 55, 58; *Deering v Earl of Winchelsea* (1787) 2 B & P 270, 273; 126 ER 1276, 1278; *Stirling v Forrester* (1821) 3 Bligh 575, 590; 4 ER 712, 717; *Pownal v Ferrand* (1827) 6 B & C 439, 442–3, 108 ER 513, 514.

was largely superseded by the language of implied assumpsit,[90] so that when, at the turn of the century, Lord Eldon acknowledged an overlap between Common law and Chancery, he was at pains to point out that money paid was a form of implied assumpsit.[91] Once relegated from the position of underlying cause, Equity was accommodated in the role of a reason for implying a contract.[92]

The close relationship with Equity was also acknowledged in money had and received.[93] In *Lewis v Campbell*,[94] Maule J observed that the actions for money paid and money had and received both rested on equitable principles. Lord Mansfield and others likened money had and received to a bill in Equity.[95] Unlike money laid out, there was no directly analogous bill in Equity but Chancery would order repayment of money as a part of its jurisdiction over mistake[96] and fraud.[97] Equity jurisdiction also extended to an order for the repayment of money where performance failed part way through.[98] In *Newton v Rowse*,[99] the plaintiff placed his son as an apprentice with an attorney and paid £120. One of the articles of the apprenticeship stated that if the attorney died within a year then the estate should repay £60. The attorney died within three weeks of the start of the apprenticeship and the father successfully recovered £100.[100] These situations are similar to those where money had and received was usually used.

---

[90] *Cowley v Dunlop* (1796) 7 TR 565, 568; 101 ER 1135, 1136.

[91] *Craythorne v Swinburn* (1807) 14 Ves Jun 160, 164; 33 ER 482, 483–4.

[92] *Davies v Humphreys* (1840) 6 M & W 153, 151 ER 361 marks the beginning of a shift away from Equity; see also *Kemp v Finden* (1844) 12 M & W 421, 152 ER 1262; *Batard v Hawes* (1853) 2 El & Bl 287, 118 ER 775.

[93] Other writers have stressed the close relationship between money had and received and Equity: B Kremer, 'The Action for Money Had and Received' (2001) 17 *JCL* 93; G Virgo, 'Restitution Through the Looking Glass: Restitution Within Equity and Equity Within Restitution' in J Getzler (ed), *Rationalizing Property, Equity and Trusts Essays in Honour of Edward Burn* (London, LexisNexis, 2003) 82, 87–8.

[94] (1849) 8 CB 541, 545; 137 ER 620, 621.

[95] *Clarke v Shee* (1774) 1 Cowp 197, 199–200; 98 ER 1041, 1042–3 (Lord Mansfield); *Straton v Rastall* (1788) 2 TR 366, 370–1; 100 ER 197, 199 (Buller J); *Master v Miller* (1791) 4 TR 320, 343; 100 ER 1042, 1054.

[96] Ibbetson (n 4) 273–4. In *Cox v Prentice* (1814) 3 M & S 344, 348, 105 ER 641 it was said that money had and received on the grounds of mutual mistake was 'not unusual'.

[97] *Colt v Woollaston* (1723) 2 P Wms 154, 24 ER 679.

[98] Both G Jeremy, *A Treatise on the Equity Jurisdiction* (London, J & WT Clarke, 1828) 365 and J Story, *Commentaries on Equity Jurisprudence* (2nd edn, Boston, MA, Little, Brown, 1839) 88–9 discuss these authorities under the heading of accident. J Newland, *A Treatise on Contracts within the Jurisdiction of Courts of Equity* (London, Butterworth, 1806) 328 thought that the court was 'in fact making a new contract for the parties'.

[99] (1687) 1 Vern 460, 23 ER 586.

[100] For other examples see *Therman v Abell* (1688) 2 Vern 64, 23 ER 650; *Hale v Webb* (1786) 2 Bro CC 78, 29 ER 44.

F. RESTRICTING THE SCOPE OF MONEY HAD AND RECEIVED

Lord Mansfield described money had and received as a 'very liberal action'.[101] It had the potential to grow into a broad remedy protecting against the unconscionable receipt of another person's money.[102] Buller J urged, 'Let us not be less liberal than our predecessors, and even we ourselves, have been on former occasions'.[103] 'Great friend' of the action though he still professed to be,[104] even Lord Mansfield became more cautious:[105]

> Great benefit results from the liberal extension of this action, but it ought not to be carried too far, nor used by way of surprise. And therefore if thrown in as of course, and the plaintiff comes prepared to try another question, he shall not by surprise be let into evidence on this, though originally the action for money had and received might have been maintained.

To begin with, the main concern seems to have been the way in which money had and received was perceived to give plaintiffs an unfair advantage in pleading, particularly when used to try warranties.[106] There were other problems too. Once it was admitted that money had and received was analogous to a bill in Equity it teetered on the borderline of property. The plaintiff recovered because the money 'belonged' to the plaintiff and the defendant was acting contrary to justice in retaining it.[107] The courts were soon making clear that money had and received could not be used to recover a specific thing as opposed to money[108] because to do so would have been to undermine trover.[109] Most difficult of all was the relationship with contract. In the aftermath of *Cutter v Powell*,[110] the courts began to tighten up the boundaries of non-contractual claims as a means of safeguarding

---

[101] *Sadler v Evans* (1766) 4 Burr 1984, 1986; 98 ER 34, 35. He used similarly expansionist terminology to describe the action for money paid around this time: *Decker v Pope* (1757) LI MS Misc 129 (unfol).
[102] *Hoam v Scott* (1767) LI MS Misc 129 f 107; *Dale v Sollet* (1767) 4 Burr 2133, 2134; 98 ER 112, 112; *Lindon v Hooper* (1776) 1 Cowp 414, 419; 98 ER 1160, 1163; *Buller v Harrison* (1777) 2 Cowp 565, 568; 98 ER 1243, 1244; *Jestons v Brooke* (1778) 2 Cowp 793, 797; 98 ER 1365, 1367; *Stevenson v Mortimer* (1778) 2 Cowp 805, 806; 98 ER 1372, 1372; *Bize v Dickason* (1786) 1 TR 285, 286; 99 ER 1097, 1097; *Straton v Rastall* (1788) 2 TR 366, 370; 100 ER 197, 199.
[103] *Master v Miller* (1791) 4 TR 320, 344; 100 ER 1042, 1055.
[104] *Weston v Downes* (1778) 1 Doug 23, 24; 99 ER 19, 20; *Towers v Barrett* (1786) 1 TR 133, 134; 99 ER 1014, 1015.
[105] *Longchamp v Kenny* (1778) 1 Doug 137, 99 ER 91; LI MS Hill 13 f 311.
[106] W Swain, '*Cutter v Powell* and the Pleading of Claims of Unjust Enrichment' [2003] *RLR* 46, 51.
[107] *Clarke v Shee* (1774) 1 Cowp 197: the plaintiff is described as the 'true owner' of the money in the head-note.
[108] *Nightingal v Devisme* (1770) 5 Burr 2589, 98 ER 361.
[109] *Longchamp v Kenny* (1778) 1 Doug 137.
[110] (1795) 6 TR 320, 1001 ER 573.

contractual liability. In modern times this has become known as the doctrine of subsidiarity.[111] Where the parties were in a contractual relationship, money had and received could only be brought when the contract was at an end.[112]

Cutter v Powell was decided just as lawyers were beginning to think more analytically.[113] Legal writers began to ponder the correct classification of the non-contractual assumpsits. Their treatment was more than a little schizophrenic. Henry Colebrooke wrote that in quasi-contract 'no consent intervenes' because such obligations were the product of law or 'natural equity',[114] which suggests that he saw contract and quasi-contract as distinct. But he qualified his remarks with the reflection that there was 'tacit or presumed consent'.[115] Joseph Chitty also included the non-contractual assumpsits in his textbook on contract.[116] At the same time Lord Mansfield's remarks in *Moses v Macferlan* prefaced a section on money had and received.[117] By the second edition Chitty was referring to the French Civil Code and suggesting that quasi-contracts were obligations formed without 'the intervention of any agreement'.[118]

Others writers were less equivocal about equating non-contractual assumpsits with implied contract.[119] Charles Addison placed the counts for money lent, money paid, money had and received and account stated alongside implied contracts of sale and implied warranty.[120] These writers were part of a tradition that included Sir William Blackstone. When Blackstone delivered his lectures in the 1750s, money had and received had appeared as a form of implied assumpsit alongside *quantum meruit, quantum valebat,* money paid, account stated and liability of an office holder.[121] In the published *Commentaries,* as a concession to *Moses v Macferlan* Lord

---

[111] Swain (n 106) 53–4. On the modern law see J Beatson, 'Restitution and Contract: Non-Cumul?' (2001) 1 *Theoretical Inquiries in Law* 83, 88; A Tettenborn, 'Subsisting Contract and Failure of Consideration—A Little Scepticism' [2002] *RLR* 1; R Cunnington, 'Failure of Basis' [2004] *LMCLQ* 234, 248–51.

[112] *Ibid,* 53–5.

[113] For the influence of this new thinking on legal literature see AWB Simpson, 'The Rise and Fall of The Legal Treatise: Legal Principles and the Forms of Legal Literature' (1983) 48 *University of Chicago Law Review* 632. The publication of JJ Powell, *Essay Upon the Law of Contracts and Agreements* (London, 1790) marks the start of this trend.

[114] HT Colebrooke, *A Treatise on Obligations and Contracts* (London, printed for the author, 1818) 15–6.

[115] *Ibid,* 16.

[116] *A Practical Treatise on the Law of Contracts not under Seal* (London, Sweet, 1826) 178–95.

[117] *Ibid,* 182.

[118] J Chitty, *A Practical Treatise on the Law of Contracts not under Seal* (2nd edn, London, Sweet, 1834) 22.

[119] S Comyns, *Treatise of the Law Relating to Contracts and Agreements not under Seal* (2nd edn, London, A Strahan, 1824) 4–5.

[120] *A Treatise on Contracts and Liabilities ex-Contractu* (London, W Benning, 1847) ch 7.

[121] All Souls MS 300 vol 18 (unfol).

Mansfield's judgment was cited verbatim,[122] but there was no attempt to generalise liability in the way that Lord Mansfield had done. Robert Chambers[123] and Richard Wooddesson,[124] who succeeded Blackstone as Vinerian Professor, continued with the implied contract analysis.

The next generation of writers was more uncomfortable with the terminology of implied contract. Leake wrote that these obligations rested in justice and equity,[125] Pollock stressed that there was not a true contract, only something analogous to one,[126] and Anson suggested that the contract classification had as much do with the historical need to use contractual forms of action as any well reasoned theory.[127] All three nevertheless retained money had and received within their treatises on contract.

Given the practical orientation of the vast majority of English legal literature in the nineteenth century, it is perhaps unsurprising that textbook writers made only oblique references to the problems associated with the implied contract analysis. Sir William Evans was much more radical. In the introduction to his translation of Pothier, he observed:[128]

> Quasi-contracts, which with us would be treated by implication, as actual contracts. They differ from contracts, as not being founded upon actual consent; and also differ from injuries. Such are the cases of receiving money which ought to be refunded, the obligation of accounting for business done for another in his absence on the one hand, and remunerating the expenses sustained in doing so on the other.

Evans begins the passage by equating quasi-contract with contract but he was quick to recognise that contract rests on assent and quasi-contract does not. The same discomfort with an implied contract analysis was evident in his commentary on Pothier, where he explained that the term 'implied contract' was 'applicable rather to the evidence than to the nature or quality of the obligation', so that 'an implied promise is deemed to have taken place'.[129] In his *Essays: On the Action for Money Had and Received, on the Law of Insurances, and on the Law of Bills of Exchange and Promissory Notes*,[130] Evans went even further. In addition to supporting Lord Mansfield's generalisation of money had and received,[131] he was the first

---

[122] Blackstone (n 55) vol 3, 162.
[123] *A Course of Lectures on English Law Delivered at the University of Oxford 1767–73*, T Curley (ed) (Oxford, OUP, 1986) vol 2, 224.
[124] *A Systematical View of the Laws of England, as Treated in a Course of Vinerian Lectures* (London, T Payne, 1792–3) vol 3, 158.
[125] *The Elements of the Law of Contracts* (London, Stevens, 1867) 38–75 esp 38–9.
[126] *Principles of Contract at Law and in Equity* (London, Stevens, 1876) 28–9.
[127] *Principles of the English Law of Contract* (Oxford, Clarendon Press, 1879) 7, 321–7.
[128] R Pothier (n 74) Introduction, 85.
[129] *Ibid* vol 1, 69.
[130] Liverpool, 1802.
[131] *Ibid*, 7.

English writer to identify the similarities with the principle of unjust enrichment.[132] Sixty years later Sir Henry Maine, in his *Ancient Law*,[133] drew a firm distinction between quasi and implied contract. In the former:[134]

> the Law consulting the interests of morality, imposes an obligation on the receiver to refund, but the very nature of the transaction indicates that it is not a contract, in so much as the convention, the most essential ingredient of contract is wanting.

By the early nineteenth century, some judges began voicing concerns that giving money had and received an equitable foundation was blurring the boundary between Common law and Equity:[135]

> In the case of *Moses v Macferlan* some principles were laid down, which are certainly too large, and which I do not mean to rely on, such as that, wherever one man has money which another ought to have, an action for money had and received may be maintained, or that wherever a man has an equitable claim he has also a legal action.

Other judges continued to find valid explanations in equity and good conscience or through the maxim *ex æquo et bono*.[136] Their remarks suggest that money had and received was still seen as a broadly based equitable type of remedy that just happened to be enforced in the Common law. At this time, the relationship between Common law and Equity was becoming increasingly fluid.[137] But behind the rhetoric a rather different picture appears.

Where it was necessary, for technical purposes, to classify the non-contractual assumpsits it was the similarities with contract and not the differences that were stressed.[138] Substantive principles also began to move across from contractual assumpsit. The courts began to apply the entire contracts rule in non-contractual assumpsit. Where the parties were in a contractual relationship and the contract was entire, a non-contractual

---

[132] *Ibid*, 8.

[133] (London, Dent, 1861) 343–4. See too Ibbetson (n 4) 284.

[134] *Ibid*, 344.

[135] *Johnson v Johnson* (1802) 3 B & P 162, 169; 127 ER 89, 93. See too *Cooth v Jackson* (1801) 6 Ves Jun 12, 39; 31 ER 913, 927.

[136] *Master v Miller* (1791) 4 TR 320, 342–3; 100 ER 1042, 1054; *Harrison v Walker* (1791) Peake 150, 151; *Cotton v Thurland* (1793) 5 TR 405, 409; 101 ER 227, 229; *Greville v Da Costa* (1797) Peake Add 113, 114; *Wright v Hunter* (1800) 1 East 20; *Surtees v Hubbard* (1802) 4 Esp 204, 170 ER 692; *Simpson v Swan* (1812) 3 Camp 291, 293; 170 ER 1386, 1387; *Foster v Stewart* (1814) 3 M & S 191, 200; 105 ER 582, 585; *Da Silvale v Kendall* (1815) 4 M & S 37, 26, 105 ER 749.

[137] As early as the 1770s Richard Wooddesson considered the difference between Common law and Equity to be mainly procedural: see R Wooddesson, *A Systematical View of the Laws of England, as Treated of in a Course of Vinerian Lectures* (London, T Payne, 1792–3) vol 1, 203.

[138] Ibbetson (n 4) 278–9.

claim was barred without the full performance of the plaintiff's obligations under the contract.[139] Something like the privity of contract principle came to restrict money had and received.[140]

With the decline of the forms of action and the eclipse of the jury, the law of contract was restructured. A ready-made framework was provided by Pothier's *Traité des Obligations*.[141] In contrast, there was no agreed framework into which money had and received could be slotted. All that lawyers had to work with was Lord Mansfield's generalisation combined with a list of examples of money had and received:[142]

> But it lies for money paid by mistake; or upon a consideration which happens to fail; or for money got by imposition, (express or implied) or extortion or oppression; or an undue advantage taken of the plaintiff's situation, contrary to the laws made for the protection of persons under these circumstances.

Sir William Evans, the only writer to inject much sophistication into his analysis of money had and received, simply adopted Lord Mansfield's list, to which he added money paid under an illegal contract.[143] In his *Abridgement*, Charles Petersdorff used a slightly different classification from that of Evans, including bank notes, rescinded contracts, money paid as fees, money paid under fraud and money paid under legal process.[144] Tindal CJ, who as late as the 1840s was still referring to the maxim *ex æquo et bono*,[145] followed up his remarks by attempting to place the case before him within one of the pre-ordained categories of relief.[146]

Some questions about the scope of Lord Mansfield's categories remained unresolved but others began firming up.[147] Describing money had and received in the 1870s, Anson wrote:[148]

---

[139] *Sinclair v Bowles* (1829) 9 B & C 92, 109 ER 35; *Roberts v Havelock* (1832) 3 B & Ad 404, 110 ER 35; *Hughes v Lenny* (1839) 5 M & W 183, 151 ER 79; *Appleby v Myers* (1867) LR 2 CP 651.

[140] Compare *Israel v Douglas* (1789) 1 H Bla 239, 126 ER 139 with *Williams v Everett* (1811) 14 East 582, 104 ER 725. See also *Baron v Husband* (1833) 4 B & Ad 611, 110 ER 586; *Howell v Batt* (1833) 5 B & Ad 504, 110 ER 877. The 'parties only' principle only became established in contractual assumpsits later, in part because of an alternative formulation based on consideration: see D Ibbetson and W Swain, 'Third Party Beneficiaries in English Law 1680–1861' in D Ibbetson and E Schrage (eds), *Ius Quaesitum Tertio* (Berlin, Duncker & Humblot, forthcoming).

[141] On the influence of Pothier on the law of contract in England see Ibbetson (n 4) 220–44; *Cox v Troy* (1822) 5 B & Ald 474, 480; 106 ER 1264, 1266; *Hoare v Cazenove* (1812) 16 East 391, 398; 104 ER 1137, 1139; *Hall v Wright* (1858) El Bl & El 746, 760; 120 ER 688, 694.

[142] (1760) 2 Burr 1005, 1012.

[143] Evans (n 64) 37–80.

[144] *A Practical and Elementary Abridgement of the Common Law* (London, 1841–4) vol 12, 670–82.

[145] *Edwards v Bates* (1844) 7 M & G 590, 597; 135 ER 238, 241.

[146] *Ibid* 598 (135 ER 241).

[147] Mistake of law was particularly problematic prior to *Bilbie v Lumley* (1802) 2 East 467, 102 ER 448.

[148] *Supra* n 127, 326–7.

This class of case, though at one time in the hands of Lord Mansfield it threatened to expand into the vagueness of 'moral obligation', is practically reducible to two groups of circumstances now pretty clearly defined. The first of these are cases of money obtained by wrong, of which payments under contracts induced by fraud, or duress, have afforded us some illustrations; the second are cases of money paid under such mistake of fact as creates a belief that a legal liability rests on the payer to make the payment.

In a note he added a third situation: consideration which had wholly failed.

G. THE MODERN HISTORY OF *MOSES V MACFERLAN* AND MONEY HAD AND RECEIVED

By the 1840s, judges were still attempting to justify money had and received on the basis of 'conscience' and 'justice and equity'. By the 1890s the terminology had been stripped of all meaning.[149] Nineteenth century judges had set their face against supposedly vague notions of this sort. Moral consideration and public policy were two other casualties.[150] With the move towards increasingly formalised judicial reasoning,[151] money had and received became trapped within pre-existing boundaries.[152] As the implied contract analysis gained ground in England, the link with Equity was lost.[153] It would never recover. In 1849, Pollock CB explained that money had and received 'is a perfectly legal action, and no good can result from calling it an equitable one'.[154]

In the early twentieth century judges became increasingly critical of the way in which Lord Mansfield had generalised money had and received in *Moses v Macferlan*. In *Bayliss v Bishop of London*, Cozens-Hardy MR commented that 'the wide language used by that great judge has not been followed'.[155] Scrutton LJ, who described the history of money had and received as 'a history of well meaning sloppiness of thought',[156] was a

---

[149] *Phillips v The School Board for London* [1898] 2 QB 447, 453; *Jacobs v Morris* [1901] 1 Ch 261, 268–9; *Re Bodega Co Ltd* [1904] 1 Ch 276, 286; *Lodge v National Union Investment Co* (1906) 76 LJ Ch 187, 193.

[150] On the brief rise and decline of moral consideration see W Swain, 'The Changing Nature of the Doctrine of Consideration 1750–1850' (2005) 54 *JLH* 47, 57–9. Judicial unease with public policy is neatly encapsulated in the description of public policy as an 'unruly horse' in *Richardson v Mellish* (1824) 2 Bing 229, 252; 130 ER 294, 303 (Burrough J).

[151] PS Atiyah, *The Rise and Fall of Freedom of Contract* (Oxford, OUP, 1979) 388–97.

[152] *Morgan v Ashcroft* [1938] 1 KB 49, 75 (Scott LJ).

[153] Winfield, *Quasi-Contract* (n 4) 12–21.

[154] *Miller v Atlee* (1849) 13 Jur 431. He made his remarks during the course of counsel's argument.

[155] [1913] 1 Ch 127, 133. At 140 Hamilton LJ observed: 'To ask what course would be *ex æquo et bono* to both sides was never a very precise guide.'

[156] *Holt v Markham* [1923] 1 KB 504, 513.

persistent critic.[157] The implied contract analysis, whilst perhaps in abeyance for a short period at the end of the eighteenth and beginning of the nineteenth centuries, had never gone away. It was unambiguously revived by the House of Lords in *Sinclair v Brougham* in 1914.[158]

During the period when the implied contract analysis reached its peak in English law, in America, claims of this sort were broken off from contract. Inspired by James Barr Ames,[159] American lawyers began to organise these authorities under the rubric of unjust enrichment.[160] Their analysis owed more to Roman than Common law.[161] This process culminated in the Restatement of the Law of Restitution in 1937.[162]

Developments in America may have been partly responsible for reinvigorating academic writing on the subject in England between the wars.[163] Judges who joined the debate were equally divided. In *Morgan v Ashcroft*,[164] Greene MR rejected Lord Mansfield's analysis in favour of the implied contract theory. But cracks were beginning to show in the implied contract analysis.[165] Lord Wright, who had expressed similar views extra-judicially,[166] put forward an alternative explanation for money had and received based on the idea of unjust enrichment.[167] Lord Wright, who admired the American Restatement,[168] also attempted to rescue *Moses v Macferlan* from obscurity, describing the decision as 'the

---

[157] In addition to *Holt v Markham* see his remarks in *RE Jones v Waring and Gillow Ltd* [1925] 2 KB 612, 637.

[158] [1914] AC 398.

[159] 'The History of Assumpsit: Implied Assumpsit' (1888) 2 *Harvard Law Review* 53. On the influence of Ames see Ibbetson (n 4) 286; A Kull, 'James Barr Ames and the Early Modern History of Unjust Enrichment' (2005) 25 *OJLS* 297.

[160] W Keener, *Treatise on the Law of Quasi-Contracts* (New York, Baker–Voorhis, 1893); FC Woodward, *The Law of Quasi-Contact* (Boston, MA, Little, Brown and Co, 1913). For a summary of the American history see G Palmer, 'History of Anglo-American Law' in P Schlechtriem (ed), *Restitution—Unjust Enrichment and Negotiorum Gestio*, part of R David *et al* (eds), *International Encyclopedia of Comparative Law* (Tübingen, JCM Mohr, 1989); Ibbetson (n 4) 285–7.

[161] Ibbetson (n 6) 46–7.

[162] For commentary on the American Restatement see W Seavey and A Scott, 'Restitution' (1938) 54 *LQR* 29; P Winfield, 'The American Restatement of the Law of Restitution' (1938) 54 *LQR* 529, P Birks, 'A Letter to America: The New Restatement of Restitution' (2003) 3 *Global Jurist Frontiers* 1.

[163] In recent times the roles may have been reversed. For a pessimistic appraisal of modern American legal development see A Kull, 'Rationalizing Restitution' (1995) 83 *California Law Review* 1191.

[164] [1938] 1 KB 49, 62.

[165] *Morgan v Ashcroft* [1938] 1 KB 49, 74–5 (Scott LJ); *United Australia Ltd v Barclays Bank Ltd* [1941] AC 1, 27 (Lord Atkin).

[166] Lord Wright, 'Sinclair v Brougham' [1938] *CLJ* 305, reproduced in Lord Wright, *Legal Essays and Addresses* (Cambridge, CUP, 1939) 1.

[167] *Brook's Wharf and Bull Wharf Ltd v Goodman Bros* [1937] 1 KB 534, 545; *Fibrosa Spolka Akcyjna v Fairbairn Lawson Combe Barbour Ltd* [1943] AC 32, 64.

[168] Lord Wright, 'Book Review of the Restatement' (1937) 51 *Harvard Law Review* 369, reproduced in Wright (n 166) 34.

basis of the modern law of quasi-contract'.[169] There were still formidable obstacles in the way of Lord Mansfield's generalisation. Even Lord Wright was forced to concede that the 'standard of what is against conscience in this context has become more or less canalized or defined'.[170]

Lord Denning was also sympathetic to Lord Wright's analysis.[171] But it was Goff and Jones, whose *Law of Restitution* appeared in 1966, who gave the subject some structure.[172] Judges were still slow to catch on.[173] Peter Birks' *Introduction to the Law of Restitution*[174] provided much needed structural coherence. In the 1990s, the House of Lords finally adopted unjust enrichment,[175] but some critics are still to be won over.[176]

H. CONCLUSIONS: THE CONTEMPORARY RELEVANCE OF EQUITY

The triumph of the unjust enrichment analysis in England has largely been achieved in spite of threadbare judicial support. In the first edition of *The Law of Restitution* Goff and Jones insisted that in *Moses v Macferlan* Lord Mansfield adopted an unjust enrichment approach.[177] Whatever the merits of unjust enrichment, *Moses v Macferlan* provides tenuous support at best.[178] The primary importance of the decision in England lies in the way in which Lord Mansfield generalised liability and avoided implied contract theory rather than the supposed acceptance of unjust enrichment.

[169] *Fibrosa* (n 167) 62; cf *Morgan v Ashcroft* [1938] 1 KB 49, 75 (Scott LJ).
[170] *Ibid* 63.
[171] *Reading v Attorney General* [1948] 2 KB 268, 275; cf the remarks of Lord Porter in the House of Lords [1951] AC 507, 513–14; *Kiriri Cotton Co Ltd v Dewani* [1960] AC 192, 204–5. Lord Denning's sympathies were evident from his argument as counsel in *United Australia Ltd v Barclays Bank Ltd* [1941] AC 1, 7. He supported this view extra-judicially in AT Denning, *The Changing Law* (London, Sweet & Maxwell, 1953) 62–5.
[172] London, Sweet & Maxwell, 1966.
[173] As late as 1977 Lord Diplock denied that English law recognised a general doctrine of unjust enrichment: *Orakpo v Manson Investments Ltd* [1978] AC 95, 104. For a summary of the English position between 1945 and 1970 see A Coleman, 'The Concept of Unjust Enrichment in English Law' (1979) 10 *Cambrian Law Review* 8.
[174] Oxford, OUP, 1985.
[175] *Lipkin Gorman v Karpnale Ltd* [1991] 2 AC 548; P Birks, 'The English Recognition of Unjust Enrichment' (1991) *LMCLQ* 473; A Burrows, 'The English Law of Restitution A Ten Year Review' in J Neyers *et al* (eds), *Understanding Unjust Enrichment* (Oxford, Hart, 2004) 11.
[176] There is still some support for the implied contract analysis, albeit in a more sophisticated form, notably in the work of Steve Hedley: *A Critical Introduction to Restitution* (London, Butterworths, 2001); *Restitution: Its Division and Ordering* (London, Sweet & Maxwell, 2001); 'Unjust Enrichment' [1995] *CLJ* 578; 'Implied Contract and Restitution' [2004] *CLJ* 435.
[177] Goff and Jones (n 172) 12; cf the most recent edition published in 2002 at para 1-013. Birks (n 174) was rather more cautious about the claims of *Moses v Macferlan* beyond Lord Mansfield's rejection of the implied contract theory. In his last book, Professor Birks explicitly rejected the view that Lord Mansfield used unjust enrichment: Birks (n 3) 14.
[178] There is some judicial support for this analysis of *Moses v Macferlan*: *Kleinwort Benson Ltd v Birmingham CC* [1997] QB 380, 386 (Evans LJ); *Westdeutsche Landesbank Girozentrale v Islington LBC* [1996] AC 669, 697 (Lord Goff).

Following the rejection of the implied contract theory,[179] developments in Australia have taken a radically different turn. Attempts have been made to create an alternative analysis with reference to unconscionability[180]— already an important principle in the law of obligations in Australia.[181] In *Roxborough v Rothmans of Pall Mall Australia Ltd*,[182] Gummow J emphasised the equitable nature of money had and received. Unconscionability was treated as a direct descendent of Lord Mansfield's principle of *ex æquo et bono*.[183] English unjust enrichment lawyers have not let the equitable analysis go unchallenged.[184] In part, these differences of opinion may reflect different attitudes towards equity in England and Australia.[185] Unconscionability prompts memories of Lord Mansfield's warning that money had and received should not be stretched too far 'lest I should endanger it',[186] but this approach also has its supporters.[187] Gummow J's judgment has revived interest in *Moses v Macferlan*, but unconscionability may be no closer to the spirit of the decision than the rival unjust enrichment theory.[188]

---

[179] *Pavey and Mathews v Paul* (1987) 162 CLR 221, discussed in D Ibbetson, 'Implied Contracts and Restitution: History in the High Court of Australia' (1988) 8 *OJLS* 312, esp 313 where he describes the 'historical learning' as 'weighty and accurate'. For earlier criticism of the implied contract theory in Australia see *Mason v New South Wales* (1959) 102 CLR 108, 146 (Windeyer J).

[180] *Baumgarter v Baumgarter* (1987) 164 CLR 137, 154 (Toohey J); *Stern v McArthur* (1988) 165 CLR 489, 526–7 (Deane and Dawson JJ); *Baltic Shipping Co v Dillon* (1993) 176 CLR 344, 359 (Mason CJ).

[181] For a summary of the role of unconscionability in Australia see M Bryan, 'Unjust Enrichment and Unconscionability in Australia: A False Dichotomy?' in Neyers (n 175) 47, 56–66; J Getzler, 'Unconscionable Conduct and Unjust Enrichment as Grounds for Judicial Intervention' (1990) 16 *Monash University Law Review* 283. The modern rise of unconscionability is generally associated with the High Court decision in *Commercial Bank of Australia v Amadio* (1983) 151 CLR 447.

[182] (2001) 208 CLR 517. For a discussion of the wider implications of the decision see Cunnington (n 111).

[183] (2001) 208 CLR 517, 545–51.

[184] P Birks, 'Failure of Consideration and its Place on the Map' (2002) *OUCLJ* 1; J Beatson and G Virgo, 'Contract, Unjust Enrichment and Unconscionability' (2002) 118 *LQR* 352; R Grantham, 'Restitutionary Recovery *Ex Æquo et Bono*' [2002] *Sing JLS* 388.

[185] For contrasting views about the ambitions of equity in England and Australia see WMC Gummow, *Change and Continuity* (Oxford, OUP, 1999) Lecture 2; The Hon Justice WMC Gummow, 'Equity—Too Successful?' (2003) 77 *ALJ* 30; A Burrows, 'We Do This at Common Law But That in Equity' (2002) 22 *OJLS* 1. In the context of unjust enrichment see P Birks, 'Equity in the Modern Law: An Exercise in Taxonomy' (1996) 26 *University of Western Australia Law Review* 1.

[186] *Weston v Downes* (1778) 1 Doug 23, 24. For these type of concerns see P Finn, 'Restitution in Australian Law' in P Finn (ed), *Essays on Restitution* (Sydney, Law Book Company, 1990) 20, 37–42; P Birks, 'Equity, Conscience, and Unjust Enrichment' (1999) 23 *Melbourne University Law Review* 1, 17–27; Virgo (n 93) 89–91.

[187] J McConvill and M Bararic, 'The Yoking of Unconscionability and Unjust Enrichment in Australia' (2002) 7 *Deakin Law Review* 225; B Kremer, 'Restitution and Unconscientiousness: Another View' (2003) 119 *LQR* 188.

[188] Faint traces of the same analysis are beginning to appear in England: see *Vedatech Corp v Crystal Decisions (UK) Ltd* [2002] EWHC 818 (Ch) [74].

3

Taylor v Plumer (1815)

LIONEL SMITH*

Si possis recte, si non, quocumque modo rem.

Honestly if possible, if not, somehow, make money.

Horace, *Epistles*

A. INTRODUCTION

THERE IS NOTHING new about fraud. Changes in banking and communications, however, have vastly enlarged the scale upon which fraud can now be committed. One of the tools which the law offers to protect the victims of fraud is tracing. Tracing is the exercise of identifying value in changed forms. This identification is usually attempted in order to permit the assertion of rights in relation to some new form in which the misappropriated value currently inheres. The practical significance of tracing is greatest in two areas. First, in the context of bankruptcy or corporate liquidation, where unsecured creditors are reduced to *pro rata* claims for a portion of the debt owing, tracing can allow a claimant to assert proprietary rights in an asset and thereby to remove it from the pool of assets subject to division among the creditors.[1] Secondly, where property has been misappropriated, tracing can allow a plaintiff to establish rights in relation to assets which have found their way into the hands of recipients who might be entirely innocent.[2]

Taylor v Plumer[3] is generally regarded as one of the root cases in this area of the law. The facts are known in outline to students of tracing. The purpose

---

* Reprinted from (1994) 15 *JLH* 1 with the kind permission of the publisher, Taylor & Francis Group (http://www.tandf.co.uk).
   [1] See eg *Barlow Clowes International Ltd v Vaughan* [1992] 4 All ER 22.
   [2] See *Agip (Africa) Ltd v Jackson* [1991] Ch 547; *Lipkin Gorman v Karpnale Ltd* [1991] 2 AC 548.
   [3] (1815) 3 M & S 562; 2 Rose 457; [1814–23] All ER Rep 167.

of this article is to examine in detail the events that engendered this litigation. This will involve some investigation of the related criminal proceedings, to which little attention has been paid. This sort of examination has its own inherent interest, but in this instance it will also lay the foundation for a more detailed legal analysis of *Taylor v Plumer*. That legal analysis, though, will barely be touched upon in what follows.

The events that led to *Taylor v Plumer* took place over a few days in December 1811. Napoleon's empire was at its height, and British goods were being excluded from Continental trade. The British had responded with a blockade, the zealous enforcement of which would soon lead to the War of 1812 with the United States. Supreme at sea, the British also retained a military foothold on the Continent with their forces in Portugal. By the time judgment was pronounced in *Taylor v Plumer* on 10 February 1815, that foothold would have been used to good advantage. Napoleon would have approached and retreated from Moscow and then been crushed at Leipzig, and his first exile would be just about to end.

George III was king, but the future George III had become Prince Regent in February 1811. The Prime Minister was Spencer Perceval, who would be assassinated in the Commons lobby by a deranged bankrupt in May 1812. Other members of the House of Commons included the Solicitor General, Sir Thomas Plumer, and an obscure stockbroker from Hackney by the name of Benjamin Walsh.[4]

---

[4] The account which follows is drawn from a number of sources. These include contemporary reports in *The Times*, *The Morning Post*, *The Morning Chronicle*, and *The Courier*; reports in the *Gentleman's Magazine* (1811: vol 81, part 2, 582; 1812: vol 82, part 1, 82, 266); the law reports of *R v Walsh* (1812) 4 Taunt 258, 2 Leach 1054, Russ & Ry 215; and the law reports of *Taylor v Plumer* (n 3). There is a record of the evidence given at the criminal proceedings, which was made from shorthand notes: J Sibly, *The Whole Proceedings of the King's Commission of the Peace Oyer and Terminer and Gaol Delivery for the City of London, and also the Gaol Delivery for the County of Middlesex, held at Justice Hall, in the Old Bailey, etc* (London, 1812?) 63–70. A copy of this book is held at the Corporation of London Records Office, Guildhall. It was particularly useful for details of Walsh's activities on the day of his defalcation. The civil proceedings proceeded on a stated case; this must be kept in mind when reading reports of them for facts. There are some inconsistencies among the various accounts, especially regarding dates and certain sums of money. I have tried to produce an edited account, generally favouring sworn evidence over other accounts, but I have not highlighted all of the points where disagreements occur. Many names appear but with a number of different spellings; I have tried to choose the most common spelling for each player in the piece. To avoid clutter, I have not cited a source for every fact in the narrative.

The newspaper accounts consulted are listed here. Within '1808: November', an entry '7: 2a' indicates that there is a relevant report in the edition of 7 November 1808 in the first column on the second page. The same system is used throughout the notes in giving references to newspaper page numbers.

The Times: 1808: November: 7: 2a; 14: 3c; 21: 4c; December: 14: 2d; 19: 3d; 1809: January: 2: 3a; February: 20: 2b; 1811: December: 10: 2e; 11: 3d, 3e (ship news); 13: 3c; 14: 3d; 16: 2a; 17: 3b (letter), 3c; 20: 4a; 1812: January: 20: 2a; 25: 3e (meeting of creditors); 27: 3a; February: 7: 4a (meeting of creditors); 21: 2e; 26: 2a; 28: 2c, 4b (letter and pardon); March: 2: 3b (letter); 3: 3c; 4: 1e; 6: 2c; November: 2: 2c; 1813: May: 10: 2e; December: 23: 2e; 1814: November: 24: 2b; 1815: February: 11: 2b.

B. BENJAMIN WALSH, MP

Although not a party to *Taylor v Plumer*, Benjamin Walsh, MP was the central figure in the story which led to it. In February 1808, at the age of 29, he was returned as one of two members for the riding of Wootton Basset in Wiltshire.[5] It would be suggested later that he bought his seat for £5,000.[6] He was involved in a number of business pursuits, including the selling of 'war insurance', a type of illegal wager under which the insured would be paid if England and France had not made peace by some future date.[7] Like other stockbrokers, he was also involved in the sale of lottery tickets. The practice of the time for the running of the State Lottery was that the Chancellor of the Exchequer received bids from brokers, and the highest bidder would purchase all of the tickets for the next draw.[8] A secondary market developed immediately, and the price of the tickets was quoted in *The Times* along with the price of Bank of England stock.[9] The rickets were treated much like other securities, and were traded through stockbrokers.[10]

At the time of his election to the House of Commons, Walsh was involved in this line of business with a partner, Thomas Nisbet. Their offices were in Angel Court, off Throgmorton Street in London. They were obviously not a great success: on 31 October 1808 they went bankrupt.[11] An arrangement was soon reached with the creditors, however; and the

---

The Morning Post: 1808: November: 7: 4a; 14: 3d; 1809: January: 2: 3b;23: 4b; 30: 3d; February: 20: 2c; 1811: December: 9: 3c; 10: 2b; 11: 3d; 12: 2c; 13: 13d; 14: 2c, 4a; 17: 3c; 18: 3c; 1813: December: 23: 3d; 1814: November: 23: 3e.

The Morning Chronicle: 1811: December: 9: 3a; 11: 2d; 12: 2d; 13: 3c (letter), 3d; 14: 3d; 16: 2a; 17: 3d; 1812: January: 20: 3b; February: 3: 3d; 15: 3d; 20: 3e; 1813: December: 23: 3d.

The Courier: 1909: January: 30: 3c; February: 20: 4b; 1811: December: 10: 3c, 3d (ship news); 11: 2d (ship news), 3b; 12: 2d; 13: 3b; 14: 3d; 17: 4b; 1812: January: 20: 1d; February: 15: 4c; 1813: December: 23: 4a.

[5] RG Thorne, *The History of Parliament: The House of Commons 1790–1820* (London, Secker & Warburg, 1986) vol V, 475; HS Smith, *The Parliaments of England from 1715 to 1847*, 2nd edn revised by FWS Craig (Chichester, Political Reference Publications, 1973) 575; *The Times*, 5 February 1808, 3c. I cannot be sure of Walsh's birth date but he was 33 on 18 January 1812: Sibly (n 4) 70.

[6] Thorne (n 5) 475; 21 *Parliamentary Debates* 1188 (Sir Francis Burdett). See also a report of the proceedings at Walsh's first bankruptcy in the *Morning Post*, 23 January 1809, 4b, where an adjournment was proposed by counsel for the creditors on the ground that 'he had some enquiries to make, connected with Mr Walsh's seat in Parliament, which, if his instructions were correct, might interfere with his retention of it'.

[7] See *Aubert v Walsh* (1810) 3 Taunt 277 (cited in *Lipkin Gorman* (n 2) 564); *Busk v Walsh* (1812) 4 Taunt 290; *Aubert v Walsh* (1812) 4 Taunt 293.

[8] See *The Times*, 22 September 1808, 3a; 14 January 1809, 2d; 16 January 1809, 3d.

[9] See eg *The Times*, 20 January 1809, 4d.

[10] See eg the advertisement by Hazard, Burne & Co in *The Times*, 1 February 1809, 1a, and that by T Bish in *The Times*, 15 October 181, 1c.

[11] See the *London Gazette* (1808) 1498. The partnership had made an unsuccessful bid on the most recent lottery: see *The Times*, 22 September 1808, 3a.

commission of bankruptcy was superseded in February 1809, contemporaneously with the dissolution of the partnership.[12] Before long, Walsh was back in Angel Court. He was expelled from the Stock Exchange by its governing committee on 22 February 1809, for 'nefarious conduct';[13] but in any event, he was working as a stockbroker in 1811, and selling lottery tickets too.[14]

In November of that year, Walsh's financial position was dire. Married in 1803,[15] he and his wife now had seven children, and number eight was imminent. His 'commission business' was not producing the income he had expected,[16] and several debts to his family and friends weighed heavily on him. He especially blamed a competitor by the name of T Bish for his predicament.[17] Bish's name crops up frequently in the newspapers in connection with the State Lottery, both as a bidder[18] and as a ticket broker.[19] He had proved as a creditor in Walsh's 1808 bankruptcy, and at that time seems to have alleged that Walsh was guilty of fraudulent practices.[20] It was these allegations that led to Walsh's censure by the Committee of the Stock exchange.[21]

Walsh had applied repeatedly to the Prime Minister for a 'situation under Government', offering 'to leave his home, his dear wife, and children; and to meet the dangers and difficulties of the worst of foreign climates';[22] but Perceval had stopped answering his letters. At any rate, Walsh came to the conclusion that desperate measures were necessary to keep his wife and children from poverty, and he formed a plan to defraud one of his clients and abscond to the United States. The client he chose was one Oldham, a man, according to Walsh, whose 'mercenary disposition would have induced no one to regret his loss'.[23] Oldham had led Walsh to believe that

---

[12] *London Gazette* (1809) 217, 220.

[13] See the letter from T Bish in the *Morning Post,* 11 December 1811, 3d; and see also 21 *Parliamentary Debates* 1188.

[14] See *The Times,* 10 May 1813, 2e. This is a report of a case in which Walsh's assignees in bankruptcy for his second bankruptcy—the same plaintiffs as in *Taylor v Plumer*—attempted unsuccessfully to recover the value of Walsh's work in selling lottery tickets from the authority running the City Lottery.

[15] 73 *Gentleman's Magazine* 282.

[16] See the letter from Walsh to his brother Joseph, written shortly after Walsh's defalcation and reproduced in 21 *Parliamentary Debates* 940–3, and in *The Times,* 2 March 1812, 3b.

[17] In another letter to his brother, Walsh said that but for the 'arch fiend' Bish, he and his family 'might at that time have been in affluence and happiness': *The Times,* 13 December 1811, 3c.

[18] See eg *The Times,* 4 November 1809, 2d; 21 June 1810, 3b; 2 March 1811, 3b.

[19] See eg *The Times,* 9 November 1808, 3d; 15 October 1810, 1c. His advertisements can be found in all of the other papers of the time as well. He is referred to as a seller of lottery tickets in a book of satirical poetry: Francis Moore, *The Age of Intellect* (London, 1819) 163.

[20] See the *Morning Post,* 14 November 1808, 3d; 2 January 1809, 3b.

[21] Letter from Bish, *Morning Post,* 11 December 1811, 3d; and see another letter from Bish in the *Morning Chronicle,* 13 December 1811, 3c, asserting that he was 'the first to detect and expose Mr W in 1808'.

[22] See *The Times,* 13 December 1811, 3c–d.

[23] See Walsh's letter to his brother (n 16).

he would soon be giving Walsh a large amount of money to buy stock. In the meantime, Walsh continued to carry on his business. Another of his customers was the Solicitor-General, Sir Thomas Plumer, KC.

C. SIR THOMAS PLUMER, KC

Thomas Plumer was born in 1753. He matriculated at University College, Oxford in 1771, and became a fellow in 1780. He took his BA in 1775, his MA in 1778, and his BCL in 1783. He had entered Lincoln's Inn in 1769, was admitted to chambers in 1775, and was called to the Bar in 1778. He took silk in 1793 and became a Bencher that same year. With the formation of the Duke of Portland's government in 1807, Plumer was elected to the House of Commons for Downtown in Wiltshire, knighted, and made Solicitor-General. He would go on to be Attorney-General,[24] the first Vice-Chancellor of England,[25] a Privy Councillor,[26] and the Master of the Rolls from 1818 until his death in 1824.[27]

Plumer's family had long been acquaintances of Walsh's, and Plumer had employed Walsh as his stockbroker for some years. In August 1811, Plumer contracted to buy Canons, an estate in Middlesex.[28] He thought that he would need the purchase price by Michaelmas,[29] and he consulted Walsh as to the wisdom of selling certain Bank of England stocks to raise the money. The stock comprised annuities paying three and four per cent; its value fluctuated based on the prevailing interest rates. Walsh advised him to wait as long as possible, as he thought that the price of the stock was likely to rise. Plumer did wait, and asked Walsh to keep him informed of changes in the market. There was then some difficulty on the part of the vendor in perfecting title to the estate, and so the money was not needed for Michaelmas.

In October, Plumer thought that the deed would be ready by Christmas, and he asked Walsh again about the wisdom of selling stock. The prices of the annuities had risen somewhat, but Walsh thought that they would rise still more, since the Commissioners for Liquidating the National Debt would be buying up stock in November. Toward the end of November,

---

[24] In 1812.

[25] From 1813 to 1818, under the statute 53 Geo III, c 24.

[26] From 1813.

[27] Sir L Stephen and Sir S Lee (eds), *Dictionary of National Biography* vol XV (London, Smith, Elder & Co, 1917) 1318; E Foss, *The Judges of England* vol IX (London, John Murray, 1864) 32–6.

[28] Although none of the contemporary accounts mentions the name of the estate, Foss (n 27) records that in 1811 Plumer purchased Canons, the former seat of the Duke of Chandos near Edgware. What remains of the house is now a school, accessible from Canons Park station on the Jubilee Line. See A Saunders, *The Art and Architecture of London* (2nd edn, Oxford, Phaidon, 1988) 264–5. Plumer's widow died at Canons on 26 November 1857: (1858) 4 *Gentleman's Magazine* (NS) 114.

[29] Ie, 29 September.

though, Walsh advised Plumer to sell out. His reasons were apparently honest: the transfer books at the Bank of England would be closed from 3 December until 7 January, and Plumer would be needing the money soon. Also, Walsh honestly thought that the value of the stock was now likely to fall. Plumer consulted a 'commercial gentleman' as to his opinion on the matter, and he agreed with Walsh.

On Thursday 28 November, Plumer authorised Walsh to sell a block of stock: four per cent stock with a face value of £13,000, and three per cent stock with a face value of £18,600. On 29 November Walsh effected a contract of sale, obtaining a price of £21,774 5s. Walsh told Plumer that the transaction would have to be completed on 4 or 5 December; that is, Plumer would transfer the stock and the purchaser would pay the price. Plumer said that 4 December would be convenient.

D. THE BREACH OF TRUST

On 29 November, pursuant to his dishonest plan, Walsh arranged to buy £11,000 worth of US government securities from the broker Dennis De Berdt, agreeing to pay on 4 December. On Monday 2 December, he arranged to buy Portuguese gold coins from Joseph Fearn, a jeweller. He was apparently still intending to pay for these purchases with Oldham's money.[30] On 3 or 4 December he booked a place on the mail coach to Falmouth, to leave on the afternoon of Thursday 5 December. He made this booking under the name of Willis. In those days, Falmouth was a very important port; it was the centre for the Post Office's packet service. Packets were small, fast ships of about two hundred tons, which carried mail and passengers to various destinations. Walsh intended to travel to Lisbon on the packet *Lady Arabella*,[31] and thence to the US.

On Tuesday 3 December, however, Oldham gave Walsh about £1,500 to invest in stock. This was far less than Walsh had expected, and far less than he needed; so in fact he applied Oldham's money properly. But Walsh must have decided straight away that he would use Plumer's money for his scheme. The next day, Wednesday 4 December, he called at De Berdt's office; but instead of paying for the US stock as had been arranged, Walsh told De Berdt that if De Berdt would call at Walsh's office the next day, he would be able to pay for the stock in bank of England notes. Also on Wednesday, Walsh told Fearn that he would want the Portuguese gold on Thursday.

---

[30] The date and amount of Oldham's payment do not appear in the contemporary newspaper accounts, and in only some of the law reports of *R v Walsh*: see 2 Leach 1059; 4 Taunt 260.

[31] See *The Times,* 11 December 1811, 3e: 'Ship News'.

That Wednesday afternoon, Plumer called at Walsh's office and effected the transfer of his stock to his buyer. On Walsh's advice, Plumer decided to invest the proceeds in Exchequer bills, which were more liquid and less volatile than the stock which had just been sold, and which would be more profitable than a bank deposit. Walsh told him, however, that it was too late to get them that day. They agreed that Walsh would receive the sale price from the buyer, pay it into Plumer's bank account, and call upon Plumer the next day to buy the Exchequer bills for him. Walsh obtained the price and paid it into his own bank; he then paid £21,500 into Plumer's account at Plumer's bank, Goslings and Sharp.[32]

Walsh's brother Joseph had been pressing him about a debt of £1,199; Joseph needed the money to pay for a lease on Friday 6 December. The brothers had dinner together on Wednesday night, and Benjamin assured Joseph that he would pay him the next day.

Thursday 5 December 1811 was a busy day for Benjamin Walsh, MP. He left his home in Hackney with necessaries for his journey, having told his wife and family that he was going to Ireland for a few days. He had a travelling greatcoat and a portmanteau, which he had packed so well that he would soon write a letter to his wife to account to her for linen that she might miss. The Hackney stage stopped outside the shop of James Webb, a hosier in Threadneedle Street, just around the corner from Walsh's office in Angel Court. Walsh alighted, entered the shop, and asked Webb whether he might leave his portmanteau and his great coat there until the evening; no doubt he did not want to be seen with these items during the course of the day.

At about 11 o'clock, Walsh called on Plumer at his chambers at No 19 Old Square, in Lincoln's Inn.[33] Plumer gave him a cheque for £22,200, with which Walsh was to buy Exchequer bills.[34] The bills were to be delivered to Plumer, or lodged on his account at Goslings. Walsh agreed to call back at about 4 o'clock.

Walsh proceeded to Goslings and cashed the cheque into Bank of England notes: 22 for £1,000 each and one for £200. Calling on a broker named William Harmon, he gave him eight of the £1,000 notes in exchange

[32] Although there is a discrepancy between the sale price (£21,774 5s) and the amount paid by Walsh into Plumer's account (£21,500), nothing is made of it in the reports. Plumer referred to it in his evidence at Walsh's criminal trial, but not in a way that suggested that he disapproved: Sibly (n 4) 65. Perhaps the difference was a commission or was to settle an earlier debt.

[33] J Wilson, *A Biographical Index to the Present House of Commons* (2nd edn, London, T Goddard, 1808) 193. Apparently Walsh's 'election' came too late for him to have an entry in this book.

[34] In some accounts the cheque is referred to as a 'draft', but it is clear that it was what we would today call a cheque. It was an order by Plumer to his bank to pay money to Walsh's order. It appears that in the idiom of the time, 'draft' was synonymous with 'bill of exchange': W Blackstone, *Commentaries on the Laws of England* vol II (Oxford, 1766; facsimile edn: Chicago, Ill, University of Chicago Press, 1979) 467.

for £6,500 worth of Exchequer bills[35] and £1,500 worth of 'India bonds'. He lodged the Exchequer bills at Goslings on Plumer's account. Shortly after noon, De Berdt called on Walsh about the US stock, and Walsh paid for it with eleven of the £1,000 notes. So nineteen of these notes were expended. He gave another to his clerk, Henry Atwright, asking him to get change at the Bank of England around the corner; the change was given to Walsh between noon and one o'clock, and he directed Atwright to remit some of the notes to a customer in the country, on account of stock sold.

Walsh's next caller was his brother, Joseph; as they had agreed the night before, Walsh paid his debt of £1,199 11s 7d, using another of the £1,000 notes and writing a cheque for the rest. He also gave his brother the £1,500 in India bonds, which related somehow to their father's estate.[36] Ironically, Joseph Walsh immediately sent his clerk to deposit these items at Goslings bank. The last £1,000 note was given to Thomas Clarke, the brother of Walsh's wife Mary. Clarke gave back cheques for £500 and £100, keeping the balance apparently for certain 'family purposes' which Walsh had asked him to attend to.

Joseph Fearn sent his clerk to call on Walsh to see exactly how much Portuguese gold Walsh wanted; Walsh sent back that he wanted £500 worth, giving the clerk the £500 cheque from Thomas Clarke. Fearn made up a parcel of £500 worth of gold coin; but, perhaps because he had distributed more money than he had foreseen, Walsh called on Fearn about half an hour later, and reduced his order to £300. Fearn gave him 71 and a half Portuguese doubloons with a value of £302 9s, and wrote Walsh a cheque for his change.

De Berdt delivered the US stock in the afternoon; the price was £10,018 10 s 6d, and he gave Walsh a cheque for the difference from the £11,000 he had paid. He advised Walsh to call on him the next day with a notary to register the stock, but Walsh put him off, saying that he was going out of town for a few days. Finally, Walsh gave his clerk, Atwright, an Exchequer

---

[35] Although all of the law reports give this figure, Plumer testified (in his evidence before the Bow Street magistrates after Walsh's arrest) that Walsh accounted for £6,645 18s 6d: *The Times*, 13 December 1811, 3c. The higher figure also accords better with the idea that Walsh cheated Plumer out of £15,500; that is the amount which Walsh confessed to having taken in various letters, and that is the number in the documents which Walsh executed at Falmouth for Plumer's attorney. It seems likely that the Exchequer bills were bought at more than face value, perhaps because there was accrued interest; they are referred to as having been bought at a 'premium' of 5s: see eg the *Morning Post*, 14 December 1811, 2c. Support for this also comes from Harmon's evidence at Walsh's criminal trial (Sibly (n 4) 66) to the effect that Walsh gave him £8,000 in Bank of England notes *and* a cheque for £171 9s.

[36] This does not come out in the newspaper accounts of the trial, but see Sibly (n 4) 67–8. Also *The Times* of 3 November 1812, 2c, gives an account of *Taylor v Walsh* in which Walsh's assignees successfully sued Joseph Walsh for the money and India bonds received from Benjamin Walsh on 5 December 1811, claiming that the payments were a fraudulent preference (that is, an illegal attempt to spare Joseph Walsh from having to prove in the bankruptcy like all other creditors).

bill worth about £300, in payment of a debt owed by Walsh to Atwright's father.

It only remained to face Plumer. Walsh called at Lincoln's Inn again at about 4:30 pm, appearing 'flurried and out of breath'.[37] Walsh gave Plumer a receipt from Goslings for the £6,500 worth of Exchequer bills that had been lodged there, and he concocted a story to account for the rest. He said that he had purchased another £15,500 worth of bills from the bankers, Coutts & Co; but the bills could not be delivered as they were locked up in the desk of Mr Trotter, a partner at Coutts & Co, who was out of town.[38] Walsh said he had arranged for the bills to be delivered on Saturday afternoon. In the meantime, he said, Plumer's £15,500 had been lodged in his account at Goslings, but the bills would earn interest from Thursday. They agreed that Walsh would call on Saturday for another cheque, with which to pay for the rest of the bills.[39]

But of course, that was not Walsh's plan. He returned to Webb's shop at about six o'clock, and purchased a dozen pairs of socks, four night caps and two pairs of gloves; and he asked Webb to have his portmanteau sent around to Angel Court. From there, Walsh proceeded to the Falmouth mail coach, which would travel through Exeter and arrive in Falmouth on Saturday. The next day, Friday 6 December, he posed several letters from Exeter. One was addressed to himself in London, but intended for his clerk; he confessed what he had done, and enclosed a letter to Plumer which the clerk was to bring to Plumer on Saturday. This letter said that Trotter had been delayed, and the Exchequer bills could not be delivered until Monday; and so, Walsh would call then. It was intended to give Walsh more breathing space before any pursuit. He also wrote to his brother Joseph.[40] He said that he had acted out of concern for his wife and children, and begged his brother to take care of them. He explained that his original intention had been to take from Oldham, but that this had not been possible, while the chance to take from Plumer had fallen into his lap:

> ... I saw that it was impossible for me to provide the means, and there was no chance of saving myself from ruin, and my dear wife and children from poverty, and my brothers and sisters from loss by me, which they could ill afford, but to

---

[37] According to Plumer's testimony at Walsh's trial: *The Times*, 20 January 1812, 2c.

[38] In fact, there was such a partner, and he was out of town; but of course there had been no such purchase. See the evidence of John Wilkinson, Coutts' clerk, reported in the *Morning Post*, 14 December 1811, 2d.

[39] An alternative version of what Walsh said appeared in several early accounts in the newspapers (*The Times*, 11 December 1811, 3d; *Morning Chronicle*, 12 December 1811, 2d; *The Courier*, 11 December 1811, 3b; *Morning Post*, 12 December 1811, 2c). In this story, Walsh had paid his own cheque (drawn on Walsh's bank, Curtis & Co) for £15,500 into Plumer's account at Goslings, and then this cheque was dishonoured the next day (Friday 6 December); but this is inconsistent with all later accounts, including evidence that Plumer would give.

[40] Above n 16.

pursue a step, which though it will bring disgrace on my name, yet will afford me the means of preventing these dreadful calamities ...

He has ever been a kind friend to me, and I fear the act will add ingratitude to the crime; but I had no other chance, and the die is now cast.—Oh! My God, pardon my heinous offence.—Sir Thomas Plumer employed me to sell a large sum of stock to pay for an estate, and I have withheld a part of the proceeds. I might have taken it all; but I thought it crime enough for my future life to answer for, to take what I conceived would be sufficient to maintain my family in competence, and pay those debts which hung the heaviest on my mind.—I have already remitted it abroad; and though my person is safe from arrest, yet I have resolved to follow it, as I can never live in this country without shame and dishonour.

It has been a heart-breaking struggle to leave you all; and I know I shall cause you great affliction, where I would bestow nothing but happiness.—What will my poor Mary say, if she hears it in her present state?—She thinks me gone to Ireland; and there is a hope it may be concealed from her till after her confinement, which she expects in about a week, if it should not get into the newspapers; though it may be possible that sir T. P. may not make it public at all—at all events it cannot be known till the beginning of next week.[41]

The letter goes on at great length, in the same tone throughout. Walsh enclosed three letters, purporting to be from Dublin, for his wife Mary, asking his brother to arrange for their delivery. He hoped that they would 'carry Mary over the first part of her confinement', which actually began on Saturday 7 December.[42]

The mail coach carried on to Falmouth. Walsh's discomfort is illustrated by the following report of the journey:[43]

The steward of the mail-coach says, that at every stage where he had to wait for a change of horses or refreshment, he walked up and down the road under apparent agitation; and, in some instances, to expedite the journey, he paid for all the passengers' meals.

The coach arrived in Falmouth on Saturday evening, and Walsh secured his passage to Lisbon on the *Lady Arabella*. Unfortunately for him, it was detained by contrary winds. He took a room at Wynn's Royal Hotel,[44] and

[41] *Ibid* 941–2; paragraph breaks have been inserted for readability.

[42] See Walsh's testimony at the trial of *Taylor v Plumer*, *The Times*, 23 December 1813, 3a.

[43] Letter to *The Times*, from an anonymous correspondent in Falmouth, 13 December 1811, 3a. This letter appears in other newspapers in slightly different forms: *Morning Chronicle*, 13 December 1811, 3c; *Courier*, 13 December 1811, 3b; *Morning Post*, 14 December 1811, 4a.

[44] The letter referred to in the last note, as it is printed in *the Times*, the *Morning Post* and the *Courier*, purports to be from the 'Vine-Inn', but this must be an error. In the *Morning Chronicle*, the same letter is shown to be from Wynn's Hotel; and another story in the *Morning Post* (14 December 1811, 2c) refers to Wynn's Inn. In J Lake, *A Falmouth Guide* (Falmouth, J Lake, 1815) 76, Wynn's Royal Hotel is listed as the best in town, and as the terminus of the London mail; there is no 'Vine-Inn' listed.

wrote again to his brother. He wrote as well to Plumer, confessing his crime and imploring him to forgive. He promised to repay the money if ever he could, and he tried to explain how he had been driven to his actions. Apparently, he was very sure of his escape. On Sunday, he went to church, and heard 'an *appropriate* sermon'.[45]

But Plumer was no fool. Immediately upon Wash's leaving him on Thursday afternoon, he noticed that while he had a receipt from Goslings for the £6,500 in Exchequer bills, there was no receipt for the £1,500 which Walsh claimed to have deposited there.[46] He strolled down Chancery Lane to Goslings in Fleet Street, where he was told that no such money had been deposited. The next day, Friday 6 December, he called at Walsh's office, only to be told that he was out. On Saturday, he went to Walsh's home in Hackney, where Mary Walsh told him that Walsh had gone to Ireland on business.

Plumer acted quickly. It is reported that he applied to the Admiralty to contact the out-ports by telegraph, but whether because this application was refused or because telegraphy was not sufficiently effective, nothing seems to have come of this step.[47] Plumer also applied to the Post Office to intercept any letters in Walsh's handwriting that might come into its possession. This measure proved fruitful: Walsh's letters from Exeter, which presumably had been sent only the day before, were found, and upon Plumer's swearing that the handwriting was Walsh's, they were opened.[48] Walsh's letters from Falmouth would be caught in the same manner.

Plumer also applied to Mr Nares, one of the Bow Street magistrates; and Mr Adkins, a Bow Street officer, was put on the case.[49] He traced Walsh's movements of 5 December, and finally spoke to a porter who told how Walsh had asked him, in the hearing of others, to take his portmanteau to the Saracen's Head, but, when they had gone part of the way, redirected him to the Swan With Two Necks, whence the Exeter mail departed. The porter also noticed that although this gentleman was travelling under the name of

---

[45] *The Times*, 13 December 1811, 3a.

[46] Roughly speaking, the £15,500 which Walsh tried to misappropriate had about the same purchasing power as £350,000 had in January 1993: see the graph in *The Economist*, vol 322, no 7747, 22 February 1992, 88. I am grateful to Mr Nick Wiseman of the Research Department at *The Economist* for providing and updating the data upon which this graph is based.

[47] The means of telegraphy would likely have been the 'shutter telegraph', established in 1795 by George Murray for the Admiralty: *The New Encyclopaedia Britannica* (15th edn, Chicago and London, Helen Hemingway Benton, 1974) Macropedia vol 18, 67.

[48] It is not clear whether permission to open these letters was granted by the Post Office or by one of the magistrates whom Plumer contacted that day. Sir Samuel Romilly considered the interception to be improper: *Memoirs of the Life of Sir Samuel Romilly* (London, John Murray, 1840) vol III, 15–16; but he added a footnote to his diary, 'I have since been informed that this letter was not intercepted at the post office, but that it was obtained by some other surreptitious means.'

[49] *Morning Post*, 14 December 1811, 2c.

Willis,[50] the name of Walsh was on a brass plate affixed to his portmanteau. Adkins reported his findings to Plumer:[51]

> who, knowing there had nearly two days and two nights elapsed since his departure, hurried ADKINS into a chaise and four, not allowing him to wait for a warrant, only sending MR JENKINS, his Solicitor, with him, to identify his person. They traced him all the way on the road in the Exeter Mail to that City, where they found he had taken his place on to Falmouth, where they arrived at four o'clock on Monday morning, in the short space of time of 35 hours from their starting from London.

The story of Walsh's defalcation first appeared in the London press on the same day that Adkins and Jenkins arrived in Falmouth. Presumably out of prudence, the early accounts did not mention Walsh by name; but there were some fairly broad hints:[52]

> WAYS AND MEANS.—A member of parliament, formerly of lottery celebrity, has lately resorted to a very singular *scheme* for raising WAYS AND MEANS. He received 22,000*l.* from Sir T.P. an eminent Law Officer, for the purpose of laying it out in Exchequer Bills; 6,000*l.* of which he only disposed of in this way, the remaining 16,000*l.* he gave notice had been placed in the hands of Sir T. P.'s banker, as he was unable to make further purchases. On enquiry, however, it was found that the *worthy member* had not *represented* the fact; and on endeavouring to procure an *explanation, he was not to be found in his place.*

Another paper initially reported the incident as a misunderstanding, caused by a clerical error.[53] The first account in *The Times* appeared on Tuesday 10 December:[54]

> Some persons doubt whether the law authorizes the arrest or detention of a Member of Parliament under the circumstances in question; but, it is supposed, that, if Adkins meets with the fugitive, he will treat him in the same manner as he would any other individual.

The matter of immunity from arrest seems to have raised some concerns:[55]

> Among the various plans suggested for laying hold of the *Honourable Member* that has absconded with a great Law Officer's money, is a Call of the House, when it meets, then if he did not attend, the Serjeant at Arms might be ordered to take him into custody.

---

[50] Some reports give 'Wallis'.
[51] *Morning Post*, 14 December 1811, 2c. The distance from London to Falmouth is about 300 miles by road.
[52] *Morning Chronicle*, 9 December 1811, 3a.
[53] *Morning Post*, 9 December 1811, 3c.
[54] At 2e.
[55] *Morning Chronicle*, 11 December 1811, 2d.

In the result, however, the issue never had to be decided. When Adkins and Jenkins arrived on Monday morning, Walsh was still at Wynn's Royal Hotel, waiting for the winds to change. Jenkins confronted him as he was eating his breakfast:[56]

> saying, as he supposed he must suspect that his business there and with him, was his running away with a considerable sum belonging to the SOLICITOR-GENERAL, which MR WALSH now acknowledged to be true.

Walsh made no resistance and surrendered the US stock and gold to Jenkins, and agreed to return to London with Jenkins and Adkins. He would later allege that Jenkins told him that if he yielded up the stock and the gold, no steps would be taken against him and something would be done for his family.[57] Jenkins would deny this; his version was that he told Walsh that no favour would be shown to him as he deserved none. Jenkins conceded that when Walsh expressed a hope that Plumer might do something for Walsh's family, he replied that he might.

At any rate, Jenkins had come to Falmouth well prepared. He had Walsh execute a number of documents, each of which was witnessed by Jenkins and by Adkins. Walsh executed (i) a deed assigning the stock and bullion to Plumer in trust to pay himself a debt of £15,500; (ii) a conditioned bond to pay a penalty of £31,000, conditioned on the payment of £15,500 to Plumer; and (iii) a power of attorney for confessing judgment on the bond. On the evening of Monday 9 December, the three left for London, arriving at about 5:30 pm on Thursday 12 December; 'they came deliberately to town to give time to SIR THOMAS PLUMER, to arrange what was to be done on their arrival'.[58]

E. THE AFTERMATH

Walsh soon found out what Plumer had arranged. As soon as Plumer learned that the travellers had arrived from Falmouth, he told Adkins to take Walsh to Bow Street. At 8:30 pm on 12 December 1811, Walsh was taken before the magistrate, where the examination was begun which would lead to his committal for trial. Walsh claimed to be astonished, as the three had travelled companionably from Falmouth and he had not considered himself to be in custody. Plumer was the first to be sworn. Jenkins gave evidence as well, and he produced the stock and gold that had been taken

---

[56] *Morning Post*, 14 December 1811, 2c. At Walsh's trial, Jenkins testified that he said (Sibly (n 4) 70): 'I am now come to desire restitution of such property as you have with you.'

[57] See the letter which Walsh wrote to a friend from Tothill-fields Prison: *The Times*, 17 December 1811, 3b; *Morning Post*, 17 December 1811, 3c.

[58] *Morning Post*, 14 December 1811, 2c.

from Walsh at Falmouth. Walsh spent the night in Tothill-fields Prison. The examination continued the next afternoon:[59]

> ... at a quarter before one o'clock, Mr Walsh was put to the bar, when he conducted himself exactly as he did on Thursday evening, hiding his face with his hands, &c. A chair was allowed him again. His sensibility was so strong, that it was thought he would have fainted, but he gave vent to his feelings by a strong cry, when he was much better.

Evidence was given by the jeweller, Joseph Fearn, and by a number of clerks and stockbrokers, including Dennis De Berdt. The examination was completed on Monday 16 December, when Walsh 'was allowed a chair and covered his face with his hands as usual'.[60] More evidence was taken, and Walsh was committed for trial. He was sent to Newgate Prison.

Not surprisingly, Walsh's flight was adjudged an act of bankruptcy. A commission of bankruptcy was issued on 10 December, and the first meeting of the creditors took place at Guildhall on 21 December.[61] At this meeting, the creditors would have chosen the assignees in bankruptcy, whose duty it was to liquidate all of Walsh's assets for the benefit of his creditors. It would be those assignees—Taylor, and another man whose name does not appear—who would later bring an action in trover against Sir Thomas Plumer, claiming the value of the US stock and the gold that was seized from Walsh at Falmouth.

F. THE CRIMINAL PROCEEDINGS: *R v WALSH*[62]

Walsh's trial took place on 18 January 1812, at the Old Bailey. It did not pass unnoticed:[63]

> Few trials have excited so much public interest as the one which is the subject of the subsequent detail. So early as eight o'clock the avenues, and vicinity of the Sessions House, were thronged with people of the most respectable appearance, eager to gain admission to the Court ...

> The melancholy appearance of the prisoner, the consideration of his situation and rank in society, the solemn gravity of the bench, on which sat the Learned Judges above-mentioned, the chief Magistrate of the City, a considerable number of Aldermen, all attired in their scarlet robes, the crowded but respectable auditory which filled every part of the Court, were all circumstances which imposed upon feeling minds, sensations that could only be justly appreciated by those who were present on this solemn occasion.

[59] *Morning Post*, 14 December 1811, 2d.
[60] *The Times*, 17 December 1811, 3c.
[61] *Ibid*, 4a.
[62] (1812) 4 Taunt 258; 2 Leach 1054; Russ & Ry 215.
[63] *Morning Chronicle*, 20 January 1812, 3b.

Walsh was tried on an indictment containing seven counts, which were framed under a statute governing prosecutions for the theft of bank notes, bills of exchange, and the like.[64] In essence, he was charged with stealing the Bank of England notes for £22,200 which he had obtained with the cheque Plumer had given him; alternatively, with stealing that cheque. The case was heard by Macdonald CB of the Exchequer and Le Blanc J of the Court of King's Bench. Walsh's counsel, Messrs Scarlett and Alley, did not dispute the prosecution's account of the essential facts, which were proved through a large number of witnesses and by the production of the seized gold and stock and twenty-two £1,000 notes. They did, however, desire to take issue on a point of law, namely whether the facts amounted to stealing under the statute.

As far as the cheque was concerned, they argued that in order for an instrument to be within the statute, it had to be of value in the hands of the alleged victim of the theft. A cheque did not qualify, because it did not create or represent a debt. In other words, if Walsh had torn up the cheque, Plumer would have lost nothing. They also argued that since Walsh used part of the cheque as he was supposed to use the whole of it—for the purchase of Exchequer bills—he could not be convicted unless misapplication of *part* of a cheque could be deemed to be theft of the whole.

The main argument with respect to the first count was that the bank notes were never the property of Plumer. Since there were no specific instructions as to what Walsh was to do with the cheque (for example, whether to cash it at Goslings or at Walsh's bank), the notes were not Plumer's when they were received by Walsh; rather, they were Walsh's, and while he was accordingly accountable to Plumer, he could not be said to have stolen Plumer's money.[65] It was also argued that there was no fraudulent 'taking' of the notes—an essential element in a charge of theft—as Plumer intended Walsh to have them and never expected to have them back:[66]

> This created a debt, and nothing but a debt, between [Walsh] and the prosecutor. Supposing for a moment, that these notes had ever been in the possession, as the property, of the prosecutor, it was no part of the contract that he should receive either the whole or any part of them back; he had no such expectation; but he expected to receive a different species of property in lieu of them, namely,

---

[64] 2 Geo III, c 25, s 3. The original records of the counts may be seen at the Corporation of London Records Office, Guildhall, in the bound minute book (SFG 216) *London Sessions of Gaol Delivery of Oyer and Terminer*, November 1809–October 1813, 333.

[65] It seems that Walsh had thought of this argument before the trial ever began: during his examination before the Bow Street magistrates, it was reported that 'MR WALSH acknowledges himself the debtor of SIR THOMAS PLUMER to the amount of the sum which he carried off; but it is probable that a somewhat different construction may be put upon the transaction by the SOLICITOR GENERAL': *Morning Post*, 13 December 1811, 3d.

[66] 2 Leach 1063. The paragraph break has been added for readability. This is actually a report of Scarlett's argument at the appeal, but the same points were made at the trial.

Exchequer bills. ... [If] he had brought an action of trover to recover [the bank notes] identically, no conversion could, under the circumstances of this case, be proved; and if there be no conversion there can be no felony.

But in truth the property of these identical notes never vested in the prosecutor, or could in any way become his property. They were received in payment of the check, and it was not in the contemplation of either of the parties, that they were to be brought back by the prisoner to the prosecutor.

Mr Garrow, for the Crown, stated that he was not prepared to make submissions on these legal arguments, and he suggested that the matter should be resolved at a higher level.

Alley, for the prisoner, indicated that he was anxious that no verdict of guilty should be returned, as then a pardon would be required if the appeal were successful. Macdonald CB could have taken a special verdict from the jury, by which they would decide essential issues of fact without pronouncing a general verdict of guilty or not guilty; and then the legal points could have been argued on appeal. But apparently it was decided that the appeal process would be faster if a general verdict were taken.[67] The jury were directed that if they found that Walsh had a fraudulent intention when he received the cheque, they should return a verdict of guilty; and Walsh was found guilty on all counts.[68] Walsh was thus a convicted felon, but no judgment was pronounced by the Court pending an appeal to the twelve judges.[69] He was sent to Newgate Prison. Eight days later, as the next step in the bankruptcy proceedings, he made a formal surrender to his creditors at the prison.[70]

The appeal was heard in two parts. On 1 February, argument began in the Exchequer Chamber before eleven judges. From the King's Bench, there

[67] *The Times*, 20 January 1812, 2d; *Morning Chronicle*, 20 January 1812, 3d. The accounts say that it was agreed to take a special verdict; but then in Macdonald CB's address to the jury, he implies that it had been decided to take a general verdict after all, as the other route 'would be attended with much greater suspense and embarrassment to the prisoner'. Further confirmation of the idea that this route was taken to speed up the process is found in the debate on the expulsion of Walsh from the House of Commons. Two members expressed the view that it was faster to take a general verdict and then appeal the point of law to the twelve judges; if a special verdict was taken, the appeal was to the King's Bench and thence to the House of Lords with the advice of the judges: see 21 *Parliamentary Debates* 1192 (Mr Abercromby) and 1197 (the Attorney General).
[68] The record of the conviction is reproduced in 21 *Parliamentary Debates* 934–9. The original is at the Corporation of London Records Office, Guildhall, SFG 216, No 19 (three sheets).
[69] That is, all of the judges of the King's Bench and the Common Pleas, and the Barons of the Exchequer. This was not formally an appeal because the jury had convicted Walsh and there remained nothing for the Court to do except pronounce judgment accordingly. Furthermore the argument before the twelve judges was technically not even a procedure in court, but simply an informal discussion. But this procedure had become part of criminal practice, and where the twelve judges felt that the conviction was incorrect, a pardon would be recommended. See JH Baker, *An Introduction to English Legal History* (3rd edn, London, Butterworths, 1990) 160, 590, 595–6.
[70] *The Times*, 27 January 1812, 3a.

was Lord Ellenborough CJ and Grose, Le Blanc and Bayley JJ; from the Exchequer, Macdonald CB and Graham, Wood and Thomson BB; and from the Common Pleas, Mansfield LCJ and Heath and Chambre JJ.[71] Lawrence J was absent from indisposition. Scarlett made his arguments on behalf of Walsh, and Mr Gurney commenced his submissions for the Crown. The argument was completed after Hilary Term, on 14 February, at Serjeant's-Inn-Hall. On this day, Lawrence J was absent again, and so too was Chambre J. Gurney completed his submissions, and Scarlett made his reply. The judges retired to consider the matter.

No judgment was pronounced that day, or ever. There was some suggestion that a public judgment would be pronounced at the next sessions at the Old Bailey;[72] and there was some excitement when those sessions began a few days later.[73] But in fact the case had already been decided. On 15 February, Macdonald CB wrote to the Home Secretary, Richard Ryder, in the following terms:[74]

> Sir,
>
> I have the honour to acquaint you, for the information of His Royal Highness the Prince Regent, that Benjamin Walsh was indicted before me at the last Session holden at the Old Bailey, for Stealing from Sir Thomas Plumer, a certain order for the payment of 22,000£, and also Stealing Bank Notes to that Amount—
>
> The facts of his having formed the design of Converting this Money to his use, and of Actually so converting much the greater part of it, were proved without contradiction—
>
> But doubts having occur'd to Mr Justice le Blanc, and myself, (Mr Justice Chambre being absent from indisposition), the Case was reserved for the Judges to Consider, whether the facts proved amounted to the Crime of Larceny—
>
> The Argument of Counsel concluded last night, and the Case was considered by Ten Judges present (two being confined by illness) who were of Opinion, that the facts proved did not in estimation of Law, amount to Felony—
>
> The prisoner having been convicted of that offence, I am humbly to recommend him as a proper object of his Majesty's pardon.

The pardon was granted by Ryder, acting in the name of the Prince Regent, who was acting in the name of King George III, on 20 February

---

[71] Foss (n 27) 213–4.
[72] *Morning Chronicle*, 15 February 1812, 3d; *Courier*, 15 February 1812, 4c.
[73] *Morning Chronicle*, 20 February 1812, 3e.
[74] 21 *Parliamentary Debates* 939–40; *The Times*, 28 February 1812, 4b. The original letter is in the Public Records Office, Kew, about one-quarter of the way through the bundle of correspondence which is HO47/49. In the rest of the letter, Macdonald CB set out another case in which a pardon was recommended.

1812.[75] Although in form Walsh had been convicted and then pardoned, he had, in substance, been acquitted on appeal.[76]

On 25 February 1812, a debate commenced in the House of Commons on the expulsion of Benjamin Walsh.[77] Walsh continually failed to obey the House's order that he should attend in his place for this debate;[78] and finally, on 5 March 1812, it was moved in his absence that Walsh was 'unworthy and unfit to continue a member of this House'.[79] By a majority of 101 to 16, Benjamin Walsh lost his seat, which he had held for four years.[80] He had never made a speech.

On the same day that the expulsion debate commenced, a bill was introduced to make it a felony for brokers and bankers to misapply securities deposited with them for safekeeping or for a special purpose.[81] The measure was enacted,[82] although the offence was made only a misdemeanour.[83] The very next chapter in the statute book is an extension of criminal liability for obtaining money or goods by false pretences to the obtaining likewise of bills of exchange, bank notes and cheques.[84] Also enacted in the same session of Parliament was a measure under which a Member who became bankrupt would, unless the bankruptcy were discharged, lose his rights to sit and vote for a year, and then lose his seat.[85] The enactment of these measures perhaps owed something to Walsh's activities.

---

[75] 21 *Parliamentary Debates* 940; *The Times*, 28 February 1812, 4b. The Home Office copy of this pardon is at the PRO: HO13/22, 342–3.

[76] See note 69.

[77] 21 *Parliamentary Debates* 943.

[78] 21 *Parliamentary Debates* 982 (27 February 1812); 1088 (2 March 1812); 1092 (3 March 1812); 1174 (5 March 1812).

[79] 21 *Parliamentary Debates* 1179.

[80] 21 *Parliamentary Debates* 1200.

[81] 21 *Parliamentary Debates* 943.

[82] 52 Geo III, c 63. This was repealed as to England in 1827 as part of an overhaul of the criminal law (7 & 8 Geo IV, c 27, s 1), and then in 1828 as to Ireland (9 Geo IV, c 53, s 1) and India (9 Geo IV c 74, s 125) in similar reforms. It was repealed in full by the Statute Law Revision Act 1887 (50 & 51 Vict, c 59).

[83] Contrary to what is said in the report of *R v Walsh* in 4 Taunt 258, 284. The bill was changed in other ways as well; notably, in response to fears that it would criminalise breach of trust (see 21 *Parliamentary Debates* 945–6 and 1214–15), it was made inapplicable to certain trustees (s 6).

[84] 52 Geo III, c 64. The reference to 'orders for the payment of money' was presumably intended to extend the act to cheques, being wider than 'warrants for the payment of money' in 2 Geo II, c 25, s 3, under which Walsh was prosecuted. 52 Geo III, c 64 was repealed by the Statute Law Revision Act 1861 (24 & 25 Vict, c 101).

[85] 52 Geo III, c 144. This measure was administratively amended in 1863 by 26 & 27 Vict, c 20, and then repealed except as to Scotland and Ireland during an overhaul of English bankruptcy law in 1869 (Bankruptcy Repeal and Insolvent Court Act 1869, 32 & 33 Vict c 83, s 20). It was finally repealed completely by the Statute Law Revision Act 1958 (6 & 7 Eliz 2, c 46). But from 1869 onwards, there has always been an equivalent provision in the various incarnations of the bankruptcy legislation: see the Bankruptcy Act 1869 (32 & 33 Vict, c 71) ss 121–3; and see now the Insolvency Act 1985 (1985, c 65), s 214(4)–(6). This became relevant in the wake of the large losses suffered by Members of Parliament who were 'Names' at Lloyd's: *The Times*, 27 May 1993, 1b; 1 June 1993, 1b.

G. THE CIVIL PROCEEDINGS: *TAYLOR V PLUMER*[86]

Walsh's assignees in bankruptcy for this, his second bankruptcy, made a considerable effort to draw together what they saw as the assets subject to division among the creditors. They managed to get from Joseph Walsh the value of the assets that Walsh had given him on 5 December 1811.[87] They failed in a claim against the committee running the City Lottery for the value of Walsh's work in selling their tickets.[88] But their most important—and most audacious—claim was in trover against Sir Thomas Plumer.

The argument was fairly simple, and not dissimilar to the arguments which had been put forward successfully by Walsh's counsel in *R v Walsh*: while Walsh might have owed Plumer £15,500, nonetheless the US stock and gold belonged to Walsh, and not to Plumer. Hence those assets must go into the pool of property subject to division among the creditors. Plumer could prove as a creditor of Walsh, but it was wrongful for him simply to take those assets for himself.

The trial took place on 22 December 1813, before Lord Ellenborough, Chief Justice of the Court of King's Bench. Benjamin Walsh gave evidence, and he changed his story slightly from that in his letter to his brother. He now omitted any claim that he had originally intended to defraud Oldham, saying instead that from the moment he ordered the US stock, he intended to pay for it with the proceeds of the sale of Plumer's stock.[89] There was a verdict for the plaintiff assignees, subject to an appeal on an agreed set of facts. The 'special argument' before the full Court of King's Bench did not take place until 22 November 1814, before Lord Ellenborough CJ and Le Blanc, Bayley and Dampier JJ. Dampier J had been appointed to replace Grose J in 1813, but the others had all heard the argument in *R v Walsh*.[90] Plumer was represented by Mr Abbott, who had been junior counsel in the prosecution of Walsh. The court gave judgment on 10 February 1815, and found for the defendant Plumer.

[86] (1815) 3 M & S 562; 2 Rose 457; [1814-23] All ER Rep 167.
[87] *The Times*, 3 November 1812, 2c. Counsel for Joseph Walsh was the new Solicitor General, Mr Garrow. He complained that he was deprived of evidence as Benjamin Walsh had failed to obey a subpoena. This was perhaps not surprising: he was the man who had appeared for the Crown at Walsh's trial (though not on appeal).
[88] *Taylor v Brewer*, *The Times*, 10 May 1813, 2e.
[89] *Morning Chronicle*, 23 December 1813, 3e; *The Times*, 23 December 1813, 2e; *Courier* 23 December 1814, 4b.
[90] Foss (n 27) 213.

H. CONCLUSION

Cyrus Redding was a traveller, an oenophile, and a prolific writer of the nineteenth century. In 1814, he was publishing a newspaper in Plymouth.[91] He wrote a number of leading articles in favour of the emancipation of Roman Catholics, and critical of the government's policies on the matters. In retaliation, the government withdrew its advertising business from his newspaper.[92] Redding decided to sell up, and a London agent put him in contact with Benjamin Walsh. Redding's impression of the new proprietor was not overwhelmingly positive:[93]

> Whether he was considered clever among the stock-brokers of the city in the mystery of money-making, I do not know; but he was a very feeble-minded man, destitute of political, as he was of literary information. His manners were mild, and on the whole, I should describe him as a weak, unreflecting person, beyond a business which flourishes or fails, like the tables of hazard.

Where Walsh obtained the money with which to buy a newspaper, only two years after his second bankruptcy, is not entirely clear. It is true that he had been granted his certificate for having complied in the bankruptcy proceedings.[94] Also, his wife's sister had published a book of poems, apparently to try to raise some money.[95] At any rate, he did not succeed in this undertaking either. Redding says: 'I never heard the particulars of his after-career, except that he set up as a merchant as well as a newspaper-proprietor, and failed.'[96] Although he seems to have avoided a third bankruptcy, Walsh made a composition with his creditors on 5 November 1816. In 1818, dividends were still being paid to creditors under this composition, and under the bankruptcy of 1811 as well.[97]

---

[91] S Lee (ed), *Dictionary of National Biography* vol XVI (London, Smith, Elder & Co, 1909) 813.

[92] Cyrus Redding, *Yesterday and Today* (London, 1863) vol I, 256–61; vol III, 317–18.

[93] Cyrus Redding, *Fifty Years' Recollections, Literary and Personal, with Observations on Men and Things* (2nd edn, London, Charles J Skeet, 1858) vol I, 222.

[94] *London Gazette* (1812) 356–7.

[95] *Poems by a Sister* (London, 1812). One of the publishers of this book was Walsh's brother, Joseph. The author's first name was Anne or Anna (see 97, 102, 104). That she was the sister of Mary Walsh can be inferred from the poem 'To My Sister Mary', at 113. The author stated (at iii) that the poems were written during an illness, and not for publication; 'but circumstances of a peculiarly interesting nature have induced her to submit them to the perusal of her friends'. The list of subscribers shows a large number of residents of Clifton, with which Mary Walsh's family seems to have had a connection: there is a poem entitled 'Clifton' (at 70), and Mary Walsh was apparently buried there (Thorne (n 5) 477). The list of subscribers also includes a disproportionate number of persons living in Clapton (where Walsh and his wife were married) and in Hackney (where they lived in 1811). A large number are also shown as members of the Stock Exchange. Included in this list are Denis De Berdt, Joseph Fearn (three copies), Thomas Nisbet (six copies) and the Duchess of York (six copies).

[96] Redding (n 93) 233.

[97] *London Gazette* (1818) 1254–5, 2084. See also *London Gazette* (1817) 1504, which shows another dividend under the 1811 bankruptcy.

How Walsh ended his days is, for now, a mystery. Perhaps at this point he did what Redding thought was fitting after the failure of the scheme to bilk Plumer: 'This individual should rather have hid his head in the obscurity of a remote place, where his conduct and person were alike strange.'[98]

The importance of tracing was touched on in the introduction. It is generally thought that there are separate rules for tracing in equity and tracing at common law, and it has been argued that common law tracing is so limited as to be irrelevant in practice.[99] But recent developments show that common law tracing cannot be ignored entirely; and *Taylor v Plumer* is said to be the basis for the possibility of tracing at common law.[100]

The legal analysis of the case, and its relevance to the modern law of tracing, are matters for another publication. The purpose of this article has been to examine the facts underlying the decisions in *R v Walsh* and *Taylor v Plumer*, beyond the dry and occasionally misleading accounts in the law reports. Benjamin Walsh was indisputably a personification of the 'rogue' who features in so many theoretical discussions of the law; but he was as pathetic and wretched a rogue as one could ever expect to find.

I. POSTSCRIPT[**]

1. Origins

This article began its life as an attempt to answer a legal question. In an important article,[101] Salman Khurshid and Paul Matthews had argued that although *Taylor v Plumer* has long been understood as a the root case for 'tracing at common law', the case was really resolved on the basis that the defendant Plumer was the beneficiary of a trust of the assets held by Walsh at the time of his bankruptcy. At the beginning of my doctoral research in the law of tracing, my supervisor, Peter Birks, suggested that I try to get to the bottom of this question. I found the story behind the litigation more and more interesting, but since I was writing a legal analysis, the human details were consigned to an ever-growing number of increasingly bloated footnotes. He suggested that the story must be rescued from the footnotes, and the result was this article. The legal analysis was published as 'Tracing in *Taylor v*

---

[98] At 222. Mary Walsh died in 1822: Thorne (n 5) 477.

[99] ELG Tyler and NE Palmer, *Crossley Vaines' Personal Property* (5th edn, London, Butterworths, 1973) 162: 'the common law right is now of academic interest'; PJ Millett, 'Tracing the Proceeds of Fraud' (1991) 107 *LQR* 71: 'the common law's remedies are inadequate and its jurisprudence defective.'

[100] See eg *Lipkin Gorman v Karpnale Ltd* [1991] 2 AC 548, 573.

[**] This postscript was written in 2005 for the present collection of essays.

[101] 'Tracing Confusion' (1979) 95 *LQR* 78.

Plumer: Equity in the Court of King's Bench'.[102] As the title reveals, I found that Khurshid and Matthews were exactly right. To my mind, the decisive piece of evidence lay in the *Times* report of the conclusion of the hearing:[103]

> *Curia advisare vult.* They would consider it (upon the authority of Lord CJ Willes) as if it were a petition before the Chancellor to have the certificates delivered up.

The case is only part of a long series of decisions that belie a common modern view that before the Judicature Acts, the courts of common law took no notice of equitable interests. The reference to Willes LCJ in the passage quoted above was to his opinion in *Scott v Surman*,[104] over seventy years before. I have heard it suggested that common law courts noticed equitable interests only because the bankruptcy statutes impliedly required them to. That does not explain cases such as *Farr v Newman*.[105] Execution was levied against an executor, in relation to his own personal debts; the sheriff seized goods that the executor held in the capacity of executor. At common law, he was the owner of those estate assets, as much as he was the owner of his own assets. Did this mean that his creditors could seize the estate assets? Said Lord Kenyon CJ, 'A more momentous question never came before this Court'. The execution was held to be unlawful; the creditors were not allowed to attach the estate property.[106]

The conclusion of the legal analysis was that *Taylor v Plumer* was decided by the recognition of Plumer's equitable rights. The case, therefore, tells us nothing about whether there are common law claims to traceable proceeds. Nor, if there are such claims, does it say anything about what rules of tracing might be applicable. It makes no suggestion that there might be rules of 'common law tracing' which are different from rules of 'equitable tracing'. That misunderstanding seems to date from *Sinclair v Brougham*.[107]

2. Subsequent Historical Evidence

After the article appeared, I learned of the existence of a set of notebooks that are held by the Lord Chief Justice of England.[108] They cover the period

---

[102] [1995] *LMCLQ* 240.

[103] *The Times,* 24 November 1814, 2c.

[104] (1742) Willes 401, 125 ER 1236.

[105] (1792) 4 TR 621, 100 ER 1209.

[106] The decision was reached with some reliance on *dicta* of Lord Mansfield in *Howard v Jemmett* (1763) 3 Burr 1368, 97 ER 878. Mansfield was an early fusionist: W Holdsworth, *A History of English Law* (London, Methuen & Co, 1938) vol XII, 584–94.

[107] [1914] AC 398.

[108] Upon the publication of DR Bentley (ed), *Select Cases from the Twelve Judges' Notebooks* (London, John Rees, 1997).

in question, and I hoped that they might shed light on the reasoning that underlay Walsh's acquittal by the twelve judges on a point of law in the criminal proceedings. It seems quite possible that the acquittal turned on the question of who held legal title to the assets in question; in general, you cannot steal something that belongs to you. In 1998 I wrote to Lord Bingham, who was at that time the Lord Chief Justice. He told me that he had caused a search to be made of the notebooks, but that no notes regarding *R v Walsh* had been found.

Details of the evidence given at Walsh's criminal trial may now be found online, at Old Bailey Proceedings Online: www.oldbaileyonline.org. Walsh's trial on 15 January 1812 is there given the number t18120115–4. This site provides digitised versions (facsimile and HTML) of the *Proceedings* that are cited in footnote 4 of the article.

3. Subsequent Legal Developments

In *Trustee of the Property of FC Jones & Sons (a firm) v Jones*, Millett LJ, as he then was, said:[109]

> In *Agip (Africa) Ltd v Jackson* [1990] Ch 265, 285, I said that the ability of the common law to trace an asset into a changed form in the same hands was established in *Taylor v Plumer* (1815) 3 M & S 562. Lord Ellenborough CJ in that case had said, at 575:
>
>> the product of or substitute for the original thing still follows the nature of the thing itself, as long as it can be ascertained to be such, and the right only ceases when the means of ascertainment fail, which is the case when the subject is turned into money, and mixed and confounded in a general mass of the same description.
>
> In this it appears that I fell into a common error, for it has since been convincingly demonstrated that, although *Taylor v Plumer* was decided by a common law court, the court was in fact applying the rules of equity: see Lionel Smith, 'Tracing in *Taylor v Plumer*: Equity in the Court of King's Bench' [1995] *LMCLQ* 240.
>
> But this is no reason for concluding that the common law does not recognise claims to substitute assets or their products. Such claims were upheld by this court in *Banque Belge pour l'Etranger v Hambrouck* [1921] 1 KB 321 and by the House of Lords in *Lipkin Gorman v Karpnale Ltd* [1991] 2 AC 548. It has been suggested by commentators that these cases are undermined by their misunderstanding of *Taylor v Plumer*, but that is not how the English doctrine of *stare decisis* operates. It would be more consistent with that doctrine to say that, in recognising claims to substituted assets, equity must be taken to have followed

---

[109] [1997] Ch 159, 169.

the law, even though the law was not declared until later. Lord Ellenborough CJ gave no indication that, in following assets into their exchange products, equity had adopted a rule which was peculiar to itself or which went further than the common law.

I have always found it difficult to understand the last three sentences of that passage. I am not sure who the commentators in question are, and I do not follow the statements about *stare decisis* at all. Sometimes equity follows the law, and sometimes the law follows equity, as it did in *Taylor v Plumer* and as it frequently has over the centuries; but these issues are not clearly related to *stare decisis*. Perhaps the argument is that if common law claims to traceable proceeds were recognised in *Banque Belge* and *Lipkin Gorman,* it follows that such claims have always been possible, and so when equity allowed them, in the eighteenth century if not long before, it was unknowingly following the law. That is not so much a question of *stare decisis* as a particular understanding of the declaratory theory of the adjudicative function. It is, however, possible to believe that judges declare the law, while still believing that the law changes over time. Be that as it may, the first and last sentences of this paragraph are surely right: proving that *Taylor* was about equitable rights does not say that the common law cannot countenance claims to traceable proceeds.[110]

Millett LJ went on to say that having different tracing rules at law and in equity was 'unfortunate though probably inevitable'; and he said:[111]

> There is, in my view, even less merit in the present rule which precludes the invocation of the equitable tracing rules to support a common law claim; until that rule is swept away unnecessary obstacles to the development of a rational and coherent law of restitution will remain.

Peter Birks long argued for the analytical distinction between tracing and claiming.[112] Tracing is the process of identifying what asset was acquired by a particular person with the purchasing power inherent in another asset; claiming is the question of what rights a claimant may have in that traceable product. I was not the only one persuaded by this view; so too was Lord Millett, which is evident not only in *Jones* but also in *Foskett v McKeown*[113] and in other cases.[114] Peter Birks also argued that the principles of tracing should be the same, whether the claim was framed at common law or in equity;[115] again, this was accepted in *Foskett*.[116] If the rules

---

[110] As I said in the conclusion to the *LMCLQ* article.
[111] *Jones* (n 9) 170.
[112] *An Introduction to the Law of Restitution* rev edn (Oxford, OUP, 1989) 358.
[113] [2001] 1 AC 102.
[114] Especially *Boscawen v Bajwa* [1996] 1 WLR 328.
[115] 'The Necessity of a Unitary Law of Tracing' in R Cranston (ed), *Making Commercial Law: Essays in Honour of Roy Goode* (Oxford, OUP, 1997) 239.
[116] By Lord Millett, speaking for the majority, albeit in *obiter dicta* on this point.

are the same in both systems, the old idea that a fiduciary relationship must be found in order to use the equitable tracing rules ceases to have any significance.

So far as concerns the claims that can be made to or in respect of traceable proceeds, the picture is less clear. As Millett LJ said in the extract from *Jones*, there seem to be examples of common law claims to traceable proceeds. These cases, however, are subject to range of different interpretations. *Jones* itself (or at least the approach taken in the case by Millett LJ) might be considered difficult to square with some basic precepts of the common law.[117] The easiest solution might be to let equity handle claims to traceable proceeds, as happened in *Taylor v Plumer,* and as Lord Browne-Wilkinson suggested in *Westdeutsche Landesbank Girozentrale v Islington LBC.*[118] On the other hand, Peter Birks used *Jones* as one of the building blocks of the view he presented in his last book, *Unjust Enrichment,*[119] to the effect that a claimant may establish common law ownership of traceable proceeds, and indeed that a claimant in unjust enrichment need not prove that he suffered any deprivation.[120]

D. CONCLUSION

Uncovering the history, and the law, behind *Taylor v Plumer* was a fascinating undertaking. In the end, it is not clear whether much light has been shed on the modern law. That is probably as it should be. I leave the final word to Oliver Wendell Holmes Jr:[121]

> The past gives us our vocabulary and fixes the limits of our imagination; we cannot get away from it. There is, too, a peculiar logical pleasure in making manifest the continuity between what we are doing and what has been done before. But the present has a right to govern itself so far as it can; and it ought always to be remembered that historic continuity with the past is not a duty, it is only a necessity.

---

[117] L Smith, *The Law of Tracing* (Oxford, OUP, 1997) 328ff.
[118] [1996] AC 669, 715–16.
[119] *Unjust Enrichment* (2nd edn, Oxford, OUP, 2005).
[120] This view was first presented in P Birks, 'At the Expense of the Claimant: Direct and Indirect Enrichment in English Law' in D Johnston and R Zimmermann (eds), *Unjustified Enrichment: Key Issues in Comparative Perspective* (Cambridge, CUP, 2002) 493.
[121] OW Holmes, 'Learning and Science', *Collected Legal Papers* (New York, Harcourt, Brace & Co, 1920) 138, 139; also in SM Novick (ed), *Collected Works of Justice Holmes* vol 3 (Chicago, University of Chicago Press, 1995) 491, 492.

4

Planché v Colburn (1831)

CHARLES MITCHELL AND CHARLOTTE MITCHELL[*]

A. INTRODUCTION

IN OUTLINE, THESE were the facts of *Planché v Colburn*.[1] The defendants, Henry Colburn and Richard Bentley, were partners in a publishing business. In June 1830 they began to publish a monthly series of children's books entitled *The Juvenile Library*, under the editorship of William Jerdan. Three books were published in the series before they decided to abandon the project, in October 1830. By this time, the plaintiff, James Robinson Planché, had written part of a volume on the history of costume, the first of two he had been commissioned to write, for a fee of £100 per volume. The defendants offered to publish Planché's work as a book for adults, if he would complete and deliver the manuscript, but he refused and sued them for breach of contract, recovering £50.

Planché is well known to contract and unjust enrichment lawyers, but seems not to have attracted the attention of literary historians, perhaps rather surprisingly, for much of the argument turned on the nature of literary work, a field of enquiry which they have long considered to be interesting and important. Moreover, the parties were prominent figures in the literary and theatrical circles of their time. Besides several reports of the case, there survives a considerable quantity of manuscript evidence relating to the events that led to the parties' dispute.[2] We shall draw on these sources

[*] We are grateful to Paul Mitchell and John Sutherland for their comments on a draft of this essay. For permission to publish manuscript material we thank the Harry Ransom Humanities Research Centre, University of Texas at Austin.
[1] (1831) 5 Car & P 58, 172 ER 876; *The Times*, 15 June 1831; *Bell's Weekly Messenger*, 19 June 1831. Subsequent proceedings: (1831) 8 Bing 14, 131 ER 305; 1 M & S 51; 1 LJCP 7; *The Times*, 7 November 1831.

[2] The archives of Richard Bentley, the publisher (who bought out his partner Henry Colburn not long after the case), are very extensive, and are held in various libraries in Britain and America. Many (though not all) have been published on microfilm as *The Archives of Richard Bentley & Son 1829–1898* (Cambridge, Chadwyck-Healey, 1977). They include authors' agreements and correspondence relating to the *Juvenile Library* series, and some notes of how far the various authors had got at the time the series folded. There is also a small collection of documents relating to the *Juvenile Library* in the Humanities Research Centre,

to describe the arrangements entered into by the parties, to explain what they expected to gain from these, and to examine why they went wrong. The legal interest of the case lies in the court's understanding of the relationship between contractual and quasi-contractual claims, and in the question whether the award made to the plaintiff was compensatory or restitutionary. From a literary perspective, the details of the story have an inherent biographical interest, and are valuable evidence of contemporary conceptions of authorship.

B. DRAMATIS PERSONAE

1. Henry Colburn (died 1855)

In September 1829, the publisher Henry Colburn went into partnership with Richard Bentley; their association ended rather acrimoniously in 1832, although both continued subsequently to play important roles in Victorian publishing. Colburn's date of birth is not known, but he was probably the elder of the two by at least twenty years, had long been a prominent publisher of books and journals, and had played an important role in developing the 'silver fork' novel popular in the 1820s: novels about high society which purported to be, and in some cases were, the work of members of the aristocracy and the fashionable set.[3] He was an enthusiastic believer in the power of advertising, which he carried to levels considered by many of his contemporaries to be sinister. He was the founder and part-owner of several periodicals, including the *Literary Gazette,* which he

University of Texas at Austin, including a draft list of proposed titles for the series, with authors, and some notes relating to the paying off of commissioned authors after its abandonment, and a series of letters from Jerdan to Colburn and Bentley. In the Croker Collection, Cork City Library, Republic of Ireland, there is an informative letter from Jerdan to Thomas Crofton Croker, enclosing a copy of a letter from Jerdan to Colburn and Bentley concerning the settlements with authors as a result of the abandonment of the project. There is also a discussion of the series (which does not mention the court case), and a transcript of Jerdan's list of the works that had been commissioned at the time of the project's abandonment, in RA Gettman, *A Victorian Publisher: A Study of the Bentley Papers* (Cambridge, CUP, 1960) 38–43. Some account of contemporary periodical response to the *Juvenile Library* is given in LA Marchand, *The Athenaeum, A Mirror of Victorian Culture* (Chapel Hill, NC, University of North Carolina Press, 1941) 124–9.

[3] MW Rosa, *The Silver-Fork School: Novels of Fashion Preceding Vanity Fair* (New York, Columbia University Press, 1936); E Engel and MF King, *The Victorian Novel Before Victoria: British Fiction During the Reign of William IV 1830–1837* (London, Macmillan, 1984). On Colburn's career see Rosa, *ibid*; Marchand (n 2) 110–20; J Sutherland, 'Henry Colburn Publisher' [1986] *Publishing History* 59; PE Garside, 'Colburn, Henry (d 1855)' *Oxford Dictionary of National Biography* (Oxford, OUP, 2004); WE Houghton *et al* (eds), *The Wellesley Index to Victorian Periodicals 1824–1900* 5 vols (Toronto, University of Toronto Press, 1966–89) vol III, 161–71.

co-owned with its editor William Jerdan and another publisher, Thomas Longman.[4]

These magazines not only carried lists of forthcoming publications, but also included in their editorial sections many rave notices of books published by Colburn, or gossip about them and their authors intended to enhance their popularity. This practice was known as puffing, and was by no means new in the 1820s. However, the inherent dishonesty of disguising promotional material as unbiased literary judgement was obvious to many observers, and the late 1820s and early 1830s saw more and more voices raised against the practice. As well as being obviously opposed to the interests of the consumer, the smaller publishers and their authors, puffing was also an issue for those who were preoccupied with the low pay and social status of professional writers. There was thus a fundamental connection between the various campaigns for copyright reform and the newspaper debates about corrupt reviewing practices: the concern was that authorship should become the kind of profession in which a respectable and reasonably prosperous gentleman could engage. And on the whole one can say that the reign of Queen Victoria did see some improvement in the respectability of authors.

These debates about reviewing practice and the behaviour of publishers in the marketplace form the backdrop to our story. In 1827 a novel called *The O'Briens and the O'Flaherties* by Sydney, Lady Morgan, had received a scathing review in the *Literary Gazette*. The reason was probably that her politics had antagonised the Tory Jerdan, rather than that he sought to pick a fight with his co-owner, whose publications he was accustomed to puffing fairly obediently.[5] Colburn, however, was furious, and, though a Tory himself, started a rival periodical, *The Athenaeum*, in 1828, writing to Jerdan to explain that he was investing in a liberal paper to protect his more radical authors from unfair treatment in the *Literary Gazette*.[6] He soon

---

[4] In 1829 Colburn founded a weekly named the *Court Journal*, whose first editor was Peter George Patmore (father of the poet Coventry Patmore). In 1832 a paragraph appeared in the journal suggesting that the Duchess of Richmond had committed adultery, and her husband laid an information for criminal libel against Colburn, who was convicted and sentenced to pay a fine of £100: *R v Colburn*, *The Times*, 25 January 1833. Colburn sacked Patmore, and sued him for reimbursement of the amount of the fine. The jury gave a verdict in his favour, but this judgment was arrested by the Court of Exchequer, on the ground that Patmore's act in inserting the libel into the journal had been separate from Colburn's act in printing it. In *obiter dicta* that were much quoted in later cases, Lord Lyndhurst CB also held that Colburn could not have recovered in any event because 'a person who is declared by the law to be guilty of a crime cannot be allowed to recover damages against another who has participated in its commission': *Colburn v Patmore* (1834) 1 CM & R 73, 83; 149 ER 999, 1003. For discussion of the present law governing illegality as a defence to claims for contribution and reimbursement, see C Mitchell, *The Law of Contribution and Reimbursement* (Oxford, OUP, 2003) 260–1.

[5] Marchand (n 2) 103, 113; A Sullivan, *British Literary Magazines: The Romantic Age 1789–1836* (Westport, CT, Greenwood Press, 1983) 244.

[6] Marchand (n 2) 113; *The Autobiography of William Jerdan* 4 vols (London, Hall, 1852–3) vol IV, 68–9.

sold his interest in the *Athenaeum*, but it survived, and in 1830, under the new editorship of Keats's friend Charles Wentworth Dilke, was positioning itself to take customers from the *Literary Gazette*; in the following year its price was halved to 4d to undercut its rival; part of its appeal lay in its editor's policy of distancing himself from the corrupt practices of the trade.[7] Another thorn in Jerdan's side was *Fraser's Magazine*, launched in 1830, which sounded the same note of contempt for magazines that were the servile mouthpieces of their publisher owners. The *Literary Gazette*'s reputation for impartiality and Jerdan's *amour propre* were in collision with Colburn's ideas about how to sell books.

2. Richard Bentley (1794–1871)

The history of publishing, especially in relation to disputes between author and publisher, has often been written by supporters of authors, and there has been a consequent tendency to cast publishers in the role of villains or heroes, which is usually an over-simplification. Colburn's partner Richard Bentley, despite a well-publicised dispute with Dickens, has had a fairly good press. After parting from Colburn in 1832, he went on to play a major part in the publishing industry for another thirty years. The copious quantity and ready availability of the surviving archives have perhaps had an influence on the point of view from which the story is usually told: unlike Colburn, Bentley had a devoted grandson (and namesake) who preserved and defended his memory, and whose example has been followed by those who have used the elaborate archives he maintained. Gettman, for example, defends the part Bentley played in the *Juvenile Library* fiasco, laying all the blame on Colburn.[8] The row with Colburn that ended their connection has always been attributed to Colburn's bad management and indecision. It is perhaps mean-spirited to observe that Colburn had long been safely dead by the time Jerdan came to write his memoirs, whereas Bentley was represented by a firm that was still very much in business.

Yet in 1830, when the *Juvenile Library* was appearing, Bentley's successes were mainly in the future, Colburn's mainly in the past. Their connection was short-lived, but it did see the beginning of what was probably Bentley's most influential publication, the *Bentley's Standard Novels* series, which reprinted fiction of the Romantic period by then out of copyright, and in

---

[7] L Brake, 'Dilke, Charles Wentworth (1789–1864)' *Oxford Dictionary of National Biography* (Oxford, OUP, 2004): 'The main principle of Dilke's editorship was to preserve a complete independence from the trade, and to criticize a book without concern for the writer or the publisher; promulgated most concertedly between 1830 and 1832 . . . Dilke withdrew from general society . . . avoiding as far as possible personal contact with authors or publishers who might seek to influence the reviews in the *Athenaeum*.'

[8] Gettman (n 2) 42–3.

doing so, it has recently been argued, determined a canon of Romantic fiction that persists to this day.[9]

3. William Jerdan (1782–1869)

Jerdan became editor of the *Literary Gazette* in 1818, and by 1830 was also part-owner, with Colburn and Thomas Longman. A noisy, touchy, overbearing man, with a keen sense of his own dignity and of the dignity of literature, he knew everybody in literary London, and liked that to be generally understood. He was a supporter of a wide range of institutions concerned with the arts, including the Royal Literary Fund and the Royal Society of Literature, which were respectively concerned with the relief of poverty and the reward of merit, and the Garrick Club, within which literary men could associate on terms of equality with actors and professional men. He lived in a large house in Brompton with his family,[10] although his wife seems to have figured little in his social life, and he was haunted by rumours of an improper association with his most successful protegée, the poet Letitia Landon. But despite his large network of acquaintances, his sociability, and the power he wielded in the literary world, he yearned for greater social status, and was acutely conscious of the poverty and indignity that was frequently the lot of the professional writer. Marchand quotes a letter he wrote to George Canning, during the brief period when the latter was Prime Minister in the summer of 1827, asking, in return for his political support, for a sinecure which would enable him to pay an efficient co-editor for the *Literary Gazette* 'and take myself a somewhat higher station in society'.[11] Marchand evidently disapproves of this readiness to sell his favour, but the episode is characteristic of the awkward situation in which Jerdan and others like him found themselves: to make a gentleman's income in the writing business one had to engage in practices that were hard to reconcile with gentlemanly behaviour or with literary honesty. Jerdan is by no means unrepresentative of his generation of writers in his touchiness on the subject of his social status, or in the fact that his statements are shot through with the language of honour and gentlemanly behaviour.

---

[9] W St Clair, *The Reading Nation in the Romantic Period* (Cambridge, CUP, 2004) 361–4.

[10] Grove House, Brompton, whose famous former inhabitant was Sir John Fielding, the blind Bow Street magistrate: FWH Sheppard (ed), *Survey of London, vol 38: The Museums Area of South Kensington and Westminster* (London, Athlone Press, 1975) 11. According to the survey, the occupant from 1806 to 1840 was JG Brett, father of the first Viscount Esher, but it may be that Jerdan had the house from him on lease. One of Jerdan's neighbours was James Robinson Planché, who lived in nearby Brompton Crescent, and who was introduced by Jerdan to various artists and literary figures: *The Recollections and Reflections of JR Planché*, 2 vols (London, Tinsley Brothers, 1872) vol II, 96.

[11] Marchand (n 2) 120.

The editorship of the *Juvenile Library*, which Jerdan undertook in return for £300 a year, was thus an opportunity for him to add to his income while distributing patronage among his many friends and hangers-on in the literary world. But it brought him into renewed contact with Colburn, a long-term business partner with whom he had recently had serious fallings-out over a particularly sensitive subject, because, as we have said, there was a rising tide of opinion against puffing and corruption in the literary world generally. The closure of the *Juvenile Library* has been attributed, by those few critics who have considered it all, to the low circulation of its few weak publications, but there is some evidence that a new dispute had arisen between Jerdan and Colburn at this precise moment. Gettman cites some malicious paragraphs in the *Athenaeum*,[12] referring to the *Juvenile Library* in disparaging terms; the second refers to rumours of a row between editor and publisher. The decision to close the *Juvenile Library* thus appears to have taken place in the context of a deteriorating relationship between editor and publisher, and may not have been made solely on commercial grounds.[13]

Some support is lent to this view by a series of references in the *Literary Gazette* to an anonymous novel entitled *The Separation*, published by Colburn and Bentley in 1830, and widely known to be the work of Lady Charlotte Bury, one of the most prominent silver-fork novelists.[14] Colburn and Bentley, like other publishers of the time, had several peers and peeresses among their authors, some of whom they were able to induce to contribute to the costs of publication. Poor Lady Charlotte, however, was not publishing for vanity's sake; though the daughter of a duke, she was burdened with many children and a much younger second husband, a clergyman; she had been writing for money for twenty years. A condescending but fairly friendly review on 21 August[15] was followed by an indignant article on 23 October, revealing that it was an old novel masquerading as a new one:[16]

> We reviewed a novel called '*The Separation*, by the author of *Flirtation*,' i.e. Lady Charlotte Bury; and we said, truly, that though the style was of the slip-slop class, the story was lively and amusing. Well, we were fairly imposed upon; and, as we helped to gull the public, we come now to explain our share of the transaction .

[12] Gettman (n 2) 40, 41, citing issues for 17 July and 23 October 1830, 129.

[13] Though it was estimated that it lost £900 in its short life: RL Patten, 'Richard Bentley (1794–1871)' *Oxford Dictionary of National Biography* (Oxford, OUP, 2004).

[14] See, for example, a puff for *The Separation* in Colburn's *New Monthly Magazine* in August, quoted by the *Literary Gazette* (23 October 1830) 689n: 'The present subject is, we understand, one of more than ordinary excitement; its incidents are said to be in themselves strictly true . . . [deriving from] a "certain case" in the "great world" which took place a few years ago, and which was more industriously than successfully attempted to be concealed.'

[15] 'The Separation: A Novel', *Literary Gazette*, 21 August 1830, 542.

[16] 'The Art of Book-Making', *Literary Gazette*, 23 October 1830, 689–90.

. . . We did not know or had forgotten, that the *new novel* of SEPARATION was only an *old novel* with a *new name*; and that, in fact the three volumes were no other than 'SELF-INDULGENCE, a tale of the nineteenth century,' in *two volumes* published in 1812, by GR Clarke, of Edinburgh, and Messrs Longman and Co, of London!! . . . The whole story is identical in both . . . the names carefully rechristened, a slight change of words here and there, and the introduction of a few dialogues to spin the work out to the necessary length. . . . We presume *Self-Indulgence* to be an anonymous production of Lady Charlotte Bury . . . [C]an there be any excuse for palming the same thing upon the public . . . as an entirely new novel? For our parts we consider it most disingenuous and discreditable; and, for the publisher's sake, we trust to have a letter from him for our next *Gazette*, disavowing any cognizance of the trick, and stating what sum he may have paid for the old-new *rifacimento* of *Self-Indulgence* . . . To be sure, one would not suspect an individual moving in this sphere . . . in which honour and principle are supposed to be peculiarly delicate, of prostituting name, rank, and character, to an unworthy deception; but really there is so much roguery in the literary world now-a-days, that we hardly know to what length *self-indulgence* may be carried; and can only do our best to promote a *separation* between the right and the wrong.

The issue for 30 October contained another reference to the business in a comment on anthologies, and a letter from Colburn and Bentley in which they denied knowing about the earlier publication of the book, printed with an unsigned letter, written on behalf of the author, defending her use of the earlier work and absolving them of responsibility.[17] It was reported on 6 November that the publishers were demanding the payment of £250 back from the author, but that the book had sold well as a consequence of the publicity.[18] Jerdan went on throwing in gratuitous references to the affair for some time. As the quotation above makes clear, issues of commercial probity, social status and moral authority could be intimately connected in the public discussion of literary matters. It is not hard to read malice into Jerdan's comments, and one can see why Colburn might not have wanted to go on paying him £300 a year while he was printing this sort of thing in a weekly magazine which they co-owned.

4. James Robinson Planché (1796–1880)

Planché was probably the most distinguished British playwright of his generation, which is faint praise, since the first half of the nineteenth century is generally reckoned to have been British drama's nadir. Planché, however, is

---

[17] *Literary Gazette,* 30 October 1830, 704 and 'The Art of Book-Making', *ibid* 706–7. A stiff letter from Colburn and Bentley to Lady Charlotte, dated 28 October 1830, survives among the firm's letter-books: Bentley Archives/British Library Reel 137, p 7 f 4.

[18] 'The Art of Book-Making', *Literary Gazette,* 6 November 1830, 722–3. Another reference to the affair appears in 'Literary Manoeuvring', *Literary Gazette,* 4 December 1830, 786.

unquestionably an important figure in the history of theatre.[19] Between 1818 and his death he wrote about 180 plays, in an astonishingly wide range of forms. Of Huguenot descent, he was brought up in a French-speaking household, and many of his plays were adaptations of French originals, notably of works by Eugène Scribe; he also adapted works by Sir Walter Scott, Thomas Love Peacock and Aristophanes. He wrote a large number of opera libretti; and because of the law confining legitimate drama to the patent theatres, musical interludes featured in almost all his plays up to 1843.[20] Much of his work falls into categories that are unfamiliar to us, such as burlesque and extravaganza, save to the extent that they prefigured the comic operas of WS Gilbert and the infinitely vulgarised modern pantomime, but he also wrote modern dramas, historical plays, farces, comedies and skits on contemporary theatrical life. One of his earliest successes was the horror play *The Vampire, or, The Bride of the Isles* (Lyceum, 1820), which introduced a theatrical device to simulate the sudden appearance or disappearance of a character through a solid wall, much used subsequently in Victorian theatre under the name 'vamp trap'.[21] It was he who wrote the dialogue of the opera *Clari, or, The Maid of Milan* (1823), now remembered only as the vehicle for the song 'Home, Sweet Home' (words by JH Payne and music by HR Bishop). In 1831, his *Olympic Revels, or, Prometheus and Pandora* (Olympic Theatre) created a wholly new genre, involving the gentle parody of mythological themes; its huge popularity resulted in a long collaboration with the actress Eliza Vestris, who was both star and theatre manager. But, as Stanley Wells remarked forty years ago, it is still true that 'If we hear anything he wrote, it is as likely as not to be in the German translation of his libretto for Weber's opera *Oberon*'.[22]

Planché became known for his innovative work on scenery and stage design, which involved both the introduction of more realistic and less

---

[19] On Planché's career see his *Recollections* (n 10), and D Roy, 'Planché, James Robinson (1796–1880)' *Oxford Dictionary of National Biography* (Oxford, OUP, 2004). For a sense of the variety of his oeuvre see P Buczkowski, 'JR Planché, Frederick Robson and the Fairy Extravaganza' (2001) 15 *Marvels and Tales: Journal of Fairy-Tale Studies* 42; K Fletcher, 'Aristophanes on the Victorian Stage: JR Planché's Adaptation of *The Birds*' (1979–81) 26/27 *Theatre Studies* 89; and R McFarland, 'The Vampire on Stage: A Study in Adaptations' (1987) 21 *Comparative Drama* 19.

[20] MR Booth in C Leech and TW Craik (gen eds), *The Revels History of Drama in English*, 8 vols (London, Methuen, 1875–83) vol VI, 44: 'because the minor theatres were forced by legal fiat into dumbshow, spectacle, melodrama, burletta and burlesque, the law shaped the whole course of nineteenth-century drama.'

[21] *Ibid* 72. A Emmet, 'The Vampire Trap' (1980) 34 *Theatre Notebook* 128, 129, cites P Fitzgerald, *The World Behind the Scenes* (1881) 58: 'two indiarubber doors or leaves, through which the performer passes, and which close behind him.'

[22] S Wells, 'Shakespeare in Planché's Extravaganzas' (1963) 16 *Shakespeare Survey* 103, 103. The role of Sir Huon in *Oberon, or the Enchanted Horn* (1826) was first sung at the Covent Garden Theatre by John Braham, a famous tenor who subsequently used some of Planché's words in a revival without his consent, leading to *Planché v Braham* (1837) 4 Bing (NC) 17, 132 ER 695, an early case on performance rights under the Dramatic Copyright Act 1833.

stylized productions and also the development of increasingly sophisticated and spectacular theatrical illusions. He was thus deeply involved in the whole theatrical event, not just the creation of the text. From early on he championed the use of historically accurate costume, notably in the performance of Shakespeare's plays,[23] and his research into this subject led him into a friendship with the antiquarian and collector Sir Samuel Meyrick, whose collection of arms and armour Planché later arranged to be displayed in public exhibitions in Manchester and South Kensington.[24] As early as 1825 Planché attended the coronation of Charles X of France, in order to create a pageant version of the ceremony in a London theatre; in 1829 he was elected a fellow of the Society of Antiquaries;[25] and later his scholarly research into historic costume and armour were acknowledged by his appointment in 1854 as Rouge Croix Pursuivant, and in 1866 as Somerset Herald, at the Royal College of Arms. In his capacity as a herald he served at various official ceremonies; he was also approached for costume advice by many of the guests at Queen Victoria's fancy-dress balls.

C. *THE JUVENILE LIBRARY*

The short life of the *Juvenile Library* can be described in some detail.[26] The earliest document is a letter from Jerdan to Colburn or Bentley, dated 29 April 1830, in which he sketches a deal between them for £200 a year while he acts as editor of the monthly *Juvenile Library*; every additional thousand copies above 4,000 will gain him an extra £25 per year. It is followed by the Memorandum of Agreement dated 30 April 1830, which survives in several copies:

> between William Jerdan Esq of Brompton on the one part, and Henry Colburn and Richard Bentley, publishers, of the other part.
>
> 1. The said Henry Colburn and Richard Bentley having undertaken to publish for their own use and benefit a Juvenile Library, and announced the same to appear in monthly volumes, and being desirous to avail themselves of the talents and Experience of the said William Jerdan Esq in the conduct thereof, the said

---

[23] JR Planché, *Costume of Shakespeare's King John, King Henry the Fourth, As You Like It, Hamlet, Othello and Merchant of Venice, selected . . . from the best authorities . . . with biographical, critical and explanatory notices*, 5 parts (London, John Miller, 1823–5). He also contributed an essay on the masques of Inigo Jones to P Cunningham, *Inigo Jones: A Life of the Architect* (London, Shakespeare Society, 1848), and served on the committee of the Shakespeare Society for some years.

[24] *Recollections* (n 10) vol I, 54–5, 232; vol II, 168–73, 268–71.

[25] *Ibid* vol I, 165.

[26] For background see L Howsam, 'Sustained Literary Ventures: The Series in Victorian Book Publishing' (1992) 31 *Publishing History* 5.

William Jerdan Esq for, and in consideration of the terms hereinafter mentioned agrees with, and on behalf of the said Henry Colburn and Richard Bentley to edit and prepare the said work for publication in the most careful manner and to the best of his ability, to use his influence to obtain the best writers for the same and in the most reasonable terms, to promote the sale and generally to further the interests of the said work as much as possible.

Jerdan was to be paid £300 per annum as long as the library continued, and once the circulation of the monthly volumes reached 5,000, this would be increased to 'Two Three Hundred and Fifty pounds per annum', with an extra £50 for every additional 1,000 copies sold. The erasure indicates that his remuneration was substantially increased in the course of negotiations. It was also provided that both parties would have power of veto, and that Colburn and Bentley could call a halt at any moment if they saw fit.[27] Some light is shed on the discrepancies between the letter and the agreement by a letter from Jerdan to the publishers (1 May 1830) in the Texas collection. Jerdan's anxiety seems to have been that the selection of authors and topics was to be collaborative, rather than his alone. He was evidently worried that he would be made to employ Colburn and Bentley's authors, and to take on books that he had no faith in. It may be that the additional pay which he seems to have negotiated was offered to persuade him to put up with this.

The first scheme seems to have been for the opening volume to be hastily composed by a 'poor Scholar', who was to 'put himself into the Mail tomorrow & proceed to the Country, whence he will not stir till he has produced the Volume', sending Jerdan bundles of manuscript week by week, 'having all ready by the 20th' of May, for publication on 1 June. The 'able Classic, a Clergyman & Member of Oxford' wanted £30 or £40 in advance for travel and accommodation. He is not named, nor is his proposed topic, and the plan does not seem to have been carried out, but it is possible that the Scholar was commissioned to write another volume in the series.[28]

The first volume, *Remarkable Youth of Both Sexes*, was published on 28 June. The main author, Don Joaquin Telesforo de Trueba y Cosío (1799–1835), a Spanish political refugee living in London since 1823 who was earning his living as a journalist and novelist, was offered work in connection with the series as early as 27 April, and he appears on Jerdan's list

---

[27] The letter is in the Harry Ransom Humanities Research Centre, University of Texas at Austin, Jerdan Collection. The agreement is BL MS Add 46611, Vol LII, f 137, microfilmed as Bentley Archives/British Library Reel 25 f 137. A copy is at Reel 35, pp 98–100, ff 63–4. Another copy is in the Harry Ransom Humanities Research Centre, University of Texas at Austin, Jerdan Collection. The copies lack the erasures that suggest Jerdan talked his price up.
[28] MS Harry Ransom Humanities Research Centre, University of Texas at Austin, Jerdan letters.

of possible future volumes as the author of works on several subjects.[29] But Jerdan wrote on 29 June complaining that a book with so many errors in it should go out 'as sanctioned by me', also at the raising of the price from 3/6 to 4 *s*.[30] This comment, in conjunction with the fact that the book had two authors, suggests that it was probably cobbled together as quickly as possible to get the show on the road.

An amusing story is told by Samuel Carter Hall in his memoirs about the preparation of Volume II:[31]

> In 1830 I produced a remarkable book: remarkable not by reason of its merit or value, but from the peculiar circumstances under which it was written. At that time monthly issues of original works were in favour with the public . . . the fashion ceased after a comparatively brief time, and they are now forgotten. . . . Mr Jerdan, who edited Colburn's [*Juvenile Library*] was 'in a fix.' He had been promised for one of the volumes a 'History of France,' but as, at the last moment, it was not forthcoming, he called upon me to ascertain if I could by any possibility write it, and have it ready for publication by the first of the month 'then next ensuing.' It was the 9th of the month, consequently there were but twenty-one days and nights in which to write, print, and publish a book of four hundred pages. Six engravings had moreover to be made—their subjects not even decided upon. There was nothing for it but to produce the book or close the series, as the work must have ceased unless the month gave its continuing part.
>
> I undertook the task, and occupied one day in collecting all the Histories of France I could obtain. Surrounded by a formidable array of volumes I began my task—working at it all night and all day, during eighteen nights and days, without interruption. The result was that, within the stipulated time, a 'History of France' . . . was written . . . The overwork led to a brain fever; I had not gone to bed for twelve nights; and the payment I received for it was very hardly, though very quickly earned.

Two rather hurried and botched volumes were thus all that had appeared when Jerdan wrote to the publishers on 18 July to promise that Miss Webb

---

[29] For the early offer of work to Trueba, see MS Harry Ransom Humanities Research Centre, University of Texas at Austin, Jerdan Letters (29 April 1830) and 'Mr Jerdan's Suggestions for Juvenile Library'. On Trueba's career we rely on the introduction by A Gonsalez Palencia to Trueba's *España Romantica* (Madrid, Saeta, 1942): born in Santander and educated in England at the Catholic college, Old Hall Green, Herts, he emigrated to England in 1823 after the failure of the progressive movement, wrote a number of plays and novels in English, which were also translated into other European languages (including Spanish), became a deputy in the Cortes after the amnesty of 1834 permitted his return to Spain, and died young in Paris in the following year. His co-author, DE Williams, seems to have been a naval officer in weak health; the following year he edited *The Life and Correspondence of Sir Thomas Lawrence*, 2 vols (London, Colburn and Bentley, 1831). The task of preparing the letters for publication was no doubt literary drudgery to be farmed out to a needy hack. See Gettman (n 2) 40.

[30] MS Harry Ransom Humanities Research Centre, University of Texas at Austin, Jerdan Letters (29 June 1830).

[31] Samuel Carter Hall, *Retrospect of a Long Life*, 2 vols (London, Bentley, 1883) vol I, 312.

would supply them with the manuscript of her *History of Africa* in plenty of time.[32] Jane Webb was a young woman who had had considerable success with her futuristic novel *The Mummy!: A Tale of the Twenty-second Century* (1827), which concerned the resuscitation of the pharoah Cheops; later, under her married name of Mrs Loudon, she became a popular writer on gardening. Whether Colburn and Bentley were reassured, and whether the statement was true, are not clear. Hall's *Historic Anecdotes of France* was published on 28 July.

D. JERDAN'S LIST

At this point, the summer of 1830, we may take a step back and look beyond these hasty stop-gap measures, to Jerdan's abortive plans for the longer-term future of the *Juvenile Library*, drawing on a manuscript list entitled 'Mr Jerdan's Suggestions for the Juvenile Library', two lists of contributors made at the time of the settlements, and other evidence from the Bentley archives.[33] They show, unsurprisingly, that he had called on a number of experienced journalists and hack-writers of both sexes whom he knew through his contacts in the literary world.

So far, as we have seen, the *Juvenile Library* consisted of: Volume 1 Joaquin de Trueba y Cosío and DE Williams, *Remarkable Youth of Both Sexes*; Volume 2 Samuel Carter Hall, *Historic Anecdotes of France*; and Volume 3 Jane (Webb) Loudon, *History of Africa*. The proposed Volume 4 was to have been a *History of Greece* by the Rev Whittington Landon, brother of the famous poet Letitia Landon; it may well be that he was the 'poor Scholar' whom Jerdan had proposed as the author of the first volume.[34] At any rate he seems to have been hard at work over the summer, because he had produced a manuscript by October. It seems likely that Volume 5 would have been *The Children of Israel* (otherwise *The History of the Jews*[35]) by the Rev Dr Daniel Guildford Wait,[36] an undoubtedly

---

[32] MS Harry Ransom Humanities Research Centre, University of Texas at Austin, Jerdan Letters f 15.

[33] 'Mr Jerdan's Suggestions' are in the collection in Texas, as is one of the lists of contributors; the other, in the British Library, is transcribed by Gettman (n 2) 38.

[34] The Rev Whittington Landon (1804/5–1883), Vicar of Slebech, Pembrokeshire 1851–77. The fact that he was the brother of Letitia Landon, whose relationship with Jerdan was the subject of gossip, might explain the suppression of his name. For Landon's career see J Foster, *Alumni Oxonienses 1715–1886*, 4 vols (London, Foster, 1887–8), citing the Rev CJ Robinson, *A Register of the Scholars Admitted into Merchant Taylors' School*, 2 vols (Lewes, Farncombe 1882).

[35] The BL list has *Children of Israel* but see Gettman (n 2) 43 for a reference to the same book as *History of the Jews*. One reason for giving it the former title would have been to avoid confusion with HH Milman's justly celebrated *History of the Jews*, published in Murray's Family Library in 1829.

[36] The Rev Daniel Guildford Wait (1789–1850) was Rector of Blagdon, Somerset, and has a brief entry, as a theologian, in *ODNB*: EI Carlyle, 'Wait, Daniel Guildford (1789/90–1850)'

learned but evidently slightly disreputable and certainly indigent clergyman, whose manuscript also seems to have been ready by the time the series folded, because Jerdan wrote to Bentley to complain that Wait had been unfairly kept in suspense about the publication of his manuscript.[37] The proposed Volume 6 is known to have been another work by Trueba, *Lives of Renowned Knights*.

Other future volumes whose authors had completed, or nearly completed, or perhaps only claimed they had completed, the commissioned work were *The History of Scotland* by Robert Chambers (the well-known author of *Vestiges of the Natural History of Creation*); *The History of Turkey* by William Henry Smith (1808–72), a journalist and lawyer; *The History of Ireland* by Thomas Crofton Croker, a close friend of Jerdan's and a prolific writer on Irish subjects; a work variously entitled *Chemistry* or *The History of Popular Science* by George Atkins, who is not identifiable; *Celebrated Commanders* by the popular novelist GPR James; *Missionaries* by Andrew Picken;[38] and *Illustrations* [or *Sayings*] *of the Seven Sages* by Isaac Cullimore, Egyptologist.

Further works in the pipeline included *Lives of the Poets* by Letitia Landon, the romantic lyricist whose name gossips coupled with the married Jerdan's; and *The History of Birds* by Anna Maria Hall, wife of Samuel Carter Hall and, like him, a prolific all-round hack writer and journalist. The Scots historian Patrick Fraser Tytler was to have contributed *The Reformation*. Dr Anthony Todd Thomson, a well-known doctor at University College Hospital, and his wife Katherine (Byerley) Thomson, close friends of Letitia Landon's, were to contribute *Botany* and *The History of England* respectively. Captain DE Williams, RN, who had part-written Volume 1, was going to write *Roman Emperors*; and another naval officer, whose name appears variously as Captain Beechey, Beecher or Becher,[39] was going to do *Circumnavigators*. Dr Robert Walsh, the former chaplain of the embassy in St Petersburg, was going to write *The History of Russia*, and the

---

revised S Agnew, *Oxford Dictionary of National Biography* (Oxford, OUP, 2004). More evidence about his career emerges from the archives of the Royal Literary Fund (case 794). He appears to have been proficient in Hebrew and Arabic, and to have written works on theology, bible history and etymology. His application in 1834, in which he claimed to have known 'the extreme of destitution' was rejected on moral grounds, suggesting sexual misconduct; he seems to have gone bankrupt at one point; the Fund gave his widow money.

[37] Another explanation may be that Jerdan respected Wait more than the rest of his contributors.

[38] Andrew Picken (1788–1833), Scots novelist, seems to have contrived to find another publisher within the year for *Travels and Researches of Eminent English Missionaries* (London, William Kidd, 1830). See also Marchand (n 2) 127 for Picken's part-authorship of an attack on the *Juvenile Library* published in the *Athenaeum* (21 August 1830). Gettman (n 2) 39 transcribes the word 'Perkin [?]' but the word appears more clearly on the Texas list. Gettman also transcribes 'Rev Mr Lander' but the reference must be to Whittington Landon.

[39] Perhaps Alexander Bridport Becher, or Frederick William Beechey.

novelist and art critic Anna Jameson was to do *Great Queens*. A work enig-
matically described as *Contrasts* by Maria Jane Jewsbury may be the same
as 'Miss Jewsbury's "Conquerors & Philanthropists"' mentioned in Jerdan's
'Suggestions', and sounds as if it would have been an interesting addition
to her short bibliography.[40] And of course, last but not least, there was
James Robinson Planché's *Dress and Costume*, which he himself called a
Chronological History of Costume, and which was described in court as 'a
volume on Costume and Ancient Armour'. This was agreed to be unfinished,
but was included among the projects on which substantial work had been
done.

E. ABANDONMENT OF THE SERIES

For some reason that is not clear—perhaps owing to the publishers' loss of
commitment, or to the lateness of one or more manuscripts—no volume
appeared in either August or September. An undated letter to Bentley probably written at about this time mentions Colburn's 'cold-water treatment of
the Juvenile' and offers to try to find another publisher for the series; he
hopes that the map and ornaments of Africa are ready.[41] On 14 October,
after a two month gap, the third and final volume of the *Juvenile Library*,
The History of Africa, was published. But even by 2 October Jerdan was
clearly worried that the publishers were losing faith in the enterprise. He
wrote to them both, complaining that they were 'not truly keeping faith
with me respecting the Juvenile Library', and that they were sacrificing it to
make room for a series for adults (the *National Library*).[42] He objected to
them having told Anna Maria Hall, one of the proposed contributors, that
it was 'to be immediately dropt': the series was not being given a fair
chance. As was very much his custom, he reminded them of how one gentleman should treat another: 'you are in honour bound'. On a more practical note, he added that he was sending the manuscript of Volume IV,
Whittington Landon's *The History of Greece*, to the printers that day, so

---

[40] The sources for this are the BL list of the state of the commissions (printed by Gettman (n
2) 39), the Texas list and the Texas 'Mr Jerdan's Suggestions'. The authors referred to are all,
except Williams, Becher and Atkins, in the new *ODNB*, which for historical reasons is especially strong on minor authors of the early nineteenth century. We think that the identifications
we have made, for example of 'Dr Walsh' and 'Mrs Hall' are safe, although there is more evidence in some cases than in others. Several of these writers are known to have been contributors to the *Athenaeum*; we cannot say whether, as is likely, many worked for the *Literary
Gazette*, because a contributor list survives for the former and not for the latter.
[41] MS Harry Ransom Humanities Research Centre, University of Texas at Austin, Jerdan to
Bentley: 'So much the enemy'.
[42] MS Harry Ransom Humanities Research Centre, University of Texas at Austin, Jerdan
Letters (2 October 1830). The *National Library* was also abandoned, at the same time as the
Juvenile Library.

that it would be ready for publication on 1 November, and added that he would be grateful for a cheque for £75 with which to pay the author.

The following day he wrote again to say that 'on account of the Juvenile Library' he had been obliged to borrow 50 guineas from Longman so as to be able to withdraw money from his bank.[43] The implication may be that he had dipped into his own pocket to pay Landon. He argued that until six or eight volumes were published it would not be possible to judge the viability of the project, and concluded that he hoped the third volume 'will do something to remove the natural dissatisfaction of dr sirs yrs truly W Jerdan'. It looks as if Landon's book turned out to be too short, because on 4 October, Jerdan sent Colburn and Bentley a book 'to complete the Vol IV Juvenile Library'. The implication seems to be that a passage (perhaps from some classical author) would be reprinted as part of Volume IV to bulk it up to the required length.[44]

By this time, though, it seems that the publishers had resolved to abandon the series altogether. At any rate, that is the implication of an interesting document which survives in triplicate. A letter from Jerdan to Colburn and Bentley beginning 'Having in order to save you from loss and annoyance . . .' exists in three different hands, and was evidently the instrument used by Jerdan to communicate this decision to his authors. Two are dated October 1830, one is dated 16 October (a Saturday).[45] The more precisely dated letter is probably the original, since it appears to be in Jerdan's own tidiest writing (and contains a few erasures). Characteristically pompous and long-winded, he writes of his own injured feelings, and objects that:

> my position appears to be utterly forgotten, and every Individual whom I have engaged with to write, is treated separately, in a manner I deeply disapprove, and without reference to what has passed between them and me—placing me in a light so ridiculous and contemptible, that I neither can nor will endure . . . I have most openly & unreservedly acted for your interest . . . (when the publication blasted in its progress and and abandoned without a fair trial, was resolved by Mr. Colburn to be given discontinued) . . . but all my efforts have been counteracted, and you seem bent on incurring the evils, pecuniary and literary, which I have been so anxious to prevent, by very fruitless, and, I think, not very creditable or high-spirited negotiations with each in their turn.

> . . . more in pity than in anger—[I] offer two lines of conduct for your <u>immediate</u> adoption

[43] MS Harry Ransom Humanities Research Centre, University of Texas at Austin, Jerdan Letters (3 October 1830). Bentley Archives/British Library Reel 1, Authors' Accounts p 41 show that Jerdan was paid a total of £100 between 8 June and 25 August for editing four volumes of the *Juvenile Library*; the last payment, on 25 August, took the form of a promissory note for £50 at two months' date for the September and October volumes.

[44] Bentley Archives/University of California, Reel 1.

[45] Two (one dated 16 October) are in Texas. The other is in the Croker collection, Cork City Library. There are only a few minor differences of punctuation and spelling between the copies.

1. I renew my proposition to settle the whole affair, (beyond what is already in your hands) for £500—taking my chance. There is no claim upon you except through me, and the moment I am a principal, your concern is over. This is legal opinion, without a doubt, and I am persuaded I can make better terms with the parties than you can;—having negotiated with them and having cogent and gentlemanlike reasons to urge for deductions, which you have not.

2. I, by a circular letter to all concerned (inclosing a copy of this my explanation) absolve myself from responsibility, and throw the parties on you. This act of justice to myself, I shall perform with regret, but I have no other means to avoid being made the complete Scapegoat, I have allowed myself to be made too far already in my endeavour to save you. As a matter of opinion, I believe that £1,000 and much odium must be the result and price of this alternative.

I now leave it to you to make your election; and by Monday shall look for your decision. On Tuesday I shall be prepared to act on as that decision dictates; and with extreme regret for the past, humiliation for the present, and, in the latter event, most unpleasant foreboding of the future.

Jerdan is not a wholly appealing figure, but there is more here than bluster. As we observed earlier, he operated at a time when the social status of the professional writer was uncertain; the sale of manuscripts to publishers looked like trade, intellectual labour was associated with the professional classes, and literature and the arts had a loosely-defined elite status. His own situation as editor, or agent, separated him from the tradesman-like publisher, but at this moment it put him in a nasty predicament, having given his word on behalf of others. He was concerned to relocate the transaction to a sphere in which the 'gentleman's agreement' holds strong, if necessary by invoking the legally-sanctioned 'verbal contract'.[46]

It seems clear that Jerdan sent out copies of his letter to many of the contributors, and we have two indications as to the format. On the second Texas copy of the letter is his signature, and a 'memorandum' which, unlike the rest of the letter, is in his writing. It states that Colburn and Bentley have chosen the second route, and he therefore asks the contributor to stop writing and send to the publishers 'the amount of your demand for what you may have done, which they have assured me will be immediately and honourably discharg^d. WJ.' This was probably a sample version.[47] The copy in

---

[46] A warmer letter, to Bentley alone, is undated except for the words 'Monday night' but may well have been written on 18 October (though it could also date from 11 October or some other date): Harry Ransom Humanities Research Centre, University of Texas at Austin, Jerdan to Bentley: 'I am much obliged'. This letter refers to 'the most degrading representations' he has had 'from Dr Thomson's' and says he has borrowed money again for the 'honour of the concern'.

[47] No contributor is named, and another letter (Jerdan Collection) indicates that it was enclosed to Bentley by Jerdan to show him what he proposed to do. But the letter to Croker suggests that the plan was indeed carried out in more or less this form.

Cork has a note of about the same length at the bottom; although it is couched in friendlier and more personal terms, the statement it makes is very similar. Croker was also asked to show the letter to a fellow contributor.[48] Jerdan wrote to Bentley that he had copied the letter to prominent figures in the literary world for the sake of his own reputation.

The reference in Jerdan's circular letter to Colburn and Bentley's botched attempts to settle the affair on their own does not make it possible to tell precisely when the two surviving lists of contributors were prepared, but they probably also belong to the first half of October. One at least seems to date from slightly before Jerdan had made this public renunciation of any further responsibility in the affair. This is an undated page of notes in the Jerdan Collection at the Humanities Research Centre in Texas, listing various *Juvenile Library* authors and estimating the total cost of paying them off; this seems to be the paper which was later produced in court and was there described as being in Jerdan's writing;[49] the authors are grouped in various categories according to the amount of work they had done. Wait, Croker, Chambers, Whittington Landon and Atkins are described as 'absolute' and the sum £375 is marked against them; we interpret this to mean that it was proposed to pay them each the full £75 in settlement.[50] The next group, Jewsbury, Smith, Letitia Landon and Planché, have '100' against them, implying that it was hoped to fob them off with £25 each. Still lower are Patrick Fraser Tytler, Katharine Thomson, Anthony Todd Thomson, Beechey and Williams, who were to be offered a mere £10 apiece.[51] A further group, consisting of Trueba, James, Anna Maria Hall, Picken and Walsh, was labelled doubtful.[52]

This list has names on it which do not appear on the list in the BL Bentley MSS printed by Gettman, and on the whole it seems likely that it preceded it in date, and that further enquiries enabled the compiler of the second list to omit various authors who had not got far with the commission. Jerdan subsequently claimed in court that it dated from the period when he was prepared to take on responsibility for negotiating with the authors on a personal basis.[53] Whoever compiled the Texas list did not know how far Trueba had got with *Renowned Knights*, whereas the compiler of the BL list describes it

---

[48] 'Captain Becher', whose subject was Circumnavigators.

[49] See nn 53, 74, and 75.

[50] MS Harry Ransom Humanities Research Centre, University of Texas at Austin, Jerdan Collection.

[51] Six names are listed, but one, 'Cullimore', is erased (perhaps by another hand). Both £60 and '100' are suggested as enough to deal with this group. In the same collection a list 'Mr Jerdan's suggestions for Juvenile Library' includes 'Cullamore' against a proposed title 'Sayings of the Seven Sages', and the reference is probably to Isaac Cullimore, Egyptologist: see HM Stephens, 'Cullimore, Isaac (1791–1852)', revised E Baigent, *Oxford Dictionary of National Biography* (Oxford, OUP, 2004). Perhaps he turned out not to have got very far with his book.

[52] Another name, which might perhaps be 'Mrs Howitt' or 'Wm Howitt', has been erased from this section.

[53] *The Times*, 15 June 1831, 6, col d; *Bell's Weekly Messenger* 19 June 1831, 198, col 1.

as 'MS on hand'. Hence it can probably be dated to before or at least not long after 16 October 1830. On that date Colburn and Bentley agreed to publish Trueba's *Satanic Records* on half-profits, and he was advanced £75 on account, in return for dropping any claim he might have had on account of the *Lives of Renowned Knights* 'intended for the Juvenile Library which is now discontinued'.[54] It appears from an entry in the author's accounts that he had already, on 17 July, received money (in the form of a post-dated draft for £50) as payment for the copyright of *Renowned Knights,* which was intended to form Volume 6 of the *Juvenile Library.*[55]

On 30 October 1830 George Atkins signed a document agreeing to relinquish his claims on Colburn and Bentley, he having been commissioned to write a *History of Popular Science* for the *Juvenile Library.*[56] Also around this time, a post-dated bill seems to have been sent to Whittington Landon, for Jerdan wrote to complain that it was no use, being 'of too long a date'.[57] There are also two surviving letters from Jerdan to Bentley relating to the deal with Dr Wait. One is undated, and sanctimonious in tone. It chides Bentley for his delay in writing to Dr Wait to end his anxiety, citing Proverbs 13:12: 'Hope deferred maketh the heart sick.' It may date from a period when it was uncertain whether Wait's *Children of Israel* was to be published. Another letter on the same subject, dated 23 October,[58] asks as a 'particular favour' from 'a personal consideration' that 'you w^d release me from £75 for the History of the Children of Israel.' He has the manuscript (except the final chapter) all ready to be sent, and he also has 'the writer's discharge ready to deliver'. This is ambiguous and not easy to interpret. It is unclear whether the money is for him or Wait, and whether publication is contemplated.

In fact the publishers seem to have been fairly successful in appeasing their authors. No doubt in other cases, as in Trueba's, other favours were extended, or, as in Landon's, dribs and drabs of money in the form of post-dated bills were used. Separate publication was offered to some of the better-known of the authors whose works were complete or almost complete: Anna Jameson's *Great Queens* appeared as *Memoirs of Celebrated Female Sovereigns,*[59] and GPR James's *Commanders* as *Memoirs of Great Commanders.*[60] However, one author made trouble, and it is tempting to attribute this to the fact that, although he was an experienced professional writer, he was not dependent, as were the others, on the goodwill of the publishing industry. This was James Robinson Planché.

---

[54] BL MS Add 46611 Vol LII, f 174.

[55] Bentley Archives/British Library, Reel 25, Authors' Accounts, f 110.

[56] *Ibid* f 178.

[57] MS Harry Ransom Humanities Research Centre, University of Texas at Austin, Jerdan letters, Jerdan to Richard Bentley, enclosing the circular letter and memorandum.

[58] This is the date on the letter, but the postmark, which is smudged, could be read October 30.

[59] London, Colburn and Bentley, 1831.

[60] London, Colburn and Bentley, 1832.

F. PLANCHÉ NEGOTIATES

On 26 October 1830 Planché wrote to Jerdan, evidently in response to the circular letter carrying the news that the *Juvenile Library* had been abandoned:[61]

My dear Sir,

I was certainly much annoyed by your communication of yesterday having very reluctantly abandoned more lucrative employments in consequence of your repeated and, I am bound to add, complimentary requests, and applied myself for upwards of two months to the collection of materials for a Chronological History of Costume in the hope that the credit it might do me in a literary point of view would balance the pecuniary disadvantage I knew must attend its production. My making any charge that would really compensate me for my loss of time and labour is, for that very reason, impossible, as I expected eventually to receive £200 for the work (100 for each vol) according to our understanding. I should think a fourth part of that sum (50) as little as Messrs Colburn and Bentley could offer me. You are aware my dear Sir that I made a journey into Herefordshire expressly to consult the fine library and avail myself of the experience of my friend Dr Meyrick in the portion allotted to antient arms and armour and you have seen and approved the drawings for ten plates made by me at Goodrich for the work and can consequently bear witness to part of the expense and trouble I have incurred.

After all I must sit down under severe disappointment as publication was my principal object—such extensive publication particularly as the exerted influence of Messrs Colburn and Bentley would have insured me.

A month later, on 24 November, Planché wrote to Colburn and Bentley:[62]

Gentlemen,

Having forwarded through Mr Jerdan, by his and your desire my claim for time and labor [sic] expended on that portion of "the Juvenile Library" I was engaged by the Editor to execute, I am anxious to learn your decision respecting it. May I request—as nearly a month has elapsed without a reply—an immediate settlement of the business. Any uncertainty respecting such matters being particularly inconvenient to

Gentlemen

your obed^t Servt

JR Planché

---

[61] Bentley Archives/University of Illinois, Reel 47.
[62] *Ibid.*

It appears that Bentley must have responded to this letter by arranging to meet Planché on 30 November.[63] It also seems likely that Bentley told Planché at this meeting that he had been unaware of the terms of Jerdan's agreement with Planché (which seem to have been slightly more generous than the terms offered to the other contributors),[64] but said that he and Colburn would publish Planché's work as a separate volume, if he would complete and deliver the manuscript, in exchange for £100, the amount that Jerdan had promised for the first volume. At the subsequent trial, Colburn and Bentley alleged that Planché had agreed to this new arrangement, although 'the form and size of the proposed new work were not settled on that occasion',[65] and that he had later changed his mind.[66] Their clerk, Charles Ollier,[67] testified that 'he had heard the plaintiff say that he would finish his treatise, if the defendants would undertake to publish it separately and as a distinct work';[68] also, that Planché had said that the subject 'was better for a separate publication than for the Juvenile Library, as in treating it for children he had been very much hampered, and there was great difficulty in adapting it for juvenile comprehension'.[69]

However, Planché himself gave a different version of events in court, denying that he had agreed to the new arrangement. Even if he had remarked that the subject was better suited to treatment for adults, the manuscript and drawings that he had prepared were unsuitable for an adult publication, and so he would have had to start writing the book all over again, or else make himself look ridiculous.[70] It is now impossible to be sure whose account of the meeting was correct. However, Tindal CJ told the jury that 'it might be, that the plaintiff considered the subject-matter was better adapted for separate publication, without admitting that the MS. and drawings already prepared were suited to such a publication',[71] and he directed them to find for the publishers only if they thought that 'the first agreement [was] entirely abandoned with [Planché's] consent . . . and an entire new agreement made between the parties'.[72] Since the jury gave a verdict for

---

[63] The law reports state that they met in November: 5 Car & P 58, 61; 172 ER 876, 878 (Tindal CJ). That 30 November was the precise date of their meeting is suggested by the reference in Planché's next letter, dated 1 December, to their having had a conversation 'yesterday': see text to n 73.

[64] £100 rather than the £75 which was paid to Samuel Carter Hall and Jane Webb. Planché's next letter corroborates this view: see text to n 73.

[65] 5 Car & P 58, 60; 172 ER 876, 877 (Serjeant Spankie, *arguendo*). See too *The Times*, 15 June 1831, 6, col d.

[66] 1 M & S 51, 52 (Serjeant Spankie, *arguendo*). See too *The Times*, 15 June 1831, 6, col d.

[67] For Ollier's life and career, see CE Robinson, 'Ollier, Charles (1788–1859)' *Oxford Dictionary of National Biography* (Oxford, OUP, 2004).

[68] 1 M & S 51, 51.

[69] 5 Car & P 58, 61; 172 ER 876, 878 (Tindal CJ).

[70] 5 Car & P 60, 172 ER 877 (Serjeant Wilde, *arguendo*).

[71] 5 Car & P 61, 172 ER 878.

[72] 5 Car & P 61–2, 172 ER 878.

Planché, we conclude that Planché did not agree to a new deal because of the additional work this would have entailed, and that his resolve hardened when Jerdan told him after his meeting with Bentley on 30 November that he had certainly commissioned Planché to do the work with Colburn and Bentley's authority.

This understanding of events is supported by Planché's next surviving letter to Colburn and Bentley, dated 1 December, within which he enclosed a letter from Jerdan bearing the same date.[73] Jerdan confirms that he engaged Planché 'to write a volume on Costume for the Juvenile Library at the price of one hundred pounds, upon which arrangement I consulted Messrs Colburn and Bentley, and which they sanctioned in common with more than ten other similar engagements'. Planché states:[74]

> As I am totally unable to reconcile his statement with the assurance you gave me yesterday that you were <u>not</u> apprized by him of the sum agreed upon, and as the work for which I was specially engaged to write is altogether abandoned I must decline any further attention to it and at once require the payment of the 50 as stated in my letter to Mr Jerdan of the 26th of October, or place the whole business in the hands of my Solicitors.

G. COURT PROCEEDINGS

Colburn and Bentley refused to pay. Perhaps they mistrusted Jerdan, whose relations with Colburn were decidedly unhappy for other reasons, as we have explained, who was at loggerheads with both of them over the abandonment of the series, and who had now lent his weight to Planché's claim for £50, although he had previously suggested that Planché might be bought off for £25.[75] Whatever their reasons, the publishers were obdurate, and Planché duly issued proceedings in the Court of Common Pleas, which came on for hearing in June 1831.[76]

The first count of Planché's declaration stated that the defendants had promised him £100 for the writing and delivery of the manuscript for

---

[73] Planché's letter to Bentley is now in Illinois but the enclosed letter from Jerdan to Planché is in Texas. Both letters are dated 1 December 1830.

[74] MS Harry Ransom Humanities Research Centre, University of Texas at Austin.

[75] Jerdan was challenged about this discrepancy when he gave evidence in court, and explained that his suggestion that Planché could be bought off for £25 was 'on the footing of an arrangement personally with himself, as a friend of the parties': *The Times,* 15 June 1831, 6, col d; *Bell's Weekly Messenger,* 19 June 1831, 198, col 1.

[76] There survives a letter (6 May 1831) from Planché's solicitor, Lythgoe, requiring all Planché's correspondence with Colburn and Bentley, and 'a certain letter written and sent to the Defendants in the month of October last by Mr William Jerdan on the subject of the present cause of action' to be produced in court: Bentley Archives/University of Illinois, Reel 47. It is endorsed 'Mr Jerdan's letter & <u>all</u> Mr Planché's', presumably by someone in the employ of Colburn and Bentley. On the whole it seems likely that the circular letter is the one referred to.

publication in the *Juvenile Library*, but had refused to accept the manuscript for publication in that series, that they had thereby prevented him from completing his obligations, even though he remained willing and able to perform, and that they had refused either to pay him the promised £100, or to compensate him or remunerate him for his time, trouble and expenses. The second count stated that the defendants were accordingly indebted to him for £100. This was a claim for damages for breach of contract, quantified by reference to the contract price. The third count stated that the plaintiff was entitled to payment of 50 guineas on an *indebitatus* count for work and labour. This was a quasi-contractual claim for a *quantum meruit* award.

In reply, the defendants pleaded the general issue, and sought to show that the parties had set the original contract aside and entered a new contract under which the plaintiff would deliver the manuscript for publication as a book for adults. According to *The Times*, Serjeant Spankie gave a 'very humorous' speech to the jury:[77]

> [He] would show that the plaintiff had admitted that costume and ancient armour were very embarrassing subjects to write about for little masters and misses, in an abridged shape, and much better adapted for a full grown volume for full grown readers. Costume was a peculiarly interesting topic, almost, though not quite, as old as the world; and all its varieties,—whether the Highlander's kilt, or the fine ladies' brocade,—were only expansions of the renowned fig-leaf, the first effort at costume. Mr Planché had no doubt studied *Albertus Magnus de re vestiariâ veterum* and *Salmasius*, and all the other authorities collected in the chapter on dress in *Tristram Shandy*; and that all this interesting learning should be lost to the world, on account of this unhappy misunderstanding with the booksellers, was much to be regretted. He trusted, however, it would still appear, to delight the jury and the adult public.

Tindal CJ put two questions to the jury: had the defendants broken their contract with Planché by refusing to publish his work in the *Juvenile Library*; and had he entered a new contract to allow them to publish the work in another form?[78] The jury found for Planché and awarded him £50.

Matters did not end there. With the court's leave, the defendants brought a second set of proceedings in November 1831, in which they asked either that the verdict should be set aside and the plaintiff non-suited, or that a new trial should be had.[79] Serjeant Spankie contended that the plaintiff could not recover £100 on the second count, since he had not completed and delivered the manuscript, and the contract specified that payment was conditional on completion and delivery. He also argued that the plaintiff

---

[77] *The Times*, 15 June 1831, 6, col d.
[78] *The Times*, 7 November 1831, 6, cols c–d.
[79] 8 Bing 14, 131 ER 305; 1 M & S 51; 1 LJCP 7.

could not recover £50 on the third count, because the contract was still open.

The court seems to have found the first of these contentions uncontroversial, Gaselee J commenting that 'if . . . the declaration had contained no other count than that founded on the special contract, the plaintiff could not have succeeded'.[80] However, the defendants' second contention required the court to revisit the facts of the case, to decide whether it had been a term of the parties' agreement that the defendants would publish the plaintiff's work as part of the *Juvenile Library*, whether they had unequivocally abandoned the series, and if so, whether the plaintiff could rescind the contract for the defendants' breach, rather than merely treat it as discharged, in which case a *quantum meruit* claim would not have been available. The court found for Planché, holding that it was a term of the parties' contract not merely that the defendants would pay the plaintiff for delivery of the manuscript, but that they would publish it 'in a suitable shape', something they had put beyond their power to accomplish 'after the abandonment of the original design'.[81] In Tindal CJ's view:[82]

> The considerations by which an author is generally actuated in undertaking to write a work are pecuniary profit and literary reputation. Now, it is clear that the latter may be sacrificed, if an author, who has engaged to write a volume of a popular nature, to be published in a work intended for a juvenile class of readers, should be subject to have his writings published as a separate and distinct work, and therefore liable to be judged of by more severe rules than would be applied to a familiar work intended merely for children. The fact was, that the Defendants not only suspended, but actually put an end to, "The Juvenile Library"; they had broken their contract with the Plaintiff . . .

H. CONTRACT AND QUASI-CONTRACT

As Patteson J later observed in *Goodman v Pocock*, the reports of *Planché* do not tell us explicitly whether the plaintiff was awarded £50 on the third, *quantum meruit* count, or as (prorated) damages for breach of contract under the second count, but Tindal CJ 'is reported as if he considered the plaintiff entitled to recover on the *quantum meruit*'.[83] Thus, we find in one report the laconic statement that in the course of argument Tindal CJ thought that the case did not turn 'upon the second count, but upon the *quantum meruit* in the third count'.[84] It is also reported that after the verdict was given in the

---

[80] 1 M & S 51, 53.
[81] 8 Bing 14, 16; 131 ER 305, 306 (Bosanquet J).
[82] 8 Bing 15–16, 131 ER 305–6.
[83] (1850) 15 QB 576, 582–3; 117 ER 577, 580.
[84] 5 Car & P 58, 61; 172 ER 876, 878.

first set of proceedings, Serjeant Spankie submitted for the defendants that 'the verdict could not be taken on the *quantum meruit*, and that the special count did not accord with the evidence', and to this Tindal CJ replied that he thought 'the plaintiff might recover on the *quantum meruit*'.[85] Taken in conjunction with Gaselee J's dictum that the plaintiff 'could not have succeeded' if he had only counted on the special contract,[86] these comments lead us to conclude that the award made was a *quantum meruit* award under the third count.

In *Hochster v De La Tour*,[87] Lord Campbell CJ subsequently asserted that Planché had 'retained his verdict on the count framed on the special contract', and relied on the earlier case as authority for the rule that an action for damages would immediately lie following an anticipatory breach of contract. In our view, however, this was a misreading of *Planché*, where the court actually held that the plaintiff could not recover damages for non-payment of the contract price because the event that would have triggered the defendants' obligation to pay—the plaintiff's delivery of the manuscript—had not occurred.[88] This is not to deny that if *Planché* were decided today, the defendants' repudiatory breach would give the plaintiff an immediate right to terminate future performance of his obligations and recover damages without having to complete and tender his repudiated performance.[89] Nor is it to deny that there are cases pre-dating *Planché* in which the seeds of the doctrine of anticipatory breach were sown.[90] Nevertheless, we do not believe that this was the basis on which *Planché* was decided,[91] and in our view the doctrine of anticipatory breach did not fully emerge until later, in a group of cases in

---

[85] 5 Car & P 58, 62; 172 ER 876, 878.

[86] See text to n 80.

[87] (1852) 2 E & B 678, 694; 118 ER 922, 927.

[88] Following *White & Carter (Councils) Ltd v McGregor* [1962] AC 413, a claimant in Planché's position might now be entitled to complete performance in the teeth of the defendants' repudiation with a view to recovering the full contract price. On the facts of *Planché*, this would have meant completing and delivering the manuscript of a book written for children, which it seems the defendants did not wish to publish. In *White & Carter*, at 431, Lord Reid held that an insistent performer can complete only if he has a 'legitimate interest' in doing so, and suggested that an 'expert' employed by a company to prepare 'an elaborate report' might not have such an interest. Did Planché have a legitimate interest in completion? He does seem to have been motivated in part by antiquarian enthusiasm and the desire to boost his literary reputation, although it must be doubted whether this would have been much enhanced by the publication of a work addressed to children, given the low status enjoyed by such works at the time: see text to n 116.

[89] See text to nn 108 ff.

[90] Eg *Jones v Barkley* (1781) 2 Doug 684, 694; 99 ER 434, 439–40 (Lord Mansfield).

[91] Cf A Kull, 'Restitution for Breach of Contract' (1994) 67 *Southern California Law Review* 1465, 1487–8: 'the *effect* of the judgment in *Planché* was the same as an award of damages for anticipatory breach, 'but contemporary contract doctrine did not permit the remedy to be so forthrightly described'.

the 1840s and 1850s—including *Hochster* itself, which was perhaps more innovatory than Lord Campbell wished to acknowledge.[92]

The law governing discharge for breach of contract in the first half of the nineteenth century also differed from the modern law in another way. It is now axiomatic that where a contracting party has accepted a repudiatory breach of contract:[93]

> the contract has come into existence but has been put an end to or discharged. Whatever contrary indications may be disinterred from old authorities, it is now quite clear, under the general law of contract, that acceptance of a repudiatory breach does not bring about 'rescission *ab initio*'.

At the time *Planché* was decided, however, the law was different.[94] When a defendant committed a repudiatory breach, the other party to the contract could sue for damages after affirming the contract or choosing to treat it as discharged, but he could also rescind the contract *ab initio*, with the result that it would 'be at an end as if it had never been'.[95] A plaintiff who did this could then bring a quasi-contractual claim to recover benefits conferred under the contract, something he could not do if the contract was merely discharged, as in this case it was thought to remain 'open', with the consequence that its continued existence precluded a quasi-contractual claim.[96]

---

[92] *Short v Stone* (1846) 8 QB 358, 115 ER 911; *Ripley v M'Clure* (1849) 4 Exch 345, 154 ER 1245; *Cort and Gee v Ambergate, Nottingham and Boston and Eastern Junction Railway Co* (1851) 17 QB 127, 117 ER 1229; *Hochster v De La Tour* (1853) 2 E & B 678, 118 ER 922; *Avery v Bowden* (1855) 5 E & B 714, 119 ER 647; (1856) 6 E & B 962, 119 ER 1122; *Reid v Hoskins* (1856) 6 E & B 953, 119 ER 1119; *Barrick v Buba* (1857) 2 CB (NS) 563, 140 ER 536. See too *Danube and Black Sea Railway and Kustendjie Harbour Co Ltd v Xenos* (1863) 13 CB (NS) 825, 142 ER 753; *Frost v Knight* (1872) LR 7 Ex 111; *Byrne & Co v Leon Van Tienhoven & Co* (1880) 5 CPD 344; *Johnstone v Milling* (1886) 16 QBD 460, 470. The emergence of the doctrine of anticipatory breach can be attributed to the development of the idea of protecting expectations as the basis of the law of contract which Patrick Atiyah dates to the period 1770–1830: PS Atiyah, *The Rise and Fall of Freedom of Contract*, paperback edn (Oxford, Clarendon Press, 1985) 212: 'It was not until the full implications of the changing rules about damages had begun to be grasped that it became somewhat clearer that the law of part executed contracts was giving way to an entirely different law of executory contract.'

[93] *Johnson v Agnew* [1980] AC 367, 393 (Lord Wilberforce).

[94] A point well made in JW Carter, 'Discharged Contracts: Claims for Restitution' (1997) 11 JCL 130. At 132–3 Carter observes that the modern law did not begin to develop until *Hochster v De La Tour* (1853) 2 E & B 678, 118 ER 922, and was not fully established for another century, with the decisions in *Universal Cargo Carriers Corp v Citati* [1957] 2 QB 401 and *Hong Kong Fir Shipping Co Ltd v Kawasaki Kisen Kaisha Ltd* [1962] 2 QB 26.

[95] *Hochster v De La Tour* (1853) 2 E & B 678, 685; 118 ER 922, 924–5 (Crompton J). See too *Bartholomew v Markwick* (1864) 15 CB (NS) 711, 716; 143 ER 964, 966 (Erle CJ); also 'Notes of Mr Dodd's Lectures at the Incorporated Law Society: Rescinding Contracts', *The Legal Observer*, January 1837, 241, esp 242–3. We are grateful to Tariq Baloch for drawing the latter account of the law to our attention.

[96] *Goodman v Pocock* (1850) 15 QB 576, 583; 117 ER 577, 580; *De Bernardy v Harding* (1853) 8 Ex 822, 824; 155 ER 1586, 1586; *Prickett v Badger* (1856) 1 CB (NS) 296, 305–7; 140 ER 123, 127; *Harrison v James* (1862) 7 H & N 804, 808–9; 158 ER 693, 695; *Boston Deep Sea Fishing and Ice Co v Ansell* (1888) 39 Ch D 339, 364–5. See too the influential note

These rules had been worked out by the end of the eighteenth century,[97] in various cases where it was held that an action for money had and received would not lie to recover money paid under a contract,[98] nor could a plaintiff who performed services pursuant to a contractual obligation recover on a quasi-contractual *quantum meruit*,[99] unless the contract had been ended by the agreement of the parties, by the operation of a contractual term, or by a breach by the defendant that was sufficiently serious to entitle the plaintiff to rescind. However, problems were then created in the early nineteenth century when *Hulle v Hightman*[100] began to be cited (erroneously) as authority for the proposition that whenever a defendant failed fully to perform his contractual obligation to pay for services, the plaintiff had to claim for contract damages, and could not bring a quasi-contractual claim for a *quantum meruit*.[101] Had it developed further, this line of cases would have created an irrational distinction between (permissible) quasi-contractual claims for money paid under a rescinded contract, and (impermissible) quasi-contractual claims for the value of services performed under a rescinded contract. Along with some other cases,[102] however, *Planché* eliminated this distinction, Tindal CJ recognising that 'when a special contract is in existence and open, the Plaintiff cannot sue on a *quantum*

on *Cutter v Powell* (1795) 6 TR 320, 101 ER 573, in successive editions of *Smith's Leading Cases*: eg the third edition by HS Keating and JS Willes (London, A Maxwell & Son, 1849) vol II, 1 ff; also H Bullen and SM Leake, *Precedents of Pleadings* (3rd edn, London, Stevens & Sons, 1868) 37.

[97] As discussed in SJ Stoljar, 'The Doctrine of Failure of Consideration' (1959) 75 *LQR* 53, 56–62; JL Barton, 'Contract and *Quantum Meruit*: The Antecedents of *Cutter v Powell*' (1987) 8 *JLH* 48, 54–5; DJ Ibbetson, 'Implied Contracts and Restitution: History in the High Court of Australia' (1988) 8 *OJLS* 312, 317–9; DJ Ibbetson, *A Historical Introduction to the Law of Obligations* (Oxford, OUP, 1999) 279; W Swain, '*Cutter v Powell* and the Pleading of Claims in Unjust Enrichment' [2003] *RLR* 46, 50–55.

[98] *Weston v Downes* (1778) 1 Doug 23, 99 ER 19; *Power v Wells* (1778) Cowp 818, 98 ER 1379; *Towers v Barrett* (1786) 1 TR 133, 99 ER 1014; *Giles v Edwards* (1797) 7 TR 181, 101 ER 920; *Payne v Whale* (1806) 7 East 274, 103 ER 105. See too J Chitty, *A Practical Treatise on Pleading* (London, W Clarke & Sons and J Butterworth, 1809) 342.

[99] *Cutter v Powell* (1795) 6 TR 320, 101 ER 573; *Peeters v Opie* (1799) 2 Wms Saund 350, n 2; 85 ER 1145. A plaintiff was also forbidden to sue on a contractual *quantum meruit* to recover the value of services if the contract under which he had performed the services laid down the amount of remuneration to which he was entitled: *Duncomb v Tickridge* (1648) Aleyn 94, 82 ER 933; *Jacob v Allen* (1703) 1 Salk 27, 91 ER 26; *Weaver v Boroughs* (1725) 1 Str 648, 93 ER 757.

[100] (1802) 4 Esp 75, 170 ER 647; 2 East 145, 102 ER 324.

[101] *Mulloy v Backer* (1804) 5 East 316, 322; 102 ER 1091, 1094 (Lord Ellenborough CJ); and other authorities cited in Ibbetson 1988 (n 97) 318, n 32. See too Chitty (n 98) 339, distinguishing the case where a plaintiff has performed all his contractual obligations (common *indebitatus* count allowed) from the case where he has not because the defendant has prevented him from doing so (special declaration on the contract required); E Lawes, *A Practical Treatise on Pleading in Assumpsit* (London, W Reed, 1810), 8–9.

[102] *Withers v Reynolds* (1831) 2 B & Ad 882, 109 ER 1370; *Phillips v Jones* (1834) 1 Ad & El 333, 110 ER 1233; *Franklin v Miller* (1836) 4 Ad & El 599, 111 ER 912 (accepting the principle).

meruit',[103] but holding that the plaintiff's claim for a *quantum meruit* under the third count was permissible because he had rescinded the contract following the defendants' repudiatory breach.

The nineteenth century distinction between 'discharged' and 'rescinded' contracts no longer forms part of the law governing breach of contract, although it remains the case that a claim in unjust enrichment to recover a *quantum meruit* award will not lie while 'an inconsistent contractual promise subsists between the parties in relation to the subject-matter of the claim'.[104] The question arises, however, whether the *quantum meruit* award made in *Planché* would now be characterised as a restitutionary award for unjust enrichment. In *Planché* modern notions of unjust enrichment were not in play, and the question of whether the defendants were unjustly enriched at the plaintiff's expense was not addressed. The case has been treated in many later cases as authority for a rule that a contracting party who starts, but who is wrongly prevented from completing, an obligation to do work can terminate future performance of his obligation and recover a *quantum meruit* award for the work that he has done.[105] However, while the defendant clearly benefited from the plaintiff's work in many of these cases, this is not something that can be said of *Planché* itself. The obvious problem is that the defendants cannot have been enriched by the plaintiff's work, since he never delivered a manuscript. Some writers have argued that *Planché* can still be regarded as an unjust enrichment case, because a defendant is always enriched when a claimant does work at his request, whether or not he receives

---

[103] (1831) 8 Bing 14, 16; 131 ER 305, 306.

[104] *Trimis v Mina* [1999] NSWCA 140 [54] (Mason P), adding: 'this is not a remnant of the now discarded implied contract theory of restitution. The proposition is not based on the inability to imply a contract, but on the fact that the benefit provided by the plaintiff to the defendant was rendered in the performance of a valid legal duty. Restitution respects the sanctity of the transaction, and the subsisting contractual regime chosen by the parties as the framework for settling disputes. This ensures that the law does not countenance two conflicting sets of legal obligations subsisting concurrently.' Recent English cases to the same effect are: *Moussavi-Azad v Sky Properties Ltd* [2003] EWHC 2669 (QB) [43]; *Mowlem plc v Stena Line Ports Ltd* [2004] EWHC 2206 (TCC) [40]; *S & W Process Engineering Ltd v Cauldron Foods Ltd* [2005] EWHC 153 (TCC) [51].

[105] *De Bernardy v Harding* (1853) 8 Exch 822, 155 ER 1586; *Prickett v Badger* (1856) 1 CB (NS) 296, 140 ER 123; *Clay v Yates* (1856) 1 H & N 73, 156 ER 1123; *Bartholomew v Markwick* (1864) 15 CB(NS) 711, 143 ER 964 (*quantum valebant*); *Inchbald v Western Neilgherry Coffee, Tea and Cinchona Plantation Co Ltd* (1864) 17 CB (NS) 733, 144 ER 293; *Appleby v Myers* (1867) LR 2 CP 651, 659; *Slowey v Lodder* (1901) 20 NZLR 321 (NZCA), affirmed on the relevant point [1904] AC 442 (PC) 453; *Chandler v Boswell* [1936] 3 All ER 179; *Thomas v Hammersmith BC* [1938] 3 All ER 203; *Clermont v Mid West Steel Products Ltd* (1965) 51 DLR (2d) 340, 356; *Hoenig v Isaacs* [1952] 2 All ER 176, 180; *Lusty v Finsbury Securities Ltd* (1991) 58 BLR 66; *Brenner v First Artists' Management Pty Ltd* [1993] 2 VR 221, 258; *Ministry of Sound (Ireland) Ltd v World Online Ltd* [2003] EWHC 2178 (Ch), [2003] 2 All ER (Comm) 823 [62]; *Len Lichtnauer Developments Pty Ltd v James Trowse Constructions Pty Ltd* [2005] QCA 214 [16].

anything.[106] In common with Andrew Burrows and many others, however, we believe that this argument entails 'an unrealistic and overinclusive notion of benefit',[107] and that in cases like *Planché*, where a claimant's work is directed towards the creation of an end-product, no part of which is ever received by the defendant, the claimant should not be entitled to a *quantum meruit* award on the ground of unjust enrichment.

This is not to say that the claimant should be denied a remedy. As we have said already, he could now be awarded damages for the defendant's anticipatory breach of contract, assessed on either an expectation or a reliance loss basis. On the facts of *Planché*, expectation damages would amount to the contract price of £100, subject possibly to mitigation on the basis that the plaintiff was saved some effort by the defendants' cancellation of the series.[108] Where a claimant has incurred costs in reliance on the defendant's promise, the law now also permits him to sue for reliance damages as an alternative to expectation damages, provided that his reliance loss does not exceed the value of the benefit that he was contractually entitled to receive from the defendant. In the latter case, the excess must be borne by the claimant, as he would otherwise be enabled to shift the consequences of his bad bargain onto the defendant.[109] It is interesting to speculate whether the award of £50 that was actually made to Planché would conform to these rules, if it were now made as an award

---

[106] P Birks, *An Introduction to the Law of Restitution* (Oxford, Clarendon Press, 1985) 126–7 and 232; P Birks, 'In Defence of Free Acceptance' in A Burrows (ed), *Essays on the Law of Restitution* (Oxford, Clarendon Press, 1991) 105, 140–1; P Maddaugh and JD McCamus, *The Law of Restitution* (2nd edn, Aurora, Ont, Canada Law Book Inc, 2004) 46–7; M McInnes, 'Enrichment Revisited' in JW Neyers *et al* (eds), *Understanding Unjust Enrichment* (Oxford, Hart Publishing, 2004) 165, 172–4. Graham Virgo argues that cases like *Planché* can be explained on the basis that D is estopped by his wrongful behaviour from denying that C's work has enriched him: G Virgo, *The Principles of the Law of Restitution* (Oxford, Clarendon Press, 1999) 91; cf *Brenner v First Artists' Management Pty Ltd* [1993] 2 VR 221, 258; *GEC Marconi Systems Pty Ltd v BHP Information Technology Pty Ltd* (2003) 128 FCR 1, 157. However, as observed in K Mason and JW Carter, *Restitution Law in Australia* (Sydney, Butterworths, 1995) 445, 'it was pointless to reject the fictional implied promise of quasi-contract as the basis for restitution, if we are to reassert it through an entirely fictional concept of acceptance [of a benefit]'.

[107] A Burrows, *The Law of Restitution* (2nd edn, London, Butterworths Lexis Nexis, 2003) 17. See too G Jones, 'Restitutionary Claims for Services Rendered' (1977) 93 *LQR* 273, 281; A Burrows, 'Free Acceptance and the Law of Restitution' (1988) 104 *LQR* 576, 588; M Garner, 'The Role of Subjective Benefit in the Law of Unjust Enrichment' (1990) 10 *OJLS* 42; J Beatson, *The Use and Abuse of Unjust Enrichment* (Oxford, Clarendon Press, 1991) 88–9; Carter (n 94) 143; A Skelton, *Restitution and Contract* (Oxford, Mansfield Press, 1998) 45–7; N Rafferty, 'Contracts Discharged through Breach: Restitution for Services Rendered by the Innocent Party' (1999) 37 *Alberta LR* 51, 64; D Harris, D Campbell and R Halson, *Remedies in Contract and Tort* (2nd edn, London, Butterworths Lexis Nexis, 2002) 236–8.

[108] In this connection, note too that Planché subsequently sold his work in a different form to another publisher: see n 118.

[109] *Bowlay Logging Ltd v Domtar Ltd* [1978] 4 WWR 105; *C & P Haulage (a firm) v Middleton* [1983] 1 WLR 1461; *CCC Films (London) Ltd v Impact Quadrant Films Ltd* [1985] QB 16; *Filobake Ltd v Rondo Ltd* [2005] EWCA Civ 563 [62].

of reliance damages for the defendants' anticipatory breach of contract. However, there are several reasons why we cannot give a sure answer to this question.

In the first place, we do not know what factors were taken into account by the jury when awarding him £50: his lost time and trouble, presumably; perhaps, too, the expense of his trip to Herefordshire to inspect Dr Meyrick's collection; less probably, but not inconceivably, his lost opportunity to spend his time more remuneratively writing for the theatre.[110] Secondly, we do not know whether he was more than halfway towards completion of the manuscript, and so we could not say whether the £50 award he received was in line with the contract price, even if the contract had stipulated that Planché should be paid for his time and labour at a particular rate. Thirdly, however, and more fundamentally, the parties had in fact made no attempt to ascribe a value to Planché's work in this way, as they were solely concerned with fixing a price for the completed manuscript; nor can it be said that the time, skill and effort that he expended had any obvious market value in themselves.

This leads us to the final observation that cases in which a claimant seeks a *quantum meruit* award on the ground of unjust enrichment are not the only cases in which it can be difficult to assign a value to services, particularly services directed towards the creation of an end-product. Similar problems can also arise where the claim is for reliance damages for breach of contract,[111] or indeed, for enforcement of a primary contractual right to payment of the fair value of work done.[112]

I. CONCLUSION

One way to look at the affair of Planché and the *Juvenile Library* would be to see it as a minor skirmish in a long-running battle to affirm the rights of authors to profit from their work, to adjust the balance of power between them and the book-trade, and to raise authorship to a rank alongside the other professions, whilst retaining the mystique of its association with

[110] Note Planché's complaint to Jerdan, quoted in the text to n 61, that he had 'very reluctantly abandoned more lucrative employments'.

[111] In *Myers v Macmillan Press Ltd* QBD 3 March 1998, which also concerned the breach of a publishing agreement, Neuberger J agreed with counsel that it was unsatisfactory to assess the claimant author's damages on a *quantum meruit* basis 'because it involves carrying out an exercise which does not reflect what happens in practice', but undertook this task nonetheless.

[112] Cf Supply of Goods and Services Act 1982, s 15. The courts do not always distinguish very clearly between *quantum meruit* claims founded on a primary contractual right to payment and *quantum meruit* claims grounded in unjust enrichment: eg *Countrywide Communications Ltd v ICL Pathway Ltd* QBD 21 October 1999; *Vedatech Corp v Crystal Decisions (UK) Ltd* [2002] EWHC 818 (Ch); *Vee Networks Ltd v Econet Wireless International Ltd* [2005] 1 Lloyd's Rep 192; *Villages of New Zealand (Pakuranga) Ltd v Ministry of Health* NZ High Ct 6 April 2005.

scholarship, celebrity and original genius. The best known of the campaigns is that which relates to changes in the law of copyright, exclusively Whiggish histories of which have recently been much challenged.[113] Peter Jaszi and Martha Woodmansee have argued that the 'Romantic conception of "authorship"' as the product of a single individual genius displaced an earlier collaborative model of composition and has been perpetuated in modern copyright law.[114] Though we may question its validity, there can be little doubt that the Romantic model was a potent weapon through which authors constituted their identities, sought to raise their own public status and their bargaining powers, and thus enhanced both the social and monetary value of literary work. Planché's persistence in pursuing his legal rights reflects, and his letter to Jerdan suggests, his eagerness to move out of the collaborative bohemian world of illegitimate drama into the arena of serious history and proper authorship.[115] There is something faintly preposterous in the proposition, considered by the court, that Planché might have added to his reputation by contributing to the *Juvenile Library*, given the low status of works addressed to children.[116] All the same, as he stands up to Colburn and Bentley, egged on by Jerdan, he is representative of the spirit of Victorian authorship, determined to be treated as a professional, not as a tradesman—paid for his time, and not just for goods produced.[117] Not

[113] Another was the movement to found trade organisations along the lines of the other professions: a line can be traced from the Royal Literary Fund and the Royal Society of Literature, promoted by Jerdan, through to the Society of Authors and PEN.

[114] P Jaszi, 'The Author Effect II' in M Woodmansee and P Jaszi (eds), *The Construction of Authorship: Textual Appropriation in Law and Literature* (Durham, NC, Duke University Press, 1994) 35.

[115] For the low status of spectacular pantomime productions see M Gamer, 'Authors in Effect: Lewis, Scott, and the Gothic Drama' (1999) 66 *English Literary History* 831, who writes of 'the two differing traditions of authorship and ownership associated with legitimate drama and pantomime. While one usually assumes legitimate drama to be authored by an individual playwright, pantomime carries with it a much stronger tradition of collective and corporate production'.

[116] Certainly the books that did come out in the series disappeared into total obscurity. *Lives of Remarkable Youth of Both Sexes* was reprinted in 1832, but it does not seem to have gained either of its authors fame or fortune (Trueba seems to have been paid £50 and Williams £31.10). Even more strikingly, neither Vols II nor III of the *Juvenile Library* is credited to their authors by the *British Library Catalogue*. Jane Loudon's biographer knows nothing of the *History of Africa*; Hall observes in his memoirs that he owned no copy of the cobbled-together *Historic Anecdotes of France*.

[117] Sutherland (n 3) 60, cites the novelist Charles Lever exclaiming, with reference to his dealings with Colburn, that 'such publishers ordered books from authors as they might breeches from tailors'. As we have seen, London in the 1830s contained many needy writers, like Trueba, Williams, Jane Loudon, SC Hall, Wait, and Washington Landon, who were only too willing to work night and day to produce breeches if wanted. We were tempted to argue that Planché required payment in guineas rather than pounds to reflect the distinction between the payment to a professional man and payment of a tradesman, as was customary, but regretfully decided that the discrepancies in the sums mentioned in the various accounts of the trial may simply be attributable to the carelessness of the reporters.

only did he get his £50, but in the end he was also able to sell the goods, or a version of them, to another buyer, for in 1834 the Society for the Diffusion of Useful Knowledge, in its *Library of Entertaining Knowledge* series, finally published *The History of British Costume*.[118]

[118] University College London, Society for the Diffusion of Useful Knowledge collection, correspondence with JR Planché. In a letter dated 9 January 1832 he proposed to the committee commissioning volumes for the Library of Entertaining Knowledge a book described as a 'Chronological History of the Civil and Military Costume of the British Islands'. A payment of £150 for the manuscript and some illustrations was agreed on 19 April (Box 12: minutes of the Entertaining Knowledge Committee). After the book's publication he was accused of plagiarism by James Logan, the author of *The Scottish Gaël, or, Celtic Manners as Preserved among the Highlanders*, 2 vols (London, Smith, Elder, 1831). The committee decided that Logan's complaint was insubstantial, given that Planché had acknowledged his book as a source; it is noteworthy that the *Scottish Gaël*'s date of publication suggests that Planché had continued to work on the *History of British Costume* after the collapse of the *Juvenile Library*. See SDUK collection, Box 12, committee minutes, October 1835, and Box 19, committee out-letters to Logan (1 December 1834 and 21 November 1835) and to Planché (1 October 1835).

5

Marsh v Keating (1834)

JAMES EDELMAN*

A. INTRODUCTION

M*ARSH V KEATING*[1] is a salacious tale of sex and gambling. It is
even more exciting for the legal historian and the restitution scholar because it also provides a perspective on three extremely difficult areas of the law of restitution. This often overlooked decision was
given by twelve of the finest common law judges in the early 19th century,
who advised the House of Lords on issues including third party recipient
liability and the ability to trace through a mixed fund at common law. It
was also the prequel—by 157 years—to the most famous restitution case of
the last century[2] and it invites comparison with that case to resolve one of
the most difficult issues in the law of unjust enrichment: the reason why a
claim can be brought for restitution of the value of the substitute for a
claimant's misappropriated asset.

B. THE STORY OF FAUNTLEROY

What should I fear in youthful days?
Why shun delicious joy?
Why not the sports of pleasure chance?
With gallant Fauntleroy?

Rejoice, O Young Man! In thy youth,
And wake thy heart to joy,
If evil—thou shalt know of truth,
The fate of Fauntleroy.[3]

* My thanks to the participants at the King's College conference and to Ms Birke Haecker
for helpful comments on an earlier draft.
[1] (1834) 2 Cl and Fin 250, 6 ER 1149; 8 Bli NS 651, 5 ER 1084; 1 Bing NC 198, 131 ER
1094.
[2] *Lipkin Gorman v Karpnale Ltd* [1991] 2 AC 548.
[3] James Usher, *The Dirge of Fauntleroy* (Whitechapel, self published, 1824).

The protagonist in the story of *Marsh v Keating* was Henry Fauntleroy, the last man hanged in England for forgery. His was a sensational trial for three reasons: Fauntleroy was a 'gentleman of position'; he had the reputation of Don Juan; and the public were beginning to doubt whether capital punishment should be imposed for anything other than murder.[4]

The story begins with Fauntleroy's father who, in 1792, became a partner in the firm of Messrs Marsh, Sibbald, Stracey and Fauntleroy. The bank of Marsh & Co had a reputation for being safe and reliable. Its partners were men of prestige: Sibbald was a baron (since 1806); Stracey was the son of Sir Henry Stracey; Marsh, although once bankrupt, had established a lucrative Naval Agency and had brought £40,000 into the firm; Fauntleroy's family roots dated to the lords of the manor at Fauntleroy Marsh in Dorsetshire. Of the four partners, William Fauntleroy, who left the banking house of Barclay to join the bank in 1792, was the bank's managing partner and driving force. When he died in 1807, Marsh & Co desperately needed a new managing partner. The choice was an obvious one. Fauntleroy's son, Henry, although only 22 years old, had been a clerk in the bank for the last seven years and was gifted with figures.

When Henry Fauntleroy assumed the position of managing partner of the bank, it was in grave difficulties. There was a scarcity of money and this had been exacerbated by the Napoleonic wars. Marsh & Co had also developed a practice of accepting and discounting bills on speculative building ventures. In 1810, the failure of one such venture left Marsh & Co with a loss of £60,000 and on the verge of bankruptcy. By 1814 things had worsened. Many of the holders of bills issued by speculative builders which Marsh & Co had accepted were demanding payment. Unless Marsh & Co obtained advances of credit they would be bankrupted. But the Bank of England began to refuse their acceptances. Perhaps to avoid the humiliation of bankruptcy and the loss of his substantial income,[5] or perhaps due to his fury at the Bank of England's refusal to accept Marsh & Co's bills,[6] Fauntleroy began an elaborate process of forgery. He would forge the signature of one of his depositors on a document giving him a power of attorney for sale of the depositor's annuity, government security or Navy loan. The sale would not be entered in the books of Marsh & Co although the proceeds would be deposited. But Fauntleroy needed to ensure that there were sufficient funds to pay dividends and interest to the defrauded depositors so that they did not discover the sale of their securities. If the depositor chose to sell the securities, Fauntleroy needed to have sufficient funds to

---

[4] H Bleackley, *Trial of Henry Fauntleroy* (London, Hodge & Co, 1824), preface.

[5] Over the five years preceding the discovery of the fraud the partnership earned £14,000 a year, of which £3,500 was Fauntleroy's share.

[6] In a letter written by Fauntleroy in 1816, which emerged at trial, he wrote, 'the Bank began first to refuse our acceptances, and thereby began to destroy our credit. They shall smart for it'.

repay the depositor. Thus, in order to hide the fraud, he would need to forge more and more powers of attorney and make more and more sales. Such was Fauntleroy's extraordinary skill as a banker that the forgeries remained undetected for a decade as they spiralled further and further out of control, eventually reaching nearly £400,000. Fauntleroy was indiscriminate as to the persons whom he defrauded—they included his mother and other members of his family.[7]

Fauntleroy's frauds were discovered when the co-trustees of the estate of Benjamin West (the President of the Royal Academy), concerned with Fauntleroy's delays in administering the estate, inquired with the Bank of England about the stock held by the estate. When they discovered that it had been sold by Fauntleroy under a power of attorney they alerted the police. On Thursday 9 September 1824 Fauntleroy was arrested. The newspapers took little time to investigate the facts and rumours were rife.[8] Of the English newspapers, the worst offender was probably *The Times*.[9] The extent of its descent into gossip was matched only (and copied) by the *Morning Post*. Although *The Times* had insisted, on 17 September 1824, that it would not publish an account of the story and the character of Fauntleroy until a public examination enabled them to give an accurate account of the facts,[10] only a week later it recanted and published the rumours circulating about the city as assertions of fact. *The Times*' purported justification for its publishing rumours was 'the great interest of the metropolis' in what Fauntleroy had done with the vast sums of money that he obtained from his forgeries.[11]

The lurid tale told by *The Times* began with speculation about Fauntleroy's background. Fauntleroy had fathered a child out of wedlock with a Miss Young but had refused to marry her. After Young's brother insisted upon a duel to defend the family's honour, Fauntleroy's family and Young's friends persuaded him to marry her.[12] But the moment the couple left the church Fauntleroy left her and they never again met until shortly before his execution. So far as his marriage, child and subsequent separation were concerned, the story was accurate. Then the wild imaginings and extraordinary rumours began.

---

[7] *The Times*, 24 September 1824, 2. His mother was defrauded of £3,550.

[8] 'Hardly any thing has been talked of either in the city or at the west end of the town, but this singular event, and all sorts of rumours are current on the subject.' *Morning Chronicle*, 17 September 1824.

[9] It may have been Thomas Barnes, editor of *The Times*, about whom James Usher was writing in *The Dirge of Fauntleroy* (n 3) that 'some writers for the public press, who cry "destroy destroy", convicted felons stand no less, than Flouted Fauntleroy'.

[10] *The Times*, 17 September 1824, 2.

[11] *The Times*, 24 September 1824, 2.

[12] Although Fauntleroy, in his speech from the dock at his trial, denied that the conduct of Young's brother influenced his decision which he said was motivated solely by a 'laudable and honourable feeling on my part'.

The Times reported that Fauntleroy fell victim to a cunning sting perpetrated by a clever gang. The gang would find attractive women of lesser moral persuasion whom they would establish in mansions in the West End of town. They would dress these women in the finest attire and take them to the opera and to the theatre. There they would introduce them to young, wealthy and inexperienced men. The leader of these women was described as Mother Bang, for in the euphemistic words of *The Times* 'she was bang up to all the arts and intrigues of her calling'.[13] As a married man, estranged from his wife, Fauntleroy was very vulnerable to the charms of such a lady. After he had been introduced to some of these women (including Mother Bang) the sting upon Fauntleroy began. He was taken to an elegant and sumptuous dinner where the finest wines and champagnes were served. As the dinner progressed the ladies would slowly drop away from the table to join a game of cards. Later in the evening a proposal was made that a card game be played by all in order to raise a few dozen bottles of champagne with which to thank the hostess. To give him confidence, Mother Bang and her women allowed Fauntleroy to win the first game. Enticed, Fauntleroy continued to gamble, loaded dice were produced and he lost vast sums of money. Another alleged sting upon Fauntleroy was that one of these women had either arranged a sham arrest or spoke of a friend who had been arrested on the basis that she owed vast sums of money. Being a man of 'generous description and humane feelings', Fauntleroy again imparted vast sums of money to secure the release of these ladies from debt.

There was barely a skerrick of truth to these rumours. The only hint of reality was that Fauntleroy did have several mistresses, including an association with a Mary Bertram (alias Mother Bang) which he eventually gave up in favour of a young girl, Maria Forbes, whom he probably seduced while she was at boarding school. Shortly after its scurrilous rumour campaign began, an informed correspondent[14] wrote to the *Brighton Gazette* pointing out that *The Times*' stories were fiction. On 8 October 1824, *The Times* disclaimed a pretence to truth, arguing that it 'undertook merely to give a condensed narrative of the various rumours afloat'.[15]

Nevertheless, these fictitious stories of Fauntleroy's philandering with the public's money served to create an atmosphere of strong public hostility toward him.[16] Although *The Times* had disclaimed any pretence of the truth of the stories, the truthful version of how the money had been lost—which Fauntleroy explained at trial in his speech from the dock—was not

---

[13] *The Times*, 20 September 1824, 4.

[14] Although published anonymously, the text of the letter was identical to passages later published by Pierce Egan in *An Account of the trial of Mr Fauntleroy for Forgery* (London, Knight & Lacey, 1824).

[15] *The Times*, 8 October 1824, 2.

[16] Indeed, one article in *The Times* on 24 September 1824 compared Fauntleroy with the cutthroat Thurtell.

believed until well after his execution. As Mr Egan observed in his 1824 account of Fauntleroy's trial, no-one could fathom the mystery surrounding what had happened to the proceeds of Fauntleroy's forgeries.[17] Although Fauntleroy had supporters, most of them were simply opponents of capital punishment or crackpots who later insisted that he had cheated the executioner by placing a pipe in his throat or a support around his neck at the time of his execution and was now living happily in America.[18] There was a great deal of resentment and personal animosity against the man who had destroyed so many lives.

Fauntleroy's trial in the Old Bailey commenced on Saturday 30 October 1824 before Justice Park, Baron Garrow[19] and a jury. Sir James Alan Park was not a stranger to such cases. He had acted for the Crown as a barrister in several forgery cases including the prosecution of the high profile forger, Joseph Blackburn, who was convicted and executed in 1815.

The indictments alleged forgeries against four people (including Miss Frances Young, Fauntleroy's sister-in-law) for values ranging between £484 and £6,000. The case against Fauntleroy was overwhelming. When Fauntleroy was arrested at the premises of Marsh & Co, he had quickly locked his private desk with a key attached to his watch. Later the officer who arrested him took the key and Fauntleroy's desk was searched. Amongst the incriminating evidence was a note in Fauntleroy's handwriting confessing that he had forged powers of attorney without the knowledge of his partners in order to keep up the credit of Marsh & Co. In the opening speech for the prosecution the Attorney General, later Lord Chancellor (Lyndhurst), remarked: 'was there ever a record of fraud more intelligible, and more negligently guarded?' After trial,[20] Fauntleroy admitted having written the note but said that it was not written with a view to flight from the country as the Attorney General had alleged but instead to absolve his partners from suspicion in the event of his sudden death.

Fauntleroy's case consisted of his speech from the dock (a prisoner not being permitted to give evidence in his own defence) and sixteen character witnesses (who were men of considerable status including a politician, a surgeon, a sheriff and an architect). In his speech from the dock Fauntleroy did not deny that he had committed the forgeries. He merely took the opportunity to deny the rumours of his extravagance, gambling and womanising.

---

[17] Egan (n 14) 2. See also Egan's reference at 30 to the 'groundless . . . rumour . . . of his having been involved in difficulties by building speculations'.

[18] These stories reached their apogee when they became part of an affidavit sworn by Fauntleroy's executors in resisting a claim in 1841. See also *The Times*, 5 April 1841, 5: 'It may seem strange but it is no less true . . .'.

[19] They were accompanied on the bench by the Lord Mayor (Robert Waithman) at the start of the trial.

[20] In a speech delivered after his first motion to arrest the judgment and sentence of death had failed.

After the jury found Fauntleroy guilty, Justice Park remarked upon capital punishment, observing that although the Crown had a prerogative of mercy, 'I am afraid that, after the many serious acts which, under your handwriting, have been proved against you, involving so many persons in ruin, you would only deceive yourself by indulging in any hope of mercy on this side of the grave'. Forgery had been a capital offence since 1729 and many lawyers and politicians believed that it should remain so. In the words of the Solicitor General:[21]

> The number and description of persons who committed the offence, went a long way to justify the law. These persons were always men of education, and they calculated on the probability of escaping with impunity. They were generally persons deeply in the confidence, and familiar with the habits of business and mode of writing of those on whom they forged. If the punishment of death were justified by the laws of God and man, it was justifiable in reference to this crime.

Fauntleroy's junior counsel, Broderick, argued a petition for arrest of the judgment before 12 judges in the House of Lords on 24 and 25 November 1824.[22] The careful argument was that the words in the statute imposing capital punishment referred to 'persons who forge any deed'[23] and that a deed at common law did not include a power of attorney and so the statute should not be so construed either.[24] The execution occurred five days after argument concluded, on 30 November 1824, and the report of the case records only that 'the judges expressed no opinion publicly, but the prisoner was executed'. As Fauntleroy was the last person executed in England for forgery, it is unlikely that there will ever be a determination of the lawfulness of his punishment.

On 5 November 1824 the other partners in Marsh & Co (Marsh, Graham and Stracey) took out an advertisement in *The Times* asking that the public not pass judgment on them until they were examined on oath.[25] Their knowledge of Fauntleroy's fraud was a matter of much debate. Although after trial Fauntleroy had confessed that he wrote the incriminating note to absolve his partners from suspicion in the event of his sudden death, he had said in his speech from the dock that 'I have never had any advantage beyond that in which all my partners participated'. Shortly before the examination, an editorial in *The Times* castigated the partners of Marsh & Co:[26]

---

[21] Parliamentary Debates 1830 NS xxiii, 676; xxv, 56.
[22] The same argument had earlier failed before Baron Garrow sitting alone (Park J had been unable to attend at short notice).
[23] 2 Geo II c 25; 31 Geo II c 22 s 78.
[24] *R v Fauntleroy* (1824) 2 Bing 413; 130 ER 365.
[25] *The Times*, 5 November 1824, 2.
[26] *The Times*, 1 December 1824, 2.

we do not, therefore, ask Messrs Stracey, Marsh and Graham whether they were privy to the precise acts of which their partner was guilty, but whether they shut their eyes to an unaccountable influx of wealth into their bank—whether they availed themselves of that influx, in aid of their private accounts, or for the support of the general concern, without ascertaining the funds from whence it accrued.

The examination took place on 18 December 1824. The partners were exonerated from any wrongdoing but they had already suffered the indignity of bankruptcy three months earlier.

C. TWO DECISIONS PRIOR TO *MARSH V KEATING*

1. *Davis v The Governor and Company of the Bank of England*[27]

Five days before Fauntleroy's execution, the Lord Chief Justice of Common Pleas, Best CJ (later Lord Wynford), delivered a decision that was to have a considerable effect upon the later litigation against Marsh & Co.[28] The claimant, Davis, was the holder of stock at the Bank of England. His brother forged his signature on a power of attorney and sold his stock. His brother later absconded from the country to avoid Fauntleroy's fate. A special action on the case was brought by Davis against the Bank of England for breach of duty by transferring his stock without authority and for refusing to pay him dividends owing.

The count for transferring his stock without authority failed because the stocks held in the claimant's name had not been transferred, and could not be transferred without the claimant's authority: 'we cannot do justice to this [claimant] unless we hold that the stocks are still his'.[29] This finding became the centrepiece to the argument for Marsh & Co in *Marsh v Keating*. In relation to the claim for the dividends, Best CJ held that they could be recovered by Davis unless the bank had a defence that to recover would not be upon the 'justice and conscience' of the claimant's case.[30] Quoting Lord Mansfield, Best CJ said that he was not speaking of a general discretion. He considered such a general discretion abhorrent.[31] To illustrate the nature of

---

[27] (1824) 2 Bing 393; 130 ER 357.

[28] One important aspect of the decision in *Davis*, which was also central to the later cases, including *Marsh v Keating*, is not dealt with in this paper. This is the scope of the rule that an owner cannot seek redress in an action arising from a felony until the felon has been prosecuted.

[29] *Davis* (n 27) 2 Bing 402–3, 130 ER 361–2.

[30] *Ibid* 2 Bing 409, 130 ER 364, quoting *Bird v Randal* 3 Burr 1345, 1353; 97 ER 866, 870 (Lord Mansfield).

[31] *Ibid* 2 Bing 410; 130 ER 364.

the defence he was describing, Best CJ gave the example of a bank that had paid out to other persons that it would otherwise have refused to pay. As will be seen below, a century and a half later the House of Lords independently recognised this defence and called it 'change of position'.[32]

Although the decision of Best CJ in the Court of Common Pleas was reversed by the Court of King's Bench upon a writ of error, this was only because there had been no allegation raised before Best CJ that the Bank of England had received any dividends on the stock from the government.[33]

2. *Stone and Gahagan v Marsh, Stracey and Graham*[34]

One of Fauntleroy's most infamous frauds was the one he perpetrated against the late magistrate, Sir Thomas Plaistoe. Fauntleroy forged a power of attorney from Plaistoe and sold £22,000 of Plaistoe's stock.[35] The question was whether Marsh, Stracey, Graham and Fauntleroy were indebted to Stone and Gahagan (who together with Fauntleroy were executors of Plaistoe's will). By order of the Lord Chancellor no complaint was raised at trial that Fauntleroy was a co-executor of the will. A verdict was given for Stone and Gahagan and the matter came before the Court of King's Bench for judgment.

Before the court, Sir (Jonathan) Frederick Pollock made a powerful argument which was later relied upon by counsel for Marsh & Co in *Marsh v Keating*. Pollock relied upon the decision in *Davis v The Bank of England*[36] to argue that because the statutory formalities[37] had not been complied with, the stock was still owned by Stone and Gahagan.[38] As a felonious transaction, the sale was also void and could not be ratified or adopted. Therefore the claim should have been brought against the Bank of England and not against Marsh & Co.

Lord Tenterden CJ, delivering the opinion of the court, affirmed the verdict he had given as trial judge. He said that it did not matter if an action could have been brought against the Bank of England because 'where an injured party has different remedies against different persons he may elect which he will pursue'.[39] Further, the claimants' action for money had and received did not require ratification of the felonious act: 'the ground of their demand is the actual receipt of the money produced by the sale and

---

[32] *Lipkin Gorman v Karpnale Ltd* [1991] 2 AC 548.
[33] See *Bank of England v Davis* (1826) 5 B & C 185, 187; 108 ER 69, 70.
[34] (1827) 6 B & C 551; 108 ER 554.
[35] See eg *The Times*, 24 September 1824, 2.
[36] *Davis* (n 27).
[37] 24 Geo III c 39 s 14
[38] *Stone* (n 34) 6 B & C 562–3; 108 ER 563.
[39] *Ibid* 6 B & C 563–4, 108 ER 559.

transfer of their annuities. The sale was not a felonious act, neither was the transfer, nor the receipt of the money.'[40]

D. THE DECISION IN *MARSH V KEATING*

1. The Findings of Fact

The facts in *Marsh v Keating* were found by a special verdict given at trial. Many of them reflected the story outlined above. Mrs Ann Keating was one of the many people who banked with Marsh & Co and who were defrauded. Mrs Keating held £12,000 of reduced 3 per cent annuities at the Bank of England. Like many others to whom he had done likewise, Fauntleroy forged Mrs Keating's signature on a document granting him a power of attorney. Pursuant to this forged power of attorney, on 29 December 1819 Fauntleroy ordered his broker Thomas Simpson to sell face value £9,000 of Mrs Keating's annuities. Simpson sold them to a Mr WB Tarbutt for £6,018 15s. Simpson then deducted from this amount half of his commission (the arrangement being that Marsh & Co would keep the other half) and wrote a cheque to Marsh & Co for £6,013 2s 6d. This was deposited into Marsh & Co's account with Martin & Co. The amount was entered into the pass-book of Martin & Co as 'Cash per Fauntleroy' (denoting that it was on Fauntleroy's behalf that the payment was made). No entry was made in any of the books of Marsh & Co (either the house book or the daily balancing book). The fraudulent sale of Mrs Keating's stock was just one of many instances in which the pass-book of Martin & Co did not correspond with the house book or daily balancing books of Marsh & Co. Fauntleroy's partners, who were wholly ignorant of the forgery, permitted him to conduct much of the banking business without their interference and although the pass-book was frequently brought to Marsh & Co from Martin & Co, when it was at Marsh & Co it was always kept locked in Fauntleroy's desk.

Upon discovery of the fraud, Mrs Keating wrote to the Bank of England asking that her stock be replaced and that she be paid the dividends for the period from when the stock was purportedly sold. The Bank paid her the dividends and agreed to pay all the expenses for her to prove in the bankruptcy of the partners of Marsh & Co (and to replace her stock if she did not recover it in the bankruptcy).

---

[40] *Ibid* 6 B & C 565; 108 ER 560.

2. The Proceedings

Marsh v Keating was plainly a test case. With the facts found by the special verdict, Mrs Keating obtained judgment without argument in the Court of King's Bench in 1832. A writ of error was brought in the Court of Exchequer Chamber and, again without argument, the court affirmed the decision of the Court of King's Bench. Marsh & Co then brought a writ of error before the House of Lords and the House summoned Common law judges to attend to hear argument and advise the House.

There were also political forces underlying the hearing of this test case. The question was essentially whether the Bank of England, which was liable for up to £400,000 and had acted with great propriety, could prove in the bankruptcies of each of the partners of Marsh & Co. Had the judges advised that it could not, it was possible that the House of Lords could have delivered a contrary decision. It was not until 1844, in a case also presided over by Tindal CJ, that the House of Lords conceded that it would not reject the advice given by judges who had been asked to hear a case.[41]

3. The Counsel and the Judges

As described, a writ of error was brought before 12 judges to advise the House of Lords. Those judges were Tindal CJ, Barons Bayley, Bolland and Gurney and Justices Park, Bosanquet, Gaselee, Littledale, Taunton, Vaughan, J Parke and Patteson.

The judges were extremely familiar with the circumstances of the case and the legal issues. As well as the extraordinary publicity given to it, the judges had been involved in the following ways: Justice Park had presided over Fauntleroy's trial; Justices Bosanquet and Bolland had been counsel for the prosecution against Fauntleroy; Justice Bosanquet had represented Stone and Gahagan against Marsh & Co[42] and had opposed Fauntleroy's petition to arrest the judgment before 12 judges of the House of Lords;[43] Sir John Gurney, Baron of the Exchequer, had been the unsuccessful lead counsel for Fauntleroy's defence; and Tindal CJ had been counsel for Davis on the writ of error in *Davis v Bank of England* and Solicitor General during much of the history of the matter.

On 23 and 24 June 1833 the case was heard. Representing Mrs Keating was Serjeant Taddy and Sir James Scarlett, KC. Taddy was one of the leading serjeants at the Bar and had appeared for Davis in the second hearing of *Davis v Bank of England* a decade earlier. Scarlett later eclipsed Taddy's

---

[41] *O'Connell v Reginam* (1844) 11 C & F 155, 422–5; 8 ER 1061, 1161–3.
[42] *Stone* (n 34).
[43] *R v Fauntleroy* (1824) 2 Bing 413; 130 ER 365.

career. Scarlett was a leading silk who was made serjeant and appointed Lord Chief Baron of the Exchequer shortly after *Marsh v Keating*. Between his appointment to silk in 1816 and his appointment as Lord Chief Baron of the Exchequer (Baron Abinger) on Christmas Eve 1834, his biographer (and son) recorded that he 'had a longer series of success than has ever fallen to the lot of any other man in the law'.[44] A joke at the Bar was that Scarlett had developed a machine which made judges nod their assent at his arguments.[45]

Representing Marsh & Co were Sir Edward Sugden (later Lord St Leonards) and Fitzroy Edward Kelly. Dr Getzler has observed that by 1830 Sugden was the leading chancery barrister in England.[46] The following year he was appointed Lord Chancellor of Ireland and was sworn as a member of the Privy Council. His junior, Kelly, was one of the most successful commercial juniors at the Bar. Kelly was made silk a year after *Marsh v Keating*, in 1845 became Solicitor General and in 1866 succeeded Sir Frederick Pollock as Lord Chief Baron of the Exchequer.

4. The Decision

The advice was given by the judges to the House of Lords on 25 June 1834[47]—almost exactly a year after the hearing—by Sir James Alan Park (who had presided over the trial of Fauntleroy a decade earlier).[48] Delivering the decision of the judges, Justice Park held that Marsh & Co were liable to Mrs Keating for the proceeds received from the sale of her shares. Justice Park summarised the four arguments for Marsh & Co:[49] (1) the transfer of shares was void and could not be affirmed; (2) it would be contrary to public policy to allow Mrs Keating to elect to affirm a sale committed by a felony; (3) the facts found by the special verdict did not show that the money was had and received to the use of Mrs Keating; and (4) by her subsequent transactions with the Bank of England, Mrs Keating lost any right of action against Marsh & Co.

As to the first and fourth arguments, Sugden had argued that Mrs Keating's stock had not been legally transferred and so, legally, she was still

---

[44] PC Scarlett, *A memoir of the right honourable James, first Lord Abinger* (London, John Murray, 1877) 71. He combined his practice with work as a parliamentarian (including a period as Attorney General in 1827).

[45] GFR Barker, 'Scarlett, James, first Baron Abinger (1769–1844)', revised EA Cawthon, *Oxford Dictionary of National Biography* (Oxford, OUP, 2004).

[46] J Getzler, 'Sugden, Edward Burtenshaw, Baron St Leonards (1781–1875)' *Oxford Dictionary of National Biography* (Oxford, OUP, 2004).

[47] *Marsh* (n 1).

[48] As a barrister, he had also prosecuted Joseph Blackburn who was convicted and executed for forgery two decades earlier.

[49] *Marsh* (n 1) 2 Cl and Fin 285; 6 ER 1162.

entitled to it. How could the money from its (void) sale be received to her use? An analogy could not be drawn with cases of waiver of tort and implied contract.[50] This was because to imply a contract[51] in circumstances plainly inconsistent with contractual intention would be a fiction.[52] The special verdict had found that Mrs Keating had never assented to the sale and had never affirmed it. She had relied upon the *absence* of any such sale when she insisted that the Bank of England credit her with the value of her shares and dividends (which it had done).

Park J held that there was no fiction because Mrs Keating did not seek to imply any contract: 'the former owner of the stock does not seek to confirm the title of the transferee of the stock. No act by her is done eo intuitû;[53] it is perfectly indifferent to her, whether the right of the transferee to hold the stock is strengthened or not. She is looking only to the right of recovering the purchase money.'[54] Park J explained that by her election to claim the traceable proceeds of the sale of her stock she could no longer bring a claim against the Bank of England for the value of the stock.[55]

The second argument was essentially that Mrs Keating could not ratify a felonious transaction and that even if she could, there was a rule preventing her from bringing a civil action without first having brought a criminal prosecution. Park J held that Mrs Keating's action was against partners of Marsh & Co who had no share in the felonious act; she was not seeking to ratify the sale, only to bring a claim for the proceeds; and it would be a nonsense to insist that she bring a prosecution when Fauntleroy had 'suffered the extreme penalty of law'.[56]

As to the third argument that Marsh & Co had not received the proceeds from the sale of Mrs Keating's stock, Park J held that it was sufficient receipt that it had been paid into the account of Marsh & Co with Martin & Co. It did not matter that there was no reference to the receipt in any of Marsh & Co's books. Further, if Marsh & Co had no actual knowledge of the receipt, they had the means of knowledge by an examination of the books of Martin & Co.[57]

---

[50] *Ibid* 2 Cl and Fin 276, 6 ER 1159.
[51] *Hunter v Prinsep* (1808) 10 East 378; 103 ER 818; *Young v Marshall* (1831) 8 Bing 43; 131 ER 316.
[52] *Marsh* (n 1) 2 Cl and Fin 272–3.
[53] 'With that intent.'
[54] *Marsh* (n 1) 1 Bing (NC) 217, 131 ER 1101.
[55] *Ibid*.
[56] *Ibid* 1 Bing NC 217–18; 131 ER 1101–2. See later *Ex parte Ball* (1879) 10 Ch D 667, 672.
[57] *Ibid* 1 Bing NC 220, 131 ER 1102.

E. THREE LESSONS FROM *MARSH V KEATING*

1. The Degree of Fault Required for Third Party Recipient Liability

> *The grave Directors of the Bank,*
> *And clerks they did employ,*
> *Had their own carelessness to thank,*
> *As much as Fauntleroy.*[58]

At the time of *Marsh v Keating*, it was clear that the common law imposed strict liability on those who received the property of another. In a case shortly before *Marsh v Keating* these principles were applied. The case was *Holiday v Sigil*.[59] Holiday lost a £500 Bank of England note. Evidence was given that Sigil was seen picking it up and had taken it to another banking house the following month. Holiday was entitled to recover the £500 in an action for money had and received against Sigil. Ironically, by the time the action was brought, Holiday's note (which came from Marsh & Co on 10 May 1823), had it still existed, would have been worthless. Counsel for Holiday included Sir James Scarlett (who represented Mrs Keating in her action against Marsh & Co) and counsel for Sigil included Sir Nicholas Tindal (who later presided in *Marsh v Keating*).

Sigil did not have any defences to the claim. The defence of *bona fide* purchase was only available if there were no 'circumstances as might fairly excite suspicion' that the property was stolen.[60] And despite the *obiter dictum* of Best CJ in *Davis v Bank of England*, there was no established defence of change of position. Sigil was held liable without any inquiry into fault or knowledge on his part.

Eight years after *Holiday v Sigil*, Sir Edward Sugden argued that fault was required before Marsh & Co could be found liable. He said:[61]

> Suppose, then, a partner of a firm robs one on the high road of a bag of money and places it in bank to the credit of the firm, and takes it out as he put it in, without the knowledge of his partners; are they to be considered as sharing in the robbery, and liable in an action for money had and received?

Scarlett did not cite *Holiday v Sigil* in reply, although as counsel for Holiday he would plainly have been aware of the case. Nor did he cite any other cases where, unlike *Holiday*, there was no suspicion at all that the money

---

[58] Usher (n 1).
[59] (1826) 2 C & P 176; 172 ER 81.
[60] *Downe v Halling* (1825) 2 C & P 11, 14; 172 ER 6, 7; *Gill v Cubitts* (1824) 1 C & P 487, 489; 171 ER 1285, 1286.
[61] *Marsh* (n 1) 2 Cl and Fin 272; 6 ER 1157.

received was stolen.[62] The reason was probably that there were two major differences between the facts before him in *Marsh v Keating* and the other cases like *Holiday*. First, Sigil and the other defendants knew of their possession of the money even if they did not know that the money belonged to the claimant. But Marsh & Co never knew that they were in possession of the proceeds of the sale of Mrs Keating's stock. Secondly, Sigil had obtained a benefit from Holiday's money by exchanging it for value. In contrast, on the authority of *Davis v Bank of England*, Mrs Keating remained the owner of her shares. Marsh & Co had received proceeds (as a credit deposit in their account at Martin & Co) from a void sale of those shares but Mrs Keating was still the legal owner of the shares. These differences raise two fundamental issues: the degree of fault required for recipient liability, and why a recipient of traceable proceeds should be liable to the owner of the original asset.

Sugden's example raised the first question: what is the degree of fault required for the recipient of another's asset to be liable to pay restitution? In his advice, Park J said that 'it is equally clear that the Defendants might have discovered the payment of the money, and the source from which it was derived, if they had used the ordinary diligence of men of business'.[63] This statement has caused much difficulty. Was it simply an observation that Sugden's arguments, even if they had merit, could not succeed? Was it a suggestion that a recipient was not liable for the receipt unless the recipient knew of it? Was it a suggestion that a recipient of another's asset was not liable unless there was knowledge of the receipt *and* a means of discovery that it was derived, without authority, from the claimant's asset? And should such principles apply beyond clear cases where a recipient had benefited from the claimant's asset at the expense of the claimant (as in *Holiday v Sigil*) to cases of receipt of the traceable proceeds of another's asset without any change to, or interference with, the claimant's assets or rights? Until 1991, various different answers had been given.

In *Jacobs v Morris*,[64] a firm called Messrs Morris paid money to the firm of Jacobs, Hart and Co after Jacobs' agent misrepresented that he had power to borrow on behalf of the firm. Morris gave the agent a cheque addressed to Jacobs' firm. The agent deposited it in the firm account and immediately withdrew it for his own purposes. Messrs Morris sought restitution of the money from Jacobs. The trial judge thought that the decision in *Marsh v Keating* meant that it was necessary to show that the partners of Jacobs knew of the deposit of the proceeds from the cheque into their account.[65]

---

[62] *Miller v Race* (1758) 1 Burr 452, 457; 97 ER 398, 401; *Clarke v Shee and Johnson* (1774) 1 Cowp 197, 98 ER 1041; *Hudson v Robinson* (1816) 4 M & S 475, 105 ER 910.
[63] *Marsh* (n 1) 2 Cl and Fin 289–90, 6 ER 1164.
[64] [1901] 1 Ch 261; [1902] 1 Ch 816 (CA).
[65] [1901] 1 Ch 261, 269, 271.

Because they did not know, or have means of knowledge, of the receipt they were not liable. In dismissing the appeal, Stirling LJ[66] and Cozens-Hardy LJ[67] agreed with the trial judge's approach to *Marsh v Keating*, although Stirling LJ thought that the trial judge had suggested that the knowledge required by the partners of Jacobs was that the deposit was 'the money of the defendants'.[68] In contrast, Vaughan Williams LJ dismissed the appeal on a different basis and doubted whether *Marsh v Keating* had imposed *any* requirement of knowledge.[69]

On the other hand, in *Reid v Rigby*,[70] in materially similar circumstances of unauthorised borrowing, but where (rather than being appropriated) the proceeds had been used to pay the wages of the defendant's workmen, the Court of Appeal held the defendant liable to make restitution. The Court of Appeal considered that *Marsh v Keating* had held that even though a defendant has *no* knowledge, liability will be imposed if the money 'came into possession of the defendants'.[71]

The most detailed consideration of this requirement in *Marsh v Keating* came from Dixon J in the High Court of Australia in *James v Oxley*.[72] The claimants were executors of an estate. The defendants were a firm of solicitors whose clerk, Rees, had power to deposit and withdraw money on the firm's partnership account. Rees received a cheque from the executors by promising them that he would invest it. He deposited the money in the partnership account and later appropriated it for his own purposes. Although finding that the firm had knowledge which was sufficient to impose liability, Dixon J (with whom McTiernan J agreed) suggested in *obiter dicta* that:[73]

The explanation of the introduction into the question of the element of 'means of knowledge' may lie in the peculiarity of the position of partners in relation to a partnership bank account upon which each partner may be empowered to draw by himself. In substance, money, though temporarily there, may never be in the actual *de facto* control of any member of the firm except the fraudulent partner. He may pay a cheque to the credit of the account and immediately draw against it. In such circumstances the technical 'receipt' by the firm may be considered as insufficient to make payment into the account a receipt to the use of the plaintiff unless the other partners knew or ought to have known of the credit and of its nature. In the same way, if an agent who operates on his principal's account free of his actual control or supervision pays in money fraudulently obtained from a stranger and forthwith draws it out again, the principal may be

---

[66] [1902] 1 Ch 816, 833.
[67] *Ibid* 833–4.
[68] *Ibid* 833.
[69] *Ibid* 830.
[70] [1894] 2 QB 40.
[71] *Ibid* 44.
[72] (1939) 61 CLR 433.
[73] *Ibid* 456.

regarded as never having really received it to the use of the stranger unless he knew or ought to have known of its presence before it was withdrawn.

This was endorsed by the High Court of Australia in *National Commercial Banking Corporation of Australia Ltd v Batty*,[74] which held that a defendant who did not know of the receipt of money in his partnership account could not be held liable.[75]

The matter was almost put to rest 157 years later by the House of Lords in the case of *Lipkin Gorman v Karpnale Ltd*.[76] The facts of *Lipkin Gorman* are extremely well known. Cass, a rogue partner of a firm of solicitors (Lipkin Gorman) withdrew £323,222 from the solicitors' client (trust) account. He gambled and lost the money at the Playboy Club (Karpnale), which was mixed with their funds and became their property.[77] Cass then absconded. Cass was later apprehended and sentenced to three years in prison, a fate far superior to that of Fauntleroy. The solicitors brought a claim against the Playboy Club.

One argument by counsel for the Playboy Club was that liability could not be imposed because the club did not know that the funds had been misappropriated by Cass.[78] Counsel argued that in equity an innocent recipient of misappropriated trust funds is not liable for the receipt and asserted that the same position existed at common law.[79] This argument had particular force because the claim in *Lipkin Gorman* could also have been brought in equity.[80] The funds misappropriated were held on trust by the solicitors for the clients. Why should the result at common law be any different from that in equity?

However, the House of Lords in *Lipkin Gorman* did not draw any comparison with equity. The Law Lords simply rejected counsel's submission that knowledge or fault was required before liability could be imposed upon the Playboy Club. In the leading speeches, Lords Goff and Templeman started from the premise that the action was a strict liability claim for restitution of unjust enrichment.[81] Lord Goff said of counsel's assertion that

---

[74] (1986) 160 CLR 251.

[75] *Ibid* 268–9.

[76] [1991] 2 AC 548.

[77] *Ibid* 572 (Lord Goff): 'at common law, property in money, like other fungibles, is lost as such when it is mixed with other money.'

[78] *Ibid* 553 (Lightman QC, *arguendo*): 'the club was an innocent recipient and had no knowledge that the money was stolen.'

[79] *Ibid* 554: 'An innocent person is not liable if trust money has passed through his hands without his knowing that there has been a breach of trust and he received it in good faith. In this respect the position is the same at common law and in equity.' Cf L Smith, 'Restitution: The Heart of Corrective Justice' (2001) 79 *Texas Law Review* 2115.

[80] *Ibid* 572 (Lord Goff): 'there is no doubt that, even if legal title to the money did vest in Cass immediately on receipt, nevertheless he would have held it on trust for his partners.'

[81] *Ibid* 564 (Lord Templeman): 'an action for money had and received is maintainable wherever the money of one man has, without consideration, got into the pocket of another.'

fault was required: 'it is plain, from the nature of his submission, that he is in fact seeking to invoke a principle of change of position, asserting that recovery should be denied because of the change in position of the respondents, who acted in good faith throughout.'[82] Ironically, Lord Goff referred to *Marsh v Keating* (which had not been cited in argument) only in relation to a different issue—tracing, which is considered below.

If the House of Lords had drawn a comparison with equity the Law Lords might have questioned whether equity's liability *should* remain fault-based. Ironically, although *Marsh v Keating* had raised the spectre of fault-based liability at common law, at that time there was authority that liability in equity was *strict*. The decision was *Harrison v Pryce*. It is reported by both Barnadiston[83] and Atkins.[84] Governor Edward Harrison had purchased £1,000 of stock in the South Sea company, but this had been placed in the name of another Edward Harrison. The other Edward Harrison sold the stock. After his death, Governor Harrison's executor brought a claim against the other Edward Harrison. When Edward Harrison died the action continued against his executor, Pryse. Barnadiston reports Lord Hardwicke's finding that although the legal title to the stock had transferred to Edward Harrison, Governor Harrison remained the equitable owner. The action by Governor Harrison's executor was based on the receipt by Edward Harrison of Governor Harrison's property. Lord Hardwicke said that the case 'may be compared to that of a man's goods coming into the hands of different persons one after the other; in which case an action of trover may be brought against any of the persons who have ever had possession of the goods'.[85] An account was ordered against Pryse.

The importance of the case lies in Barnadiston's report and Lord Hardwicke's analogy with trover. In cases of trover, liability for possession and disposal of the goods of another was strict. The pleading of finding and loss could not be traversed.[86] On this account, receipt (and possession) of another's asset, however *innocent*, attracted a strict liability to account for its value in equity just as it did at law for trover. Although Best CJ in *Davis v Bank of England*[87] preferred Atkins' very abbreviated report in relation to a different issue (Atkins had suggested that legal title had not passed to Edward Harrison), Barnadiston is more accurate. Apart from its very abbreviated nature, the Atkins report also incorrectly records the order.[88]

---

[82] *Ibid* 578.
[83] *Harrison v Pryce* (1740) Barnadiston 324; 27 ER 664.
[84] *Harrison v Harrison* (1740) 2 Atkins 121; 26 ER 476.
[85] (1740) Barnadiston 324, 324; 27 ER 664, 664.
[86] *Hartop v Hoare* (1743) 2 Str 1187; 93 ER 1117; *Cooper v Chitty* (1756) 1 Burr 20; 97 ER 166.
[87] *Davis* (n 27) 2 Bing 406–7, 130 ER 363.
[88] This observation was also made by Sir Edward Sugden in *Marsh* (n 1) 2 Cl and Fin 267, 6 ER 1155.

After *Lipkin Gorman,* it is clear that liability in unjust enrichment is strict, subject to defences such as change of position. But this does not mean that Park J's statement is entirely redundant. A key difference might be that the Playboy Club's knowledge of *its receipt of the money* might be relevant even if its knowledge of the provenance of the money was irrelevant. Suppose Fauntleroy's fraud, like the fraud in *National Commercial Bank v Batty,* could not have been detected by Marsh & Co so that the firm could not have known that it received the money. Lack of knowledge is relevant to whether the *receipt* by the firm is an enrichment. For if the firm did not know and could not reasonably discover its receipt of an asset, it cannot receive beneficially[89] or, at least, it can later disclaim the receipt.

Because Marsh & Co had constructive knowledge of their receipt, if the case were argued today their only chance of avoiding liability in unjust enrichment would depend upon the application of the defence of change of position.[90] Could Marsh & Co argue that despite their negligence they should have a defence of change of position? The answer is unclear. In favour of such a defence it has been said that the defence does not require that the defendant act in reliance upon the receipt to have changed position.[91] Further, the Privy Council recently adopted arguments of Professor Birks[92] and said that they will not inquire into relative fault except to ask whether the defendant's change of position was in good faith.[93] On the other hand, the Court of Appeal have recently said that a defendant will not be permitted to raise the defence where it would be 'inequitable' or 'unconscionable' to do so,[94] raising the possibility that negligence (or 'means of knowledge' of the nature of the payment) could be a bar to the defence or, at least, that the defence might be barred in cases of something less than bad faith of the defendant. Much will depend upon what courts identify as the nature and rationale of the defence.

---

[89] *Port of Brisbane Corp v ANZ Securities* [2003] 2 Qd R 661.

[90] It seems that Australian courts also now treat the element of knowledge as relating to a defence: *David Securities Pty Ltd v Commonwealth Bank of Australia* (1992) 175 CLR 353 [59]; *Custom Coaches (Sales) Pty Ltd v Frankish* [2002] NSWSC 795 [6].

[91] *Scottish Equitable plc v Derby* [2001] EWCA Civ 369, [2001] 3 All ER 818 [30]–[31] (Robert Walker LJ); *Lipkin Gorman* (n 76) 581.

[92] P Birks, 'Change of Position and Surviving Enrichment' in W Swadling (ed), *The Limits of Restitutionary Claims: A Comparative Analysis* (London, UK National Committee of Comparative Law, 1997) 36, 41.

[93] *Dextra Bank and Trust Limited v Bank of Jamaica* [2002] 1 All ER 193.

[94] *Niru Battery Manufacturing Company v Milestone Trading Limited* [2003] EWCA Civ 1446, [2004] 1 All ER (Comm) 193 [148]–[149], [162], [182]–[185], [192]. See also the reference to 'inequitable' by Lord Goff in *Lipkin Gorman* (n 75) 580, which Munby J said in *Commerzbank AG v Price Jones* [2003] EWCA Civ 1664 [2005] 1 Lloyd's Rep 298 [56] there was no need to 'gloss or refine'.

2. The Nature of Recipient Liability for Receipt of a Traceable Substitute

In *Marsh v Keating,* Park J did not give any reason why Mrs Keating was able to claim the value of the substitute of her property in the hands of the third party recipient. In *Lipkin Gorman,* Lord Goff explained that the reason why the defendant was required to make restitution to the claimant of the proceeds received was because the defendant was unjustly enriched at the expense of the claimant.[95] Neither the speech of Lord Goff nor that of Lord Templeman contained explicit discussion of why the enrichment was 'unjust'. However, the requirement of 'unjust' could be satisfied either because of the solicitors' ignorance of the transaction[96] or because there was no basis upon which the Playboy Club could retain the notes.[97] However, the nature and meaning of 'unjust' is not the concern of this chapter.[98]

In *Lipkin Gorman*, the House of Lords held that when Cass withdrew money from Lipkin Gorman's client account he became the legal owner of the notes.[99] Although he was not authorised to gamble with money from the client account, he was authorised to withdraw it. How, then, could the Playboy Club have been unjustly enriched *at the expense of Lipkin Gorman* if the funds it received belonged to Cass? In the only speech that addressed this point, Lord Goff said:[100]

> There is in my opinion no reason why the solicitors should not be able to trace their property at common law in that chose in action [ie their client account], or in any part of it, into its product, ie cash drawn by Cass from their client account at the bank. Such a claim is consistent with their assertion that the money so obtained by Cass was their property at common law.

The case Lord Goff relied upon for this reasoning was *Marsh v Keating*[101] and, in particular, the advice that Mrs Keating had a right to the value of proceeds received (the traceable product) from the sale of her shares. One qualification must be made to Lord Goff's reasoning. Merely because the value can be traced from a bank account into the cash withdrawn does not explain why the holder of the bank account (the solicitors) had proprietary rights in the traced substitute (the notes withdrawn). Tracing is merely a process of identifying the passage of value through transactions; it does not

---

[95] *Lipkin Gorman* (n 76) 578.

[96] See A Burrows, *The Law of Restitution* (2nd edn, London, Butterworths LexisNexis, 2003) 191.

[97] P Birks, *Unjust Enrichment* (2nd edn, Oxford, OUP, 2003) 103, 155.

[98] See the discussion in R Stevens, 'The Proper Scope of Knowing Receipt' [2004] *LMCLQ* 421, 425.

[99] Following *Union Bank of Australia Ltd v McClintock* [1922] 1 AC 240 and *Commercial Banking Co of Sydney Ltd v Mann* [1961] AC 1.

[100] *Lipkin Gorman* (n 76) 574.

[101] *Ibid*.

explain the reason why a claimant obtains new rights in the substitute.[102] In 1991, Professor Birks argued that the solicitors had a proprietary right (although not ownership) in the money withdrawn by Cass which arose because of the unjust enrichment of Cass when he substituted the solicitors' chose in action for banknotes.[103] The proprietary right was a *power* to rescind the transfer to Cass and to revest the proceeds of his withdrawal from the solicitors' account. This point had been conceded by counsel for the Playboy Club.[104]

The answer to why the Playboy Club's enrichment was 'at the expense of' the solicitors is that the solicitors had property rights in the cash (the traceable substitute from their client account) that Cass gambled. Although that property right of the solicitors was not lost when Cass passed the ownership of the notes to the Playboy Club, this did not prevent a claim for unjust enrichment. The requirement of 'at the expense of' does not require impoverishment. It is simply a requirement that the immediate source of the defendant's unjust enrichment must be the assets of the claimant. Because the Playboy Club received notes in which the solicitors had property rights, this sufficed to show that the receipt was at their expense.

3. The Law of Tracing

Marsh v Keating has another important lesson for the law of tracing generally: it is possible, at common law, to trace value through a mixed fund.

The starting point is the decision of the Court of King's Bench in *Taylor v Plumer*[105] in 1815. Sir Thomas Plumer wished to purchase £22,200 of Exchequer bills. He wrote a cheque for this sum to his stockbroker who purchased only £6,500 of bills and absconded to the United States with the rest of the money, much of which he used to purchase US stock and gold coins. Plumer's agent located the stockbroker and seized the stock and gold for Plumer. But the stockbroker was bankrupt when Plumer's agent had seized the stock and gold. The stockbroker's trustees in bankruptcy brought an action against Plumer for trover, arguing that he had converted the stock and gold. They were unsuccessful. In the course of his Lordship's decision, Lord Ellenborough said:[106]

[102] L Smith, *The Law of Tracing* (Oxford, Clarendon Press, 1997) 11–14 and the authorities cited therein.
[103] P Birks, 'The English Recognition of Unjust Enrichment' [1991] *LMCLQ* 473. There were actually three substitutions: the chose in action held by the solicitors for cash, the cash for a chose in action against a building society, and then later that chose in action for cash.
[104] *Lipkin Gorman* (n 76) 555: 'Cass's title is liable to be displaced by the solicitors' claim.'
[105] (1815) 3 M & S 562; 105 ER 721. For discussion of the background to this case, see Professor Smith's chapter in the present volume.
[106] *Taylor* (n 105) 3 M & S 575, 105 ER 726.

It makes no difference in reason or law into what other form, different from the original, the change may have been made, whether it be into that of promissory notes for the security of the money which was produced by the sale of goods of the principal, as in *Scott v Surman* [1742] Willes 400, or into other merchandize, as in *Whitecomb v Jacob* [1710] Salk 160, for the product of or substitute for the thing still follows the nature of the thing itself, so long as it can be ascertained as such, and the right only ceases when the means of ascertainment fail, which is the case when the subject is turned into money, and mixed and confounded into a general mass of the same description. The difficulty which arises in such a case is a difficulty of fact and not of law, and the dictum that money has no ear mark must be understood in the same way; ie as predicated on an undivided and undistinguishable mass of current money.

The prevailing interpretation placed on this passage in the twentieth century was that where a claimant's money is deposited into a bank account which then, or subsequently, reflects credit from other sources, the common law cannot trace beyond the deposit.[107] Professor Smith has shown why this interpretation is incorrect. Explaining from both principle and authority, he has conclusively shown that *Taylor v Plumer* was a case about equitable rights, not common law rights.[108] The reason why the stockbroker's trustees in bankruptcy did not succeed was not because the stockbroker was not the legal owner of the stock and gold (which he was). Instead, the claim failed because he was not the equitable or beneficial owner. As Professor Smith has explained, Lord Ellenborough was speaking in the context of an equitable claim; his remarks are best understood as relating to whether a claimant was entitled to claim property rights in a traceable product, not when the product was traceable;[109] and there are many cases subsequent to *Taylor v Plumer* that permit the common law to trace though a mixed fund.[110] One of those is *Marsh v Keating*.

In *Marsh v Keating* it will be recalled that after the stockbroker, Mr Simpson, purported to sell Mrs Keating's shares, he received £6,018 from the purported purchaser, Mr Tarbutt. This payment would presumably have been by cheque issued to Simpson. Simpson must have deposited the cheque into his account because he wrote a new cheque to Marsh & Co for the same amount, less half of his usual commission.[111] That cheque was then deposited in the account that Marsh & Co had with Martin & Co. In his address in reply in *Marsh v Keating* (delivering the junior's reply) Kelly

---

[107] *Banque Belge pour l'Etranger v Hambrouck* [1921] 1 KB 321, 328 (Bankes LJ) and 330 (Scrutton LJ); *Re Diplock* [1948] Ch 465, 518; *Agip (Africa) Ltd v Jackson* [1991] Ch 547, 566 (Fox LJ).

[108] L Smith, *The Law of Tracing* (Oxford, Clarendon Press, 1997) 168–174. See also R Pearce, 'A Tracing Paper' (1976) 40 *Conv* (NS) 277; S Khurshid and P Matthews, 'Tracing Confusion' (1979) 95 *LQR* 78.

[109] *Ibid* 279.

[110] *Ibid* 278 and cases cited therein.

[111] *Marsh* (n 1) 1 Bing (NC) 204, 131 ER 1096.

argued that *Taylor v Plumer*[112] was an authority which had decided that because the money had been mixed in Simpson's account, it could not be traced into the cheque paid to Marsh & Co. Kelly was interrupted in his reply by Scarlett, who rose to say that this would only be a good argument if the action were for trover. In other words, in an action for trover—wrongful conversion of the money—Mrs Keating would have needed to establish that particular notes belonged to her and to follow those notes into the hands of Marsh & Co to show that they had been converted. By allowing recovery in *Marsh v Keating*, although not expressly referring to this argument, the judges implicitly agreed that this limitation did not apply to a claim for money had and received based on tracing.

One hundred and fifty seven years later, counsel for the Playboy Club in *Lipkin Gorman v Karpnale Ltd*,[113] presumably with an eye to *Marsh v Keating,* conceded that the mixing of the money did not prevent the solicitors tracing the value from their client account into the cash gambled by Cass.[114] This was despite the fact that Cass had deposited cheques drawn on the solicitors' client account into his accounts at building societies in which he had some of his own money and had withdrawn cash from those accounts for the gambling.[115]

Despite explicit acceptance of Smith's arguments by the Court of Appeal[116] and two Law Lords,[117] some contemporary judges unfortunately still insist that it is not possible to trace through a mixed fund at common law.[118] *Marsh v Keating* is a valuable testament that this is not good law.

F. CONCLUSION

Marsh v Keating is far more than just an interesting historical case. It is a decision which has implications for three very difficult areas of restitutionary liability. The first is the law concerning recipient liability at common law and in equity. Although a full discussion of the development of recipient liability in equity is beyond the scope of this chapter, it is clear that, like the common law, equity has oscillated between strict liability and fault (with different degrees of fault imposed in different cases). Whilst the prevailing understanding is that the liability of a third party recipient in equity is based

---

[112] *Taylor* (n 105).
[113] *Lipkin Gorman* (n 76) 553 (Lightman QC, *arguendo*): 'even if the claim lies the money received from C has been mixed with other money and is unidentifiable.'
[114] *Ibid* 572.
[115] *Ibid* 568–9.
[116] *Trustee of FC Jones & Son (a firm) v Jones* [1997] Ch 159, 169.
[117] *Foskett v McKeown* [2000] UKHL 29, [2001] 1 AC 102, 113 (Lord Steyn) and 129 (Lord Millett).
[118] *Shalson v Russo* [2003] EWHC 1637, [2005] Ch 281 [103].

on some (unclear) requirement of fault,[119] several Law Lords, following the lead of Professor Birks,[120] have now expressed the opinion that the principle is one of unjust enrichment and the rule should be strict liability subject to the defence of change of position.[121] This would not only put to rest this vexed issue in equity but it would also be a conclusion coterminous with that of the same vexed issue at common law which was encountered in *Marsh v Keating*. Once a new—and clearer—test for liability emerges, the focus will shift to the defence of change of position. There is much more work to be done in relation to understanding the nature and operation of that defence.

The second lesson that can be taken from *Marsh v Keating* lies in the approval of the decision by the House of Lords in *Lipkin Gorman* and the recognition of the underlying nature of claims relating to receipt of a traceable substitute (from the claimant's asset) as based also on unjust enrichment. Recognition that a claim in unjust enrichment can arise from the receipt of the substitute of an asset to which the claimant had property rights does not mean that alternative claims are not available. For example, in *Foskett v McKeown*[122] a majority of the House of Lords said that the retention of an asset (proceeds of a life insurance policy) in which the claimants had equitable property rights enabled the claimants to bring an action to vindicate their property rights.[123] In the words of Lord Browne-Wilkinson, the claim 'is based on the assertion by the purchasers of their equitable proprietary interest in identified property'. Again, in *Criterion Properties plc v Stratford UK Properties llc*, Lord Nicholls (with whom

---

[119] The many cases are comprehensively discussed in A Burrows, *The Law of Restitution* (2nd edn, London, Butterworths Lexis Nexis, 2003) 194–206. Examples are *Carl Zeiss Stiftung v Herbert Smith & Co (No 2)* [1969] 2 Ch 276, 302 and *Re Montagu's Settlement Trusts* [1987] Ch 264 (want of probity); *Belmont Finance Corporation v Williams Furniture Ltd (No 2)* [1980] 1 All ER 393 and *International Sales and Agencies Ltd v Marcus* [1982] 3 All ER 551 (negligence); *Ministry of Health v Simpson* [1951] AC 521 (strict liability).

[120] P Birks, *Introduction to the Law of Restitution* (Oxford, OUP, 1985) 140–6. See also P Birks, 'Misdirected Funds: Restitution from the Recipient' [1989] *LMCLQ* 296. Birks' final statement on the subject is *Unjust Enrichment* (2nd edn, Oxford, OUP, 2005) 156–8. Before Professor Birks, there had been a similar suggestion by Denning J in *Nelson v Larholt* [1948] 1 KB 339.

[121] Judicially: *Criterion Properties plc v Stratford UK Properties llc* [2004] UKHL 28, [2004] 1 WLR 1846 [4] (Lord Nicholls; Lord Walker agreeing); *Twinsectra Ltd v Yardley* [2002] UKHL 12, [2002] 2 AC 164 [105] (Lord Millett). Extrajudicially: Lord Hoffmann, 'The Redundancy of Knowing Assistance' in P Birks (ed), *The Frontiers of Liability* (vol 1, Oxford, OUP, 1994) 29; Lord Nicholls, 'Knowing Receipt: The Need for a New Landmark' in W Cornish *et al* (eds), *Restitution Past, Present and Future* (Oxford, Hart, 1998) 231; Lord Walker, 'Dishonesty and Unconscionable Conduct in Commercial Life: Some Reflections on Accessory Liability and Knowing Receipt' (2005) 27 *Sydney Law Review* 187; Lord Millett, 'Proprietary Restitution' in S Degeling and J Edelman (eds), *Equity in Commercial Law* (Sydney, Thomson, 2005) ch 12.

[122] [2001] 1 AC 102.

[123] *Ibid* 108 (Lord Browne-Wilkinson) and 129 (Lord Millett, with whom Lord Hoffmann agreed).

Lord Walker agreed) said that where B is in possession of assets in which A has property rights:[124]

> A will have a proprietary claim, if B still has the assets. Additionally, and irrespective of whether B still has the assets in question, A will have a personal claim against B for unjust enrichment, subject always to a defence of change of position.

Lord Millett has explained that the alternative claim to vindicate a claimant's property right (which relies on the possession of the claimant's asset by the defendant) is based on a policy of protection of property rights.[125] Although Professor Birks argued that such vindication claims cannot be brought at common law as they can in equity, there is authority to the contrary[126] and the action for detinue was historically such a proprietary claim, certainly prior to the expansion of conversion in 1596.[127]

Does this mean that a claimant can prevent a defence of change of position by bringing a claim to vindicate a property right in an asset retained by the defendant rather than by bringing the claim for unjust enrichment? This is a difficult question which is well beyond the scope of this chapter. On the one hand, the claims are plainly different: a vindication claim is based upon the receipt and possession of a thing in which the claimant has property rights, whereas unjust enrichment does not require that the claimant retain the property, merely that he has been enriched by its receipt.[128] On the other hand, the development of the defence of change of position may show that it is not inextricably bound up with the enrichment of the defendant. Although in *Foskett v McKeown* Lord Millett said that the vindication claim was not subject to the defence of change of position, he has recently emphasised that he chose those words carefully and did *not* intend to suggest that change of position would be unavailable in *all* cases where the claim is one to vindicate a property right.[129]

The third and final lesson of *Marsh v Keating* for restitution scholars is, as Professor Smith has proved, that at common law it is possible to trace value that has passed through a (mixed) bank account which also reflects credit from other sources.

---

[124] [2004] UKHL 28, [2004] 1 WLR 1846 [4].

[125] Millett (n 121).

[126] Speaking of the *actio personalis* rule in *Phillips v Homfray* (1883) 24 Ch D 439, Bowen and Cotton LJJ said that an action will lie 'where the defendant has something in his hands representing the plaintiffs' property or the proceeds or value of it. But if there were any such it could be recovered at law as well as in equity'.

[127] J Baker, *An Introduction to English Legal History* (4th edn, London, Butterworths, 2002) 398–400.

[128] *Criterion* (n 124) [4].

[129] Lord Millett has recently suggested that change of position is excluded only from property claims of the particular type in *Foskett* and not all claims to traceable substitutes: Millett (n 121).

G. POSTSCRIPT

Although the result and reasoning in *Marsh v Keating* direct attention to these three controversial contemporary restitutionary issues, the result today would nevertheless be wholly unexceptional for entirely different reasons. The case would easily succeed as one of vicarious liability.

Principles of partnership law developed after *Marsh v Keating* and codified in the Partnership Act 1890 recognise the vicarious and strict liability of partners for wrongdoing by a co-partner in the course of business. Section 10 of the Partnership Act 1890 reads:

> Where, by any wrongful act or omission of any partner acting in the ordinary course of the business of the firm, or with the authority of his co-partners, loss or injury is caused to any person not being a partner in the firm, or any penalty is incurred, the firm is liable therefore to the same extent as the partner so acting or omitting to act.

The principle first arose eight years after *Marsh v Keating*, in *Brydges v Branfill*.[130] The Vice-Chancellor heard a case involving a solicitor in a partnership with two others who had fraudulently paid out proceeds from the sale of a life estate. An action was brought against the partners of the solicitor by the remainderman after the death of the tenant for life. The Solicitor General, representing the partners, argued that there was no case in which an innocent partner had been held liable for the fraud or misconduct of another partner.[131] Counsel for the other partners referred to *Marsh v Keating* and argued that the other partners had means of knowledge of the transaction, particularly through entries in the partnership books. The Vice-Chancellor found that although the 'moral characters' of the co-partners were unaffected because they did not have 'the least knowledge or suspicion', it was their duty to have ascertained what was going on under their names, and inquiry would have led to discovery of the fraud.[132]

By 1860, the principle was well recognised. For this reason, in *The Law of Partnership*, Lord Lindley disapproved of the reference by Park J to 'means of knowledge' in *Marsh v Keating*:[133]

> it was the business of the firm there to sell through their broker stock belonging to their customers and to receive and remit the proceeds: and the money for which the firm was held answerable did arise from the sale of the stock of a customer though it was sold under a forged power of attorney.

---

[130] (1842) 12 Sim 369, 59 ER 1174.
[131] *Brydges* (n 130) 12 Sim 377, 59 ER 1177.
[132] *Ibid* 12 Sim 390–1, 59 ER 1182.
[133] N Lindley, *A Treatise on the Law of Partnership: including its application to joint-stock and other companies* (Philadelphia, T & JW Johnson & Co, 1860) 244 and 249.

Twenty years later Lindley's pupil, Sir Frederick Pollock, in his *Digest of the Law of Partnership*, said of Lord Lindley's comment:[134]

> If his comment is right, as it clearly is, one can hardly see what the knowledge or means of knowledge of the partners had to do with it; they were liable because money representing their customer's property had come, in an apparently regular course, though in truth by wrong, into the custody of the firm. The point is treated as material in the opinion of the judges. The truth is that the rule as above given, by which the ordinary course of business is the primary test of the firm's liability, was developed only by later decisions.

It is a small irony that Pollock's grandfather (Sir (Jonathan) Frederick Pollock) had made the contrary argument (against vicarious liability) in 1827.[135] Nevertheless, from 1842 onwards, there has been little doubt that in a case with the facts of *Marsh v Keating* an argument of vicarious liability would succeed. Indeed, in the most recent decision on section 10 of the Partnership Act Lord Millett, affirming the principle of the irrelevance of knowledge, expressly endorsed *Brydges v Branfill*.[136]

---

[134] F Pollock, *Digest of the Law of Partnership* (2nd edn, London, Stevens, 1880) 47 n 3.
[135] *Stone* (n 34) 6 B & C 559, 108 ER 557–8.
[136] *Dubai Aluminium Co Ltd v Salaam* [2002] UKHL 48; [2003] 2 AC 366.

6

Erlanger v The New Sombrero Phosphate Company (1878)

MICHAEL LOBBAN*

A. AN ISLAND AND A COMPANY

IN MAY 1871, Henry Chatteris, the official liquidator of the bankrupt Sombrero Phosphate Company Ltd, put the company's main asset—a lease for the island of Sombrero—up for sale. The northernmost island of the Lesser Antilles, Sombrero is 'a barren flat rock', one mile long and up to 500 yards across, constantly battered by spray from the sea and waves which can wash over the whole island. Today, it is home to a lighthouse and many Caribbean birds. In 1871, no birds inhabited the island, but it was home to four Europeans, two 'creoles', and 254 West Indian miners, migrant workers from nearby St Martin. The island's treasure was phosphate of lime, a rich agricultural fertilizer, which had been mined here since 1857. In 1865, a year that saw 287 joint stock companies launched, of which 49 were mining companies,[1] the lease was acquired from the Crown by the newly formed Phosphate of Lime Company Ltd. As with so many companies launched that year, this one struggled,[2] and was reformed in 1867 as the Sombrero Phosphate Company Ltd.[3] Short of working capital and burdened by debt, the company went into liquidation in May 1870.[4] Chatteris's advertisement caught the attention of Thomas Miller Mackay, a London shipbroker, and Thomas Westall, his solicitor. They saw

* Research for this paper was done during my tenure of a British Academy Research Readership, as part of work on the law of obligations in the nineteenth century. The support of the British Academy is gratefully acknowledged. Thanks also to Catharine MacMillan for her valuable comments.

[1] *The Economist*, 10 March 1866.
[2] For the launch of the company, and its subsequent difficulties in floating (which involved the promoters in share rigging), see *The Times*, 13 June 1865, cols 5a, 12f, and *Bradshaw v Green*, *The Times*, 29 June 1868, 11 col d.
[3] *The Times*, 9 March 1867, 11 col a.
[4] Aspects of its failure can be traced in *Phosphate of Lime Company v Green and Nichols*, *The Times*, 20 April 1871, 11 col d, and 13 November 1871, 11 col c.

an opportunity to acquire a valuable asset cheaply: but as individuals, they lacked the means to make a bid for an asset, whose reserve price was set at £55,000. They therefore approached Sir James Anderson, who in turn introduced them to Baron Emile Erlanger, a German financier who ran banking businesses in both London and Paris.

Despite the failure of Overend, Gurney & Co in 1866, and the crisis in public confidence about commercial morality that followed the subsequent collapse of many more firms, the early 1870s saw many more speculative businesses formed, by promoters whose commercial morality was often dubious. The conduct of notorious speculators such as Albert Grant soon served to blacken the name of professional company promoters and to encourage investors to seek remedies against them. Born Abraham Gottheimer in Dublin in 1831, Grant had floated numerous companies in the 1860s and 1870s, most of which generated litigation raising accusations of fraud. At his peak, Grant became an MP, built a mansion in Kensington and cleared and donated Leicester Square to the Metropolitan Board of Works. But when the markets fell after 1873, Grant's fortune and reputation ebbed away, and his main monument to posterity would be the character of Augustus Melmotte in Trollope's *The Way We Live Now*.[5] By contrast, Emile Erlanger's career was much more respectable and stable. Born in 1832, he had entered his father's banking business in Frankfurt-am-Main at the age of 17. Ten years later, in 1859, he founded a banking firm in Paris, before opening a branch in London in 1870. His business was solid, and his sons followed in his footsteps as bankers.[6] Nonetheless, even a respectable businessman like this could find himself engaged in projects which raised awkward questions about how strictly a successful business could be expected to observe the demands of commercial morality. The dispute with the New Sombrero Phosphate Company was not the first time he had been engaged in litigation over speculative ventures. In 1861, Erlanger bought land at Auteuil, which he sold on to a set of company promoters, who were to create a company to build a Universal Exhibition Hall on the site. When the project went awry, Erlanger withdrew, and in 1866 he was sued by investors who had lost their money in the venture. The case went to the French Imperial Court, where the Advocate-General recognised the Baron's good faith, but held that he should indemnify innocent debenture holders who had lost money while he had profited from the sale of his land. The Imperial Court however declined to follow the Advocate-General's advice, and found for Erlanger, observing that no man of standing would take part in useful enterprises if they ran the risk of a loss of reputation and fortune if they failed.[7] A few years later, the

---

[5] George Robb, *White Collar Crime in Modern England* (Cambridge, CUP, 1992) 99–102; PL Cottrell, 'Albert Grant', *Dictionary of Business Biography*, 3 vols (London, Butterworths, 1984–6) vol 2, 623–9.

[6] Obituary, *The Times*, 25 May 1911, 13 col e.

[7] *The Times*, 6 March 1866, 10 col a.

Baron's concept of what was acceptable business practice was considered to strain at the limits by a parliamentary committee investigating his flotation of a loan to the Costa Rican government in 1872.[8] Moreover, in 1905, Kleinworts told Goldman Sachs that the nature of the business of Emile Erlanger & Co 'is much too speculative & unknown to render their acceptance desirable & we recommend you to completely avoid the name in the course of your exchange business'.[9]

Erlanger was tempted by the proposition to acquire Sombrero, and set about assembling a syndicate that would bid for the asset.[10] The business certainly looked attractive: this was no bubble speculation. Both previous companies had paid six figure sums for the island,[11] and it had a history of profitability. In the early 1860s, its profits had run at £20,000 per annum, while Chatteris's advertisement had spoken of 'large profits' made from the mine under his administration.[12] In July 1871, Chatteris told the Vice-Chancellor that these profits would reach £15,000.[13] Moreover, there seemed to be plentiful phosphate reserves. In an era when phosphate seemed to be money waiting to be mined, Erlanger's syndicate was not the only interested bidder. Julian Goldsmid MP, who later bought 1,700 shares in the company formed by the syndicate, himself offered £49,000 for the lease. Erlanger's syndicate, which had earlier submitted lower bids, offered £50,000 on 29 August, but hurriedly increased it to the reserve price on the following day, when another buyer threatened to beat them to the post with the full price of £55,000. Erlanger was pleased with his deal, for in his view the property was worth at least £120,000.[14]

What was to be done with the asset? Erlanger claimed later that while it had always been the syndicate's intention to convert it into a limited liability company, there was no initial decision taken as to whether shares in the company would be offered to the public. Members of the syndicate therefore paid for the property with their own money, a point which would be of some significance in the litigation. However, although the evidence is not conclusive, there are some signs that the syndicate may not originally have anticipated paying in full until a company had been floated and shares sold,

[8] Report from the Select Committee on Loans to Foreign States, Parl Papers 1875 (367) XI 1 xxxii–xxxv, xlvi–l; see also his defence of his conduct at qq 3896ff.

[9] David Kynaston, *The City of London. Volume II: Golden Years 1890–1914* (London, Chatto & Windus, 1995) 279.

[10] His own stake was just over 30%, while Westall and his associates took a stake over 27%.

[11] The Sombrero Phosphate Company Ltd had valued the island at £100,000, while the Phosphate of Lime Co Ltd had been formed to buy both this property and another in Spain, for £250,000.

[12] *The Times*, 29 June 1871, 4 col f.

[13] House of Lords Record Office, HL/PO/JU/4/3/317 (henceforth cited as 'HLRO Erlanger'), Bill of Complaint, 31.

[14] HLRO Erlanger, Case of the Appellants and Appendix, Document 3 (Answer of Baron Emile Erlanger).

for a public company was formed at the earliest opportunity. The contract to buy the island was signed on 30 August, between Chatteris and John Marsh Evans, a business acquaintance of Erlanger's, who acted as purchaser and trustee for the syndicate. Erlanger put up the 10% deposit. The contract was approved on 15 September by the Vice-Chancellor, the balance of the payment being due by 15 November. On 16 September, Erlanger began to collect money from his fellow members, and on 20 September a contract was signed between Evans and Francis Pavy (as trustee for the company to be formed), to sell the asset to the company for £110,000, of which £30,000 would be in fully paid-up shares. In the contract of sale, the contract of 30 August was referred to, but the fact that the syndicate had paid only £55,000 was not. The New Sombrero Phosphate Company itself was registered on 21 September. However, any plan the syndicate may have had to raise the money for the purchase by selling shares in the company was frustrated: for when they sought to register the new company on 20 September, the Registrar said he would only register a company with a name so similar to the one in liquidation if the official liquidator agreed. While Chatteris agreed, it was on condition that the full purchase price was paid at once. Full payment was duly made before shares were sold to the public.

A board of five directors was appointed. Three of them were in effect Erlanger's nominees. The first was Evans, who was simply Erlanger's agent.[15] The second was the president of the Société des Agriculteurs de France, M Drouyn de Lhuys, who never once came to England to learn about the company. The third was Admiral Ronald John Macdonald, an impecunious old sailor who had written to Erlanger to see if something could be found in the City to help him out. He did not have the money to buy the qualification shares, and so Erlanger told him that '[i]t is quite understood that we lend you the 50 shares necessary for your qualification'.[16] Of the other two, EB Eastwick was away in Canada. He only agreed to join the board on the understanding that he would quit if he did not approve of the scheme on his arrival home; which he duly did. Only Thomas Dakin, the Lord Mayor, who had some connections with the trade in chemicals, was in any way independent; but even his powers were limited, since the company's articles allowed two of three directors present at a meeting to have a binding voice. In any event, on 29 September, at their first meeting, the directors endorsed the contract for the purchase of the mine, with Dakin (who claimed to be ignorant of the earlier £55,000 purchase) concurring.

A prospectus was issued which gave a highly optimistic impression of the property. The information in the prospectus was largely derived from

---

[15] He was not a member of the syndicate and had only been made the purchaser of the mine, since he (unlike the Baron) was a British subject.
[16] HLRO Erlanger, Case of the Respondents, 110.

Chatteris, who by September was even more hopeful regarding the mine's prospects than he had been in July. Chatteris reported a ten months' profit of over £23,000, premised on a market price of £5 per ton. The prospectus claimed that with more efficient working practices than could be achieved in a liquidation, annual profits of £42,000 could be anticipated, reaching £50,000 a year with increased production. The company also promised an annual set-aside of £9,000, to be returned to shareholders on a lottery basis each year, so that each investor would have all his capital returned by the time the 14 year lease expired. If all went well with increased production, investors could thus look to a 38% annual dividend. Little wonder the issue was greatly oversubscribed:[17] as the leading dissident shareholder later put it, 'we all thought we were going to make our fortune'.[18] During the flotation, Erlanger spent over £6,000 in what was considered to be a rigging of the market, keeping up the share price: but his main interest here does not seem to have been in speculating in the shares as much as ensuring a safe flotation.[19]

If the prospectus was sanguine, it may safely be assumed that the promoters felt they had bought a good asset. But no independent checks had been made; and once the company was formed, and Captain Pavy was sent out to survey, things began to look less rosy. In December, his report arrived, stating that all previous owners of the island had 'looked to the present without any regard to the future', mining the easiest seams without properly clearing away debris.[20] More investment was needed. Moreover, when the company's London manager, Mackay, urged increased production, the manager on the ground, George Fassnidge—who had to be talked out of resigning when the new company was formed—replied that, given the problems of productivity, no more than 15,000 tons could be expected in 1872, 10,000 tons short of what had been held out as possible in the prospectus.[21]

Despite these difficulties, at the first general meeting of the company at the start of February 1872, Sir Thomas Dakin felt able to declare a profit of £6,000 on the first three months' operation. At this meeting, one shareholder, HP Stephenson, said that he had heard a rumour that the property had been bought by the promoters for around £50,000. This worry was

---

[17] 22,332 applications were received for the 10,000 available shares, though by an error 10,325 were allotted.

[18] HLRO Erlanger, Appendix, 543.

[19] £80,000 of the purchase price was paid in cash, and £3,250 of the sum due from shares was also paid in cash. Erlanger held 313 shares in January 1872, and 263 in July 1877: National Archives [TNA] BT 31/1647/5708.

[20] HLRO Erlanger, Appendix, Document 40: Report of Captain Francis Pavy to the New Sombrero Phosphate Company, December 1871, 523.

[21] He pointed out that the 1869 production of 18,662 tons was untypical, and resulted from the old company's efforts to extract the most accessible material in the cheapest way. Quoted in the Report of the Committee of Investigation, HLRO Erlanger, Appendix, Document 20, 363.

brushed aside: with the company promising to pay its £9,000 bonus warrants and reporting a profit, the rest of the shareholders voted their satis-
faction with the company. In fact, in May, Mackay was still estimating the
company's profitability to be £5,204.[22] However, it soon turned out that
these estimates had been too optimistic and at the June annual general
meeting, a committee of investigation was appointed by the shareholders.
By the time its report was delivered two months later, it was clear that the
company had losses to June amounting to over £4,000; and the prospects
for the future looked bleak.[23] The shareholders' committee reported that
the company's claims relating to its profitability, made both in the prospectus and at the February meeting, were false. It also noted that the property
had been bought by the promoters for half the price at which they sold it
to the firm.[24] Having sought the advice of J Napier Higgins QC, they
resolved to recover the £55,000.

HS Stephenson was the moving force behind the shareholders' revolt. At
the end of August 1872, he was appointed to the board, becoming chairman. He later admitted that 'if we had made 50 per cent. dividend the
shareholders would never have filed this bill';[25] but once the chance of high
profits receded, he took an increasingly hawkish and litigious view. But
some of his fellow directors wanted a settlement, and it was agreed initially to pursue an amicable solution. In September, the board therefore wrote
to Erlanger seeking the return of the £55,000. He replied on 23 October:
'we are quite willing under the disappointing circumstances which have
occurred to give the Company the benefit of the full amount of profit which
we personally derived in cash and in shares from the transaction.'[26] But the
offer was refused, since Erlanger was referring only to his own proportion
of the profits (amounting to £13,230), rather than guaranteeing the return
of the full sum. Stephenson dismissed the offer as 'a drop in the pan', considering 'the fraud that had been committed on us'.[27]

By late summer, when shares were trading at £4 and there was little
prospect of any profit, Stephenson was clearly keen to get *all* the investment
returned, and not merely the secret profit made by the Baron and his associates. Erlanger's delayed response may have helped to swing the company's

[22] Quoted in the Report of the Committee of Investigation, HLRO Erlanger, Appendix, Document 20.
[23] Indeed, by the end of 1874, the company had made an overall loss of over £7,600. The figures are in the cross examination of HP Stephenson, HLRO Erlanger, Appendix Document 21, 426–7, 429–30.
[24] The committee reported that it was 'surprised and astonished that the original directors as men of business acting as trustees for the shareholders should have without the most minute inquiry consented to give to one of their own colleagues £110,000 for a property which they were aware was purchased by him for £55,000 only a few days previously'. Report of the Committee of Investigation, HLRO Erlanger, Appendix, Document 20, 367.
[25] HLRO Erlanger, Cross Examination of Stephenson, 393.
[26] *Ibid*, Answer of Emile Erlanger (Document 3), 145–6.
[27] *Ibid*, Cross Examination of Stephenson, 405.

mood in Stephenson's favour. With a falling share price, the company became ever more determined to litigate. When in spring 1876 the case came before the Vice-Chancellor, Stephenson was convinced that the company would never be profitable. The shares were now worth only £2, and were being kept at that artificially high level (he claimed) by the Baron, who was seeking to buy shares in the market, in order to secure the votes, which (he implied) would allow the company to be wound up.[28] In 1875, the company resisted attempts by some shareholders to wind up the company, but at the same time—while short of working capital—refused to invest in the island, preferring to keep funds for the forthcoming Chancery litigation.

B. INTO EQUITY: THE CASE BEFORE SIR RICHARD MALINS

The company's case against the syndicate came to court in March 1876, just as a flood of cases arising from failed companies launched by dubious promoters in the early 1870s entered the courts. The New Sombrero Company's claim to rescind their contract with Erlanger's syndicate was based on two principal arguments. The first—and in fact weaker—claim was that the prospectus contained wilful misrepresentations, particularly concerning the island's profitability, and the quantity of phosphate to be found there. Though the shareholders were clearly upset at having a less profitable asset than they had hoped, it was hard to pin responsibility for this on Erlanger and his colleagues. If Chatteris's claims about profitability (quoted in the prospectus) seemed over-optimistic, they represented his genuine view in September 1871, which he confirmed separately to the phosphate merchants Pickford and Winkfield. To all intents and purposes, the island had appeared in the summer of 1871 to be a good investment: the decline in profitability was attributable to other causes subsequent to the formation of the firm. Erlanger argued that the decline was due to operational factors. These included Fassnidge's mismanagement on site. Under increasing pressure to produce, he began to send poorer quality material, which was then rejected by the buyers. While Dakin had indeed over-estimated the company's profitability in February 1872, this was because he assumed that shipments which had been sent by Fassnidge would fetch a high price. But potential profit had turned to loss when the consignment was rejected for being of low grade and had to be sold cheaply. A second factor that hit the firm was the decline in demand for phosphate of lime, and the consequent drop in price. The price quoted in the prospectus of £5 a ton had been charged by Chatteris; but from November 1871 the price began to fall, reaching £4 per ton. It was only from 1874,

---

[28] *Ibid*, Cross Examination of Stephenson, 405–6.

when the commodity price began to rise again, that the company returned to modest profitability.[29]

The plaintiffs also claimed that the prospectus was misleading in its assertion that there were 700,000 tons of phosphate on the island. This claim was made on the basis of a report from a civil engineer, EB Webb, made for the Crown in 1865. Insofar as it gave the impression that this was a *recent* report, this might have been misleading. Nonetheless, there was much evidence to support the claim that the island remained rich in phosphate. Indeed, in August 1872, Webb confirmed to Mackay that in his view, the island contained a million tons of phosphate.[30] Although he had not been back to recheck, Pavy's report from December 1871 spoke of extensive deposits, while Chatteris in February 1872 reiterated that there were plentiful deposits on the island which could be worked at a profit. Even the shareholders' committee reported that there was good phosphate to be obtained on the island, while at the trial, the merchant William Pickford told the court that 'the island is capable of producing very large quantities of phosphate now'.[31] If investment was needed to obtain the phosphate and if the easiest seams had been exhausted, it could hardly be said that the prospectus had given a misleading impression when describing the quantity of material.

The second of the plaintiffs' arguments was more important: that the contract was vitiated because the directors had suppressed details of their own initial purchase of the asset. The defendants claimed that they had no obligation to disclose this. To support this view, they claimed that the asset had been sold to the company at a fair price. As Dakin told the February meeting:[32]

> I did not ask the question whether the purchaser made money by a good bargain. The question is whether the thing is fairly stated in the prospectus, whether it is worth what is given for it, and whether it is likely to produce a profit to the shareholders.

Moreover, it was claimed that it had been very well known in the summer of 1871 that the mine was being sold for £55,000, while the fact that Evans was both the vendor of the mine to the company and a director was evident from the prospectus. Finally, it was claimed that the syndicate bought the mine at their own risk, and not as agents of the company: they had bought cheap and were perfectly entitled to sell at a fair price.[33]

---

[29] *Ibid*, Cross Examination of Stephenson, 216. In the first half of 1875, when the price was £4 15s, the company made a profit of £479.

[30] EB Webb to TM Mackay, 28 August 1872, HLRO Erlanger, Appendix, Document 87, 682.

[31] HLRO Erlanger, Appendix 524, 533, 646.

[32] *Ibid*, Appendix, 387.

[33] *Ibid*, Appendix, 108

This was a contentious issue. The *Erlanger* case came to court at a time of great uncertainty about company promoters' duties to disclose their own interest. There had been a great deal of recent discussion about the meaning of section 38 of the Companies Act of 1867. Passed in the aftermath of notorious suppressions of information in the prospectus of Overend, Gurney & Co Ltd, this section enacted that any prospectus which failed to give information regarding 'any contract entered into by the company, or the promoters, directors or trustees thereof' before its issuing was to be deemed a fraud on shareholders taking on the faith of the prospectus. The discussion of promoters' duties in cases on this section provided an important background to the arguments in the *Erlanger* case; though since the latter was a suit by a company, rather than individual shareholders, the legislation did not itself apply.

The meaning of section 38 had been disputed since it was unclear from its wording whether mention had to be made only of prior contracts which would bind the company being formed (such as had been omitted in the case of Overend, Gurney & Co), or whether it covered any contract, the knowledge of whose existence might influence potential shareholders. When the question was first raised, courts held to the former position, believing that it was acceptable for promoters to buy cheap and sell dear. In March 1875, Sir James Bacon V-C had heard *Gover's Case*,[34] in which a shareholder sought to rescind her contract to buy shares in a gas producing company. The company had bought a patent for the manufacture of gas from its promoter, WS Mappin, for £125,000, but had failed to mention in its prospectus that the promoter had himself bought the patent for £65,000. Even though Mappin's contract to buy the patent was conditional on his forming a company to work it, and the patent was to be paid for partly in shares, Bacon held that he was not a promoter at the time he bought the patent. This was because Mappin might equally have sold the patent to *another* company to be formed by *others*, rather than forming one himself. It was for the plaintiff to establish by proof that his first agreement pointed unequivocally to an intention to *form* a company, which would make him a promoter. Without such proof, his purchase of the patent was to be considered an entirely separate transaction from the sale, so that Mappin stood in no fiduciary relationship with the company, and had no obligation to disclose the contract.[35] 'It is not inequitable,' Bacon ruled, 'that a man should buy as cheap and sell as dear as he can.'[36] The seller was under no obligation to disclose the price at which he bought an asset, for purchasers could make up their own minds as to its value. The case went to the Court

---

[34] *Re Coal Economising Gas Co, Gover's Case* (1875) LR 20 Eq 114.
[35] *Ibid*, 123–4: 'what trust or confidence exists in the case of a man who buys a patent for £60,000 and offers to sell it for £120,000?'
[36] *Ibid*, 124.

of Appeal in December. A divided court upheld Bacon's decision. James LJ took a line similar to Bacon's:[37]

> It is surely open to any man, in point of law, to sell his property to a joint stock company, and to invite persons to form themselves into a joint stock company to purchase from him, just as it is open to any man to sell to any persons in the world the right to become his partners in any property or undertaking. Until the formation of the partnership he is simply a vendor of the wares.

The dissenting Brett J held that while Mappin was not a promoter at the time of the first contract (when the company did not exist)—so that his non-disclosure of the first contract in the second could not be intentional fraud—he was liable under section 38, since the two agreements were part of one continuing transaction, and since knowledge of the first was bound to influence any potential shareholder. Mellish LJ, in the majority, upheld Bacon's decision, on the ground that the plaintiff had no right to have her name removed from the list of contributors to the company, which was the remedy she sought. But he agreed with Brett that section 38 would give her a remedy against Mappin, since it was (in his view) not designed to cover only contracts entered into by promoters after they had become promoters. At the same time, he was clear that Mappin was not a promoter at the time he made the first contract, and that there was no fiduciary duty towards the company later formed at that time.[38] Brett's and Mellish's view was to suggest that any duty incurred by the promoter could only be based on section 38 of the Act.

When the *Erlanger* case came before Malins V-C, *Gover's Case* had recently been decided. Malins had also recently heard *Phosphate Sewage Company v Hartmont*,[39] in which the promoters of a company were held bound to repay the full purchase price of a mining concession sold to the company (at an inflated price), after the concession was cancelled by the government which granted it. Both cases were present in the Vice-Chancellor's mind when deciding—the first for its legal arguments, the second as an example of clearly fraudulent commercial conduct by unrespectable professional promoters. Malins found in favour of Erlanger's syndicate.[40] He rejected the idea that the defendants had to restore their £55,000 profit, for breach of a fiduciary duty to the company, as having been their agent when they bought the asset. Echoing Bacon's words in *Gover*, he asked: 'what fiduciary relation is there between a man or body of men who buy an island for £55,000, and sell it to a company for £110,000?'[41] Malins accepted Erlanger's contention that they were

---

[37] *Re Coal Economising Co* (1875) 1 Ch D 182, 187.
[38] *Ibid*, 191.
[39] (1877) 5 Ch D 394.
[40] *New Sombrero Phosphate Company v Erlanger* (1877) 5 Ch D 73.
[41] *Ibid*, 93.

undecided at this point whether to sell to a public company or not. Having (unlike Mappin) paid cash for the property, Erlanger and his associates were absolute owners, and were free either to work it themselves, or sell it on. The question of whether they might be liable for their profit as promoters at the time of the sale was not raised, as this was not a case covered by section 38 of the Companies Act.[42]

The second issue was whether the contract could be rescinded on the ground of fraudulent misrepresentation.[43] Malins, oddly, commented that it would not be justifiable to sell a property to a company at double its original price 'without clearly satisfying themselves that it was worth the increased price'.[44] But he was satisfied that the price was fair. This was a case where the vendors might have made 'highly coloured and sanguine' statements about the prospects of the mine, but—unlike the vendors in *Phosphate Sewage Company v Hartmont*—they were perfectly *bona fide*. Nor did the failure to mention the contract of 30 August constitute a misrepresentation. The shareholders might after all have asked to see the contract; 'and I cannot think that persons who join joint stock companies are justified in forbearing all inquiry and investigation as to documents which they are told may be seen.'[45]

C. IN THE COURT OF APPEAL

By February 1877, the moral view of company promoters had altered, thanks partly to the disgrace of Albert Grant, who was now facing ruin.[46] On 14 February, the judges of the Common Pleas Division pronounced a judgment in *Twycross v Grant*,[47] one of the many cases brought against him, which endorsed Brett's earlier view that company promoters were required by section 38 of the Companies Act to include in the prospectus details of all prior contracts they had entered into which might affect the judgment of potential shareholders. In this judgment, Grant was made to pay back to 88 shareholders in the Lisbon Steam Tramway Company the cost of the (now worthless) shares they had bought in reliance on a

---

[42] Since this was a case between the company and its promoters, section 38 (which applied to shareholders) did not apply (though it was mentioned by the plaintiffs' original bill of complaint of 1872). But compare *Craig v Phillips* (1876) 3 Ch D 722, decided in the month after *Erlanger*, on the meaning of section 38: Sir James Bacon V-C held that a man who purchased a coal mine for £16,125 on 10 May 1873 was entitled to sell it to a company on 29 May for £23,275, despite the fact that the first contract was not mentioned in the prospectus.

[43] *New Sombrero* (n 40) 97 (Malins V-C): 'I do not find that they are in express terms charged with fraud, but wilful misrepresentation and suppression of known facts to induce persons to act in the belief of the facts which are misrepresented, and in ignorance of others which are suppressed, is clearly fraud, and the bill must therefore, I think, be treated as founded on fraud.'

[44] This seems odd since, if they were not fiduciaries, it is unclear on what basis the failure to verify a fair price would justify rescission on the grounds of misrepresentation.

[45] *New Sombrero* (n 40) 100.

[46] Robb (n 5) 100–1.

[47] (1877) 2 CPD 469.

prospectus which failed to mention a contract under which Grant made a secret profit.[48] Eight days later, the Court of Appeal pronounced its judgment in *New Sombrero Phosphate Company v Erlanger*. Before this court, the defendants continued to argue that the transaction was fair; but they now added two new arguments. First, it was contended that the company had lost its right to sue by its laches or acquiescence, having been aware of the original purchase price as early as February 1872. Secondly, it was argued that the only remedy in such a case was for individual shareholders to sue for damages, rather than the company seeking rescission.

On the principal issue, Jessel MR ruled that 'the promoters of a company stand in a fiduciary relation to that company which is their creature' and that in this case, at the moment (on 29 September 1871) when the company ratified the contract of purchase, there were no independent directors raising a voice.[49] He added that 'persons in a fiduciary position must make a full and fair disclosure when they are about to sell property to those towards whom they stand in that relation', and that it was obviously not fair not to disclose that the property being sold was one's own.[50] Jessel's remedy for this failure to disclose was to rescind the contract: the contract of 20 September, notionally ratified by the nominee directors nine days later was 'nothing more than a mere sham contract, a thing entered into by one agent of the promoter to sell, with another agent of the promoter to buy; there really was nothing more in it when it had been adopted than when it was entered into; and it was not a transaction which could in any sense bind the company'. He noted that the directors of the company owed a duty to 'future shareholders who were to form the real company', a duty that could not be fulfilled when they were the nominees of the promoters. For Jessel, 'the promoters being . . . in a fiduciary position, not only having avoided making a complete disclosure, not only having concealed material facts, but having also misrepresented material facts, there was no binding contract on the company'.[51] This was to give the company the kind of remedy *Twycross*

---

[48] It should be noted that in this action, Grant was not required to account for the secret profit he had made: but was held liable, as in fraud, for the financial loss of the investors.

[49] Of the three present, Evans was Erlanger's nominee, Macdonald's shares were supplied by Erlanger, and Dakin had yet to purchase his shares.

[50] *New Sombrero* (n 40) 112.

[51] *Ibid*, 113. Jessel claimed that there was a material misrepresentation insofar as (he claimed) the prospectus misleadingly stated that the 'directors'—which could only mean all five—had entered into a provisional contract to purchase the property from Evans (which he said must refer to the contract of 20 September entered into by Erlanger's nominees). This was not a misrepresentation initially identified by the plaintiffs (though much stress was later made in argument on the point that 'directors' should be read as meaning all five, rather than the three present on 29 September). In fact, the prospectus was more ambiguous, reading: 'The Directors have entered into a provisional contract to purchase the property . . . as from 29 September . . . Copy of this contract, which is dated the 20th September 1871, and made between John Marsh Evans of the one part, and Francis Pavy on behalf of the Company, may be seen at the office of the Company's solicitors.'

v Grant had given shareholders: putting them back into the position they were in before the promoter had misled them into a purchase by not giving the information he was obliged to divulge.

James LJ, who had given the leading judgment in *Gover's Case*, reiterated his view that a man could buy cheap and sell dear. But he now stressed the fact that company promoters owed fiduciary duties to the companies they formed:[52]

> If that promoter has a property which he desires to sell to the company, it is quite open to him to do so; but upon him, as upon any other person in a fiduciary position, it is incumbent to make full and fair disclosure of his interest and position with respect to that property. I can see no difference in this respect between a promoter and a trustee, steward or agent.

Since he had not made the full disclosure required by equity, that he was the real vendor, the contract could be set aside. In coming to this decision, the Court of Appeal stressed that both Evans (the nominal vendor) and Captain Pavy (the purchaser for the company) were Erlanger's nominees. There was no sale through an independent party.

The Court of Appeal also rejected the argument as to laches. As Jessel saw it, the rumours that circulated in February were not strong enough to attach knowledge to the company: once they found out the true position, they acted quickly enough. Jessel also dismissed two other arguments against rescission. The first was that it would be unfair to give the company the original purchase price, since that would reward the guilty parties who had kept their shares as well as the innocent. The second was the objection that to rescind the contract would undermine the objects of the company. The argument that a *restitutio in integrum* was not possible does not seem to have been raised in the Court of Appeal. This issue was raised only before the House of Lords. The arguments in the Court of Appeal, as has been seen, were to some degree informed by the thinking that had informed a majority in the same court in *Twycross v Grant*. If the result seemed just in the context of the panic over speculative company promotions in the 1870s, it nevertheless left doctrine vague in an area where promoters did not have the statutory duties imposed by section 38. If promoters were fiduciaries, it was still unclear precisely what this entailed. Things were complicated by the fact that the term 'promoter' 'is a term not of law but of business, carefully summing up in a single word a number of business operations familiar to the commercial world by which a company is generally brought into existence'.[53] When *Erlanger*

---

[52] *Ibid*, 118.
[53] *Whaley Bridge Calico Printing Co v Green* (1879) 5 QBD 109, 111 (Bowen J), quoted in (1886) 82 *Law Times* 78.

came to the Lords, the court had to grapple with the precise nature of the
relationship of the promoter to the company, for the determination of this
question—which turned on the nature of agency—was central to settling
the remedy.

D. *ERLANGER* AND THE PROBLEM OF AGENCY

It was clearly settled that agents owed fiduciary duties to their principals.
An agent was bound to look solely to the interests of the person who had
bargained 'for the exercise of the disinterested skill, diligence and zeal of the
agent for his own exclusive benefit';[54] and the property transactions of
agents were therefore closely regulated.[55] While an agent was permitted to
buy the property of his principal, he had first to make a full disclosure of
his position and of all information in his possession; and the transaction
had to be fair.[56] Equally, an agent was permitted to sell his own property to
the principal, though the latter had the right to rescind or affirm on discovering the agent's interest. An agent who made any secret profits from his
agency was bound to restore them to his principal, whose property such
profits were considered to be.

In *Erlanger*, the nature of the remedy available to the plaintiffs turned in
large part on the nature of the relationship between the syndicate and the
company that was formed. The promoters were clearly agents by the time
of the sale of their asset to the company: Evans, Erlanger's nominee, was
after all a director of the company. But what was their position vis-à-vis the
company when they acquired the asset? If their relationship with the New
Sombrero Phosphate Company began only after they acquired the asset,
then they would be seen as agents selling their own property to their principals. This would be a transaction which might be vitiated by rescission

---

[54] See Joseph Story, *Commentaries on the Law of Agency,* 7th edn by Isaac F Redfield and
William A Herrick (Boston, MA, Little, Brown & Co, 1869) § 210.

[55] Thus, an agent who bought property during his agency, intending to keep it for himself,
was regarded as trustee of the property for his principal. *Lees v Nuttall* (1829) 1 Russ & My
53, 39 ER 21; *Taylor v Salmon* (1838) 4 My & Cr 134, 40 ER 866.

[56] See *Lowther v Lord Lowther* (1806) 13 Ves Jun 95, 33 ER 230; *Murphy v O'Shea* (1845)
8 Ir Eq R 329, 2 Jo & Lat 422; *Dunne v English* (1874) LR 18 Eq 524. Even if the principal
was perfectly willing to sell, the agent still had to show that the transaction had been fair: see
Dally v Wonham (1863) 33 Beav 154, 55 ER 326. Unlike cases of trust, the agent did not need
to prove the positive assent of his principal, but he did have to show that the principal was
given sufficient information to imply consent. For the position of trustees, see *Gibson v Jeyes*
(1801) 6 Ves Jun 266, 277, 31 ER 1044, 1049–50. See also *Coles v Trecothick* (1804) 9 Ves
Jun 234, 246–7, 32 ER 592, 597; *Fox v Macreth* (1788) 2 Bro CC 400, 29 ER 224; *Ex parte
Lacey* (1802) 6 Ves Jun 625, 31 ER 1228. See also *Whelpdale v Cookson* (1747) 1 Ves Sen 9,
27 ER 856; *York Buildings Co v Mackenzie* (1795) 8 Brown PC 42, 3 ER 432; *Ex parte James*
(1803) 8 Ves Jun 337, 32 ER 385.

(regardless of whether the price was fair),[57] but not by an account of profits. By contrast, if the syndicate could be considered to be the agents of the company at the time they acquired the island, then the asset would have been purchased by them on behalf of the company: and the company's remedy would have been the refund of the private profit of £55,000.

Courts had long been keen to protect the principal where he bought property from the agent. 'Where a man undertakes to buy for me in the most beneficial manner, what my colliery shall want,' Sir Pepper Arden ruled in *Massey v Davies* in 1794, 'can it be possible, that I can trust him to sell those articles to me himself? The clearest evidence is necessary to shew consent. It is opening a door to a monstrous fraud.'[58] In this case, Arden ordered the profit made by the agent to be handed over. Similarly, in 1845, in *The York and North Midland Railway v Hudson*, Sir John Romilly ruled that George Hudson was not permitted to keep the profit arising from the rise in the market price of iron, when he sold on to his company iron he had bought in the market to sell to them.[59] Where an agent was employed to purchase an item for his principal, but sought to make a profit by acting himself as intermediate purchaser and vendor, there was little question of setting aside the transaction: for the agent was clearly already acting for the principal.[60] Where an agent bought property which he then sold on to the firm, equity also treated the intermediate sale as a fiction, and held that the agent had been acting for the principal all along. In such cases, the fairness of the second transaction was not considered relevant, and the agent had to account for his profit.[61]

If this was obvious enough when agents bought for existing principals, matters were less clear when property was sold to a company yet to be formed (as in *Erlanger*). Nonetheless, courts from the 1830s to the 1850s treated the purchaser of the asset as already an agent of the company. In *Hichens v Congreve* in 1831, three entrepreneurs agreed to buy some Irish

---

[57] In *Gillett v Peppercorne* (1840) 3 Beav 78, 84, 49 ER 31, 33, Lord Langdale set aside a contract with a stockbroker to buy shares, when it turned out that the broker in fact owned the shares being sold. The court refused to look at the question of whether the price was fair or whether fraud was intended, holding that the broker was simply 'in such a situation of trust with regard to the Plaintiff that the transaction cannot, in the contemplation of this Court, be considered valid'.

[58] *Massey v Davies* (1794) 2 Ves Jun 317, 321–2; 30 ER 651, 653.

[59] The case was reported on a different point—that Hudson could not keep the profit on shares sold, which had been allocated by the company to be 'at the disposal of the directors': (1845) 16 Beav 485, 51 ER 866. The unreported point was discussed by Romilly MR in *Great Luxembourg Railway Co v Magnay* (1858) 25 Beav 586, 595; 53 ER 761, 764. See also *Bentley v Craven* (1853) 18 Beav 75, 76–7; 52 ER 29, 30.

[60] Thus, in *Benson v Heathorn* (1842) Y & CCC 326, 62 ER 909 the defendant, employed to buy a vessel for a partnership, who had bought it for £1,350 himself and sold it on for £1,500 was thus forced to return the profit made to the partners.

[61] See the comments in *Aberdeen Railway Company v Blaikie Brothers* (1854) 1 Macq 451, 471.

mines for £10,000, which they intended to sell on to a newly formed company (of which they were directors) for £25,000. The company's shareholders subsequently sought to recover the £15,000 profit. Sir Lancelot Shadwell V-C ruled that the promoters could not claim this as fair profit: 'if they fairly exercised their judgments, which as directors they were bound to exercise', they could not have come to this conclusion. For the judge, the company was effectively misled as to the real purchase price. He rejected as irrelevant the contention that the mines were worth £25,000 (which he admitted they might have been): for there was a misrepresentation about the price in fact paid for the mine. He addressed a second objection:[62]

> Strictly speaking, it is true that there was no company in existence [at the time of the initial purchase]: but these gentlemen were endeavouring to form a company, and they had taken upon themselves the character of directors for the benefit of all persons who had agreed to be, or might afterwards become, members of the company. The £25,000 was to be paid out of the funds which should be subscribed by persons who might, thereafter, become members of the company.

Shadwell also dismissed the defendants' arguments that the only remedy available was rescission. He held there was no other way to give relief than making them account for profit, 'for it would be no relief to make Flattery take back the mines; that would destroy the company altogether'.[63] Shadwell was here clearly treating the three promoters as agents of the company who had made a secret profit, treating the intermediate sale to their nominees as ineffective, and treating it as akin to cases where partners sought to make secret profits from transactions entered into for the partnership.[64]

In 1859, a similar approach was taken in *Bank of London v Tyrrell*.[65] Here, a solicitor, who was one of the original promoters of the plaintiff bank, joined with ER Read in buying the Hall of Commerce in Threadneedle Street, which premises were later sold to the bank. In this case, Sir John Romilly MR held that Tyrrell had to account for the £6,000 profit he made on the transaction. Since the bank had paid out considerable sums in fitting the building out, and since it had bought the property jointly from Read (against whom no equity lay), rescission of the contract was not an option. For Romilly, this was a property acquired via the defendant's agency, rather than a case of an agent selling his own property to his principal. His answer to the problem that the company did not yet exist at the time of the purchase was to suggest that:[66]

---

[62] *Hichens v Congreve* (1831) 4 Sim 420, 427; 58 ER 157, 160.

[63] *Ibid*, 4 Sim 428, 58 ER 160. The judge did not address how Flattery could have been expected to repay £25,000, rather than the £10,000 received: but this may have added to his views against rescission.

[64] See *Fawcett v Whitehouse* (1829) 1 Russ & My 132, 39 ER 51.

[65] (1859) 27 Beav 273, 54 ER 107; affirmed by the House of Lords (1862) 10 HLC 26, 11 ER 934.

[66] *Ibid*, 27 Beav 291–2; 54 ER 114.

One person may be made the agent of another by acts done *ex post facto* . . . [A]s Mr Tyrrell was adopted as the solicitor or agent of the company, he must be considered as having been the agent of the company in all matters in which he professed to act as such agent, that is, in all matters relating to the company which was afterwards formed.

The notion that a promoter was agent for the company at the time of his purchase was also seen in *Beck v Kantorowicz* in 1857. In this case, a syndicate of five promoters agreed to buy a German mine, which was then sold on to a company formed by them. Four of them were deceived by the fifth, who told them that the vendors of the mine would not take less than £85,714 for it, without mentioning that this sum included a £20,000 share for himself. The mine was sold on to the company for £125,000, a sum which (according to the prospectus) included 'all preliminary expenses, and a premium to the parties who incurred the risk and responsibility of the original purchase'. Page Wood V-C had no hesitation in saying that Kantorowicz could not keep his secret profit and had to make good the sums: but the question was whether the money was to go to the company or to his fellow promoters. The Vice-Chancellor noted that the mine was worth the £125,000 and could be worked at a profit; and so he had to overcome the problem of how any shareholder could 'say he is defrauded in having to pay a fair price for a fair profit'.[67] Noting that two of the five promoters were members of the company's committee of management, and therefore its agents, as well as being agents of the syndicate, he ruled that they were bound, when dealing for the company, to keep the purchase price within reasonable bounds. They had (he said) formed the view that £30,000 for the promoters was a reasonable sum. Without Kantorowicz's fraud, the promoters would have got their £30,000 and the company would have bought the mines £20,000 more cheaply. 'Here the company get their whole bargain,' he said, 'even if they pay £125,000 for the mine; but they had a right, as against the members of the committee of management, *to the best bargain* that the latter, had they known the facts, would have been in a position, acting fairly and rightly, to give them.'[68] Here the company was not seeking rescission of the contract for purchase of the mines, but a declaration that Kantorowicz was not entitled to the benefit of shares he had secretly acquired. This was in effect to treat the syndicate as agent for the company in the purchase of the mines, entitled to remuneration for their labour.

In the cases discussed so far, it was clear that the promoter had bought an asset with the intention of selling it on. But what of cases where the agent sold to his principal something which was originally his, rather than

---

[67] *Beck v Kantorowicz* (1857) 3 K & J 230, 247; 69 ER 1093, 1100.
[68] *Ibid*, 3 K & J 250–1, 69 ER 1101.

something acquired to be sold on? In such a situation, the defendant clearly could not be regarded as agent for the principal at the time of the original acquisition. According to long-established rules of equity, in such cases the principal had a choice as to whether to rescind or affirm, with affirmation being evidenced by acquiescence or lapse of time.[69] But could the vending agent be made to account for his profit in the sale if rescission was no longer possible, as was done in *Hichens v Congreve*? This question was raised in 1858, in *The Great Luxembourg Railway Company v Magnay*, where the ruling of Sir John Romilly suggested that he could not. In this case, a director of the plaintiff company was sent to Belgium to acquire a concession for branch lines feeding the Brussels-Namur railway and was given £25,000 of company shares to effect the purchase. Unbeknown to the company, Magnay was himself already holder of the concession, which he transferred to the company for the shares. The concession turned out to be useless for the plaintiffs, who sought the return of the £25,000; but while the suit was in progress, they sold the concession to a third party, agreeing to reimburse them whatever they won against Magnay. Romilly refused to give the company a remedy, since by selling the concession they made it impossible to rescind the contract.[70] In his view, the company was attempting to 'repudiate the contract, as far as they are to pay for it, but they adopt it as far as they are to get anything by it'. He considered it impossible to force the defendant 'to repay £25,000 to the Plaintiffs, without having restored to him a particle of that which was the consideration for it'.[71] The case appears to establish the proposition that where rescission is impossible, no account of profits should be given: but the crucial consideration here does not seem to have been the impossibility of rescission so much as the fact that the company had covered their losses (and by implication affirmed the transaction) by selling the concession on: so that (to use terms not used by the Master of the Rolls) Magnay had not been unjustly enriched at the company's expense.

Nevertheless, in 1872 in *Kimber v Barber*, Romilly endorsed the wider view that once rescission was impossible a purchaser was stuck with his purchase. Here, the plaintiff had asked the defendant to acquire 264 shares in the Colonization Assurance Company, which Kimber sought to relaunch. The shares were to be transferred to other directors for their qualification shares, and 200 were duly transferred to his nominees. The shares were bought at £3 each, but it later transpired that Barber had already acquired the shares for £2, with the intent of selling them on. Unlike the

---

[69] See *Wright v Vanderplank* (1856) 8 De GM & G 133, 44 ER 340 (concerning a transaction between parent and child).

[70] They could in any event not simply return the property, since as a railway concession this needed the assent of the Belgian government.

[71] *Great Luxembourg Railway Company v Magnay* (1858) 25 Beav 586, 598; 53 ER 761, 765.

Court of Appeal, which overturned his decision, Romilly did not feel that Barber was Kimber's agent when making the original purchase. In his view, the appropriate form of relief would have been to set aside the transaction and order the repayment of the money; but this was no longer possible, given that the shares had been transferred to others. While this suggests a peremptory rule that where rescission was impossible, all other remedies were lost, Romilly may have considered that, having transferred the shares on, Kimber had gained a benefit and implicitly affirmed the contract.

He was clear, however, that he had no power to order restoration of the £1 per share profit since that would be 'making a new contract for the parties, which I have no right to do'.[72] By this view, only the parties could set the price for any asset: it was not for a court to impose its agreement on the parties by determining a 'fair' price, since the agent might not have agreed to sell at that price. Fairness to the vendor, this seemed to suggest, required the purchaser either to accept or reject. But if the purchaser was not in a position to reject the goods, it was hardly fair to allow a fiduciary in breach of his duties to retain the benefit of an inflated sale. If the principal had elected to keep the asset, or disposed of it for value, and thereby affirmed the agreement, to make the agent account for profit might indeed involve the court rewriting the agreement in a way that was unfair to the vendor; but where the asset could no longer be restored to the vendor without the purchaser's fault, and without affirmation by the purchaser, it was hardly fair to the purchaser to leave him without any remedy.

That Romilly may have been aware of this problem might be indicated by other comments he made in *Great Luxembourg* about the kinds of profits agents could not keep. Having noted that a railway director like Hudson, when selling his iron to a company, could not sell it 'as if it were his own property', Romilly turned to the example of an agent or trustee who, when asked to buy an estate containing ore for a mining company, sold his own estate to them 'for double its value'. Such a transaction, he said, could not stand; and if it became impossible to restore the estate, the trustee would only be 'entitled to the full value of the estate sold' or its 'proper value'.[73] In the examples given by Romilly, the (unarticulated) suggestion appeared to be that where the property remained in the plaintiff's hands but could not be restored—as with real property in the hands of a mining company (or indeed with raw materials such as iron sold and consumed)—the principal could recover any profit above the fair market price; whereas where

---

[72] *Kimber v Barber* (1872) LR 8 Ch App 56, 57n. For such arguments, see also *Re Cape Breton* (1885) 29 Ch D 795 (discussed in text to nn 132 ff); *Marler's Case* (1913) 114 LT 640n, 641; *Tracy v Mandalay Pty Ltd* (1953) 88 CLR 215, 241.

[73] *Great Luxembourg Railway Company v Magnay* (1858) 25 Beav 586, 595; 53 ER 761, 764–5. In *Bank of London v Tyrrell* (1859) 27 Beav 273, 295 (54 ER 107, 115) he explained his meaning to be that the company could in such case recover any sum 'over and above the full value of the property'.

the principal had sold the asset on for value, he could not, the implication here being that the further sale covered any loss from the initial transaction. If this were the view to be followed, the principal would be forbidden from seeking an account for profit where the asset could not be returned only if he had affirmed the sale. As shall be seen, this unresolved problem was raised again after *Erlanger*.

In *Erlanger* itself, the House of Lords rejected the line taken by early nineteenth century company cases.[74] The Lords took the view that when the syndicate bought the asset, they were not agents for the New Sombrero Company. They stood in no fiduciary position to anyone, but were free to retain the island, to sell it to another party, or to promote a company to buy it.[75] They were thus considered to be in the position of agents who sold their own property to the company: like the promoter in *Gover* and unlike the men in *Hichens*. This meant that the profit they made was not the money of the company: and therefore no account of profits could be ordered. As Lord Cairns LC put it:[76]

> The part of the case of the Respondents, which, as an alternative, sought to make the Appellants account for the profit which they made on the re-sale of the property to the Respondents, on an allegation that the Appellants acted in a fiduciary position at the time they made the contract of the 30th of August, 1871, is not, I think, capable of being supported, and this, as I understand, was the view of all the Judges in the Courts below.

However, since they were in a position to exert undue influence at the time of the sale, they were bound 'if they wished to make a valid contract of sale to the company, to nominate independent directors and fully disclose the material facts'[77] to ensure that the purchase had been properly assented to. Nor was it any defence to assert that the price had been fair.[78] In the view

---

[74] *Erlanger v New Sombrero Phosphate Company* (1878) 3 App Cas 1218.
[75] *Ibid*, 1267 (Lord Blackburn).
[76] *Ibid*, 1235.
[77] *Ibid*, 1229.
[78] This defence had sometimes been available in fiduciary cases involving solicitors, removing the need for independent advice. In *Edwards v Meyrick* (1842) 2 Hare 60, 67 ER 25, a solicitor was entitled to retain an estate bought from his client, whose value rose dramatically when the building of a railway opened up the possibility of extracting coal on the property. At 2 Hare 68, 67 ER 28, Sir James Wigram stated that in the case of a solicitor there was not 'the positive incapacity which exists between a trustee and his *cestui que trust*; but the rule the Court imposes is, that inasmuch as the parties stand in a relation which gives, or may give, the solicitor an advantage over his client, the onus lies on the solicitor to prove that the transaction was fair'. See also *Gibson v Jeyes* (1801) 6 Ves Jun 266, 278, 31 ER 1044, 1050, where Lord Eldon said that in such a case, if the attorney did not ensure that the vendor obtained independent advice, he had to show that he had given her the independent advice he would have given a third party. In *Harries v Tremenheere* (1808) 15 Ves Jun 34, 42, 33 ER 668, 671, Lord Eldon said that 'the Defendant must be required to shew, that he made as good a bargain for his employer, as against himself, as a provident, well-managing, honourable, steward, acting most adversely, in a fair sense, would'. See also *Montesquieu v Sandys* (1811) 18 Ves Jun 302, 34 ER 331.

of the Lords, the fiduciary duty owed by the syndicate was not fulfilled by the ratification of the purchase by a board dominated by nominees. The contract could thus be vitiated. But since the Lords (who did not consider the position hinted at by Romilly in his *obiter* comments in *Great Luxembourg*) felt that no account for profit could be ordered in such situations, the remedy of the firm hinged for the Lords on whether the right to rescind remained.

E. *ERLANGER* AND THE PROBLEM OF RESCISSION

When did a contracting party lose the right to rescind? At common law, rescission was a self-help remedy, seen primarily in two contexts.[79] Firstly, where there was total failure of consideration in a contract, it was possible to return the goods delivered, and sue for recovery in an action for money had and received. Thus, if faulty goods were delivered, they could be returned and the price recovered.[80] But where there had been partial performance of the contract, or if the non-breaching party accepted any benefit under the contract—such as occupation of land for a time—he lost his right to rescind and had to sue on the contract.[81] Secondly, where one of the contracting parties had been guilty of fraud, the innocent party was entitled to rescind, once he became aware of the fraud, by returning the goods.[82] As Crompton J put it in 1858: 'If you are fraudulently induced to buy a cake you may return it and get back your price; but you cannot both eat your cake and return your cake.'[83] Where goods could not be returned, the innocent party's remedy was to sue in an action of deceit for his damages, rather than an action for money had and received. Where a party had entered into a contract on the basis of an innocent misrepresentation, he could neither

[79] For recent discussion see J O'Sullivan, 'Rescission as a Self-Help Remedy: A Critical Analysis' (2000) 59 *CLJ* 509; J Poole and A Keyser, 'Justifying Partial Rescission in English Law' (2005) 121 *LQR* 272.

[80] *Grimaldi v White* (1802) 4 Esp 95, 170 ER 654, discussed in M Lobban, 'Contractual Fraud in Law and Equity, c 1750–c 1850' (1997) 17 *OJLS* 461.

[81] See *Hunt v Silk* (1804) 5 East 449, 102 ER 1142, explaining *Giles v Edwards* (1797) 7 TR 181, 101 ER 920, and *Blackburn v Smith* (1848) 2 Ex 783, 792; 154 ER 707, 711. See also W Swain, '*Cutter v Powell* and the Pleading of Claims of Unjust Enrichment' [2003] *RLR* 46.

[82] The innocent party here was prevented from rescinding if he made a clear election to affirm the contract: but if no such election was made, the issue remained open until such time as the innocent party had notice of the fraud. See the rule articulated in *Clough v The London and North West Railway Co* (1871) LR 7 Ex 26, 34–5. It was noted that lapse of time might be taken as evidence of an intent to affirm.

[83] *Clarke v Dickson* (1858) EB & E 148, 152–4; 120 ER 463, 465–6. The case concerned the purchase of shares in a cost book mine which was later converted to limited liability.

rescind the contract at common law[84] nor get damages consequent on innocent misrepresentations.

Courts of equity were more generous. Unlike common law courts, which decided whether a party's action to rescind was legally valid, the courts of Chancery were the instruments through which rescission was effected in situations where the parties could not do it themselves: notably in setting aside purchases of property. Besides intervening in cases of fraud, equity also had the power to set aside contracts where rescission was not possible at common law, where there had been breaches of fiduciary duties or unconscionable conduct, such as the use of undue influence.[85] From the middle of the nineteenth century, courts of equity had become increasingly willing to rescind contracts where misrepresentations had been only negligent or even innocent, rather than fraudulent.[86] However, the development of this doctrine left the problem that while rescission was available for non-fraudulent as well as fraudulent misrepresentations, damages were not.[87] This meant that while the victim of a fraud, who was no longer in a position to rescind by being unable to offer *restitutio in integrum*, could be adequately compensated in damages, the victim of a non-fraudulent misrepresentation unable to restore would get no remedy.

The problem was eased, however, by the fact that equity had a less strict view of *restitutio in integrum* than did the common law courts. Where property had been partly consumed, equity still offered rescission. This can be seen from Lord Lyndhurst's judgment in *Small v Attwood* in 1832. In this case, the plaintiffs, having formed a partnership called the British Iron Company, bought some mines and works in Staffordshire from the defendant, but were misled by false representations as to its value. Lyndhurst held that the contract could be set aside on the ground that they had acted on the misrepresentation (a judgment overturned in the Lords). He also answered the defendant's objection that 'great alteration has taken place in the property' as a result of the working of the mines by the plaintiffs. This,

---

[84] As Sir George Jessel summarised it in *Redgrave v Hurd* (1881) 20 Ch D 1, 13: 'There were, indeed, cases in which, even at Common Law, a contract could be rescinded for misrepresentation, although it could not be shewn that the person making it knew the representation to be false. They are variously stated, but I think, according to the later decisions, the statement must have been made recklessly and without care, whether it was true or false, and not with the belief that it was true.' Rescission for innocent misrepresentation at common law was limited to cases where there had been a total failure of consideration: *Kennedy v The Panama, New Zealand and Australian Royal Mail Company Ltd* (1867) LR 2 QB 580.

[85] This is described as the 'auxiliary and exclusive' equitable jurisdiction in R Meagher, D Heydon and M Leeming, *Meagher, Gummow and Lehane's Equity: Doctrine and Remedies* (4th edn, NSW, Chatsworth, 2002) [24-075].

[86] See the arguments in M Lobban, 'Nineteenth Century Frauds in Company Formation: *Derry v Peek* in Context' (1996) 107 *LQR* 309.

[87] *Redgrave v Hurd* (1881) 20 Ch D 1, 12. Although there were efforts in the later nineteenth century to develop a rule that there could be damages awarded for non-fraudulent misrepresentations, this was curtailed by the House of Lords in *Derry v Peek* (1889) 14 App Cas 337.

he noted, was no bar to rescission, for they had only 'acted fairly in the management of the property' as owners.[88] In his decree, Lyndhurst ruled:[89]

> the agreement must be vacated; . . . the money that has been paid must of course be returned with interest; and . . . the parties who have been in possession of this property must account for the profits of that property; of course, in that account, they must be considered as having held that property during that period on account of Mr Attwood.

Given that it was the court of equity which rescinded the contract, rather than the parties, it was able to do so on terms which overcame the problem that pure *restitutio in integrum* was not possible. Similarly, in *Gillett v Peppercorne*, where a stockbroker had sold his own shares to a client, the client was able to rescind the purchases, some of which dated back to 1826, subject to his also returning all dividends received.[90]

Equity also allowed rescission even though the value of the asset had diminished. This can be seen from cases involving the return of shares whose value had fallen. In *Blake v Mowatt* in 1856, Sir John Romilly set aside a contract, despite the fact that the shares bought under it were now worth much less. 'It is the leading principle of the equity administration in this Court,' he ruled, 'that truth shall govern all transactions, and that one who deludes another in a contract, or permits him to be deluded, and takes advantage of that delusion, cannot afterwards complain that, if the contract be set aside, he will be in a worse situation than if the contract had never been entered into.'[91]

By the time *Erlanger* was decided, the question of when rescission was available had been put in issue once more in *Western Bank of Scotland v Addie*, a Scottish appeal to the Lords where the pursuer sought either rescission of a contract to buy shares in a joint stock company (which in England would have been a matter for equity) or alternatively damages (which would have been a common law matter). Rescission, Lord Cranworth held, 'can only be had where the party seeking it is able to put those against whom it is asked in the same situation in which they stood when the contract was entered into'.[92] Echoing the decision in *Clarke v Dickson*, he noted that as the bank had converted to limited liability after he had bought his shares, the shareholder was unable to return shares in the original company and so had lost his right to rescind. This was to say that if the plaintiff had disposed

---

[88] *Small v Attwood* (1832) You 407, 506; 159 ER 1051, 1092.

[89] *Ibid*, You 507, 159 ER 1092.

[90] *Gillett v Peppercorne* (1840) 3 Beav 78, 49 ER 31. See also *Maturin v Tredennick* (1864) 12 WR 740.

[91] *Blake v Mowatt* (1856) 21 Beav 603, 613–4; 52 ER 993, 997. The defendant's conduct in this case would probably not have sustained an action of deceit.

[92] *Western Bank of Scotland v Addie* (1867) LR 1 Sc & Div 145, 164–5. Cranworth ruled that the same principles applied south as well as north of the border.

of the asset that was the subject of the contract, he could not rescind, having nothing to return.

Western Bank of Scotland v Addie did not, however, settle the question of what should be done where the asset had diminished in value but still existed. On this point, the Lords in *Erlanger* were divided. Lord Cairns ruled (in a dissenting opinion) that the contract could not be rescinded, since the parties could not in his view be returned to the *status quo ante*.[93] By contrast, Lord Blackburn felt that rescission was available, and he stressed the power of equity here. Blackburn noted that it was a condition of rescission that there had to be a *restitutio in integrum*, for it would be 'obviously unjust' to allow a person who had had the benefit of property transferred under a repudiated contract to retain those benefits without accounting for them, or to return deteriorated property without compensating for the deterioration. At common law, where there was no power to take accounts, the defrauded party had to keep the altered property and sue for deceit, which secured a full indemnity. By contrast, 'a Court of Equity could not give damages, and, unless it can rescind the contract, can give no relief'. Equity solved the problem by ordering an account of profits and allowance for deterioration, so that property could be returned even in an altered condition. It gave the relief by rescission 'whenever, by the exercise of its powers, it can do what is practically just, though it cannot restore the parties to the state they were in before the contract'.[94] In deciding whether rescission was to be allowed, he went on, 'it must always be a question of more or less, depending on the degree of diligence which might reasonably be required, and the degree of change which has occurred'.[95] Convinced that there could be no accounting for profits where an agent had sold his own property to a principal, the Lords in effect endorsed a broad view of the power of the court to order rescission. This was done in order to effect a just solution for the shareholders in the New Sombrero Phosphate Company, and in a context in which the courts and public opinion were happy to make promoters bear the losses arising from their misconduct.

Emile Erlanger and his associates were ordered to repay £80,000 with 4% interest, to return the shares that had not been disposed of, and to

---

[93] Cairns's comments in *Erlanger* (n 74) 1240 indicate a certain sympathy for the position of the syndicate for, having noted that a commercial concern was the subject matter of the contract, and that it was evident to shareholders that the board was not wholly independent, he spoke of their 'duty of taking steps at the earliest possible moment' to inquire into and repudiate the contract.

[94] *Erlanger* (n 74) 1278–9.

[95] Blackburn drew on the dictum of Sir Barnes Peacock in the Privy Council in *Lindsay Petroleum Company v Hurd* (1873–4) LR 5 PC 221, 239 concerning laches. Peacock spoke of the court refusing to intervene only where it would be 'practically unjust' to do so. In that case, the argument turned on delay, rather than any deterioration of the property, on which '[n]othing appears to have been done beyond the sinking of a single well, by way of trial, upon the ground': *ibid*, 240.

account for the proceeds of shares that had been sold. In return, the company had to account for its profits, which in 1877 ran only to some £4,500.[96] The island was duly returned to Erlanger, and by the beginning of 1879, the company had recovered its money in full.[97] Unlike promoters such as Grant and Hartmont, Erlanger remained solvent and kept his engagements. Moreover, the syndicate itself formed a new limited company, the Phosphate Company of Sombrero, to purchase the lease. But this time the company remained a private one, and continued to operate, with Erlanger remaining the largest shareholder. The company was finally wound up in 1899.[98]

If the outcome of the case satisfied public opinion in the 1870s, the judgment left two issues unsettled. Firstly, there was concern in the decades which followed that the remedy of rescission might be used to make morally innocent promoters bear the burden of failed commercial ventures, in cases where they would not be liable to damages at common law. Secondly, some courts also worried about the injustice to shareholders of denying them any remedy when, through no fault of theirs, rescission was impossible.

F. AFTER *ERLANGER*: REINING IN EQUITABLE RESCISSION

Ten years later, the House of Lords endorsed *Erlanger*'s generous approach to rescission, and seemed to take it even further, in *Adam v Newbigging*. This case was not one involving fiduciary duties, but concerned an investor in a worsted spinning firm, who sought to rescind his contract to join the partnership. Colonel William Newbigging claimed that he had been induced to join on the basis of (non-fraudulent) misstatements concerning the partnership's profitability and solvency, as well as the value of its machinery and stock in trade. Since he had joined, the firm had deteriorated further in value, and was now hopelessly insolvent. Having joined the partnership for a year, this was not a case of a contract that could be rescinded for total failure of consideration, and equity's assistance was required. However, the defendants claimed that rescission was no longer available, since the parties could not be put into the position they were in before the contract was made, as the value of the business had deteriorated and new liabilities had been incurred. The Lords however confirmed that rescission was available. The defendants had sold a failing business, and would recover a failing business, whose failure was in no way Newbigging's fault. This was to rule that rescission was available where the property in question deteriorated without the plaintiff being at fault.[99]

---

[96] *The Times*, 15 March 1877, 6, col e.
[97] *The Times*, 29 January 1879, 7, col d.
[98] TNA BT 31/2483/12747.
[99] *Adam v Newbigging* (1888) 13 App Cas 308.

This being a partnership, Newbigging had incurred liabilities to its customers, and so a second question arose: could he rescind, and also be given an indemnity? In the Court of Appeal, it was stressed that an indemnity was needed to return Newbigging to the *status quo ante*. The defendants claimed that to impose liabilities on them which they did not have antecedent to the contract would be equivalent to awarding damages for a non-fraudulent misrepresentation. This was rejected by the appeal judges, Cotton LJ holding that the plaintiff here 'does not recover damages as in an action of deceit, but gets what is the proper consequence in equity of setting aside the contract into which he has been induced to enter'.[100] This effectively followed a well-established equitable doctrine, whereby rescission could be accompanied by indemnities for losses incurred as a result of the rescinded transaction.[101]

The generous approach this seemed to herald was reined in by the Court of Appeal, in the 1899 case of *Lagunas Nitrate Company v Lagunas Syndicate*.[102] This case had many echoes of *Erlanger*. A syndicate was formed in 1889 to buy land with nitrate deposits in Chile, for £110,000. In 1894, a decision was taken to form a new company to buy part of the property, the sale price being £850,000. The seven promoters became the original directors of the firm, and issued a prospectus on its behalf. As in *Erlanger*, the property was generally agreed to be worth the price at the time of the sale, and for a time the share price rose; but, after a fall in the price of the raw material, things deteriorated. In 1895, the company began to suspect that the asset had been bought too dearly, and an investigation was launched after three directors were forced from the board. In June 1896 an action was commenced which sought rescission, or alternatively an account for profits, or damages for the misrepresentations. Meanwhile, mining continued. As in *Erlanger*, the plaintiff company in its action did not claim that there had been fraud, but pointed to a number of misrepresentations in the prospectus which affected the value of the property.[103] However, it also asserted that the price was exorbitant and that this sum would not have been paid if the syndicate had not 'excluded from the directorate of the company all persons except directors of the syndicate, these directors holding practically the whole of the shares of the syndicate'.[104]

The case came before Romer J in the Chancery Division. He ruled first that since there had been full disclosure in the prospectus of the fact that

---

[100] *Newbigging v Adam* (1886) 34 Ch D 582, 589.
[101] See *Edwards v M'Leay* (1815) G Coop 308, 35 ER 568, where however the Master of the Rolls found fraud. The plaintiff was allowed to rescind and to be compensated for money spent on improvements.
[102] [1899] 2 Ch 392.
[103] It was claimed that the property was not as rich in nitrates as had been asserted; that the oficina (or works) were not, as claimed, in full working order but needed investment; and that the water supply was not sufficient.
[104] *Lagunas* (n 102) 401.

the asset was being sold 'at a profit' by the syndicate, whose directors were to be directors of the firm, there was no action in respect of any breach of fiduciary duty. Nor had the directors been guilty of the gross negligence which alone would make them liable *qua* directors.[105] In Romer's view, there could be no complaint about the price, since the directors had acted in good faith and had reasonable grounds to believe that the company paid a reasonable price. Romer then turned to the complaint of misrepresentations in the prospectus, and ruled that, in the absence of fraud—which had not been charged— it would be inequitable to rescind the contract, since there had been a working of the property. In coming to this view, Romer drew on the old equitable doctrine in land purchase cases—ignored in *Erlanger*—that while the court would refuse specific performance for any misrepresentation, once a conveyance had been executed it would only be set aside on proof of actual fraud.[106] This doctrine had not been followed by the Chancery in company cases in an era of misleading prospectuses, though it had been endorsed with respect to land.[107] The remedy ordered by Romer was damages for breach of contract, sustained by defects in the property that had been represented to have been in full working order. This was to give a common law, contractual solution, but one which offered a far smaller remedy to the company, effectively allowing the promoters to retain their profit.

The Court of Appeal, by a majority, endorsed this approach, and in so doing separated out the fiduciary (equitable) aspects from the misrepresentation aspects (which were approached in a common law way). Given the time interval between the purchase and sale, the promoters could not be regarded as agents of the company at the time of the purchase of the property. They were thus (like Erlanger) agents selling their own property to their principal. Under the rule enunciated in the earlier case, the principal could reject the contract if the agent failed to disclose the full nature of his interest, even if the price had been fair. In the *Lagunas* case, the dissenting Rigby LJ followed the approach taken in *Erlanger*, noting that the 'equitable rule' relating to fiduciaries 'does not in any way depend upon fraud or any presumption of advantage actually taken; indeed, it applies equally, even though it be shewn that no advantage has been taken'.[108]

---

[105] *Ibid*, 409–10, 416–18.

[106] *Wilde v Gibson* (1848) 1 HLC 604, 9 ER 897. For the eighteenth and early nineteenth century equitable approach, see Lobban (n 80) 446–57.

[107] In *Hart v Swaine* (1877) 7 Ch D 42, Fry J appeared to depart from the older doctrine by setting aside a conveyance induced by a *bona fide* misrepresentation, on the grounds that the defendant had thereby committed a 'legal fraud'. The fact that this decision was made several months before the House of Lords gave their judgment in *Erlanger* may explain why the doctrine was not discussed there. However, the older position regarding land was restated by Lord Selborne LC in the Scottish appeal of *Brownlie v Campbell* (1880) 5 App Cas 925, 937–8, and continued to thrive into the twentieth century, as discussed in the text below.

[108] *Lagunas* (n 102) 442.

But the majority of the Court of Appeal appeared to be unhappy that the broad approach of *Erlanger*, which allowed rescission for breach of fiduciary duty even where the value of an asset had fallen, in effect threw the risk of loss on the agent who had failed to disclose as he should have. This seemed unfair when the promoters had been *bona fide*, and the company had failed in large part because of market problems rather than bubble speculation. The *Lagunas* majority judgment reflected a view that to force an innocent promoter to bear the loss would constitute a form of punishment, and that promoters as such should not be made to bear the risk of losses.

In his judgment, Sir Nathaniel Lindley MR turned first to the question of whether the promoters had performed their fiduciary duties to the company. Since the directors appointed were aware of all the facts, the issue turned on whether promoters had a duty to ensure that the company had an independent board of directors. Although this seemed to be implied by the decision in *Erlanger*, Lindley held that there was no such duty. After the decision in *Salomon v A Salomon & Co*,[109] it was 'impossible to hold that it is the duty of the promoters of a company to provide it with an independent board of directors, if the real truth is disclosed to those who are induced by the promoters to join the company'. The trouble in *Erlanger*, he noted, was that the share buyers were not made aware that the directors who endorsed the purchase were not independent.[110] This problem could be solved (as here) by ensuring that the shareholders were made aware of the potential conflicts of interest.[111]

Lindley noted that the company might nonetheless be able to obtain a remedy if there were material misrepresentations or any non-disclosure of material facts in the prospectus which had been issued to the public.[112] Since issuing the prospectus was the final act of promotion, it was to be seen as the act of the promoters, rather than an act of the nitrate company.

---

[109] [1897] AC 22.

[110] *Lagunas* (n 102) 425. But contrast Lord Cairns' comment in *Erlanger* (n 74) 1240, that the shareholders 'are content to ignore the fact both that they have not had the independent judgment of all the directors exercised for their protection in making the contract, and also the further fact, still more calculated to prejudice them, that one of the directors sitting at the board has been a person with an interest entirely antagonistic to their own'. For the majority, the key problem in *Erlanger* was that the board was not independent—whether the shareholders might have been aware of this or not.

[111] Contrast the view of Jessel MR in *New Sombrero* (n 40) 113, that the board's ratification would only be valid if all future shareholders assented as well—that is, 'if it could be shewn that every human being who came into the company took his shares upon a full disclosure of every material fact'.

[112] Lindley's comment ([1899] 2 Ch 431) that 'I do not consider the non-disclosure of the price paid by the syndicate for the Lagunas and of the profit made by the sale to the nitrate company as fatal to the validity of the sale' acknowledged that there *was* a non-disclosure. But he looked at this issue not with a view to establishing whether a fiduciary duty to disclose had been breached, but rather to see whether the non-disclosure rendered the prospectus misleading.

Nor could the company lose its right to rescind because its non-independent directors had affirmed the contract. Since the prospectus was misleading, and 'a clear breach of duty on the part of the directors', it would be against 'well-settled legal principles, to hold that [the directors] could, whilst they concealed the facts from the members of the nitrate company, deprive that company of the rights acquired by the concealment of those very facts'.[113] But should the contract be rescinded here, where a *restitutio in integrum* was not possible? Lindley saw the solution to this problem through the lens of common law misrepresentation, rather than through the lens of fiduciary duties, which led him to focus on fraud. In *Erlanger*, he ruled, rescission had been justified, since that case 'was one of fraud'. But 'there being in this case no fraud, the reasoning which in a case of fraud would justify such an order is inapplicable'. Lindley's comments about *Erlanger* were patently incorrect: it had been accepted by all that Erlanger's syndicate had acted in perfect good faith. But the effect of his ruling was to turn an equitable rule allowing broad rescission for failure to perform fiduciary duties of disclosure into a common law rule, where rescission would only be available for a fraudulent misrepresentation.[114]

The need for actual fraud to be present in order to rescind an executed contract was taken further in 1904 by Joyce J in the Chancery Division in *Seddon v The North Eastern Salt Company Ltd,* in which the plaintiff had bought shares in the defendant company on the basis of misrepresentations as to the size of its trading loss. There being no allegation of fraud, Joyce J treated it as an innocent misrepresentation and, drawing on the equitable doctrine in *Wilde v Gibson*[115] and the common law doctrine in *Kennedy v Panama, New Zealand and Australian Royal Mail Company Ltd,*[116] held that the absence of fraud was a fatal objection to the action.[117] The doctrine had a long afterlife. It was applied once more in *Angel v Jay,*[118] a land case heard in 1911, and in 1917 McCardie J acknowledged (and regretted) the existence of the rule that where a contract had been executed, there could be no rescission in equity for innocent misrepresentation.[119] In 1939, the House of Lords endorsed the view that 'the Court will be more drastic in exercising its discretionary powers in a case of fraud than in a case of

---

[113] *Lagunas* (n 102) 432–3.
[114] This is to suggest, in contrast to the view of Peter Birks in *An Introduction to the Law of Restitution* (Oxford, OUP, 1989), 422, that Lindley did have in mind '*Derry v Peek* deceit' rather than the 'equitable meaning of unconscionable conduct'.
[115] See n 106 and text.
[116] See n 84.
[117] *Seddon v The North Eastern Salt Company Ltd* [1905] 1 Ch 326. This decision was doubted by Scrutton LJ in *Lever Brothers Ltd v Bell* [1931] 1 KB 557, 588, who added that the comments regarding rescission in *Kennedy* were no longer applicable after the fusion of judicatures.
[118] *Angel v Jay* [1911] 1 KB 666.
[119] *Armstrong v Jackson* [1917] 2 KB 822, 825.

innocent misrepresentation' since the latter involved no moral obloquy.[120] It was only in 1950, in *Solle v Butcher*,[121] that Denning LJ held that the doctrine was incorrect, opening the way for rescission for innocent misrepresentations in executed contracts and, with it, clearing a path for equity's broader approach to the problem of *restitutio in integrum*.[122]

In the context of the late nineteenth century common law, this doctrine appeared to have a certain plausibility. Given that (after *Derry v Peek*) damages were only to be given for a fraudulent misrepresentation, it was considered that where misrepresentations were innocent, losses should lie where they fell, unless there was a total failure of consideration, and the parties could be put into the exact *status quo ante*. To do otherwise, and allow rescission in cases where complete restitution was not possible, might effectively have transferred a loss to an innocent party, and undermined the principle of not giving damages without fraud.[123] Yet these arguments were scarcely relevant to cases involving fiduciaries acting in breach of their duties, as was realised by judges after the outbreak of the First World War,[124] and confirmed by the Court of Appeal in 1985.[125]

G. AFTER *ERLANGER*: REMEDIES WHEN RESCISSION WAS IMPOSSIBLE

In treating the syndicate in *Erlanger* as agents selling their own property to the New Sombrero Company, the House of Lords made a decision of fact which was questionable, but which had beneficial consequences for the company. For in any case, where the amount of loss made by the purchasing company on the asset exceeded the secret profit made by the promoter,

---

[120] *Spence v Crawford* [1939] 3 All ER 271, 288. *Alati v Kruger* (1955) 94 CLR 216 was also a case where rescission was given without strict *restitutio in integrum* being possible in a case of a fraudulent misrepresentation.

[121] *Solle v Butcher* [1950] 1 KB 671.

[122] It should be noted however that the dissenting Jenkins LJ was not prepared to overrule it.

[123] This was not in itself a convincing argument if rescission was simply a matter of voiding a contract, for as Lord Wright put it in *Spence v Crawford* [1939] 3 All ER 271, 288–9 (while endorsing the distinctive nature of fraud): 'Though the defendant has been fraudulent, he must not be robbed nor must the plaintiff be unjustly enriched, as he would be if he both got back what he had parted with and kept what he had received in return. The purpose of the relief is not punishment, but compensation.' The argument would only be convincing if it was held that the misrepresentor might have been unjustly enriched in cases of fraud, but not unjustly enriched when morally innocent.

[124] *Armstrong v Jackson* [1917] 2 KB 822: the case concerned transactions by a broker. Four years later, the same judge noted (in *First National Reinsurance Company, Limited v Greenfield* [1921] 2 KB 260) that the principle did not apply to contacts for the taking of shares, something which should have been evident to Joyce J from the nineteenth century case law, but which he had somehow overlooked. See also Viscount Sankey's comments in *Regal (Hastings) Ltd v Gulliver* [1942] 1 All ER 378, 381.

[125] *O'Sullivan v Management Agency and Music Ltd* [1985] QB 428.

as here, it was clearly in the interests of the company to rescind. The court's generous approach to rescission gave the company a remedy that seemed harsh for *bona fide* promoters, but which was in line with the tough approach of the 1870s. By contrast, where the company had not made a loss equivalent to the secret profit of the promoter, it was in its interests to seek an account of profits, treating the promoter as its agent at the time of the sale, while retaining the asset. Where companies wished to carry on trading (as in *Hichens*), they sought an account for profits; where they did not (as in *Erlanger*), they sought rescission. But even where a firm had ceased trading, it might prefer to seek an account for profits rather than rescission, for instance if the asset acquired could be disposed of for value in a liquidation. In the later nineteenth century, the courts thus faced the problem of dealing with cases where companies sought to treat promoters differently, depending on what was the value of the asset in their hands. As shall be seen, the cases came to the courts in a context in which the latter sought to be less harsh on *bona fide* promoters than they had been in the 1870s.

Where the promoter was a third party, courts were happy enough to treat that person as an agent for the purchase, since this was the only way to make him disgorge his secret profit. This is evident from *Lydney and Wigpool Iron Ore Company v Bird*. Here, the defendants, who had been approached by the owners of a mine in difficulties, suggested the formation of a company to buy the mines. Under an arrangement made on 15 December 1871, the property was to be sold for £100,000, of which £10,800 was to go to the promoters. On 19 December the property was sold to a trustee for the company to be formed, and a prospectus was subsequently issued which made no mention of the £10,800. In the Chancery Division, Pearson J ruled that Bird & Co were not promoters of the company but merely agents for the vendors, and that they made no secret profit.[126] The Court of Appeal disagreed. In contrast to the approach taken in *Erlanger* and *Lagunas*, Lindley LJ ruled that while the defendants were not strictly speaking agents or trustees of the company before its formation, 'the old familiar principles of the law of agency and of trusteeship have been extended, and very properly extended, to meet such cases'. They did constitute promoters, and:[127]

> it is perfectly well settled that a promoter of a company is accountable to it for all moneys secretly obtained by him from it just as if the relationship of principal and agent or of trustee and cestui que trust had really existed between them and the company when the money was so obtained. Nor in such a case is it necessary for the company to rescind the whole transaction of which the payment by the company of the money in question is found to be part.

[126] *Lydney and Wigpool Iron Ore Company v Bird* (1885) 31 Ch D 328.
[127] *Lydney and Wigpool Iron Ore Company v Bird* (1886) 33 Ch D 85, 94.

In taking this view, Lindley LJ reiterated the position he took in 1879 in *Emma Silver Mining Co v Lewis*, a case brought against a firm of metal brokers which had acted as promoters in the launching of the plaintiff company.[128] Moreover, in 1877, one year before the Lords heard *Erlanger*, the Court of Appeal ruled in *Bagnall v Carlton* that a company could sue its professional promoters for a return of secret promotion moneys even when it had compromised its dispute with the original vendor, electing not to rescind the contract. In that case, Bacon V-C noted in the Chancery Division that the promoters were agents of the company, liable to make good 'the whole benefit which has been obtained without the sanction of the principals'.[129] In the Court of Appeal, Cotton LJ agreed, holding that the promoters were trustees for the company and as such were liable to repay.[130] In cases involving third parties, there was no other way for the company to obtain any remedy: since 'third party' promoters were not agents of the purchaser selling their own property to the principal, the contract could not be rescinded for breach of fiduciary duty.

If there was doctrinal scope to take a tougher approach against company promoters, it was not an approach that courts by the 1880s were keen to take, at least where the promoter was not a 'third party'. In *Erlanger*, since the plaintiffs had asked for rescission, and the majority of the judges agreed that rescission was possible, they did not have to explore whether alternative remedies might be available for breaches of fiduciary duty (as had been hinted at in *Great Luxembourg* by Romilly). But in the 1880s, a number of cases came to court in which the company had been liquidated and the asset disposed of. In these cases, it had to be decided whether the promoter could be held liable for breaches of its fiduciary duties. Led by Cotton LJ (who took up Cairns's views in *Erlanger*), the courts took the view that in these cases no remedy remained.

Cotton set out his views first in *In re Ambrose Lake Tin and Copper Mining Company* in 1880. In this case the Vice Warden of the Stannary Courts had held owners of shares in a cost book mine liable to the official liquidator of a company for the difference between the value of their shares in a new limited liability company which they formed to buy their mine, and the value of their shares in the old mine. Cotton rejected this approach. Since they were not trustees for the new company when they acquired their initial interest, the profit they made was not the property of the new company.

---

[128] In this case, Lindley ruled that the company did not have to rescind its contract with the vendor on whose behalf the promoters were acting, rejecting the argument that until they did so, the payment by the vendor to the promoters was his own affair: *Emma Silver Mining Co v Lewis* (1879) 4 CPD 396, 408–9.

[129] *Bagnall v Carlton* (1877) 6 Ch D 371, 385.

[130] *Ibid*, 407–8. See also *Whaley Bridge Calico Printing Company v Green* (1879) 5 QBD 109. *Bagnall v Carlton* was cited before the Lords in *Erlanger* but was not considered relevant by the judges.

While the new company could have set aside the flawed contract with its agents, it could not 'make another contract' to buy the asset at the price originally paid by the vendor.[131] The two other judges concurred in the result, but on different grounds.

Cotton's views were not shared by James LJ in this case;[132] but they were taken up in the Chancery Division four years later by Pearson J, in *Re Cape Breton Company*. The case concerned the purchase of property in Nova Scotia by six men in 1871 for £5,500, which was sold on two years later to a company they had formed for £42,000. The company was ordered to be wound up in 1875, and it was effected by a scheme of arrangement agreed by the shareholders. Under this arrangement, in 1878, the shareholders were given the choice of seeking to rescind the contract or adopting the purchase and seeking to sell the property to the best advantage. The latter option was taken and in 1880 the property of the company was sold for £14,500. In 1882, a contributory in the winding up sought to make one of the original vendors liable for the amount of his profit.

In this case, as the property had been sold, rescission was not an option. Moreover, it was accepted by the plaintiffs that the defendant, Thomas Fenn, had not stood in a fiduciary relation to the company when the original purchase had been made, but that he had later become an agent selling his own goods to the company without their knowledge.[133] In the Chancery Division, Pearson J (following Cotton LJ in *In re Ambrose* and Lord Cairns in *Erlanger*) ruled that he could not order an account for profits against a person 'whose only fault' was to sell to his principals without disclosing his interest. This was confirmed by Cotton LJ in the Court of Appeal, who ruled that an account for profit was only available where the original purchase was made by the agent on behalf of the company, and that where an agent (as here) sold his own property to his principal, rescission was the only remedy.[134]

For Cotton, a key objection to offering financial compensation when rescission was no longer possible was the difficulty, where a trustee sold his own property, of fixing the market price. If the promoter had not been the company's agent when the property had initially been bought, he could not be liable for the difference in price between that at which he bought the asset and that at which he sold it to the company: for the property was legitimately his, and he was entitled to any rise in price between his original purchase

---

[131] *In re Ambrose Lake Tin and Copper Mining Company, ex parte Taylor, ex parte Moss* (1880) 14 Ch D 390, 398–9.

[132] *Ibid*, 394, ruling that a sale made by a fiduciary could be set aside, and that 'if there is any difficulty in the way of restoration, if it is made out that they had received something beyond the proper price of the property, there ought to be no difficulty in making them pay that extra value'.

[133] *Re Cape Breton Company* (1884) 26 Ch D 221, 228.

[134] (1885) 29 Ch D 795, 803. Cotton LJ cited *Erlanger* as his authority.

and subsequent sale. The court would thus have to put a fair value on the asset at the time of the sale to the company, something which was (he felt) almost impossible to do where (as here) the asset had no market value, but was worth what people chose to pay for it. If the court set a price, it would be making the bargain for the parties, which he found unacceptable.[135]

A second argument for barring the plaintiff's rights in this case was the fact that the firm had elected not to seek rescission when it had the option to do so. This in effect constituted an affirmation of the contract. This explanation of *Cape Breton* would not rule out financial compensation in other circumstances, where there had been no act of affirmation. It is notable, therefore, that Fry LJ's judgment stressed the point of affirmation most clearly, with this significant rider:[136]

> Nor, again, is this the case of an agent who, by any subsequent acts of his own, has rendered the rescission of the contract by his principal impossible. I express no opinion whether or no, in that case, the principal would have a right against the agent, notwithstanding the non-rescission of the contract.

The common lawyer Bowen LJ dissented, arguing that the right of the principal or cestui que trust to claim a profit made by his trustee when acting on his behalf was wholly independent of the right to rescind: indeed, the principal's ability to recover secret profits was precisely valuable where he could not rescind. If a victim of fraud could at common law affirm and sue for deceit, he could not see why one who had been deceived by his trustee should not be able to seek an account of profits. Bowen admitted that it might not be easy to establish the price due: but this, he observed, was a problem faced on a daily basis by common law courts dealing with damages.[137] Bowen's disquiet was shared in the Lords by Lord Macnaghten, who concurred with the rejection of the appeal (on the grounds that the plaintiff had failed to prove an interest), but who observed that 'if a person in the position of Mr Fenn abstained from disclosing his interest, and thus led the board to purchase the property for more than it was really worth, it would be very difficult for him to escape from the charge of fraud'.[138] Thus, paradoxically, at a time when equity lawyers were redefining fiduciary duties in terms of common law fraud, common lawyers were prepared to attach the consequences of common law fraud to breaches of fiduciary duty as defined in an equitable way.

---

[135] The decision was upheld in the Lords, sub nom *Cavendish-Bentinck v Fenn* (1887) 12 App Cas 652; like Cotton LJ, Lord Herschell was worried about how one could correctly determine the value of the asset, nor was there proof (he felt) that the asset had been bought at a price which was not considered fair.
[136] *Cape Breton* (n 134) 811.
[137] *Ibid*, 808–9.
[138] *Cavendish-Bentinck* (n 135) 671.

Nonetheless, there was a further difficulty implicit in the approach of Bowen LJ and Lord Macnaghten which was not explored. If the market price at the time of sale could be established, there remained another problem: ensuring that the amount of compensation effectively recovered would not differ, depending on whether rescission was effected or not. Was the measure of compensation to be an account of profits (as Bowen seemed to suggest) or damages in deceit (as Macnaghten seemed to suggest)? As was evident from the debates in *Erlanger,* an account of profits generated a different value from that generated by rescission. Had the company in *Cape Breton* been in a position to rescind the contract, they would have recovered the £42,000 spent on the asset. But if the promoters were held to account for their profits, the company would have recovered a different amount which would have left them with either a loss or a profit on the transaction, depending on questions of valuation.[139] The pecuniary equivalent to rescission (where it was no longer available) would have required returning the parties to the *status quo ante*, by making the promoters return the purchase money, and the company returning to the promoters the sums recovered in liquidation for the asset. This would have solved any difficulties of making a new contract for the parties, for it would merely have cancelled the contract. This would have been equivalent to a remedy in damages, rather than an account of profits.

The view hinted at by Lord Macnaghten suggested giving damages for the breach of fiduciary duties. Had damages been given for the breach of such duties as (under the rule in *Erlanger*) justified rescission—such as the mere failure to disclose an interest—it in effect would have been an extension of the rule in section 38 of the 1867 Act beyond the limits of the statute: for it would have treated any breach of fiduciary duties as equal to fraud. Neither late nineteenth century judges nor commercial opinion had the stomach for such an extension of constructive fraud to throw heavy losses onto *bona fide* businessmen. Thus, where pecuniary remedies were offered to a company whose asset could no longer be restored, as in *In re Leeds and Hanley Theatres of Varieties, Limited,* it was as a result of a finding of fraudulent misrepresentations on the part of promoters.[140] However, this reluctance to expand the penalties for breaches of fiduciary duties may in turn help to explain the approach of Lindley and the Court of Appeal in *Lagunas,* when they limited the remedy of equitable rescission to cases of

---

[139] If the company recovered the difference between the price at which the agents bought and sold, they would have made a profit of £9,000. If the asset had been differently valued at the time of its sale to the company, however, and the profit of the promoters had been valued at less than £27,500, they would have made a loss.

[140] As Vaughan Williams LJ put it, the company could not 'in reference to this breach of fiduciary duty by their promoters, maintain an action in the nature of an action for money had and received. I think the safer way of putting it is to say that their remedy is in damages': *In re Leeds and Hanley Theatres of Varieties, Limited* [1902] 2 Ch 809, 825.

fraud. For this effectively made the remedy of rescission operate in the same way in these cases as the remedy of damages.

By the early twentieth century, academic commentary had noted that when dealing with the profits of promoters, the key distinction turned on whether the promoter had been agent at the time of the original purchase.[141] The doctrinal distinctions seemed clear enough, and there appeared to be certain tests of whether a promoter was an agent of the company at the time of his purchase.[142] But in practice, what shaped the approach of the judiciary most clearly was whether they felt that the promoter had been a fraudster or *bona fide*. If judges were convinced of the *bona fides* of promoters, then even if there was a very short period between the acquisition and formation of the company, and even if it had been intended all along to form a company, the decision could be made in the promoter's favour, treating him as an agent in the sale to the company of the asset, but not its agent in the purchase.[143] By contrast, where the promoters were deemed to have been engaged in a plain scam, then the courts took a different view. Much therefore turned on the view of the facts taken by the courts.[144] Thus a new paradox emerged: in effect, courts held those promoters to be agents of the company at the time of the purchase in cases where they were convinced of their *mala fides*: but the remedy consequentially given was only an account of their profit, and not an award in damages.

This is perhaps most clearly evident in the decision of the Court of Appeal in *In re Olympia Ltd* in 1898 (affirmed later by the House of Lords). In this case, one of four promoters was held liable to account for his profits in acquiring and disposing of a mortgage and debentures relating to the Olympia exhibition hall, prior to purchasing the hall and selling it on to a company. At first instance, Wright J, who reluctantly accepted *Cape Breton*,[145] dismissed the summons, holding the defendants not to be promoters at the time they profited from the debentures. But in the Court

---

[141] See 45 *Solicitors Journal* 234 (2 February 1901); Sir Francis Palmer, *Company Precedents* (10th edn, London, Stevens & Son, 1910) part 1, 118.

[142] These tests included whether there had been an intention at the outset to form a company, and whether the company's money was later used in the purchase.

[143] Eg *Ladywell Mining Co v Brookes* (1887) 35 Ch D 400.

[144] Even the determination of fact could be contentious, when judges made it dependent on intentions. See Sargant J's comments in *Omnium Electric Palaces Ltd v Baines* [1914] 1 Ch 332, 347: 'Whether promoters are in fact acquiring any assets as trustees for a company must, in my judgment, be a question of fact; and where as here the whole scheme has throughout been that they are to sell to the intended company at a profit the assets which they are acquiring, the natural inference of fact is that, qua those assets, they are not intending to be trustees for the company, but are intending to occupy the relationship to the company of vendors.'

[145] Wright was unhappy with the rule in *Cape Breton*, preferring Bowen's dissent, but he felt bound by it: see his comments in *In re Lady Forrest (Murchison) Gold Mine Ltd* [1901] 1 Ch 582, holding that there was no remedy for breach of fiduciary duty when rescission was no longer possible.

of Appeal, Lord Lindley MR disagreed, describing the scheme as an ingenious mechanism to bleed the company of £20,000. Although Lindley did not directly address the question of whether they were agents when they bought the assets, he did note that they were clearly the creators of the company, whose existence was essential to their scheme. Citing *Erlanger*, he ruled:[146]

> [T]he persons who then agreed to form a company, and ultimately did form it in order to carry the agreement into effect, owed duties to that company when it came into existence. One of such duties was not to make a profit out of it without informing it of the fact and giving the company an opportunity of declining to allow such profit to be made at its expense.

In apparent contrast to his approach in *Lagunas*, Lindley ruled that in deciding whether there had been adequate disclosure, one needed to bear in mind 'the habits and practical necessities of ordinary business men', rather than looking at '[r]efined equitable doctrines of constructive notice'. The vague mention in the prospectus of interim investments made by the promoters was not enough: it was not sufficient to give a company the *means* to discover the transaction; the transaction had to be explicitly stated. Equally, the ratification by the board of directors was vitiated by the fact that the directors (who were also the promoters) were not independent. Finally, Lindley rejected the argument that since rescission was no longer possible here, there could be no other remedy. 'The same people who saddled the company with the property have prevented its restitution in the condition in which the company acquired it,' he ruled: since the company acquired the property *nolens volens*, 'its inability to return it as it got it does not justify the conclusion that the company has elected to keep it'. There was nothing to prevent the company from claiming the secret profit.[147] *Cape Breton* was to be distinguished on the ground that in that case, the property had originally been bought with the promoters' own money, rather than (as here) with the company's money.[148]

Collins LJ (a common lawyer, but much of whose work at the bar had dealt with business matters) added that in *Cape Breton*, there was 'an election with full knowledge to adopt the contract'. He noted that unlike *Cape Breton*, this was a case of misrepresentation. He went on:

> In holding . . . that to give the relief claimed would be to make a new contract between the parties, Cotton LJ clearly could not have meant to decide that in the case of a contract induced by fraud there is no remedy in damages where

---

[146] *In re Olympia Ltd* [1898] 2 Ch 153, 165–6.

[147] *Ibid*, 169.

[148] *Ibid*, 170: 'No one decided in that case that as a general proposition the mere fact that a contract for purchase by a company cannot be rescinded precludes the company from obtaining from the vendor if he is a promoter.'

rescission is impossible . . . The objection, therefore, that to enforce against a fraudulent vendor repayment of a part of the sum which in his capacity as purchaser in the name of the company he has paid to himself as a secret profit out of the purchase-money is to make a new contract, does not seem to rest on any solid foundation.[149]

These judgments seem to smudge a number of issues which earlier decisions had distinguished. On the one hand, Lindley in effect treated the four promoters as agents at the time of their purchase, who therefore had to account for profits. This was uncontroversial enough: but it rendered redundant his discussion of their fiduciary duty to disclose information about their interest, which would only be relevant if they were to be seen as selling their own property to their principal. Equally, his comments on the inability to rescind were not relevant to a case where the promoter was already agent at the time of the purchase. Collins' stress on the fraudulent conduct of the promoters was also irrelevant in this context, being relevant only in cases where the agent was selling his own property which could no longer be restored. But in such a case, the remedy would not have been an account for profits, but damages in deceit. *In re Olympia* was upheld by the House of Lords, which saw the venture as fraudulent, but treated the promoters as agents.[150] The decision was not held to cast any doubt on the approach taken in the *Lagunas* case or *Cape Breton*, whose doctrine continued to be applied.[151] These cases reveal that the question of whether a promoter was agent for the company at the time of his purchase turned less on 'objective' factors such as whether he was using his own money or had planned to form a company, and more on whether the court regarded the project as fraudulent. Once more, the language of fiduciary duty had been translated into the language of fraud.

H. CONCLUSION

Erlanger's broad approach to rescission had indicated that a tough approach would be taken against company promoters. By not treating the promoters as agents at the point of purchase, but instead focusing on their fiduciary duty at the time of sale to the company, the House of Lords forced the syndicate not merely to return the sum by which they had been unjustly

---

[149] *Ibid*, 178–9.

[150] Lord Macnaghten commented: 'The point was settled more than sixty years ago by the decision in *Hichens v Congreve*, and, so far as I know, that case has never been questioned.' *Gluckstein v Barnes (Official Receiver and Official Liquidator of Olympia, Limited)* [1900] AC 240, 249.

[151] In *Burland v Earle* [1902] AC 83 (PC), 99, Lord Davey held that, since rescission was no longer possible, there could be no remedy: 'To rescind the sale is one thing, but to force on the vendor a contract to sell at another price is a totally different thing.'

enriched—their undisclosed profit—but to bear the loss of the entire venture. The House of Lords took a broad, equitable view of rescission, though it was not confronted with the problem of what remedy might be available if the asset had been destroyed. In the era of *Derry v Peek*, when a narrow reading of fraud and damages consequent to it was in the ascendant, courts in company cases thus reined back the liability of promoters, recasting it in common law terms. After *Erlanger*, the refusal to allow some form of pecuniary equitable compensation after rescission became impossible, while rescission was allowed where the asset had diminished and could not be purely restored, seemed anomalous: and *Lagunas* and *Cape Breton*[152] thus reined in the broad approach of the earlier case. But this risked throwing the baby out with the bathwater: for it threatened the very notion of promoters' *fiduciary* duties which *Erlanger* had established.

The alternative route would have been to focus more strongly on these fiduciary duties and the consequences of their breach. *Erlanger's* solution, of returning the parties to the *status quo ante* by combining a return of the asset with financial adjustments, could have been extended to a remedy by a purely financial adjustment to that *status quo*, when the asset had disappeared—provided that such disappearance was not the result of the company's fault or choice. The need for the actual asset to exist in a returnable state was a remnant of the common law remedy of returning items where there had been a total failure of consideration. Such an approach appeared unthinkable in the years before the First World War. But in the twentieth century, some steps were taken down this path, beginning in 1914 with the recognition in *Nocton v Ashburton* that equitable compensation could be given for non-fraudulent conduct on the part of fiduciaries, 'to compensate the plaintiff by putting him in as good a position pecuniarily as that in which he was before the injury'.[153] The eclipsing of fiduciary duties by the

---

[152] This case is interestingly discussed in R Nolan, 'Dispositions Involving Fiduciaries: The Equity to Rescind and the Resulting Trust' in P Birks and F Rose (eds), *Restitution and Equity, volume one: Resulting Trusts and Equitable Compensation* (London, LLP. 2000) 119 and *id*, 'Conflicts of Interest, Unjust Enrichment and Wrongdoing' in WR Cornish *et al* (eds), *Restitution Past, Present and Future: Essays in Honour of Gareth Jones* (Oxford, Hart, 1998) 87. Nolan argues that since the promoters here merely failed to disclose their interest—in breach of the fiduciary dealing rule—they had not committed any wrong against the company. In his view, the company lost its rights by its own voluntary act of affirmation. It should be noted, however, that in *Ladywell Mining Company v Brookes* (1887) 35 Ch D 400, 407–8, Cotton LJ rejected this interpretation of *Cape Breton* (also given by Lindley LJ in *Lydney and Wigpool Iron Ore Company v Bird*). Nolan also argues that 'In circumstances such as those of *Re Cape Breton Co*, there is no obligation on a fiduciary to desist from making a profit, so there is no reason why he should account for that profit' ('Dispositions', 122) (as suggested in G Jones (ed), *Goff and Jones on the Law of Restitution* (6th edn, London, Sweet & Maxwell, 2002) 721). Against this, it may be suggested that a breach of a fiduciary duty may be seen as a wrong (see P Birks, *Unjust Enrichment* (Oxford, Clarendon Press, 2003) 11). However, as discussed in the text above, there are problems with making an account for profit the remedy for this wrong.

[153] *Nocton v Ashburton* [1914] AC 932, 952 (Viscount Haldane LC).

great shadow of fraud was slowly lifted.[154] The twentieth century also saw the (sometimes hesitant) acceptance in a number of jurisdictions of the principle that financial compensation can be awarded for a breach of fiduciary duties, to return the parties to the position they were in prior to the sale of the asset, even where the subject-matter of the contract has been disposed of.[155]

---

[154] See also, of course, *Hedley Byrne & Co Ltd v Heller & Partners Ltd* [1964] AC 465.

[155] See *Mahoney v Purnell* [1996] 3 All ER 61 (an undue influence case), where May J said that '[p]ractical justice requires an award which is akin to damages' though the award given would not be damages but 'fair compensation in equity as an adjunct to setting aside the agreement'. This decision is discussed with approval in *Goff and Jones* (n 152) 359. For Commonwealth approaches, see also *McKenzie v McDonald* [1927] VLR 134 and *Canson Enterprises Ltd v Broughton & Co* (1992) 85 DLR (4th) 129. Nonetheless, some judges have continued to articulate a more cautious view of the scope of rescission: see eg Colman J in *de Molestina v Ponton* [2002] 1 Lloyd's Rep 271 [6.2].

7

Phillips v Homfray (1883)

WILLIAM SWADLING*

A. INTRODUCTION

IN THAT PART of the law of restitution called 'Restitution for Wrongs', where the cause of action is some wrongdoing on the part of the defendant, one case stands out as anomalous. It is the decision of the Court of Appeal in 1883 in *Phillips v Homfray*.[1] The common perception of the majority judgment of Bowen and Cotton LJJ is that it is 'anti-restitution' in that it lays down an arbitrary and illogical requirement that only positive accretions to the defendant's wealth can be made the subject of a restitutionary claim based on wrongdoing. Where the defendant's wrong has resulted in a mere saving of expense, restitution will be denied. In other words, restitution for wrongs is only available for positive enrichments, not negative ones. So, while a trespasser who charges third parties for the use of another's land can be forced to give up his profits, a trespasser who makes use of the land himself, and thereby saves himself the expense of renting out other land, will be immune from any demand for restitution. This interpretation of *Phillips v Homfray* was used by Lloyd LJ in *Ministry of Defence v Ashman*[2] to deny a restitutionary claim against the wife of a tenant who remained in possession beyond the end of a lease; the same thinking has surfaced in a number of American jurisdictions.[3]

The rule so formulated is clearly illogical, and on that basis has been almost universally condemned. Successive editions of *Goff and Jones* have

---

* This is a lightly revised version of 'The Myth of *Phillips v Homfray*' which first appeared in W Swadling and G Jones (eds), *The Search for Principle: Essays in Honour of Lord Goff of Chieveley* (Oxford, Oxford University Press, 1999). It is reprinted here by kind permission of the publisher.
[1] (1883) 24 Ch D 439.
[2] (1993) 66 P & CR 195, 202.
[3] Examples include *Adsit v Kaufman* 121 F 355 (1903); *Bradford v Indiana Harbor Belt Rlwy Co* 16 F 2d 836 (1927); *Shell Petroleum Corp v Scully* 71 F 2d 772 (1934).

called for it to be overruled;[4] Professor Burrows has described it as a 'major and unfortunate obstacle' in the development of restitution for wrongs;[5] and a number of American courts have declared themselves openly to be departing from it.[6] Apart from the supposedly irrational distinction it draws between positive and negative benefits, *Phillips v Homfray* is also said to be inconsistent with a number of later decisions, including *Penarth Dock Engineering Co Ltd v Pounds*,[7] where damages based on the cost of user were awarded in respect of trespass to a dock, and *Bracewell v Appleby*,[8] where a similar award was made in respect of the use of an easement. Furthermore, it is said that the positive/negative distinction has never been drawn with respect to chattels, as witness the decision of the Court of Appeal in *Strand Electric and Engineering Co Ltd v Brisford Entertainments Ltd*,[9] where damages for the retention of lighting equipment by a theatre beyond the hire period were assessed on the basis of the gain thereby made by the wrongdoer.[10] All in all, the almost unanimous[11] view is that the decision in *Phillips v Homfray* cannot be defended and should be overruled.

The thesis of this essay is that that view of *Phillips v Homfray*, which is the interpretation adopted by most writers on Restitution, in England as

[4] In the first edition of *The Law of Restitution* (London, Sweet & Maxwell, 1966) 433, the learned authors take the view that *Phillips v Homfray* should be overruled, or, if not, that its *ratio decidendi* should not extend beyond its material facts. Similar comments can be found in later editions.

[5] AS Burrows, 'Contract, Tort and Restitution—A Satisfactory Division or Not?' (1983) 99 LQR 217, 237–8. Similar views are expressed in AS Burrows, *The Law of Restitution* (London, Butterworths, 1993) 391. His view in the second edition of the last-mentioned work (London, Butterworths/Lexis Nexis, 2002) 473–5, written after this essay was first published, is more muted.

[6] Two examples are: *Edwards v Lee's Administrators* 96 SW 2d 1028 (1936); *Raven Red Ash Coal Co v Ball* 99 SE 2d 213 (1946).

[7] [1963] 1 Lloyd's Rep 359.

[8] [1975] Ch 408.

[9] [1952] 2 QB 246.

[10] While it is true that only one member of the court, Denning LJ, said that damages were restitutionary, the attempt of Somervell and Romer LJJ to explain the award as compensating the plaintiffs for a loss was clearly fictitious, for it was proven that there was no market for the goods in question.

[11] One notable exception is WMC Gummow, now a justice of the High Court of Australia, who, in an essay written in 1990, drew attention to the fact that many commentators had misinterpreted the case: The Hon Mr Justice WMC Gummow, 'Unjust Enrichment, Restitution and Proprietary Remedies' in PD Finn (ed), *Essays in Restitution* (Sydney, Law Book Company, 1990) 47, 60–67. He stops short, however, of trying to rehabilitate the case and incorporating it within the wider law of restitution. There is also a brief reference by Hedley to the fact that the case was only concerned with the effect of the *actio personalis* rule: S Hedley, 'Unjust Enrichment as the Basis of Restitution—An Overworked Concept?' (1985) 5 LS 56, 64; and by Sharpe and Waddams in their influential piece attempting to analyse many of the cases in this area as involving awards of compensatory damages for lost opportunities to bargain: RJ Sharpe and SM Waddams, 'Damages for Lost Opportunity to Bargain' (1982) 2 OJLS 290, 294–5.

well as the United States,[12] is a myth. At the very least, the case can be seen to have been correctly decided on the basis of the rules then governing the survival of actions on death. But more importantly, far from being a 'significantly anti-restitution case',[13] the decision is actually authority for the very opposite proposition for which it is said to stand. Careful analysis will show that *Phillips v Homfray* is in fact a decision *in favour* of restitutionary damages for trespass to land, even where that trespass results in a mere saving of expense rather than a positive accretion to the defendant's wealth. Moreover, the case can also be demonstrated to provide authority for the long-held view of *Goff and Jones*, contrary to the 'independent claim' theorists, that there is indeed a category in the law called 'Restitution for Wrongs'.

B. THE LITIGATION

It is important at the outset to notice that there were three stages to the *Phillips v Homfray* litigation. Criticism has focused on the decision of the Court of Appeal handed down in 1883, in what was in fact the second stage of the proceedings. One mistake many commentators make is to examine this judgment in isolation. In order not to repeat this, we will label the second round of litigation *Phillips v Homfray (No 2)*. And so as to present the whole picture, we will begin with *Phillips v Homfray (No 1)*,[14] decided some twelve years earlier, in 1871. But since we are only concerned with the correctness of *Phillips v Homfray (No 2)*, there is no need for any detailed examination of the final instalment, *Phillips v Homfray (No 3)*,[15] decided in 1892.

1. *Phillips v Homfray (No 1)*

The defendants, Forman, Homfray and Fothergill, were partners in a coal-mining business. The plaintiffs owned a farm surrounded on all sides by the

---

[12] According to Keener, 'It has been held that it is not sufficient for the plaintiff to prove that the defendant has committed a tort whereby he has enriched himself. It must further appear that what has been added to the defendant's estate has been taken from the plaintiff's. That is to say, the facts must show, not only a plus, but a minus quantity': WA Keener, *A Treatise on the Law of Quasi-Contracts* (New York, Baker, Voorhis & Co, 1923) 163.

This is also the interpretation of Palmer. 'When the trespasser merely uses the land, without removing any of its physical substance, he has received the benefit of such use and one might expect that courts would allow recovery of its value in quasi contract . . . But the traditional view . . . rejects the restitution claim against the trespasser': GE Palmer, *The Law of Restitution* (Boston, Little, Brown, 1978) vol I, 74. A similar view is expressed in the *Restatement*: 'A person who has trespassed upon the land of another is not thereby under a duty of restitution to the other for the value of its use': American Law Institute, *Restatement of Restitution* (St Paul, Minn, American law Institute, 1937) § 129.

[13] Burrows (1993) (n 5) 390.

[14] (1871) LR 6 Ch App 770.

[15] [1892] 1 Ch 465.

defendants' mine. For a number of years the defendants had been trespassing under the plaintiffs' farm. They mined coal from under the farm, which they brought to the surface and sold. They also used the workings under the farm to carry their own coals from their outlying workings to their pithead. The plaintiffs brought a bill in equity, seeking, *inter alia*:

(a) an account of all coal and ironstone extracted by the defendants from under the farm, and an order that the defendants pay for the coal and ironstone so gotten; and

(b) an account of all coal and ironstone conveyed from the defendants' mines through passages under the farm, and an order that the defendants pay for all underground wayleave and privileges which they had used under the farm in getting coal and ironstone from their own mines.

Before the cause came on for hearing in 1871, one of the defendants, Forman, had died, and the suit was revived against his executor. The relief sought by the plaintiffs was granted by Stuart V-C as against the still living defendants, but as against Forman's estate only the first enquiry was allowed. The Vice-Chancellor's decision on these points was affirmed by Lord Hatherley LC in the Court of Appeal.

We should notice two things about *Phillips v Homfray (No 1)* immediately. First, though a distinction between positive and negative benefits was made in respect of the claim against the executor of Forman's estate, it was not drawn in the case of the living defendants, Homfray and Fothergill, where recovery of both positive and negative gains was allowed. Secondly, no appeal was taken from the decision of the Lord Chancellor. *Phillips v Homfray (No 1)* is therefore authority in favour of a restitutionary award in respect of both positive and negative benefits, at least where living defendants are concerned.

2. *Phillips v Homfray (No 2)*[16]

The enquiries ordered were not carried out immediately. There was a further but related dispute between the plaintiffs in this action, who were only copyholders, and the lord of the manor, as to who had the better right to minerals found under copyhold land. That dispute was eventually resolved in favour of the plaintiffs, but not until 1881.[17] In that same year, another of the partners, Fothergill, died. The question for the court in *Phillips v*

---

[16] (1883) 24 Ch D 439.
[17] *Llanover v Homfray* (1881) 19 Ch D 224.

Homfray (No 2) was whether the same enquiries previously ordered against Fothergill in *Phillips v Homfray (No 1)* could now be revived against his executor. In effect, therefore, the dispute in *Phillips v Homfray (No 2)* was whether Stuart V-C and Lord Hatherley LC had in 1871 been right to draw a distinction between claims against living defendants and those against executors, the point not having been contested in that case.

(a) The Dissenting Judgments

At first instance, Pearson J held that both enquiries could be continued against Fothergill's executor. The question turned on the operation of the rule *actio personalis moritur cum persona* (a personal action dies with the person) and in this regard Pearson J purported to follow the judgment of the Court of King's Bench, led by Lord Mansfield, in *Hambly v Trott*, given over a century before.[18] Pearson J said that the only actions that died with the defendant were those in which the defendant was alleged to have caused loss to the plaintiff. Where the action was for the price to be paid by a wrongdoer for the use of a plaintiff's property, that action could still be maintained against an executor. In this case, the claim was not for damages for loss, but was:[19]

> really and truly paying back to the Plaintiffs part of the profit which the Defendants themselves received from using the wayleave instead of raising their coal by a more expensive and difficult way . . . [It] is not damages in the ordinary sense for personal injuries inflicted, but simply compensation which has to be paid out of the estate of the testator, because that estate, in one way or another, derived profit from the use of the wayleave . . .

On appeal, Baggallay LJ agreed. He too thought the issue decided by *Hambly v Trott*, which, he said, only barred claims for compensatory damages, not actions in respect of gains brought against executors.[20]

(b) The Majority Judgments

Bowen and Cotton LJJ delivered a joint judgment, allowing the appeal. They took a different view of the operation of the *actio personalis* rule, and it was here that the positive/negative distinction was introduced. They said that a remedy for a wrongful act could be pursued against the tortfeasor's estate where that act had added to his own estate or moneys:[21]

> But it is not every wrongful act by which a wrongdoer indirectly benefits that falls under this head, if the benefit does not consist in the acquisition of property or its

---

[18] (1776) 1 Cowp 371, 98 ER 1136.
[19] *Phillips (No 2)* (n 16) 446.
[20] *Ibid*, 471.
[21] *Ibid*, 454–5.

proceeds or value. Where there is nothing among the assets of the deceased that in law or in equity belongs to the plaintiff, and the damages which have been done to him are unliquidated and uncertain, the executors of a wrongdoer cannot be sued merely because it was worth the wrongdoer's while to commit the act which is complained of, and an indirect benefit may have been reaped thereby.

The words of Lord Mansfield in *Hambly v Trott* relied upon by Pearson J were said to be ambiguous and in any case *obiter*, and the case was distinguished as being one in which the particular tort concerned, in that case trover, could be waived, whereas the wrong in the instant case, trespass to land, could not.[22] As we shall see, it is this pronouncement which has led at least one commentator to argue that Bowen and Cotton LJJ would have denied a restitutionary claim in respect of a negative benefit even were the defendant still living.

C. *HAMBLY V TROTT*[23]

Clearly, then, everything turns on *Hambly v Trott*. Two questions arise. First, was the majority in *Phillips v Homfray (No 2)* right to distinguish it as they did? Secondly, even if they were not, was *Hambly v Trott* itself an accurate statement of the law? The view that will be put forward, albeit with some trepidation in that it calls into question the judgment of the father of much of the modern law of restitution, is that *Hambly v Trott*, though correctly decided, contains *obiter dicta* which cannot be supported. In order to sustain that argument, we need to look at the case itself.

In *Hambly v Trott* a claim was brought for trover and conversion in respect of some sheep, goats, pigs, oats and cider. The trover and conversion was alleged to have been committed by the defendant in his lifetime, but the claim was brought against his administrator. The plaintiff obtained a judgment which the administrator sought to set aside, relying on the rule *actio personalis moritur cum persona*. A strong Court of King's Bench, led by Lord Mansfield, and including Acton and Ashurst JJ, held that the claim was indeed barred. In the course of so doing, they laid down a set of rules as to which actions could, and which could not, be brought against a deceased's estate.

Lord Mansfield correctly pointed out that the maxim *actio personalis moritur cum persona* was not generally true, for there were many personal actions which could be brought against an executor or administrator. A claim might be barred, he said, for one of two reasons: either because of the nature of the *cause* of action itself, or because of some procedural limit

---

[22] *Ibid*, 461.
[23] (1776) 1 Cowp 371, 98 ER 1136.

contained in the *form* of the action. As to the former, Lord Mansfield said:[24]

> where the cause of action is money due, or a contract to be performed, gain or acquisition of the testator, by the work and labour, or property of another, or a promise of the testator express or implied; where these are the cause of action, the action survives against the executor. But where the cause of action is a *tort*, or arises *ex delicto* supposed to be *by force* and *against the King's peace*, there the action dies; as battery, false imprisonment, trespass, words, nuisance, obstructing lights, diverting a water course, escape against the sheriff, and many other cases of the like kind.

So far as the *form* of the action was concerned:[25]

> In some actions the defendant could have waged his law; and therefore, no action in that form lies against an executor. But now, other actions are substituted in their room upon the very same cause, which do survive and lie against the executor.—No action where in form the declaration must be *quare vi et armis, et contra pacem*, or where the plea must be, as in this case, that the *testator* was *not guilty*, can lie against the *executor*. Upon the face of the record, the cause of action arises *ex delicto*; and all private criminal injuries or wrongs, as well as public crimes, are buried with the offender.

In the instant case the plaintiff's claim died with the defendant because the cause of action as pleaded was in tort.

But Lord Mansfield went on to say that the claim would not have failed had a different form been used. He said that in most, if not all, cases where trover lay against the testator, another action could be brought against the executor which would answer the purpose:[26]

> If a man take a horse from another, and bring him back again; an action of trespass will not lie against the executor, though it would against him; but an action for the use and hire of the horse will lie against the executor.

And later:[27]

> If it is a sort of injury by which the offender acquires no gain to himself at the expense of the sufferer, as beating or imprisoning a man, etc., there, the person injured has only a reparation for the *delictum* in damages to be assessed by a jury. But where, beside the crime, property is acquired which benefits the testator, there an action for the value of the property shall survive against the executor. As for instance, the executor shall not be chargeable for the injury done by

[24] *Ibid*, 1 Cowp 375, 98 ER 1138.
[25] *Ibid*.
[26] *Ibid*.
[27] *Ibid*, 1 Cowp 376, 98 ER 1139.

his testator in cutting down another man's trees, but for the benefit arising to his
testator for the value or sale of the trees he shall.

It was these last two passages which the dissentients in *Phillips v Homfray
(No 2)* relied upon to hold that even negative enrichment claims could be
brought against the tortfeasor's estate. And though, as Bowen and Cotton
LJJ notice, the second passage is ambiguous in that it does not state whether
the benefit need be positive or negative, when read in conjunction with the
passage regarding the use of the horse, that ambiguity disappears. There
seems to be no doubt whatsoever that Lord Mansfield would have allowed
a claim for a negative benefit, even against an executor.

Unfortunately, Bowen and Cotton LJJ's attempt to explain away the
example of the horse is not convincing:[28]

> The case [Lord Mansfield] puts is the case of a horse taken and restored, not of
> a horse taken and held under an adverse claim, and we are not prepared to say
> that, if absolutely nothing appeared in evidence except that a horse was taken
> and was afterwards brought back again, the owner might not recover for the use
> and hire of the horse on the hypothesis of an implied contract to pay for him.

This attempt to explain recovery on the basis of a contract implied in fact
rather than one implied by law is probably due to the now discredited
implied contract theory of restitution prevalent at the end of the nineteenth
century.[29] But it is well known that Lord Mansfield himself was no sub-
scriber to the implied contract theory of restitution, as his judgment in
Moses v Macferlan[30] makes clear, and it is therefore highly unlikely that this
is what he had in mind.

At this point, therefore, the dissentients would seem to have the upper
hand. But if we go back further, to the origins of the *actio personalis* rule,
we will discover that it is Lord Mansfield who was wrong and not the
majority in *Phillips v Homfray (No 2)*.

D. *ACTIO PERSONALIS MORITUR CUM PERSONA*

The rules on the survival of actions on death, and within that, the operation of the maxim *actio personalis moritur cum persona*, are obscure.[31] The
traditional explanation is that given in *Hambly v Trott*, which, as we have
seen, starts from the position that a claim against a deceased's executor

---

[28] *Phillips (No 2)* (n 16) 460.
[29] G Jones (ed), *Goff & Jones on the Law of Restitution* (6th edn, London, Sweet &
Maxwell, 2002) 4–11.
[30] (1760) 2 Burr 1005, 97 ER 676.
[31] According to Bowen LJ in *Finlay v Chirney* (1887) 20 QBD 495, 503, 'we are still left in
the dark as to the maxim's exact meaning and source'.

might be barred either because of the particular form of action used, or because of the nature of the cause of action. But, as we shall see, the form in which the action was brought was not originally determinative, and at first all personal claims did indeed die with the defendant. However, we start with the thinking behind *Hambly v Trott*.

The reason why the particular *form* of action might make a difference was because different methods of proof attached to different forms of action. Some forms of action were subject to wager of law, while in others, those which came later, proof was by way of jury trial. Claims in respect of debts, whether promissory or non-promissory, were originally enforced through the action of debt, where proof was by wager of law. It was thought that the forms of action to which the defendant might wage his law could not survive his death because it was not possible for one person to wage another's law. Wager of law was concerned with the question whether the defendant's oath that he was innocent could be trusted. The executors were not in a position to know whether a liability had been discharged or not, and therefore could not be admitted at their souls' peril to swear an oath on a subject about which they had no knowledge.[32] It was for this reason that debt could not be brought against executors. But those actions to which wager of law was never available, amongst which were included all actions of trespass,[33] were not barred for this reason.

The fact that debt was subject to wager of law meant that, from a plaintiff's point of view, it was an unpopular action, not only because it could not be brought against executors, but because, even against the living, the ability of the defendant to wage his law made the bringing of successful claims very difficult. Wager of law involved the defendant procuring eleven men to swear the truth of his oath that he was not guilty, and it was apparently not difficult to find men who were willing to sell their souls for this purpose. Creditors therefore sought to take advantage of the more modern action of assumpsit, a species of the action upon the case, itself a species of trespass, in which the obligation arose because of an undertaking by the defendant to do something, and where the method of proof was jury trial. But creditors faced two problems in trying to take advantage of this new form of action. First, there was the subsidiarity rule, under which actions on the case were not available to plaintiffs who already had the benefit of existing forms of action.[34] The action on the case was designed to fill the gaps in the older forms of action, not to supplant them altogether, and those who were owed a sum certain already had the action of debt. Secondly, there might not always be present on the facts of a particular

[32] AWB Simpson, *A History of the Common Law of Contract* (2nd edn, Oxford, OUP, 1986) 558.
[33] *Rempston v Morley* (1383) YB Mich 7 Ric II, 30, pl 11.
[34] *Anon* (1522) YB Pas 14 Hen VIII, fo 31, pl 8.

case an express undertaking on the part of the debtor to pay the sum in question.

So far as debt claims against living defendants were concerned, both of these problems were overcome in the case of promissory debts by 1602. Around the middle of the sixteenth century it was held that assumpsit would lie where there was an express promise to pay the sum due.[35] That finding was both confirmed and extended by *Slade's Case* in 1602, a case of goods sold and delivered, where it was held that assumpsit could be brought even where debt could have been brought on the same facts, and that even where an express undertaking to pay was lacking, such an undertaking was implicit in the contract of sale. And to the objection that this would deny the defendant the benefit of wager of law, this was no bad thing, for in the words of Coke (as counsel), 'experience now proves that men's consciences grow so large that the respect of their private advantage rather induces them to perjury'.[36]

Although *Slade's Case* involved living parties, the fact that a form of action could be used which did not involve wager of law opened the way for promissory debts to be brought generally against executors. This was acknowledged nine years later in *Pinchon's Case*,[37] in which executors were successfully sued in assumpsit in respect of a loan of £200 made to the deceased. Coke CJ held that *Slade's Case* had in effect overruled the point that debt did not lie against executors:[38]

> a man shall never have an action against executors where the testator in his life-time might have waged his law; and the reason thereof is because the executors shall be deprived of the benefit of waging law, if an action will lie against them; which reason strongly proveth, that in the case at bar the action will lie against the executors, because the testator, in an action on the case on this assumpsit, could not wage his law; and therefore his executors shall not be deprived of it.

So, by 1611 the availability of wager of law was no longer a problem when consideration was given to the question whether claims could be brought against executors. In other words, so far as the survival of actions on death was concerned, the *form* of action was no longer an issue. But even with the demise of wager of law, some actions were still not enforceable against executors. This was no longer a matter of form; it was one of substance, and it was here that the *actio personalis moritur cum persona* rule came into play. But the maxim was not literally true, for it would otherwise have barred the claim in *Pinchon's Case* itself.

---

[35] *Norwood v Reed* (1558) 1 Plowd 180, 75 ER 277. The claim here, however, was against an executor, and the question whether assumpsit could have been brought against the deceased in his lifetime seems not to have been argued.

[36] (1602) B & M 420, 441.

[37] *Pinchon's Case* (1611) 9 Co Rep 86b, 77 ER 859.

[38] *Ibid*, 9 Co Rep 87b, 77 ER 861.

So, to what claims did it apply? This is a difficult question. According to Willes CJ in *Sollers v Lawrence*, '*actio personalis* is always understood of a tort'.[39] The rule, it was said, 'never extended to personal actions founded on any obligation, contract, debt, covenant, or any other duty to be performed'.[40] The reason why tort actions died, but no others, given by Newton CJ in a case in 1440 concerning an action by churchwardens for things carried off from a church, was that the executor himself had committed no wrong: 'if one doeth a *trespass* to me and dieth, the action is dead also, because it would be improper to recover against one who was not a party to the wrong.'[41] But this is unsatisfactory, for it does not explain the continuance of all other actions; just as the executor was not a party to the tort, nor was he a party to any other obligation of the deceased.

A more probable explanation is given by Street.[42] If we go back to the thirteenth century, to the time of Bracton, we see the *actio personalis* rule being applied to all personal obligations without exception. The first exception to be made concerned contracts under seal to which the deceased's successor, who was usually the heir, was expressly bound. According to Street, 'The solemnity of the instrument and the fact that the obligor expressly bound his heir were accepted as affording a sufficient reason for changing the ordinary rule'.[43] Later, the fact that the contract was under seal was itself enough to make the contract binding on the successor (now executor) even in the absence of express words to that effect. The orthodox explanation, and that adopted by Lord Mansfield in *Hambly v Trott* itself, for the difference between contracts under seal and simple contracts was that only in respect of the latter was wager of law available, and that since the deceased could not wage his law where the contract was under seal, the executor would not be being denied this privilege.

But according to Street this explanation, which first gained currency around 1433, is wrong, and in fact, in an anonymous case decided in 1535,[44] Fitzherbert said that assumpsit was subject to the same perishability as debt. Although there was a decision of Fyneux CJ and Coningsby J in 1520, *Cleymond v Vyncent*,[45] in which Fitzherbert, as counsel, had managed to obtain assumpsit against an executor, he said: 'But I hold that the law is clearly otherwise, and that [the judges] acted without taking any advice, but only on their own opinions.' When told that *Cleymond v Vyncent* was reported in the Year Books, Fitzherbert replied: 'Put that case

[39] (1743) Willes 413, 421; 125 ER 1243, 1247.
[40] *Wheatley v Lane* (1668) 1 Wms Saund 216a, 85 ER 228.
[41] (1440) YB 19 Hen VI, 66, pl 10.
[42] TA Street, *The Foundations of Legal Liability* (Northport, NY, Edward Thompson Co, 1906) vol 3, 60–71.
[43] *Ibid*, 65–6.
[44] *Anon* (1535) YB Trin 27 Hen VIII, fo 23, pl 21; B & M 447.
[45] (1520) YB Mich 12 Hen VIII, fo 11, pl 3; B & M 446.

out of your Year books, for it is not law without doubt. (Note that.)' In this view, Fitzherbert was not alone. Seven years later, in *Sukley v Wyte*, Shelley J described *Cleymond v Vyncent* as a 'doubtful case', and reaffirmed the view that 'the action on the case does not lie against executors on a promise made by their testator'.[46]

This immunity of executors at law must, however, be placed in context. Holdsworth points out that it was common practice for testators to direct executors to pay their debts and to make good their wrongs, that in the case of persons dying intestate the administrator was bound to employ part of the deceased's estate in pious uses for the good of his soul, and that the payment of debts and the making good of injuries were recognised as such pious uses.[47] But pressure for reform of the common law came with the decline in influence of the ecclesiastical courts, which originally had jurisdiction in this area. Chief among those advocating change was Coke, both as counsel and as a judge, and, as we have seen in *Pinchon's Case*, he used the non-availability of wager of law as his cover for extending the reach of the common law.

The position seems to have been that by 1611, contractual debts of all kinds, whether or not under seal, survived against executors, while all other claims died with the defendant. The next development related to non-contractual debts. Once *Slade's Case* had sanctioned the bringing of assumpsit for promissory debts, and *Pinchon's Case* had seized on the non-availability of wager of law to make promissory debts binding on executors, the way was now clear for non-promissory creditors to proceed down the same route. This was done in *City of London v Goree*,[48] where a claim was made by the City in assumpsit for customary dues levied upon foreign goods offered for sale within their boundaries. The court held that because the City could have brought debt, there also lay indebitatus assumpsit, which is of course a complete inversion of the proposition laid down in *Slade's Case*. But whatever doubts there may have been as to the validity of this reasoning, from then on the way was open for restitutionary plaintiffs to bring indebitatus assumpsit rather than debt and, in the process, to ensure that those restitutionary claims could be brought against executors.

But what of restitutionary claims founded on a tort? If claims for compensation for torts did not survive the death of the tortfeasor, could a restitutionary plaintiff whose action depended on the commission of a wrong circumvent this by 'waiving the tort' and framing his action in assumpsit? This, in fact, is the very issue at the heart of *Phillips v Homfray (No 2)*. Before this case, there seems to have been no instance of it having been

---

[46] (1542) B & M 404, 405.
[47] Sir W Holdsworth, *A History of English Law* (London, Methuen & Co, 1903) Vol III, 582–3.
[48] (1677) B & M 476; 2 Lev 174.

done, though, as we have seen, there are dicta in *Hambly v Trott* which indicate that it was a possibility. A modern lawyer knows from *United Australia Ltd v Barclays Bank Ltd*[49] that the claim to restitution in such a case depends on the commission of the tort, and that if the tort disappears, then so too does the restitutionary claim. For as Viscount Simon LC there observed:[50]

> When the plaintiff 'waived the tort' and brought assumpsit, he did not thereby elect to be treated from that time forward on the basis that no tort had been committed; indeed, if it were to be understood that no tort had been committed, how could an action in assumpsit lie? It lies only because the acquisition of the defendant is wrongful and there is thus an obligation to make restitution.

So nowadays we would say that the majority in *Phillips v Homfray (No 2)* were perfectly correct in holding that the restitutionary claims based on the wrong of trespass to land could not be continued against the tortfeasor's estate, and that Lord Mansfield in *Hambly v Trott* seems to have been uncharacteristically beguiled by form over substance. And from a reading of Bowen and Cotton LJJ's joint judgment, there is abundant evidence to show that they did indeed decide the case on this basis, that the claim was based on a wrong, and that the foundation for that claim had disappeared with the death of the defendant. They twice, for example, described the claim as involving a 'remedy for a wrongful act'.[51] But more importantly, towards the end of their judgment they said that 'The claim of the Plaintiffs is in *substance*, so far as these inquiries are concerned, an action for trespass', and later, that 'the claims of the Plaintiffs . . . are claims for unliquidated damages in respect of a wrong done' and such claims 'abated . . . upon the death of the deceased, R Fothergill'.[52] Thus, it is Lord Mansfield in *Hambly v Trott* who was mistaken about the survival against executors of restitutionary claims based on wrongdoing, and Pearson J and Baggallay LJ who went wrong in applying his dictum to the facts of *Phillips v Homfray (No 2)*: Bowen and Cotton LJJ simply anticipated by nearly sixty years the reasoning of the House of Lords in *United Australia* and should be applauded for so doing.[53]

---

[49] [1941] AC 1.

[50] *Ibid*, 18.

[51] *Phillips (No 2)* (n 16) 454 and 455. The relevant passage is set out below in the text to n 63.

[52] *Ibid*, 466; emphasis added.

[53] This, of course, means that the reasoning of Edmund Davies J in *Chesworth v Farrer* [1967] 1 QB 407, in which a plaintiff evaded the limitation period laid down by s 1(3) of the Law Reform (Miscellaneous Provisions) Act 1934, the statute which abolished the *actio personalis* rule, by framing his action for the profits of a conversion as a claim for money had and received, cannot be supported. It is notable, however, that neither *Phillips v Homfray (No 2)* nor *United Australia* was cited to the learned judge.

E. THE CLAIM IN RESPECT OF THE POSITIVE ACCRETIONS

But what of the first inquiry? It will be recalled that only the second and third claims were disallowed against the deceased tortfeasor. If Bowen and Cotton LJJ were truly saying that restitutionary claims for torts could not survive the death of the tortfeasor, how do we explain the continuance of the first inquiry against the deceased's estate in respect of the positive accretions? Was that not also a claim based on the tortious conduct of the deceased?

There has always been said to be one exception to the *actio personalis* rule so far as claims in tort were concerned. The claim was not barred where the deceased had during his lifetime taken property from the plaintiff which at the time of his death still formed part of the defendant's estate. So, for example, detinue could be brought against executors upon a bailment made to their testator.[54] And in *Sherrington's Case*[55] executors were held liable for one hundred oaks and twenty oxen which the testator had wrongfully taken from the plaintiff's land. No satisfactory reason for this exception has ever been found, Winfield's suggestion that the taint of trespass did not attach to an obligation to return property[56] requiring that we read *poenalis* for *personalis*.[57]

A simpler explanation is that this was no exception at all. The rule is that personal actions die with the defendant. But not all actions are personal actions. Some are actions *in rem*. If I lend you a book, that book remains mine even if you die while it is in your possession; your executors will commit the wrong of conversion if they deal with it in any way inconsistent with my rights. The claim is one against the executors *personally*, not in their capacity as executors. This is demonstrated by a number of pieces of evidence. First, detinue could be brought against the executor of a bailee without the plaintiff having to say that the defendant executor was being sued in that capacity. The mere fact that the chattel had been bailed to someone and had now come into the defendant's possession was enough.[58] Secondly, detinue was an action to which the defendant could wage his law. But as we have seen, one man could not wage another's law, and so if detinue were brought against an executor it must have been against him in his personal and not his representative capacity. Thirdly, where there was more than one executor, there was no need to join them all; where only one had possession, it was enough to sue him alone. Indeed, where there were three

---

[54] YB 11 Hen IV 46, 20.

[55] (1583) Savile 40, 123 ER 1000.

[56] PH Winfield, *A Text-Book of the Law of Tort* (London, Sweet & Maxwell, 1937) 196.

[57] See too P Birks, 'Restitution for Wrongs' in EJH Schrage (ed), *Unjust Enrichment: The Comparative Legal History of the Law of Restitution* (Berlin, Duncker & Humblot, 1995) 171, 176, n 19.

[58] *Wagworth v Halyday* (1355) B & M 267.

executors and only one had possession, the action lay against him alone.[59] This should be contrasted with the normal rule that where there was more than one executor, all had to be joined and made defendants.[60] Fourthly, the 'exception' seems to have applied only where the goods still formed part of the testator's estate at the time of his death. The continued existence of the goods is presupposed by the statement in *Le Mason v Dixon* that 'if the executors have the goods in their possession, then detinue lies against them *on their own possession*',[61] and in *Hambly v Trott* itself it would seem that the real reason the claim in trover failed was because neither the goods nor their traceable value were present in the estate at the time of the testator's death. As Aston J pointed out in argument:[62]

> Where goods come into the hands of the executor *in specie*, *trover* will lie; where in *value*, an action for *money had and received*. But the difficulty with me is, that here it does not appear whether the goods came to the hands of the defendant in specie or in value.

So, the exception to the *actio personalis* rule in respect of positive accretions was really no exception at all. The claim was not one in respect of profitable wrongdoing by the defendant, but instead one in respect of the detention by the executor of a *res* belonging to the plaintiff. That this is how Bowen and Cotton LJJ viewed the first inquiry is evident from the following passage in their judgment:[63]

> The only cases in which, apart from questions of breach of contract, express or implied, a remedy for a wrongful act can be pursued against the estate of a deceased person who has done the act, appear to us to be those in which property, or the proceeds or value of property, belonging to another, have been appropriated by the deceased person and added to his own estate or moneys. In such cases, whatever the original form of action, it is in substance brought to recover property, or its proceeds or value, and by amendment could be made such in form as well as in substance. In such cases the action, though arising out of a wrongful act, does not die with the person. The property or the proceeds or value which, in the lifetime of the wrongdoer, could have been recovered from him, can be traced after his death to his assets, and recaptured by the rightful owner there.

---

[59] Vin Abr Detinue D1: 'If the Bailee of a Thing Dies, Detinue lies against his Executors if they take it'; Vin Abr Executors Ab7.9: 'If three are Executors and the one has the Possession, Action lies against him alone'.

[60] Vin Abr Executors Ab4.4, 15; *Ryalls v Bramall* (1848) 1 Ex 734, 154 ER 312; *Cabell v Vaughan* (1669) 1 Wms Saund 291 *m*; 85 ER 389, 398.

[61] (1626) W Jones 173, 174; 82 ER 92, 93; translation supplied and emphasis added. The original reads: '*si le executors ount les biens en lour possession, donque detinue gist vers eux, sur lour possession demesne.*'

[62] *Hambly* (n 23) 374.

[63] *Phillips (No 2)* (n 16) 454.

Thus, the continuance of the first inquiry is explicable on the ground that it was simply a tracing exercise designed to identify an asset belonging to the plaintiff still in the executor's hands; it was not a claim dependent on the commission of a wrong by the deceased.

F. TRESPASS TO LAND CANNOT BE WAIVED

The argument made above, that *Phillips v Homfray* is simply a case concerned with the operation of the *actio personalis moritur cum persona* rule, and not with restitution for wrongs generally, has been rejected by Professor Burrows. Although he finds such an argument generally attractive, he says:[64]

> Unfortunately, on a fair reading of the judgments it appears that while the issue in point was whether an action could be brought against the deceased's executors, the reasoning was also directed to claims against the wrongdoer himself. For example, Bowen LJ said, 'the true test to be applied in the present case is whether the plaintiffs' claim against the deceased . . . belongs to the category of actions *ex delicto* or whether any form of action against the executors of the deceased, *or the deceased man in his lifetime,* can be based upon any implied contract or duty.

Thus, says Professor Burrows, *Phillips v Homfray* really is the anti-restitution case it was always thought to be.

But this view can be challenged. First, it takes no account of the fact that the proceedings in *Phillips v Homfray (No 1)* gave a restitutionary award for negative enrichments against the defendant when alive, and that Bowen and Cotton LJJ cast no doubt on that decision. Secondly, it is clear that Bowen and Cotton LJJ were talking only of the *form* of the action through which the claim to restitution might be made, as the sentences which immediately follow the passage cited by Professor Burrows make clear. They go on to say:[65]

> In other words, could the Plaintiffs have sued the deceased at law in any form of action in which 'Not guilty' would not be the proper plea? If such alternative form of action could be conceived it must be either an action for the use, by the Plaintiffs' permission, of the Plaintiffs' roads and passages, similar in principle, though not identical, with an action for the use and occupation of the Plaintiffs' land. Or it must be in the shape of an action for money had and received, based upon the supposition that funds are in the hands of the executors which properly belong in law or in equity to the Plaintiffs. We do not

---

[64] Burrows (1993) (n 5) 391; emphasis in original. The view adopted in the second edition (2002) is less emphatic.

[65] *Phillips (No 2)* (n 16) 461.

believe that the principle of waiving a tort and suing in contract can be carried further than this—that a plaintiff is entitled, if he chooses it, to abstain from treating as a wrong the acts of the defendant in cases where, independently of the question of wrong, the plaintiff could make a case for relief.

In other words, what Bowen and Cotton LJJ are there saying is that the tort of trespass to land is not one for which waiver of tort was available. But, as we shall see immediately below, while they are undoubtedly correct in saying this, it does not mean that a restitutionary claim would be barred, for, as *Phillips v Homfray (No 1)* itself shows, waiver of tort is only one route to restitution for wrongdoing.[66] There, an account of profits lay in respect of the wrong, even though waiver of tort was not available. But we should nevertheless explain why trespass to land was not a tort which could be 'waived'.

To modern eyes, the true nature of waiver of tort is as described in *United Australia Ltd v Barclays Bank Ltd*.[67] As we have seen, when the plaintiff 'waives the tort' he is not electing between causes of action, between tort and unjust enrichment, but between responses to the same cause of action, between compensation and restitution. But in an era still dominated by the *forms* of action, an era in which the first textbooks dividing the subject matter of the law by *causes* of action were only just beginning to appear,[68] the phrase 'waiver of tort' meant simply a choice between forms of action. And the problem in *Phillips v Homfray* was that there was no appropriate count to which the plaintiff could have switched. Indebitatus assumpsit for money had and received to the use of the plaintiff was obviously out, for the defendant had not received money. As long ago as 1770 in *Nightingall v Devisme*,[69] Lord Mansfield himself held that when an action said 'money' it meant 'money'. Moreover, there was no indebitatus assumpsit count for the use and occupation of land, and therefore no alternative form of action to which the plaintiff who 'waived' his tort could go. The reasons for this are complex.[70] We have already seen that, at first, claims for debts, whether promissory or non-promissory, were enforced through the action of debt and that, from a plaintiff's point of view, this was unattractive because of the defendant's ability to wage his law. We have also seen how the more attractive action of assumpsit was made generally available for the enforcement of contractual debts by *Slade's Case* in 1602.

But claims in respect of the use and occupation of land were different. In debt for rent against a tenant, wager of law had never been available, with

---

[66] Cf Birks (n 57) 173–5.
[67] *United Australia* (n 49).
[68] P Birks, 'Adjudication and Interpretation in the Common Law: A Century of Change' (1994) 14 *LS* 156, 160–6.
[69] (1770) 5 Burr 2589, 98 ER 361; 2 Wm Bl 684, 96 ER 401.
[70] The history is traced by JB Ames, 'Assumpsit for Use of Occupation' (1889) 2 *Harvard LR* 377.

the result that there was no justification for the court ignoring the old rule about the subsidiarity of the action on the case and not confining landlords to the more ancient action of debt. And if promissory claims for rent could not be brought in assumpsit, non-promissory claims for debts which arose from the use and occupation of land were also denied this action, for there was then no promissory action to fictionalise. There was thus no indebitatus count for the use and occupation of land, with the consequence that waiver of tort could not get the plaintiff into indebitatus assumpsit for the simple reason that there was no alternative form of action to which to go.

The position on promissory debts regarding land was later relaxed, first by the common law, and then by statute. Where there was an express promise to pay rent the courts in 1683 held that assumpsit could be brought.[71] Where the agreement was to pay a reasonable rent, the subsidiarity point never arose, for there debt was never available, there being no sum certain. In such a case a claim in *quantum meruit* could be brought. But had a sum certain been agreed, then any claim by the landlord in *quantum meruit* would be nonsuited. The equivalent of *Slade's Case*, where the court would imply an undertaking to pay from the fact of a contract of lease, was supplied by statute in the early part of the next century. A statute of 1738[72] extended *quantum meruit* to the case where the rent was certain but there was no express promise to pay. It provided:

> [To] obviate some difficulties that many times occur in the recovery of rents, where demises are not by deed . . . it shall and may be lawful to and for the landlord or landlords, where the agreement is not by deed, to recover a reasonable satisfaction for the land, tenements, or heriditaments held or occupied by the defendant or defendants, in an action on the case, for the use and occupation of what was so held and enjoyed; and if in evidence on the trial of such action any parol demise or agreement (not being by deed) whereon a certain rent was reserved shall appear, the plaintiff in such action shall not therefore be nonsuited, but may make use thereof as an evidence of the quantum of damages to be recovered.

Thus, promissory debts, both express and implied, relating to the use and occupation of land were now actionable within assumpsit. The next logical step would have been for the courts to have brought non-promissory debts for the use and occupation of land within the ambit of indebitatus assumpsit too. But this step was never taken. The reason is that while in the non-land cases the indebitatus assumpsit counts were the creation of the courts, with land, indebitatus assumpsit was the creature of statute, and according to Ames:[73]

---

[71] *Johnson v May* (1683) 3 Lev 150, 83 ER 624.
[72] II Geo II c 19 s 14.
[73] Ames (n 70) 381.

the courts could not, without too palpable a usurpation, extend the count to cases not within the act of Parliament. The statute was plainly confined to cases where, by mutual agreement, the occupier of land was to pay either a defined or a reasonable compensation to the owner. Hence the impossibility of charging a trespasser in assumpsit for use and occupation.

This explains why, in the passage cited above, Bowen and Cotton LJJ say that the alternative form of action 'must be either an action for the use, by the Plaintiffs' permission, of the Plaintiffs' roads and passages, similar in principle, though not identical, with an action for the use and occupation of the Plaintiffs' land' or money had and received. But in saying this they were not denying altogether the availability of a restitutionary claim for negative enrichments; they were simply being faithful to legal history. Only the *form* such a claim might take was in issue, and, as we have seen, their lordships cast no doubt on the alternative route of an account of profits. Thus, Professor Burrows is wrong when he says that the denial of waiver of tort against a living tortfeasor means that *Phillips v Homfray (No 2)* is authority preventing a restitutionary claim in respect of negative benefits against a living tortfeasor.

G. CONCLUSION

Phillips v Homfray (No 2) is not the anti-restitution case it is painted to be. It should not be overruled, or banished to a dark corner of our law, but should instead be set out in lights. It is a decision concerned solely with the operation of the maxim *actio personalis moritur cum persona*, and therefore tells us nothing of the restitutionary liability of living wrongdoers. But when it is read in conjunction with *Phillips v Homfray (No 1)*, it is in fact authority *against* the very proposition for which it is said to stand, namely, that a restitutionary claim in respect of the wrong of trespass to land yields only positive benefits, for in the first stage of the litigation Stuart V-C at first instance, and Lord Hatherley LC on appeal, allowed a restitutionary claim for expense saved by the then living defendants.[74] But most importantly, it is also authority for the view that there is indeed a part of the law of restitution in which the plaintiff's restitutionary claim is dependent on the commission of a wrong by the defendant. The only thing that needs to be buried is the myth of *Phillips v Homfray*, not the decision itself.

---

[74] This is confirmed by a later decision of the Court of Appeal, where negative benefits were recovered in respect of a trespass to land. In *Whitwam v Westminster Brymbo Coal and Coke Co* [1896] 2 Ch 538 the defendant colliery owner had for many years used the plaintiff's land as a tip. The Official Receiver found that the diminution in the value of the land was £200, but that the saving of expense to the defendant was over £1,000. Chitty J applied *Phillips v Homfray (No 1)* and made an award based on the saving of expense, which was upheld by the Court of Appeal (Lindley, Lopes and Rigby LJJ, who had been counsel in *Phillips v Homfray (No 2)*).

8

Allcard v Skinner (1887)

CHARLOTTE SMITH

A. INTRODUCTION

*A*LLCARD V SKINNER[1] lies at the heart of the modern doctrine of undue influence relating to *inter vivos* transactions. It is known to generations of law students as authority for the proposition that an *inter vivos* transaction may be set aside in certain instances where there is a relationship of trust and confidence between the parties. If such a relationship exists then relief may be granted where the claimant can prove that the transaction was obtained by the exercise of 'actual' undue influence; or where, though the claimant has not proved 'actual' undue influence, she has successfully proved that the relationship between herself and the defendant raises a presumption (not successfully rebutted by the defendant) that the transaction was procured by undue influence.

The doctrine of undue influence has, in recent years, been the subject of considerable controversy as both the judicial and academic communities have attempted to elucidate the rational basis for relief. In their attempts both academics and judges have regularly referred to *Allcard v Skinner*, and in this sense it is a leading case. Given this, the aim of this chapter is to examine the light that it can shed, as a legal authority, upon the basis of the doctrine of undue influence. The chapter will examine the judgments handed down in *Allcard v Skinner* and also their use in recent articulations of the doctrine. Having examined the case as a legal authority, attention will then turn to an exploration of its identity as a historical event taking place at a particular time and in a particular place. This exploration will focus on the religious content and context of the case. It will explore three aspects of that context: general themes in religious attitudes and religious change; controversies within the Church of England; and the resurgence of the organised religious life in nineteenth century England.

---

[1] (1887) 36 Ch D 145.

B. THE SEARCH FOR THE BASIS OF RELIEF

The doctrine of undue influence is only applicable as a ground for relief where a relationship of trust and confidence existed between the parties at the time of the transaction against which relief is sought. The 'undue influence which the Courts of Equity endeavour to defeat is the undue influence of one person over another'.[2] It is the necessary presence of this relationship which confounds efforts to determine and articulate the basis and rationale of relief.

The question for consideration is whether relief for undue influence is claimant-focused or defendant-focused. Put another way, the question is whether relief is granted because the claimant's ability to consent was impaired; or because the defendant has behaved in an unconscionable or unfair way. Alternatively, it may be argued that relief is granted because public policy demands that relationships characterised by trust and confidence should be protected from the possibility of abuse.

The difficulty inherent in any attempt to articulate the basis of relief is that, given that a relationship must be present in order for the doctrine to arise, the quality of the consent given cannot ever be entirely divorced from the position or conduct of the defendant. As Bigwood writes:[3]

> The jurisdiction is subject, first and foremost, to the liberty principle (utmost freedom to dispose of one's property as one chooses), but it also assists to define what 'liberty' means in this connection by reference to the processes by which transferees of property may, relative to equity's 'conscience', legitimately procure or accept the assent of their transferors.

Given this, the question of whether relief is claimant-centred or defendant-centred is necessarily one of focus or emphasis. Yet the debate about the proper basis of relief continues, and has obvious consequences for such basic issues as treatment of the defendant who has not acted in a blameworthy or unconscionable manner. As Mummery LJ stated in the recent case of *Pesticcio v Huet*:[4]

> The continuing confusions matter. Aspects of the instant case demonstrate the need for a wider understanding, both in and outside of the legal profession, of the circumstances in which the court will intervene to protect the dependant and the vulnerable in dealings with their property.

---

[2] *Ibid*, 162 (Lindley LJ).

[3] R Bigwood, 'Undue Influence in the House of Lords: Principles and Proof' (2002) 65 *MLR* 438.

[4] [2004] EWCA Civ 372 [2].

Yet at the present time neither judicial precedent nor academic commentary yields a coherent and consistent account of the basis for relief.[5] A prominent example of continued disagreements and controversies is provided by the judgments handed down in the recent case of *Attorney General v R*,[6] and in the subsequent decisions of the Court of Appeal in similar cases. In *Attorney General v R* Lord Hoffmann, carrying with him the support of the majority, gave a predominantly defendant-centred account of relief. He focused on the unconscionable or improper behaviour of the defendant, and the correlative need to protect the claimant made vulnerable by their subjection to the influence or relationship concerned. Thus he held that:[7]

> Like duress at common law, undue influence is based upon the principle that a transaction to which consent has been obtained by unacceptable means should not be allowed to stand. Undue influence has concentrated in particular upon the unfair exploitation by one party of a relationship which gives him ascendancy or influence over the other.

In contrast, Lord Scott, speaking in dissent, favoured a more distinctly claimant-centred account of relief. He focused less specifically upon the possibility of unfair exploitation of a trusting relationship, and to a greater degree upon the quality of the consent given to the impugned transaction. He characterised relief in the following terms:[8]

> It is well established that the relationship between parties to a contract, coupled with the nature of the contract and, sometimes, the circumstances in which consent to it by one party was obtained by the other, may give rise to a presumption that the consent of the former was obtained by undue influence. The presumption is an evidential presumption requiring the dominant party, seeking to enforce the contract, to introduce some additional evidence to show that the consent to the contract of the subservient party was a true consent fairly obtained.

Despite the defendant-centred approach taken by the majority in the House of Lords in *Attorney General v R* it is the claimant-centred approach of Lord Scott which seems to have been most prominent in recent Court of Appeal decisions. In *Pesticcio v Huet*[9] Mummery LJ, giving the judgment of the

---

[5] For detailed discussion of the opposing views and the relevant case law see Bigwood (n 3); P Birks and Chin NY, 'On the Nature of Undue Influence' in J Beatson and D Friedmann (eds), *Good Faith and Fault in Contract Law* (Oxford, Clarendon Press, 1997) 57; P Ridge, 'The Equitable Doctrine of Undue Influence Considered in the Context of Spiritual Influence and Religious Faith: *Allcard v Skinner* Revisited in Australia' (2003) 26 *University of New South Wales Law Journal* 66.

[6] [2003] EMLR 24. See also *National and Commercial Bank (Jamaica) Ltd v Hew* [2003] UKPC 51.

[7] *Ibid* [21].

[8] *Ibid* [41].

[9] [2004] EWCA Civ 372.

court, was clear that relief could be granted even though the defendant had not acted in a wrongful manner. The court intervened to set aside the transaction in order to prevent disadvantage to the claimant.[10]

These differences of opinion are echoed in many of the recent decisions on undue influence. In reaching them many judges have appealed to the decisions handed down in *Allcard v Skinner*. Thus, in characterising the doctrine of undue influence as a response to the need to protect relationships of trust and confidence from abuse, Sir Martin Nourse referred in *Hammond v Osborn* to Cotton LJ's assertion that:[11]

> the Court interferes . . . on the ground of public policy, and to prevent the relations which existed between the parties and the influence arising there from being abused.

Similarly, in formulating his claimant-centred account of relief in *Attorney General v R*, Lord Scott cited with approval Bowen LJ's assertion that where a gift has been procured under influence it should be set aside:[12]

> unless it is shewn that the donor, at the time of making the gift, was allowed full and free opportunity for counsel and advice outside—the means of considering his or her own worldly position and exercising an independent will about it.

In fact, an examination of the judgments delivered in *Allcard v Skinner* yields support for each of the three justifications for relief outlined above. Had he chosen to do so, Lord Hoffmann could have found support for his defendant-centred account of relief in Lindley LJ's assertion that:[13]

> to protect people from being forced, tricked or misled in any way by others into parting with their property is one of the most legitimate objects of all laws; and the equitable doctrine of undue influence has grown out of and been developed by the necessity of grappling with insidious forms of spiritual tyranny and with the infinite varieties of fraud.

However, while the judgments in *Allcard v Skinner* provide authority for different conceptions of the doctrine of undue influence, they are unified by a recognition of the relevance of both the defendant's position and conduct and the quality of the claimant's consent. One of the most famous and obvious examples of this duality is found in Bowen LJ's distinction between the

[10] *Ibid* [20].
[11] [2002] EWCA Civ 885 [1]. See also *Pesticcio* (n 4) [20] (Mummery LJ).
[12] *Attorney General* (n 6) [40]. He also cited with approval other parts of the various judgments which supported relief on the ground that there was a need to prevent the potential for abuse in relationships of trust and confidence.
[13] (1887) 36 Ch D 162.

donor's absolute freedom of disposition and the duties and restraints placed upon the donee who was in a position of influence. He asserted:[14]

> It seems to me that persons who are under the most complete influence of religious feeling are perfectly free to act upon it in the disposition of their property, and are not the less free because they are enthusiasts . . . Passing next to the duties of the donee, it seems to me that, although this power of perfect disposition remains in the donor under circumstances like the present, it is plain that equity will not allow a person that exercises or enjoys a dominant religious influence over another to benefit directly or indirectly by the gifts which the donor makes under or in consequence of such influence, unless it is shewn that the donor, at the time of making the gift, was allowed full and free opportunity for counsel and advice outside . . .

It seems, then, that an examination of the judgments handed down in *Allcard v Skinner* highlights the longevity of the uncertainty surrounding the doctrine of undue influence, rather than resolving it.

C. SETTING THE SCENE: AN INTRODUCTION TO *ALLCARD V SKINNER*

The facts of *Allcard v Skinner* are well known but are most entertainingly reprised by *The Times*:[15]

> Miss Allcard's story is not an uncommon one, and in few families is not some such tale told. Her father died in 1861 . . . In 1868 she was moved to devote herself to the religious life, and made the acquaintance of the Rev Henry Nihill . . . Events took their natural course; that which generally happens when a wandering irresolute spirit meets those fully convinced. Miss Allcard joined the sisterhood . . . For a time she was in full sympathy with her companions . . . In course of time there came weariness, disillusion, and restlessness; the spell of Mr Nihill's influence waned. Her associates became uncongenial to her, and she perhaps to them, and we have reason to conjecture that petty worldly troubles were not unknown within the convent walls, pushing some of the principles of her directors to their logical result. She quitted the convent in May, 1879, and on the 10th of the month sought rest in the Church of Rome.

This contemporary summary indicates that the religious content of the case was relevant to public attitudes towards it. *Allcard v Skinner* was relatively unusual in terms of the degree of public attention it attracted, but it was only one of a number of cases in the later nineteenth century in which religious devotees or their representatives sought to rely upon the doctrine of

---

[14] *Ibid*, 166.
[15] *The Times*, 1 February 1887.

undue influence. These cases included a variety of religious organisations and movements, including spiritualism,[16] Roman Catholicism,[17] the Plymouth Brethren,[18] and a religious community led by a maverick Anglican curate who claimed to be the new messiah.[19]

Allcard v Skinner stands out amongst these cases for a number of reasons which, taken together, may explain its contemporary and current significance. As noted above, the case attracted far more interest from the press and the public than most of the other cases of its kind. This seems odd given that it concerned an Anglican institution, while others involved far more contentious religious organisations. The attention given to the case is perhaps at the same time both explicable and unexpected given the facts and arguments upon which it was decided. Most of the cases involving religious persons were examples of clear wrongdoing by the defendant, and usually of influenced parties of a particularly vulnerable nature. In *Lyon v Home*, for example, though it was clear that the claimant was not wholly truthful, the defendant had acted in an extremely questionable manner when he accepted large cash gifts from a lonely old woman whom he had only just met. In *Whyte v Meade*,[20] the defendant had acted improperly in breaking a promise that the plaintiff would not have to take vows before her twenty-first birthday, in compelling her to take those vows, keeping her captive and denying her family intercourse with her. Similarly, in *Morley v Loughan* the defendant had accepted gifts consisting of the greater part of the property of a man who relied upon him for care and was in a feeble mental and physical condition. The defendant in that case also acted in a highly suspicious manner in destroying all evidence of his financial transactions. In *Nottidge v Prince* the defendant was the beneficiary of a will made by a woman only recently released from a lunatic asylum and subject to the delusion that he was the new messiah. By contrast, allegations that the defendant in *Allcard v Skinner* had acted immorally were rejected.[21] This meant that relief turned explicitly upon the presence and effect of the religious influences and context in question.

The case is unusual amongst later nineteenth century cases in that the judgments handed down contain clear and express statements of suspicion, caution and even antipathy towards religion and its influence. Kekewich

---

[16] *Lyon v Home* (1868) LR 6 Eq 655.
[17] *Parfitt v Lawless* (1868–72) LR 2 PD 462; *Whyte v Meade* (1840) 2 Ir Eq Rep 420.
[18] *Morley v Loughan* [1893] 1 Ch 736.
[19] *Nottidge v Prince* [1843–60] All ER Rep 764.
[20] *Whyte* (n 17).
[21] In *Parfitt* (n 17), a probate case, the claim of undue influence failed.
[22] Described as 'a strong Churchman and a Conservative' in JB Atlay, 'Kekewich, Sir Arthur (1832–1907)' revised H Mooney, *Oxford Dictionary of National Biography* (Oxford, OUP, 2004).

J,[22] for example, asserted that religious influence was 'the most subtle of all, and may be exercised by means and channels which for other purposes might be of little avail',[23] while Lindley LJ[24] stated that 'of all influences religious influence is the most dangerous and the most powerful'.[25]

Perhaps such overt statements of suspicion towards religion are explicable, given that *Allcard v Skinner* was unusual in turning explicitly upon the religious nature of the relationship and influence in question. As demonstrated above, other later nineteenth century authorities upon religious influence can be explained without reference to the religious context in which they arose. Yet in *Allcard v Skinner* that context was decisive in the determination to grant relief. Given this, statements about the power of religious influence are explicable as attempts to justify judicial intervention to set aside transactions in situations where there is a relationship of religious influence, but where no other evidence of undue influence or unconscionable conduct has been found.

D. THE WIDER RELIGIOUS CONTEXT OF *ALLCARD V SKINNER*

While statements of judicial caution towards religion are explicable as a preliminary attempt to justify judicial intervention in the case of transactions made under such influence, they also act as a prompt for an examination of the broader religious context within which the case was set. This context must have shaped, perhaps unconsciously, the attitudes of the judges concerned and the decision that the court should intervene where religious influence was evident.

1. A History of Caution in Respect of Religion and its Influences

Grim pictures of the consequences of unchecked ecclesiastical power and pretensions formed part of the popular historiography of the Tudor Reformation. They were perpetuated in the popular memory of more recent periods of constitutional strife and upheaval, including the actions of the

---

[23] *Allcard* (n 1) 151.
[24] Lindley was the son of the botanist John Lindley, who is described as 'formally an Anglican . . . [who] disliked the church, and refused all discussion of religious matters' in R Drayton, 'Lindley, John (1799–1865)' *Oxford Dictionary of National Biography* (Oxford, OUP, 2004). This dislike of the church was demonstrated in his choice of establishment for the education of his son: Lindley LJ was educated at University College School and University College London, both avowedly secular foundations.
[25] *Allcard* (n 1) 163.

non-juring clergy[26] at the time of the Glorious Revolution and the actions of Anglican bishops in voting against the Reform Act 1832.[27]

One of the most prominent manifestations of a continuing need to control ecclesiastical power and influence was found in nineteenth century defences of the constitutional position of the Church of England as an Established Church. So, for example, in its defence of Establishment the *Edinburgh Review* urged that the relationship between Church and State was the best possible means by which to suppress ecclesiastical pretensions and tendencies towards tyranny. It asserted:[28]

> Happily the existing jurisdiction of the Queen in Church and State affords to the nation an ancient and efficient barrier against the pretensions of the clerical party on the one hand, and the levelling tendencies of the enemies of religion on the other: by that alone the discipline of the Church may be maintained without encroaching on her freedom; and she may continue to unite, as she has done for three centuries, stability with progress.

Such arguments were not only advocated by those of a distinctly Protestant and anti-Catholic persuasion. Lord Selborne LC, for example, a High Churchman and one of the foremost defenders of Establishment, wrote:[29]

> Regarded apart from their higher moral and social effects, the relations between the Church of England and the State, which constitute the Establishment of the Church, are in their true nature securities taken against possible excesses of ecclesiastical power . . .

While such statements were redolent of a pervasive sense of the dangers inherent in religion and religious influence, the context in which they were given, idealising and defending the Church of England, illustrated that what was feared was not religion per se, but religion that was not constrained and channelled to proper ends. Thus, though some rejected its place in the

---

[26] Who refused to take the oath of obedience to the new king after James II fled to France.
[27] Examples of this can be seen in a general survey of articles concerning the Church of England, its courts and discipline in *The Times* during the debate about the Public Worship Regulation Act 1874. Other examples can be found in numerous articles in the Whig-influenced *Edinburgh Review*, including: 'The National Church' (1868) 128 *Edinburgh Review* 251 and 'The Ecclesiastical Jurisdiction of the Crown' (1865) 121 *Edinburgh Review* 154. See generally O Chadwick, *The Victorian Church* vol 1 (London, A and C Black, 1966); vol 2 (London, A and C Black, 1970); WR Ward, *Religion and Society in England, 1790–1850* (London, Batsford, 1972).
[28] 'The Ecclesiastical Jurisdiction of the Crown' (1865) 121 *Edinburgh Review* 180.
[29] R Palmer, *A Defence of the Church of England Against Disestablishment* (5th edn, London, Macmillan and Co, 1911) 73–4.

constitution and framework of the state, and though many advocated caution towards it, most were also convinced of the importance of religion in the life of the nation. The *Edinburgh Review*, for example, asserted the:[30]

> . . . conviction that religion is a matter of public and national concern. It is a determination that the Church shall not be in name but in reality national, and that the clergy shall obey the will of the whole nation.

Thus, while one of the factors that might have influenced attitudes towards *Allcard v Skinner* was a fear of uncontrolled religion and its influences, another was the conviction that religion was important and necessary in the life of the nation and its citizens. In the context of the later nineteenth century this led in turn to another influencing factor: the fear of religious apathy or irreligious tendencies.

2. Anxieties about Irreligious Tendencies and the Value and Necessity of Religion

While it would be wrong to characterise nineteenth century England as a secular and irreligious nation, there was much contemporary concern about what was perceived to be a rising tide of agnosticism, atheism and apathy. Such was the consternation caused by this in the early years of the nineteenth century that considerable grants were made from state funds to build churches.[31]

Agnosticism and atheism, though far from commonplace, increased slowly across all sections of society as scientific advances and liberal theology placed traditional beliefs under novel strains.[32] However, it was religious apathy and hostility among the working poor massed in the industrial cities that caused greatest concern. It was the plight of the urban poor, who were inadequately served by the traditional parochial system of the Church of England, which prompted church building initiatives, home mission societies and innovations such as outdoor services and services in music halls and theatres.[33] The need to reach and Christianise these people, and to galvanise

---

[30] 'Convocation, Parliament and the Prayer Book' (1874) 140 *Edinburgh Review* 427.
[31] Chadwick vol 1 (n 27) 46–7, 99 and 146ff.
[32] On this see generally A Symondson (ed), *The Victorian Crisis of Faith* (London, SPCK, 1970); P Corsi, *Science and Religion: Baden Powell and the Anglican Debate, 1800–1860* (Cambridge, CUP, 1988); and O Chadwick, *The Secularisation of the European Mind in the 19th Century* (Cambridge, CUP, 1975).
[33] For a panoramic picture of religious life in England at this time see generally J Wolffe, *God and Greater Britain: Religion and National Life in Britain and Ireland, 1843–1945* (London, Routledge, 1994) and Chadwick vol 2 (n 27).

the laity into action in this respect, was a war cry for Anglican Church reformers.[34] So, for example, writing a dedication at the beginning of a book advocating an increased role for the laity in Church government, one activist warned:[35]

> Such are the exigencies of the times,—such the menacing attitude assumed by the various enemies of the Crown, of the social institutions, of our Church, and even of Christianity itself,—that defensive measures, involving action among Churchmen of all orders and degrees, seem specially called for.

In large part the impetus towards efforts to Christianise the nation, and to reach the urban poor, came from religious concerns to bring people into a closer relationship with God and increase the influence of the churches. Yet the fear of such a large proportion of people living outside of the influences of Christianity was prompted in part by a belief that this struck at the very foundations of civilised society. Thus Gladstone wrote:[36]

> I suppose the low tone of spiritual life to be the source of our prevailing evils . . . I feel a strong conviction that every one of these blots would be removed, and that speedily, from our escutcheon, when a more intelligent and more active spirit of Church-membership should have been matured among us, by the serious, regular, and authorised discharge of important functions appertaining to us as the laity of the Church.

Such beliefs were influenced by the link commonly made in the nineteenth century between religion, morality and law. Once again, defences of the relationship between the Church of England and the state provided prominent examples of this. Lord Selborne, for example, in his defence of Establishment asserted that:[37]

> The mainstay of all law . . . is . . . the moral sense of mankind; religion, wherever it is truly professed, is . . . powerful in the direction and reinforcement of that moral sense.

This echoed a conviction, famously asserted by Gladstone,[38] that there was a direct link between morality and the maintenance of society; the idea

---

[34] See eg R Oastler, *The Church and the People* (London, CW Reynell, 1860).

[35] H Hoare, *Hints on Lay Co-operation. A Collection of Documents Showing How Co-operation of Clergy and Laity May be Most Readily Obtained; the Synods of the Clergy Remaining Intact, and the Royal Supremacy Inviolate* (London, Francis and John Rivington, 1858) lii.

[36] WE Gladstone, *A Letter to the Right Rev William Skinner DD, Bishop of Aberdeen, and Primus, on the Functions of Laymen in the Church* (London, John Murray, 1852) 23–4.

[37] Palmer (n 29) 73.

[38] WE Gladstone, *The State in its Relations to the Church* (4th edn, London, John Murray, 1841) 50, 60–3.

being that the society in question was founded upon law, and that law depended, in some sense, on the moral sense of man. Such arguments themselves followed in the footsteps of the maverick philosopher and poet Samuel Taylor Coleridge, who had argued that the office of the national Church was:[39]

> to form and train up the people of the country to be obedient, free, useful, organisable subjects, citizens, and patriots, living to the benefit of the State, and prepared to die for its defence. The proper object and end of the national Church is civilization with freedom . . .

In making this statement Coleridge set forth the fundamental argument that the national Church had a vital role in fitting men to be citizens of a free and civilised society, being a society ruled according to law and justice rather than force. It was in accordance with this tradition that Spencer Holland, a High Church Anglican barrister, later defended the place of an Established Church in a democratic state. A democratic state, he argued, was one based on the will of the majority. This sort of state depended on law. The law, in turn, depended upon the moral sense of man, and religion played a vital role in fostering this. In his own words:[40]

> The moral sanction of justice is necessary to the State's authority, and this alone calls forth the virtuous activity of its members. In a word, a State lives and prospers, not by wealth alone or force alone, but by morality . . .

The picture drawn is one in which a traditional distrust of uncontrolled religious bodies and influences is amalgamated with a belief that religion is necessary to a democratic state founded upon law. The fear of generalised apathy and hostility towards religion equalled the fear of clerical tyranny.

3. Changes to the Religious Composition of the Nation

In the later nineteenth century the complexity of traditional attitudes towards religion was further exacerbated by radical changes to the religious composition of the nation. That nation, though it remained predominantly Christian, was far removed in character from that of former ages. Since the Reformation of the sixteenth century England had been very largely an Anglican nation. By the later nineteenth century such religious uniformity was a distant memory. The effects of revitalised Roman Catholicism and the

---

[39] ST Coleridge, *On the Constitution of Church and State According to the Idea of Each* (3rd edn, London, William Pickering, 1869) 58.
[40] SL Holland, *The National Church of a Democratic State* (London, Rivingtons, 1886) 5.

immigration of Roman Catholics from Ireland, together with the Evangelical Revival and the growth of Protestant bodies outside of the Church of England, meant that, while still Christian, England was comprised of many different religious communities. This plurality was witnessed in the variety of religious bodies represented in the cases listed above. Only in the case of *Allcard v Skinner* itself was the institution in question part of the Church of England.[41]

The growth of religious diversity went hand in hand with constitutional reform which recognised the religious and political rights of dissenters. A series of ad hoc Indemnity Acts had for some years protected them from the civil penalties attaching, under the Tests Acts of 1673 and 1678 and the Corporation Act of 1661, to being out of conformity with the Church of England. In the nineteenth century the repeal of the Tests and Corporation Acts in 1828, the Roman Catholic Relief Act 1829, and the Jews Relief Act 1858, finally recognised Protestant Nonconformists, Roman Catholics and Jews as full citizens of England.

The admission of pluralism as a constitutional principle, taken together with the increasingly diverse character of England's religious life, posed new challenges for the judiciary. Judges had to deal with an increasingly wide range of religious bodies—not to suppress or penalise them, but to recognise and enforce their legal rights and those of their members. Judicial statements in religious influence cases illustrated both attempts to adjust to this change and, perhaps, the difficulty that some judges experienced in making that adjustment. Thus in *Lyon v Home* GM Giffard V-C took pains to avoid the impression that he was passing judgment on spiritualism. He asserted:[42]

> I know nothing of what is called 'spiritualism' otherwise than from the evidence before me, nor would it be right for me to advert to it, except as portrayed by that evidence. It is not for me to conjecture what may or may not be the effect of a peculiar nervous organisation, or how far that effect may be communicated to others, or how far some things may appear to some minds as supernatural realities, which to ordinary minds and senses are not real.

Yet he could not resist saying:[43]

> [T]he system as presented by the evidence, is mischievous nonsense, well calculated, on the one hand, to delude the vain, the weak, the foolish, and the superstitious; and on the other, to assist the projects of the needy and of the adventurer . . .

[41] For a picture of religious diversity in nineteenth century England see generally MA Noll, DW Bebbington and GA Rawlyk (eds), *Evangelicalism: Comparative Studies of Popular Protestantism in North America, the British Isles, and Beyond, 1700–1900* (Oxford, OUP, 1994) and G Parsons (ed), *Religion in Victorian Britain* vol 2 (Manchester, Manchester University Press in association with the Open University, 1988).
[42] *Lyon* (n 16) 681–2.
[43] *Ibid*, 682.

Similar evidence of a judiciary somewhat torn between the pluralism and tolerance of the age and their own beliefs and conceptions is found in the case of *Parfitt v Lawless*, which concerned an unsuccessful attempt to set aside a testamentary disposition by a Roman Catholic woman in favour of her chaplain and confessor. In seeking to prove undue influence counsel argued:[44]

> It is notorious that a Roman Catholic confessor claims the highest authority over the conscience and actions of the penitent, and such influence is progressive, and cannot be shewn at any particular moment . . . The bequest shews a morbid feeling, and there can be no doubt who raised that state of mind.

Lord Penzance, in rejecting this attempt to find the degree of compulsion and subjection necessary to found a claim of testamentary undue influence, was an exemplar of judicial impartiality. It was not enough for counsel to plead grave suspicions arising simply from the fact that the donee was a Roman Catholic priest. He held:[45]

> Unless . . . it is right and just to conclude in all cases that a Roman Catholic priest, holding the position of confessor, must be held to possess and exert over those whom he confesses such a dominion as to extinguish their free will in the disposition of their property, there were no materials . . . from which such a conclusion could be drawn in the present case, and therefore no evidence for the jury.

However, while Lord Penzance appeared immune to efforts to sway his judgment by reference to old suspicions and calumnies against Roman Catholic priests, Pigott B was less sure. Though he concurred in Lord Penzance's judgment, he did so with some hesitation and expressed the view that the case was redolent of 'suspicion' and 'mystery'.[46]

Most of the judges in *Allcard v Skinner* took some trouble to proclaim their impartiality in respect of the religious body concerned. Thus Kekewich J asserted:[47]

> There are issues of law . . . and I have considered and intend to decide them without regard to any claims which, were I not deciding them, either party might have had on my sympathy.

He concluded his judgment by stating:[48]

> I have endeavoured, to the best of my ability, to treat this as a question of law, regardless of feelings which might otherwise sway the judgment, and, so far as I

---

[44] *Parfitt* (n 17) 467.
[45] *Ibid*, 475.
[46] *Ibid*.
[47] *Allcard* (n 1) 149.
[48] *Ibid*, 156.

could control thoughts or command language, I have endeavoured to express my conclusions so as to avoid wounding susceptibilities or causing pain to any person directly or indirectly interested in the matter.

While such judicial proclamations of impartiality might justifiably have provoked suspicion that the disclaimed bias existed, certain unreported remarks by Kekewich J appeared both to confirm the presence of bias, and to show once again the difficulty that some judges experienced in their dealings with unfamiliar religious bodies. The *Church Times* reported Kekewich J, a judge famed for unfortunate and ill-considered remarks from the bench, as having given the following opinion of Miss Allcard and religious converts like her:[49]

> She gave her evidence on the whole well. It exhibited far less than I expected that deterioration of moral character which almost invariably follows change of faith, and especially religious faith.

Similarly, while Bowen LJ,[50] like Kekewich J, disclaimed any bias, he did appear to damn the institution in question by the faintness of his praise:[51]

> Now I offer no sort of criticism on institutions of this sort; no kind of criticism upon the action of those who enter them, or those who administer them. In the abstract I respect their motives . . .

4. Ritualism: A Challenge from Within the Church of England

Thus far this survey of the religious context of *Allcard v Skinner* has focused on challenges and changes coming from outside of the Established Church of England. The case, however, concerned members of an Anglican institution which was under the aegis of an Anglican clergyman well known as a protagonist of the High Church Ritualist party of the Church of England. The significance of this affiliation was unlikely to have been lost on the judges.

The High Church tradition, explained in the most simplistic of terms, was a tradition focused on institutional religion and the authority of the Church. Traditionally it was concerned most closely with justifying and

---

[49] *Church Times*, 4 February 1887. The resulting outcry in the Roman Catholic press was both indignant and vociferous. See eg *Weekly Register*, 5 February 1887.
[50] Bowen was the son of an Irish Evangelical clergyman (see the *ODNB* entry on his brother: Anon, 'Bowen, Edward Ernest (1836–1901)' revised MC Curthoys, *Oxford Dictionary of National Biography* (Oxford, OUP, 2004). His lack of enthusiasm for sisterhoods would suggest that he inherited at least some of his father's Evangelical beliefs.
[51] *Allcard* (n 1) 166.

proving the identity of the Church of England as a true and spiritually authoritative Church, and thus as part of the universal Church of which Rome was one branch. One of the chief characteristics of the High Church tradition, which arose from this quest for authority, was an emphasis upon the doctrine of Apostolic Succession. This was the belief that the Holy Spirit, bestowed upon the Apostles at Pentecost, was passed down to the present bishops of the Church by the laying on of hands during the ordination service. An emphasis upon this led to a further emphasis upon some form of sacerdotal religion, that is, religion in which the clergy mediated in some sense between individuals and God. Sacraments, which could only be performed by the ordained clergy, were thus placed at the heart of faith and worship.[52]

The ethos of the historic High Church tradition was essentially moderate and promoted unity and compromise with other elements of the Church of England. As such, though not to the taste of all, it was relatively unproblematic. In the nineteenth century, however, two different movements or revivals within the High Church marked an increasingly absolutist and less compromising development of its doctrines and traditions.[53] The earliest of these was the Oxford Movement. This was a revival of institutional religion characterised by a quest for holiness within the life and organisation of the Church. Like the historic High Church it was concerned most deeply with the authority of the Church. Crucially, however, while the historic High Church had lauded the traditional relationship between Church and State, the Oxford Movement, reacting to the exigencies and uncertainties of the time, emphasised the spiritual identity and authority of the Church outside of Establishment. This was problematic given that it was Establishment which rendered safe and acceptable the spiritual influence of the Church.[54]

The second High Church revival of the later nineteenth century, Ritualism, was in some sense continuous with the Oxford Movement and shared many of its doctrinal preoccupations. However, while the Oxford Movement focused on the internal aspects of faith and the holy life, Ritualism focused on the externals of worship—upon liturgy, ritual, ceremony and vestments. It was this manifestation and development of High Church doctrine which attracted notoriety in the later nineteenth century. Ritualism, with its militancy, open expressions of sacerdotal religion, and

---

[52] See P Nockles, *The Oxford Movement in Context: Anglican High Churchmanship, 1760–1857* (Cambridge, CUP, 1994).

[53] See P Avis, 'The Tractarian Challenge to Consensus and the Identity of Anglicanism' (1986) 9 *Kings Theological Review* 14.

[54] See generally Nockles (n 52); also O Chadwick, *The Spirit of the Oxford Movement* (Cambridge, CUP, 1990) and G Faber, *Oxford Apostles: A Character Study of the Oxford Movement* (London, Faber, 1933).

its emphasis upon the spiritual authority of the Church, was seen by many more moderate Churchmen as being extremely dangerous. It appeared to threaten the work of the Reformation and to undo the very constraints upon the Church of England which made it a 'safe' religious institution.[55]

Whatever their own religious inclination, it would have been almost impossible for the judges in *Allcard v Skinner* to have been unfamiliar with Ritualism, its chief preoccupations, and their consequences. In the later nineteenth century many Ritualist clergy appeared before secular and ecclesiastical courts as a result of their ceremonial practices and their refusal to recognise the authority of ecclesiastical courts constituted by statute and staffed by judges without ecclesiastical qualifications. Throughout the period much legislative time and effort was devoted to attempts to suppress or otherwise regulate Ritualism.[56]

E. THE PARTICULAR RELIGIOUS CONTEXT OF *ALLCARD V SKINNER*: ANGLICAN SISTERHOODS

The organised religious life was unknown in England from the dissolution of the monasteries in the sixteenth century until the Roman Catholic Relief Act of 1829 legalised convents. The years between 1829 and the end of the nineteenth century witnessed a rapid proliferation of religious communities. In 1865 the House of Commons was informed that:[57]

[I]n England and Wales there were religious houses of men in 1841 but one; of convents, 16; of colleges, 9. But in 1851 there were religious houses of men, 17; convents, 53; colleges, 10 . . . In 1865 there are religious houses of men 58; convents 187; colleges, 10: and if to the account we add 14 convents for Scotland, there are 201 convents established in this country, and possessing, to my knowledge, in the midland counties, considerable real property as well as personal estate.

In Britain the increase in religious communities, together with a new brand of Ultramontane, ebullient and very public Roman Catholicism, caused great consternation.[58] Across continental Europe many governments legislated in

---

[55] See generally LE Ellsworth, *Charles Lowder and the Ritualist Movement* (London, Darton, Longman and Todd, 1982); JEB Munsen, 'The Oxford Movement by the End of the 19th Century' (1975) 44 *Church History* 382; JS Reed, *Glorious Battle: The Cultural Politics of Victorian Anglo-Catholicism* (Nashville, Tennessee, Vanderbilt University Press, 1996).

[56] See CL Smith, *Assessing the Impact of Establishment upon Attempts to Reform Clergy Discipline, c 1840–1883* (unpublished PhD thesis, London, 2003).

[57] Parl Debs (series 3) vol 177, cols 150–1.

[58] For an introduction to religious change in the nineteenth century see generally Wolffe (n 33) and Ward (n 27).

restraint of religious communities, subjecting them to state control and inspection.[59] In Britain repeated attempts were made in Parliament, between 1850 and 1877, to secure the regulation of religious communities. Large parliamentary majorities voted for state inspection of convents in 1853 and 1854.[60] When such initiatives failed, attempts were made to secure inquiries into convents and monasteries,[61] resulting in the appointment of a select committee in 1870 to inquire into the law relating to convents and the amount of property held by them.[62]

Attempts, in 1872, 1873 and 1876, to secure a more detailed inquiry failed,[63] largely as a result of the efforts of Irish Roman Catholic MPs.[64] However, the resultant publicity given to allegations of abuses had a lasting impact.[65] The instances of abuse raised for the attention of the House added to the many stories which appeared in the press[66] and popular literature[67] throughout the nineteenth century, causing one Member of Parliament to complain that:[68]

> while on other questions the English were the most scrupulously truthful people in the world, they appeared on the single subject of religion to be wholly reckless as to the truth or falsehood of their assertions. Nothing could be lower than the standard of morality of religious journalism; nor did men care what they said of each other in social life on religious matters.

Against this backdrop of controversy, and caught up in it,[69] the Anglican sisterhoods, including that at the centre of *Allcard v Skinner*, were born. They, too, attracted suspicion and hostility from some because they were

---

[59] Newdegate MP sought a return on these foreign initiatives in 1874, 1875 and 1876. See Parl Debs (series 3) vol 218, col 1097; Parl Debs (series 3) vol 222, col 397; and Parl Debs (series 3) vol 228, col 1002.

[60] See eg Parl Debs (series 3) vols 126, 127, 128 and 129.

[61] See eg Parl Debs (series 3) vol 177.

[62] *Report of the Select Committee on Conventual and Monastic Institutions* (25 July 1870).

[63] See Parl Debs (series 3) vol 210, cols 1632ff; Parl Debs (series 3) vol 214, cols 526ff; and Parl Debs (series 3) vol 228, col 1002.

[64] The debates on convents were characterised by rifts between Irish Roman Catholics and Evangelical MPs. They were characteristically bad-tempered and irritable and initiatives were often defeated by somewhat underhand means—such as Irish MPs walking out of the House en masse, forcing the House to be counted, and leaving it without the required quorum to transact business. This may explain the anxiety of the judges not to be seen to have been influenced by the particular religious context of *Allcard v Skinner*.

[65] See eg Parl Debs (series 3) vol 177, col 1057ff (Newdegate MP).

[66] See eg *The Times*, 9 March 1865, 1 March 1869, and 31 July 1869.

[67] See eg *The Awful Disclosures of Maria Monk*, *The Cadiere Case*, and RT Reed, *Six Months' Residence in a Convent* (all published in numerous cheap editions in the nineteenth century).

[68] Parl Debs (series 3) vol 128, col 575.

[69] They were subjected, for example, to the select committee inquiry of 1870.

associated most frequently with the problematic Ritualist movement.[70] This, together with certain aspects of their life and organisation, undermined the respectability which might otherwise have attached to them as Anglican associations.[71] The remaining part of this chapter will explore the case of *Allcard v Skinner* in the context of attitudes towards the organised religious life.

1. Stolen or Undutiful Daughters

Most of the judges in *Allcard v Skinner* referred to the domestic situation that might have contributed to Miss Allcard's decision to join the sisterhood. They were also concerned with the effect that her decision had upon her family relationships. Kekewich J, for example, indicated that her decision had been influenced by her unhappiness at home. Further, he drew a link between her integration into the life of the sisterhood and her progressive alienation from the influences and ties of home and family.[72] Lindley LJ recounted the story of that process in the following terms:[73]

> In 1870 the Plaintiff became a postulant, and later in the same year a novice, and finally in August, 1871, a sister. Each of these steps was accompanied by religious services and bound the Plaintiff more and more closely to the sisterhood, and alienated her more and more from the world at large.

The court's concern with this alienation from home and family was easily explicable. It indicated that Miss Allcard was vulnerable to exploitation and unable to seek external help and guidance. However, it also echoed a popular complaint against sisterhoods. It was often alleged that they acted immorally, 'stealing' wives and daughters away from their proper domestic duties and encouraging them to live an unnatural life.[74]

The inference that sisterhoods stole women from their proper and ordained role in the household coloured their activities with a tinge of

---

[70] The community of which Miss Allcard was a former member was no exception. The advanced Ritualist practices of their spiritual director were the subject of frequent complaints to his bishop. See eg *Fulham Palace Papers (Bishop Frederick Temple)* vol 36, ff 152–5 (Lambeth Palace Library).

[71] For a historical introduction to the resurgence of the organised religious life in England see S Mumm, *Stolen Daughters, Virgin Mothers: Anglican Sisterhoods in Victorian Britain* (London, Leicester University Press, 1999) and M Hill, *The Religious Order: A Study of Virtuoso Religion and its Legitimisation in the Nineteenth-Century Church of England* (London, Heinemann, 1973).

[72] *Allcard* (n 1) 150–4.

[73] *Ibid*, 159.

[74] See eg *Archiepiscopal Papers (Archbishop Tait)* vol 200 ff 432–5 and *Archiepiscopal Papers (Archbishop Benson)* vol 17 ff 36–7 (Lambeth Palace Library).

impropriety, making it easy to infer unconscionable conduct on their part. For many the alleged wrong was compensated for by their provision of trained nurses and teachers.[75] For others, however, no charitable or benevolent work could justify the evil represented by the organised religious life.[76]

The imputation of wrongful conduct on the part of sisterhoods was potentially a double-edged sword for those seeking relief against them. Claimants were not themselves entirely untouched by charges of impropriety. *The Times*, for example, opined that:[77]

> English opinion is dead against the substitution of such artificial modes of life for those which PROVIDENCE has put in the way of most of us, if not all. It believes that in general people enter into these institutions to escape duties rather than to seek them, and to exchange the difficulties of their lot for those of their choice.

While it was willing to accept that many women entered sisterhoods because they were denied the opportunity to experience marriage, *The Times* believed that many wilfully deserted their proper duties. They had, in part, been the creators of their own difficulties. Thus, while it was easy to impute wrongdoing on the part of the sisterhoods, it was not easy to ignore the part that claimants had played in their own 'downfall'. Lindley LJ clearly felt this, admitting:[78]

> Everything that the Plaintiff did is in my opinion referable to her own willing submission to the vows she took and to the rules she approved, and to her own enthusiastic devotion to the life and work of the sisterhood. This enthusiasm and devotion were nourished, strengthened and intensified by the religious services of the sisterhood and by the example and influence of those about her. But she chose the life and work; such fetters as bound her were voluntarily put upon her by herself; she could shake them off at any time had she thought fit, and had she had the courage so to do; and no unfair advantage whatever was taken of her. Under these circumstances it is going a long way to hold that she can invoke the doctrine of undue influence . . . I am by no means insensible to the difficulty of going so far.

Further difficulties were created by the apparent contrast between the portrayal of sisters as weak defenceless women, and the very real freedom which the life and work of sisterhoods offered to their members. Most Anglican sisterhoods undertook various forms of charitable work. In this women were offered unparalleled opportunities to order their own existence, receive

---

[75] See eg the Rev William Durst (Rector of Alverstoke and Hon Canon of Winchester) speaking at the Church Congress of 1888 (*Report of Church Congress*, 1888).
[76] See eg *The Times*, 1 March 1869.
[77] *The Times*, 3 April 1876.
[78] *Allcard* (n 1) 163.

practical training, do useful work, travel, and interact with different elements of society.[79] As one woman commented:[80]

> The great bulk of unmarried women are a very helpless race, either hampered with duties, or seeking feebly for duties that do not come; miserably overworked, or disgracefully idle; piteously dependent on male relations, or else angrily vituperating the opposite sex for their denied rights or perhaps not undeserved wrongs. Between these two lies a medium class, silent and suffering, who have just enough money to save them from the necessity of earning it, just enough brains and hearts to make them feel the blankness of their life without the strength to obviate it—to strike out a career for themselves, and to cheat Fate by making it neither a sad nor useless one. It is for these stray sheep, sure to wander if left alone, but safe enough in a flock with a steady shepherd to guide them, that I open up for consideration the question of Sisterhoods.

These attributes attracted suspicion from a patriarchal society and contributed to a portrayal of those who had freely chosen the life as wilful and determined women who had abandoned their proper sphere of life and activity. Hints of this can be seen in the judgments in *Allcard v Skinner*. Kekewich J asserted that:[81]

> The more powerful influence or the weaker patient alike evokes a stronger safeguard, and there can be no case more urgently requiring it than one of the influence of a priest, director, or mother superior of a convent, on an emotional woman residing within the convent walls, and subject to its discipline.

However, he was also satisfied of Miss Allcard's capabilities and competence, stating:[82]

> Though, as I have said, an emotional woman, she [Allcard] gave her evidence calmly and shewed no lack of memory. Above all, she satisfied me that she possessed intelligence, educated intelligence above the average . . . Perhaps she acted rashly in associating herself with Miss Skinner . . . but that Miss Allcard appreciated the full meaning of devotion to the poor and a life of hard work . . . and realised that in joining the sisterhood she would 'forsake all', no one who, having watched her in the witness-box . . . can for a moment doubt.

2. Isolation and Absolute Power

The absolute and unqualified nature of the power apparently exercised by the directors of sisterhoods caused considerable concern. Their authority

---

[79] See RT Davidson and W Benham, *The Life of Archibald Campbell Tait Archbishop of Canterbury* (3rd edn, London, Macmillan and Co, 1891) vol 1, 453ff.

[80] DM Craik, *On Sisterhoods* in the Pickering Women's Classic Series edited by Elaine Showalter with textual notes by Penny Mahon (London, William Pickering, 1993) 53 (first published in *Longman's Magazine* in 1883).

[81] *Allcard* (n 1) 151.

[82] *Ibid*, 154.

was not subject to systematic supervision and there was obvious potential for abuse. Anglican sisterhoods were particularly open to criticism on this basis. They were a vibrant but unsystematic development in the life of the Church, which had developed despite its efforts and not because of them. Though belated attempts were made to remedy this,[83] they were never fully integrated into the disciplinary and regulatory structures of the parochial system.[84]

Many sisterhoods recognised the fundamental character of the objection to the lack of external checks and oversight, and sought to mitigate its effects. They frequently invited bishops to act as visitors and sought to establish structures and links which fitted into the territorial organisation of the Church.[85]

Allcard v Skinner provides an example both of objections to the absolute concentration of power, and of attempts to undermine such objections. The absolute concentration of power was manifested in the rule that forbade sisters from consulting with externs without the consent of the mother superior. This played a significant role in the judicial decisions handed down. The judges were unanimous in their distaste of it. Lindley LJ, for example, commented:[86]

> The rule against obtaining advice from externs without the consent of the lady superior invites great suspicion. It is evidently a rule capable of being used in a very tyrannical way, and so as to result in intolerable oppression.

In evidence (unsuccessful) efforts were made to mitigate the effect of this rule by demonstrating authoritative supervision. The spiritual director, Rev Nihill, asserted that the bishop had held a Confirmation service in their chapel in the previous year and that the Bishop of Bedford had visited the community.[87] Yet even had there been regular episcopal visitation it was unlikely, given a general distrust of untempered ecclesiastical authority, that it would have wholly countered the objections. A famous protagonist of state inspection of convents, for example, had previously argued that:[88]

> this exclusively clerical visitation is the very thing of which Protestants are suspicious, and not without good reason. They are equally suspicious of it as exercised by their own clergy . . .

---

[83] See eg Bishop Blomfield to Archbishop Tait (14 January 1873) in *Tait* (n 74) vol 92 ff 7–10.

[84] The bishops had to bear the brunt of this and received many complaints from disgruntled parochial clergy. See eg *Tait* (n 74) vol 187 ff 4–9.

[85] See eg *Tait* (n 74) vol 108 ff 98–9.

[86] *Allcard* (n 1) 160.

[87] *The Times*, 21 January 1887.

[88] *The Times*, 29 April 1870.

3. Physical Abuses, Convents and Sisterhoods

Stories abounded of false imprisonment, corporal punishment, and harsh physical conditions behind convent walls. Combined with the fear of absolute and unfettered religious power they formed the basis for the numerous calls for the inspection and regulation of convents.

Those calls derived much of their force from the secrecy surrounding the inner life and discipline of those institutions. This secrecy fostered supposition and fear, affirmed when news escaping from the cloister shocked and scandalised the nation. In the nineteenth century disillusioned 'escapees' wrote highly coloured accounts of the suffering and depravity common in convents. They wrote of beatings, abductions, starvation, incarceration and even murder, and alluded to the lewd behaviour of the clergy.[89]

Every so often the newspapers reported incidents that supported such allegations. So, for example, the general public was regaled with the tale of a mad Polish nun who had been incarcerated in darkness and filth for twenty years.[90] Similar tales were brought before Parliament. In a single debate Newdegate MP informed the House of instances of child abduction, breach of the law relating to lunatics, the escape and recapture of starved and cowering nuns, subterranean cells with iron bars, and secret burials.[91]

By the 1880s, however, such allegations were confined to sensational novels and the extreme Protestant press. By as early as 1876 even *The Times* was happy to admit that there was no reliable evidence to support general claims of ill usage.[92] Convents and sisterhoods had been accepted, albeit grudgingly, into the religious life of the nation.

Allcard v Skinner, occurring as in did in 1887, provided an interesting example of an appeal to the old fears regarding religious communities. In evidence Miss Allcard spoke at length of the hardships of sisterhood life, of the confiscation of her keys when she confessed that she wished to leave the community, of being compelled to do laundry[93] from dawn until the dead of night, of meagre rations, and harsh discipline. She further alleged that the spiritual director and mother superior ate rich food, that they very frequently went to Scotland at the expense of the sisterhood, and that the spiritual director was in the habit of eating breakfast with the mother superior in her bedroom.[94] The reaction to such claims, however, appeared to reflect the

---

[89] See eg *The Awful Disclosures of Maria Monk*.
[90] *The Times*, 31 July 1869.
[91] Parl Debs (series 3) vol 177, cols 1057–9.
[92] *The Times*, 3 April 1876.
[93] Counsel made much of the fact that it was the custom of the sisters to do all of their own housework.
[94] *The Times*, 21 and 22 January 1887.

increasing tolerance with which the public treated religious communities. *The Times* recorded laughter in court and the press was generally dismissive of such allegations. *The Evening Standard* commented:[95]

> We do not hear that the energetic Superior actually chastised nuns with her own hands, or even that there were any dark cells for the interment of disobedient sisters under the pavements of Mark Street Finsbury.

4. Vows and the Destruction of Private Judgement

Though dismissive of stories of systematic abuse, the public remained concerned by the effect that the religious and spiritual regime and beliefs of sisterhoods had upon the ability of inmates to exercise independent and autonomous judgement. It was this consequence of the religious life that was most to be feared and deprecated. Thus *The Times* asserted:[96]

> Convents and monasteries are very pernicious institutions, but their evil and their cruelty lie, not in bolts and iron bars, but in moral and spiritual oppression.

In part, the concerns related to the effect of any strict regime of religious worship and work upon the will of adherents. Thomas Chambers, for example, complained that within the walls of convents:[97]

> the rigours of ascetic discipline, and the burdensome rites of a ceremonial religion, are wearing away the reason and the lives of those who are entitled to be free and happy, but who are suffering miseries the nature of which is imperfectly understood, enduring penances and priestly inflictions . . .

Similar concern was evident in the judgment of Lindley LJ. He found a valid claim of undue influence based on the effect alone of the religious life and rules of the sisterhood.[98] He recognised that Miss Allcard had willingly submitted to the life and rules of the sisterhood, and that no wrongful advantage had been taken of her, but found that her enthusiasm had been strengthened by the religious devotions of the sisterhood.[99]

It was the effect of the rules and devotions of the religious life which most animated the press. *The Times* commented at length on the detrimental

[95] *Evening Standard*, 1 February 1887.
[96] *The Times*, 14 March 1865.
[97] Parl Debs (series 3) vol 127, cols 80–1.
[98] *Allcard* (n 1) 159–60.
[99] *Ibid*, 163.

effect of the organised religious life upon the free will and judgement of its adherents. In a leading article on *Allcard v Skinner*, it commented:[100]

> Life in a sisterhood . . . may favour the growth of some virtues; undoubtedly it is apt to be baneful, even fatal, to others. The process of deterioration is slow, insidious, and sure. The will grows limp and flaccid, and the moral decay which often sets in may be concealed by fervour of speech and demeanour and some of the apparent signs of strength. Certain emotions are abnormally active and absorbing; self-abnegation seems a necessity; and, unless in rare instances, there comes a time when the devotee is little more than an automaton, when the sister's speech is but the word of the director and her acts but his.

It further urged:[101]

> Imperceptibly the horizon of the devotee contracts to that which can be seen within the convent precincts; there appears to be an attractive simplicity to all duties, which in the end are merged in one supreme duty—annihilation of self and prostration before the feet of some director.

The article concluded with this warning:[102]

> How vain to hope for the free exercise of judgment in regard to anything earthly, least of all property, when, with no calm, disinterested adviser at hand, the will is paralyzed by alternate visions of bliss if only secular goods be sacrificed, and of eternal misery if a thought of the outer world and its claim visit the mind.

Such strong opinions reflected in great part an acute anxiety about the role played by vows and rules in the organised religious life. Vows were one of the most controversial and fiercely contested elements of life in a sisterhood.[103] Concerns about their effects stood at the heart of the judgments delivered in *Allcard v Skinner*. Upon profession as a full sister Miss Allcard had taken 'perpetual' vows of poverty and obedience.[104] The latter was supported by the Rule of the community, which defined it as follows:[105]

> First, it consists in regarding the voice of your Superior as the voice of God . . . The letter of your Rule and the living voice of your Superior are nothing else but helps and guides to the end that ye may more perfectly do the will of God.

---

[100] *The Times*, 1 February 1887.
[101] *Ibid.*
[102] *Ibid.*
[103] See eg Parl Debs (series 3) vol 177, col 1082.
[104] Vows of this species, at least if intended to be perpetual, were contrary to the accepted teaching of the Church of England. The taking of vows by those seeking entry to religious communities was not accepted by the Convocations of the Church until 1891. Even then vows were subject to stringent controls and limitations. See the speech of WJ Butler (Dean of Lincoln) at Church Congress in 1893 (*Reports of Church Congress*, 1893).
[105] *Allcard* (n 1) 150.

Therefore, as in seeking to obey your Superior ye seek to obey God, so in the command of your Superior ye must necessarily hear the voice of God.

In formulating their *prima facie* findings in favour of relief, the judges unsurprisingly focused closely on the vow and rule of obedience. Cotton LJ,[106] for example, emphasised the importance of the rule of obedience to the Superior[107] and deprecated the terms in which it was expressed, holding:[108]

although it is necessary that a sister should be obedient to the orders of the superior in any work like that in which the sisterhood was engaged, yet I cannot but express my doubt as to the propriety of the absolute submission required by the rules to the will of the superior, and I regret the terms in which the rules expressed the obedience which was required. Certainly the rules imposed the most absolute submission by the sisters to the superior . . .

Bowen LJ also relied on the presence of the vow and rule of obedience in finding for the claimant on the question of undue influence,[109] while Lindley LJ argued that:[110]

The vow and rule obliging implicit obedience to the lady superior, and the exhortation or command to regard her voice as the voice of God, produce very different effects on different minds. There can, however, be no question that the Plaintiff felt bound by the vow and by the rule until she emancipated herself from both of them, which she did when she left the sisterhood.

Though concerns about vows can be understood as a reflection of arguments about the importance of personal autonomy and independent judgement, it was evident that the Protestant Christian ethics and preconceptions of those examining them moulded attitudes towards them. These preconceptions included the belief that perpetual vows in general, and vows of obedience in particular, were contrary to human nature and conscience. This was an argument first employed against Roman Catholic convents.[111]

---

[106] Cotton was the son of a high Anglican family with links to such strong traditional High Church figures as Thomas Acland. See the *ODNB* entry on his father: AC Howe, 'Cotton, William (1786–1866)' *Oxford Dictionary of National Biography* (Oxford, OUP, 2004).

[107] Mumm (n 71) 32ff notes that the vow of obedience was much misunderstood and was, contrary to its popular description, primarily a promise to abide by the Rule of the community. It was only secondarily a vow of obedience to particular people, and only then insofar as the demands of those people were consonant with the constitution of the community.

[108] *Allcard* (n 1) 156.

[109] *Ibid*, 166.

[110] *Ibid*, 160.

[111] It is reminiscent of the argument for excluding Roman Catholic clergy from the civic life of the nation on the ground that compulsory celibacy was unnatural and barred the clergy from the full (family) life and relationships of society. See most famously Coleridge (n 39). For examples of similar objections being made to sisterhoods, see *The Times*, 27 July 1848 and 12 May 1853.

It appears to have had two concrete foundations. The first, directed at vows of obedience, was based on Protestant objections that such vows caused individuals to neglect their proper duty to exercise their own independent moral judgement. *The Times* urged that:[112]

> By imposing vows of irrevocable obedience to a human authority they create an artificial conscience, which gradually undermines every healthy moral principle . . . A person who has once taken such vows has no will and no judgment of his own. The most tremendous spiritual influence is brought to bear on him, not merely to submit his actions to the command of his superior, but to suppress every movement of his mind and conscience which opposes his superior's judgment.

Further, vows of absolute obedience to human authority were unacceptable because they placed the voice and authority of a human being between the individual and the will of God.[113]

The judgments in *Allcard v Skinner* reflected some of these attitudes. They seemed to be at the root, for example, of Cotton LJ's disapproval of the vow and rule of obedience. His judgment also appeared to express another essentially Protestant idea. This was the idea that God's work should be done by willing hands, and that individuals should trust God to give them the strength to do it, rather than relying on vows to hold them to the task.[114] Cotton LJ rejected the argument that relief should be denied because of the detrimental effect that it would have upon the work of the sisterhood, arguing that:

> Such work to be effectual must be done with a willing mind, and in my opinion it would be productive of evil to attempt to retain in such a society as the sisterhood, by the pressure of loss of property, those whose hearts and will are no longer in the work, and who desire to exercise their legal right of withdrawing.[115]

F. CONCLUSION

Modern judges, formulating their own accounts of relief, very frequently appeal to the judgments in *Allcard v Skinner*. Yet it has been shown that these judgments, taken out of context, add nothing new to the present

---

[112] *The Times*, 30 March 1869.

[113] This sounds like an attack on the Ultramontane Roman Catholic doctrine of Papal Infallibility. See Davidson and Benham (n 79) vol 1, 453ff.

[114] This appears to relate to a typically Evangelical notion of the world as a testing or proving ground for the soul and the faith of the individual. For an introduction to Evangelical eschatology see generally Noll *et al* (n 41) and DN Hempton, 'Evangelicals and Eschatology' (1980) 31 *Journal of Ecclesiastical History* 179. For a contemporary example of this argument see *The Times*, 5 October 1889.

[115] *Allcard* (n 1) 157.

debate. An examination, however, of the religious attitudes and controversies within which they were embedded helps to illuminate the judicial attitudes and concerns which influenced the rule laid down in that case.

The religious context revealed in this chapter has been shown to have been incredibly complex, with historical and popular fears of unrestrained religious influence combining with equally venerable traditions supporting the necessity of religion as a vital component of a society founded upon law and democratic principles. In the nineteenth century fears aroused by what was perceived to be a rising tide of irreligious sentiment combined with the difficulties created by an unprecedented degree of religious pluralism and change to contribute to a volatile mixture of attitudes. To this was added the controversy and legal strife provoked by the growth of Ritualism within the Church of England and the uncontrolled growth and development of its sisterhoods.

Each element of this tapestry can add something to our understanding of the legal rule laid down in *Allcard v Skinner*. The controversy, for example, surrounding Ritualism, and the tales of stolen daughters and unsavoury and abusive practices behind convent walls, might easily have created a feeling that Miss Skinner's sisterhood was in some sense improper. This would have helped to focus judicial attention upon the conduct of the defendant and the possibility of unconscionability. So, too, if given prominence, would stories of the physical abuse and restraint of sisters.[116] Such an emphasis might, in fact, have suggested a construction of the doctrine of undue influence similar to that of Lord Hoffmann in *Attorney General v R*, equating it to the common law doctrine of duress.

By contrast, an emphasis upon the seclusion of sisters away from the influences of family and society, together with a focus upon the absolute authority and spiritual power claimed by their superiors, would have supported the formulation of undue influence as a doctrine concerned crucially with the application of intangible influence and the protection of parties in relationships of trust and confidence. Similarly, a concentration upon the effect of the rules and vows by which sisters bound their actions would have supported a formulation of undue influence focused upon the quality of the claimant's consent and their ability to exercise independent judgement.

It appears that an examination of the religious context and content of *Allcard v Skinner* bears out the relevance of several factors in the formulation of the doctrine of undue influence. However, I would conclude by arguing that it is most strongly suggestive of an emphasis upon the autonomy of the claimant, set against a backdrop of public policy concerns relating to the potential for abuse of relationships of trust and confidence.

---

[116] See *Toogood v Clark*, *The Times* 7, 8, 12 and 13 June 1907.

In 1887 claims of physical abuse and imprisonment were treated with derision. It was factors reflecting concerns with the autonomy of the claimant and the lack of external oversight or intercourse, rather than claims of physical compulsion, restraint and abuse, which were accorded greatest significance. The evidence in *Allcard v Skinner*, the judgments and commentary upon them, focused upon the threat posed by the vows and rules of the sisterhood to the autonomy and independent judgement of its inmates. It was this, together with the danger of abuse inherent in the absolute power of the mother superior, and the lack of external advice and intercourse, which most concerned judges, counsel and commentators.

Further, in the late nineteenth century's climate of ever increasing religious toleration and pluralism, and given the express finding by the judges that the spiritual directors had not acted in an unconscionable manner, it would have been highly problematic to base relief upon unconscionability or immorality. To have done so would have been tantamount to a finding that the life of the sisterhood was itself unconscionable and immoral. This was difficult given that sisterhoods, though not to everyone's taste, were broadly accepted as part of the religious life. Such a finding would also have run counter to the spirit of toleration given that it would have amounted to an indictment of practices central to Roman Catholicism.

Finally, it can be noted that in the two claims of undue influence brought against Miss Skinner's sisterhood, claims which turned upon the evidence of many of the same witnesses, the focus of counsel's arguments and the emphasis of the evidence given were strikingly different. In *Allcard v Skinner* the evidence and arguments of counsel focused upon the rules and life of the sisterhood and their effect on the claimant's will. Allegations of wrongdoing, such as those concerning harsh treatment and holidays to Scotland, were made but were peripheral to the main issues. In contrast, in the testamentary case of *Toogood v Clarke*,[117] where counsel had to prove undue influence amounting to compulsion and an element of unconscionability on the part of the defendant, the evidence taken emphasised the alleged violent temper, irrationality and brutality of the mother superior.

A comparison with the evidence given in *Toogood v Clarke* is necessarily inconclusive. The case was settled before it went to the jury. Further, the very fact that it was a jury trial might have influenced counsel's examination of witnesses. Perhaps in the context of a jury trial counsel were more inclined to play on old fears about what happened behind convent walls. Perhaps, also, the tenor of the evidence is explicable as a reflection of the fact that twenty years on from *Allcard v Skinner* sisterhoods had become such a respectable and established part of the religious life that arguments based on their life and vows were perceived as being doomed to failure. By

---

[117] *Ibid.*

1907 the sisterhood in question was under Episcopal visitation and religious vows had been recognised and sanctioned, albeit with reservations and limitations, by Convocations. It is arguably a mark of the changed status of sisterhoods that, in 1907, the discharged jury in *Toogood v Clarke* raised a collection for the sisterhood so that its work might not be inconvenienced by the financial loss it suffered as a result of the settlement reached.[118]

Though the comparison between the cases is inconclusive, I would conclude that the different emphases of the evidence would, taken together with the other factors outlined above, suggest that insofar as *Allcard v Skinner* is a leading case on undue influence, it advances a view of that doctrine which is distinctly claimant-centred, though reinforced by clear public policy concerns about the inherent potential for abuse.

---

[118] *The Times*, 13 June 1907.

9

Sinclair v Brougham (1914)

EOIN O'DELL*

Whom the Mad would destroy, they first make Gods.[1]

A. INTRODUCTION: THE LOVE OF MONEY IS THE ROOT OF ALL EVIL?[2]

SOME ARE BORN great, some achieve greatness, and some have greatness thrust upon them.[3] As with people, so with cases. *Sinclair v
Brougham*[4] was probably born to greatness; something of a *cause
célèbre* of its time,[5] it reached a division of the House of Lords of exceptional ability, who produced forthright speeches of elegance and style, characterised by legal precision tempered with an equitable eye to a just
outcome. In many ways, therefore, it was a virtuoso performance which
deserved its plaudits and the pre-eminence which it enjoyed for more than
eighty years.[6]

---

* This chapter first appeared as 'The Case that Fell to Earth. *Sinclair v Brougham*' (1914)
in Eoin O'Dell (ed), *Leading Cases of the Twentieth Century* (Dublin, Thomson Round Hall,
2001). It is reprinted here by kind permission of the publisher.

[1] Reworking the more traditional rendering, this is Bernard Levin, of Mao Zedong: *The
Times*, 21 September 1987.

[2] 1 Timothy 6:10.

[3] W Shakespeare, *Twelfth Night*, II:5.

[4] [1914] AC 398; discussed in Lord Wright of Durley, '*Sinclair v Brougham*' in *Legal Essays
and Addresses* (Cambridge, CUP, 1939) 1; SJ Stoljar, 'Re-examining *Sinclair v Brougham*'
(1959) 22 *MLR* 21.

[5] There were full reports of the arguments and speeches in *The Times*: 9, 10, 11, 13 and 16
December 1913, and 13 February 1914. See also the notes (brief and unsigned in the contemporary style) in (1914) 48 *ILT* 294; (1914) 30 *LQR* 263 and 385.

[6] For example, Stevens has written that it was part of a 'clear' trend in private law adjudication in the House of Lords at the time when after 'a shaky beginning, the House of Lords
moved into a golden period in private law': R Stevens, *Law and Politics. The House of Lords
as a Judicial Body, 1800–1976* (London, Weidenfeld and Nicolson, 1979) 20. Again, Lord
Wright wrote that it 'has been generally regarded as an authority of first rate importance':
Wright (n 4) 1. For Hanbury, it was 'the great case of *Sinclair v Brougham*': HG Hanbury,
'The Recovery of Money' in *Essays in Equity* (Oxford, Clarendon Press, 1934) 1, 12. Stoljar
wrote that '*Sinclair v Brougham* has always, and rightly, been thought as of fundamental

History teaches us that, however they have achieved greatness, the mighty can fall, and often do, for reasons as Shakespearean as hubris or as mundane as the vagaries of fashion. Again, as with people, so with cases. *Sinclair v Brougham*, from its great height, had far to fall, and, over the last decade or so, it has fallen far. From a perspective which sees the decline as merited, the influence of the case, though profound, was at best coquettish, at worst malign. On this view, then, it has been not so much a leading case as a misleading[7] or even a bad one. Bad cases, Dworkin says, have no staying power; they don't fit, and the law—eventually—works itself pure.[8] Even if there are problems with this analysis,[9] as Allen Hutchinson has discussed,[10] nevertheless, in many ways it is an excellent description of the rise and fall of *Sinclair v Brougham*. Decided in 1914, early in the twentieth century but displaying a distinctly nineteenth century cast of mind, its comeuppance eventually arrived in the shape of the decision of the House of Lords in *Westdeutsche*,[11] decided in 1996, late in the twentieth century but heralding for the twenty-first century a fresh start and a firmer footing for the law.[12]

There are many similarities between the England of Queen Victoria and that of Margaret Thatcher. In Victorian England, what we now call classical economics were then newly in vogue and application; Thatcher's England saw the apotheosis of neo-classical economics. As a consequence, both periods saw the growth of financial markets and investment products, sophisticated by contemporary standards: investing in a building society in the former era was as sophisticated a financial transaction as investing in interest rate swaps would be in the latter.[13] Unsurprisingly, the similarity of

importance': Stoljar (n 4) 21. In Ireland, Barton J was of a similar opinion, observing that the 'celebrated speeches are the most remarkable illustration . . . of the meticulous care with which that House approaches the task of reconciling what is called "abstract justice" with the strict rule of law': *Re Cummins* [1939] IR 60, 71.

[7] With apologies to AP Herbert, *Uncommon Law. Being Sixty Misleading Cases* (London, Methuen, 1935).

[8] R Dworkin, *Taking Rights Seriously* (London, Duckworth, 1977) chapter 4; *Law's Empire* (London, Fontana, 1986); *A Matter of Principle* (Oxford, OUP, 1986) chapter 6.

[9] See eg M Cohen (ed), *Ronald Dworkin and Contemporary Jurisprudence* (London, Duckworth, 1984). For a more sympathetic treatment, see S Guest, *Ronald Dworkin* (2nd edn, Edinburgh, Edinburgh UP, 1997).

[10] AC Hutchinson, 'The Importance of Leading Cases. A Critical Analysis' in E O'Dell (ed), *Leading Cases of the Twentieth Century* (Dublin, Round Hall Sweet & Maxwell, 2000) 1. See also AC Hutchinson, 'The Last Emperor?' in A Hunt (ed), *Reading Dworkin Critically* (New York, Berg, 1992) 45.

[11] *Westdeutsche Landesbank Girozentrale v Islington LBC* [1996] AC 669.

[12] It might be said that, in this area of the law at least, there has been, as in history, a short twentieth century. See E Hobsbawm, *The Age of Extremes. The Short Twentieth Century 1914–1991* (London, Abacus, 1995) 5–11.

[13] "The impetus leading to the formation of these societies was not so much the desire of the 'industrious class' to obtain funds by 'periodical subscriptions' (as stated in the preamble of the Building Societies Act, 1836), but the desire on the part of capitalists to invest at a higher rate of interest than the usury laws then allowed": Stoljar (n 4) 21–2, n 5 referring to Lord Cranworth LC's decision in *Fleming v Self* (1854) 3 De GM & G 997, 43 ER 390.

economic background gave rise to similarity of economic legal problems. In each case, some of these flagship modes of investment would founder on the rock of legal incapacity: in *Sinclair v Brougham*, a building society operated as an *ultra vires* bank; in *Westdeutsche*, a local authority had entered into *ultra vires* interest rate swaps.

What *Sinclair v Brougham* and *Westdeutsche* have in common, therefore, is that they arise out of, and seek solutions for, sophisticated financial transactions that went wrong. Operating successfully, such sophisticated financial instruments can generate untold wealth; George Soros famously made a fortune on the European currency markets at a time of great volatility in 1992.[14] When things go wrong, there is great scope for financial destruction. Nick Leeson famously lost a fortune on the Far Eastern derivatives markets and bankrupted Barings Bank in the process in 1995.[15] There are many who would see in these cautionary tales some support for the biblical injunction[16] that the love of money is the root of all evil. Unlike Leeson and Barings, however, the transactions underlying *Sinclair v Brougham* and *Westdeutsche* went wrong, not because of financial incompetence, but because of the legal incapacity of a major player in each transaction. The problem was of the law's making, and, on this view, it was incumbent upon the law to find an appropriate solution. *Sinclair v Brougham* was its first attempt, denying a legal and personal remedy to the depositors in the *ultra vires* bank, but giving them a partial equitable proprietary one. In truth, this was not a particularly good solution; indeed, in some quarters, it came to be demonised as the root—if not of all evil—then at least of much legal error. *Westdeutsche*, on the other hand, seems to have made a much better fist of things, affording a legal and personal remedy to the local authority but denying an equitable proprietary one, and in the process correcting many of the errors perpetuated by *Sinclair v Brougham*, though not without arousing controversies in its turn.

The controversies of *Sinclair v Brougham* are the theme of this paper, and the approach taken is purely formal[17] to demonstrate the decline of the once-great case by considering the course of the litigation in the case (part

[14] Betting against sterling, he made US $1 billion when the pound collapsed on 16 September 1992. See eg 'Turning Dollars into Change' *Time Magazine*, 1 September 1997.

[15] Trading derivatives on the Singapore International Monetary Exchange, Nick Leeson lost more than US $1 billion of Barings' money. See eg 'Going for Broke' *Time Magazine*, 13 March 1995. Less than three months earlier, Orange County, California, having suffered a US $1.5 billion loss in a US $20 billion derivatives investment pool, had filed for bankruptcy protection in the largest municipal collapse in US history. See eg 'The California Wipe-out' *Time Magazine*, 19 December 1994.

[16] On the legal fate of another, more famous 'biblical injunction [that] you should love your neighbour' ([1932] AC 562, 580 (Lord Atkin)), see S Hedley, '*M'Alister (or Donoghue) (Pauper) v Stevenson* (1932)' in O'Dell (n 10) 64.

[17] Though, I hope, not formalist. Although I am more convinced by the theories which have replaced it than by those embodied in the case itself, the decline of *Sinclair v Brougham*, like its original rise, was by no means inevitable.

B), the unsuccessful personal claim (part C) and the successful proprietary one (part D), and by assessing the greatness to which the case was born but from which it has now been decisively evicted (part E), all the while considering the corrective impact of the *Westdeutsche* case but leaving for another day (and perhaps for the leading cases of the twenty-first century[18]) the resolution of many of the replacement *Westdeutsche* controversies.

B. THE *SINCLAIR V BROUGHAM* LITIGATION: DIARY OF A MADMAN?[19]

It all began innocuously enough with the formation, in 1851, of a building society, the Birkbeck Permanent Benefit Building Society. As its business expanded, it increased its deposits and began also to operate what soon became 'an extensive banking business'.[20] Hence, from 1871, it began to call itself the Birkbeck Bank, and by 1910 the bank was 'much the larger part of the enterprise'.[21] However, it was contrary to the provisions of the Building Societies Act 1836 for a building society to carry on the business of a bank, and its borrowing from its depositors was therefore *ultra vires*.[22] That became apparent in 1911 when the Society was wound up.[23] The outside creditors,[24] and those shareholders whose shares were to have matured, were paid off. What remained was enough to pay either the permanent shareholders or the depositors, but not both; and the liquidator sought directions.

The depositors argued that their deposits were money had and received by the society to their use, or represented money which they had always owned and which therefore had never properly formed part of the society's assets and could be traced into the hands of the society's liquidator; the intended effect of these arguments was to constitute the depositors as creditors who would then be paid off ahead of the shareholders. On the other hand, the shareholders argued that the deposits were *ultra vires* and invalid

---

[18] Though see, generally, P Birks and FD Rose (eds), *Lesson of the Swaps Litigation* (London, Mansfield Press/LLP, 2000).

[19] With apologies to Nikolai Gogol, *Diary of a Madman,* R Wilks (trans) (Harmondsworth, Penguin, 1972) and G de Maupassant, *The Diary of a Madman, and other Tales of Horror,* A Kellett (trans) (London, Pan Books, 1976).

[20] *Sinclair* (n 4) 439 (Lord Parker).

[21] *Ibid*, 411 (Viscount Haldane LC).

[22] *Ibid*, 411 (Viscount Haldane LC), 418 (Lord Dunedin), 439 (Lord Parker), and 451 (Lord Sumner).

[23] 'In 1911, however, there was a run on the bank which drove it into liquidation': Stoljar (n 4) 21. 'Heavy losses were incurred and the society went into liquidation': Wright (n 4) 4. See too *Re Birkbeck Permanent Benefit Building Society* [1912] 2 Ch 183, 187.

[24] These outside creditors were 'inconsiderable in number and value': *Sinclair* (n 4) 427 (Lord Dunedin) and, as such, 'they were rightly paid, under the circumstances of the actual case, and had they not been, they would stand, after the expenses of the liquidation, at first in the ranking': *ibid*, 437 (Lord Dunedin).

and could therefore give rise to no obligation on the part of the Society to repay them. At first instance and in the Court of Appeal,[25] the remaining shareholders prevailed over the depositors,[26] but the House of Lords divided the spoils between them, ordering that the liquidator should apportion the entirety of the remaining assets between depositors and remaining shareholders in proportion to the amounts originally paid by them.[27] They reached this conclusion, not on the basis of the depositors' legal personal claim—the money had and received argument, which was dismissed, but on the basis of the depositors' equitable proprietary claim—the tracing argument.

The outcome in *Sinclair v Brougham* seems fair. The means by which it was reached seemed unimpeachable at the time; but, after *Westdeutsche*, very little, if anything, of the reasoning in the speeches now remains. That case also began innocuously enough, with local authorities seeking to take advantage of the financial markets, and in particular of interest rate swaps, to generate extra income at a time when other sources of funding were capped. In *Hazell v Hammersmith and Fulham LBC*[28] the House of Lords held that interest rate swaps transactions were *ultra vires* local authorities. In *Westdeutsche*, at first instance,[29] Hobhouse J held that a net payor on such an *ultra vires* swap—in this case a bank—was entitled to restitution of the net payment. He reached this conclusion on the basis of a legal personal claim, notwithstanding *Sinclair v Brougham*. The Court of Appeal affirmed.[30] The defendant

---

[25] *Re Birkbeck Permanent Benefit Society* [1912] 1 Ch 183 (Neville J and CA).

[26] At first instance, Neville J ordered that the assets be applied: first, in payment of costs; second, in paying outside creditors; third, in paying off the shareholders; and fourth, what remained, proportionately, to depositors. The Court of Appeal, by a majority, affirmed. 'This order [had] the effect, so far as the . . . shareholders [were] concerned, of paying them in full': *Sinclair* (n 4) 428 (Lord Dunedin). As Lord Wright pointed out, this 'was clearly illogical . . . Logically the shareholders if entitled to priority would have been entitled to divide up *all* the remaining assets of the society': Wright (n 4) 5 (emphasis added). He is followed in this by Oakley who also thought it 'difficult to follow the logic of this order': AJ Oakley, 'The Prerequisites of an Equitable Tracing Claim' (1975) 28 *CLP* 64, 75 n 47. However, Neville J had followed the Court of Appeal's earlier decision in *Re Guardian Permanent Benefit Building Society* (1883) 23 Ch D 440 (varied in part, sub nom *Murray v Scott* (1883–4) 9 App Cas 519, but not in any particular which would affect Neville J's order), and he must have been influenced by the concern that that would later motivate the House of Lords, that to have held entirely in favour of the shareholders and entirely against the depositors, though logical, would have been unjust.

[27] After the decision in the Court of Appeal, the liquidator had made payments accordingly; after the decision of the House of Lords, it was clear that they were overpayments, and in a subsequent action, Neville J held that he was entitled to recover them as mistaken payments: *Re Birkbeck Permanent Building Society* [1915] 1 Ch 91.

[28] [1992] 2 AC 1.

[29] [1994] 4 All ER 890 (Hobhouse J and CA).

[30] *Ibid* (Hobhouse J and CA); [1994] 1 WLR 938 (CA).

local authority did not appeal this matter to the House of Lords, but their Lordships plainly considered it to be right, and overruled *Sinclair v Brougham* on this point. Such a personal action carried an award of only simple interest; but the bank wanted compound interest, which would have been available had there been an equitable claim. So it sought to rely on the successful equitable claim in *Sinclair v Brougham*. This hare had been started in the Court of Appeal,[31] was given added legs in the House of Lords by the enthusiasm of Viscount Haldane LC in particular,[32] and the argument prevailed at first instance and in the Court of Appeal in *Westdeutsche*. However, the local authority did appeal this matter to the House of Lords, and succeeded in having *Sinclair v Brougham* overruled on this point as well.

It is clear, therefore, that *Sinclair v Brougham* made two entries in the diary of legal madness: denying a legal personal claim, and awarding an equitable proprietary one instead. They—and their quite proper repudiation in *Westdeutsche*—are treated in the next two parts.

C. THE PERSONAL CLAIM: THE ONCE AND FUTURE KING

The depositors claimed that they had paid the society on foot both of a mistaken belief in the society's capacity to accept deposits as a bank and for a consideration which had wholly failed, so that their deposits amounted to money had and received by the society to their use, and the society was thus under a duty to repay the sums deposited. They relied upon a tradition which conceived of the action for money had and received as a means of achieving restitution and preventing unjust enrichment. It drew its inspiration from the judgment of Lord Mansfield in *Moses v Macferlan*,[33] who took an open-textured and flexible approach to the action,[34] and the tradition constructed upon it saw the implied contract as no more than a fiction which should have faded away with the mid-nineteenth century reforms of the procedure[35] to which it had given rise, to be replaced with an obligation imposed by law to make restitution, just as the obligation to compensate for tortious behaviour is imposed by law.

---

[31] The Court of Appeal, in having recourse to equity, 'started a line of reasoning which was to become most troublesome' (Stoljar (n 4) 23) and which would attain 'new levels of complexity' in the House of Lords (*ibid*, 27).

[32] *Sinclair* (n 4) 404 *arguendo*.

[33] (1760) 2 Burr 1005; 97 ER 676.

[34] *Ibid*, 2 Burr 1008–10; 97 ER 678–9; see also n 127.

[35] Eg Common Law Procedure Act 1852; Supreme Court of Judicature Act 1873.

Such arguments were not necessarily doomed to failure.[36] Indeed, just before the House of Lords came to decide *Sinclair v Brougham*, in *Re Irish Provident Assurance Co*,[37] the Court of Appeal in Ireland held that an insurance company which had carried on an *ultra vires* life assurance business could, in principle, recover back *ultra vires* payments, subject to making counter-restitution of the premiums received, which was a complete defence on the facts. But this view of the law was never going to command the assent of Lord Sumner. As Hamilton LJ in the Court of Appeal the previous year, he had dismissed this view of the action for money had and received:[38]

> whatever had been the case 146 years ago [when *Moses v Macferlan* was decided], we are not now free in the twentieth century to administer that vague jurisprudence which is sometimes attractively styled 'justice as between man and man'.

In the House of Lords in *Sinclair v Brougham*, he returned to this theme:[39]

> I cannot but think that Lord Mansfield's language has been completely misunderstood . . . I think it is evidence that Lord Mansfield did not conceive himself to be deciding that this action was one in which the courts of common law administered 'an equity' in the sense in which it was understood in the Courts of Chancery. . . . There is no ground left for suggesting as a recognisable 'equity' the right to recover money *in personam* merely because it would be the right and fair thing that it should be refunded to the payer.

Rejecting the open-textured view of the action for money had and received should not of itself have necessarily been fatal to the depositors' claim. Yet the House of Lords unanimously held that it could not be maintained. On their Lordships' view, the common law of obligations had only two branches—tort and contract—within which an obligation to repay of the sort relied upon by the depositors against the society had to be accommodated.

---

[36] 'Brice, the nineteenth-century English authority, in his treatise on *Ultra Vires*, acknowledged that no action could be brought to enforce an *ultra vires* agreement, but then went on to state as a general proposition of English law that benefits received by the corporation under such agreements must be restored': PD Maddaugh and JD McCamus, *The Law of Restitution* (Aurora, Ontario, Canada Law Book Inc, 1991) 327, citing SW Brice, *Ultra Vires* (3rd edn, London, Stevens & Haynes, 1895) 641 ff. Thus, for example, in *Re Phoenix Life Assurance* (1862) 2 J & H 441, 70 ER 1131 and *Flood v Irish Provident Assurance* (1912) 46 ILTR 214, [1912] 2 Ch 597n, it was held that premiums paid to an insurance company on *ultra vires* policies were recoverable for total failure of consideration. See also *Confederation Life Association v Howard* (1894) 25 OR 197 where money paid on *ultra vires* debentures was recovered as money had and received.
[37] [1913] 1 IR 352. See E O'Dell, 'Incapacity' in Birks and Rose (eds) (n 18) 113, 146–50.
[38] *Baylis v Bishop of London* [1913] 1 Ch 127, 140; compare his comments just a short time later sitting in the Court of Appeal in *R Leslie v Sheill* [1914] 3 KB 607, 613; though cf some less critical views on his part as Hamilton J in *Evanson v Crooks* (1911) 106 LT 264, 269.
[39] *Sinclair* (n 4) 454–6 (Lord Sumner). As a consequence, Scrutton LJ described the history of the action for money had and received as a 'history of well-meaning sloppiness of thought': *Holt v Markham* [1923] 1 KB 504, 513.

Such an obligation, described as *quasi-contractual*, could only be imposed on the society by means of a contract implied by law; and since the society could not in fact make such a contract, one could not be imposed by law. The point is summed up best in a sentence in the speech of Lord Parker of Waddington: 'The implied promise on which the action for money had and received is based would be precisely that promise which the company or association could not lawfully make.'[40] Other speeches were more expansive. Viscount Haldane LC, with whom Lord Atkinson concurred, put it thus:[41]

> [So] far as proceedings *in personam* are concerned the law of England really recognizes (unlike the Roman law) only actions of two classes, those founded on contract and those founded on tort. When it speaks of actions arising *quasi ex contractu* it refers merely to a class of action in theory based on a contract which is imputed to the defendant by a fiction of law. The fiction can really only be set up with effect if such a contract would be valid if it really existed. . . . Consideration of the authorities has led me to the conclusion that the action [for money had and received] was in principle one which rested on a promise to pay, either actual or imputed by law. . . . I think that it must be taken to have been given only . . . where the law could consistently impute to the defendant at least the fiction of a promise.

Lord Dunedin's reasoning on this point was similar:[42]

> The English common law has various actions which . . . are divided into actions in respect of contract and of tort . . . . [The] English law, having no *quasi contract*, got over the difficulty in such cases as the action for money had and received by the fiction of a contract. . . . That there can be no resulting proper contractual obligation [in the case of an *ultra vires* contract] is clear . . . . It is here that the difficulty comes in extending the action for money had and received to such a case. . . . [How] is it possible to say that there is a fictional contract which is binding in circumstances in which a real contract is not binding? . . . I have come to the conclusion that the action for money had and received cannot be stretched to meet the situation.

But the most strident and striking rhetoric rejecting the common law actions was that of Lord Sumner:[43]

> All these causes of action are common species of the genus assumpsit. All now rest, and long have rested, upon a notional or imputed promise to repay. The law cannot *de jure* impute promises to repay, whether for money had and received or otherwise, which, if made *de facto*, it would inexorably avoid.

---

[40] *Ibid*, 440 (Lord Parker).
[41] *Ibid*, 415–7 (Viscount Haldane LC). Heuston described this speech as 'an authoritative survey of the scope of the doctrine of restitution or quasi-contract': RFV Heuston, *Lives of the Lord Chancellors* (Oxford, Clarendon Press, 1964) 239.
[42] *Sinclair* (n 4) 432–4 (Lord Dunedin).
[43] *Ibid*, 452 (Lord Sumner).

The persuasive power of an opinion is an important factor in establishing a judgment as leading,[44] and this passage has an epigrammatic[45] quality rendering it instantly memorable and quotable. I remember being struck by this passage as a student, and it has never failed to grab my attention whenever I have encountered it since. I do not believe myself to be alone in this: many of my own students quote it as easily as they remind me that promissory estoppel acts as a shield and not a sword;[46] it has been followed in the House of Lords,[47] and it was chosen as representative of the reasoning of the House of Lords on this point by Hobhouse J at first instance[48] and by Lord Goff in the House of Lords[49] in *Westdeutsche*.[50] This passage is by no means the whole of the reason for the importance of *Sinclair v Brougham*, but it must surely have played a not insignificant part.

The speeches are working on many levels: the rejection of a flexible approach to unjust enrichment, the denial of restitution as a third head of obligations separate from contract and tort, the insistence on restitutionary obligations being imposed by means of an implied contract, and the reification of the implied contract fiction in the conclusion that if a valid contract could not have existed in fact, one could not be implied in law. Even though each conclusion does not flow inexorably from the one before—the rejection of a flexible approach to unjust enrichment does not necessarily entail the denial of restitution as a third head for obligations, any more than subscribing to an implied contract explanation for the obligation to make restitution does not entail the conclusion that a contract cannot be implied if it could not have existed in fact—they have come to be regarded as a package deal: buy one, get the others free. And their heady mix proved extraordinarily potent: there were many buyers at the time and subsequently. Thus, its rejection of *Moses v Macferlan* and its strong version of the implied contract theory were sometimes enthusiastically embraced, as in *Holt v Markham*,[51] and, in more temperate language, in *Morgan v Ashcroft*.[52]

---

[44] See eg W Twining, *Rethinking Evidence* (London, Blackwell, 1990) 219, especially his discussion of Lord Denning (232–8).

[45] Wright (n 4) 24.

[46] *Coombe v Coombe* [1951] 2 KB 215, 224 (Birkett LJ), adopting the 'vivid' description given by counsel for the husband; on which see O Breen, 'Dusting Down Equity's Armour. *High Trees* (1947) in Perspective' in O'Dell (n 10) 164, text with n 39.

[47] *Boissevain v Weil* [1950] AC 327, 341 (Lord Radcliffe).

[48] [1994] 4 All ER 980, 919.

[49] *Westdeutsche* (n 11) 687, describing it as a 'much-quoted passage'.

[50] See also *United Australia Ltd v Barclays Bank Ltd* [1941] AC 1, 45 (Lord Porter); *Fibrosa Spolka Akcyjna v Fairbairn Lawson Combe Barbour* [1943] AC 32, 64 (Lord Wright) (on which see text to n 68).

[51] [1923] 1 KB 504, 513 (Scrutton LJ). And, in an excellent example of the reification of the implied contract, it became common to include claims based upon so called quasi contracts within those paragraphs of RSC Order 11 covering contracts: *Bowling v Cox* [1926] AC 751. See A Briggs, 'Jurisdiction under Traditional Rules' in FD Rose (ed), *Restitution and the Conflict of Laws* (Oxford, Mansfield Press, 1995) 49.

[52] [1938] 1 KB 49, 62 (Lord Greene MR). Compare *Re Cleadon Trust* [1939] Ch 286, 299–300 (Lord Greene MR), 315 (Scott LJ), and 319 (Clauson LJ); *Re Diplock* [1948] Ch

Hanbury, for example, wrote that to 'allow an action for money had and received here would be unhistorical and nonsensical'.[53]

Sinclair v Brougham seemed, therefore, to have put paid to the possibility of restitutionary remedies for *ultra vires* contracts, and many subsequent cases simply set up a dichotomy between enforceability and non-enforceability of the *ultra vires* transaction, without asking whether there are any legal alternatives to enforceability. Remedies consequent upon non-enforceability are simply not considered. Indeed, this has led, on at least one occasion, to the *non sequitur* that because the contract is unenforceable, there must be no remedy. In the Irish case of *Re Cummins*[54] Johnston J held that the 'theory of the law is that the whole transaction is null and void and can give rise to no legal rights or claims whatever'.[55]

But these conclusions did not go unchallenged. Lord Wright led the counter-charge against this aspect of *Sinclair v Brougham*,[56] defending the concept of unjust enrichment,[57] arguing for restitution as a third head of obligations,[58] and deprecating the misuse of the language of *quasi-contract*[59] and of the implied contract fiction[60] as:[61]

465, 480 (Lord Greene MR). Similarly, in cases such as *Hirsch v Zinc Corp* (1917) 24 CLR 34, *Smith v William Charlick* (1924) 34 CLR 38, and *Turner v Bladin* (1951) CLR 463, the implied 'contract theory was dutifully adopted by the High Court of Australia': S Erbacher, *Restitution Law: Text, Cases and Materials* (London and Sydney, Cavendish, 1998) 7; see also K Mason and J Carter, *Restitution Law in Australia* (Sydney, Butterworths, 1995) 20.

[53] Hanbury (n 6) 12.

[54] *Re Cummins* [1939] IR 60.

[55] *Ibid*, 70.

[56] In Wright (n 4), which Lord Atkin subsequently described as 'a valuable contribution to the discussion': *United Australia* (n 50) 26.

[57] Lord Wright of Durley, 'The Study of Law' in *Legal Essays and Addresses* (Cambridge, CUP, 1939) 387, 404: 'not implied contract but unjust enrichment'. Similarly, a 'careful study of the English reported cases at law or in equity will, I think, show that the basis of the doctrine of unjust enrichment is, as has been so often here stated, that the defendant has received some property of the plaintiff or received some benefit from the plaintiff, for which it is just (as shown in the precedents) that he should make restitution': Wright (n 4) 26.

[58] '[Unjust] enrichment has no relation as a juristic conception with contract at all . . . the dichotomy [of contract and tort] does not correspond to any juristic classification . . . . even if the term "contract implied by law" is retained as meaning quasi-contract, and if the equitable rights and remedies are ignored, still "contracts implied by law" signify a third head apart from contract and tort. The specific character of restitution as a legal category may be disguised but cannot be destroyed by confusing and inappropriate terminology': Wright (n 4) 15–16. 'I cannot understand why it is not more generally recognised that quasi-contract or restitution involves a definite system of rules, just like the rules of contract or tort': ibid, 26. See also Lord Wright of Durley, 'The Common Law in its Old Home' in *Legal Essays and Addresses* (Cambridge, CUP, 1939) 327, 345–6; Wright (n 57) 403.

[59] The term *quasi-contract* 'is not very apt, but it does no harm if it is understood to be a label, and to refer to the peculiarity of the action, though there is no promise in fact, the defendant is ordered by the court to pay the money just as much as if he had promised to pay it': Wright (n 58) 356; see also *ibid*, 384. That is, the substance is the prevention of unjust enrichment: *ibid*, 358.

[60] 'The old common lawyers [who utilised the fiction] were a robust people, and if a fiction was convenient under the old rigid forms of pleading they did not worry about its correspondence to reality or to juristic concepts. But it does not follow that they did not realise the true

... such unfortunate and misleading terminology. The room of the fiction is better than its company. Not only is it undesirable that English law should be defaced by superfluous solecisms and illogical phrases, but the ghost of this fiction has, I fear, actually delayed and hindered in England the systematic and scientific study of this important branch of law. I should like to see it forgotten for good and all here and now. But it is certainly doomed. Another generation of lawyers will have forgotten it, or if they ever remember it, will wonder why people troubled to discuss it except as a matter of obsolete history.

He cited authorities from 1699[62] to 1908[63] in which the obligation to make restitution was seen simply as one imposed by law and not by means of an implied contract, and he continued, rather disingenuously, that he did not believe 'that the House of Lords in *Sinclair v Brougham* had any intention of overruling these authorities';[64] and he sought to limit the fallout from the speeches in *Sinclair v Brougham*:[65]

it is the decision which is the precedent. Here no decision was based on the Lords' views about legal history or about the old forms of action. It was already settled that in such a case as that before them the legal claim did not lie.[66] ... Decisions,

---

nature of the concept': Wright (n 4) 20. Again, 'the old common lawyers did not always take their fictions seriously. They used them for their practical value': Wright (n 4) 30. Hence, 'a fiction was adopted in the past merely as a device to justify a court in less enlightened days when it was applying a novel doctrine and was doing so on the analogy of, and by way of extending, a familiar rule. Hence the crop of absurd and outrageous fictions, now mostly forgotten, which it is almost indecent to exhume, fictions which can never have deceived anybody': Wright (n 58) 384–5. See also (1949) 65 *LQR* 295. See now, generally, JH Baker, 'The History of Quasi-Contract in English Law' in WR Cornish *et al* (eds) *Restitution: Past, Present and Future* (Oxford, Hart Publishing, 1998) 37, 40–2; and DJ Ibbetson, *A Historical Introduction to the Law of Obligations* (Oxford, OUP, 1999) chapter 14.

[61] Wright (n 4) 33.
[62] *Starke v Cheesemann* (1699) 1 Ld Raym 538; 91 ER 1259 (Holt CJ).
[63] *Nash v Inman* [1908] 2 KB 1.
[64] Wright (n 4) 22, see also *ibid*, 24: 'the House of Lords cannot have intended to overrule the established authorities'. He also refers to the later House of Lords decision of *Jones v Waring & Gillow* [1926] AC 670 as not setting the restitutionary obligation imposed in that case on an implied contract; ironically, he relies in particular on Lord Sumner's speech in that case ([1926] AC 696) and he even manages to extract some solace from *Baylis v Bishop of London* [1913] 1 Ch 127, 140 (Hamilton LJ) despite the comments in that case set out at the text with n 38. As Tunney points out in 'The Search for Justice. *Mabo* (1992)' in O'Dell (n 10) 445, text after n 9, the devil can cite scripture for his purpose, and there is something of that in Lord Wright's selective citation of Lord Sumner's views in *Baylis*, *Jones* and the later *Hirji Mulji v Cheong Yue Steamship Co* [1926] AC 497, 510 and even *Sinclair v Brougham* itself (!): Wright (n 4) 25, citing [1914] AC 458.
[65] Wright (n 4) 32.
[66] *Ibid*, 19. That the legal personal claim did not lie had been settled in *Re National Permanent Building Society ex p Williamson* (1869) 5 Ch App. 309; *Cunliffe Brooks & Co v Blackburn and District Benefit Building Society* (1884) 9 App Cas 857; *Baroness Wenlock v River Dee Co* (1885) 10 App Cas 354, discussed by Lord Parker in *Sinclair* (n 4) 440, and referred to by Lord Wright earlier in the essay: Wright (n 4) 16. However, in the consequent remedy fashioned in *Cunliffe Brooks*, it was overruled in *Sinclair v Brougham*, and this entire line of authority, holding against the personal claim, is no longer good law after *Westdeutsche*.

I repeat, are decisions. Views on legal history are not legal decisions. They may form the basis of decisions, though they did not in *Sinclair v Brougham*.

In the *Fibrosa* case, he went even further:[67]

> [Serious] legal writers have seemed to say that the words of Lord Sumner in *Sinclair v Brougham* closed the door to any theory of unjust enrichment in English law. I do not understand why or how. It would indeed be a *reductio ad absurdum* of the doctrine of precedents. In fact the common law still employs the action for money had and received as a practical and useful, if not complete or ideally perfect, instrument to prevent unjust enrichment . . .

There is a large measure of wishful thinking in all of this. Lord Wright's essay on the case had drawn from Holdsworth's pen[68] a strong defence of *Sinclair v Brougham* in all its rigour, and, from his reference to 'serious legal writers', Lord Wright must have had Holdsworth's defence in mind in that passage from *Fibrosa*. In fact, Lord Sumner's words do fairly bear the interpretation rejected by Lord Wright but defended by Holdsworth. Whether the law ought to maintain that position is an entirely different matter. It is now clear that it has decided not to. First, in England, there are some examples of restitution of benefits transferred pursuant to an *ultra vires* contract notwithstanding *Sinclair v Brougham*.[69] More than that, an alternative

---

[67] *Fibrosa* (n 50) 64.

[68] See Sir WS Holdsworth, 'Unjustifiable Enrichment' in *Essays in Law and History*, AL Goodhart and HG Hanbury (eds) (Oxford, Clarendon Press, 1946) 238 (see also (1932) *JSPTL* 41; (1937) 53 *LQR* 302, 304). The editors of this collection of Holdsworth's papers point out in their preface that 'this article . . . is in the nature of reply to Lord Wright's paper on *Sinclair v Brougham*': *ibid*, xiii. And Lord Wright seems to have been taken aback by it. In his preface to his *Legal Essays and Addresses* (Cambridge, CUP, 1939) he confesses that he had not 'appreciate[d] what criticism and opposition my humble extra-judicial expression of opinion would provoke' (xii). He goes on: 'in the United States, as I understand, it is generally accepted that *quasi-contract*, or restitution as the Restatement calls it, is a separate category in the law . . . Why, I wonder, is the view so strongly held in England that in the Common Law there are not three but only two categories of civil liability, contract and tort? That view has recently received its most complete expression in a recent article in the *Law Quarterly Review*, but, with all the respect that I feel for that great lawyer, I cannot in this matter agree with his arguments' (xiv).

[69] See generally AL Street, *The Doctrine of Ultra Vires* (London, Sweet & Maxwell, 1930) 376–89: '. . . restitution is a wholly distinct relief. It is, if possible, granted in all cases of true *ultra vires* to all parties affected by the finding of nullity' (376). Hence, parties 'to an *ultra vires* transaction will so far as possible be restored to their original position' (377, citing, *inter alia*, *Re Irish Provident Assurance Co* [1913] 1 IR 352, on which see n 37). Thus for example, in *Craven Ellis v Canons* [1936] 2 KB 403 a managing director whose appointment was *ultra vires* nevertheless got a *quantum meruit*; in *Linz v Electric Wire Co of Palestine*, Lord Simonds for the Privy Council did not 'question the general proposition that, where an *ultra vires* issue of shares has been made, the subscribers are entitled to recover their money' in an action for money had and received for total failure of consideration ([1948] AC 371, 377); in *Bell Houses Ltd v City Wall Properties Ltd* [1966] 1 QB 207, 226, Mocatta J at first instance affirmed the availability of both the *quantum meruit* and the action for money had and received; and in *Simmonds v Heffer* [1983] BCLC 298 an *ultra vires* political donation was recovered. A peculiar species of subrogation—of which the leading Irish example is *Re Lough Neagh Ship Co*

view of the history of the implied contract has judicially prospered,[70] the fiction has been rejected in favour of a largely descriptive principle against unjust enrichment, and restitution has become established as a third head of obligations alongside tort and contract.[71] As Keane J put it in the *Bricklayers' Hall* case:[72]

> It is clear that, under our law, a person can in certain circumstances be obliged to effect restitution of money or other property to another where it would be unjust for him to retain the property. Moreover, as Henchy J noted in *East Cork Foods v O'Dwyer Steel*,[73] this principle no longer rests on the fiction of an implied promise to return the property which, in the days when the forms of actions still ruled English law, led to its tortuous rationalisation as being '*quasi-contractual*' in nature.

The modern authorities in this and other common law jurisdictions, of which *Murphy v Attorney General*[74] is a leading Irish example, have demonstrated that unjust enrichment exists as a distinctive legal concept, separate and distinct from tort and contract, which in the words of Deane J in the High Court of Australia in *Pavey & Matthews v Paul*:[75]

> . . . explains why the law recognises, in a wide variety of distinct categories of cases, an obligation on the part of the defendant to make fair and just restitution for a benefit derived at the expense of a plaintiff and which assists in the determination, by the ordinary process of legal reasoning, of the question of whether the law should, in justice, recognise the obligation in a new and developing category of case.[76]

> . . . the law, as it has developed, has avoided the dangers of 'palm tree justice' by identifying whether the case belongs in a specific category which justifies . . .

[1895] 1 IR 533—has also been pressed into service: see Street 379–83; G Jones (ed), *Goff and Jones on the Law of Restitution* (5th edn, London, Sweet & Maxwell, 1998) 153–69; C Mitchell, *The Law of Subrogation* (Oxford, Clarendon Press, 1994) 154–61.

[70] See especially the speech of Lord Atkin in *United Australia* (n 50) 29, rejecting 'fantastic resemblances of contracts'; the speech of Lord Wright in *Fibrosa* (n 50); and the judgments of the High Court of Australia in *Pavey & Matthews v Paul* (1987) 162 CLR 221, on which, for this point, see DJ Ibbetson, 'Implied Contracts and Restitution: History in the High Court of Australia' (1988) 8 *OJLS* 312.

[71] I have attempted elsewhere to describe this process: see E O'Dell, 'The Principle against Unjust Enrichment' (1993) 15 *Dublin University LJ* (ns) 50; *id*, 'Bricks and Stones and the Structure of the Law of Restitution' (1998) 20 *Dublin University LJ* (ns) 101.

[72] *Dublin Corporation v Building and Allied Trades Union* [1996] 1 IR 468, 483–4. On the case see E O'Dell [1996] *Restitution Law Review* § 134; *id*, 'Restitution and *Res Judicata* in the Irish Supreme Court' (1997) 113 *LQR* 245; and *id*, 'Bricks and Stones' (n 71).

[73] [1978] IR 103, 110: the implied contract fiction was no more than 'a pleader's stratagem . . . it would be an affront to truth and reality to say that the basis of that cause of action is an implied promise to repay the money'.

[74] [1982] IR 241, on which see generally Y Scannell, 'The Taxation of Married Women. *Murphy v AG* (1982)' in O'Dell (n 10) 327.

[75] *Pavey* (n 70).

[76] *Ibid*, 256–7 (Deane J).

describing the enrichment [as unjust]: possible instances are money paid under
duress or as a result of a mistake of fact or law or accompanied by a total failure of consideration.

Such a development undercuts all of the main planks of the denial of the
personal action at law in *Sinclair v Brougham*. In retrospect, its overruling
by the House of Lords in *Westdeutsche* has an aura of inevitability about
it, not least because there were Canadian and Irish harbingers.

Canadian courts have 'demonstrated a remarkable capacity for finding
excuses for failing to follow'[77] *Sinclair v Brougham*. It was almost immediately doubted,[78] and it was soon held that:[79]

> the principle that a corporation which has received benefit from an *ultra vires*
> contract must account for the benefit received . . . [is] long and firmly established
> . . . [and] applicable to any case in which by reason of an *ultra vires* engagement,
> a corporation has received benefit.

The recovery is now explained on the basis of 'the recent revival of the law
related to restitution based on unjust enrichment'.[80] Consequently, *Sinclair
v Brougham* does not seem to form part of the law in Canada.[81]

As to the Irish harbinger, in the *PMPA* case,[82] Murphy J pointed out that
the significance of the development of a law of restitution predicated upon
the principle against unjust enrichment and not the implied contract fiction
'is that by eliminating the need for an express or imputed promise to pay as

---

[77] Maddaugh and McCamus (n 36) 28 and generally, chapter 14. The case 'had no effect on
American Law': JW Wade, *Restitution: Cases and Materials* (2nd edn, New York, Foundation
Press, 1966) 852.

[78] *Trades Hall Co v Erie Tobacco* (1916) 29 DLR 779, 794 (Cameron JA); *Gnaedinger v
Turtleford Grain Growers* (1922) 63 DLR 498; *Re General Finance Corp (Yarmouth)* [1941]
1 DLR 754; *Machrays Department Store v Zionist Labour* (1965) 53 DLR (2d) 657.

[79] *Halton County v Trafalgar Township* [1927] 4 DLR 134, 142 (Grant J). Similarly, a borrower under an *ultra vires* contract must return the money so borrowed to prevent unjust
enrichment: *Caledonia Community Credit Union Ltd v Haldimand Feed Mill* (1974) 45 DLR
(3d) 676, 679 (Van Camp J). See also *La Caisse Populaire Notre Dame Limitée v Moyen*
(1967) 61 DLR (2d) 118; *Breckenridge Speedway v The Queen in right of Alberta* (1970) 9
DLR (3d) 142; *Provincial Treasurer of Alberta v Long* (1975) 49 DLR (3rd) 695; compare *Re
KL Tractors* (1961) 106 CLR 318.

[80] *First City Development Corp v Regional Municipality of Durham* (1989) 67 OR (2d) 655,
689 (Craig J).

[81] *Parkland Mortgage Corporation Ltd v Therevan Developments* (1981) 130 DLR (3d)
682, 696 (Feehan J). However, Maddaugh and McCamus are more circumspect, merely commenting that it has been confined to its own particular facts; see Maddaugh and McCamus (n
36) 324 ff.

[82] *Re PMPA Garage (Longmile) Ltd (No 2)* [1992] 1 IR 332, on which see E O'Dell,
'Estoppel and *Ultra Vires* Contracts' (1992) 14 *Dublin University LJ* (ns) 123, and O'Dell (n
37) 140–1. Hence, Murphy J could avoid the 'monstrous injustice' that would flow from the
'audacious' and 'unattractive' proposition (*ibid*, 336) that there could be no remedy; thereby
correcting the error in *Re Cummins* (n 55).

an ingredient of the action for money had and received it overcomes the problem faced by the House of Lords in *Sinclair v Brougham*'.[83]

Unsurprisingly, therefore, for Lord Browne-Wilkinson in *Westdeutsche*, the development of the law of restitution demonstrated that the reasoning in *Sinclair v Brougham* was no longer sound and ought to be overruled, so that the depositors should have been entitled to restitution of their deposits on the ground of failure of consideration.[84] Lord Slynn agreed that *Sinclair v Brougham* should be departed from,[85] and Lord Lloyd agreed that it was wrongly decided.[86] Lord Woolf expressed no opinion on the point. Only Lord Goff demurred, thinking *Sinclair v Brougham* 'basically irrelevant to the decision of the present appeal',[87] for two reasons. First, he identified 'the problems which arose in *Sinclair v Brougham*'[88] as the exclusion of a personal remedy in restitution 'on the grounds of public policy'[89] and held that it did not arise in the present case as it was not concerned with a borrowing contract.[90] Secondly, he regarded the decision in *Sinclair v Brougham* as confined to '*ultra vires* borrowing contracts, and as not intended to create a principle of general application'.[91] Consequently he was not for overruling *Sinclair v Brougham*.

There is a respectable pedigree for Lord Goff's first point that the personal remedy in restitution was excluded in *Sinclair v Brougham* on the grounds of public policy. There is support in the speeches in the case itself. Viscount Haldane LC was of the opinion that to 'hold that a remedy will lie *in personam* of a statutory society, which by hypothesis cannot in the case in question have become a debtor, or entered into any contract for repayment, is to strike at the root of the doctrine of *ultra vires* as established in the jurisprudence of this country'.[92] Lord Sumner and Lord Parker of Waddington were of the same opinion.[93] Indeed, Hobhouse J at first instance and Leggatt LJ in the

---

[83] *Ibid*, 352.
[84] *Westdeutsche* (n 11) 710.
[85] *Ibid*, 718.
[86] *Ibid*, 738.
[87] *Ibid*, 686.
[88] *Ibid*, 688.
[89] *Ibid*. See generally S Arrowsmith, 'Ineffective Transactions, Unjust Enrichment and Problems of Policy' (1989) 9 *LS* 307.
[90] *Ibid*.
[91] *Ibid*.
[92] *Sinclair* (n 4) 414 (Viscount Haldane LC). Similarly, 'the law of England cannot now, consistently with the interpretation which the courts have placed on the statutes which determine the society the capacity of statutory societies, impute the fiction of such a promise where it would have been *ultra vires* to give it': *ibid*, 417 (Viscount Haldane LC).
[93] 'To hold otherwise would be indirectly to sanction an *ultra vires* borrowing': *Sinclair* (n 4) 452 (Lord Sumner). 'It is not . . . open to the House to hold that in such a case the lender has an action against the company or association for money had and received. To do so would in effect validate the transaction so far as it embodied a contract to repay the money lent': *ibid*, 440 (Lord Parker). This line of reasoning seems to have commenced with the judgment of Cozens-Hardy MR in *Re Guardian Permanent Benefit Building Society* (1883) 23 Ch D 440: see Stoljar (n 4) 28 n 35.

Court of Appeal in *Westdeutsche*[94] were prepared to support the result in *Sinclair v Brougham* on that ground. But the policy underlying the *ultra vires* rule must be carefully excavated. It is not monolithic, but instead has two aspects, each designed to increase the funds available for disbursement to company shareholders or local authority ratepayers: there is the retention policy at issue in *Sinclair v Brougham* which allows the retention of *ultra vires* receipts by the company or local authority acting *ultra vires*, and there is a parallel restitution policy which allows restitution of *ultra vires* expenditure by the company or local authority acting *ultra vires*; in both cases, the effect of that policy is to swell the coffers of the *ultra vires* company or local authority.[95]

The retention policy has its critics. Goff and Jones observe that, at times, 'the courts have tended too readily to deny a restitutionary claim on this ground'.[96] Even in *Sinclair v Brougham* itself, Lord Dunedin thought that the *ultra vires* doctrine could not allow an *ultra vires* borrower to retain the borrowing: to do so would be 'to run the doctrine mad. It was a doctrine which was introduced in order to let societies keep their own money, not to appropriate other people's'.[97] The rigour of other rules for the maintenance of capital has been much mitigated;[98] and if the law is not strict on capital maintenance even where the capital is validly obtained, there can be little if any justification for its retention where it is invalidly obtained.

By contrast, there is no such objection to a restitution policy which allows societies to recover their own money paid away *ultra vires*—indeed, in *Brougham v Dwyer*,[99] the liquidator of the Birkbeck Building Society succeeded in just such an action—and every reason in principle to support it.

Moreover it seems that the retention policy is being supplanted by a restitution policy even in the case of *ultra vires* receipts: it was canvassed briefly by Birks in his discussion of Hobhouse J's judgment in *Westdeutsche*[100] and

---

[94] [1994] 4 All ER 890, 918 (Hobhouse J); [1994] 1 WLR 938, 952 (Legatt LJ). See also P Birks, *An Introduction to the Law of Restitution* (rev edn, Oxford, Clarendon Press, 1989) 396: restitution would have 'flatly contradicted the *ultra vires* rule'. Compare *Kasumu v Baba-Egbe* [1956] AC 539, 551 (Lord Radcliffe).

[95] See O'Dell (n 37) 162–7.

[96] Goff and Jones (n 69) 68, criticising *Sinclair v Brougham* on this ground, but defending *R Leslie v Sheill* [1914] 3 KB 607. Cf A Burrows, *An Introduction to the Law of Restitution* (London, Butterworths, 1993), 458–60, convincingly refuting the reliance by the House of Lords on such policy in the former case, and 452, seeing a consequently 'overwhelming' case to overrule the latter.

[97] *Sinclair* (n 4) 438.

[98] For example, the rule in *Trevor v Whitworth* (1887) 12 App Cas 409 has progressively been relaxed (see, in Ireland, the Companies Act 1990, Part XI, and, in England, the Companies Act 1985, chapter VII). On the modern justifications, if any, for such rules, see J Armour, 'Share Capital and Creditor Protection: Efficient Rules for a Modern Company Law' (2000) 63 *MLR* 355.

[99] (1913) 108 LT 504, 505 (Lush J). See also *Re Coltman* (1881) 19 Ch D 64. Compare *Re Irish Provident Assurance* [1913] 1 IR 352.

[100] P Birks, 'No Consideration: Restitution after Void Contracts' (1993) 23 *University of Western Australia Law Review* 195, 206, *semble* changing his mind since Birks (n 94).

taken up by Waller LJ in *Guinness Mahon v Kensington LBC* who suggested that there was therefore 'no injustice in the council [the receiving incapax] being bound to repay'.[101] As the co-author of a commentary upon *Guinness Mahon*,[102] Birks has returned the compliment: for him, the proper basis for restitution after an *ultra vires* swap is now 'to be found by asking whether the policy behind the nullity dictates that there must be restitution',[103] and he finds various passages in *Guinness Mahon*—and in the subsequent decision of the House of Lords in *Kleinwort Benson v Lincoln City Council*[104]—which imply that there has to be restitution in order to uphold the policy behind the *ultra vires* rule.[105] These passages are significant because they appear in cases in which it is the defendant who seeks to retain what has been received *ultra vires*, circumstances in which the retention policy would previously have denied restitution. If this is correct, then the focus of policy in the context of *ultra vires* receipts will have flipped from justifying retention to justifying restitution. Hence, the tide of policy seems now to be running strongly in favour of restitution not only of payments made *ultra vires* the payor but also of payments received *ultra vires* the payee. In both cases, by allowing restitution to unwind any performance of the *ultra vires* contract, the void nature of the contract is emphasised and the policy of the *ultra vires* rule is supported and not subverted. Consequently, the ground has been cut out from under Lord Goff's first point in defence of *Sinclair v Brougham*.

His second point, intimately bound up with his first,[106] was that it is confined to the narrow context of precluding the indirect enforcement of *ultra vires* borrowing contracts. It too has a respectable pedigree, and support in the speeches in *Sinclair v Brougham*. For example, Lord Parker of Waddington was of the opinion that if:[107]

---

[101] [1998] 3 WLR 829, 843–4, relying on *Westdeutsche* [1994] 1 WLR 938, 951 (Leggatt LJ).

[102] P Birks and WJ Swadling, 'Restitution' [1998] All ER Rev 390, 393–5. See also P Birks, 'Private Law' in Birks and Rose (eds) (n 18) 1, 17–18, making the same point.

[103] Birks and Swadling (n 102) 394.

[104] [1999] 2 AC 349, 382 (Lord Goff) and 415 (Lord Hope).

[105] Birks and Swadling (n 102) 394.

[106] For example, the comments of Viscount Haldane LC, Lord Sumner and Lord Parker quoted in nn 92 and 93 and those of Hobhouse J and Leggatt LJ cited in n 94 might as easily be cited here.

[107] *Sinclair* (n 4) 440, on which see Wright (n 4) 14–15. See also *Westdeutsche* [1994] 4 All ER 890, 919 (Hobhouse J). However, though confined, the policy can still catch the unwary, as seems to have occurred in *South Tyneside BC v Svenska International* [1995] 1 All ER 454. Clarke J held that where a net payor on a void swap was entitled to restitution, the net payee could not rely on payments in advance as constituting a change of position because to do so 'would in effect be relying upon the supposed validity of a void transaction': *ibid*, 465. However, the decline of this policy (discussed in the text to nn 112–15) must call this reason for rejecting the defence into question: if restitution of benefits transferred does not amount to enforcing a borrowing contract, then *a fortiori* neither does a change of position defence.

the *ultra vires* contract . . . was not a contract of borrowing . . . the implied promise on which the action for money had an received depends would form no part of, but would be merely collateral to, the *ultra vires* contract.

In truth, this offers two routes by which to escape the shackles of *Sinclair v Brougham*'s denial of restitution: a claimant can argue that the contract in the instant case is not a borrowing one, or that the policy against indirect enforcement is inapplicable. The judgment of Murphy J in the *PMPA* case[108] provides an excellent example of the first route: in *Sinclair v Brougham* 'their Lordships had to consider problems which by coincidence bear an extraordinary resemblance to the facts of the present case with the crucial distinction that in *Sinclair v Brougham* it was the borrowing which was *ultra vires* whereas in the instant case it is the lending which was incompetent'.[109] As to the second route—that the policy against indirect enforcement of *ultra vires* borrowing is inapplicable—it is no more than a consideration in the specific context of *ultra vires* borrowing of the general question already discussed of whether the policy underlying the *ultra vires* rule is better served by retention of restitution.

The judgment of Lardner J in the Irish High Court in *Re Frederick Inns*[110] seems to provide an example: in the case of a company making an *ultra vires* payment to the Revenue Commissioners in attempted settlement of a debt of related companies, Lardner J held that an action for money had and received lay against the Revenue on the ground of their unjust enrichment, and that 'the considerations relating to the *ultra vires* nature of the transaction of deposit-taking which existed in *Sinclair v Brougham* . . . do not exist in the present case'.[111] Before *Westdeutsche*, it was an increasingly common strategy.[112] However, in truth, it is an unnecessary one. Restitution of an outstanding balance is a very different from repayment according to the detailed repayment schedule and other terms of a contract. More generally, even if the value of the defendant's enrichment and the contract price correspond,[113] then restitution in the amount of the benefit transferred under an

[108] [1992] 1 IR 332.
[109] *Ibid*, 336. See also *ibid*, 339. Indeed he had noticed this at an earlier stage in the proceedings when he determined the *ultra vires* point: *Re PMPA Garage (Longmile) Ltd (No 1)* [1992] 1 IR 315, 331. The same distinction is drawn in *La Caisse Populaire Notre Dame Limitée v Moyen* (1967) 61 DLR (2d) 118, 147–51 (Tucker J).
[110] [1991] ILRM 582.
[111] *Ibid*, 593. In an extraordinarily selective citation from *Sinclair v Brougham*, Lardner J simply set out Viscount Haldane LC's quotation of *Moses v Macferlan* (*Sinclair* (n 4) 415) without referring to its fate in the Lord Chancellor's speech or to the views on the action for money had and received set forth in all of the speeches. However, Lardner J had also held that the Revenue held the *ultra vires* payment on constructive trust ([1991] ILRM 591–2), and on appeal, this was the only mechanism of recovery discussed: [1994] 1 ILRM 387.
[112] See eg *Dynevor v The Proprietors, Centre Point Building Units Plan No 4327*, unreported, Queensland CA, 12 May 1995, digested [1996] *Restitution Law Review* § 20.
[113] As they often will, but not invariably: if the benefit is a service, its value may be different from any contract price.

invalid contract may look like enforcing the contract,[114] but emphatically it is not—it is giving a remedy in restitution. Since the contract is not being enforced, there is no conflict with the *ultra vires* doctrine. Indeed, in the House of Lords in *Westdeutsche*, Lord Goff himself 'incline[d] to the opinion that a personal claim in restitution would not indirectly enforce the *ultra vires* contract'.[115] The ground therefore seems also to have been cut out from under the second of Lord Goff's reasons for not overruling *Sinclair v Brougham*.

Neither of Lord Goff's reasons to support *Sinclair v Brougham* holds. Nothing beside remains. Its overruling in *Westdeutsche* is therefore to be welcomed as placing the law, at last, upon a sounder footing. On this point at least, a once-great case has therefore quite properly fallen. Though hubris may be a realistic aspersion to cast upon the speeches in *Sinclair v Brougham*, the displacement of the implied contract theory by the principle against unjust enrichment, described in the long extract from the *Bricklayers' Hall* case set out above,[116] is much more likely to be a result of the changing winds of academic and judicial fashion and a judicial adoption of the principle against unjust enrichment as the flavour of the month theory. More profoundly, it may be that the principle against unjust enrichment is an idea whose time has come.

---

[114] There is another context in which such concerns have been articulated. In the context of an *ultra vires* contract performed, or partly so, on one side, while *Sinclair v Brougham* obscured the availability of restitution of the benefits transferred in that purported performance, the question was raised as to whether the party who had performed could prevent the other from taking the *ultra vires* point and so in effect enforce the contract to have a remedy for that performance (see eg M Furmston, 'Who Can Plead that a Contract is *Ultra Vires*?' (1961) 24 *MLR* 715). This view had some attraction (see eg *Cabaret Holdings v Meeanee Sports and Rodeo Club* [1982] 1 NZLR 673, 675 (Somers J); *Re PMPA* (n 82) 341–3 (Murphy J)) but was ultimately rejected as inconsistent with the *ultra vires* doctrine (see eg *Kathleen Investments v Australian Atomic Energy Commission* (1976–77) 139 CLR 117, 148–9 (Stephen J); compare *Commonwealth Homes and Investment Co v Smith* (1937) 59 CLR 443, 460 (Dixon J). This was the position taken by Mocatta J at first instance in *Bell Houses Ltd v City Wall Properties Ltd* [1966] 1 QB 207, 224–6; on appeal, Salmon LJ was attracted to the distinction, but found it unnecessary to 'consider the interesting, important and difficult question which would arise were the contract *ultra vires*, namely, whether, the plaintiff company having fully performed its part under the contract and the defendants having obtained all the benefit of the contract, the defendants could successfully take the point that the contract was *ultra vires* the plaintiff company and so avoid payment. It seems strange that third parties could take advantage of a doctrine, manifestly for the protection of shareholders, in order to deprive the company of money which in justice should be paid to it by the third parties': [1966] 2 QB 656, 693–4. Consistently with the *ultra vires* doctrine, there is no contract, and on Salmon LJ's example the defendant could so plead, but a remedy in restitution would prevent the injustice he identified. Had it been appreciated that restitution does not amount to the enforcement of the contract, it would not have been necessary to flirt with the heresy of enforcing an *ultra vires* contract to provide an appropriate remedy in the context of a performed or partly-performed *ultra vires* contract.

[115] *Westdeutsche* (n 11) 688. Compare Street (n 69) 376: 'restitution is a *wholly distinct* relief' (emphasis added). And in Canada, where *Sinclair v Brougham* had been rejected, there seems to be no difficulty with restitution of benefits transferred under an *ultra vires* borrowing contract: see n 79.

[116] Text following n 72.

There may be nothing so powerful as an idea whose time has come. It must first, however, displace the idea whose time has passed. Thus has the principle against unjust enrichment displaced the implied contract theory. But once the idea's time has come, it must defend itself against other ideas or in turn be vanquished. Thus must the principle against unjust enrichment defend itself against various charges: that it does not organise the subject of restitution, because unjust enrichment ideas are broadly dispersed throughout the realm of private law, or because the law of restitution does not have an organising principle, or because, if it does, it is something other than the principle against unjust enrichment, or because, if the principle does organise the subject, it does not do so in an exclusive way but shares that function with other principles.[117] As Lord Wright found support for the principle against unjust enrichment in the speeches in *Sinclair v Brougham*, so also— and with perhaps greater justification—may some support for another competing idea be found in them.

Stoljar has suggested that in the action for money had and received, the claimant recovers 'on what is in effect a proprietary basis'[118] by asserting that the money in the defendant's hands belongs to him (ie the claimant) and that the defendant came to it without the claimant's consent.[119] Lord Haldane may have taken a similar approach in *Sinclair v Brougham* when he said that the 'common law looked simply to the question whether the property had passed'.[120] Certainly, this is how it is represented by Lord Wright: 'Lord Haldane puts the remedy of law as being based on the fact that no property in the money has passed.'[121] The property explanation is attractive, but modern writers[122] do not ground their theories upon *Sinclair v Brougham*. Lord Wright, having discerned in *Sinclair v Brougham* a theory other than the implied contract fiction, nevertheless rejected it as an insufficiently comprehensive explanation of the decided cases in favour of the principle against unjust enrichment,[123] and the modern versions of the

---

[117] These alternative theories are considered and rejected in the articles cited in n 71.

[118] SJ Stoljar, *The Law of Quasi-Contract* (2nd edn, Sydney, Law Book Co, 1989) 18. See also p 20.

[119] *Ibid*, 6.

[120] *Sinclair* (n 4) 420.

[121] Wright (n 4) 11; and he finds further support for this in the speech of Lord Dunedin: *ibid*, 12.

[122] It has been taken up not only by Stoljar, but in various ways by P Watts, 'A Property Principle and a Services Principle' [1995] *Restitution Law Review* 49; N McBride and P McGrath, 'The Nature of Restitution' (1995) 15 *OJLS* 33; and, to a lesser extent, J Dietrich, *Restitution: A New Perspective* (Sydney, Federation Press, 1998).

[123] Wright (n 4) 12–13. See also p 24: 'However, I feel a difficulty in limiting the concept to ideas of property. The cases of services rendered or debts discharged certainly afford frequent examples of unjust enrichment. I think it is safer to state the claim for unjust enrichment in such cases as depending on an obligation imposed by law in all the circumstances of the case in order to satisfy the requirements of justice, that is, to avoid what is unconscionable or unconscientious . . .'

proprietary theory do not entirely meet these objections. However, even if a modern version were to displace the principle against unjust enrichment, *Sinclair v Brougham* is not necessary for this displacement.[124]

Under Lord Mansfield, who professed himself a great friend of the action for money had and received,[125] it prospered mightily. If it was not king of all it surveyed, it was certainly a prince among actions. If, by circumscribing the action, *Sinclair v Brougham* did not quite commit regicide, it certainly consummated a successful coup. And if *PMPA* and *Westdeutsche* did nothing else, they may have helped to restore the law of restitution, incorporating the action for money had and received, to its rightful place among the heads of obligation at common law.

D. THE PROPRIETARY CLAIM: BAD CASES MAKE HARD LAW?

Not only did the denial of the personal claim in *Sinclair v Brougham* set the law on the wrong path, it also had the potential to work an injustice on the facts. If the case had rested with the depositors' loss on the personal claim, then the permanent shareholders would have got everything. This would have resulted in a five-fold windfall for them.[126] For the House of Lords, this was unthinkable. When the common law finds itself in times of trouble, principles of equity come to it, speaking words of wisdom (frequently). Unsurprisingly, therefore, their Lordships appealed to equity to mitigate the harshness of their decision on the common law point. Thus, Lord Sumner thought that 'the present case must be decided upon equitable principles upon which there is no direct authority';[127] while for Lord Dunedin, it was not:[128]

> necessary that the claim should be one capable of being made good by action at common law. It will suffice if there is an equitable remedy. Precisely the same difficulty was felt and met in the Roman Law . . . Is English Equity to retire defeated from the task which other systems of Equity have conquered?

[124] Even more, Lord Haldane's speech may not be a secure basis for the property theory of the action for money had and received, because in the passage cited at n 120 Lord Haldane was dealing not with the depositors' personal claim at law, but with their tracing claim.

[125] *Weston v Downes* (1778) 1 Doug 23, 24; 99 ER 19, 20.

[126] 'The appalling result in this very case would be that the society shareholders having got the proceeds of the depositors' money in the form of investment . . . [would be] enriched to the extent of 500 per cent': *Sinclair* (n 4) 436 (Lord Dunedin).

[127] *Ibid*, 458 (Lord Sumner).

[128] *Ibid*, 434 (Lord Dunedin). On the Roman learning discussed by Lord Dunedin, and intended by him as a guide to the solution of the problem in Scots law, see A Rodger, 'Recovering Payments under Void Contracts in Scots Law' in G Jones and WJ Swadling (eds), *The Search For Principle: Essays in Honour of Lord Goff of Chieveley* (Oxford, OUP, 1999) 1, 5–7, 10–14.

Rousing rhetoric; stirring stuff. Unfortunately, it is difficult to discern precisely what the equitable remedy was.[129] Lord Sumner called it 'the 'tracing' equity',[130] and the word 'tracing' appears in the other speeches,[131] but this seems to have been the occasion upon which this child of equity was christened.[132] Like all infants, it suffered somewhat from its lack of maturity.[133] Indeed, only in recent years has it become clear that the tracing exercise proceeds in two stages: a claimant must first identify his property or its exchange product in the defendant's hands, and then, secondly, make a claim to it.[134] It is commonplace in this context to distinguish between tracing at law and tracing in equity.[135] However, this ought to be understood as applicable not to the identification stage of the tracing exercise but to the claiming stage; there is no justification for having two sets of identification rules:[136] either the claimant's property or its exchange product is to be found in the defendant's hands or it is not; once it has been identified, the claimant's claim to it can then be made either at law or in equity. Not only do these separations bring order to a notoriously chaotic field of law, but they supply a useful tool with which to analyse the speeches in *Sinclair v Brougham* on this point.

The House of Lords ordered that the depositors and remaining shareholders should share in the proceeds *pari passu*, and then congratulated themselves on a job well done. It has been left to subsequent generations to

---

[129] Nevertheless, it has been applied not only generally in subsequent tracing cases, but also in the context of *ultra vires* contracts; see eg *Re PMPA* (n 82); *Tauranga Borough v Tauranga Electric Power Board* [1944] NZLR 155.

[130] *Sinclair* (n 4) 460 (Lord Sumner).

[131] *Ibid*, 418 (Viscount Haldane LC), 437 (Lord Dunedin), and 441 (Lord Parker).

[132] PH Winfield, 'Equity and Quasi-Contract' in *Select Legal Essays* (London, Sweet & Maxwell, 1952) 226, 235: a curious feature of the 'tracing order' was that 'although it is well represented in Equity, there is an almost total lack of reference to it *eo nomine* in the treatises and textbooks on equity, in which its baptismal name is some phrase like 'following trust property'. In the law reports its christening as a 'tracing order' seems to be as modem as the decision of the House of Lords in *Sinclair v Brougham*'.

[133] For Hanbury, it represented a 'somewhat rough-and-ready principle': Hanbury (n 6) 13; while for Lord Wright, though it worked substantial justice (Wright (n 58) 358), it was also 'a sort of rough justice, in the form of a tracing order' (Wright (n 4) 2), even 'a rough sort of tracing order' (*ibid*, 5).

[134] LD Smith, *The Law of Tracing* (Oxford, OUP, 1997) chapter 1. See *Boscawen v Bajwa* [1996] 1 WLR 328, 334 (Millett LJ); *Trustees of the Property of FC Jones and Son (a firm) v Jones* [1997] Ch 159, 169–70 (Millett LJ); *Foskett v McKeown* [2001] 1 AC 102, 109 (Lord Browne-Wilkinson), 113 (Lord Steyn), and 128 (Lord Millett). Indeed, there would seem to be some measure of support for this separation of the tracing exercise into identification and claiming in the speech of Viscount Haldane LC in *Sinclair* (n 4) 419 (discussed by Smith, 12): 'So long as the money . . . can be *traced* into what has been procured with it, the principal can . . . *claim* that his money is invested in a specific thing' (emphasis added).

[135] This distinction is drawn in the speeches in *Sinclair* (n 4) 420 (Viscount Haldane LC) and 436–7 (Lord Dunedin).

[136] Smith (n 134) 120–30, 277–9, and 342–7; P Birks, 'The Need of a Unitary Law of Tracing' in R Cranston (ed), *Making Commercial Law: Essays in Honour of Roy Goode* (Oxford, OUP, 1997) 239; *Jones* (n 134) 169–70 (Millett LJ); *Foskett* (n 134) 113 (Lord Steyn) and 128–9 (Lord Millett).

work out whether such a conclusion is justifiable. It is not enough simply to assert that the depositors and shareholders were able to trace their money into the society's funds; it is necessary to show both that such money was identifiable in the society's hands and that it could be claimed by the depositors and shareholders.

In the course of argument,[137] Viscount Haldane LC suggested that the principle in *Re Hallett's Estate*[138] would help in this regard. In that case Hallett, a solicitor, died insolvent. Upon his death, it was discovered that by selling bonds, he had misappropriated funds first from his marriage settlement and then from a client, and lodged the proceeds to his bank account. Fry J at first instance took the view that Hallett had misapplied trust funds in both cases, and that the client and the trustees of the settlement could, in principle, identify the proceeds of their bonds in the bank account and claim accordingly. However, he applied the rule in *Clayton's Case*,[139] and concluded that the trustees' claim was completely defeated by subsequent withdrawals, and the client's claim was partially so.

The Court of Appeal affirmed the finding that Hallett's misappropriation of the client's bonds was a misapplication of trust funds and that the client could, in principle, claim in the bank account the identifiable proceeds of her misapplied bonds. Jessel MR laid down some basic principles of identification and claiming. First, if the misappropriated trust funds are applied to a purchase, the beneficial owner 'is entitled at his election either to take the property, or to have a charge on the property for the amount of the trust money'.[140] Secondly, if the misappropriated trust funds are mixed with the trustee's own funds for the purchase, the beneficial owner is 'entitled to a charge on the property purchased, for the amount of the trust money laid out in the purchase; and that charge is quite independent of the facts of the amount laid out by the trustee'.[141] Furthermore, he confirmed that these rules applied not only where the trustee purchased land or goods with the misappropriated funds, but also where he lodged them in his bank account,[142] and applied not only to express trustees, such as the trustees of the marriage settlement, but also to other fiduciary relationships, such as that between a solicitor and his client.[143]

---

[137] See n 32.

[138] (1880) 13 Ch D 696.

[139] (1816) 1 Mer 529; 35 ER 767. The rule presumes that, in the absence of contrary intention or countervailing circumstances, the first debt in time is discharged by the first incoming credits, and so on, and *vice versa*. See generally DA McConville, 'Tracing and the Rule in *Clayton's Case*' (1963) 79 LQR 388.

[140] *Re Hallett's* (n 138) 709 (Jessel MR).

[141] *Ibid*.

[142] *Ibid*, 711 (Jessel MR), approving *Pennell v Deffell* (1853) De GM & G 372, 43 ER 551, and doubting *Ex parte Dale* (1879) 11 Ch D 772. Baggallay LJ concurred at 721–2.

[143] *Ibid*, 709–10 and 720 (Jessel MR) and 721 (Baggallay LJ, concurring).

In a separate judgment on the applicability of the rule in *Clayton's Case*, Jessel MR held that 'where a man does an act which may be rightfully performed, he cannot say that the act was intentionally and in fact done wrongly'.[144] Applying this to Hallett's lodgment of trust money to his bank account from which he subsequently made drawings, it was to Jessel MR 'perfectly plain that he cannot be heard to say that he [Hallett] took away the trust money when he had a right to take away his own money'.[145] The rule in *Clayton's Case*, though a very convenient one, applied 'unless there is evidence either of agreement to the contrary, or of circumstances from which a contrary intention must be presumed and then, of course, that which is a mere presumption of law gives way to those other considerations',[146] as in this case. Since the account at all times had sufficient credit to meet the claim both of the trustees and of the client, the trustees' appeal was allowed.

Quite what all this has to do with identifying money in the society's hands which could be claimed by the depositors and shareholders in *Sinclair v Brougham* is unclear. *Re Hallett's Estate* states two rules to be applied when an errant trustee misapplies trust funds to aid in the identification of the beneficiary's funds, and uses a presumption against a wrongdoer to decline to apply the rule in *Clayton's Case* in the same identification process. On the other hand, in *Sinclair v Brougham*, trust funds may have been mixed but they were not misapplied; there was no wrongdoer; and *Clayton's Case* would have been unusable on the facts.[147]

Sinclair v Brougham boils down simply to a case in which two funds were mixed through no fault of either of the contributors.[148] Where property has been mixed through no fault of the contributors to the mixture, the general rules seem to be that each party 'can assert that her contribution exists in any part of the mixture, *subject to* the right of other contributors to do likewise'[149] and reductions in the mixture are borne in proportion to

---

[144] *Ibid*, 727. Again, whenever 'an act can be done rightfully the man who has done it is not allowed to say, as against the persons entitled to the property or the right, that he has done it wrongfully. That is the universal law': *ibid*.

[145] *Ibid*. See also *Shanahans Stamp Auctions v Farrelly* [1962] IR 386, 425–9, and 443 (Budd J); *Re Irish Shipping* [1986] ILRM 518, 521 and 523 (Carroll J).

[146] *Ibid*, 728 (Jessel MR). Baggallay LJ concurred at 738–9. See also *Re Chute's Estate* [1914] 1 IR 180, 185 (Ross J); *Re Hughes* [1970] IR 237, 243 (Kenny J); *Re Money Markets International*, unreported, Irish High Court, 20 July 1999, 13 (Laffoy J).

[147] *Barlow Clowes International v Vaughan* [1992] 4 All ER 22; see also *Re Securitibank Ltd* [1978] 1 NZLR 97; McConville (n 139) 406–7. For Viscount Haldane LC, the enthusiast for *Hallett* in the House of Lords in *Sinclair v Brougham*, 'the really relevant part of the judgment in *Hallett's Case* is that which stresses how the difficulty of following money into a debtor and creditor account like a banker's is got over in equity': *Sinclair* (n 4) 422. That is, he regarded *Hallett* as relevant at the identification stage of the process, whereas the analysis above demonstrates otherwise.

[148] *Sinclair* (n 4) 437–8 (Lord Dunedin). Compare *Re Diplock* (n 52) 532 (Lord Greene MR).

[149] Smith (n 134) 73; emphasis in original.

the original contribution.[150] Assuming that these principles apply not only to mixtures but also to bank accounts and applying them to the facts of *Sinclair v Brougham*, it is plain that, in principle, the depositors and shareholders could each identify the proceeds of their money in the society; and the House of Lords readily—perhaps too readily—concluded that they could in fact so identify their money.[151]

On the question of whether they could then claim the money so identified, Viscount Haldane LC was of the view that if property in the money had not passed at law, the owners of the money could claim at law.[152] But, money being currency,[153] property passes easily—as it does when it is lodged into a bank account and is therefore replaced with a debt owed by the banker to the customer—and the basis of this claim at law disappears.[154] Where there was a claim at law, equity 'exercised a concurrent jurisdiction based upon trust';[155] where there was no claim at law, equity:[156]

> gave a further remedy. The Court of Chancery could and would declare, even against the general creditors of the wrongdoer, that there was what it called a charge on the banker's debt to the person whose money had been paid in to the latter's account in favour of the person whose money it really was. And as Jessel MR pointed out in *Re Hallett's Estate*, this equity was not confined to cases of trust in the strict sense, but applied at all events, to every case where there was a fiduciary relationship. . . . I see no reason why the remedy explained by Jessel MR

[150] *Ibid. Hallett* is relevant to neither principle, but Smith posits a third, of which he instances *Hallett* as an example—that 'when a contributor withdraws from a mixture, his contribution is followed into his withdrawal; in other words, what he takes out is counted first against his contribution': Smith (n 134) 76. But, as has already been said, the facts of *Sinclair v Brougham* do not fall within the terms of this principle.

[151] The application to bank accounts of general principles relating to mixtures is a large and controversial matter, but it is the correct position in principle: Smith (n 134) 183–215. As to the overly easy application of identification principles by the House, see Smith (n 134) 227–34.

[152] 'The common law . . . looks simply to the question whether the property had passed, and if it had not, for instance, where no relationship of debtor and creditor had intervened, the money could be followed, notwithstanding its normal character as currency, provided that it could be earmarked or traced into assets acquired with it': *Sinclair* (n 4) 420 (Viscount Haldane LC). If by this he meant, as it seems he did, that the claimant could make a proprietary claim to the money paid, it is at best an overstatement. See *Re Diplock* (n 52) 519: 'Specific relief, as distinct from damages (the normal remedy at common law), was confined to a very limited range of claims. See also Stoljar (n 4) 28–30, and more generally, Smith (n 134) 320–38.

[153] Where it is not currency, then it is treated like any other chattel. Furthermore, 'if money in a bag is stolen, and can be identified in the form in which it was stolen, it can be recovered *in specie*': *Sinclair* (n 4) 418. This seemingly simple case of the stolen bag of coins in fact causes great difficulties of analysis: see nn 189–90.

[154] *Sinclair* (n 4) 420: 'But while the common law gave the remedy I have stated, it gave no remedy when the money had been paid by the wrongdoer into his account with his banker, who simply owed him a debt, so that no money was or could be, in the contemplation of a court of law, earmarked.'

[155] *Ibid*.

[156] *Ibid*, 420–1.

in *Re Hallett's Estate* of declaring a charge on the investment in a debt due from bankers on balance, or on any mass of money or securities with which the plaintiff's money had been mixed, should not apply in the case of a transaction that is *ultra vires*. The property was never converted into a debt, in equity at all events, and there has been throughout a resulting trust, not of an active character, but sufficient, in my opinion, to bring the transaction within the general principle.

However, the funds to be distributed by the liquidator represented money which not only the depositors but also the society (and thus its shareholders) were entitled to follow; and, since the depositors could 'only claim the depreciated assets which represent[ed] their money, and nothing more',[157] it followed that 'the principle to be adopted in the distribution must be apportionment on the footing [that] depreciation and loss are to be borne *pro rata*'.[158] Lord Sumner 'agree[d], without recapitulating reasons, that the principle upon which *Re Hallett's Estate* is founded justifies an order allowing the appellants [the depositors] to follow the assets'[159] and make a claim, subject to the equal rights of the shareholders similarly to identify and claim.

It is difficult to make sense of these passages, but they seem to come to this. In *Hallett*, Jessel MR had held that once the client could identify the proceeds of the sale of her bonds in Hallett's bank account, since he stood in a fiduciary relation to her and was bailee of the bonds, she could claim such proceeds in the account. Similarly, here, since the society owed fiduciary duties to the depositors—who could identify the proceeds of their money in the society—they could claim those proceeds. Hence, though it was not relevant on the identification leg of the tracing exercise, *Hallett* proved relevant on the claiming leg of the exercise.

So much is tolerably clear from these passages. However, they contain at least three difficulties. First, the *pro rata* distribution of the funds to the depositors and shareholders is made to sound as though it were a consequence of the claiming rules at issue. On the reading presented here, it was just as much if not more so a consequence of the identification rules at issue. The fiduciary relationship asserted to subsist between the depositors and the society allowed the depositors to claim in equity the proportion of the funds that had already been identified; both the depositors and shareholders could identify proceeds of their money in the society, and since each group can in such circumstances assert that its contribution exists in any part of the mixture, *subject to* the right of any other group to do likewise,[160] what the

---

[157] *Ibid*, 424.
[158] *Ibid*. Heuston (n 41) 215–6 comments that in 'the field of equity Haldane was particularly strong . . . [especially] in the uncertain area where the principle of common law and equity overlap . . . [and in this speech] he expounded with masterly learning the circumstances in which equity would permit a beneficiary to trace misapplied trust funds'. Cf n 206.
[159] *Ibid*, 459.
[160] See text with n 149. Compare *Sinclair* (n 4) 438 (Lord Dunedin) and 448–9 (Lord Parker).

depositors could identify and therefore claim was limited by what the share-holders could similarly identify and claim.

Secondly, Viscount Haldane LC seemed to hold that the society owed fiduciary duties to the depositors.[161] This proposition is startling, because the relationship of banker and customer is usually one of debtor and creditor, and not fiduciary in nature,[162] and there was nothing more on the facts of the relationship between the depositors and the society[163] to alter this conclusion.[164] Hence, it is, as Chambers notes:[165]

> difficult to understand why the directors were in a fiduciary relationship with the depositors, and, if so, why they were in breach of their duties when the depositors had consented to the investment of their money. It is also difficult to accept the classification of shareholders as innocent recipients and directors as fiduciaries in breach, when the . . . shareholders included all of the directors of the society.

The third difficulty arises from the fact that Viscount Haldane LC justified the depositors' equitable claim not only on the basis of the fiduciary relationship but also because the facts gave rise to 'a resulting trust'—though it was 'not of an active character'. In *Westdeutsche* the bank latched on to this, and claimed that the net payments on the *ultra vires* swaps were held

---

[161] In allowing the parties to trace and claim, he based himself on *Re Hallett's Estate* which he held 'applied to all events to every case where there was a fiduciary relationship': *Sinclair* (n 4) 421. Since he held that *Hallett* applied, it follows that he must have regarded the relationship between the parties as fiduciary, though he was careful to hold that the society had not breached its fiduciary duty: *ibid*, 422–3. Lord Atkinson concurred, and Lord Parker delivered a speech to similar effect: *ibid*, 441 (fiduciary relationship). Lord Sumner agreed that *Hallett* justified the tracing order: *ibid*, 459. This presumably amounts to a concurrence that a fiduciary relationship subsisted on the facts. Only Lord Dunedin disagreed, holding at 439 that neither 'party is here in any fiduciary position to the other'.

[162] *Foley v Hill* (1848) 2 HLC 28; *Kinlen v Ulster Bank* [1928] IR 171. See eg Oakley (n 26) 76–7: 'The relationship between the depositors and the society was clearly that of creditor and debtor and, therefore, it is difficult to see how the depositors retained any legal or equitable proprietary interest in the money deposited—a creditor retains no proprietary interest in the money advanced.' Again, 'it is by no means clear why the directors of the building society owed fiduciary duties to members, let alone to lenders of money borrowed *ultra vires*', that is, let alone to the depositors: RP Meagher, WMC Gummow and JRF Lehane, *Equity: Doctrines and Remedies* (3rd edn, Sydney, Butterworths, 1992) para 505.

[163] Indeed, MA Donnelly, *The Law of Banks and Credit Institutions* (Dublin, Round Hall Sweet & Maxwell, 1999) 127–8 sees the principle in *Foley v Hill* as applicable as between customer and credit institutions generally, and in chapter 3 she includes building societies within that category of credit institutions.

[164] However, in *Re Diplock* the Court of Appeal argued that in *Sinclair v Brougham* 'a sufficient fiduciary relationship was found to exist between the depositors and the directors by reason of the fact that the purposes for which the depositors had handed their money to the directors were by law incapable of fulfilment': *Re Diplock* (n 52) 540–1.

[165] R Chambers, *Resulting Trusts* (Oxford, OUP, 1997) 156, citing *Sinclair* (n 4) 422–3 and 458 for the proposition that the depositors had consented to the investment, and [1912] 2 Ch 183, 222–3 for the directors' status as shareholders! See also Mason and Carter (n 52) 100 n 228.

by the local authority on resulting trust. Lord Goff concluded that there
was no basis for imposing a resulting trust,[166] as did Lord Browne-
Wilkinson, who described the inactive resulting trust posited by Viscount
Haldane LC as an unconventional one of which there was no trace in any
other authority[167] and for which there was no justification in principle.[168]
Whether or not their Lordships in *Westdeutsche* were correct in rejecting a
resulting trust in principle,[169] they were surely right to hold that the reasoning in *Sinclair v Brougham* provides no support for such a trust.

If neither a fiduciary relationship nor a resulting trust justified the depositors' claim, the question arises: what else in the case—if anything—
does?[170] Another equitable proprietary interest was touched on by Viscount
Haldane LC when he said that he could see 'no reason why the remedy
explained by Jessel MR in *Re Hallett's Estate* of declaring a charge . . .
should not apply in the case of a transaction that is *ultra vires*'.[171] Lord
Parker[172] and Lord Sumner[173] spoke to the same effect.[174] In this identification of a charge[175] there is a credible equitable proprietary base for the
depositors' claim. And, as a matter of Irish law, it is clear that a claimant
who can identify and claim in equity 'has a charge on the account to which
the money or cheques have been lodged or on property on which the

---

[166] *Westdeutsche* (n 11) 690.

[167] *Ibid*, 712.

[168] *Ibid*, 712–13. Lord Slynn agreed that 'no resulting trust could arise': *ibid*, 718. Compare
Lord Lloyd at 738. Similarly, it 'is hard to see how a resulting trust, even one of an inactive
character, whatever that may be, can arise in a situation where a person intentionally places
money on deposit with another, both parties intending that the property in the money should
pass to the depositee': Oakley (n 26) 77. See also Stoljar (n 4) 32; and Chambers (n 165)
156–63 and 167. Cf S Worthington, *Proprietary Interests in Commercial Transactions*
(Oxford, OUP, 1996) 148–61.

[169] On the nature of the resulting trust after *Westdeutsche*, see O'Dell (n 71) 170–1 with references, to which should now be added W Swadling, 'The Law of Property' in Birks and Rose
(n 18) 242; and P Birks and FD Rose (eds), *Restitution and Equity: Resulting Trusts and
Equitable Compensation* (London, Mansfield Press/LLP, 2000).

[170] See also G Virgo, *Principles of the Law of Restitution* (Oxford, OUP, 1999) 634, who
speculates that a constructive trust might be appropriate on the facts; whether or not that is
correct in principle, it was not canvassed in the case.

[171] *Sinclair* (n 4) 421; though, in fact, this was more by way of a prelude than an alternative
to the resulting trust point.

[172] *Ibid*, 441–2.

[173] *Ibid*, 459–60.

[174] Hence, the House of Lords in *Sinclair v Brougham* based 'the remedy available in equity
on a right of property recognised by equity as vested in the plaintiff throughout, not lost by
payment into a banking account, nor by the mixture of moneys, nor by merger in a mass of
assets. In all these cases the equitable remedy by way of declaration of charge is available': *Re
Diplock* (n 52) 540.

[175] Lord Wright called it a lien. 'Equity in such cases gives a partial right, which has been
called an equitable lien, on the total property to the extent that the total property represents
the plaintiff's property': Wright (n 4) 7. On whether it should more properly be called a lien,
see Worthington (n 168) 175. On the accuracy of the concept, see Smith (n 134) 200–1; as to
when it is appropriate and possible for a claimant to claim such a charge or lien, see Smith (n
134) 347–51, and, generally, *Foskett* (n 134).

monies received have been spent'.[176] Certainly, a charge was imposed in
Hallett, and this aspect of it may finally provide the reason for Viscount
Haldane LC's championing of it in *Sinclair v Brougham*; but if *Hallett* is
secure as an authority justifying such a charge, the deeply problematic
speech of Viscount Haldane LC is unnecessary for this purpose. In the end,
therefore, although a charge might justify the depositors' equitable claim in
Sinclair v Brougham, that decision is not necessary to justify the availability of a charge in equity's armoury.

Much else has been taken from the speeches in *Sinclair v Brougham* on
the tracing issue. For example, it has been said that, as a consequence:[177]

> [In] England, at least, it is apparently clearly established . . . that a subsisting
> fiduciary relationship is a necessary precondition of the equitable right to trace.

That is, in *Sinclair v Brougham*:[178]

> Lord Parker and Viscount Haldane both predicate the existence of a right of
> property recognised by equity which depends on there having existed at some
> stage a fiduciary relationship of some kind.

The requirement of a subsisting fiduciary relationship is often easily satisfied,[179] as it was at first instance in *Westdeutsche* by Hobhouse J[180] and in
the Court of Appeal.[181] But for so long as it persists, it will preclude an
equitable claim in support of a purely legal interest, and if strictly interpreted could preclude an equitable claim in support of another species of equitable interest, such as one subsequently raised to reverse an unjust
enrichment in a relationship which is not fiduciary. If however, the fiduciary limitation is not found in *Sinclair v Brougham*, or if it is no longer to

---

[176] *Re Shannon Travel Ltd*, unreported, Irish High Court, 8 May 1972, Kenny J at 8–9 of
the transcript.
[177] Meagher, Gummow and Lehane (n 162) para 505, commenting that it is clearly established by '*Re Diplock* relying on the speech of Lord Parker in *Sinclair v Brougham*'. To like
effect, see H Delany, *Equity and the Law of Trusts in Ireland* (2nd edn, Dublin, Round Hall
Sweet & Maxwell, 1999), 634–5 and 643–7; Goff and Jones (n 69) 103. The requirement
seems to have been rejected in Canada and Australia: Smith (n 134) 128. But the position in
New Zealand is unclear: Smith (n 134) 120 n 2 and 128 n 33.
[178] *Re Diplock* (n 52) 540. Compare the earlier defence of 'the necessity of establishing as a
starting point the existence of a fiduciary or a quasi-fiduciary relationship or of a continuing
right of property recognised in equity': *ibid*, 520.
[179] See eg *Chase Manhattan Bank NA v Israel British Bank (London) Ltd* [1981] Ch 105;
Re Irish Shipping [1986] ILRM 518; *Agip (Africa) Ltd v Jackson* [1990] Ch 265, 280 (Millett
J) (a point not taken on appeal: [1991] Ch 547).
[180] [1994] 4 All ER 890, 937: 'the present case is indistinguishable from *Sinclair v
Brougham*. The fiduciary relationship comes into existence and the equity is created at the time
that the payee receives the money.'
[181] [1994] 1 WLR 938, 949 (Dillon LJ) and 953 (Leggatt LJ). The objections to the finding
of a fiduciary relationship in *Sinclair v Brougham*, considered at nn 162–5 above, apply with
equal if not greater force here.

be followed on this point, then these limitations can fall away, though it will then be a separate question as to whether they should.

The fiduciary requirement seems to have had no friends since Lord Greene MR's decision in *Re Diplock*.[182] Oakley argues that *Hallett* supported the right of the holder of *any* equitable proprietary interest to identify his property in its exchange product and claim it on the basis of an equitable proprietary interest,[183] and that properly interpreted, apart from Lord Dunedin,[184] the House of Lords in *Sinclair v Brougham*[185]did likewise.[186] On this reading, having identified their money in the society, the depositors' equitable proprietary claim was based simply upon an equitable proprietary interest in the money, of which not one species (the fiduciary relationship) but three (that relationship, resulting trust, and charge) were identified,[187] and there is nothing in the speeches to confine the claim to only one species or source of equitable proprietary interest such as a fiduciary relationship.[188] In *Westdeutsche*, Lord Browne-Wilkinson accepted that the owner of a stolen bag of coins lodged in a bank account could trace into the bank account, ie identify the coins in their exchange product and claim accordingly, notwithstanding the absence of a fiduciary relationship between the claimant and the thief.[189] This has probably, and quite rightly, sounded the death-knell for the fiduciary relationship as a matter of English law.[190] Similarly, in Ireland Budd J in the *Bricklayers' Hall* case in the High Court commented that '[i]t is questionable whether *Sinclair v Brougham* is authority for the proposition that a fiduciary relationship is essential before

---

[182] See the careful analysis in Smith (n 134) 120–30 (demonstrating that the requirement is founded upon misunderstanding) and 340–7; see also Worthington (n 168) 184–5.

[183] Oakley (n 26) 72. In this respect, in *Hallett,* the fiduciary relationship was a *sufficient* basis for an equitable proprietary claim, but not a *necessary* one: see Smith (n 134) 124–5.

[184] Who simply looked to a 'superfluity' in the defendant's hands: *Sinclair* (n 4) 437. This 'unworkable principle' is 'extraordinarily difficult to apply—what constitutes a superfluity for these purposes?' (Oakley (n 26) 79 and 80). Lord Browne-Wilkinson was very wary of it in *Westdeutsche* (n 11) 711.

[185] Oakley (n 26) 76–7; see also AJ Oakley, 'Proprietary Claims and their Priority in Insolvency' [1995] *CLJ* 377; and Smith (n 134) 123–5.

[186] For example, Viscount Haldane LC commented that the depositors' money 'was never converted into a debt, in equity at all events': *Sinclair* (n 4) 421. Lord Parker said that his approach was based upon the creation by equity of 'rights of property, though not recognised as such by the common law': *ibid*, 422.

[187] A similar argument as to *Diplock* is also more than possible: Oakley (n 26) 80–2; Oakley (n 185) 383–4; RA Pearce, 'A Tracing Paper' (1976) 40 *Conv* 277. But it is probably rather more sound to argue instead that if the fiduciary limitation is not properly to be found in *Sinclair,* or if it is but *Sinclair* is no longer regarded as good law on the point, limitation should wither away notwithstanding *Diplock*. Compare G Jones, '*Ultra Vires* Swaps: The Common Law and Equitable Fall-Out' [1996] *CLJ* 432, 435, and cf *Westdeutsche* (n 11) 714 (Lord Browne-Wilkinson).

[188] Compare Smith (n 134) 125–6; Worthington (n 168) 184.

[189] *Westdeutsche* (n 11) 716.

[190] See Virgo (n 170) 649, and LD Smith, 'Tracing' in Birks and Rose (n 18) 233 and 234–5.

property can be followed in equity'.[191] This should similarly sound the death-knell for the fiduciary requirement as a matter of Irish law.

It is therefore difficult to abstract anything of value from *Sinclair v Brougham* on the so-called 'tracing' issue. Indeed, for Stoljar, it 'cannot be really explained on the basis of the tracing doctrine. What was here called "tracing" or "following" property, was nothing more than a question-begging method to make the society return some of the lenders' money'.[192] It comes as no surprise then that it did not survive *Westdeutsche* on this issue either: Lord Browne-Wilkinson held that 'the decision as to rights *in rem* in *Sinclair v Brougham* should . . . be overruled'.[193] Lord Slynn agreed that *Sinclair v Brougham* should be departed from,[194] and Lord Lloyd agreed that it was wrongly decided.[195] Given the infirmity of *Sinclair v Brougham* on the whole tracing process, both as identification and as to claiming, this must be right. Furthermore, to my late twentieth century eyes, raised on the distinction between ownership and obligation,[196] it is strange indeed that, where a personal action failed, a proprietary one should have succeeded! This outcome has been described as 'somewhat irrational',[197] not least because, in the case of an insolvency, it could result in an unfair priority over other creditors, and this was one of the concerns relied upon by Lord Browne-Wilkinson to justify overruling *Sinclair v Brougham* on this point.[198]

Lord Goff, however, was reluctant to adopt this course, not least because:[199]

> Lord Wright, who wrote in such strong terms indorsing the just result in *Sinclair v Brougham*, would turn in his grave at any such suggestion.

For Lord Wright:[200]

> The importance of the substantial and affirmative decision and of the actual discussion in the judgments lies in the exposition of the *equity* of restitution.

---

[191] Unreported, Irish High Court, 6 March 1996, at 41 of the transcript. The point did not arise on appeal: [1996] 1 IR 468. It might be objected that Budd J was bound by the contrary authority of his father's judgment on the point in *Shanahan's Stamp Auctions v Farrelly* [1962] IR 386. However, this may not necessarily be so. In *Shanahan's*, though he quoted them extensively, the elder Budd J did not consider *Sinclair v Brougham* and *Re Diplock* for what they themselves might have held but only for whether they supported his interpretation of *Re Hallett's Estate* (see eg [1962] IR 428, 438 and 443).

[192] Stoljar (n 4) 32.

[193] *Westdeutsche* (n 11) 713.

[194] *Ibid*, 718.

[195] *Ibid*, 738.

[196] Eg RM Goode, 'Ownership and Obligation in Commercial Transactions' (1987) 103 *LQR* 433.

[197] RH Maudsley, 'Proprietary Remedies for the Recovery of Money' (1959) 75 *LQR* 234, 234–5.

[198] *Westdeutsche* (n 11) 713–4. A similar point motivated Lord Goff's more limited rejection of the resulting trust: *ibid*, 690.

[199] *Ibid*, 689.

[200] Wright (n 4) 19; emphasis added. Compare *Fibrosa* (n 50) 64.

Pointing to passages from the speeches of Lord Dunedin and Lord Parker[201] in which the so-called 'tracing' claim was justified to prevent the unjust enrichment of the shareholders at the expense of the depositors,[202] he tries to spin *Sinclair v Brougham* as supportive of unjust enrichment reasoning, if not at common law, then at least in equity:[203]

> I regard the case as primarily significant as embodying the leading principles on which the Court acts in exercising its equitable jurisdiction to give relief in order to prevent unjust enrichment, or to achieve restitution.

There is just as much wishful thinking in this, however, as there is in Lord Wright's attempts to spin the common law. The common law has subsequently developed a coherent law of restitution based upon the principle against unjust enrichment, its unfinished business is the integration of equity,[204] and it would better achieve that integration without the distorting effects of *Sinclair v Brougham*.

Bad cases make hard law.[205] *Sinclair v Brougham* is doubly hard; first, hard in the sense that it is difficult to follow,[206] and secondly, hard in the sense of unfair, not necessarily to the parties, but potentially to creditors in subsequent cases in which it is cited.[207] As Burrows and McKendrick

---

[201] 'Of the four speeches, I have found those of Lord Parker and Lord Dunedin most illuminating': Wright (n 4) 6. Notice that he says that there were four speeches, of which two were illuminating, trying to create a spurious equality between these favoured views and the disfavoured views in the other two speeches. He glosses over the point that one of the other two speeches—that of Viscount Haldane LC—commanded the assent of Lord Atkinson, so that the disfavoured views were in fact not equal but in the majority.

[202] 'The shareholders are entitled to share among them the proper assets of the society. But they are not entitled to be made rich at the expense of the depositors by swelling the assets of the society by means of the proceeds of moneys to which they themselves never contributed': *Sinclair* (n 4) 437–8 (Lord Dunedin). 'The equity lay in this, that it would be unconscionable for the society to retain the amount by which its assets had been increased by, and in fact still represented, the borrowed money': *ibid*, 444 (Lord Parker).

[203] Wright (n 4) 1.

[204] J Beatson, 'Unfinished Business: Integrating Equity' in *The Use and Abuse of Unjust Enrichment* (Oxford, OUP, 1991) 244.

[205] *Sinclair v Brougham* also demonstrates that hard cases make bad law. This is a maxim almost as much beloved of lawyers as those referred to in the text to n 46 above: eg RFV Heuston, 'Hard Cases Make Bad Law' (1978) *Dublin University LJ* 31; Dworkin (n 8). Compare *Sadler v Evans* (1766) 4 Burr 1984, 1990; 98 ER 34, 37 (Lord Mansfield): 'the granting [of] this rule would be a bad precedent; though in a favourable case. Favourable cases make bad precedents.'

[206] 'We should, however, be lacking in candour rather than showing respect if we refrained from saying that we find the opinions in *Sinclair v Brougham* in many respects not only difficult to follow but difficult to reconcile with one another': *Re Diplock* (n 52) 518. 'Like others before me, I find Lord Haldane LC's reasoning difficult, if not impossible, to follow': *Westdeutsche* (n 11) 712.

[207] Of course, the proprietary remedy is limited to the identifiability of the claimed *res*. As Lord Sumner is reported to have observed in the course of argument (*The Times*, 11 December 1913, 3a) that if there is no personal claim, and the proprietary one is lost because the money is no longer identifiable, then 'the way to get rich quick is to act *ultra vires*, and keep no accounts'!

observe, 'the obscurity of the reasoning of their Lordships in *Sinclair v Brougham* on the finding of a proprietary interest means that few will mourn its passing'.[208]

E. CONCLUSION: *SINCLAIR V BROUGHAM*: MAD, BAD AND DANGEROUS TO KNOW[209]

Apart from getting things so comprehensively wrong, all that the litigation in *Sinclair v Brougham* achieved was to dissipate in legal fees a large portion of the money otherwise available for disbursement to the depositors and the remaining shareholders:[210] the litigation only benefited the lawyers in the case itself and baffled generations of lawyers since.

The contrast between their Lordships' insistence upon detailed precision (and misguided if not misunderstood detail at that) at law, and their tolerance of (even revelling in) untrammelled discretion in equity is decidedly odd. It is all the more odd when one realises that the precision was applied to the relatively puny legal personal claim, whilst the discretion was applied to the vastly potentially more powerful equitable proprietary claim. Indeed, the woolliness on the proprietary claim is a whirlwind still being reaped in subsequent attempts to generate unwarranted proprietary claims to gain priority over outside creditors on an insolvency. In neither *Sinclair* nor *Westdeutsche* was this reason in play—the outside creditors in *Sinclair v Brougham* had already been paid off, and in *Westdeutsche*, the local authority, though strapped for cash, was not insolvent—in both cases the important point was that it was equitable, and the fact that it was proprietary was somewhat beside the point. It is difficult to escape the conclusion that if they had got it right on the personal claim at law, the House of Lords would not have had to distort the proprietary claim in equity to achieve a just result.

Part of the problem on the equitable point seems to have been that Viscount Haldane LC wanted to talk about *Hallett*, and manufactured the opportunity to do so in *Sinclair v Brougham*,[211] thereby managing to give it 'something of a new mystique, as if it held untold possibilities'.[212] In fact, it added very little to the outcome, apart from supplying the source for the charge as one of the three equitable proprietary claims canvassed in the speeches.

---

[208] A Burrows and E McKendrick, *Cases and Materials on the Law of Restitution* (Oxford, OUP, 1997) 676.

[209] This is Lady Caroline Lamb's description in her *Journal* of Lord Byron.

[210] Costs came first out of the fund, even in the House of Lords: *Sinclair* (n 4) 427 (Viscount Haldane LC).

[211] In much the same way, Lord Browne-Wilkinson manufactured an opportunity to discuss constructive trusts in *Westdeutsche*, and having helped to still the controversies surrounding *Sinclair v Brougham*, thereby constructed a whole new set: O'Dell (n 71) 170–80.

[212] Stoljar (n 4) 30.

For all its problems, however, if *Sinclair v Brougham* hadn't happened, we'd probably have had to invent it. Its statement of a hard-line thesis generated as an anti-thesis the modern principle against unjust enrichment. Strange though it is to say, the modern law of restitution needed *Sinclair v Brougham*. Without it, the law could have gone the way of discretion rather than principle and been all the less important for that. But this having occurred, its usefulness is now past. Holmes, according to Lord Wright, thought that cases have a shelf-life of about half a century.[213] In this light, the eighty or so years of the *Sinclair v Brougham* hegemony is a very good innings, and it is unsurprising that this once-great case should have fallen to earth.

The decline of *Sinclair v Brougham* is an excellent example of the tradition of transformation which Hutchinson argues is at the heart of the common law.[214] But it can also be pressed into other jurisprudential service. For those who disagree with the reasoning in the speeches, the decline of *Sinclair v Brougham* could be seen as an important example of the law working itself pure.[215] Whether one agrees with it or not, as a matter of observation, its decline provides an example of narrative which did not prove compelling.[216] The story of that decline is one of the displacement of the implied contract fiction and the rise of the principle against unjust enrichment, which could be presented as an important paradigm shift[217] in the alignment of the common law of obligations.

The Chief Justice of Ireland has written that *Sinclair v Brougham* 'must share with *Donoghue v Stevenson* the distinction of being the most intensively raked over judicial decision of the [twentieth] century'.[218] But whilst it can confidently be predicted that *Donoghue* will retain its iconic status in the twenty-first, *Sinclair v Brougham*—as the case that fell to earth—quite properly will not.

---

[213] 'That great American lawyer, Mr Justice Holmes, said that every half-century the case-law is rewritten so that earlier cases may be put aside': Wright (n 57) 382. See also Wright (n 58) 45.

[214] Hutchinson (n 10).

[215] Above, text with nn 8–10.

[216] A central concern of branches of the law and literature movement. For various views on this issue, see eg JB White, *The Legal Imagination* (Chicago, IL, University of Chicago Press, 1985); P Brooks and P Gewirtz (eds), *Law's Stories, Narrative and Rhetoric in the Law* (New Haven, Conn, Yale UP, 1996); M Freeman and A Lewis (eds), *Law and Literature* (Oxford, OUP, 1999). Contra RA Posner, *Law and Literature* (revised ed, Cambridge, MA Harvard University Press, 1998); RA Posner, 'Relations between Law and Literature' (1999) 34 *Irish Jurist* (ns) 18.

[217] TS Kuhn, *The Structure of Scientific Revolutions* (3rd edn, Chicago, IL, University of Chicago Press, 1996).

[218] R Keane, *Equity and the Law of Trusts in the Republic of Ireland* (Dublin, Butterworths, 1988) 282.

10

Fibrosa Spolka Akcyjna v Fairbairn Lawson Combe Barbour, Limited (1942)

PAUL MITCHELL

A. INTRODUCTION

WHAT STANDS OUT as a landmark depends on the observer's position. From the modern perspective the claim that the House of Lords' decision in *Fibrosa Spolka Akcyjna v Fairbairn Lawson Combe Barbour, Limited*[1] is a 'landmark' in the law of unjust enrichment is questionable. At first glance the case may look important. Their Lordships recognised a new general principle that a party who had made a pre-payment under a subsequently frustrated contract could recover the pre-payment, provided that there had been a total failure of consideration. In doing so they reversed previous Court of Appeal authority.[2] But the significance of their decision seems to be entirely overshadowed by the almost immediate enactment of the Law Reform (Frustrated Contracts) Act 1943. The statute, described as 'the most important statute in the law of restitution' by one commentator,[3] introduced a completely new regime to regulate the consequences of frustration. That new regime meant that the House of Lords' decision in *Fibrosa* was, for all practical purposes, redundant.

It is therefore not surprising that the modern view of *Fibrosa* is that it is a case of marginal importance. Its main significance is seen as being that the House of Lords' criticisms of the common law were the catalyst for Parliamentary action. As Robert Goff J put it in *BP Exploration Co (Libya) Ltd v Hunt (No 2)*,[4] 'no doubt stimulated by the observations made in the

---

[1] [1943] AC 32.
[2] *Chandler v Webster* [1904] 1 KB 493.
[3] A Burrows, *The Law of Restitution* (2nd edn, London, Butterworths LexisNexis, 2002) 359.
[4] [1979] 1 WLR 783.

Fibrosa case, in the following year the legislature enacted the Act of 1943'.[5] The editors of *Chitty on Contracts* put it slightly higher: the defects in the common law identified in *Fibrosa* 'compelled Parliament to intervene'.[6] Whether Parliament was cajoled or coerced, the focus is on the political process, as distinct from the judicial prompting.

This essay argues, however, that the distinction between the political and judicial contributions to the reform of the law on the consequences of frustration is mistaken. The decision in *Fibrosa* should be seen, not as initiating a separate political process, but as *part of* the political process. Furthermore, the political story begins, not with *Fibrosa*, but with the Law Revision Committee's consideration of pre-payments under frustrated contracts in 1937–9.[7] Each of these three, apparently discrete, events—the Committee, the case and the Act—were linked by continuity of purpose and personnel; each casts light on the other two; and they can only be fully understood if considered together.

B. THE CONSEQUENCES OF FRUSTRATION AT COMMON LAW: THE RULE IN *CHANDLER V WEBSTER*

The Law Revision Committee, the House of Lords in *Fibrosa* and Parliament were each trying to answer the same question: how should the common law rules about the consequences of frustration be reformed? Those common law rules were simple: the loss lay where it fell. If one party had paid in advance and the return performance had been frustrated, he could not recover his payment.[8] If, conversely, work had been started for which payment was due on completion, but the frustrating event prevented completion, no payment could be recovered for the work done.[9]

The rule about pre-payment had been elaborated in a series of cases[10] arising out of the cancelled coronation procession for Edward VII, most famously in the Court of Appeal's decision in *Chandler v Webster*.[11] There a contract had been made for the use of a room overlooking the route of

---

[5] *Ibid*, 798.

[6] H Beale (ed), *Chitty on Contracts* (29th edn, London, Thomson Sweet and Maxwell, 2004) 23-072.

[7] Law Revision Committee, *Seventh Interim Report (Rule in Chandler v Webster)* (Cmd 6009/1939).

[8] *Chandler v Webster* [1904] 1 KB 493.

[9] *Appleby v Myers* (1867) LR 2 CP 651.

[10] *Krell v Henry* (1902) 18 TLR 823 (KBD), [1903] 2 KB 740 (CA); *Blakeley v Muller & Co* [1903] 2 KB 760n; *The Civil Service Co-Operative Society, Limited v The General Steam Navigation Company* [1903] 2 KB 756; *Clark v Lindsay* (1903) 88 LT 198.

[11] [1904] 1 KB 493.

the procession on the day it was due to take place. Payment of the entire fee of 141l was to be in advance. The defendant complied as to 100l, but had failed to pay the balance by the time that the procession was cancelled. The claimant sued for the balance; the defendant counterclaimed for the return of the 100l advance payment. 'This case,' argued counsel for the defendant, 'is simply one of a total failure of consideration.'[12] The Court of Appeal disagreed, finding for the claimant on both the claim and the counterclaim.

The Court of Appeal's reasoning analysed the situation in terms of the law of contract. As Collins MR put it in the first sentence of his judgment, 'The question appears really to depend upon the terms of the contract made by the parties'.[13] Counsel's attempt to persuade the court that it was a simple case for the return of payment on the ground of total failure of consideration was unsuccessful because it did not take account of the legal effect of frustration. As Collins MR explained:[14]

> from the time when the fact of [frustration] had been ascertained, the contract can no further be performed by either party, it remains good up to that point, and everything previously done in pursuance of it must be treated as rightly done, but the parties are both discharged from further performance of it. If the effect were that the contract were wiped out altogether, no doubt the result would be that money paid under it would have to be repaid as on a failure of consideration. But that is not the effect of the doctrine; it only releases the parties from further performance of the contract. Therefore the doctrine of failure of consideration does not apply.

Romer LJ put the same point slightly differently:[15]

> the parties . . . are both free from any subsequent obligation cast upon them by the agreement; but, except in cases where the contract can be treated as rescinded ab initio, any payment previously made, and any legal right previously accrued according to the terms of the agreement will not be disturbed.

This idea that accrued contractual rights could not be circumvented by restitutionary claims had significant historical support. In *Appleby v Myers*,[16] for example, it had been held that, where a contract provided for payment on completion of the work, and completion was prevented by frustration, the contractor could not resort to a *quantum meruit* claim to recover the value of the work done. Similarly, in *Stubbs v The Holywell Railway Company*,[17] when a contract of personal services for a fixed term

---

[12] *Ibid*, 495.
[13] *Ibid*, 496.
[14] *Ibid*, 499.
[15] *Ibid*, 501.
[16] (1867) LR 2 CP 651.
[17] (1867) LR 2 Exch 311.

had been frustrated by the death of the contractor, payment had to be made on the contractual basis (per quarter), rather than—as the employer would have preferred—for the value of the work done. The decision that a claim for total failure of consideration was not available to the claimant in *Chandler v Webster* was, therefore, orthodox.

Whether it was convincing was another matter. Buckland, for instance, was not persuaded, commenting that 'no obvious reason appears why the mere accrual of the right should save this particular claim from the general wreck'.[18] It might not have been obvious, but the most likely explanation for the position adopted in *Chandler v Webster* (and earlier authorities) was that, at the time, contract was the dominant scheme of analysis. Indeed, restitutionary claims were classified as a sub-species of contract: quasi-contract or contracts implied in law.[19] Given this prevailing assumption about the status of restitutionary claims it was not surprising to find the Court of Appeal prioritising the express contractual obligations of the parties. Nor was this prevailing assumption about the subordinate nature of restitutionary claims short-lived: ten years later, in *Sinclair v Brougham*,[20] the same assumption led the House of Lords to the conclusion that no action could lie for money had and received against a recipient who had had no contractual capacity to receive it.

The precise rule in *Chandler v Webster*, therefore, was that the loss lay where the contract provided. Such provision might be an express term of the contract, as it was in *Elliott v Crutchley*.[21] There, three weeks after *Chandler v Webster*, an identically constituted Court of Appeal demonstrated that it was prepared to interpret such terms liberally. The term provided that there should be 'no liability' if the coronation naval review was cancelled 'before any expense is incurred by the caterer'.[22] The caterer had incurred such expense, but the Court of Appeal held that the term required the return of the pre-payment, with a deduction for expenses incurred.

A term might also, more controversially, be implied. Thus, for instance, in *Krell v Henry*[23] the trial judge implied a term that a pre-payment made under a contract to hire a room to see the Coronation procession should be returned if the procession was cancelled. Before an appeal was heard, the trial judge's reasoning was censured by the Lord Chief Justice in *Blakeley v Muller & Co*.[24] He commented that:[25]

---

[18] W Buckland, '*Casus* and Frustration in Roman and Common Law' (1932–3) 46 *Harvard Law Review* 1281, 1290.

[19] D Ibbetson, *A Historical Introduction to the Law of Obligations* (Oxford, OUP, 1999) 277–81.

[20] [1914] AC 398.

[21] [1904] 1 KB 565.

[22] *Ibid*, 566.

[23] (1902) 18 TLR 823.

[24] [1903] 2 KB 760n.

[25] *Ibid*, 761.

The learned judge seems to have thought that *Taylor v Caldwell* justified him in constructing for the parties the contract they would probably have made if they had contemplated the event which happened; but in my opinion it does not.

When the appeal in *Krell v Henry* was finally heard,[26] the defendant's claim to recover his pre-payment was dropped.[27]

The difficulty with implying a term about the financial consequences of frustration was that it risked becoming too speculative. As Wills J explained in *Blakeley v Muller & Co*:[28]

> The process of constructing a hypothetical contract by supposing what terms the parties would have arrived at if they had contemplated the possibility of what was going to happen is, to my mind, very unsatisfactory. It is very difficult to construct such a contract for them. Probably . . . the defendants would have stipulated for compensation for their outlay, and the plaintiffs for a return of their money; but it is impossible to say with any certainty what the result of their bargaining would have been.

In *Chandler v Webster* Collins MR quoted this passage with approval,[29] although both he and Mathew LJ contemplated that, in suitable cases, such a term could be implied.[30]

Whilst the point about speculation was a powerful objection, it was not conclusive: a certain amount of speculation was unavoidable where terms were being implied. Furthermore, the doctrine of frustration itself was, at the time, seen as based on an implied term following the decision in *Taylor v Caldwell*.[31] It was also thought to require an event outside the contemplation of the parties.[32] So, every time a court held that a contract was frustrated it was using this 'very unsatisfactory' technique to 'construct' a contract covering a situation not contemplated by the parties.

It was really a question of degree: having implied a term to bring the relationship to an end, could the court go further and imply a term for ancillary relief? In *Russkoe Obschestvo D'Lia Izgsbovlenia Snariadov I'Voennick Pripassov v John Stirk & Sons, Ltd*[33] Bailhache J felt that he could do so, and held that a proportionate part of a pre-payment should be returned in a situation where some of the goods to be supplied had been

[26] [1903] 2 KB 740.
[27] *Ibid*, 754.
[28] [1903] 2 KB 760n, 762.
[29] [1904] 1 KB 493, 500.
[30] *Ibid*, 497 and 502 respectively.
[31] (1863) 3 B & S 826, 122 ER 309.
[32] *Krell v Henry* [1903] 2 KB 740, 751; *Maritime National Fish Ltd v Ocean Trawlers Ltd* [1935] AC 524, 529.
[33] (1921) 8 Ll L Rep 394 (KBD), (1922) 10 Ll L Rep 214 (CA).

manufactured by the seller, but sold elsewhere following a direction of the
British government. The Court of Appeal's response was scathing. Bankes
LJ asserted that it was contrary to principle to imply any term regulating
the consequences of frustration;[34] this was an extreme position that would
have surprised the Court of Appeal in *Chandler v Webster*.[35] Younger LJ
agreed with both Bankes LJ and Atkin LJ. Atkin LJ took a more sophisticated approach which attacked the implied term theory of frustration and,
therefore, took away the foundation for implying a further term to deal
with the consequences of frustration. For him it was 'a little unfortunate'[36]
that implied term analysis had ever been used for frustration. Rather, both
it and the rules regulating its consequences should be seen as 'positive rules
of law imposed upon contracting parties',[37] with no dependence on the parties' intentions. Certainly, in his view, the rule in *Chandler v Webster* could
not be seen as flowing from the parties' intentions:[38]

> I venture to doubt whether any two business people in the world would ever real-
> ly make a contract that if certain unforeseen events happen the contract should
> be at an end and that moneys paid should remain exactly as they were. It seems
> to me impossible that that should be deliberately done by business men: they
> would be practically certain to try to make some arrangement as to the adjust-
> ment of their rights.

The judgment of Atkin LJ in the *Russkoe* case was a sign that the tide of
judicial opinion was starting to turn against *Chandler v Webster*. It also
hinted at an option for reform: a rule of positive law that defeated commercial expectations should be changed to meet those expectations. Indeed, the
passage quoted above was also quoted by the Law Revision Committee in
their Report on *Chandler v Webster*,[39] which advocated such a reform.

It is, therefore, particularly important to note that Atkin LJ was completely mistaken.

C. THE CONSEQUENCES OF FRUSTRATION IN MARITIME LAW

For over two hundred years businessmen had consistently agreed that pre-
payments should be retained, despite a frustration of contractual performance, when they were contracting to have goods carried by sea. The earliest

---

[34] (1922) 10 Ll L Rep 214, 215.
[35] See text accompanying n 30.
[36] (1922) 10 Ll L Rep 214, 216.
[37] *Ibid*, 217.
[38] *Ibid*.
[39] *Seventh Interim Report* (n 7) 4.

case, a report of a ruling by Saunders CJ in 1683,[40] established that the ship owner was not bound to pay the wages of his crew if the ship was lost on the voyage and, therefore, earned no freight. The position was different, however, where there was 'advance-money paid before, if in part of freight, and so named in the charter-party'.[41] Then wages were due even if the ship failed to reach its destination, 'according to the proportion of the freight paid before; for the freighters cannot have their money'.[42]

Payment of at least part of the freight in advance was not 'impossible' to imagine; quite the reverse. In a case in 1800[43] Serjeant Shepherd assured the Court of Exchequer that 'it is always customary in the carriage of goods to India to contract for payment of the freight previous to the sailing of the ship'.[44] Brett J, in *Allison v Bristol Marine Insurance Company*,[45] attributed the origin of the rule to Indian voyages, explaining that '[the] length of the voyage would keep the shipowner for too long a time out of money; and freight is much more difficult to pledge, as a security to third persons, than goods represented by a bill of lading'.[46] In 1871 the Court of Exchequer Chamber (reluctantly) acknowledged that the non-recoverable nature of advance freight payments was too well established to be reversed.[47]

The rule does not seem to have caused hardship to the freighter. Although its effect was to transfer risk to him in relation to a perilous venture, that shift in risk could be reflected in the price, insurance arrangements or, more typically, both. *Andrew v Moorhouse*[48] illustrates the effect on price. There the voyage was from London to the Cape of Good Hope, and the ship owner offered a choice: either 5l per ton paid in London, or 7l per ton at the Cape. The defendant opted for the 5l per ton arrangement, but failed to pay immediately. He then refused to pay absolutely once he heard that the ship had been lost. Serjeant Best submitted that 'no man would be so unjust to himself as to pay his money with the chance of obtaining nothing for it'.[49] But the King's Bench disagreed: the payment was due in London immediately and unconditionally.

The advance freight rule also prompted adjustments in insurance arrangements, and these influenced the price. If advance freight was paid in full, the shipowner would be overpaid because, had he been forced to wait

---

[40] *Anon* (1683) 2 Show KB 283, 89 ER 941.
[41] *Ibid.*
[42] *Ibid.*
[43] *Blakey v Dixon* (1800) 2 Bos & Pul 321, 126 ER 1304.
[44] *Ibid*, 322.
[45] (1876) 1 App Cas 209.
[46] *Ibid*, 226.
[47] *Byrne v Schiller* (1871) LR 6 Ex 319.
[48] (1814) 5 Taunt 435, 128 ER 758.
[49] *Ibid*, 5 Taunt 437, 128 ER 759.

until the end of the voyage for payment, he would have insured his freight. Equally, the burden of insuring under a contract with payment of advance freight moved to the freighter.[50] The parties, therefore, typically made a deduction for insurance from the advance freight payment. Indeed, this deduction of insurance came to be seen as a reliable indicator that the contract required payment of advance freight, as opposed to a mere loan to the shipowner, because a mere loan was not insurable.[51]

The case law on shipping also provided illuminating illustrations of how a more flexible approach to the consequences of frustration might function. One potentially useful technique was the doctrine of freight *pro rata itineris*, which allowed courts to award a proportion of the total freight where the voyage had been cut short by frustration, and the ship had been forced to stop at an intermediate port. Thus, for instance, in *Luke v Lloyd*[52] a vessel was seized by an enemy ship, then retaken by a British vessel and returned to a British port. Seventeen days of a twenty-one day voyage had been completed; half of the cargo had been taken by the British vessel to pay salvage. Lord Mansfield CJ held that the shipowner could recover damages equivalent to 17/21 of half the total freight.

The precise basis of the doctrine was contentious, and Lord Mansfield CJ's analysis in *Luke v Lloyd* could be read in two ways. One possibility was that the benefit conferred on the shipper of the goods called for compensation. The second possibility was that the conduct of the shipowner and the shipper waived their existing contractual obligations, and substituted a new contractual agreement. The former explanation was essentially restitutionary, the latter contractual. The practical difference between the two was that they gave different answers if the shipper refused to accept his goods at the intermediate port. If the restitutionary analysis applied, the key factor was the benefit conferred. But if the contractual explanation was correct, there could be no liability to pay pro rata freight, since the shipper's conduct did not indicate a willingness to waive the existing obligations and enter into a new contract.

In *Osgood v Groning*[53] both rationales for pro rata freight could be seen. Lord Ellenborough CJ emphasised that a new contract had to be found, and the shipper's agreement to take the goods at an intermediate port expressly without prejudice to his rights could not be seen as the foundation for a promise to pay pro rata freight.[54] The Lord Chancellor, however, to whom

---

[50] *Allison v Bristol Marine Insurance Company* (1876) 1 App Cas 209, 223.
[51] *Hicks v Shield* (1857) 7 El & Bl 633, 119 ER 1380.
[52] (1759) 1 W Bl 190, 96 ER 102.
[53] (1810) 2 Camp 466, 170 ER 1220.
[54] *Ibid*, 2 Camp 470, 170 ER 1221.

the case was returned, ruled that 'if it should appear that the plaintiff could not have been reasonably required to proceed on the voyage, the defendant should admit that he had accepted the goods in the [intermediate] port'.[55] On this analysis, the shipper's willingness to accept delivery short of the destination became a question of law, not fact.

Even when the doctrinal basis was unambiguous, its requirements could be manipulated to give surprising results. In *The Soblomsten*[56] Dr Lushington set out a classic contractual approach, but then proceeded to find that silence and inactivity on the part of the shipper amounted to a waiver of the existing obligation coupled with an implied promise to pay pro rata freight. It is difficult to see the new contract here as anything other than a fiction.[57]

The analytical basis of pro rata freight was finally settled in favour of the contractual approach.[58] Thus it was held in *Metcalfe v Britannia Ironworks Company*[59] that there was no liability on a shipper whose goods were to be carried from Middlesborough to Taganrog (on the Black Sea), when they were carried as far as Kerch (another Black Sea port) and further progress was prevented by the sea being frozen.[60] The crucial point was that on arrival at Kerch the shipper had initially refused to take the goods, and eventually took them under protest: it was therefore impossible to imply a new contract. As Bramwell LJ commented, the shipper's conduct 'might not have been very generous, but it was very discreet'.[61]

Although the decision in *Metcalfe* settled the basis of the doctrine, it was not unanimous. In the Divisional Court Cockburn CJ had put forward a compelling case for playing down the strict contractual dimensions of the doctrine. Rather, a contract should be implied 'where justice and equity require it'.[62] The present facts, in his view, were just such a case:[63]

Nothing could apparently be more unjust than that, having had the benefit of the conveyance of the cargo so far on its way, the owner, if he has derived benefit from its conveyance so far, should be released from the obligation of paying a proportionate part of the freight.

It followed that if a shipper took his goods at the intermediate port and disposed of them, he was automatically under an obligation to pay.

---

[55] *Ibid*, 2 Camp 471, 170 ER 1221.
[56] (1866) LR 1 Add & Ecc 293.
[57] Cf *The Hannah Blumenthal* [1983] 1 AC 854; *The Leonidas D* [1985] 1 WLR 925.
[58] *Metcalfe v Britannia Ironworks Company* (1876) 1 QBD 613 (DC), (1877) 2 QBD 423 (CA); *St Enoch Shipping Company, Limited v Phosphate Mining Company* [1916] 2 KB 624.
[59] (1876) 1 QBD 613 (DC), (1877) 2 QBD 423 (CA).
[60] *Ibid*.
[61] (1877) 2 QBD 423, 429.
[62] (1876) 1 QBD 613, 619.
[63] *Ibid*, 620.

The Court of Appeal dismissed this approach as the invocation of 'a sort of general equity',[64] but, with the benefit of hindsight, Cockburn CJ can be seen to have been ahead of his time: his approach was almost exactly the same as the approach adopted over fifty years later in the Law Reform (Frustrated Contracts) Act 1943.

The majority in the Divisional Court (Quain and Mellor JJ) took the contractual approach to pro rata freight. But they, too, referred to the possibility of equitable adjustment in an intriguing aside. They acknowledged that the point about benefit was a powerful one, and said that, had they heard more evidence about benefit to the shipper, "a question might have arisen whether we might not now be called upon to administer in favour of a shipowner . . . some of that 'larger equity' . . . as exercised by Courts of Admiralty in similar cases".[65]

The Courts of Admiralty dealt with the consequences of frustration in an entirely different way to their common law counterparts. As Sir Samuel Evans put it, in *The Corsican Prince*:[66]

> the Prize Courts deal with claims in accordance with the law of nations, and upon equitable principles freed from contracts, which almost always cease to have effect upon capture or seizure, by reason of the non-performance or noncompletion of the contract of affreightment; whereas common law Courts would only determine the consequences of the strictly legal obligations of the parties. The King's Bench Courts would either give the claimants for freight the whole or nothing according to whether the contract of affreightment had been performed or not; but the Prize Court takes all the circumstances into consideration, and may award, as it has done in decided cases, the whole, or a moiety, of the freight, or a sum pro rata itineris, or it may discard the contract rate altogether, even as a basis for assessment or calculation . . .; or it may withhold or diminish the sum by reason of misconduct, as, eg, by resistance to search, or spoliation, or non-disclosure of papers.

The contrast with *Chandler v Webster* ('The question appears really to depend upon the terms of the contract made by the parties'[67]) could not be more striking.

Thus, for instance, in *The Friends*,[68] where a voyage to Lisbon had been frustrated by the vessel being captured by a Spanish privateer, retaken by a British cruiser, then sold to pay salvage, the Court of Prize was asked to decide what freight, if any, was due. Sir William Scott explained that he

---

[64] (1877) 2 QBD 423, 427.
[65] (1876) 1 QBD 613, 635.
[66] [1916] P 195, 202.
[67] [1904] 1 KB 493, 496.
[68] (1810) Edw 246.

could not give effect to the contractual obligations of the parties, because the contract had not been performed. Rather, the Court's role was 'to discover what was the relative equity between the parties'.[69] He concluded that the equitable solution was to share the loss; in other words, that the charterer should pay half of the freight. Other courts adopted a more complex approach to ascertaining the relative equity. In *The Juno*, for example, Sir Samuel Evans insisted that in making the assessment, regard must be had to:[70]

> the rate of freight originally agreed (although this is not necessarily conclusive in all cases), to the extent to which the voyage has been made, to the labour and cost expended, or any special charges incurred in respect of the cargo seized before its seizure and unlivery, and to the benefit accruing to the cargo from the carriage on the voyage up to the seizure and unlivery.

In 1871 the Court of Admiralty, in *The Teutonia*, offered a sophisticated justification for its distinctive approach to the consequences of frustration:[71]

> The law . . . justifies what it commands; if, on the one hand, it commands, in these circumstances, the dissolution of the contract, does it not, on the other hand, justify the command by placing the parties as nearly as possible in statu quo ante contractum? Does it give to one party, both being equally innocent, a manifest advantage over the other?

Both the date and the content of the justification are significant. In 1871 the leading common law case was *Taylor v Caldwell*,[72] and the doctrine of frustration was based on an implied term. At common law, the law did not 'command' the dissolution of the contract; it was, in theory, the will of the parties. Similarly, any rule about the consequences of frustration had to be attributed to the will of the parties. This gave rise to the problem that a court implying a term to regulate the consequences of frustration could be criticised for being too speculative, as we have seen. The maritime cases illuminate different aspects of the common law position. The advance freight cases showed that there were justifications for a rule that a pre-payment was irrecoverable. The pro rata freight decisions showed that a contractual analysis was not inconsistent with some flexibility. But, most importantly, the Admiralty authorities showed how restrictive it was to insist upon a contractual explanation for everything, particularly if 'contractual' meant based on the will of the parties.

---

[69] *Ibid*, 247.
[70] [1916] P 169, 175.
[71] (1871) LR 3 Ad & Ecc 394, 417; affirmed by the Privy Council on different grounds (1872) LR 4 PC 171.
[72] (1863) 3 B & S 826, 122 ER 309.

D. THE CONSEQUENCES OF FRUSTRATION IN SCOTLAND

Ultimately reform of the English common law was prompted by a case highlighting the contrast between the restrictive common law contractual analysis and the approach taken in a system permitting recourse to a wider range of principles. The system in question was not the law of nations as administered in Admiralty; it was the Civil Law, as administered in Scotland.

The facts in *Cantiare San Rocco SA v Clyde Shipbuilding and Engineering Company Limited*[73] were, for all practical purposes, identical to those in *Chandler v Webster*. Indeed, the case reached the House of Lords precisely because Scottish judges applied *Chandler*'s case, and held that a pre-payment under a subsequently frustrated contract could not be recovered. The House of Lords unanimously disagreed. Scots law was different: it recognised the Roman *condictio*, the underlying principle of which was that:[74]

> a person had received from another some property, and . . . by reason of circumstances existing at the time, or arising afterwards, it was or became contrary to honesty and fair dealing for the recipient to retain it.

The recipient was required to return the property to the extent that he would be unjustly enriched if he retained it.[75] Crucially, the basis of the *condictio* was not contractual; it was restitutionary.

Their Lordships made it clear that the different approach of Scots law was not a cause for regret. The Earl of Birkenhead pointed out that the English authorities could be reviewed by the House of Lords.[76] Viscount Finlay commented that 'the Scottish doctrine of restitutio ascertains more accurately the rights of the parties respectively'.[77] Lord Dunedin also emphasised the restitutionary approach, but added that he was 'not at all concerned to criticize English law'.[78] His self-restraint was not shared by Lord Shaw of Dunfermline: the English law result was 'monstrous' and was rightly regarded with 'a feeling both of uneasiness and of disrelish'.[79] Leaving the loss to lie where it fell was appropriate only 'among tricksters, gamblers and thieves'.[80] For any other parties, it was a dereliction of the law's duty not to attempt some adjustment of rights.

[73] [1924] AC 226.
[74] *Ibid*, 234 (Earl of Birkenhead).
[75] *Ibid*, 235 (Earl of Birkenhead) and 252 (Lord Shaw of Dunfermline).
[76] *Ibid*, 233.
[77] *Ibid*, 244.
[78] *Ibid*, 248.
[79] *Ibid*, 258.
[80] *Ibid*, 259.

As a matter of strict Roman law, their Lordships' application of the *condictio causa data causa non secuta* to the consequences of frustration was mistaken: the *condictio* technically applied only to property transferred under unenforceable agreements.[81] A more accurate Roman analysis would have pointed to a contractual remedy, based on the payee's general obligation of good faith. Such a contractual solution was identical, in all but name, to the implication of a contractual term to regulate the consequences of frustration. In other words, English and Roman law were not so different after all. But the House of Lords' reasoning in *Cantiare* had set Scots law on an entirely different path, distinct from both English and classical Roman law, by asserting that the consequences of frustration should be regulated by the principles of restitution.

The importance of this distinctive approach was not to remain confined to Scotland for long: in 1937, when the Law Revision Committee was asked to report on the rule in *Chandler v Webster*, the terms of reference specifically required a response to the observations of Lord Dunedin and Lord Shaw.

E. THE LAW REVISION COMMITTEE

The rule in *Chandler v Webster* was referred to the Law Revision Committee at the prompting of its chairman, Lord Wright.[82] Although the precise terms of reference were drafted by a civil servant in the Lord Chancellor's Office,[83] Lord Wright had final approval.[84] The Committee was to consider:

> Whether and, if so, in what respect the rule laid down or applied in *Chandler v Webster* [1904] 1 KB 493 requires modification, and in particular to consider the observations made thereon in *Cantiare San Rocco, SA v Clyde Shipbuilding and Engineering Co, Ltd* [1924] AC 226 by Lords Dunedin and Shaw at pp 247, 248 and 259.

As the Committee was also directed (also on Wright's prompting) to consider reform of the law of contributory negligence, it was decided, at a plenary meeting of the Committee in July 1937, to form two Sub-Committees.[85] The

---

[81] Buckland (n 18) 1284–6; R Evans-Jones, 'Roman Law in Scotland and England and the Development of One Law for Britain' (1999) 115 *LQR* 605, 612.
[82] Lord Wright to Sir Claud Schuster, Lord Chancellor's Office, 2 April 1937. LC 02/1989 ('Law Revision Committee—Extended terms of reference').
[83] Sir Claud Schuster to John Foster, 8 April 1937. LC 02/1989.
[84] Sir Claud Schuster to Lord Wright, 12 April 1937. LC 02/1989.
[85] Plenary meeting of Law Revision Committee, 21 July 1937. LC 02/1990.

Chandler v Webster Sub-Committee consisted of Lord Wright, Lord Romer, Goddard LJ, Professor Goodhart, AD McNair, WE Mortimer, Asquith J, Judge Topham, HU Willink and Professor Gutteridge. The first draft of the Sub-Committee's Report was to be prepared by a Drafting Committee consisting of Goodhart, McNair, Asquith and Gutteridge. It was circulated in mid-February 1938.

The first draft[86] contained much material that was to remain in the final version. For instance, the vivid description of the rule's consequences—'The guillotine falls with faultless precision but often with ruthless effect'[87]—was there right from the start. Similarly, the basic structure of the Report was to remain unaltered: introduction, exposition of *Chandler v Webster*, critique of the reasoning in *Chandler*, possible solutions, recommendation.

But the tone of the first draft was rather different from the final version: it was more restrained, less partisan. For instance, in the final draft, the Report states that a rule of the law of contract which fails to share benefits and burdens between the parties is *prima facie* suspect. 'But,' the Report continues, 'this is the result which the existing rule is calculated to produce.'[88] In the first draft, the same sentence read: 'But this is the result which, in an extreme case, the existing rule produces.'

The more even-handed approach of the first draft was particularly striking in the discussion of advance freight. As we have seen above,[89] pre-paid freight was not recoverable if the voyage was frustrated, a rule which had operated for over two hundred years. From its first draft to its final version, the Report set out the rule, acknowledged its seventeenth century basis, then quoted from *Byrne v Schiller*,[90] where Cockburn CJ had grudgingly felt forced to hold that the courts could not reverse the rule. In the first draft, the Report continues:

> On the other hand the rule has been defended on the ground that that it embodies a business practice by which the cargo-owner takes the risk and covers himself by insurance so that he obtains a more favourable rule of freight. (See the observations of Lord Sumner on the rule in *French Marine v Compagnie Napolitaine d'Eclairage* (1921) 2 AC at p 519.)

In the second draft, dated 5 May 1938, this sentence had been deleted, and the reference to *French Marine* now supported the proposition that the existing law caused hardship. The manuscript note of this change, on paper headed 'Trinity Hall Camb', reveals it to be the work of Professor HC

---

86 LC 02/1990.
87 *Seventh Interim Report* (n 7) 3.
88 *Ibid.*
89 Section C.
90 (1871) LR 6 Ex 319.

Gutteridge. His more critical, edited account of the advance freight rule was the account that ultimately appeared in the Report.[91] His Cambridge colleague, Professor PH Winfield,[92] added the erudite reference to a sixteenth century indication that advance freight was recoverable.[93]

The tone of the first draft was also reflected in its conclusion. In a passage found in early drafts of the Report, but deleted from the final version, the Committee emphasised that there might be a term regulating the consequences of frustration, and that such a term would still conclusively define the parties' rights. Furthermore, 'contracts which fall within a well-known trade practice such as the case of advance freight and charter parties' should also remain untouched. For other frustrated contracts, the Committee recommended that:

> any money paid by one party to another shall be recoverable less any expenses which the other has reasonably incurred in the performance of the contract. This rule is not to apply where the contract makes a specific provision on the point or where there is a well-recognised trade practice to the contrary.

This final recommendation cannot have proved satisfactory to the Committee, because the final recommendation in the second draft was radically different:

> When performance of a contract has been frustrated in whole or in part owing to supervening impossibility any money paid by the one party to the other in pursuance of the contract shall be recoverable less the greater of the two following amounts (1) the amount of all expenditure, liabilities, and losses directly incurred for the purpose of performing the contract by the party to whom the money has been paid (2) the value of any benefits received under or by virtue of the contract by the party who has made the payment.

Deducting the value of benefits received by the payor if those benefits exceeded the expenses incurred by the payee was a completely new way of approaching the problem. There is nothing on the file to explain why the Committee adopted this unusual approach, but the most likely explanation is that it was inspired by a comparative perspective. Whilst there was no precedent in English law for deducting whatever was the greater of expenses incurred or benefits conferred, that approach was mirrored in French law. There the appropriate cause of action for a payor under a frustrated

---

[91] Appendix B 10–11.

[92] Winfield was a member of the Law Revision Committee, but he had been deliberately appointed to sit on the contributory negligence sub-committee. Wright to Schuster, 2 April 1937. LC 02/1989.

[93] Winfield to Sir Claud Schuster, 22 May 1938. LC 02/1990.

contract was the *actio de in rem verso*.[94] The action required both an enrichment of the defendant and an impoverishment of the claimant without legal cause. The award of damages was, therefore, assessed with both the enrichment of the defendant and impoverishment of the claimant in mind. As Planiol and Ripert put it, in their *Traité Pratique de Droit Civil Français*:[95]

> La condemnation étant subordonnée à l'existence à la fois d'un enrichissement et d'un appauvrissement, le montant en sera déterminé par le chiffre le moins élevé des deux.

If the Committee's new approach was comparative, it is easy to see who was behind it. Gutteridge, Professor of Comparative Law at Cambridge 1934–41, was on the Drafting Committee, and had been responsible for an Appendix to the Report dealing with Continental Law. Indeed, we know that he was responsible because he included incorrect page references for Planiol-Ripert's *Traité Pratique* in the first draft of the Appendix, and wrote to the Committee's Secretary to apologise for his mistake.[96] Furthermore, an article in the *Cambridge Law Journal* that was cited in the Appendix without naming its authors, was in fact co-authored by Gutteridge.[97] It was an exposition of the French *actio de in rem verso*, including the method of assessing damages,[98] with a section by Gutteridge on what English law could learn from the French. His view was that direct doctrinal transplant would probably be inappropriate:[99]

> but we can find much in the experience of the French Courts which will be of service to us if and when the time comes to endeavour to remove the injustices which admittedly arise from the present state of our law.

The best solution would be legislation. 'It is here', he concluded:[100]

> that French law can help us by indicating the nature of such problems and by demarcating the area within which they are likely to arise. In default of some such guide there is a danger that attempts to revise our existing rules may either go too far or else not go far enough.

With the benefit of hindsight, we can read Gutteridge's helpful suggestions to the legislature in another way, as a declaration of intent.

---

[94] Sir MS Amos and FP Walton, *Introduction to French Law* (Oxford, Clarendon Press, 1935) 204–7.
[95] Planiol-Ripert, *Traité Pratique de Droit Civil Français* (Paris, 1931) vol VII, 63.
[96] Gutteridge to Barbara Sharp, 15 February 1938. LC 02/1990.
[97] H Gutteridge and R David, 'The Doctrine of Unjustified Enrichment' (1933–5) 5 *CLJ* 204.
[98] *Ibid*, 221.
[99] *Ibid*, 227.
[100] *Ibid*, 229.

The final recommendation was still in the form of deducting either expenses incurred or benefits conferred when a further draft was circulated in the middle of June 1938. At the meeting to consider that draft, however, a new difficulty was raised, which Lord Wright considered important enough to call for a further, better attended, meeting. As he put it in his letter to Sir Claud Schuster, of the Lord Chancellor's Office:[101]

> It will be necessary at the Meeting to discuss a new matter that was raised, which was what the position in law is or should be when the consideration given in advance is not money but shares, options, licenses or other valuable assets. The chairman was provisionally of the opinion that this question was outside the terms of reference, but the Committee will have to consider that and also be prepared to discuss any relevant authorities.

Lord Wright added that he 'should like to know what is the official view as to the construction of the terms of reference'.

Eight months later, on 28 February 1939, Lord Wright had his answer. The 'strict terms of reference' did not require consideration of cases where the payment was non-financial, and, without any apparent embarrassment, one should have regard to 'the desirability of a report being made at an early date'. The Committee did not, therefore, address cases of non-pecuniary benefits in their Report,[102] an omission which prompted two Committee members to make a formal protest.[103] Lord Wright's response, when warned that the protest was to be included, is interesting. 'I quite understand Mr Mortimer's criticism',[104] he replied. Perhaps he regretted not devising a broader remit.

Once the Lord Chancellor's ruling had been obtained, progress was reasonably swift. By 3 March 1939, when a near-final draft of the Report was circulated, the proposal had reverted to the terms of deducting expenses: the alternative of deducting benefits had gone. There was some debate about the precise form of words,[105] but by May 1939 the Report was finalised.

The recommendation was now that pre-payments should be recoverable:[106]

> subject to a deduction of such sum as represents a fair allowance for expenditure incurred by the payee in the performing of or for the purposes of performing the contract.

---

[101] Wright to Schuster, 30 June 1938. LC 02/1990.

[102] Although they did discuss freight pro rata itineris, which involved conferment of non-pecuniary benefits, in Appendix B. See *Seventh Interim Report* (n 7) 11.

[103] *Seventh Interim Report* (n 7) 11.

[104] Wright to Barbara Sharp, 20 March 1939. LC 02/1990.

[105] See in particular the suggestions of Lord Porter (Porter to Barbara Sharp, 5 March 1939) and H Willink (Willink to Barbara Sharp, 6 March 1939), both in LC 02/1990.

[106] *Seventh Interim Report* (n 7) 7.

The maximum amount recoverable from the payee was limited to the sum agreed to be paid as a pre-payment under the contract.

F. IMPLEMENTING THE LAW REVISION COMMITTEE'S RECOMMENDATION (1)

The Law Revision Committee's Report was published in the second week of May 1939, when it was noted in a leading article in *The Times*.[107] At the end of the same week, the Lord Chancellor, Lord Maugham, sent a memorandum to the Cabinet asking permission to have a Bill drafted to implement the Committee's recommendation.[108] The Cabinet agreed to approve the adoption of the Report 'in principle',[109] but decided that a Bill should not be drafted until 'the present congestion of legislative business was relaxed'.[110]

In August 1939 the Treasury agreed to have a Bill drafted, and by 2 September 1939 a first draft was completed. Like the Report, it dealt solely with money payments, as its short title—Law Reform (Payments under Frustrated Contracts) Bill—made clear. A senior civil servant in the Lord Chancellor's Office, called Napier, organised a committee to consider the Bill. It consisted of himself, AL Goodhart and AD McNair (both of whom had been on the Drafting Committee for the Law Revision Committee's Report).

Two aspects of the Bill immediately caused difficulty. The first was the attempt, in its opening section, to define the doctrine of frustration. This stated:

> Where a party to a contract is discharged from the performance after the happening of any event of the provisions of the contract, on the ground that it was an implied term of the contract that on the happening of that event the parties thereto should be discharged from its performance thereafter.

The draftsman himself, in his covering letter, expressed 'serious doubt' as to whether this definition was correct.[111] Napier, in his letters to Goodhart and McNair, echoed those doubts.[112] McNair's response left in place the reference to an implied term, but added that the contract could be discharged

---

[107] *The Times*, 12 May 1939.
[108] 17 May 1939. LC 02/1991.
[109] Minutes of Cabinet, 23 May 1939.
[110] *Ibid*.
[111] Ellis (Parliamentary counsel) to Napier (Lord Chancellor's Office), 2 September 1939. LC 02/1991.
[112] Napier to Goodhart, copy to McNair, 4 September 1939. LC 02/1991.

by an event failing to happen. The draftsman was unconvinced, and in the second draft opted for the vaguer expression, 'having become impossible of performance or having been otherwise frustrated'. As he described it in his covering letter to Napier:[113]

> I have evaded the various difficulties that arise from trying to describe the event, or 'non-event', or what-not, that gives rise to the frustration of a contract. I think that it is desirable to use general words, as it seems to be possible to do so, in order to give the court some elbow-room.

This form of general words was to be employed in the 1943 Act. McNair, who had deprecated the use of the word 'Frustrated' in the short title of the Bill because it was too imprecise, would make the same criticism of the wording of the Act in his article in the *Law Quarterly Review*: 'The sense in which the word "frustration" is used is now changing and widening and cannot yet be said to be uniform.'[114]

The second difficulty concerned terms regulating the consequences of frustration. The first draft did not mention them. But, following a meeting of the Committee on 8 September 1939, a new clause 2(2) was added to the Bill:

> Where such a contract contains any provision inconsistent with any enactment in the preceding sub-section, being a provision which is upon the true construction of the contract intended to have effect in the circumstances constituting the ground for the discharge of the parties to the contract, the preceding section shall have effect subject to that provision.

Again, the draftsman was unconvinced, writing to Napier that he was 'still very much puzzled'[115] by how to implement the Law Revision Committee's recommendation. The underlying problem was that frustration was still seen as depending on an implied term. 'As I understand the frustration cases', he explained:[116]

> they depend to a very great extent on the proposition that, where frustration occurs, the express terms of the contract ought not to be carried out. The sense of the subsection as I have drafted it is intended to be that the terms of the contract are to prevail in so far as it can be found that the parties visualised the event or 'non-event' which has occurred and dealt with it. This may be right, but I am not so sure that I understand how, where that can be found, the court will hold a contract to have been frustrated.

---

[113] Ellis to Napier, 13 September 1939. LC 02/1991.
[114] A McNair, 'The Law Reform (Frustrated Contracts) Act 1943' (1944) 60 *LQR* 160.
[115] Ellis to Napier, 13 September 1939. LC 02/1991.
[116] *Ibid.*

Goodhart agreed.[117] McNair, however, offered a trenchant explanation of why the clause was necessary:[118]

> Supposing I obtain from the MCC a ticket for the pavilion at Lords for the Eton v Harrow match, and the ticket contains upon it the following words (amongst others): 'Money not returnable in any event.' This contract might become impossible or be frustrated by any one of numerous events—eg destruction of the pavilion by fire, deluge of rain and no play, cancellation of match owing to epidemic at one of the schools, prohibition of cricket under Defence of the Realm Act, etc etc. The parties to the contract have not visualised specifically any of these events. All they know is that various events can happen which prevent cricket matches from being played; they wish to provide that, come what may, the money shall not be returned; and therefore they insert in their contract a term to that effect. That seems to me to give a reasonable explanation of the occurrence in the report of the expression 'unless a contrary intention appears from the terms of the contract'. It seems to be wrong, as was suggested by somebody at the recent conference, to say that where a contract contains a term like that it cannot be frustrated.

It is perhaps too much of a coincidence that Viscount Simon LC, in his speech in *Fibrosa Spolka Akcyjna v Fairbairn Lawson Combe Barbour, Limited*,[119] was to speak of the 'true construction' of such a term, and to give as an illustrative example a spectator buying a ticket for a cricket match.[120]

The machinery of law reform seemed to be in motion. But the day after the second draft of the Bill had been circulated, the Attorney General (Sir Donald Somervell) wrote to Sir Claud Schuster (of the Lord Chancellor's Office) saying that it was 'inadvisable to proceed with the Bill'.[121] The problem was that the outbreak of war had rendered many contractual obligations more onerous, and the government was not yet 'in a position to state its policy'[122] on the matter. As Somervell put it:[123]

> Members in all quarters of the House would, I think, at once say that they were interested not so much in contracts which had been frustrated as in contracts not frustrated, the fulfilment of which had become impracticable or likely to inflict great hardship owing to war circumstances.

---

[117] Goodhart to Napier, 16 September 1939. LC 02/1991.
[118] McNair to Napier, 18 September 1939. LC 02/1991.
[119] [1943] AC 32.
[120] *Ibid*, 42–3.
[121] Somervell to Schuster, 14 September 1939. LC 02/1991.
[122] *Ibid*.
[123] *Ibid*.

The government was therefore anxious to avoid being pressed on the point. The Lord Chancellor, Viscount Caldecote, took the hint. As Napier later described it:[124]

> Lord Caldecote . . . was impressed with the difficulty and danger of legislating at all on frustration, and no further instructions were given to Ellis as to revising the draft in the light of criticisms which the earlier draft had received.

Reforming the law of frustration had turned into a political liability.

G. IMPLEMENTING THE LAW REVISION COMMITTEE'S RECOMMENDATION (2)

There was no legislative progress for over two years, and a further obstacle appeared when the Home Policy Committee insisted that Bills should not be introduced into Parliament 'unless they were definitely war time Bills'.[125] The position appeared hopeless. But, during this period of stagnation, two events took place which would have a profound influence on later developments. First, Viscount Caldecote was replaced as Lord Chancellor by Sir John Simon when Churchill formed a new government in May 1940.[126] Simon was a man of extraordinary talent and energy, who had held most of the great offices of State. His political abilities were unmatched. Second, *Fibrosa Société Anonyme v Fairbairn Lawson Combe Barbour, Limited*[127] was decided by the Court of King's Bench and Court of Appeal.

Fibrosa was a Polish company, whose buying agent, the British and Foreign Trading Co, had agreed to purchase two sets of flax hackling machines from Fairbairn Lawson Combe Barbour, Limited, of Leeds. Delivery was to be at Gdynia, in Poland. The cost was 4800l, one third of which was to be paid in advance.[128] Fibrosa paid 1000l. But, at the end of August 1939 Germany invaded Poland and occupied Gdynia. The parties failed to reach a compromise, and their dispute reached the courts in March 1941. Fibrosa advanced two important arguments. First, the contract was not frustrated by the German occupation of Gdynia, because clause 7 of Fairbairn's standard terms and conditions provided:

> Should despatch be hindered or delayed by your instructions, or lack of instructions, or by any cause whatsoever beyond our reasonable control, including

---

[124] Napier to Swan (Law Officers' Department), 16 May 1941. LC 02/1991.
[125] Schuster to Sir Donald Somervell, 8 October 1941. LC 02/1991.
[126] Visount Simon, *Retrospect* (London, Hutchinson, 1952) 255.
[127] [1942] 1 KB 12.
[128] The full text of the contract was printed for the House of Lords proceedings. It can be found in Appeal Cases, 1942 HL/PO/JU/4/3/971 (House of Lords Record Office).

strikes, lock-outs, war, fire, accidents, defective material or approval of drawings, a reasonable extension of time shall be granted.

If this was incorrect, and the contract had been frustrated, the advance payment was recoverable.

Both points failed before Tucker J and the Court of Appeal. Tucker J held that clause 7 was void, as being against public policy, because it would hamper trade and limit the resources of the kingdom in wartime.[129] The Court of Appeal's approach was different, and focused on the construction of the term. In their view, it should be interpreted as applying only to short delays, for which a 'reasonable extension of time' would be appropriate.[130]

The two courts' approach to the pre-payment question, by contrast, was identical. *Chandler v Webster* was binding, so the pre-payment was not recoverable. The Court of Appeal regretted that this was the position, remarking that if the implied term enunciated in *Taylor v Caldwell*[131] had included:[132]

> as part of the implied term a provision that a party to the contract who, by part performance, had received a benefit should compensate the other for that benefit, it might well have been thought a reasonable addition.

It envisaged that the House of Lords would 'substitute a rule like the more civilized rule of Roman and Scottish law'.[133]

Of course, criticism of *Chandler v Webster* was not new. Noting the Court of Appeal's decision in *Fibrosa*, Winfield observed that:[134]

> Like Major Bagstock's native servant in *Dombey and Son*, [*Chandler*] exists in a rainy season of missiles hurled at it by its employer who nevertheless seems to be unable to get rid of it.

He doubted whether even the House of Lords could legitimately reverse it, since the reference to the Law Revision Committee suggested that reversal could only be achieved by legislation.

The official response to *Fibrosa* in the Court of Appeal was, initially, muted. The first reference to it in correspondence seems to be a letter from EH Hodgson (Board of Trade) to Sir Claud Schuster.[135] Hodgson reminded Schuster that the attempt to reverse *Chandler v Webster* by statute had

---

[129] [1942] 1 KB 12, 19.
[130] *Ibid*, 26.
[131] (1863) 3 B & S 826, 122 ER 309.
[132] [1942] 1 KB 12, 27.
[133] *Ibid*, 28.
[134] P Winfield (1941) 57 *LQR* 439.
[135] Hodgson to Schuster, 11 October 1941. BT 15/190.

stalled, and that it had been thought that there was no pressing need for reform, since 'business people did not anticipate any difficulties which could not be resolved by goodwill on both sides'.[136] He cited *Fibrosa* as a case where such goodwill would have been appropriate. However, he continued, a new problem had now arisen, which had been raised by the Textile Machinery and Accessories Export Group. The Inland Revenue had begun to take an interest in pre-payments, taxing them as excess profit. This intervention made it 'impossible for a manufacturer to put himself right with his customer after the war'.[137]

The timing of Hodgson's letter was fortuitous. Schuster had just been discussing the Frustration Bill with the Attorney-General[138] and, the day before, the Lord Chancellor had received a letter from Reginald Purbrick MP, which referred to the Bill and asked, 'Would it be possible to have something DONE in the matter?'[139]

Schuster prepared a minute for the Lord Chancellor.[140] The MP's letter, he said, 'comes at a very awkward moment'. He explained why the legislative progress of the Bill had been halted, and was inclined to dismiss the letter as 'based on [nothing] except the desire which comes upon people in war time to DO something'. He also related the tax problem, but concluded that:[141]

> the introduction of a Bill to reverse *Chandler v Webster* would be attended by the difficulties which I have noted . . . and would give rise to a ragged discussion in which almost every form of commercial transaction . . . would once again come in question.

Viscount Simon, however, was not a man to be daunted by civil servants advising caution. Indeed, he later admitted in his autobiography that he had left the House of Commons with regret, and regarded the Lord Chancellorship as something of a backwater.[142] Perhaps he welcomed the prospect of a contentious Bill. Certainly, with his political experience, he would not have been intimidated by the task of guiding such a Bill through Parliament. Whilst Viscount Simon's reply to the MP was a masterpiece of

---

[136] *Ibid.*
[137] *Ibid.*
[138] Schuster to Hodgson, 13 October 1941. BT 15/190. See also Schuster to the Attorney-General, 13 October 1941, enclosing Hodgson's letter: 'Please see the enclosed which comes oddly at this moment just after you and I had discussed the frustration question generally.' LC 02/1991.
[139] Purbrick to Simon, 10 October 1941. LC 02/1991.
[140] 14 October 1941. LC 02/1991.
[141] *Ibid.*
[142] *Retrospect* (n 126) 258: 'no Minister in the Upper House can have more than a secondary influence.'

evasion,[143] a letter from Schuster to the Attorney-General of the same date reveals that the legislative process had entered a new phase: the Lord Chancellor 'inclined to the view that it might be desirable to legislate'.[144] The Attorney-General's reply hinted at how they might avoid the objection that the Bill was not a wartime measure: 'the case in the TLR [ie *Fibrosa*] might afford ground for our proceeding with the Bill during the war if we are satisfied that it is all right.' The legislation was immediately back on the agenda, and *Fibrosa* had become part of the political process.

Although the tax point was soon resolved informally,[145] a Parliamentary question about legislation, tabled by Purbrick, prompted further action. On 7 January 1942, Viscount Simon held a meeting with three of his senior civil servants—Schuster, Napier and Coldstream.[146] He had read the Law Revision Committee's Report and the draft Bill, and drew the meeting's attention to the fact that both dealt only with pre-payments, and did not consider beneficial services received before frustration. He also thought that:[147]

> the Law Revision Committee were wrong in concluding that the doctrine in *Chandler v Webster* was concerned only with the former class of case, and that the latter class of case was, in fact, within their terms of reference.

The Court of Appeal's decision in *Fibrosa* was also referred to.

The Lord Chancellor decided that a definite decision had to be made about legislation, and telephoned Purbrick to ask him to withdraw his question so as to allow time for consultation. Purbrick agreed. The Lord Chancellor then told his civil servants that he proposed to consult Lord Wright, Lord Romer, Lord Porter 'and possibly also'[148] Lord Atkin. But he also made it clear that he had not ruled out other options:

> The Lord Chancellor said that he would have enquiries made to see whether the *Fibrosa* case was being appealed to the House of Lords. He expressed the view that, if that case came to the Lords, and, in the event, the doctrine in *Chandler v Webster* was rejected, he would consider that a more satisfactory method of disposing of the matter than by legislation. He made it clear that he did not necessarily agree that

---

[143] '. . . you may feel assured that I am fully alive to the importance of reaching a decision as to whether we could legislate, and, if so, how': Simon to Purbrick, 16 October 1941. LC 02/1991.

[144] Schuster to Somervell, 16 October 1941. LC 02/1991.

[145] The Inland Revenue agreed to treat any tax liability as being in suspense until after the War. If the pre-payment was then returned, there would be no tax liability. Somervell to Schuster, 3 November 1941; Hodgson to Schuster, 11 November 1941. LC 02/1991.

[146] See Coldstream's note of the meeting, headed LAW REFORM (PAYMENTS UNDER FRUSTRATED CONTRACTS) BILL, 7 January 1942. LC 02/1991.

[147] *Ibid.*

[148] *Ibid.*

Chandler v Webster ought to be reversed; but that, at the same time, he was not definitely opposed in principle to a Bill limited to dealing only with the recommendations of the the Law Revision Committee.

In a manuscript addition to the civil servant's note of the meeting, made the following day, Viscount Simon wrote:[149]

> It has now been ascertained that the *Fibrosa* cases are expected to be filed very shortly and it will then be in the public interest to appoint an early hearing of the appeal. In the meantime, this prospect gives an excellent ground for *not* introducing legislation at the moment.

So, far from being 'stimulated'[150] or 'compelled'[151] to act by the House of Lords' decision in *Fibrosa*, the legislator was in fact waiting for it with some impatience. At least one member of the Judicial Committee, and probably also those consulted by Viscount Simon, was considering his judgment before the parties had even lodged their printed cases. In short, what the House of Lords should say in *Fibrosa* had assumed an urgent political significance six months before judgment was given.

H. THE HOUSE OF LORDS' DECISION IN *FIBROSA*

The *Fibrosa* case was argued in April, before a panel of seven Law Lords. Judgment was handed down on 15 June 1942.[152] Their Lordships unanimously held that an action to recover a pre-payment under a subsequently frustrated contract lay, if the payor could show that there had been a total failure of consideration. They also upheld the Court of Appeal's interpretation of the contractual provision allowing for reasonable delay.

Viscount Simon LC gave the leading speech. His analysis began by emphasising that one must always start with 'the terms of the particular contract'.[153] Thus:[154]

> If the contract itself on its true construction stipulates for a particular result which is to follow in regard to money already paid, should frustration afterwards occur, this governs the matter. The ancient and firmly established rule that freight paid in advance is not returned if the completion of the voyage is frustrated . . . should, I think, be regarded as a stipulation introduced into such contracts by custom, and not as the result of applying some abstract principle.

---

[149] *Ibid.*
[150] *BP Exploration Co (Libya) Ltd v Hunt (No 2)* [1979] 1 WLR 783, 798.
[151] *Chitty* (n 6) 23-072.
[152] *Fibrosa Spolka Akcyjna v Fairbairn Lawson Combe Barbour, Limited* [1943] AC 32.
[153] *Ibid*, 42.
[154] *Ibid*, 42–3.

By way of further illustration, he referred to a cricket spectator paying for admission, who 'cannot recover the entrance money on the ground that rain has prevented play if, expressly or by proper implication, the bargain with him is that no money will be returned'. It was 'tempting'[155] to go further, and hold that a term could always be implied to regulate the consequences of frustration. But ultimately it was impossible to be confident about what the parties would have agreed upon.

He then turned to the decision in *Chandler v Webster*, and made two criticisms of it. First, the question of recovering money paid under a contract was not exclusively a question of construing the contractual obligations: where there had been a total failure of consideration, a non-contractual obligation could arise 'from the circumstances'.[156] Second, if *Chandler v Webster* was based on the idea that there was no total failure of consideration where one party had received the other's promise, it was mistaken.[157] A promise was sufficient consideration for the purposes of contract formation; but to prevent a claim for total failure of consideration, some performance of that promise was required. There was, therefore, no analytical obstacle to a claim to recover the pre-payment on the ground of total failure of consideration.

Viscount Simon LC concluded his speech on a note of dissatisfaction. The ability of the payor to bring a claim for total failure of consideration was not a panacea. It would cause unfairness wherever the recipient of a payment had done work or incurred expenditure. What was really needed was some mechanism for apportionment. But that would have to come from the legislature.[158]

The other speeches echoed and elaborated upon these themes. Lord Roche, for instance, emphasised the importance of the contractual terms in determining whether a payment was recoverable. On the facts of the case before them, the contract terms showed that the payment was provisional only, 'no more than a payment on account of the price'.[159] In the future, 'parties to contracts will know that as the law stands, the contract between them is the matter of crucial or final importance'.[160]

The criticism of the Court of Appeal's analysis in *Chandler v Webster* was unanimous. Lord Atkin found it incomprehensible;[161] Lord Macmillan and Lord Wright thought it was just wrong.[162] Lord Wright added that it had

---

[155] *Ibid*, 43.
[156] *Ibid*, 47.
[157] *Ibid*, 48.
[158] *Ibid*, 49–50.
[159] *Ibid*, 75.
[160] *Ibid*, 76.
[161] *Ibid*, 52.
[162] *Ibid*, 60 and 70 respectively.

not been followed in the United States,[163] and could find no basis in Roman law either.[164] There was also unanimity about apportionment: it was the ideal solution, but was not an option open to the House. 'Some day,' said Lord Wright, 'the legislature may intervene to remedy these defects.'[165]

It might be thought that the House of Lords' analysis required the defendants to return the pre-payment to the claimants. However, it did not. As Viscount Simon LC pointed out, any payment due as a matter of common law would be regulated by the Trading with the Enemy Act 1939.[166] For this reason their Lordships not only ordered that judgment be entered for Fibrosa for £1,000, but also that the case be 'remitted back to the King's Bench Division of the High Court'.[167] No further proceedings seem to have taken place, and that is not surprising, since making the payment would undoubtedly have been an offence under the Act.[168] Given that the criminal law forbade the payment, it is also not surprising that the claimants did not pursue a claim for interest.[169]

The outcome of the House of Lords' decision in *Fibrosa* was, therefore, purely academic. It might also have been incorrect on the facts. Their Lordships, in particular Viscount Simon LC and Lord Roche, had emphasised the importance of 'the terms of the particular contract'[170] in their abstract analyses, but had paid very little attention to the terms of the contract actually before them. Such a lack of attention was understandable. Counsel had directed their attention only to clause 7 of the contract, providing for a reasonable delay in delivery should war break out. Furthermore, Viscount Simon LC, Lord Wright, Lord Porter and, possibly, Lord Atkin had the bigger question of legislative reform in mind. As we have seen, for them the issue in *Fibrosa* was whether the House of Lords could implement the Law Revision Committee's proposals. The precise facts of the case that raised this question would have seemed of secondary importance.

---

[163] *Ibid*, 71.
[164] *Ibid*, 73.
[165] *Ibid*, 72.
[166] *Ibid*, 40.
[167] Order of House of Lords following printed speeches. Appeal Cases, 1942—HL/PO/JU/4/3/971 (House of Lords Record Office).
[168] 'Trading with the enemy' was defined in s 1(2)(a) as including financial dealings 'for the benefit of an enemy'. Enemies included corporations controlled by persons resident in enemy territory (s 2(1)(c)); enemy territory included occupied territory (s 15(1)).
[169] Exchange between the Lord Chancellor and counsel for the appellant after the speeches had been delivered. See Appeal Cases, 1942—HL/PO/JU/4/3/971 (House of Lords Record Office). Cf *BP Exploration Co (Libya) Ltd v Hunt* [1979] 1 WLR 783, 835–6, where, discussing *Fibrosa*, Robert Goff J said: 'I observe that the appeal to the House of Lords in that case was against an order refusing to allow a claim for recovery of £1,000 with interest; but although the appeal was allowed, it is not clear from the report whether the order included an award of interest, although I should be very surprised if it did not do so.'
[170] [1943] AC 32, 42 (per Viscount Simon LC).

A closer examination of the contract in its factual matrix indicates a common intention that the payment should be retained in the event of war. Three important details—the date, the parties and the contractual structure—cumulatively show that this was not a conditional payment. The date of the contract was 12 July 1939. War did not break out break out between Germany and the United Kingdom until September 1939; but it was obvious what was coming. Indeed, in *Monarch Steamship Co Ltd v Karlshamns Oljefabriker (A/B)*[171] the House of Lords held that as early as April 1939 the likelihood of war was such that reasonable businessmen must have been taken to contemplate it. The analyses of Lord Porter and Lord Wright were particularly eloquent. So, the situation in *Fibrosa* was significantly different to *Chandler v Webster*: the parties were fully aware that the frustrating event was likely to occur. It was in fact the same, in all material respects, as the situation in *Clark v Lindsay*,[172] another Coronation case, where a contract for a room to view the procession had been made knowing of the King's ill health. As Channell J there put it, holding that a pre-payment could not be recovered, 'The doubt was known, and each party took his chance'.[173]

The parties and the contractual structure indicate that war was precisely what the payment was intended to guard against. The contract was concluded by the British and Foreign Trading Co, buying agents for Fibrosa.[174] As the agent of a foreign principal, it was personally liable on the contract under the law as it then stood.[175] Fairbairn effectively had a guarantor against Fibrosa's insolvency. Furthermore, the contractual structure suggests that Fairbairn was not generally concerned about customers' reliability to the extent of requesting payment in advance. The term requiring pre-payment from Fibrosa was an amendment to their standard terms and conditions; the standard term relating to payment did not require it to be made until shipment of goods.[176] In other words, if Fairbairn's insistence on pre-payment was to protect them against Fibrosa becoming insolvent, it was both unnecessary and uncharacteristic. But, in the political climate of July 1939, with war looming, it was eminently sensible.

The main importance of the House of Lords' speeches was not to be found in their detailed analysis of the facts. Rather, it lay in their exposition

---

[171] [1949] AC 196.
[172] (1903) 88 LT 198.
[173] *Ibid*, 202.
[174] The full text of the contract was printed for the House of Lords proceedings. It can be found in Appeal Cases, 1942—HL/PO/JU/4/3/971 (House of Lords Record Office).
[175] *Chitty* (n 6) 31-086.
[176] Condition 9, headed TERMS OF PAYMENT, stated that 'payment in full in respect of any of the goods shall be due upon presentation of shipping documents and invoices in the United Kingdom'.

of principles; in particular, the principle that restitutionary remedies might be available to parties to a frustrated contract. The emphatic assertions that the actions for money had and received, and money paid under a mistake of fact, were not in any way contractual were particularly valuable in clearing the ground for future developments.

But commentators, both now[177] and then,[178] found the speeches lacking in ambition. Surely, it was said, their Lordships could have gone further. As Glanville Williams pointed out, there would be no remedy for a party who had received any of the contractual performance before frustration. Nor was there any way of compensating a party who had conferred non-pecuniary benefits.[179] Similarly, as Ewan McKendrick has observed, the House of Lords asserted that it could not take account of expenses incurred, despite the Court of Appeal's belief that such a rule could be introduced. Nor did the House of Lords take the opportunity to recognise a defence of change of position.[180]

The modest improvement in the law effected by *Fibrosa* is all the more surprising when one considers the personnel involved. Viscount Simon LC, as we have seen, wanted *Fibrosa* to implement the Law Revision Committee's recommendations. Lord Atkin was not a judge to hold back if he felt that the common law needed developing.[181] Lord Porter had been a member of the Law Revision Committee that proposed the change. Most strikingly, Lord Wright had been the chairman of the Committee, and was, at the time, 'the leading advocate of the existence of a law of restitution'.[182]

Extrajudicially Lord Wright had made his views clear. In his admiring review of the American Law Institute's *Restatement of the Law of Restitution*, for instance, he had written that:[183]

> where a contract is rescinded for breach or illegality or supervening impossibility, the right to restitution (if any) for benefits received depends as a rule on the principles of quasi-contract, if as is generally the case the express contract is silent on the matter.

In lectures to students at Birmingham and Harvard, he had expressed the view that English law should be brought into line with Scots law,[184] as espoused in *Cantiare San Rocco SA v Clyde Shipbuilding and Engineering Company,*

---

[177] E McKendrick, 'Frustration, Restitution and Loss Apportionment' in A Burrows (ed), *Essays on the Law of Restitution* (Oxford, OUP, 1991) 147, 151–2.
[178] G Williams, 'The End of *Chandler v Webster*' [1942] MLR 46, 52–3.
[179] *Ibid*.
[180] McKendrick (n 177) 151–2.
[181] Eg *Donoghue v Stevenson* [1932] AC 562.
[182] McKendrick (n 177) 153 n 31.
[183] Lord Wright of Durley, *Legal Essays and Addresses* (Cambridge, CUP, 1939) 50.
[184] *Ibid*, 257 and 359 respectively.

Limited.[185] Furthermore, in practice he had seen the Admiralty rule of loss apportionment following frustration being applied, having appeared as counsel in virtually every reported case on the subject.[186] Nor, if his extrajudicial writings are any guide, was he afraid of developing the law. As he put it to an audience of students at the London School of Economics, 'from the earliest times the judges have really made laws, that is legislated, even though they pretended to be merely declaring law which already existed'.[187]

It is difficult to believe that their Lordships were not tempted to go further than they did. What ultimately held them back was, perhaps, the Law Revision Committee's Report. This might seem to be a paradoxical claim—we tend to think of the Committee's Report as signposting the way forward, not barring it—but participants in the reform process seem to have seen the reference to the Law Revision Committee as a sign that the common law could develop no further. Thus, Winfield, noting the Court of Appeal's decision in *Fibrosa*, was pessimistic about what the House of Lords could do, precisely because the Law Revision Committee had considered the point. As he put it:[188]

> the mere fact that the doctrine . . . was referred to the Law Revision Committee for consideration implies a conviction in high quarters that the only way of getting rid of it was by legislation.

Lord Wright probably shared this view; several years earlier he had described the Committee's work as:[189]

> recasting particular rules which appear to be ill-conceived but which can only be altered by legislation, because they are based on binding authorities.

Judicial reform of *Chandler v Webster*, on this view, was no longer an option.

I. LEGISLATION

The only option left was legislation. Before the speeches in *Fibrosa* were handed down on 15 June 1942, the Lord Chancellor was already pondering

---

[185] [1924] AC 226.
[186] *The Corsican Prince* [1916] P 195; *The Iolo* [1916] P 206; *The St Helena* [1916] 2 AC 625. These cases made Wright's career at the Bar; before the First World War he had had such little work that he had been driven to contemplate academia. See the entry (by Lord Devlin) in Williams and Nicholls (ed), *The Dictionary of National Biography 1961–1970* (Oxford, OUP, 1981) 1116–17.
[187] *Essays and Addresses* (n 183) 193.
[188] P Winfield (1941) 57 *LQR* 439, 440.
[189] *Essays and Addresses* (n 183) 349–50.

the Bill's content.[190] He remained convinced that any Bill had to deal with non-pecuniary benefits, and, shortly after the speeches were handed down, he formulated two propositions that any legislation should reflect:[191]

I. Where owing to the frustration of a contract in the course of its performance, money which has been paid by one party to another in part performance thereof is liable to be returned on the ground that the recipient holds it as money had and received to the use of the payer, the court may direct that the money paid, or such part thereof as it thinks just, may be retained by the recipient (notwithstanding the frustration) to the extent that the recipient has suffered loss or incurred expense in connection with his duties under the contract before the date of frustration.

II. Where a contract is frustrated in the course of its performance and there has been no pre-payment, but the situation is such that owing to the expenditure or outlay by one party, the other party has received a benefit which he cannot or ought not to return, the first party ought to be in a position in which he, himself is rewarded on a quantum meruit basis.

The second proposition was later amended. Its revised version deleted the reference to *quantum meruit* as the basis of calculation, and replaced it with:[192]

a payment to the party which has done the work or conferred the benefit which the court considers to be equivalent to the benefit thus received, provided that the court shall have regard to any disadvantage suffered by the party so benefited from the non-completion of the performance of the contract, and to all the circumstances of the case.

A meeting of the Law Lords was called to discuss these propositions. Lord Atkin immediately drew attention to a situation not covered by either rule: what would happen if a party had not received a pre-payment, nor conferred a benefit on the other party, but had incurred expenditure in performing the contract?[193] Lord Macmillan said that such a case would require a completely new principle. Such a principle would be 'not one of restitution but of adjustment'.[194] The mood of the meeting seemed to be against such a principle.

---

[190] Note by Schuster, 11 June 1942. LC 02/1991.

[191] Minute from Coldstream to Simon, 8 July 1942: 'You may like to have, in writing, the two propositions which you propounded this morning.' LC 02/1991.

[192] Note circulated by the Lord Chancellor to the Law Lords before their meeting on 21 July 1942.

[193] Notes of a Meeting in the Lord Chancellor's Room, House of Lords, 21 July 1942, para 2. LC 02/1991.

[194] *Ibid.*

The Lord Chancellor then explained that:[195]

> from a Parliamentary standpoint he had no doubt that it would be impossible to pass a Bill which did not make provision for both sides, ie dealt with the cases covered both by propositions 1 and 2 of his memorandum.

Lord Wright, perhaps slightly on the defensive, added that the Law Revision Committee had not dealt with questions of non-pecuniary benefit because they did not appear to fall within the terms of reference. The Lord Chancellor kept his previously expressed view[196] to himself.

The next question was how to move forward. Lord Macmillan, who in *Fibrosa* had made a rather sardonic allusion to legal academics mourning the demise of *Chandler v Webster*,[197] now suggested that their Lordships should wait until 'the learned contributors to the Law Quarterly Review and other eminent legal critics had . . . an opportunity of commenting on the case'.[198] Lord Roche suggested consulting the British Chambers of Commerce.[199] The meeting resolved to do so, and also to press ahead with a draft Bill.

The Association of British Chambers of Commerce had already taken an interest in the matter, having written to the Lord Chancellor immediately after *Fibrosa* to urge the introduction of legislation.[200] 'It is a matter of considerable importance to the commercial community,' wrote the Association's President, 'that the law should enable equitable settlements to be made between the contracting parties in the absence of a provision in the contract itself.'[201] The Lord Chancellor met the President to discuss the consultation process, but there was a problem: the President wanted to consult members about adjustments between the parties when there was no pre-payment received or benefit conferred.[202] The Lord Chancellor asserted that such legislation would be 'unsound',[203] but the Association insisted.

---

[195] *Ibid*, para 3.

[196] See text accompanying n 147 above.

[197] [1943] AC 32, 60. Winfield found the suggestion rather hurtful, observing that Lord Macmillan's statement 'does less than justice to most teachers of, and writers upon, the law': P Winfield (1942) 58 *LQR* 442. Glanville Williams shrugged it off: 'those of us who obtained pleasure from discussing *Chandler v Webster* will now be just as happy to discuss the decision of their Lordships that supersedes it': Williams (n 178) 46.

[198] Notes of a Meeting in the Lord Chancellor's Room, House of Lords, 21 July 1942, para 5. LC 02/1991.

[199] *Ibid*.

[200] President of the Association of British Chambers of Commerce to Lord Chancellor, 18 June 1942. LC 02/1991.

[201] *Ibid*.

[202] Note from Schuster to Simon, 6 August 1942. LC 02/1991.

[203] Simon to Secretary of Association of British Chambers of Commerce, 15 September 1942. LC 02/1991.

The letter ultimately sent to Chambers of Commerce across the country sought their view on that situation.[204]

The reason for the Association's defiance is intriguing. It had consulted AD McNair about adjustment between the parties in the absence of pre-payment or benefit. McNair's advice was characteristically incisive, and compelling:[205]

> Why does justice require this result? A and B are not partners or co-adventurers, so that they should share losses and gains equally. They stand in no relation of confidence. They are at arms' length . . . Just because during a war such as this the prevailing urge is to share losses and bear one another's burdens and so forth, is that a sound reason for introducing what seems to me to be a fundamentally new principle into the relation of vendor and purchaser? In fact, is not your approach somewhat emotional?

The Association, however, sought a second opinion. Justin Lynskey gave them the answer they wanted, advising that:[206]

> Frustration is not the fault of either party to the Contract. In my view therefore the fairest thing is that they should equally share the loss caused by the frustration.

Glanville Williams expressed the same view in print.[207]

The Chambers of Commerce themselves, however, were not convinced. Whilst they unanimously supported reforming the law on pre-payments and benefit, there was little support for going further. When the Law Lords met again, they agreed that 'legislation on the lines of the wider proposal should not be pursued for the moment'.[208]

The Lord Chancellor now felt that he was in a position to get Cabinet approval for the Bill. His memorandum to the Legislation Committee of the War Cabinet set out the common law position, the Law Revision Committee's proposal, and referred to his own speech in *Fibrosa*.[209] The Legislation Committee was persuaded. A draft Bill was circulated on 4 May 1943.[210]

The provision for pre-payments was in exactly the form that was ultimately enacted. The provision about benefits was very different. Particularly striking was clause 1(3)(b), dealing with the effect of frustration on the benefit:

---

[204] President of the Association of British Chambers of Commerce to members of the Association, 21 September 1942.

[205] McNair to Dean (Chairman of the Association of British Chambers of Commerce Finance and Taxation Committee), undated. LC 02/1991.

[206] Lynskey to Dean, 28 August 1942. LC 02/1991.

[207] Williams (n 189) 50.

[208] Note of meeting of the Law Lords, 16 March 1943, para 2. LC 02/1993.

[209] Memorandum from Simon to Legislation Committee, 24 March 1943. LC 02/1993.

[210] Law Reform (Frustrated Contracts and Contributory Negligence) Bill. LC 02/1993.

this subsection shall not apply to any benefit which is wholly destroyed by the circumstances constituting the ground for the discharge of the parties to the contract, and, in estimating in any other case the value of the benefit, regard shall be
had to the effect of those circumstances.

The draftsman drew the Lord Chancellor's attention to this provision in
his covering letter:[211]

Clause 1(3) proviso (b) excludes benefits accruing before the frustration occurred
but destroyed by the frustration. This narrows the field considerably and seems
to me to be right in principle. The party who has given credit, either by a payment in advance or by performing valuable services without payment, takes the
risk of the destruction of the subject matter. He can only recover where he can
show that after the frustration has occurred the party to whom the payment was
made or the services were rendered is still enjoying a net benefit from the contract, whether in the form of money or value received . . . Admittedly this is a
debateable point, but if benefits accrued immediately before the frustration and
subsequently destroyed by the frustration are to be included, the door opens very
wide because in nearly every case one party or the other has, while the contract
is still in being, gained some advantage. It seems to be better and simpler, and
probably what is wanted, to examine the position immediately after the guillotine
has fallen, and see what benefits have survived.

Clearly the Lord Chancellor was not convinced. He suggested that the subsection be redrafted in a less rigid form.[212] This was the result:

Where any party to the contract has, by reason of anything done by any other
party thereto in, or for the purpose of, the performance of the contract, obtained
a valuable benefit which accrued before the time of discharge and survived thereafter, there shall be recoverable from him by the said other party such sum, if any,
as the court or arbitrator by or before whom the matter falls to be determined
considers just having regard to—

  (a)   the value of the said benefit,
  (b)   the amount of any expenses incurred before the time of discharge by the ben-
        efited party in, or for the purpose of, the performance of the contract . . .
        . . . and to all the other circumstances of the case.

He was still not satisfied. The third draft finally achieved what he wanted,
deleting the phrase 'which accrued before the time of discharge and survived thereafter', and adding to s 1(3)(a) 'immediately after the time of discharge'. As the Lord Chancellor commented when he circulated the third
draft to the Law Lords, 'I have already had several interviews with the

---

[211] HS Kent (Parliamentary counsel) to Simon, 4 May 1943. LC 02/1993.
[212] HS Kent to Simon, 1 June 1943. LC 02/1993.

draftsman (Mr Kent) who seems to me to have done very well'.[213] Lord Wright agreed.[214] The subsection was enacted without amendment.[215]

Later judges and commentators have not shared the Lord Chancellor's view of the draftsman's efforts; and the lack of Parliamentary scrutiny of s 1(3) has also been a cause of concern.[216] Whilst both are legitimate criticisms of the Act, they are, perhaps, tempered by the evidence presented here. Before, during and after *Fibrosa* the Law Lords were giving the question of legislation close attention. They were consulted at every stage. Furthermore, the final form of words in s 1(3) was not chosen lightly. The option of *quantum meruit*—later advocated by Robert Goff J in *BP Exploration Co (Libya) Ltd v Hunt (No 2)*[217]—had initially been advanced by the Lord Chancellor, then altered. The opposite extreme—entirely disregarding benefits destroyed by the frustrating event—had also been mooted, only to be rejected. The end result was a carefully crafted compromise, deliberately leaving scope for judicial discretion. As the Lord Chancellor put it on the Second Reading of the Bill:[218]

> the Judge is to intervene and is to decide what is the right thing . . . It is not like deciding who is right or wrong in law; it is a question of the distribution of responsibility.

J. CONCLUSION

Fibrosa's significance for legal doctrine was that it marked a stage in the process of disentangling restitution from contract: the exclusively contractual approach in *Chandler v Webster* made way for restitutionary options. But its doctrinal significance was its least important aspect. Far more important was its political dimension. Here its importance went far beyond the law of unjust enrichment and highlighted the intricate patterns of law reform.

In particular it shows us that the standard account of *Fibrosa*, which allocates separate roles to the Law Revision Committee, the House of Lords and Parliament, is misconceived because the three theoretically distinct institutions were all interconnected, often by the same personnel. Thus, Lord Wright chaired the Law Revision Committee, gave a speech in *Fibrosa*

---

[213] Simon's covering note accompanying the third draft of the Bill, 4 June 1943. LC 02/1993.
[214] Wright to Simon, 5 June 1943. LC 02/1993.
[215] CLXXV *Journals of the House of Lords* (1943) 154, 6 July 1943; 198 *Journals of the House of Commons* (1943) 162, 28 July 1943.
[216] McKendrick (n 177) 154.
[217] [1979] 1 WLR 783, 802.
[218] *Hansard* HL (series 5) vol 128 cols 149–50 (29 June 1943).

and was there in Parliament to support the Bill.[219] Viscount Simon LC tried
to avoid legislation by getting the House of Lords in its judicial capacity to
solve the problem. When that failed, he delivered a speech in *Fibrosa*, which
he then cited to the War Cabinet's Legislation Committee in support of a
Bill. The same point about theoretical distinctions could also be made about
academics. Gutteridge, as draftsman of the Appendix to the Law Revision
Committee's Report, drew on his own article: his helpful suggestions
about legislation were, as events turned out, addressed to himself. One of
McNair's criticisms of the 1939 draft Bill, made as consultant to the Lord
Chancellor, re-appeared in his *Law Quarterly Review* article on the 1943
Act. The Lord Chancellor probably borrowed the example about cricket in
his speech in *Fibrosa* from McNair's other main criticism. Winfield was,
variously, a member of the Law Revision Committee, an academic commentator on *Fibrosa* in the Court of Appeal and House of Lords, and a consultant to the Lord Chancellor. In this latter capacity it is interesting to note
that he interpreted s 1(3) in the same way that Robert Goff J was to do thirty years later,[220] ie that the recipient of a benefit destroyed by the frustrating event would pay nothing.[221] When the same people are involved
throughout a process, it does not much matter what formal capacity they
happen to be acting in at any particular time.

   The one apparent exception to this was the distinction between the judicial and the legislative functions of the Law Lords. As Lord Wright had put
it, extrajudicially, 'there are certain definite limits beyond which no judge
would go'.[222] The Law Lords' refusal to implement the Law Revision
Committee's proposals in *Fibrosa* could be seen as illustrating the point.
But this is a rather technical way of analysing events. Immediately after
Fibrosa the Law Lords met to decide what the legislation should say. The
records of their meetings are even entitled FIBROSA.[223] Parliament made
no amendment to any of their substantive proposals. Driving the process
along was the Lord Chancellor, whose office conflated the judicial and the
executive. He expertly manipulated both roles to achieve the result he
wanted.

   So, *Fibrosa* may not be a leading case on unjust enrichment, but it is
undoubtedly a landmark. Once its full significance is understood, it stands
as tall as the 1943 Act. Indeed, it could be said that the Act was the product of the House of Lords' further proceedings in *Fibrosa*, which did not

---

[219] *Hansard* HL (series 5) vol 128 col 148 (29 June 1943).
[220] *BP Exploration Co (Libya) Ltd v Hunt (No 2)* [1979] 1 WLR 783, 801–2.
[221] Winfield to Simon, 13 June 1943. LC 02/1993.
[222] *Essays and Addresses* (n 183) xx.
[223] The notes of the meetings on 21 July 1942 (LC 02/1991) and 16 March 1943 (LC
02/1993) both have this heading.

appear in the Law Reports, and took place after the speeches allowing the appeal had been handed down. Furthermore, it should not be seen only as a landmark in unjust enrichment. Anyone who is tempted to believe in the separation of powers should read it too; it must be one of the most important authorities on the point.

11

Re Diplock (1948)

TIM AKKOUH AND SARAH WORTHINGTON*

A. INTRODUCTION

CALEB DIPLOCK PROBABLY had more impact in death than he did in life. In life, he amassed an enormous fortune running the Lion Steam Brewery in Eastbourne, described as the town's 'most successful venture'.[1] When he died on 23 March 1936 at the ripe old age of ninety-five, he had no close relatives and intended to leave much of his fortune to charity. A single crucial clause of his will became the subject of protracted and hostile litigation that raged over fifteen years, visited the House of Lords in both 1944 and 1950, and was a significant factor in the implementation of an Act of Parliament.[2] In the second phase of this long litigation, Diplock's next-of-kin attempted to recover huge sums wrongly paid by his executors to institutions such as hospitals and schools. The determinations of the Court of Appeal, reported in *Re Diplock*,[3] are re-examined here in the light of modern unjust enrichment doctrine. First, however, it is instructive to recall the detailed factual backdrop.

Diplock left a will that he had made on 3 November 1919 and which was proved soon after his death. Under it, he left legacies of £5,000 to each of his three executors 'for acting in such capacity'; his property, South Down Hall, to Sophie Watkin; £5,000 to her sister, Ada Calder; and legacies to his gardener (£100), cook (£50), and housemaids (£10 and £5).[4] Diplock also left £5,000 to the Princess Alice Memorial Hospital, and £20,000 for 'such

---

* The authors acknowledge joint and several responsibility for this paper. Tim Akkouh takes credit for the historical research and the analysis presented in the '*in personam*' section of the paper; Sarah Worthington for the '*in rem*' section. Both, however, endorse the final product and, as a corollary, share equal responsibility for any shortcomings. We would like to thank Charles Mitchell, Nicholas Le Poidevin, Lionel Smith and Charlie Webb for their helpful comments on early drafts of this paper.

[1] John Surtees, *Eastbourne's Story* (Seaford, SB Publications, 2005).
[2] Charitable Trusts (Validation) Act 1954.
[3] *Re Diplock* [1948] Ch 465, [1948] 2 All ER 318.
[4] Unfortunately, and despite extensive enquiries, no details of the favoured Sophie Watkin, or of the nature of Diplock's relationship with her, have been found.

Hospitals Homes and Institutions for Officers and Soldiers wounded maimed blinded and disabled in the [First World War]' as his executors should select. Sophie Watkin predeceased Diplock, and so her interest lapsed. The residuary estate clause in Diplock's will therefore assumed a heightened importance. This clause stated that the residue was to be applied 'for such charitable institution or institutions or other charitable or benevolent object or objects in England'[5] as his executors, in their absolute discretion, should select. The amount available to the executors to distribute in accordance with this instruction amounted to almost £263,000, which, in today's money, would total a staggering £9.37 million.[6]

Diplock's obituary did not appear in *The Times*, although the paper reported his death on the 25 March 1936. *The Times* also gave brief details of his will in their Wills and Bequests column on 17 June 1936 under the now somewhat ironical headline, 'A Fortune to Charity'.[7] Caleb's executors—Leslie Wintle, Dr Lionel Handson and Charles Thomas—assumed office and paid his funeral expenses and the various legacies. They then turned their attention to the residuary estate, dealt with by clause 6 in Diplock's will. Wholly ignorant of this clause's now obvious invalidating feature—the fact that it referred to 'charitable *or* benevolent' instead of 'charitable *and* benevolent'—the executors proceeded to distribute £203,067 amongst 139 charitable institutions between the years of 1936 and 1938. These distributions were made by way of cheque accompanied by a letter from the executors' solicitors, a small firm named Wintle and Hodgson, which summarised the residuary estate clause in Caleb's will and requested the return of an enclosed form of receipt. The largest single payment appears to have been the £21,000 paid to Guy's Hospital. Other institutions received smaller distributions. For example, Westminster Hospital received £4,000, the Heritage Crafts School received £2,000, and the Prince of Wales' Hospital, Plymouth, received £1,000. The smallest distribution made was £10. In discussions in this chapter, the recipients of the Diplock money are collectively referred to as 'the institutions'.

In 1939, several people claiming to be Diplock's next-of-kin informed the executors that they planned to challenge the validity of the residuary bequest. Whilst it would be presumptuous to delve too deeply into their motives for so doing, the fact that these next-of-kin only learned of Diplock's death in 1939 gives some indication of their relationship with him during his life.[8] In response, the executors' solicitors wrote 'warning letters' to each of

---

[5] *Re Diplock* (n 3) 470.
[6] This figure was reached using the Retail Price Index values for 1936 (5.3) and 2005 (188.9).
[7] Many thanks to Catharine Morris of *The Times*' obituary division for her help in tracking down these entries.
[8] See the Statement of Facts agreed between the parties prior to the first instance hearing before Wynn-Parry J at para 11. Thomas Simpson only learned of Caleb's death in 'early 1940'.

the selected institutions on 18 October 1939 informing them of the challenge and calling upon them not to deal with the distributed sums still in their hands until the matter had been resolved. On 3 January 1940, the next-of-kin issued a writ against the executors and four charitable institutions. This action was eventually stayed in June of that year when the executors took out a summons to determine the validity of the 'charitable or benevolent' clause.

Farwell J heard what would now be called a Part 8 claim and held the clause to be valid in 1940. A unanimous Court of Appeal overturned his judgment the next year. The House of Lords upheld the Court of Appeal in 1944 (*sub nom Chichester Diocesan Fund and Board of Finance (Inc) v Simpson*[9]). Lord Simonds held that the clause 'charitable or benevolent' could not be read conjunctively, and that it therefore created an invalid non-charitable purpose trust because all those purposes which were benevolent were not necessarily charitable.[10] Lord Wright dissented, on the basis that nobody 'would seriously contest that what was meant was "other charitable objects also capable of being characterised as benevolent"'.[11] The net effect of this first phase of the litigation was that eight years after Diplock's death, and five to seven years after over £203,000 had been distributed to many recognised charities, those distributions were held to be wrongful dispositions from Diplock's estate.[12]

The next important event was the settlement in 1944 of the action against the executors (or their personal representatives) for £15,000.[13] Simonds J (as he then was) approved the settlement and ordered that it should bind the executors or their personal representatives, all persons beneficially entitled to an interest in Diplock's intestacy, and the overpaid institutions. As the three executors each received £5,000 under the will for acting as executors, the settlement of the claim against them recovered the same sum as they had initially received from the estate. One can only speculate as to why the next-of-kin did not seek a more generous settlement, given that at the time they did not know how likely they were to succeed against the institutions. One plausible explanation is that the next-of-kin were worried about the executors being relieved of liability under s 61 of the Trustee Act 1925 on the basis that they acted honestly, reasonably and ought fairly to be excused from liability.[14] Another is that the executors did not have any other significant assets. This curious feature of the case must remain unresolved.

---

[9] [1944] AC 341.

[10] *Ibid*, 367.

[11] *Ibid*, 351 and 362.

[12] A rather tragic part of the history of the litigation has been brushed over. Lionel Handson, one of the executors, died on 14 July 1940. Leslie Wintle, another, died on 7 May 1942. We have it on good authority that one of these two executors committed suicide as a result of the pressure of the litigation.

[13] See the Schedule ((A) of '1st Part') to Simonds J's order dated 5 April 1944. This figure today equates to £390,827. The Retail Price Index had risen to 7.25 by 1944.

[14] This section applies to personal representatives by virtue of s 68(1)(17).

Despite the settlement of the claim against the executors, and the House of Lords' decision that the recipient institutions had received money to which they were not entitled, no further progress had been made in the next-of-kin's action against the institutions by 1945. This lull in the litigation was not to last, however, with the next-of-kin issuing a writ against the President, Vice-President, Treasurer and Governors of the Westminster Hospital in July of that year. By this time the ranks of the next-of-kin had swollen to 48, with the action being brought by three representatives. Other institutions were then joined to the action. The matter was tried before Wynn-Parry J in late 1946 and early 1947. He rejected the claimants' claims *in personam*, but allowed their claims *in rem*, at least in part. The next-of-kin appealed to the Court of Appeal.

It is this decision of the Court of Appeal that is the main focus of this chapter. The court had the invidious task of attempting to resolve a dispute between two innocent parties—the next-of-kin and the institutions. The Court of Appeal heard argument over twenty-two days and had the assistance of submissions from fourteen counsel (including four silks). A senior member of Lincoln's Inn recollects that the Court of Appeal was not persuaded by the silk appearing on behalf of the next-of-kin, and invited his junior, JL Arnold (later Arnold P), to 'follow'. His submissions were clearly more effective.[15] After almost four months' consideration, Lord Greene MR delivered an oral summary of his judgment, since the full version ran to over 89 pages.[16] Wrottesley[17] and Evershed LJJ concurred. Lord Greene concluded that Wynn-Parry J had been wrong to reject the next-of-kin's *in personam* claims. Instead, he held that a personal equity arose when the institutions were paid money to which they were not entitled. This equity arose in favour of those who were properly entitled to the deceased's assets, either because they were creditors of the deceased, or because they were entitled under the rules of testate or intestate succession. Interestingly, and rather controversially, a curious limitation was placed on this equity: it could only be exercised after the claimants' remedies had been exhausted against the personal representatives responsible for the improper payments. This *in personam* aspect of the Court of Appeal's decision was appealed to the House of Lords. The appeal received short shrift, however. Lord Simonds' brief leading judgment began with the words 'My Lords, I think that the reasoning and conclusion of the Court of Appeal are unimpeachable . . .'.[18]

[15] Many thanks to John Macdonald QC, JL Arnold's former pupil, for this recollection.
[16] *Re Diplock* (n 3) 470–559.
[17] Legend has it that the case was a significant factor behind the retirement of Wrottesley LJ, a common lawyer, in the autumn of 1948, a matter of months after the judgment was handed down.
[18] [1951] AC 251, 265.

Before the Court of Appeal, the next-of-kin's claims *in rem* were also allowed, at least to the extent that the money paid out by the executors remained traceable. In deciding whether this was so, the Court of Appeal reached several interesting conclusions. It held that the rule in *Clayton's Case*[19] applied in respect of any payments out of charity bank accounts into which the Diplock money had been paid. It also held that the ability to trace ceased where Diplock money had been spent in discharging loans (whether secured or unsecured) or in effecting building improvements to properties already owned by the charities. There was no appeal from these *in rem* aspects of the Court of Appeal's decision.

Finally, it should be noted that the Charitable Trusts (Validation) Act 1954 was, to a large extent, enacted as a result of the problems highlighted by the *Diplock* saga.[20] This Act applies to trusts in existence before 16 December 1952 under which 'property could be used exclusively for charitable purposes, but could nevertheless be used for purposes which are not charitable'.[21] The effect of the Act is to validate any dispositions made under such a clause prior to 16 December 1952, and to permit trusts containing such clauses to continue after that date so long as no distributions were made to causes that were not charitable. This Act is still used to save old trusts from invalidity, the most recent example being in the case of *Ulrich v Treasury Solicitor*.[22]

Now that the background detail has been sketched, it is possible to analyse the Court of Appeal's substantive decision. This chapter re-examines the *Re Diplock* conclusions on *in personam* and *in rem* claims. In particular, it investigates whether the findings accord with modern unjust enrichment doctrine, and, more controversially, whether and how a change of position defence should be applied.

B. CLAIMS *IN PERSONAM*

There are three aspects of the Court of Appeal's *in personam* decision that call for discussion. The first is the court's rejection of the next-of-kin's argument that the institutions had notice of the invalidity of the distributions from the moment they received them. The second is the condition that the next-of-kin exhaust their remedies against the personal representatives responsible for the improper distributions before looking to recover from the overpaid recipients. And the third is the court's acceptance of the rule

---

[19] (1816) 1 Mer 572, 35 ER 781.
[20] See further J Warburton (ed), *Tudor on Charities* (9th edn, London, Sweet & Maxwell, 2003) 162.
[21] See s 1(1).
[22] [2005] 1 All ER 1059.

that the overpaid institutions were under a duty to repay the received funds to the next-of-kin to the extent that recovery from the personal representatives was impossible. It will be argued that while the Court of Appeal's reasoning on the first issue is unimpeachable, its conclusions on the second and third issues are likely to cause injustice. This section will conclude by offering a modern reformulation of the *Diplock* personal claim.

1. The Importance of Notice of the Next-of-Kins' Claim

The distributions to the institutions were made by way of cheque, accompanied by an acknowledgement form and covering letter which, although it did not quote the residuary clause from Diplock's will, paraphrased it in such a way as to 'retain the original vice of the . . . disjunctive formula'.[23] As the first part of their *in personam* submissions,[24] the next-of-kin argued that this letter had the effect of putting the institutions on notice of the invalidity of the payments made to them. Lord Greene did not agree. He observed that despite having 'some attraction',[25] this argument led to 'startling'[26] results. He continued:[27]

> if the respondents can be said to be put upon inquiry then they must have been under some duty to inquire. What . . . would be the duty of one who is told by executors that he is a legatee under a testator's will and paid that which he is told he had been given? Must he call for and examine the will to satisfy himself of its validity? Must he inquire whether all claims ranking in priority to his own have been satisfied? In the present case it is to be noted that the letter which the respondents received came, on the face of it, from the executors' solicitors. Moreover, even though the language used in the letter might be said to convey to the tutored mind some suspicion of the validity of the disposition, it would not follow that such language though taken verbatim from the will would necessarily in its context result in invalidity. In our judgment persons in the position of the respondents, themselves unversed in the law, are entitled . . . to assume that the executors are properly administering their estate: and if, as is admitted in this case, they took the money bona fide believing themselves to be entitled to it, they should not have imposed upon them the heavy obligations of trusteeship.

This reasoning is wholly convincing. On the particular facts of the case it was not, at the time, clear that the now infamous residuary clause in Diplock's will was invalid. Indeed, when the courts came to determine the matter both Farwell J at first instance and Lord Wright in the House of

---

[23] *Re Diplock* (n 3) 477.
[24] *Ibid*, 476–7.
[25] *Ibid*, 478.
[26] *Ibid*.
[27] *Ibid*.

Lords took the opposite view. Further, it would seem that there is a strong efficiency argument in favour of allowing the recipient of money from a personal representative to assume that the office-holder has properly performed his duties. Were the law otherwise, the transaction costs associated with probate would soar as all those who receive a benefit from a deceased person's estate would be well advised to seek legal advice to confirm either the validity of the clause under which they benefited or, on intestacy, their status and rights as an intestate successor.

This reasoning is also consistent with the modern approach of the law of unjust enrichment in determining when a person who has been enriched can legitimately claim the benefit of the defence of change of position. Thus, a person who is mistakenly paid £500 will not automatically be barred from claiming change of position on the basis that he should have known that the money was not his. Instead, he will only be precluded from the benefit of the defence if he acts in bad faith, which he would no doubt do if he spent the £500 knowing that it had been mistakenly paid to him. But the modern law does not impose on every bank account holder the duty of checking account statements meticulously to ensure that every penny can be properly accounted for. And the policy justification for this rule is, in part at least, one of efficiency.[28]

A further parallel with the modern law of unjust enrichment arises from the institutions' concession that they had notice of the next-of-kin's claim after they received the 'warning letters'. Lord Greene noted that the effect of such notice was to render the institutions 'accountable in respect of any balance of the sums originally paid to them which remained in their hands unexpended or undisposed of'.[29] In modern terminology, it would be said that once the parties' attention is drawn to the fact that they have been unjustly enriched, they can no longer claim the defence of change of position in respect of subsequent expenditure. To do so would involve acting in bad faith, which precludes reliance on the defence.

But, having accepted in his discussion of the *in personam* claim that the recipients only received notice of the improper payments when the warning letters were sent out, Lord Greene proceeded to find that this did not much matter, as the claim was best analysed as one of strict liability without any substantive defences.[30] Perhaps this can be explained on the basis that Lord Greene thought that fairness was achieved by the requirement that the primary action be brought against the personal representatives. This novel requirement is analysed next.

---

[28] The 'fairness' justification for the change of position defence is examined below, 301 ff.

[29] *Re Diplock* (n 3) 477.

[30] One explanation for this may be that what Lord Greene meant when he referred to 'notice' is what is usually understood as 'knowledge' in the context of a claim for knowing receipt, since he also referred to constructive trusts in this section of his judgment dealing with the notice issue: *ibid*, 477.

2. The Requirement that the First Claim be Brought Against the Executors

Lord Greene explained why the first action should be brought against the executors:[31]

> Since the original wrong payment was attributable to the blunder of the personal representatives, the right of the unpaid beneficiary is in the first instance against the wrongdoing executor or administrator: and the beneficiary's direct claim in equity against those overpaid or wrongly paid should be limited to the amount which he cannot recover from the party responsible. In some cases the amount will be the whole amount of the payment wrongly made, eg, where the executor or administrator is shown to be wholly without assets or is protected from attack by having acted under an order of the court . . . . In our judgment the absence or exhaustion of the beneficiary's right to go against the wrongdoing executor or administrator ought properly to be regarded as the justification for calling upon equity to come to the aid of the law by providing a remedy which would otherwise be denied to the party who has been deprived of that which justly is his.

Lord Greene therefore held that it was a necessary condition of a successful claim against the institutions that the next-of-kin had exhausted their claims against the executors. He conceded that this was a novel requirement, and that 'no direct authority for the qualification is to be found in any of the other decided cases'.[32] In reaching this conclusion, he may have been attracted by the intuitive resonance of the question 'Why shouldn't those primarily responsible for the loss be the first to face legal proceedings?' The simple response to this question is, however, that the law generally does not make it a condition for bringing a claim against B that a prior claim has already been brought against A, even when A seems to be the more morally culpable party. The most obvious example arises wherever people share joint and several liability. Thus a partner is liable on a contract entered into and breached by another partner. Other specific examples can easily be identified. For example, a guarantor is liable to be sued on the principal debtor's default before any claim is made against the principal debtor, even though the guarantor only assumes a secondary liability,[33] and an employer is vicariously liable for the dishonest acts of its employee (carried out in the course of his employment) even though the employer is innocent of any dishonesty.[34]

---

[31] *Ibid*, 503–4.
[32] *Ibid*, 503. Lord Greene explained this absence of authority on the basis that 'in none of those cases where the direct claim was allowed, did it appear in fact that there was an executor or administrator against whom a claim might have been made or successfully made' (*ibid*, 503).
[33] See eg *Yeoman Credit Ltd v Latter* [1961] 1 WLR 828 (CA).
[34] *Dubai Aluminium Co Ltd v Salaam* [2002] UKHL 48, [2003] 2 AC 366 [43]–[49] (Lord Nicholls) and [153]–[161] (Lord Millett). See further C Mitchell, *The Law of Contribution and Reimbursement* (OUP, Oxford, 2003), paras 10-43 to 10-52.

Indeed, there is no requirement for pre-emptive action against the morally culpable party in claims that are closely analogous to the *Diplock* personal claim. Take the common law claim for money had and received. If A takes my money and pays it to B, I have a claim against B in money had and received even though I have not first pursued my claim against A.[35] Equity uses a slightly different model: so long as the more stringent test of unconscionability[36] is made out, a knowing recipient of trust property is personally liable regardless of whether an action is commenced against the defaulting trustee. Debate rages over whether we need two models rather than one,[37] but the effect of the Court of Appeal's decision is to introduce yet another model—and one that is radically different from the other two—to cater for the relatively unusual situation where a personal representative improperly pays away a deceased's assets.

In addition to its unnecessary complexity, a practical criticism can be levelled at the pre-emptive approach adopted by the Court of Appeal. As the law then stood, it was often impossible for personal representatives to recover improper payments made from an estate because of the mistake of law and other bars.[38] Nevertheless, the first-action rule demanded that wealthy personal representatives compensate the next-of-kin to the full extent of any improper distributions. This was unfortunate for the personal representatives, but extremely fortunate for the overpaid recipients, who were then immune from any claim by the personal representatives (because of the operation of legal bars) or by the next-of-kin (because of the rule against double recovery). This strict approach applied even in cases where the improper distribution was identifiable as an unused deposit in the recipient's bank account.

On the other hand, as the Court of Appeal realised,[39] it may not always be possible to pursue a claim against the personal representatives in full or even at all; they might be impecunious or entitled to a total defence under s 61 of the Trustee Act 1925. It is in such situations that the 'equity' vested in the next-of-kin to sue the overpaid recipients assumes a crucial importance.

---

[35] The claimant must of course show that the money that B received from A was originally the claimant's at common law. This personal claim against B depends solely upon receipt of the funds by B (so long as B has not changed his position); it does not depend on those funds remaining traceable in B's hands. See further Lord Goff in *Lipkin Gorman v Karpnale Ltd* [1991] 2 AC 548, 572.

[36] *BCCI (Overseas) Ltd v Akindele* [2001] Ch 437, 455 (Nourse LJ).

[37] See the later discussion in various parts of this chapter. The authors find themselves resolutely on opposite sides in this debate.

[38] See JHG Sunnucks (ed), *Williams, Mortimer and Sunnocks on Executors, Administrators and Probate* (18th edn, London, Sweet & Maxwell, 2000) para 80-06.

[39] *Re Diplock* (n 3) 503.

3. The Nature of the 'Equity' Vested in the Next-of-Kin

Lord Greene held that an 'equity' which vested in the next-of-kin allowed them to bring a personal claim against the institutions once they had exhausted their rights against the executors. This decision was in stark contrast to the reasoning of Wynn-Parry J at first instance, who held that the next-of-kin:[40]

> could only sue the wrongly paid recipient in equity in the same circumstances as those which would enable him in the name of or by joining the personal representative to sue at law, that is, when the wrong payment had been made under a mistake of fact.

As it was clear that the mistake that the executors had made lay in their incorrect decision to treat the residuary estate clause as creating a charitable trust, Wynn-Parry J held that no further rights lay against the institutions.

For Lord Greene, determining the nature and extent of the next-of-kin's equity required 'research into cases over a period of more than two hundred and fifty years',[41] in order to ascertain whether it had 'an ancestry founded in history and in the practice and precedents of the courts administering equity jurisdiction'.[42] Lord Greene therefore launched into a lengthy analysis of the authorities relied upon by the appellants. The earliest notable decision was that of *Noel v Robinson*, in which Lord Nottingham LC held that:[43]

> though there be no provision made for refunding, yet the common justice of this court will compel a legatee to refund. It is certain that a creditor shall compel the legatee to refund and so shall one legatee compel the other where the assets become deficient.

The subsequent cases of *Newman v Barton*[44] and *Orr v Kaines*[45] place a slight qualification on this general principle: recovery is possible only where the payment is improper at the time it is made, not where it merely becomes improper subsequently by reason of 'waste by the executor'. Lord Greene summarises this qualification as whether 'at the time when the payment was made, the legatee received anything more than, at the time, he was properly entitled to receive'.[46] Thus if an executor mistakenly pays A and B £15,000 each when in fact he should have divided the £30,000 residuary

---

[40] *Ibid.*
[41] *Ibid*, 479.
[42] *Ibid*, 482.
[43] (1682) 1 Vern 90, 93–4; 23 ER 334, 336.
[44] (1690) 2 Vern 205, 23 ER 733, 28 ER 125.
[45] (1750) 2 Ves Sen 194.
[46] *Re Diplock* (n 3) 488.

estate amongst A, B and C in equal shares, C will be able to recover £5,000 from both A and B. However, if the executor is correct in determining that A, B and C are to receive one-third shares of a £30,000 estate, and pays A £10,000 but subsequently negligently loses £10,000, neither B nor C can recover any sum whatsoever from A. This reasoning seems sensible. As Lord Greene put it:[47]

> in the absence of an original deficiency the first paid legatee got no more than what he was properly entitled to receive: and so, it may be added, there was nothing in respect of which equity could affect his conscience.

In unjust enrichment terminology, the same example might now be explained as follows: when A receives £10,000 from the executor, he is fully entitled to it; no unjust factor exists that can possibly suggest that A should be required to repay all or part to any third party. To then hold that the executor's future acts—acts that are completely unconnected with the payment to A—are somehow sufficient to create an unjust factor would be unfair because the factor would only arise *ex post facto*. Even if one tried to argue that the executor's payment to A was a result of the executor's misprediction that he would remain able to pay B and C in full (which is in itself a somewhat difficult task), any potential claim would fall foul of the Privy Council's holding in *Dextra v Bank of Jamaica*[48] that mere mispredictions (rather than mistakes) will not support claims in unjust enrichment.

Lord Greene went on to consider other authorities[49] before concluding that the next-of-kin themselves should be able to recover in a direct personal action against the recipient institutions:[50]

> it seems to us, first, to be established that the equity may be available equally to an unpaid or underpaid creditor, legatee, or next-of-kin. Second, it seems to us that a claim by a next-of-kin will not be liable to be defeated merely (a) in the absence of administration by the court; or (b) because the mistake under which the original payment was made was one of law rather than fact; or (c) because the original recipient, as things turn out, had no title at all and was a stranger to the estate; though the effect of the refund in the last case will be to dispossess the original recipient altogether rather than to produce equality between him and the claimant and other persons having a like title to that of the recipient. In our judgment there is no authority either in logic or in the decided cases for such limitations to the equitable right of action. In our judgment also there is no justification for such limitations to be found in the circumstances which gave rise to the equity. And as regards the conscience of the defendant upon which in this as in other jurisdictions equity is said to act, it is *prima facie* at least a sufficient

---

[47] *Ibid*, 487.
[48] [2001] UKPC 50, [2002] 1 All ER (Comm) 193 [29] (Lords Bingham and Goff). See too T Akkouh and C Webb, 'Mistake, Misprediction and Change of Position' [2002] *RLR* 107.
[49] In particular, *Peterson v Peterson* (1866) LR 3 Eq 111 and *In re Rivers* [1920] 1 Ch 320.
[50] *Re Diplock* (n 3) 502–3.

circumstance that the defendant, as events have proved, has received some share of the estate to which he was not entitled. 'A party' said Sir John Leach in *David v Frowd* 'claiming under such circumstances has no great reason to complain that he is called upon to replace what he has received against his right'.

The breadth of the *Diplock* claim so formulated is worthy of note, in terms of both who can use it (namely creditors, legatees, and next-of-kin), and against whom it can be used (namely legatees or those in analogous positions, and strangers to the estate).

Of course, the next-of-kin's rights against the institutions were only for those sums that could not be recovered from the executors. The amounts so recovered:[51]

> ought to be credited rateably to all the one hundred and thirty-nine charities so that the amount which in equity can be recovered by the next-of-kin from any [institution] is thus limited . . . . For example, if the amount so recovered [from the executors] is one-fourth of the total sum paid away, then the maximum liability of any [institution] to refund to the next-of-kin would be three-fourths of that which the [institution] received.

As has been noted, the next-of-kin compromised their claim against the executors for £15,000. This left the institutions liable to repay approximately 92% of the sums that were initially distributed to them.[52] As small consolation, the Court of Appeal held that interest should not be added to the required repayments (although the issue was only considered in passing).[53]

---

[51] *Ibid*, 504.

[52] The total sums distributed were £203,000, and the sum recovered from the executors was £15,000. Charles Mitchell makes an important point in relation to this issue. He asks why the recipients should be bound by the terms of a settlement to which they were not party if this was too generous to the executors. On the facts of *Diplock*, the simple answer is that the next-of-kin's settlement with the executors bound the recipients because of the order of Simonds J (see text to nn 13–14). But this does not answer the question as a matter of principle. If the next-of-kin do not take reasonable care in pursuing their primary cause of action, it is difficult to justify their full loss nevertheless being recoverable from the overpaid recipients. There is an analogy between this and the duty of parties to a contract to take reasonable steps to mitigate their losses, with failure to do so rendering such losses irrecoverable. For discussion of a similar problem under the Civil Liability (Contribution) Act 1978 see C Mitchell, *The Law of Contribution and Reimbursement* (OUP, Oxford, 2003) paras 12.10 ff.

[53] This is in contrast to the courts' modern trend of routinely awarding interest and not enquiring into what the defendant has in fact done with an enrichment (see eg *La Pintada Cia Navegacion SA v The President of India* [1983] 1 Lloyd's Rep 37, 43). There is certainly something to be said for the Court of Appeal's approach in a situation where money is mistakenly paid to a recipient who, not knowing of the payment, leaves it in an account bearing a paltry rate of interest. Under the modern law, any such a recipient would *prima facie* be liable to pay the mistaken payer interest at a rate of 8% per annum. Even over a limited time, this could amount to a considerable sum. Given that the whole point of an unjust enrichment claim is to strip a defendant of his enrichment (and no more), this result would leave the recipient worse off. The *Diplock* solution of refusing to award any interest may be preferable to the modern solution, at least when the modern solution causes the defendant a loss.

Now that the nature of the equity vested in the next-of-kin has been outlined, it is possible to analyse it in further detail. Of particular interest is Lord Greene's explanation for why repayment should be made by those who have been overpaid: he says it is because the payment was received against such a person's 'right'. Lord Greene expanded upon this, holding that:[54]

> so far as concerns the conscience of the recipient . . . the fact that he has received something to which in truth he was never entitled . . . may well sufficiently affect his conscience for the purposes of the jurisdiction of the court of equity. . . . [C]omplaints of hardship come with little force from the party who seeks to support a wrong.

This last passage is crucial. It suggests that liability in equity for receipt of property may be strict. It also rejects any defence based on hardship. These two propositions merit closer scrutiny.

(a) Strict Liability in Equity

Lord Greene's reasoning appears to recognise the existence of strict liability personal claims in equity against those who receive property to which they are not entitled. Traditionally these 'knowing receipt' claims have been seen as requiring the recipient of trust property to have some degree of knowledge that the property has been transferred in breach of trust, although there is considerable disagreement about how this knowledge requirement should be defined.[55] Reforming recipient liability so that it is receipt based would often seem to yield fairer results. Lord Nicholls supports such a change in the law.[56] When explaining why, he uses the example of a defendant innocently receiving an unauthorised payment of trust money and spending it on an everyday item—say on rent—so that it becomes untraceable. So too does Lord Walker. He uses the example of an innocent recipient of trust property who uses it to pay off his overdraft.[57] In these circumstances, the beneficiary has no proprietary claim (because he cannot trace his trust property), and no personal claim (because of the traditional requirement of 'knowing' receipt). The recipient is clearly enriched, and able to remain so. The result seems unfair. It also seems contrary to the tenor of Lord Greene's reasoning in *Diplock*.

---

[54] *Re Diplock* (n 3) 492–3.

[55] See eg A Burrows, *The Law of Restitution* (2nd edn, London, Butterworths, 2002) 194–201.

[56] Lord Nicholls, 'Knowing Receipt: The Need for a New Landmark' in WR Cornish *et al* (eds), *Restitution: Past, Present and Future* (Oxford, Hart, 1998) 231.

[57] Lord Walker, 'Dishonesty and Unconscionable Conduct in Commercial Life: Some Reflections on Accessory Liability and Knowing Receipt', (2005) 27 *Sydney LR* 187, 202.

A majority of modern commentators favour recognition of a strict liability claim in unjust enrichment either instead of or in addition to the traditional knowing receipt claim.[58] In other words, they favour extending the ambit of the *Re Diplock* reasoning. As judged by recent judicial utterance, this academic standpoint is becoming more widely accepted.[59] Others, however, oppose the change. They deploy at least two arguments against the strict liability revolution. The first is that a strict liability claim does not fall within the traditional subtractive unjust enrichment framework because the recipient is not enriched as he only acquires legal title to the assets (or, conversely, that there is no subtraction from the beneficiary, who only ever had, and still retains, equitable title to the trust property). The second, made by Professor Lionel Smith in particular,[60] is that the current law is justified by the undoubted differences that exist between equitable and legal title. While space does not permit these counter-arguments to be examined in great depth, it is necessary to consider some of the possible responses to them.

There are a number of responses to the first argument. The recipient clearly obtains a factual enrichment by receipt of trust property, as he is able to use and enjoy it. Thus a recipient who hangs the trust's Picasso painting in his drawing room clearly benefits from possession. Indeed, the fact that the recipient has both possession and legal title to the trust property is beneficial, as it confers on him good title against anyone else in the world save the trust's beneficiaries. Alternatively, the recipient's use of trust property may result in the recipient's undoubted enrichment if he deals with the property in such a way as to render it untraceable. For example, there is a clear enrichment in Lord Nicholls' example of a recipient using trust money to pay rent that he would otherwise have paid from his salary.

The second part of the first argument is that strict liability in equity should not be recognised since the recipient's enrichment is not at the beneficiaries' expense as the latter (i) obtain a cause of action against their trustee and (ii) retain equitable title. While these two propositions are indisputable, there are a host of reasons suggesting that the beneficiaries are nevertheless worse off. The trustee may be impecunious or entitled to a defence, in which case it can be said that although the trustee remains legally liable (despite there being no prospect of him discharging this liability), the recipient's enrichment is *factually* at the beneficiaries' expense.[61] Furthermore, the beneficiaries lose their collective right to have the trustee transfer possession and legal title in the trust property to them under the rule in *Saunders v Vautier*[62]

[58] Listed in Burrows (n 55) 202, note 13.

[59] See, for instance, Lord Millett in *Twinsectra v Yardley* [2002] UKHL 12; [2002] 2 AC 164 [105].

[60] See especially LD Smith, 'Unjust Enrichment, Property, and the Structure of Trusts' (2000) 116 *LQR* 412, 431–3. See also S Worthington, *Equity* (Oxford, OUP, 2003) 164–74.

[61] Smith, *ibid*, 441–2.

[62] (1841) 4 Beav 115, 49 ER 282.

when a third party intervenes, as the trustee no longer holds the trust property. The beneficiaries also lose their rights to the specific assets once they become untraceable. Although this last argument only shows that the loss to the beneficiary occurs when his equitable property becomes untraceable, this is of no particular concern for it is only at this point that the personal claim against the recipient becomes crucial.

The arguments recited in the preceding paragraphs show that recognising strict liability in equity for the improper receipt of trust property is not doctrinally impossible. But there is a different and potentially more persuasive argument raised by Professor Smith. He suggests that it would be unfair to hold recipients of trust property to a strict liability standard because:[63]

> trust interests tend to be hidden. Indicia of title, such as possession, control, and registration are lacking. Of course, legal ownership can also be undetectable, as in the case of a stolen chattel; but the difference is that for equitable interests, this is the normal state of affairs. The generally undetectable nature of equitable interests justifies a general doctrine of bona fide purchase, and a requirement of fault for personal liability for wrongful interference.

In this passage, Professor Smith rightly points out that equity protects those who purchase trust property from a proprietary claim in respect of that property by recognising the defence of bona fide purchaser. The common law offers no equivalent. The equitable rule ensures that no unfairness results to the purchaser of a legal interest who will often have a harder job of spotting that the trustee is improperly selling trust property than his common law counterpart who purchases property from a thief. This is because a trustee who sells an item of trust property in breach of trust will often have the indicia of ownership (ie receipts or other registration documents) whereas the thief will probably have no such documentary evidence of title.[64] Hence the bona fide purchaser rule makes good sense in relation to equitable proprietary claims.

But the bona fide purchaser rule is also a defence to personal unjust enrichment claims.[65] A bona fide purchaser of trust property from a trustee selling in breach of trust will be immune from both proprietary and personal claims. Two justifications are commonly given for the role of the bona fide purchaser defence in relation to personal claims. The first is that the

---

[63] Smith (n 60) 432.

[64] Thus a trustee who purchases a painting as an investment for a trust with that trust's money will appear to do so wholly legitimately. He may well obtain a receipt for the painting in his own name. When he decides to sell the painting in breach of trust, it is far easier for him to represent that he has good title to it than if a thief sells a stolen painting. Of course, this is a rule of thumb that will not hold good in all cases, as it is quite conceivable that in specific instances trustees have no such indicia of title, or that thieves forge such documentary evidence. But it is a rule that will probably hold good in the majority of cases.

[65] *Lipkin Gorman v Karpnale Ltd* [1991] 2 AC 548, 580–2 (Lord Goff).

law of unjust enrichment is quite properly subservient to the law of contract; it cannot be engaged until any underlying contract has fallen away.[66] The second is that, in the words of Professor Birks, 'within [a] valid contract, it is impossible to say that the values exchanged [are] not exactly equal'.[67] These justifications do not revolve around the 'generally undetectable nature of equitable interests'. They rather concern the proper ambit of the law of unjust enrichment and the appropriate method of computing a recipient's enrichment.

The real disagreement, then, is about whether those recipients who are volunteers should be exposed to a claim in unjust enrichment.[68] The best argument in favour of adopting such an approach is that it is not unfair to require a person who is enriched to give up any extant enrichment when the payor's intent is somehow vitiated. One cannot improve on the explanation given by Professor Birks:[69]

> Suppose that you receive change for a £50.00 note when in fact you had paid with a £20.00 note. You are chatting to your friend and put the money in your purse without so much as looking at it. Before you reach the door of the shop they ask you to give back the surplus £30.00. It is no good you saying that they were very careless or that you were absolutely innocent. Fault on either side is irrelevant. The reason is that there is no question of making you bear a loss. You are only being asked to return a surplus that you were never intended to have.

As has been argued above, there is good reason to have different rules that apply to title claims in law and at equity. But it is a wholly different thing to assert that separate rules should apply to personal claims at law and in equity that are concerned with returning an extant enrichment. So long as the bona fide purchaser rule is observed so that the law of unjust enrichment is kept within proper bounds, there can be no proper distinction between a mistaken recipient of a payment of £500 from my bank account

---

[66] P Birks, *Unjust Enrichment* (2nd edn, Oxford, OUP, 2005) 241; Burrows (n 55) 585–91.

[67] Birks, *ibid*, 243.

[68] Lionel Smith's insightful comments on this paper have identified another issue which needs to be resolved if recipient liability is to be based on the unjust enrichment model, namely that the recognised unjust factors rely on the person who enriches a recipient acting under some type of misapprehension of what he is doing. This might be because he is mistaken, because he has some form of mental/physical/economic pressure exerted on him, or because he is 'ignorant' of what has happened to his property. But where a trustee pays away money to a non-beneficiary deliberately, he is not acting under any of these states of mind; rather, he positively intends the recipient to have the enrichment that is transferred. This is, as Professor Smith points out, a different situation: the trustee's intention is not vitiated—it is fully efficacious. The simple answer to this objection is that the beneficiary, who is the ultimate owner of the trust property (and not its mere custodian), is ignorant as to what has happened to it; he thinks it is happily ensconced in, say, a trust bank account when in fact it is in the hands of a third party. Thus the strict liability claim in equity can be brought within the traditional regime of unjust factors.

[69] P Birks, 'Receipt' in P Birks and A Pretto (eds), *Breach of Trust* (Oxford, Hart, 2002) 229.

and the payment of £500 by my trustee that is used by its recipient to repay his overdraft or pay his rent. Both recipients are clearly enriched; neither was intended to have that benefit by the person at whose expense it was conferred (ie the mistaken payor or the trust beneficiary). Both cases therefore fall within the principle underlying the law of unjust enrichment.

(b) The Change of Position Defence

Within the law of unjust enrichment, strict liability is tempered by the defence of change of position. But Lord Greene rejected this defence in *Re Diplock*. He said that 'complaints of hardship come with little force from the party who seeks to support a wrong'.[70] Nowadays it is appreciated that the improper recipient does not seek to support a wrong, in the sense of asserting that the payment received was proper and should be retained in its entirety. Rather, the change of position defence is designed to alleviate the unfairness caused when people spend money on things that they would not have bought 'but for' their enrichment.[71] As Burrows argues, if a person who is enriched 'uses money received to buy benefits which he would not otherwise have bought, liability to make restitution to the payor in effect forces him to pay for benefits that he did not want'.[72]

Clearly not all expenditure is treated as being subject to the change of position defence: the expenditure has to be extraordinary for the individual who has incurred it.[73] This is an important qualification. As Lord Goff stressed in *Lipkin Gorman*:[74]

---

[70] *Re Diplock* (n 3) 493.

[71] *Lipkin Gorman v Karpnale Ltd* [1991] 2 AC 578, 580 (Lord Goff): 'where an innocent defendant's position is so changed that he will suffer an injustice if called upon to repay or to repay in full, the injustice of requiring him so to repay outweighs the injustice of denying the plaintiff restitution. If the plaintiff pays money to the defendant under a mistake of fact, and the defendant then, acting in good faith, pays the money or part of it to charity, it is unjust to require the defendant to make restitution to the extent that he has so changed his position.'

[72] Burrows (n 55) 512.

[73] Although the word 'extraordinary' can itself lead to the assumption that the defence is overly circumscribed. See further Burrows (n 55) 519 ff. Note, too, that the defence of change of position can be relied upon where the recipient's enrichment is removed because it is destroyed in a fire or is stolen by a thief: *Rose v AIB Group (UK) plc* [2003] 1 WLR 2791 [49] (Nicholas Warren QC sitting as a deputy High Court judge).

[74] [1991] 2 AC 578, 580. Perhaps this mistaken view of the change of position defence was also present in Lord Greene's reasoning. When explaining why the primary action should be brought against the personal representatives, he went on to mention what would happen if the personal representatives turned out to be men of straw, stating that 'if the executor is insolvent, an unpaid legatee is admitted to claim direct from the wrongly paid recipient because "there is no other way"': *Re Diplock* (n 3) 503. Carnwath J treated this portion of Lord Goff's judgment with caution in *Gray v Richard Butler (a firm)* 140 SJ LB 194: 'It is true that in *Lipkin Gorman* . . . Lord Goff referred to [a passage in Lord Simonds' judgment] as reflecting the mistaken assumption that the mere expenditure of money can be regarded as amounting to a change of position. However, Lord Simonds' speech, which was accepted by the other members of the House, appears to be good authority for the proposition that, at least in the context of a claim against recipients of a legacy under a will, the only equitable defences available are those relating to the conduct of the plaintiff.'

the mere fact that the defendant has spent the money, in whole or in part, does not of itself render it inequitable that he should be called upon to repay, because the expenditure might in any event have been incurred by him in the ordinary course of things. I fear that the mistaken assumption that mere expenditure of money may be regarded as amounting to a change of position for present purposes has led in the past to opposition by some to recognition of a defence which in fact is likely to be available only on comparatively rare occasions. In this connection I have particularly in mind the speech of Lord Simonds in *Ministry of Health v Simpson* [1951] AC 251, 276.

So, one explanation for Lord Greene's rejection of any form of change of position defence may have been that he misunderstood the defence's proper ambit. But Lord Greene had a further explanation for the solution he propounded: the jurisdictional differences between the common law claim for money had and received and the equitable *Re Diplock* type claim justified differences in approach. He reasoned as follows:[75]

> there are marked and important differences between the claim here put forward on the part of the appellants and a claim at common law for money had and received. In the latter the proper claimant is normally the person who originally made the payment or . . . that person's principal or representative: and the claim is made against him who received the money or his representative . . . . In the present case the payments were originally made by the executors and it is in our judgment impossible to say that in making the payments the executors were acting as agents or in any way on behalf of the next-of-kin, of whose rights and existence the executors were entirely ignorant. Plainly, nothing that the next-of-kin have done can be said to have involved any ratification or acceptance on their part of the executors' acts. Further . . . the next-of-kin have never made any mistake at all whether or law or of fact. . . .. Equity here, as in other places, comes in as Maitland has observed, 'not to destroy the common law but to fulfil it'. Since . . . the common law can only recognise the two parties to the transaction, payer and payee, or at most third parties asserting the rights of one or other of them, the common law does not, to borrow again from the language of Maitland, 'comprehend the whole truth'.

It is, of course, right that there are important differences between the next-of-kin's claim and a traditional claim for money had and received. But, as argued earlier, these differences do not explain why the institutions should be required to repay almost all of the sums received regardless of what they were motivated to do as a result of their receipt. The institutions are innocent parties, too; this status is not simply the preserve of the next-of-kin. And the requirement that any action must first be brought against the executors does not afford the institutions protection against this practical injustice. If the executors are impecunious or entitled to a defence, then the institutions will be required to repay the sums in full, with no consideration given to their innocent dealings with the received funds. In *Re Diplock*

---

[75] *Re Diplock* (n 3) 480–1.

itself, the existence of a first claim against the executors patently failed to assuage the hardship caused to the institutions: they remained liable to repay 92% of the sums received, regardless of any expenditures they had made on the reasonable assumption that the receipts were theirs to spend at will.

Finally, the notion that equity might fulfil the common law by insisting on such injustice seems wholly antithetical to the jurisdiction's jurisprudential foundations of remedying hardship caused by the common law. Indeed, the reluctance to provide the institutions with any substantial defence stands in stark contrast to the modern law of knowing receipt where, it has been argued, the rules are overly generous to recipients.

If recipient liability were remoulded so as to become strict but subject to the defence of change of position, would any unfairness result? Recall that Professor Smith argues that unfairness might result because of the different nature of legal and equitable property. But if a recipient cannot possibly be left *worse off* because of the protection afforded by the defence of change of position, then no unfairness can result. Strict liability coupled with the defence of change of position would therefore provide a fair compromise between the *Diplock* and knowing receipt extremes.

4. Conclusion

A number of criticisms have been made of the Court of Appeal's *in personam* reasoning. Two are fundamental. The first is that the requirement that the next-of-kin make their initial claim against the personal representatives exposes these representatives to potentially massive claims which, if successful, will leave the unauthorised recipients free to retain their enrichment. The second is that, to the extent that the personal representatives are unable to make good the next-of-kin's loss, the recipients of improper distributions remain personally liable for the amounts that they have received regardless of whether they have, in modern terms, changed their position.

The solution advocated here is far simpler. It would refocus the primary claim so that it is one in unjust enrichment—with modern defences—brought against the overpaid recipients by the next-of-kin. Unfairness to the recipients is prevented by the change of position defence. A secondary claim might then be brought against the personal representatives, but limited to those sums not recovered from the overpaid recipients. In this way the secondary action against the personal representatives also appears fair as it seeks to recover a loss from the personal representatives that can sensibly be imputed to them. In practice, the two claims might be launched together so that matters can be dealt with efficiently. The same reasoning should also apply to a person who receives trust property transferred in breach of fiduciary duty.

C. CLAIMS *IN REM*

The next-of kin did not simply rely on their claims *in personam*. They also pursued claims *in rem*, alleging that they were entitled to 'follow' and 'trace' the money that had been paid to the charities into any assets held by the charities that might be regarded as wholly or partly attributable to the *Diplock* funds. The cheques paid to the charities were credited to the charities' bank accounts (usually being mixed there with the charities' own funds). Using these accounts, the charities made various payments, discharging debts, purchasing assets and investments, improving their real estate and such like. Both sides accepted without question that the next-of-kin had a proprietary claim to the notional unmixed fund of 'money' paid to the charities (if such a fund could be identified).[76] But the next-of-kin went further, claiming a proprietary interest of some sort in the various assets derived from the use of this fund of Diplock money.

The trial judge, Wynn-Parry J, rejected this further advance on the initial proprietary claim to the unmixed moneys on the basis that such further claim could only be made where the mixing took place in breach of trust or some other fiduciary relationship, and the claim was made against the defaulting fiduciary. Here, however, the mixing was effected by an innocent volunteer. The Court of Appeal disagreed. It rejected this narrow interpretation of the power of equity to deal with the claims of two innocent parties (here, the next-of-kin and the charities), and found that both *Re Hallett's Estate*[77] and *Sinclair v Brougham*[78] (the two authorities principally relied upon by Wynn-Parry J) were adequate to support this wider approach. This conclusion is not now controversial, and the analysis need not be revisited here.[79]

What is controversial is the approach the Court of Appeal then took to the application of equity's detailed rules. Three separate issues merit further discussion. These concern the perceived problems associated with tracing, claiming and equitable defences. Other issues that were material in the *Re Diplock* appeal have been overtaken by subsequent judicial

---

[76] Interestingly, it is this non-controversial assumption that might now be seen as most controversial, especially given the decision of the House of Lords in *Westdeutsche Landesbank Girozentrale v Islington LBC* [1996] AC 669, and the doubt there expressed in relation to *Chase Manhattan Bank v Israel British Bank* [1981] 1 Ch 105.

[77] (1880) 13 Ch D 696.

[78] [1914] AC 398.

[79] And, on the basic tracing issues, Lord Greene MR's detailed analysis of the difference between common law and equitable approaches to tracing remains much cited, although now the more modern approach favours only one set of tracing rules: see eg *Foskett v McKeown* [2000] UKHL 29, [2001] 1 AC 102, 113 (Lord Steyn) and 128–9 (Lord Millett), both *obiter*; and LD Smith, *The Law of Tracing* (Oxford, OUP, 1997) 123–30 and 168–74.

developments, and in any event are incidental to the principal focus of this chapter.[80]

1. Tracing: Problems Associated with Mixed but Non-Homogeneous Inputs

Significant sums from the Diplock funds were spent by the charities on redevelopment and improvement of their real estate. For example, Guy's Hospital spent over £14,000 of Diplock money on reconstruction work to create two children's wards, known as the 'Caleb' and 'Diplock' wards. This was the largest single sum spent in this way, but these claims were undoubtedly the most important to the next-of-kin in terms of the total amounts in issue.

The goal pursued by the next-of-kin was simple. They wished to assert a proprietary interest in the real estate into which their funds had been fed in redevelopment work. The Court of Appeal rejected these claims outright. In its view, it was impossible to trace in equity into substitute assets derived from mixed but non-homogeneous inputs (ie here, derived from money from the Diplock estate together with real property from the charities). Further, even if this conclusion were wrong, the court held that since the only possible remedy was the grant of a charge over the charities' properties, and since this remedy would operate inequitably in the circumstances, it would not be granted in equity.[81]

The Court of Appeal was in no doubt that tracing in these circumstances presented insurmountable obstacles. In describing these obstacles, modern eyes now see clearly that the court failed to distinguish between tracing problems and claiming problems. Instead, the two were rolled together, as was common practice until relatively recently. First, the court was troubled by the notion that it might sometimes be necessary to conclude that the investment money had 'disappeared', in the sense that the expenditure had

---

[80] Two issues are notable in this context. First, there are the presumptions in dealing with disbursements from a mixed fund (using the rule in *Clayton's Case*, or *Re Hallett* presumptions, or a pro rata presumption in favour of innocent contributors, unless, in any of these cases, the relevant presumption is displaced by the defendant's own allocation—although presumably such an allocation may not be allowed to work to the detriment of a claimant, at least when the defendant is not an innocent volunteer): see *Re Diplock* (n 3) 549–54. Secondly, there is the law relating to subrogation. The Court of Appeal denied the possibility of reviving subrogation (*ibid*, 548–9), suggesting that it would produce the same undesirable ends for the charities as tracing into substitutes derived from mixed inputs (see the discussion below, 305–306). This outcome is surely simply fortuitous: tracing allows one asset to stand in the place of another; subrogation allows one claimant to stand in the place of another. In any event, the law of subrogation is not now so restrictive, although the developments are not without their own problems: S Worthington, 'Subrogation Claims on Insolvency' in F Rose (ed), *Restitution and Insolvency* (London, LLP, 2000) 66; and, more generally, C Mitchell, *The Law of Subrogation* (Oxford, OUP, 1994).

[81] *Re Diplock* (n 3) 548.

resulted in no added value to the land;[82] at other times, the added value could well be less than the sum actually spent. What remedy should the next-of-kin then have? Secondly, how would a court assess the *charity's* contribution to the substitute asset?[83] Would it be the entire parcel of charity land, or only the small and specific portion of it that had been improved? In this context, the court seemed perturbed that any lien securing the next-of-kin's money investment might be over the entire estate belonging to the charity, and not restricted to some smaller area. Finally, the court felt it inequitable that the innocent charity, having contributed land (not money) to the substitute asset might be confined to a remedy that would return not the land, but only money (by way of a charge over the land to secure the charity's interest).[84]

As against this, there is the intuitive sense that the next-of-kin's Diplock money *is* represented in the improved buildings owned by the charities, and that the law should recognise this and act accordingly. Indeed, Millett LJ seemed to suggest as much, in *obiter dicta*, in *Boscawen v Bajwa*:[85]

> If the plaintiff's money has been applied by the defendant, for example, not in the acquisition of a landed property but in its improvement, then the court may treat the land as charged with the payment to the plaintiff of a sum representing the amount by which the value of the defendant's land has been enhanced by the use of the plaintiff's money.

And, a few pages later, in specific discussion of the *Diplock* case:[86]

> Justice did not require the withholding of any remedy, but only that the charge[87] . . . should not be enforceable until the hospital had had a reasonable opportunity to obtain a fresh advance on suitable terms from a willing lender, perhaps from the bank which had held the original security.[88]

This careful approach seems to address all the concerns expressed by the *Diplock* Court of Appeal in valuing the next-of-kin's contribution to the substitute asset, and in being fair to the charities by controlling the enforcement of the proprietary remedy awarded to protect the claimants' interests.

---

[82] *Ibid*, 547.

[83] *Ibid*.

[84] *Ibid*, 548. The risk at issue was that the next-of-kin might enforce their charge against the charities' real estate, thereby forcing a sale of the land unless the charities had surplus funds with which to meet the claim.

[85] [1996] 1 WLR 328 (CA), 335. To the same effect: *Foskett v McKeown* [2000] UKHL 29, [2001] 1 AC 102, 109 (Lord Browne-Wilkinson).

[86] *Ibid*, 341.

[87] Here by subrogation, but the practical problems were seen by the *Diplock* Court of Appeal as identical in subrogation and tracing.

[88] Adding, in the next sentence: 'Today, considerations of this kind would be regarded as relevant to a change of position defence rather than as going to liability.'

Unfortunately, a little serious thought suggests that the position is by no means so simple. The problem of 'mixed but non-homogeneous inputs' requires us to think very carefully about what, precisely, tracing is designed to do.[89] At its most fundamental, tracing is simply a legal technique for proving that Asset B is the exchange product, or substitute asset, for Asset A.[90] There is little need for sophisticated 'legal techniques' when Asset A is £100, which is handed over in cash to purchase Asset B, a painting. We say, without pause, that the cash can be traced into the painting. But special legal rules are clearly necessary if X's £100 is first deposited in Y's bank account, which is already £100 in credit, and a painting costing £100 is then purchased using Y's debit card. Then it is more difficult to say whether the entire painting, or some part of it, or none of it, is the 'exchange product' of X's £100.[91] For the purposes of this chapter, it is not the legal rules themselves that are in issue, but precisely what it is that 'tracing' is designed to do.

Before pursuing this line, it is worth reiterating the crucial difference between 'tracing' and 'following'. The distinction becomes especially important, and sometimes difficult, in the context of non-homogeneous inputs, but in simple cases it is clear. Suppose X's £100 is paid to Y to purchase Y's painting, and Y then uses this £100 to purchase a sculpture from Z. We can focus on one party, and 'trace' the *exchanges* of property. Consider X. In X's hands, X's £100 is exchanged for a painting: X's £100 can be *traced* into the painting, its direct substitute. Or consider Y: Y's painting is exchanged for £100, which is exchanged for a sculpture: Y's painting can be traced into £100, and from there into a sculpture. These are all simple direct exchanges. The problems are magnified if there are mixed

---

[89] In this context it is now common to cite Millett LJ in *Boscawen* (n 85) 334: 'Equity lawyers habitually use the expressions "the tracing claim" and "the tracing remedy" to describe the proprietary claim and the proprietary remedy which equity makes available to the beneficial owner who seeks to recover his property in specie from those into whose hands it has come. Tracing properly so-called, however, is neither a claim nor a remedy but a process. Moreover, it is not confined to the case where the plaintiff seeks a proprietary remedy; it is equally necessary where he seeks a personal remedy against the knowing recipient or knowing assistant. It is the process by which the plaintiff traces what has happened to his property, identifies the persons who have handled or received it, and justifies his claim that the money which they handled or received (and, if necessary, which they still retain) can properly be regarded as representing his property.' But this does not advance the matters in debate here. Indeed, in some respects the passage fails to differentiate sufficiently between 'tracing' an asset into its substitutes and 'following' an asset as it passes, in unaltered form, from hand to hand.

[90] Once this has been done, a second issue becomes material: if the claimant has a property interest in Asset A, will she also be regarded as having a property interest in Asset B?

[91] Clearly X's £100 *could* have provided the entire purchase price; equally clearly, so too could Y's £100. The truth is impossible to discover. In these circumstances, equity operates on the basis of legal presumptions which differ depending upon whether Y is an innocent party (if so, pro rata contribution to the exchange is presumed) or a wrongdoer (in which case the presumption of entire contribution by X or by Y is left to X's election, to be effected in whichever way best benefits X, bearing in mind the present value of the painting and any alternative tracing options that may be afforded on the particular facts).

inputs, as when Y uses only £50 of the receipts from X, and £50 from another source to purchase the sculpture. But in every case tracing remains an exercise in identifying *exchange products*.

'Following' is different. With following, the focus remains on a single asset as it is transferred from hand to hand, with the goal being discovering who has had any dealings with it. So X's original £100 can be *followed* into Y's hands and then into Z's; equally, the painting can be followed from Y's hands into X's. With following, too, there can be mixing difficulties. If X's £100 is paid into Y's bank account which is £100 in credit, and Y then uses funds from this account to purchase the sculpture, can X's initial £100 be followed from X to Y and then to Z, or only from X to Y, or not at all because the absence of a means of identification of precisely which notes are X's is prohibitive? Again, whatever the difficulties, following remains an exercise in identifying a specific asset as it passes through the hands of successive recipients.

Finally, to complete the picture, notice that both of these processes are ultimately directed at allowing one party to establish a claim against another, although neither process, of itself, suggests anything about the existence of an effective claim. X's £100 may be followed into Y's hands and then into Z's, given the right facts. If this is the consequence of a chain of legitimate purchases, however, X cannot possibly mount any claim to the funds that are now held by Z. A great deal has been written attempting to explain precisely how tracing and following are related to claiming.[92]

Bearing in mind these fundamental differences, what were the tracing difficulties in *Re Diplock*? Recall that the next-of-kin wished to trace the Diplock funds into the charities' improved real estate. In equity, Asset A can be *traced* into Asset B because A has been *exchanged* for B.[93] The assets need not be tangible assets, but the goal of tracing is to discover which item of property is the substitute for another. Where the facts are unclear, and

---

[92] See any standard textbook on equity, unjust enrichment or personal property. The first and second of these tend to focus on the way that tracing may preserve or enhance claims (whether these are claims in equity or in unjust enrichment); the last (ie personal property texts) usually provide an account, however brief, of both tracing and following. For an outline of some of the central issues, see Worthington (n 60) ch 4, and also S Worthington, 'Justifying Claims to Secondary Profits' in EJH Schrage (ed), *Unjust Enrichment and the Law of Contract* (The Hague, Kluwer, 2001) 451.

[93] Again, note very carefully the difference between tracing and following. The goal of tracing is to track *exchanges*; it is not to *follow* the initial asset and conclude that it *remains* physically (or intangibly) present in the second asset. Put another way, in tracing, Asset A will *not* remain intact as a physical or intangible part of Asset B; Asset A will generally continue to exist independently, perhaps now in some third party's hands, transferred in exchange for Asset B. In *following* cases, however, Asset A either remains intact and independent, or intact but physically part of Asset B: this is the problem the common law addresses in confusion and co-mixing cases. The distinction between tracing and following becomes particularly fraught in accession and manufacturing cases: is Asset A properly *traced* into the manufactured exchange product, or *followed* there? Does the distinction matter? See the discussion that follows, 310–313.

Asset A *could* have been exchanged for Asset B, but could equally have been exchanged for some other asset (as in the earlier examples where funds from different sources are mixed before a purchase is made), then presumptive rules must be applied. These legal rules attempt to effect the fairest outcome between the parties when the true facts are undiscoverable—this is the role of the 'rules' in *Clayton's Case*,[94] or the *Re Hallett* presumptions,[95] or the *pro rata* presumption in favour of innocent contributors. In this way, a presumptive assessment is made of the different parties' respective contributions to the exchange product. Crucially, however, the tracing trail ends if there is no practical way that Asset A could *possibly* have been exchanged for Asset B. This is seen in its most familiar guise in the 'intermediate balance' rule,[96] and in the more controversial 'no backwards tracing' rule.[97] Put bluntly, equitable tracing's most significant feature is its complete commitment to 'real exchange'.[98]

This requirement of a 'real exchange' is, in truth, what is being tested in the *Diplock* case. With mixed non-homogeneous inputs, has the next-of-kin's money been exchanged for the substitute asset (the reconstructed hospital site), and, if so, to what extent?[99] Given all that has been said so far, it seems to follow naturally, intuitively indeed, that if the next-of-kin contribute £10,000 to the redevelopment of the hospital's site, and the hospital contributes its site, then each should be able to assert that their contribution to the substitute asset (the improved site) is in proportion to the respective value of their initial contributions. This, surely, is a simple case of mixed inputs being used to acquire a single asset substitute. The sums might work out as follows: £10,000 contribution in money from the next-of-kin,

---

[94] (1817) 1 Mer 575, 35 ER 781.
[95] *Re Hallett's Estate* (1879) 13 Ch D 696.
[96] *James Roscoe (Bolton) Ltd v Winder* [1915] 1 Ch 62.
[97] *Bishopsgate Investment Management Ltd v Homan* [1995] Ch 211.
[98] This is notwithstanding the suggestion in *Re Diplock* (n 3) 520, that equity's 'metaphysical approach' stands in stark contrast to the common law's 'physical approach'. The point of the assertion there was that equity can deal with uncertainties, and resolve them by presumptions, in a way that the common law was not prepared to do.
[99] Before considering this in detail, notice two further features of the very familiar tracing rules. First, the treatment of mixed *homogeneous* inputs is well-developed and uncontroversial. No one disputes the outcome if money from both the claimant and the defendant is mixed and used to purchase Asset B. It is the same if another identical asset, such as premium grade oil, from both claimant and defendant is mixed and sold on the market, so that Asset B is itself money. Secondly, the tracing analysis is conducted without reference to the *value* of Asset B. That may be material at the *claiming* stage of the analysis, but tracing, in these mixed input cases, is designed simply to establish the *extent* to which the claimant can assert that Asset B is the substitute for the claimant's contribution (Asset A), and the extent to which she has to concede that other parties are entitled to make similar assertions in respect of their contributions to the substitute. For example, if a painting is purchased for £10,000, with the purchase fund made up of £4,000 from X and £6,000 from Y, then the tracing rules will allow X to assert a 40% contribution to Asset B (the painting) and Y a 60% contribution. These tracing rules do not determine what *claim* X or Y can make once they have traced their funds into the painting; that depends upon other rules, discussed to a limited extent later in this chapter. The issues assume significance if, at the time of claiming, the painting is worth vastly more, or less, than its purchase price.

and £200,000 in value of the site from the hospital, giving a 1:20 split of interests in the substitute asset.

Why did the Court of Appeal find this approach impossible? Indeed, why are they not alone is seeing difficulties? In *Borden (UK) Ltd v Scottish Timber Products Ltd*, Bridge LJ had to decide whether resin (sold subject to a retention of title clause, and so clearly the claimant's asset until it was paid for) could be traced into the chipboard that it was used to make. He had this to say:[100]

> Suppose cattle cake is sold to a farmer, or fuel to a steel manufacturer, in each case with a reservation of title clause, but on terms which permit the farmer to feed the cattle cake to his herd and the steelmaker to fuel his furnaces, before paying the purchase price. Mr Mowbray [counsel for the seller] concedes that in these cases the seller cannot trace into the cattle or the steel. He says that the difference is that the goods have been consumed. But once this concession is made, I find it impossible to draw an intelligible line of distinction in principle which would give the plaintiffs a right to trace the resin into the chipboard in the instant case. What has happened in the manufacturing process is much more akin to the process of consumption than to any simple process of admixture of goods. To put the point in another way, if the contribution that the resin has made to the chipboard gives rise to a tracing remedy, I find it difficult to see any good reason why, in the steelmaking example, the essential contribution made by the fuel to the steel manufacturing process should not do likewise.

There may be legitimate debate about the accuracy of the analogies drawn here, and a sneaking suspicion that following and tracing have been confused.[101] Nevertheless, taking the statement at face value, what is clearly at issue is the need, in tracing, for 'real exchange': one asset must be the *substitute* for another; it must not simply enable the production of the subsequent asset, or its maintenance.[102]

---

[100] [1981] Ch 25 (CA), 41–2.

[101] Recall that 'following' seeks to identify the location of a specific asset. If the issue is following, rather than tracing, then it is easy to say that the fuel has 'disappeared' and cannot be followed (identified in its original form) into any end product; so too with the cattle cake. These examples may be contrasted with the mixing of two containers of wheat in a silo. Both sources of wheat are clearly present in the silo—they can be 'followed'. Which model is more apt when resin is mixed with woodchips to make chipboard? Has the resin 'disappeared', or can it be followed? Logical responses may differ, but the common law has opted for the former answer when new products are manufactured: the common law says that the resin has 'disappeared'; it cannot be followed into the newly manufactured product. But is it also true that the resin has 'disappeared' and cannot be *traced* into the manufactured product? This is, in part, the *Diplock* problem.

[102] The same difficulties arise in cases where money is expended on repairs to property which are designed to prevent deterioration that would otherwise result in a fall in value. There is authority suggesting that these expenditures leave no traceable residue (*Re The Esteem Settlement* [2002] JLR 53), but also commentary criticising this response (C Mitchell, 'Tracing, Following, and Claiming the Proceeds of Stolen Assets' (2003) *Jersey Law Review*, published online at http://www.jerseylegalinfo.je/publications/jerseylawreview/feb03/jlr0302_mitchell.aspx).

As against this, there is an alternative approach that suggests itself as equally fair, or maybe even more fair, to the contributing parties. It is an approach that traces the *value* of contributions: Asset A can be traced into Asset B because the *value* inherent in Asset A is used to create the *value* inherent in Asset B. On this approach, there is no difficulty tracing cattle cake into the cattle, or fuel into steel. Indeed, the suggestion that this *is* the goal in tracing may be read into the words used by Lord Millett in *Foskett v McKeown* (although, equally, the words can bear a more restrictive interpretation):[103]

> We also speak of tracing one asset into another, but this too is inaccurate. The original asset still exists in the hands of the new owner, or it may have become untraceable. The claimant claims the new asset because it was acquired in whole or in part with the original asset. *What he traces, therefore, is not the physical asset itself but the value inherent in it.*

There is no material slippage in outcome with these two different versions of tracing if the problem concerns mixed homogenous inputs. If a mixed fund of money derived from X and Y is used to buy eggs and flour, and these ingredients are used to make a cake, then X and Y can trace their money into the cake. If the parties contributed funds in the ratio 80:20, for example, then those same proportions will determine the extent to which the cake is the traceable substitute of their funds. Now change the facts slightly. If, instead of first mixing X and Y's funds and then buying the ingredients, X and Y each purchases one of the ingredients themselves (with the value ratio remaining as 80:20), and then the cake is made with X's eggs and Y's flour, the answer is surely no different.[104] It must be acceptable to say that X and Y's different inputs are physically exchanged for the substitute asset. It should follow that X and Y can trace their mixed non-homogeneous contributions (eggs and flour) into the substitute asset (the cake). It would seem to do our law no harm to allow this, and earn it some disrepute if it were incapable of such a conclusion. Indeed, despite earlier cases to the contrary,[105] *Foskett v McKeown*[106] might be regarded as opinion from the highest court that this is possible.

---

[103] [2000] UKHL 29, [2001] 1 AC 102, 128 (emphasis added).

[104] And this is a consequence of *tracing*, not following. As noted earlier, it is uncontroversial that in these circumstances the eggs and the flour will be regarded as 'disappearing', so that *following* is impossible. What is at issue, then, is whether the initial inputs can be *traced* in equity into the substitute asset. At common law, of course, the matter would be put differently: the common law needs to attribute legal ownership of the substitute asset to *someone*, and its rules are therefore directed at determining the resolution of this (often difficult) problem. Equity's tracing rules assume that common law title rests wherever the common law directs, but tracing conclusions may work to assist any claims that are available to the different contributing parties.

[105] For example, *Borden* (n 100) 41–2 (Bridge LJ) is directly to the contrary.

[106] *Foskett* (n 103). There the mixed inputs were money (from the claimant beneficiaries) and a chose in action under a contract of insurance (from the defaulting trustee and, through him, his dependants).

Now change the scenario slightly. Suppose X and Y's funds are mixed and used to buy eggs and flour, as before, and also to pay for the labour to make the cake. Assuming the same total fund, this cake will clearly be smaller (made with fewer ingredients, given labour costs), but X and Y will be able to trace their funds into the cake in precisely the same 80:20 proportion as before (and could also trace their funds into the expenditure on labour, but this delivers no traceable end product). This is not controversial, but it does throw into sharp relief the issue that arises with mixed non-homogeneous inputs. If the initial asset is not a mixed fund of money, but the non-homogeneous inputs of eggs, flour and labour contributed by X, Y and Z, say, then how are the different inputs to be traced into the resulting cake? Orthodox tracing rules suggest that the outcome is the same as before for X and Y; they share 80:20. But Z's contribution of labour does not deliver a 'physical exchange', and so Z's input delivers no traceable substitute. Moreover, it must follow that the resolution cannot be any different simply because X provides *both* the eggs *and* the labour, and Y provides the flour. Nor can it be any different if X provides the eggs and the *money* for the labour, and Y provides the flour. This is one aspect of the problem that worried Bridge LJ in *Borden*, as noted earlier. The same analysis is also readily applied to the *Re Diplock* problem. The money provided by the next-of-kin was not used to supply 'eggs'; it was used to supply 'eggs and labour'. This affects the tracing exercise.

Admittedly, this is not at all how the analysis was pursued by Lord Greene. His approach was much more factual and pragmatic, and bundled together issues of tracing and claiming without any thought of doctrinal distinctions. Now we insist on distinguishing the different steps in the reasoning. This forces us to draw on different resources. In doing so, we have to determine the real function of tracing. Do we mean that 'one asset can stand for another because it is the exchange product'; or do we meant that 'one asset can stand for another because it was acquired in whole or in part with the value inherent in the original asset'? The latter approach would dramatically expand the scope of tracing—indeed, every transfer of 'value' that merited a claim in unjust enrichment would seem to give rise to tracing options, with all the proprietary consequences that then ensue.

The 'eggs, flour and labour' example used earlier assumes that tracing is a legal technique for identifying *exchanges of property*, not simply contributions of value. But has the law moved on? In particular, will contributions of *value* (whether by way of money or labour) expended on the improvement of property allow their supplier to trace this value into the improved property? Lord Browne-Wilkinson suggested as much in *obiter dicta* in *Foskett v McKeown*. He said:[107]

---

[107] *Ibid*, 109.

Tracing is a process whereby assets are identified. . . . [T]he rules of tracing . . . [include rules that regulate] the position when moneys of one person have been innocently expended on the property of another. . . . [I]t is . . . clear that money expended on maintaining or improving the property of another normally gives rise, at the most, to a proprietary lien to recover the moneys so expended [rather than proportionate ownership, as when tracing is through a mixed fund].

The inference is that contributions of *value* can be *traced* into exchange products, although the resulting claim will be for a lien only, ensuring recovery of the value of the original financial input rather than a proportionate interest in the improved asset. The precedents marshalled in support suggest that if money is spent improving a plot of land, the supplier of the funds will acquire a lien over the land; similarly, the person paying an artist to sculpt a block of marble will acquire a lien over the sculpture.

If this outcome is accurately characterised, it is enormously significant. It suggests a substantial change in the scope of tracing, and a consequential expansion in potential claims that may be brought by claimants. The *Diplock* problem, or the 'eggs, flour and labour' problem, will be answered differently. Yet Lord Browne-Wilkinson does not suggest that he is advancing a change in the law; he says he is simply describing current law. Crucially, then, is this part of the law of tracing, or is it something else?

To pre-empt what follows, these liens seem best characterised as unrelated to tracing, not as new (or newly recognised) rules about tracing value. Take a simple example. Suppose X pays £1,000 to Y to erect a fence on Z's property. Ignoring any claiming difficulties, can X's £1,000 be traced into Z's property?[108] Indeed, it should make no difference if X builds the fence himself, rather than paying Y to do the work. Orthodox rules of following and tracing would lead to the following analysis. In X's hands, X's use of £1,000 leads to no traceable substitute asset: what X receives in exchange for the £1,000 is a contract right enforceable against Y, but not exchange *property*. An alternative is to *follow* the £1,000 into Y's hands, and trace from there. The £1,000 is then traced into whatever assets may be purchased by Y using these funds. This process of tracing may lead to traceable substitutes (a purchased painting, or shares, for example) or untraceable substitutes (food that is consumed, or rent paid, for example). Fortuitously, Y may spend the funds on fence posts for the new fence, but this will not necessarily be the case. In further tracking X's £1,000, which of the traceable assets in Y's hands can then be followed into Z's hands, and from there traced into the property improvements effected by the new fence? The difficulties with the assertion that the initial provider of value

---

[108] Put in Lord Browne-Wilkinson's terms, can X trace his £1,000 into the improvements on Z's property and claim a lien on Z's property to secure recovery of the value of the improvement (whether that is more or less than the £1,000 spent)?

may trace value into the improvements to Z's property are clear. And these are just the following and tracing difficulties; the separate claiming difficulties are equally significant.

And yet, Lord Browne-Wilkinson is right. We do know of cases where liens are granted in favour of X to protect X's contribution to improvements in the value of Z's property.[109] But this is not done by way of an expanded tracing regime. It is done to effect a *primary* remedy between X and Z, not a tracing process contingent on some other separate self-standing primary claim. These cases are all instances of proprietary estoppel. These estoppel rules are complicated—controversial, even—but they have nothing to do with tracing.[110] Perhaps the estoppel label hides a lack of formal rigorous analysis, but what is hidden is not a process of tracing property, or even tracing value, but a process of remedying situations of formal contract failure or of unjust enrichment. Equity's estoppel rules provided remedies where the common law contract or unjust enrichment rules could not (then) meet the justice of the situation. Equity achieved this, not by ordering the payment of damages or some other money remedy (it could not do this), but by equity's typical *in personam* orders directed to the defendant, and by its property-based rules. So, despite formal contract failures, equity regarded some promises as enforceable by means of constructive trusts, or as reversible (ie effecting restitution) by means of equitable liens entitling the claimant to recover unintentionally conferred benefits.[111] But the prerequisites for establishing these primary proprietary claims are far more demanding than those that enable a claimant to follow or to trace into substitutes once the claimant has established a primary proprietary interest against the defendant. The former cases insist on stricter reasons to strip the recipient of received benefits than the mere fact of receipt, especially when it is proposed to do this by way of lien in favour of the donor in the manner suggested by Lord Browne-Wilkinson. Even a personal remedy to effect restitution in these circumstances has its difficulties, as is recognised in the now familiar discussions of the 'uninvited shoe-cleaner'.[112]

In summary, the *Diplock* tracing problem, or the 'eggs, flour and labour' problem, is not one that should be approached carelessly. It may well be

---

[109] See eg *Unity Joint Stock Mutual Banking Association v King* (1858) 25 Beav 72, 53 ER 563 (lien for expenditure on improvements); *Dillwyn v Llewelyn* (1862) 4 De GF & J 517, 45 ER 1285 (constructive trust over the improved property); *Amalgamated Investment and Property Co Ltd (in liq) v Texas Commerce International Bank Ltd* [1982] QB 84, 103 (Robert Goff J suggesting that the principle of equitable estoppel was 'surely one of the most flexible'). For more modern authority, see the cases cited in S Worthington, 'Equitable Estoppel: Unpacking a Doctrine' (2000) 27 *Journal of Malaysian and Comparative Law* 227.

[110] Although, of course, once the initial lien has been established, *it* may be traced into substitutes. But establishment of the *initial* lien is not a result of tracing the supplier's funds into the land or the marble.

[111] Worthington (n 60) 221–32, and the cases and commentary cited above.

[112] *Falcke v Scottish Imperial Insurance Co* (1886) 34 Ch D 234.

right to reconsider the *Diplock* analysis, and allow tracing of the Diplock funds into the charities' improved property, but establishing precisely how that is done requires a rigorous commitment to clearly articulated tracing rules. The essential policy question is whether the law should remain wedded to the idea that tracing maps 'exchanges of property' or whether it should move to a new paradigm where tracing maps 'exchanges of value'.[113] The latter would radically enlarge the impact of tracing, and if the claiming practice at the end of such a tracing chain were to remain proprietary, then the commercial impact would be enormous.

2. Claiming: Whether the Remedy Following Tracing is a Charge or an Ownership Interest

The second issue of importance in relation to the *Re Diplock in rem* claims is the nature of the claim that follows successful tracing. It has become modern orthodoxy to separate the processes of tracing and claiming, and to insist that the second is not an automatic corollary of the first. This is often pointedly illustrated by the simple example of the sale of a car. Suppose X sells her red sports car to Y, and Y then re-sells the car and successfully invests the entire proceeds in a painting and shares. X can *follow* her car into Y's hands and from there *trace* it into the resale cash and then into the painting and the shares (tracing being merely a technique for identifying substitutions), but in these circumstances she has no *claim* to any interest in the substitute assets. She lost all claiming rights following the valid sale of her car.

Insisting that tracing and claiming are distinct suggests that the same tracing path can generate different claims depending upon the context in which a remedy is being sought. Were it otherwise, there would be no point in keeping the processes separate. But the modern approach of the House of Lords is completely at odds with this. According to the Lords, provided the claimant can establish a proprietary interest in an original asset in the defendant's hands, the tracing consequences (ie the permissible *claims*) are then automatic. As was said in *Foskett v McKeown*:

> The transmission of a claimant's property rights from one asset to its traceable proceeds is part of our law of property, not of the law of unjust enrichment. . . . Property rights are determined by fixed rules and settled principles. They are not discretionary. They do not depend upon ideas of what is 'fair, just and reasonable'. Such concepts, which in reality mask decisions of legal policy, have no place in the law of property.[114]

---

[113] See eg S Evans, 'Rethinking Tracing and the Law of Restitution' (1999) 115 *LQR* 469.
[114] *Foskett* (n 103) 127, *per* Lord Millett.

. . . If, as a result of tracing, it can be said that certain of the policy moneys are what now represent part of the assets subject to the trusts of the purchasers' trust deed, then as a matter of English property law the purchasers have an absolute interest in such moneys. There is no discretion vested in the court. There is no room for any consideration whether, in the circumstances of this particular case, it is in a moral sense 'equitable' for the purchasers to be so entitled. The rules establishing equitable proprietary interests and their enforceability against certain parties have been developed over the centuries and are an integral part of the property law of England. It is a fundamental error to think that, because certain property rights are equitable rather than legal, such rights are in some way discretionary. This case does not depend on whether it is fair, just and reasonable to give the purchasers an interest as a result of which the court in its discretion provides a remedy. It is a case of hard-nosed property rights.[115]

In the earlier example, *if* the vendor can establish any form of proprietary claim to the original asset (the car) *when it is in Y's hands*, then she will be able to trace and claim, asserting equitable ownership of the resale purchase fund, and, later, equitable ownership of the substitute painting and the shares. The conclusion, it seems, follows automatically and ineluctably from the rules of English property law. Put another way, the common understanding of these modern authorities on tracing and claiming is that the claimant's equitable ownership interest in the original asset will deliver equitable ownership of any traceable proceeds; a lesser initial equitable interest, by way of charge, will deliver only the same lesser interest in the substitutes.[116]

It is not clear that these conclusions are in complete accord with the conclusions of the *Diplock* Court of Appeal. Although the court allowed very few tracing claims, those it did allow involved tracing Diplock funds into bonds and other investments returning contractually agreed rates of interest. In some parts of the court's judgment the assertion is made that the claimants are 'entitled to a *charge* on the funding loan [the substitute asset] in respect of their claim to £3,000 [the initial Diplock sum being claimed]'.[117] On the other hand, these *in rem* claims were also held to carry

---

[115] *Ibid*, 109, *per* Lord Browne-Wilkinson.

[116] *Ibid*, 127. In fact, even the House of Lords implicitly concedes that the rules are not so clear-cut. It was assumed in *Foskett* that an initial *ownership* interest in a fund would deliver only a *lien* over the asset that the fund was used to improve (but see also the earlier discussion on whether this is a result of tracing at all). In any event, whether such a limitation is ultimately significant may be a matter for debate. In *Sinclair v Brougham* [1914] AC 398, now overruled on the initial proprietary claim, it was assumed that both parties' charges over the funds would effectively divide ownership of the funds between the chargees. As Lord Parker noted (*ibid*, 442): 'Each [innocent volunteer] is entitled to a charge on the property for his own money, and neither can claim priority over the other. It follows that their charges must rank *pari passu* according to their respective amounts. Further, I think that *as against the fiduciary agent* they could by agreement claim to take the property itself, in which case they would become tenants in common in shares proportionate to amounts for which either could claim a charge' (emphasis added).

[117] *Re Diplock* (n 3) 553.

an entitlement to interest on the sums claimed, unlike the *in personam* claims. In this context, the court suggested that the next-of-kin were entitled to sums 'representing the interest in fact earned by the investments into which the Diplock money[118] is so traced'.[119] This does not explicitly give the next-of-kin an ownership interest in the substitute assets, but its effect is certainly an entitlement to the accrued benefits of ownership. A further contradiction arises in the analysis of the improvements made to the charities' properties. As already noted, although the next-of-kin could assert initial equitable ownership of the Diplock moneys in the charities' hands, the Court of Appeal was clear that they would at most be entitled to a lien over any property improved as a result of spending this money. In the event, even a lien was denied.

Deciding whether the proper approach is one that delivers ownership of the traceable substitutes or something less is clearly crucial. The outcome for claimants may be vastly different depending upon the analysis adopted. According to the modern approach advocated by the House of Lords, the process of tracing enables a claimant's initial claim to be amplified, purely fortuitously, by what the defendant happens to have done with the initial asset.[120] It does not matter whether the basis of the initial claim is a priority dispute in property law, or an unjust enrichment claim, or a claim against a wrongdoing fiduciary or an abuser of intellectual property rights. Nor does it matter whether the defendant is a fraudster, a wrongdoer, or a person completely innocent and ignorant of the claimant's interests. All that matters is the initial assertion of a property right. *If* X has a claim to an interest in property in Y's hands, then that interest can be traced, and property consequences (property rights) follow automatically for X.

Using tracing to generate these potentially advantageous ends seems unacceptable. The purpose of tracing, surely, is simply to *preserve* and protect a claimant's *initial* claim, not to amplify it in an arbitrary fashion unrelated to the particular harm being remedied.[121] This is why tracing and claiming are separate processes. And yet the modern view of tracing and claiming is completely at odds with this. Again, this is an area where the modern law merits revisitation.

---

[118] Reduced by an amount representing the sums recovered from the next-of-kin's settlement with the executors: *Re Diplock* (n 3) 557. This issue is discussed below, in conjunction with the analysis of change of position.

[119] *Re Diplock* (n 3) 557.

[120] The unjust enrichment approach to claims following a tracing exercise delivers precisely the same outcomes, despite the non-proprietary doctrinal foundations. The unjust enrichment approach is preferred by many restitution scholars: eg P Birks, 'Tracing, Property and Unjust Enrichment' (2001) 54 *CLP* 231; Burrows (n 55) 527–8.

[121] See the discussion in Worthington, 'Secondary Profits' (n 92) 451. Note that tracing is not inevitably a secondary protective device; it can also be used to *identify* the profits that have been made by wrongdoers, and, where the claimant is entitled to bring a primary claim for recovery of such profits, it assists.

3. Defences: Application of the Change of Position Defence to the *In Rem* Claims

The modern approach to tracing and claiming does not simply offer the possibility of augmenting the subject matter of a claim; it may also deny the operation of certain defences. In this chapter the focus is on the change of position defence.

At the time that *Re Diplock* was decided, there was no judicial recognition of change of position. Despite this, the Court of Appeal refused to accept any *in rem* claims if the charities might thereby be unfairly treated. This was most evident in the court's treatment of the charities' improvements to buildings. These days, an alternative approach would be to admit the *prima facie* possibility of continuing proprietary protection of the claimants' claims in a much wider range of circumstances, permitting tracing whenever the physical reality suggests that the claimant's original asset has been exchanged at least in part for the substitute asset, but then protecting the innocent defendant's position by permitting a change of position defence to reduce the value of the proprietary claim.

The potential unfairness of doing otherwise is easily illustrated, even without any tracing complications. Suppose £5,000 of Diplock money is paid into the charity deposit account and, as a result of this bequest, the charity decides to offer £5,000 worth of support to sister ventures that might not otherwise be funded. Suppose it does this from its current account, leaving the Diplock deposit untouched. If the claim for return of the £5,000 were recognised as a personal claim in unjust enrichment, the charity would have a complete defence because of change of position. This is a paradigm example of the way the defence operates. A pure *in rem* claim, on the other hand, would result in full recovery of the funds by the claimant. After all, the funds are physically traceable into the charity's bank account, and remain there untouched. The anomaly seems indefensible if both remedies seek to repair the problem of unjust enrichment.

The '*if*' is critical. It is this that makes the doctrinal analysis supporting introduction of a change of position defence more difficult than first impressions would suggest. The change of position defence operates only in relation to unjust enrichment claims.[122] It is therefore essential to classify the *Diplock* claims as unjust enrichment claims. This is not self-evident. The *in personam* claims brought by the next-of-kin against the charities are, at most, *indirect* unjust enrichment claims. These personal claims have already been discussed in detail earlier in this chapter. The simple direct unjust enrichment claim is that of the executors against the charities, now made possible because of removal of the mistake of law bar. Whether these direct and indirect claims should be treated in the same way is open to debate. As

---

[122] Although this assertion may be increasingly under attack.

highlighted earlier in this chapter, there are many commentators who agree that direct and indirect claims are equivalent; but others disagree, arguing that equity's orthodox 'knowing receipt' limitations are warranted;[123] and the Court of Appeal in *Re Diplock* adopted yet a third way. This is not an easy debate.[124] The issue is not *whether* the next-of-kin should have a claim in unjust enrichment against the charities. It is whether they should have such a claim *when their trustee or executor would not.* The trustee/executor now has a direct claim in unjust enrichment against the charities: the mistake of law bar has been removed, and with it the historical unfairness in this area of the law that allowed unintended recipients to sit on windfall gains without being exposed to claims from either the trustee/executor or (until *Re Diplock*) the next-of-kin. If the trustee/executor has a claim, then the next-of-kin can ensure that this claim is pursued for their benefit, and perhaps it does no great harm if they can pursue this claim directly. But the real controversy centres on whether the next-of-kin can bring a strict liability (subject to defences) claim in unjust enrichment against the charities when the trustee/executor cannot. In any other case the option of strict liability in relation to this indirect claim adds nothing to the existing rights of the next-of-kin. Orthodox equity (perhaps pejoratively described as the old-fashioned approach) suggests that the next-of-kin should only have this right to bring additional direct personal claims against the charities where the charities are 'knowing recipients' of the unintended benefits. The modern view, adopted by the majority, as noted earlier in this chapter, is that strict liability in any event (subject to defences, of course) should be the order of the day even with these indirect claims.

If that is the difficulty with the personal claims, the *in rem* claims are equally difficult. Since these claims may be seen as equity's proprietary equivalent of the *in personam* claims, their justification could also be said to be unjust enrichment. On this basis, with the same justification in favour of the claimant, there seems to be little reason not to insist on the same protections for the defendant. The problem, if this is the approach, is to confirm that the *in personam* claims (and, by analogy, their *in rem* equivalents) are indeed unjust enrichment claims. Is there any alternative classification of these claims? One view is that these *in rem* claims are simply mechanisms for mediating priority disputes to an asset (the Diplock funds). The next-of-kin (on this analysis) must have *prior* equitable ownership of the money. The charities have subsequently acquired legal ownership, but not as bona fide purchasers for value, so they take subject to the earlier equities (ie subject to the prior interests of the next-of-kin). Change of position is not a defence to a priority dispute, so the strict property analysis determines the outcome between the parties.

---

[123] Smith (n 60) 428 ff.
[124] The authors of this chapter disagree on where the merits lie.

This 'priority-issue' categorisation of the *in rem* claims delivers a knock-out-blow to any suggestion that change of position may be relevant to these claims. But, on this analysis, it is vital to show that the next-of-kin had an equitable interest in the Diplock money *before* it reached the hands of the charities. The priority dispute can only be between the next-of-kin's *prior* equity and the charity's subsequent acquisition of legal title as a volunteer. On the *Diplock* facts, this is not the case. The accepted analysis is that potential beneficiaries under a will do *not* have this type of equitable proprietary interest in the undistributed estate.[125] The possibility of classifying the next-of-kin's claim as a priority dispute therefore disappears. This highlights the importance of accurately analysing the initial position between the parties. If the next-of-kin's claim is not a priority dispute, then is it an unjust enrichment claim?

An agreed accurate characterisation of the *in personam* claim (and, by analogy, the *in rem* claim) is beyond the scope of this chapter. The debate between the authors has been noted. Assuming for the sake of argument, however, that the *Re Diplock in rem* claims *are* responding to unjust enrichment, then should a change of position defence apply? The issue is usefully considered in two stages. First, does the change of position defence apply to the claimant's *initial* proprietary claim to the original receipt by the charities? Secondly, does the defence apply to the claimant's later claim to any traceable proceeds?

The first stage is more easily dealt with. The practical problem in issue was indicated earlier: a charity receives £5,000, which it retains intact, but it spends £5,000 of its own funds on projects that would not have been funded but for the receipt. Will a change of position defence be available to protect the charity against a *proprietary* claim to the intact £5,000? The defence would, of course, protect the charity against a personal claim for that amount. *Re Diplock* itself pre-dates any formal recognition of the change of position defence, even in relation to personal unjust enrichment claims. Nevertheless, there is at least a hint that the Court of Appeal was alert to the possibility, albeit in a different context. Once the court had decided that the next-of-kin could successfully assert a small number of proprietary claims against different charities, the court had to consider how to bring into play the sums the next-of-kin had already received by way of settlement from the executors. This is not a change of position issue (which looks to the sensible calculation of the real enrichment received by the defendant), but rather an 'at the expense of' issue (which looks to the source of the defendant's enrichment, but also, many would argue, to the 'loss' to the claimant that ought to be remedied by the unjust enrichment

---

[125] *Commissioner of Stamp Duties (Qld) v Livingston* [1965] AC 694.

claim[126]). These factors might be seen as two sides of the same coin: the 'plus', or enrichment, of the defendant; and the 'minus', or detriment, to the claimant. In considering the latter issue, albeit not explicitly, the Court of Appeal thought that the settlement sums ought to be credited rateably to all the charities for all purposes—that is, for the purposes of the claims *in rem* as well as the claims *in personam*.[127] This possibility of *in rem* claims abating is significant. It provides judicial approval for the notion that *in rem* remedies are not immune to such arguments.

The same suggestion is implicit in the analysis suggested by Millett LJ in *Boscawen v Bajwa*:[128]

> [In cases where the claimant attempts to trace into substitutes] . . . the defendant will either challenge the plaintiff's claim that the property in question represents his property (ie, he will challenge the validity of the tracing exercise) or he will raise a priority dispute (eg, by claiming to be a bona fide purchaser without notice). If all else fails he will raise the defence of innocent change of position. This was not a defence which was recognised in England before 1991 but it was widely accepted throughout the common law world. In *Lipkin Gorman v Karpnale Ltd* [1991] 2 AC 548 the House of Lords acknowledged it to be part of English law also. The introduction of this defence not only provides the court with a means of doing justice in future, but allows a re-examination of many decisions of the past in which the absence of the defence may have led judges to distort basic principles in order to avoid injustice to the defendant.
>
> If the plaintiff succeeds in tracing his property, whether in its original or in some changed form, into the hands of the defendant, *and overcomes any defences which are put forward on the defendant's behalf*, he is entitled to a remedy.

Distinguished academic comment is of the same view.[129] It is difficult to support the contrary argument. If the remedy is founded on a particular moral and social justification that affords the defendant certain defences in relation to the personal claim, then it would require strong arguments, not so far advanced, to see the position operating differently in relation to proprietary claims.

---

[126] This remains controversial. For a long time the English view was that restitution was not capped by the minus to the claimant; the Canadian view was to the contrary (*Pettkus v Becker* [1980] 2 SCR 834, 117 DLR (3d) 257). There were a few dissenters (eg S Worthington, 'Reconsidering Disgorgement' (1999) 62 *MLR* 218, and the references cited). More recently, however, the minority view has received powerful support from Professor Peter Birks, previously one of the most vocal advocates of the opposite view: P Birks, *Unjust Enrichment* (2nd edn, Oxford, OUP, 2005) ch 4.

[127] *Re Diplock* (n 3) 557, although admittedly without the benefit of argument.

[128] *Boscawen* (n 85) 334–5 (emphasis added).

[129] See the references cited in Burrows (n 55) 527; P Birks, 'Overview: Tracing, Claiming and Defences' in P Birks (ed), *Laundering and Tracing* (Oxford, OUP, 1995) 289, 319–22 and 326–7.

The second stage is marginally more complicated. Recall that the issue is whether the change of position defence applies to claims to traceable proceeds. Again, the practical problem is readily illustrated. Suppose, as in the earlier example, that a charity receives £5,000. This time, however, it invests the funds in a series of exchanges that may see the initial £5,000 traced through shares, cash, and into a painting, now worth £10,000. Suppose, too, that during this investment activity the charity spends £5,000 from other sources on projects that would not have been funded but for the initial receipt. Will a change of position defence be available to protect the charity against a *proprietary* claim to the painting? For all the reasons already outlined, it would seem indefensible to suggest otherwise.[130] The only doctrinal impediment might be seen to come from the analysis advanced in *Foskett v McKeown*, as outlined (and criticised) earlier. This case suggests that the benefits of tracing are part of English property law; they have nothing to do with unjust enrichment. It is faintly arguable, therefore, that a change of position defence in these circumstances is completely out of the question. The claimant's initial unjust enrichment claim to £5,000 in the charity's hands is proprietary, and (at that stage) not subject to any defences. When the investment exchanges are effected, the *law of property* allocates these new properties, in equity, to the claimant. Any unjust enrichment defence comes too late to impinge on these property rules. The better argument, however, would seem to be that the claimant's claim is, and remains throughout, a primary claim in unjust enrichment for a sum determined by the law of unjust enrichment, but its proprietary attributes are preserved and protected by the ability of the claimant to trace into substitutes to preserve the security of its claim.[131] The ultimate choice between these approaches must await the courts' further determinations.

But, finally, and to bring this analysis full circle, it is crucial to reiterate that the logic in favour of the change of position defence limiting *both* the personal and the proprietary claims of the next-of-kin against the charities is conditional on these claims being accurately characterised as unjust enrichment claims. This is still a matter for debate. The same logic would not favour a change of position defence if these claims were, for example, claims in respect of accessory liability.

---

[130] Indeed, it is arguable that the claimant should be restricted to a claim of no greater value than the *personal* unjust enrichment claim, although secured against any traceable proceeds. In the illustration used here, the personal claim is nil, being effectively cancelled by the change of position defence. See Worthington, 'Secondary Profits' (n 92) 451.
[131] This is *not* the same as the argument put by many unjust enrichment scholars that each traceable exchange raises a new claim in unjust enrichment, with the claimant being entitled to claim that the enhanced value of the new investment is liable to be recovered by way of restitution. Again see Worthington, 'Secondary Profits' (n 92) 451; and contrast Burrows (n 55) 527–8.

4. Conclusions on the *In Rem* Claims

The *Re Diplock in rem* claims clearly raise far more questions than they answer. This chapter suggests that neither the *Re Diplock* case itself, nor any subsequent case, has yet delivered a convincing analysis of the ambit and objectives of tracing, the links between tracing and claiming, and the operation of defences when tracing is in issue.

D. CONCLUSION

This chapter has mounted various criticisms of the *Re Diplock* reasoning. Viewpoints still differ on most of the issues raised. In other words, almost sixty years after Lord Greene decided *Re Diplock*, and fifteen years after judicial recognition of an English law of unjust enrichment, very few of the issues that troubled Lord Greene have yet been satisfactorily resolved by modern courts or commentators. In fact, as the chapter demonstrates, Lord Greene's judgment remains sufficiently cogent and provocative to warrant careful scrutiny in any modern re-assessment of the *in personam* and *in rem* claims that might be brought by disappointed indirect claimants. This chapter is a conscious attempt to move the debate forward by proposing what appear to be principled and advantageous potential modern analyses of these *in personam* and *in rem* claims and their related defences.

12

Solle v Butcher (1950)

CATHARINE MACMILLAN

A. INTRODUCTION

T HE EFFECT OF a mistake upon a contract is difficult to gauge due to the uncertain application of the law. Nowhere is this uncertainty greater than when the mistake is as to the assumptions made by the parties to the contract relating to a quality of the subject matter of the contract. The reason is simple: the contracting parties have received something like what they bargained for. Modern English law has largely chosen to uphold this 'something like' contract rather than disturb the general sanctity of contracts with the perceived effects of commercial uncertainty and consequent insecurity. The House of Lords' decision in *Bell v Lever Brothers*[1] is largely responsible for this state. Within twenty years of the decision, however, the Court of Appeal in *Solle v Butcher*[2] attempted to develop a counterbalance. In this case, the court found that the mistaken, shared assumption about a quality of the subject matter of the contract rendered the contract voidable in equity. The contract could be rescinded, and rescinded on terms. In *Great Peace Shipping Ltd v Tsavliris Salvage (International) Ltd*[3] the Court of Appeal recently rejected *Solle v Butcher* and reaffirmed *Bell v Lever Brothers*. The result has been to revive interest in an area long bypassed by commentators. The focus here will be on what the Court of Appeal was attempting to do in *Solle v Butcher* and why they were attempting to do this. *Solle v Butcher* has long been seen as an important case in the law of contract, but it has significance for the law of restitution as well. The purpose of this chapter is to examine *Solle v Butcher* in the extraordinary context in which it belongs: set against a backdrop of

---

[1] [1932] AC 161.
[2] [1950] 1 KB 671, [1949] 2 All ER 1107, 66 TLR (Pt 1) 448, [1949] EGD 346. All further references to the case are to [1950] 1 KB 671 unless expressly noted.
[3] [2002] EWCA Civ 1407, [2003] QB 679.

war, consequent housing shortages and the legislative response to these shortages. In this historical context, the case has the company of other ground breaking cases such as *Central London Property Trust Ltd v High Trees House Ltd*[4] and *Davis Contractors Ltd v Fareham UDC*,[5] both of which are further legal responses engendered by modern war and its deleterious effect upon housing.

Mistake in contract stands at the border of two areas of law: contract and restitution.[6] If the mistake is sufficiently fundamental, then the consent to contract is absent and this results in a paradox: the void contract. The absence of consent is, in this sense, similar to the absence of intent which may allow a mistaken payer to recover his payment.[7] But the significance for restitution is greater than this similarity, because the mistake has left the apparent contract void. As contractual obligations will not exist absent this apparent contract, the parties may turn to restitutionary remedies for the recovery of benefits conferred pursuant to the void contract.[8] The situation is more complicated where the mistake results in a voidable contract.[9] The complications arise because 'the remedy of rescission of a contract makes no clean divide between attacking the contract (the law of contract) and recovering benefits rendered under it (the law of restitution)'.[10] It is recognised that while in some circumstances a rescission on terms ensures a full counter-restitution of benefits to the defendant, in other cases it is probably non-restitutionary where the terms are to enter a new contract.[11]

One of the significances of *Solle v Butcher* is that it lies at the boundary between contract and restitution. The Court of Appeal found that the contract

---

[4] [1947] KB 130.

[5] [1956] AC 696.

[6] Exactly where the border is can be difficult to establish in any given case. See eg A Burrows, *The Law of Restitution* (2nd edn, London, Butterworths/LexisNexis, 2002) 128–30.

[7] *Kelly v Solari* (1841) 9 M & W 54, 152 ER 24. The case is described by Peter Birks as 'the core case': P Birks, *Unjust Enrichment* (2nd edn, Oxford, OUP, 2005) ch 1. At 102–5, he discusses the point that there were two possible explanations as to why the payee's enrichment in the case was unjust: first, that there was an incomplete intent to benefit the payee; and secondly, that the payee had no entitlement to the payment.

[8] Although the mistake was of a different nature, this was the point established by the swaps cases: *Hazell v Hammersmith & Fulham BC* [1992] 2 AC 1; *Kleinwort Benson Ltd v Sandwell BC* [1994] 4 All ER 890; *Westdeutsche Landesbank Girozentrale v Islington LBC* [1994] 4 All ER 924, varied [1996] AC 669; *Guinness Mahon & Co Ltd v Kensington and Chelsea Royal London BC* [1998] QB 215; *Kleinwort Benson Ltd v Lincoln CC* [1999] 2 AC 349. This position is taken in Birks (n 7) 122 and 126.

[9] It is recognised, without discussing the point at this stage, that it is possible to argue, as many have (eg Birks (n 7) 123), that the result of *The Great Peace* is that such voidability in equity no longer exists.

[10] Burrows (n 6) 128–9.

[11] *Ibid*, 59–60.

was voidable and ordered a rescission on terms. A finding that the contract was void would have opened up the possibility of restitutionary claims. The case is of interest for two reasons: first, why did the Court of Appeal find the contract voidable; and, secondly, why did Sir Gerald Hurst, in the county court, uphold the contract but allow the repayment of moneys made pursuant to an illegal obligation?[12] The balance of this chapter will consider these issues in relation to the legal, social and military context in which they arose. It is when these issues are so considered that they can be best resolved. The dispute between the tenant Solle and the landlord Butcher as to the rent which could be paid for a particular flat occurred within a social and legal environment that has not survived the changes which occurred in the last two decades of the twentieth century.

B. MODERN WARFARE AND ITS PHYSICAL AND SOCIAL CONSEQUENCES

There are so many intriguing legal issues present in *Solle v Butcher* that it is easy to overlook the essential fact that the case is a fragment from a much larger historical picture. The case is concerned with the resolution of a legal problem that occurs in extraordinary social circumstances. The immediate circumstances that gave rise to our small fragment began in 1940. But the circumstances of 1940 were largely created by the events of the First World War. In the later stages of that war, German airships and aeroplanes reached London and were able to drop bombs, on one occasion in full view of the horrified staff of the newly formed Air Board stationed on the Strand. This was a comparatively small affair, in that the damage inflicted over the entire First World War amounted to the worst night experienced by London in the Second World War.[13] The significance of the raids was, however, that without suffering casualties themselves the Germans had inflicted death and destruction upon civilian Britons.[14] The greatest damage was the terror instilled in the civilian population.[15] The events of 1917 caused an Italian General, Giulio Douhet, to expound a theory of mass demoralisation

---

[12] Birks (n 7) 123.

[13] N Longmate, *The Bombers* (London, Hutchinson, 1983) 21.

[14] 200 German airships and 430 German aeroplanes created 4,400 casualties: T Harrison, *Living Through the Blitz* (London, Collins, 1976) 20.

[15] This was particularly true of an island that had stood apart from all continental conflagrations since the Norman Conquest. The result produced a series of apocalyptic works of literature and dire predictions from government ministries of the evils contained in future wars. Britain was particularly concerned with the issue of air disarmament in the inter war period. See M Smith, *Britain and 1940: History, Myth and Popular Memory* (London, Routledge, 2000) ch 2 for a discussion of this environment.

brought about by droves of bombers wreaking havoc upon civilian popula-
tions.[16] The purpose of this inhuman havoc was to hammer the enemy into
submission. Douhetism was decidedly contentious and different views of its
efficacy were adopted.[17] It influenced both the Luftwaffe and the Royal Air
Force. Lord Trenchard, Marshal of the recently formed Royal Air Force,
was much impressed with the potential of aerial bombardment and developed a theory similar to Douhet's, arguing that it could destroy both the
ability of a nation to wage war and its morale to continue. Trenchard's
approval of aerial bombardment was prompted by his overwhelming ambition to create an air force in the new RAF which was independent of both
the navy and the army.[18] His views on aerial bombardment were controversial not only when he first expounded them but also when they were later
implemented to devastating effect upon Germany. Trenchard's ideas influenced Winston Churchill during the Second World War and Churchill was
a firm supporter of Bomber Command.[19]

    The difficult moral issues of this campaign of aerial bombardment
remain. In contrast to Trenchard, Air-Marshal Goering was less impressed
with Douhetism and the death of Germany's leading Douhetist, General
Walter Wever, led the Luftwaffe to concentrate upon a different aerial strategy based around fighter planes rather than long range bombers. While
much is made of the bombing of Britain, the different effects of Douhetism
between the RAF and the Luftwaffe was to mean that the Luftwaffe pos-
sessed limited capacity for mass bombing and that the German populace
would, ultimately, suffer far greater casualties.[20] The result of aeronautical
advances and new military theories led two European nations into battles
to destroy and demoralise the populace of each other's nation. Ultimately,
the effect of the demoralisation was never severe enough to cause either
nation to capitulate. Even the London Blitz and the Hamburg firestorms,
Die Katastrophe, failed to produce mass civilian demoralisation. The massive death tolls which had been forecast in Britain were not, mercifully,

---

[16] G Douhet, *The Command of the Air* (tr D Ferrari) (London, Faber & Faber, 1943). The
original, *Il dominio dell' aria*, was published in 1921.

[17] Harrison (n 14) 22–4.

[18] On the development of this air force, see Longmate (n 13) ch 3 and M Hastings, *Bomber
Command* (London, Michael Joseph, 1979) ch 1.

[19] The firmness of his support may have been brought about by political and strategic necessities. See T Davis Biddle, 'Bombing by the Square Yard: Sir Arthur Harris at War, 1942–1945'
(1999) 21 *International History Review* 626.

[20] A Calder, *The Myth of the Blitz* (London, Jonathan Cape, 1991): 'Bomber Command had
to be left out of the Myth of the Blitz, or mythology would have ceased to be efficacious. The
heroism of the British under bombardment was quasi-Christian—its great symbol, after all,
was St Paul's dome flourishing above the flames. The Myth could not accommodate acts, even
would-be acts, of killing of civilians and domestic destruction initiated by the British themselves, however they might be justified strategically.'

realised. However, while people were not killed in the numbers expected,[21] they were rendered homeless in unforeseeable numbers.[22]

The Luftwaffe had not set out to do this in the summer of 1940. What they had intended to do was gain control over British skies, and with this objective, a summer of aerial combat constituted the Battle of Britain.[23] The RAF, although ill prepared for such a battle, won. One of the reasons for their success was that on 7 September 1940, the Luftwaffe, on Hitler's orders, made the first of the attacks that were to form the Blitz. Night after night, until mid November 1940, the planes returned. 13,000 tons of explosive were dropped on London before the Luftwaffe switched its attention to Coventry.[24] Beckenham, on the south-eastern outskirts of London, suffered extensively from aerial bombardment.[25] It was near a major military target at Biggin Hill airbase, it lay on the main rail line into London, and it was the home of a major electronics factory and several smaller ones. It was also on the bombers' route over to London and thus formed a ready place to unload bombs for any bomber unable to reach the capital.

During one of these bombardments a landmine damaged Maywood House. As a part of its aerial bombardments the Luftwaffe dropped magnetic mines, originally designed for sea use, by parachute:[26]

huge cylinders, eight feet long and two feet in diameter, which swung silently down at about forty miles per hour, but seemed to float like sycamore seeds. They

[21] See Harrison (n 14) ch 2 for discussion of the British predictions and precautions concerning air raids.

[22] The difficulties attendant in homelessness caused Lord Cherwell, Churchill's scientific advisor, to predict that a deliberate campaign of aerial bombardment to 'de-house' the German population would introduce such significant strains as to break the spirit of the German people. The prediction was disputed but ultimately accepted: C Messenger, *Bomber Harris and the Strategic Bombing Offensive 1939–1945* (London, Arms and Armour, 1984) 69–70; M Connelly, *Reaching for the Stars: A New History of Bomber Command in World War II* (London, IB Tauris, 2001) 66. It is estimated that over half a million German civilians died as a result of Allied bombing, with another million receiving serious injury and the destruction of three million homes: SA Garrett, *Ethics and Airpower in World War II* (New York, St Martin's Press, 1993) 21.

[23] It would appear that the then inhabitants of Maywood House, the property involved in *Solle v Butcher*, would have been able to watch aerial dog fights from the House. See the account of a long-time member of the adjacent cricket club: T Thomas, 'Memories of Tennis at Beckenham', 2000, published online at http://www.beckenhamtennisclub.co.uk/tennis_memories.php.

[24] Harrison (n 14) 127.

[25] ER Inman and N Tomkin, *Beckenham* (Chichester, Phillimore, 1993) 109: 'During the war nearly 1,000 high explosive bombs, 10,000 incendiaries and 79 V1 and V2 rockets rained down on the borough, killing 360 people and injuring almost 1,800 more.' For further information on the damage to Beckenham see Graham Reeves, *Undaunted: The Story of Bromley in the Second World War* (Bromley, Bromley Leisure Services, 1990) ch 5.

[26] A Calder, *The People's War: Britain 1939–1945* (London, Jonathan Cape, 1969) 172. See also Philip Ziegler, *London at War 1939–1945* (London, Sinclair-Stevenson, 1995) 125.

did not penetrate the earth and their blast, which was not muffled by the soil, could blow a man a quarter of a mile and throw thirty-five ton train cars into the air like shoe-boxes.

South East London received the brunt of the parachute mine attacks. The mines were particularly feared because, suspended by parachute, they landed and usually detonated after people thought that the bombers had passed. Containing between half a ton and a ton of explosives, they caused a great amount of damage to property and a high number of casualties: 'in a matter of days the mine became feared as the most awesome weapon of the Blitz.'[27] It appears that the mine which damaged Maywood House fell on the tennis courts of the adjacent Beckenham Cricket Club. The mine had become detached from its parachute and exploded on impact. This lessened the blast, which would otherwise have destroyed several of the nearby houses.[28] The complete destruction of Maywood House might have prevented the problems English contract law was to encounter. It is probable that the mine fell in mid November 1940.[29] Maywood House, a block of five flats, was badly damaged and rendered uninhabitable. Its occupants departed: they joined, for an unknown period, the vast numbers of people who were dispossessed and left homeless as a result of the Blitz.[30]

[27] L Blake, *Red Alert: South East London 1939–1945* (London, Lewis Blake, 1992) 28. If the mine failed to explode, it was particularly dangerous. The bomb disposal units needed to deal not only with the mechanical impact fuse but also the possibility that the magnetic trigger could be activated by vibration or metal: *ibid*, 29. Further information on parachute mines can be found in WG Ramsey (ed), *The Blitz Then and Now* (London, After the Battle Publications, 1987) vol 1, 157–8.

[28] Thomas (n 23).

[29] It has not proven possible to fix the exact date that the land mine fell. The law report in the *Estates Gazette Digest* records that the damage occurred in November 1940, and one of the tenants of Maywood House, Alfred Layman, died on 8 November 1940 at Maywood House: *The Times*, 11 November 1940. His death certificate records a cause of death unrelated to bombing and the house must have been standing at that date. The Register of Civilian War Dead does not include casualties at Maywood House. The most likely date is the night of 15/16 November 1940. That night saw a heavy attack on London with land mines dropped at Beckenham: WG Ramsey (ed), *The Blitz Then and Now* (London, After the Battle Publications, 1988) vol 2, 278, and the Bromley Local Archives contain a photograph (F4/199) dated 16 November showing land mine damage to Beckenham Place Park.

[30] The problems of a citizenry rendered homeless had not been considered before the war. As it had been thought that people would be killed in the raids, there was little provision to house the homeless. It formed a pressing problem. While it has not proven possible to follow Howard Taylor, the tenant of the flat that assumed such significance later, the experiences of one of his neighbours, Dr W Graham Scroggie who inhabited flat number 3 in 1939 are recorded. Dr Scroggie, a Baptist clergyman, had left Edinburgh for health reasons in the 1930s. He not only lost his flat, but appears also to have lost his wife (an engagement between himself and a Miss Hooker of nearby Foxgrove Avenue was announced in *The Times*, 2 April 1941, 7) and also lost the church to which he ministered in a fire caused by an air raid (*The Times*, 30 June 1941, 2). Dr Scroggie himself was to survive the war, dying in Wimbledon at the age of 81: *The Times*, 30 December 1958, 8.

C. THE RENT ACTS: A LEGISLATIVE CONSEQUENCE OF MODERN WARFARE[31]

1. World War I

While the aerial bombardments failed to realise Douhet's theory of demoralisation, they did destroy substantial amounts of British housing. Vast numbers of homeless people had not been envisaged in British war plans. The people, it had been anticipated, would simply die in the aerial bombardments.[32] The ensuing housing shortage was a surprise. By the end of the war, an estimated three and three-quarter million homes had been damaged or destroyed: in other words, two houses in every seven.[33] Nowhere was this shortage more acute than in and around London. The shortage of housing was complicated by pre-war housing problems and by other problems with their origins in the First World War. This war was the first in which Britain was required to undertake a mass mobilisation of men and resources.[34] An enormous expansion of industry was required to maintain the guns of war. Such expansion necessarily required the co-operation of the citizenry and the working class members of this citizenry faced housing problems. While it is misleading to discuss Victorian and Edwardian housing as a constant over time or geography, certain observations can be made.

The most significant is that housing was largely provided by private landlords. At the outbreak of the First World War about 10 per cent of the population lived in a house they owned.[35] Working class housing was largely provided by private enterprise for commercial gain, with limited provision by philanthropic individuals. While some of the work of the social reformers had been dedicated to improving conditions, they were far from ideal. There was little incentive on the part of private landlords to improve conditions for their tenants. Housing did, however, exist for the labouring classes and the years 1896 to 1906 had seen something of a boom in property building.[36] The introduction of Land Values Duties in 1910 acted to

---

[31] A comparative account of the history of rent control can be found in JW Willis, 'A Short History of Rent Control Laws' (1950–1) 36 *Cornell Law Review* 54.

[32] While official estimates of casualties during aerial bombardment had risen as high as 60,000 per day, by early 1940 these had been reduced to 16,000 per day: Smith (n 15) 23 and 26.

[33] Calder (n 20) 223.

[34] For some of the other legal oddities which resulted from this, see GR Rubin, *Private Property, Government Requisition and the Constitution, 1914–27* (London, Hambledon Press, 1994).

[35] J Doling and EM Davies, *Public Control of Privately Rented Housing* (Aldershot, Gower, 1984) 13. This figured varied from region to region within Britain according to local conditions and was as high as 60 per cent owner-occupation in some areas.

[36] *Ibid*, 21.

reduce output, and in London between 1911 and 1915 the number of rooms actually decreased as a result.[37] These shortages were masked by the outbreak of war in 1914. Initial estimates of the war's duration turned out to be overly optimistic and a year after Britain had declared war, social and economic strains began to appear. Unsurprisingly, one such strain was housing: building the equipment of modern warfare resulted in large numbers of workers being moved into areas of industrial production. Inevitably, housing shortages occurred.[38] Landlords faced increased charges as a result of the war when rates, insurance and maintenance charges rose. They responded to increased costs and demand for accommodation by raising rents. The result was industrial unrest: an unrest which, unlike previous problems involving working class housing, could not be ignored. Industrial output had to be maintained and for this the willing co-operation of the working class was needed.

The impetus for legislative control of rents was formed when workers in the Clyde shipyards undertook industrial action in response to rising rents.[39] Parliament, fearing social unrest, hastily passed the Increase of Rent and Mortgage Interest (War Restrictions) Act 1915.[40] Two purposes underlay the Act: first, to provide housing for workers in wartime industries; and secondly, to ensure that military recruitment was not impaired by the fear that the families of the enlisted would be dispossessed due to their inability to pay increased rents. The Act sought to achieve these aims by restricting rent to the amount recoverable in August 1914. The effectiveness of rent restriction was facilitated by a prohibition on the eviction of tenants. Rent restrictions were initially aimed at working class housing, which was defined by the rateable value of the property.[41] In fairness to those landlords who had borrowed to finance their capital investments, increases in mortgage interest were capped and a prohibition on the calling in of mortgages introduced. The 1915 Act was introduced as a wartime measure

---

[37] J Burnett, *A Social History of Housing 1815–1870* (Newton Abbott, David & Charles, 1978) 217.

[38] The unpleasantness of this situation was exacerbated by the restrictions faced by workers in the munitions industries who could not leave their employment without the permission of their employer or a Munitions Court. That these Munitions Courts were sometimes sympathetic to applications for a leaving certificate due to the impossibility of the worker finding affordable housing can be seen in LF Orbach, *Homes for Heroes: A Study of the Evolution of British Public Housing, 1915–1921* (London, Seeley, 1977) 13–14.

[39] Actions against rising rents had occurred in other parts of the country. There were rent strikes in Glasgow, Birkenhead, Birmingham, Coventry, Dudley, London and Northampton. Although all parts of the country were subjected to rent raises to some degree, action was generally undertaken in areas where trade unionism was rife.

[40] During the war, the Act was amended by the Courts (Emergency Powers) Act 1917 ss 4, 5 and 7, and by the Increase of Rent &c Act 1918.

[41] The 1915 Act applied to houses not exceeding an annual rent or rateable value of £35 in London (Metropolitan Police District), £30 in Scotland and £26 elsewhere.

intended to be of temporary duration (the war and a further six months). From the outset, however, it was observed by some that the Act would have permanent consequences. One contemporary, Sir Walter Essex, observed:[42]

> I think that those who harbour the comforting thought that this is a temporary measure, temporary in its entirety, temporary in its acceptance of a principle, are hugging a delusion which they are certain to find is a delusion before they are many years older . . .

Essex was correct. Even with rent restrictions, war had done little to improve housing conditions. Although bomb damage had been slight due to the limited carrying capacity of Zeppelins and Gothas, meeting the exigencies of war had severely impaired the building of civilian housing. It was also apparent that the end of war would unleash new economic and social forces. The result was the formation of a Committee chaired by Lord Hunter, charged with the task of considering rent restriction legislation in relation to the provision of working class housing and to recommend any steps necessary to remove related difficulties. The Hunter Committee was the first of many committees charged with examining this supposedly temporary situation of rent restrictions. The Committee heard evidence from a variety of sources. On the one hand, certain interests advanced on behalf of working class tenants advocated the state provision of housing for such people given the lamentable nature of facilities provided by private landlords. On the other hand, landlords pointed to huge increases in the cost of building and maintaining property and the unfairness inherent in restricting returns from rental investment when other such investments were not so restricted. The Hunter Committee issued its report at the very end of 1918.[43] It had now become apparent that because the legislation controlled prices in a market with significant social and economic dimensions, it was impossible to remove these controls quickly without suffering social disruptions. The report consequently sought to balance the interests of landlords and tenants by essentially delaying the inevitable day of decontrol. The Committee was concerned that the end of war would result in various unsettling social factors: demobilisation, industrial unemployment brought about by the end of the war, a reduction in wage earners' incomes, and increased expenses for landlords. However, allowing these dislocations to be accompanied by an increase in rents would create unacceptable results.

---

[42] Quoted in AA Nevitt, 'The Nature of Rent Controlling Legislation in the UK' (1970) 2 *Environment and Planning* 127.

[43] Report of the Committee on the Increase of Rent and Mortgage Interest (War Restrictions) Acts (1919) Cmnd 9235, hereafter the 'Hunter Report'.

The Committee found that while it was desirable to return to 'economic conditions as soon as possible' and that the restrictions could not form a permanent measure, it would be unwise to remove all restrictions on the expiry of the Act.[44] Their recommendations resulted in the Increase of Rent and Mortgage Interest (Restrictions) Act 1919 which extended the duration of the restrictions for a further three years and increased the ambit of restricted properties.[45]

Peace produced its own difficulties: rent control had the effect of decreasing the available housing stock as landlords sold uneconomic properties[46] and the cost of building houses was greatly increased. Lloyd George's government had embarked upon an ambitious programme of 'Homes fit for Heroes' in an attempt to alleviate the dreadful conditions of working class homes. The nation would gratefully repay the services given to it by a generation of men.[47] It became apparent, in part due to the interest generated in the subject by rent control, that it would be unrealistic to rely upon private landlords to undertake this programme. The result was a period of state intervention in an attempt to increase both the quantity and the quality of working class housing.[48] These schemes took time to have effect and one result of this slowness was a continuation of rent restriction in an attempt not to exacerbate the situation.

In 1920 a further committee, chaired by the Marquis of Salisbury, observed that removing restrictions would allow rents to rise to a level considered inequitable. Landlords, however, were discouraged from undertaking repairs because of the greatly increased cost of building materials and labour and the devaluation of money. Rent restriction also acted as a disincentive to private building.[49] The committee recommended that 'though, therefore the restriction of rent must be continued, the evidence is decisive that some relief to the house owner is requisite and should not be longer delayed'.[50] The result was the Increase of Rent and Mortgage Interest

---

[44] *Ibid*, para 30.

[45] The Act allowed limited increases in rent up to 10 per cent and allowed mortgage interest increases not exceeding half a percent. Rent control, almost always introduced as a temporary measure, proved very difficult to remove in every country in which it was introduced. The essential difficulty was that the control of results destroyed the pre-war price/rent relationship in such a way as to make it impossible to restore: Willis (n 31) 71–2.

[46] Where a landlord sold a controlled property a new owner, as a tenant, could dispossess an existing protected tenant. There were concerns that such actions were widespread in London. See Orbach (n 38) 74.

[47] The influence of war in precipitating change in housing conditions is explained in Burnett (n 37) 215–16.

[48] It is beyond the scope of this paper to discuss these programmes at length. For detailed discussion see Orbach (n 38).

[49] Report of the Committee on the Increase of Rent and Mortgage Interest (War Restrictions) Acts 1920 Cmd 658 (hereafter referred to as the Salisbury Committee) 3.

[50] *Ibid*.

(Restrictions) Act 1920, which formed the basis of rent restriction for decades to come. The 1920 Act increased, again, the number of houses within the restrictions by trebling the rental value of the houses affected,[51] allowed increases in rent up to 40 per cent over the 1914 rentals, and permitted an increase in the rate of mortgage interest of up to one per cent. It was not the end of housing problems. Three years later the Onslow Report[52] formed the basis for the Rent and Mortgage Interest Restrictions Act 1923. By 1920, about 98 per cent of houses within Britain were within rent control.[53] The government's programmes of subsidised building of the kind of houses desired for modern living could not keep pace with demand; ultimately the Homes for Heroes campaign was abandoned as being too costly.[54]

It is important to note that the Rent Acts had two basic objectives. The first was to ensure that landlords could only charge a 'standard rent' (1920 Act, s 1); the standard rent was determined by reference to the rent charged in August 1914 with such increases as were permitted by the legislation. To ensure that this primary objective was met, a secondary objective was to provide tenants with a security of tenure which prevented landlords from evicting them without a court order. Courts, in turn, were forbidden from making orders for possession except on certain specified grounds enumerated in the legislation (1920 Act, s 5).

2. The Inter-War Years: Attempts at Control

While government schemes were not successful, private schemes were enormously successful. An increasing pool of labour and materials, minimal land usage control, changes in public transportation with the advent of the motor car, and increased finance through building societies to purchase houses combined to create an explosion of suburban properties for the middle class. House building in inter-war Britain proceeded at the greatest pace the nation had ever known.[55] The problem was that these kinds of houses would not solve the housing crisis. Working class needs remained largely unaddressed and it was very difficult for the average working class family

---

[51] The Act covered houses of a rent or rateable value of £105 in London, £90 in Scotland and £78 elsewhere.

[52] Final Report of the Departmental Committee on the Increase of Rent and Mortgage Interest (Restrictions) Act 1920 (1923) Cmd 1803.

[53] Report of the Inter-Departmental Committee on the Rent Restrictions Acts (1931) Cmd 3911 (hereafter 'Marley Report') para 19.

[54] M Bowley, *Housing and the State 1919–1944* (London, Allen & Unwin, 1945) 24 and 26.

[55] Peter Hennessy, *Never Again: Britain 1945–51* (London, Jonathan Cape, 1992) 169.

to find housing.[56] Two further inter-war committees cast doubt on the ability of rent restriction legislation to solve these housing difficulties.[57] The Marley Committee noted that by 1930 a million and a half homes had been built but that the shortage of working class homes remained acute.[58] Rent restrictions contributed to this process and acted as a great disincentive for working class families to move into the properties vacated by the new group of middle class owner-occupiers. The vacant properties were necessarily outside rent control and working class families were thus required to give up their secure, rent controlled tenure[59] and place themselves in a market where the rent increases could be as much as 90 per cent.[60] The problem was how to change the situation without disruption. The Marley Report recommended complete decontrol of the most expensive houses, partial decontrol of an intermediate group of houses and the retention of control for the least expensive houses.[61] The Ridley Report of 1937 recommended a scheme for the gradual and total decontrol of all rent restrictions.[62] While it is tempting to portray rent restriction legislation as a self-perpetuating problem, and there is no doubt that it affected the market, such a portrayal is misleading. Other forces were at work. One was that investment in own-to-let property, a primitive investment strategy, was replaced with different investment plans after the First World War.[63] Another was that the owner-occupier filled most of the housing void and through the development of a building society system, purchasing to own had never been easier.[64] By 1938, Britain was finally emerging from the dilemma of rent control.

3. World War II and the Expansion of Control

The Ridley Report of 1937 had noted that the happening of certain events, 'such for instance as a major European war',[65] might necessitate the

---

[56] *Ibid*, 54.
[57] Marley Report (n 53); also the Ridley Report of 1937 (n 62).
[58] Marley Report (n 53), para 28.
[59] *Ibid*, para 33.
[60] *Ibid*, para 21.
[61] These were known in the Report, respectively, as Class A houses (those with a rateable value of or over £45 in London, £35 in England and Wales, and £45 in Scotland), Class B houses (those with a rateable value of between £20 and £45 in London, between £13 and £35 in the England and Wales, and between £26 5s but less than £45 in Scotland), and Class C houses (£20 or less in London, £13 or less in England and Wales, and £26 5s or less in Scotland).
[62] Report of the Inter-Departmental Committee on the Rent Restrictions Acts (1937) Cmd 5621 (hereafter 'Ridley Report'). The Report was the basis for the Increase of Rent and Mortgage Interest (Restrictions) Act 1938.
[63] Bowley (n 54) 88. She also observed that rent control should not have acted as a disincentive to new building because such buildings were free from restrictions.
[64] *Ibid*, 93.
[65] Ridley Report (n 62) para 60.

imposition of rent control. When war broke out, this is what occurred: the Rent and Mortgage Interest Restrictions Act 1939 both suspended the programme of decontrol and brought virtually all British housing within rent control.[66] All houses existing at the time of the 1939 Act and any built after it came into existence fell within the Act. Local authority housing, as usual, was outside the scope of the legislation. The rent a landlord could charge his tenants was the standard rent and was determined by reference to one of two points in time: the rent fixed by reference to the rent charged on 3 August 1914 (old control), or the rent fixed by reference to the rent charged on 1 September 1939 (new control).

The 1939 Act brought the five flats in Maywood House within the scheme of rent restriction. The flats, which were created from the original Maywood House, had been outside the scheme as they were created in 1931. This conversion reflected the social changes that were sweeping England as a whole as demand for large houses dropped. Two changes to middle class life contributed to this process: pressures upon middle class income led to economising in relation to large expenditure, and a shortage of domestic servants meant that large houses were difficult to maintain.[67] There was, consequently, great demand for small houses and flats. The flats in Maywood House appear to have been desirable accommodation for middle class couples.[68] On 1 July 1938, Howard Taylor rented flat 2 for £140 per annum. Taylor occupied the property with his wife, Joan;[69] they must have liked Maywood House because prior to occupying flat 2, they had lived in flat 5 for two years.[70]

4. Damage by Enemy Action and the Need for Post-War Control

Almost as many houses were lost in the Second World War as had been built during the inter-war period.[71] The damage done to Britain's housing

---

[66] Properties with a rateable value of £100 in London, £90 in Scotland and £75 elsewhere.

[67] AE Holmans, *Housing Policy in Britain: A History* (London, Croom Helm, 1987) 72. In the case of Maywood House, the Stevens family who occupied the property prior to its conversion into flats advertised in 1919 for a between maid. The advertisement details that the family of four employed four maids and a houseboy: *The Times*, 12 May 1919, 1.

[68] The rateable value for flat 1 before the war was £45, which placed it at the boundary of the Class A and Class B divide in 1931. The flats were not subject to rent control at that time, having come into existence after 1919. The titles of some of the occupants are indicative of middle class occupancy, including as they did retired naval officers and a clergyman. The local directory (below, n 70) indicates full occupancy of all five flats except for the year 1936. Maywood House was located in a desirable spot on a quiet, wooded lane next to the Beckenham Cricket Club and the Foxgrove Golf Course. It was a short walk away from Central Beckenham and the train station.

[69] Register of Electors 1939–40, Beckenham North Electoral Division Polling District U, Copers Cope Ward, 6.

[70] *Kelly's Directory of Beckenham Penge and Neighbourhood* (41st edn, London, 1936) 144, (42nd edn, London, 1937) 145.

[71] Hennessey (n 55) 169.

stock was concentrated in London, which had borne the brunt of bombing in the Blitz of 1940 and the V1 and V2 rocket attacks of 1944–5. It was estimated that 218,000 houses had been destroyed, a further 250,000 had been damaged beyond habitation[72] and almost as many habitable abodes had been severely damaged.[73] It had been apparent from the outset of the Blitz that another housing crisis loomed.[74] In 1945, the situation was worse than anticipated. Not only had the damage to housing been severe, but there was also a shortage of the materials needed for rebuilding. The workers necessary to build with these inadequate materials were still in the army.[75] The war also caused profound social and demographic changes. The world was not the same in 1945 as it had been in 1939. The great mid-century baby boom was underway: marriages were up by 11 per cent and births were up by 33 per cent over 1939 in the first three post-war years.[76] More complex changes such as an increase in younger marriages, smaller family size and greater life expectancy combined to create more separate households and an even greater demand for housing.[77] The extent of the housing shortage can be seen in the background to this case: during the period in which the reconstruction of Maywood House was undertaken by Charles Butcher, he and his wife appear to have been living with her mother.[78]

In the 1945 election, housing, unsurprisingly, was a key concern and Labour made elaborate promises. The influence of social reformers such as the Webbs, who had been involved in the rent restriction committees, was evident. Housing was too important a social issue to be left in the hands of private enterprise and under Aneurin Bevan, the focus would be upon local authorities building permanent council houses to a high standard and with affordable rents. Labour, however, had manifold problems in rebuilding

---

[72] Ministry of Reconstruction, *Housing* (1945) Cmd 6609 para 34.

[73] *Ibid.*

[74] Lord Wooton wrote in his diary at the time: 'We are telling them now that they are heroes for the way in which they are standing up to the strain of the mighty bombardment—and it's true. I think they will keep on being heroes, but when the war is over they will demand the rewards of heroism: they will expect to get them very soon and no power on earth will be able to rebuild the homes at the speed that will be necessary . . . . I think there's going to be grave trouble, and the danger is that if the machine of government which can spend money so recklessly engaging in a war, fails to be equally reckless in rebuilding, there will be both the tendency and the excuse for revolution.' Lord Wooton, 1940—Lord W Diary Entry for 1 November 1940 Wooton MS 2, Department of Western Manuscripts, Bodleian Library, Oxford, quoted in Hennessey (n 55) 163.

[75] The workforce in the building industry had been halved, with the remaining men concentrated in construction for the armed forces and munitions work: Holmans (n 67) 91.

[76] Hennessey (n 55) 169.

[77] The situation is considered in detail in Holmans (n 67) ch 10.

[78] Electoral Register for the Parliamentary Borough of Kingston upon Thames, Parish of New Malden, Polling District S: 1945, 10; 1946, 10; and 1947, 11. See too *Kelly's Directory of Kingston Malden & Coombe* (London, 1948) 422 and 473. Mr and Mrs Butcher appear to have moved away by 1951.

Britain. The political structure meant not only that responsibility for housing was divided between government and the local authorities but also that several different government ministries were involved. The shortages of materials, particularly timber, were aggravated by the post-war currency crisis. Labour struggled to meet its target of 900,000 new homes and the struggle went on for years.[79] Its failure to construct sufficient houses was one of the reasons for electoral defeat in 1951.

As had happened at the end of the First World War, rent control again played a part in housing policy. In 1945, as the war was ending, Lord Ridley chaired another Rent Control Committee. The resulting Report observed that almost all British housing was covered by rent restrictions, although the standard rent recoverable differed widely between similar houses because they had been let at different dates. Pressure on housing, brought about by war damage, a largely non-existent replacement of building, demobilisation and an increasing number of families meant that rent control, once again, could not be 'safely reduced'.[80] The Committee recommended that rent control needed to continue unchanged where it applied but that any new houses constructed after the war should not be controlled.[81] The difficulty in ascertaining the relevant rents was also noted.[82] The problem that Solle and Butcher were to face—determination of the relevant rent—was a common one. The Landlord and Tenant (Rent Control) Act 1946 retained the 1939 limits and extended restrictions to include furnished accommodation. The longevity of the problem of rent control can be seen in the continuation of the legislation for a further four decades.[83]

D. MAYWOOD HOUSE

1. Repairs, Refurbishments and Rentals

We turn now to how this complicated machinery applied to Solle and Butcher. Solle, a surveyor, and Butcher, a builder, were engaged in a business

---

[79] For a discussion of the problems facing the reconstruction of housing, see KO Morgan, *Labour in Power 1945–51* (Oxford, Clarendon Press, 1984) 163–170; R Eatwell, *The 1945–51 Labour Governments* (London, Batsford, 1979) 64–6; Hennessey (n 55) 174; Holmans (n 67) 276–95.

[80] Report of the Inter-Departmental Committee on Rent Control (April 1945) Cmd 6621 para 18.

[81] *Ibid*, para 20.

[82] *Ibid*, para 38.

[83] The curious reader is referred to the summary in JS Collyer and Sir R Megarry (gen eds), *The Rent Acts* (11th edn, London, Stevens, 1988) 1–3. Ultimately rent control was slowly diminished by largely refusing to allow its application to new tenancy agreements and by changing the nature of leaseholds in 'shortholds' and 'assured tenancies': Housing Act 1980 and the Housing and Planning Act 1986. The effect is, over time, slowly to decrease and ultimately eliminate the number of controlled properties.

designed to remedy the housing shortage. Following the mine damage to Maywood House, the building remained derelict for the remainder of the war. After the war Universal Estates, Ltd bought Maywood House. Universal Estates submitted claims to the War Damage Commission and, after putting forward plans for the reconstruction of the house, received £6,420.[84] Butcher was the managing director of CP Butcher & Co Ltd, a firm of building contractors based in Kingston upon Thames, a London suburb about three quarters of an hour's drive from Beckenham.[85] In 1947, he was introduced to Universal Estates by Solle, who was the surveyor employed on the Maywood House reconstruction. Butcher was engaged to undertake the reconstruction. The pair worked together closely on the project. They formed an estate agent's business, 'Godfrey and Charles'. After determining the feasibility of the project, Butcher decided to take a long lease of the war damaged property and he bought this for £1,000. Solle negotiated the mortgage for the purchase; indeed, 'while they were partners the whole question of Mr Butcher taking over the building, letting the flats, arranging new rateable values, etc, was largely dealt with by Mr Solle on Mr Butcher's behalf'.[86] In their undertaking, the pair considered whether or not the Rent Acts applied to these flats. On this point, the county court judge, Sir Gerald Hurst, preferred the evidence of Butcher where there was a conflict. Solle later testified that he cautioned Butcher that the flats might be covered by the Rent Acts and that he (Butcher) needed to seek legal advice. Sir Gerald Hurst accepted Butcher's testimony that Solle presented him with a part of a counsel's opinion and advice that the flats were outside the Rent Acts. Butcher relied upon Solle in this matter. After the rent for flat 1 had been set at £250 per annum, Solle asked Butcher to let it to him.[87]

The rental difference between controlled and non-controlled accommodation was great. Once accommodation was within the Rent Acts, landlords could not raise the rent by more than a permitted amount above the

---

[84] There is a discrepancy between the law reports of this case. Universal Estates is mentioned in only one account of the case, in the *Estates Gazette Digest*: [1949] EGD 346, 347; this account maintains that they received the sum to reconstruct the building. The reports of the case in the Times Law Reports and the All England Reports record Bucknill LJ as stating that the evidence indicates that Butcher had expended this sum to repair the building: [1949] 2 All ER 1107, 1112; 66 TLR (Pt 1) 448, 451. This portion of Bucknill LJ's judgment is not reproduced in the official reports, but it is provided by the law reporter: [1950] 1 KB 671, 674. It is also unclear whether Universal Estates was the freehold owner of the property or the head lessor of the property. It may be that Universal Estates submitted the claim for the war damage but it was paid to Butcher. The War Damage Commission had originally offered payment of £2,600 on a total loss basis: [1949] EGD 347.
[85] *Kelly's Directory of Kingston, Malden & Coombe* (London, 1948) 473 and 497.
[86] [1949] EGD 346, 347. The other three law reports substantiate the extent of Solle's managerial role and Butcher's comparative absence. Butcher was based and resident outside the immediate locality, in Kingston upon Thames.
[87] *Ibid.*

standard rent and, in addition, tenants were provided with security of tenure. Landlords were unable to evict tenants without a court order and an order for possession was forbidden except on certain specified grounds. In short, 'the main objects of the Acts [were] to give tenants "fair rents" and "a status of irremovability"'.[88] It was impossible to contract out of the Acts[89] and the Acts operated *in rem*, attaching to properties rather than persons.[90] It was not easy to ascertain the application of the Acts: 'one of the most important and difficult of the questions which arise under the Rent Acts is whether any particular premises are within the Acts, and, if so, whether they are subject to old control or new.'[91] The Acts applied only to a dwelling house let as a separate dwelling.[92] In certain instances, the premises might fall within a list of exceptions to the Act. Flat 1[93] in Maywood House was a dwelling house,[94] and it was let by Butcher to Solle for seven years at £250 per annum by a written lease dated 29 September 1947. It was to be used as a dwelling by Solle and his wife, Frances. While Solle and Butcher considered the application of the Rent Acts, they believed that the property came within one of the recognised exceptions to the Acts. At the outset of their agreement, the foundation for this belief came from the repairs undertaken to the property.[95] The particular exception was the doctrine of change of identity, a doctrine created by judicial development. The 1920 Act did not extend to houses built after 2 April 1919 and it further provided that it did not apply to properties reconstructed by way of conversion into two or more separate flats or tenements.[96] From this basic provision the doctrine of change of identity emerged. As the pre-eminent author of the day explained, there was:[97]

> a general principle, applicable alike to old control and new, that if a house within the Acts is subjected to such 'substantial structural alteration' that it becomes 'a new and separate dwelling-house in fact' by reason of change of identity, the new premises shed all the attributes of the old. . . . To fall under this head, there

---

[88] RE Megarry, *The Rent Acts* (6th edn, London, Stevens & Sons, 1951) 7.

[89] *Ibid*, 12.

[90] *Ibid*, 13–18.

[91] *Ibid*, 31.

[92] *Ibid*, ch 3.

[93] During the course of the refurbishments, the numbers of Taylor's flat 2 and the original flat 1 were switched.

[94] 1920 Act, s 12(2); 1939 Act, s 3(1).

[95] By the time the matter was litigated a further ground was advanced, that Solle's lease included the use of a garage not included in the lease of the previous tenant who used it with the permission of the previous landlord. The inclusion of additional premises within a property subject to rent control could, in some circumstances, change the identity of the property. The additional premises had to result in 'a substantial variation (and not merely a small or incidental change) between the physical entities comprised in the two lettings': Megarry (n 88) 83.

[96] 1920 Act, s 12(9).

[97] Megarry (n 88) 81–62.

must be 'something fundamental, transforming the general structural character of the house as an entire entity'. The change must be more radical than mere improvements or structural alterations; the court 'must be astute to see that the landlord is not evading the restrictions upon increases of rent imposed by the statute by . . . small, and possibly colourable, alterations of the structure, or by a mere sub-dividing of the tenement'.

Exactly when a change of identity occurred was a question of fact and the question was attended by uncertainty. The extensive damage caused by bombing presented its own challenges to this legislation. Repairs were obviously necessary, but at what point did the repaired premises become new premises? There was authority that when half a flat had been destroyed and the other half reconstructed, the resulting premises were no longer bound by the previous rent.[98] The burden of proving this change of identity lay upon the landlord. Unusually in *Solle v Butcher*, the basis for the landlord's belief was his reliance upon the apparently knowledgeable opinion of his tenant. Butcher's work upon the flat was fairly significant, particularly in light of the then current difficulties in obtaining labour and materials. He expended £6,240[99] on repairing the war damage and a further £1,000 on further alterations and decorations to the flats. In relation to flat 1, he had removed two broken walls and in so doing altered the internal arrangement of the rooms. The work was substantial enough to require underpinning in the cellar and steel joists in the ceiling: 'This was a substantial alteration and the work was difficult and expensive.'[100] The structural element of the changes appears to have been largely overlooked by the county court judge but was noted by the Court of Appeal with some sympathy.

Thus it was that Solle and Butcher contracted on the shared assumption that the flat was outside the Rent Acts. For this reason, Butcher did not take steps to calculate certain permitted additions to the standard rent which were permitted under the 1938 Act.[101] Had this been done, Butcher would have been able to recover almost the entire rent of £250.[102] His failure to do so was to have significant consequences because once the lease was entered into, it was impossible to have the additional rent added. The standard rent for flat 1 was the rent charged to the tenant who occupied the flat on 1 September 1939: this was the £140 per annum Taylor had agreed to

---

[98] *Langford Property Co Ltd v Sommerfield* [1948] WN 287, affd (1947) 151 EG 41.
[99] It may have been that Butcher received these moneys from the War Damage Commission directly or from Universal Estates.
[100] [1950] 1 KB 671, 675.
[101] Rent and Mortgage Interest (Restrictions) Act 1938, s 7(4).
[102] [1950] 1 KB 671, 690.

pay.[103] It was possible to raise the standard rent for new control houses in circumstances where the landlord had effected an improvement or structural alteration after 2 September 1939,[104] or where the rates payable on the property increased and the landlord paid the rates.[105] A landlord in possession of a dwelling house to which the Acts applied could charge a new tenant the full increases from the start of the tenancy by serving upon the prospective tenant a notice of increase of rent in the prescribed form.[106] If the prospective tenant took the flat, the permitted increases applied from the beginning of the tenancy[107] and similarly applied to all subsequent tenancies without the necessity of further notice.[108] Permitted increases could only be recovered if notice was served in the prescribed form. Thus, when Butcher rented the flat to Solle without serving the notice, he could not recover any of the increases that would otherwise be permitted for the entire currency of the lease. In addition, Butcher could not evict Solle from the flat during the period of the lease. A small procedural defect, based on a shared mistake, was to have enormous consequences.

2. Litigation

Within a year, Solle and Butcher had a falling out; the reasons are not recorded. Solle subsequently claimed to have discovered Taylor's rental receipt for the flat for May 1939. Solle brought suit against Butcher in the county court, alleging that the standard rent was £140 and seeking to recover the overpayment of rent. Butcher, in his defence, argued that he had rented the flat to Solle on Solle's assurance that the flat was not controlled by the pre-war rent because of the damage it had suffered. Butcher both denied that the premises were subject to rent restrictions and alleged that Solle was estopped by his conduct from asserting that the rent restrictions relieved him of his personal obligation to pay the rent of £250. By way of counter-claim, Butcher sought rescission of the lease on the ground that the lease had been entered into under a mutual mistake of fact.

---

[103] The relevant legislation is the Rent and Mortgage Interest Restrictions Act 1939 (2 & 3 Geo VI c 71), s 3, Sched 1 and the amendment which this Act affected to the principal legislation, the Increase of Rent and Mortgage Interest (Restrictions) Act 1920 (10 & 11 Geo V, c 17), s 1.

[104] 1920 Act, s 2(1)(a); 1939 Act, 1st Sched. The rental increase permitted was an amount equal to 8 per cent per annum.

[105] 1920 Act, s 2(1)(b); 1939 Act, 1st Sched. The amount which could be recovered was the actual amount of the increase of rates.

[106] Increase of Rent and Mortgage Interest (Restrictions) Act 1938 (1 & 2 Geo VI c 26), s 7(4).

[107] *Ibid.*

[108] 1920 Act, s 3(2).

It is important to set the social and legal context in which the case arose. Homelessness and the acute shortage of housing facing England as a whole has been noted above. At the time, one third of Britons cited housing as the single greatest problem facing the nation.[109] The winter of 1947 had been one severely cold; it became the 'yardstick' by which all future winters would be measured.[110] The cold had been exacerbated by a fuel crisis which resulted in domestic and industrial cut backs in coal and electricity. Output was severely hampered. As Britain slowly shrugged off the effects of this crisis, Butcher began his work on Maywood House. It could not have been easy. The fuel crisis meant that production in the essential building industries of glass, brick, cement and non-ferrous metals was greatly diminished for months.[111] Lower industrial production severely hampered Britain's ability to export; this, in turn, created a balance of payments problem, followed by the convertibility crisis. By summer, emergency measures were put in place to restrict imports. The effect on housing was particularly deleterious. In Beckenham extensive damage during air raids had caused a particularly acute shortage and the populace struggled to repair, rebuild and build houses following the war.[112] The situation was so grave that in 1947 Beckenham was one of only three local authorities which had refused to re-open its register of applicants for housing accommodation for applicants who had resided in the borough on or before 1 September 1939. The Council refused to re-open the list because to do so would give the applicants an entirely false hope of securing housing.[113]

The shortage of accommodation can be seen in the fact that throughout 1947, the classified pages of the local newspaper contained far more advertisements for accommodation wanted than for accommodation to let.[114] In

---

[109] *Gallup International Public Opinion Polls: Great Britain, 1937–75* vol I, January 1947, quoted in AJ Robertson, *The Bleak Midwinter 1947* (Manchester, Manchester University Press, 1987) 104.

[110] Robertson (n 109) 108.

[111] *Ibid*, 149.

[112] *Beckenham Journal*, 1 February 1947, 3. At least 16,000 houses had been damaged: Beckenham Cator Townsmen's Guild, *Survey of Beckenham—June, 1949*.

[113] *Beckenham Journal*, 3 May 1947, 3.

[114] A random sampling will suffice to make the point. The relevant advertisements were for 'Houses, Flats, Rooms and Apartments Wanted' and 'Houses, Flats, Rooms and Apartments to Let'. It was commonly the case that the former greatly outnumbered the latter in any given week. This was the case in the *Beckenham Journal* of 27 September 1947, two days before Solle and Butcher executed their lease. A random sample of other dates will suffice to make the point. See the *Beckenham Journal* of 30 August 1947, 12–13, and 7 June 1947, 12–13. On the latter date, twenty flats were wanted, primarily by couples and small families, whilst six forms of accommodation were available for let, primarily bed sitting rooms and guest houses. The post-war exigencies can be seen in that one of these advertisements was from a widower with a young son who sought to let accommodation within his home to a widow with a similarly aged child.

August 1947, the Chairman of the Health Committee in Beckenham told the council that 'the housing situation in Beckenham, as in the rest of the country, still remains desperately serious and that with a grave shortage of houses it is essential to get existing houses into a habitable condition'.[115] This was exactly the task that Solle and Butcher were engaged in that summer. They undertook this work in an environment in which the Council had urged residents to employ private builders in an attempt 'to get on with their war damage repairs'.[116] Given the shortage of materials and the fact that they would have been competing with the local authority and its power to requisition bomb damaged premises,[117] they succeeded admirably in their endeavour. Five flats were created in the bomb damaged Maywood House within five very difficult months in England; homes were provided for at least eleven people by 1948.[118] In short, Butcher had responded to a vital public need. He had obviously done so for gain, but in relation to flat 1 he had charged no more than the market rent.[119] Solle, a surveyor, was not only knowledgeable about this market but was entrusted with advising Butcher on the rental of the flats and making suitable arrangements. It is unlikely that his task in finding tenants was a difficult one.[120]

We turn now from strictly social considerations to their interface with legal considerations. Two points are worth emphasising. The first is that the Rent Acts were not, on the whole, popular with the judiciary. As has been considered, the legislation had been enacted on an emergency basis and in a piecemeal fashion; overarching codification was still awaited this area of

---

[115] *Beckenham Journal*, 2 August 1947, 2. The shortage of housing was continually expressed in the *Beckenham Journal* of 1947. See eg the issues of 4 January 1947, 12; 1 February 1947, 3; and 19 April 1947, 3. In one extreme example, an account was given of a family (two parents and three young children) who inhabited a garage: *Beckenham Journal*, 11 January 1947, 1. The family was given a notice to quit when the owner was informed by the council that she would be required to submit a change of user of premises under the Building Restrictions (Wartime Contraventions) Act 1940.

[116] *Beckenham Journal*, 1 February 1947, 3.

[117] The *Beckenham Journal*, 3 May 1947, 3 records that the council was actively seeking the owners of bomb damaged premises to establish whether or not they would be amenable to a requisitioning of their properties. The same article records a severe shortage of building materials. Such a shortage can be seen in the account of two women who had waited two years for builders to replace their war damaged roof, only to have it almost immediately ripped off in a freak gale: *Beckenham Journal*, 22 March 1947, 1.

[118] The Register of Electors 1948–49, Parliamentary Borough of Bromley, Copers Cope Ward East, 1 records eleven adults as eligible to vote. It is possible that children were also resident in the flats.

[119] That the market rent was charged was accepted in the Court of Appeal. In addition, in one of the few advertisements for accommodation offered in 1947 similar accommodation described as a 'self-contained, newly furnished freshly decorated flat to let in Beckenham' with a lounge, double bedroom, kitchen and bathroom was offered to rent for £280 per annum: *Beckenham Journal*, 22 March 1947, 13.

[120] The author has been unable to locate any advertisements for the flats in question.

law in 1947. One member of the Court of Appeal referred to the Acts in 1945 as an 'obscure mass of words' and the problem before him as 'yet another almost insoluble problem arising from that welter of chaotic ver-biage which may be cited together as the Rent and Mortgage Restrictions Acts, 1920 to 1939'.[121] Lord Porter referred to:[122]

> the difficult and elusive wording of the Rent Restriction Acts. Whether it will ever be possible to consolidate and redraft their provisions I do not know, but the difficulty to which their language gives rise undoubtedly calls for their recon-sideration.

The author of the leading treatise on the Rent Acts collected instances of 'judicial vituperation' of the Acts and used them to preface his work.[123] A more direct author described the Acts bluntly in his introduction:[124]

> Rent control has nevertheless continued to be regarded as a subject for emergency measures, with the result that the relevant legislation has merged in the form of a string of miscellaneous and hastily drafted statutes, devised to meet particular points as they arise, with little if any attempt to integrate the whole into a consis-tent system or to bring about even a minor degree of consolidation. The conse-quent welter of confusion has been exposed to ceaseless criticism from judges, practising lawyers, and laymen alike . . .

In short, the Rent Acts were viewed as poorly drafted measures, confusing and difficult to apply with certainty and justice.

The second point that needs to be emphasised is that the problem of when a flat or a house ceased to be the same flat or house by reason of war damage and was removed from the ambit of rent control was a troublesome one and one with widespread relevance in London. The problem could not be resolved by reference to the previously existing body of case law given the comparatively low level of aerial bombardment in the First World War. *Solle v Butcher* was one of the first significant cases to be considered on the issue of whether or not there had been a change of identity brought about by the refurbishment and repair of war damaged property.[125] As the ques-tion was one of fact rather than law, the perimeters of the doctrine were still being established in these instances. Two cases existed to provide guidance: *Ellis & Sons Amalgamated Properties, Limited v Sisman*[126] and *Hemns v*

---

[121] *Vaughan v Shaw* [1945] KB 400, 401 (Mackinnon LJ).
[122] *Langford Property Co v Batten* [1951] AC 223, 231.
[123] Megarry (n 88) xvii–xix.
[124] D Lloyd and J Montgomerie, *Rent Control* (2nd edn, London, Butterworth & Co, 1955).
[125] The *Estates Gazette Digest* recorded it under the section on 'War Damage' rather than 'Rent Restrictions and Rent Control Acts'.
[126] [1948] 1 KB 653.

Wheeler.[127] In the former case the house in question had been entirely destroyed by enemy action and the landlord was in the process of constructing a new house on the same site. The county court judge found that this was really no more than a repair and that consequently the house still fell within the Rent Restriction Act 1920 and had not been altered into something substantially different. The Court of Appeal allowed the landlord's appeal and found that the original house had 'quite clearly ceased to exist altogether'.[128] In *Hemns v Wheeler*, a bomb damaged cottage had been repaired and certain structural alterations and improvements carried out which resulted in a change, and an extra 103 square feet added, to the cottage and a backyard added to the property. The court held that there had been no sufficient change to make the house a different one, although the repairs were such as to allow a permitted increase of rent.

The difficulty facing post-war courts was that so many properties had been bomb damaged and that owners, in the process of repairing them, usually took the opportunity to refurbish and modernise them. If anything other than a stringent test was taken as to when a change of identity occurred, a substantial number of properties would be removed from the Rent Act protection.[129] It became accepted that there could be no change of identity without physical alteration and that this alteration had to involve substantial effort and expenditure:[130]

> The line of demarcation . . . has now been plainly established: there must have been substantial structural alteration before the dwelling can be said to have shed its identity and become a new entity.

For anything short of substantial alteration, the recompense of the landlord in such refurbishments lay in the entitlement recognised in the Rent Acts to increase the rent accordingly.[131] In general terms, alterations short of complete reconstruction tended to be decided in favour of the tenants, whether their tenancy pre-dated the war damage or occurred subsequently. Courts cannot have been completely oblivious to the plight of those who undertook such work. As counsel for the landlord in one such case asked, 'Why, then, should a landlord be penalized if he carries out what is his public duty by making as many flats for homeless people as possible?'[132]

In summary, *Solle v Butcher* arose in circumstances where there would be some sympathy for the plight of a landlord in attempting to ascertain whether his alterations and repair did create a change of identity. Courts, however,

---

[127] [1948] 2 KB 61.
[128] *Ellis* (n 126) 665.
[129] See eg *Hazell, Watson & Viney v Malvermi* [1953] 1 WLR 782, 785 (McNair J).
[130] *Capital & Provincial Property Trust Ltd v Rice* [1952] AC 142, 150 (Lord Porter).
[131] *Mitchell v Barnes* [1950] 1 KB 448, 451 (Denning LJ).
[132] *Rice v Capital & Provincial Property Trust Ltd* [1950] 2 KB 481, 483.

were faced with literally thousands of properties which had suffered such damage and anything other than a strict interpretation of a change of identity would have resulted in even greater levels of homelessness. Private landlords, however, clearly needed some encouragement to repair and improve and justice demanded that they receive some recompense for their efforts. The recompense, however, lay in allowing the increases in rent permitted by the Rent Acts in these circumstances. The question in *Solle v Butcher* was how to do this in such a way as to benefit Butcher without possibly depriving countless tenants of Rent Act protection. We turn now to the case itself.

E. THE COUNTY COURT

Solle succeeded at the Bromley County Court where Sir Gerald Hurst declared that the flat was subject to rent restrictions because there had not been a change of identity. If the flat had not changed identity, the only rent that could be levied under the Rent Acts was the standard rent of £140 per annum.[133] It will be recalled that the twin objectives of the Rent Acts were to fix the rent which could be levied and to ensure security of tenure for tenants. In order to facilitate the first objective, the Rent Acts also provided that where a landlord charged sums in excess of the permitted rent the tenant could bring an action to recover the overpayment. This was, in part, what Solle sought in his action. Sir Gerald Hurst thus made an order for the repayment of £137 10s, the amount of rent overpaid. The actual decision of Sir Gerald Hurst does not seem to have survived. However it appears that the repayment would have been ordered on the basis of section 14(1) of the 1920 Act.[134] The section specifically provided that any amounts charged by a landlord in excess of the standard rent could be recovered by the tenant if the tenant brought his action within two years.[135] The section

---

[133] Section 1 of the Increase of Rent and Mortgage Interest (Restrictions) Act 1920 and Schedule 1 to the Rent and Mortgage Interest Restrictions Act 1939 applied to restrict the rent recoverable to that which was the standard rent. The standard rent in the case of this flat was set by the rent paid by the tenant in occupation on 1 September 1939: 1920 Act, s 12(1)(a) and 1939 Act, Sched 1.

[134] As amended in relation to this property by Schedule 1 to the 1939 Act.

[135] The sub-section was labelled with the seemingly nonsensical heading 'Recovery of sums made irrecoverable, &c'. What the draftsman referred to was the ability of a tenant to recover sums which had been paid, but which were in excess of the standard rent permitted by the Rent Acts (and thus irrecoverable by the landlord). The subsection, as amended, read: 'Where any sum has, whether before or after the passing of this Act, been paid on account of any rent or mortgage interest, being a sum which is by virtue of this Act, or any Act repealed by this Act, irrecoverable by the landlord or mortgagee, the sum so paid shall be recoverable from the landlord or mortgagee who received the payment or his legal personal representative by the tenant or mortgagor by whom it was paid, and any such sum, and any other sum which under this Act is recoverable by a tenant from a landlord or payable or repayable by a landlord to a tenant, may, without prejudice to any other method of recovery, be deducted by the tenant or mortgagor from any rent or interest payable by him to the landlord or mortgagee.' The two year limitation period was set by the 1923 Act, s 8(2) and the 1938 Act, s 7(6).

was integral to the scheme of the Rent Acts. Without such provision, a landlord who obtained excess payments from his tenant could succeed in defeating the primary purpose of the Rent Acts: to set a standard rent which could not be overcome by any contractual device between the parties. The ability of a tenant to recover overpayments was not as contested as many of the other provisions of the Acts and Megarry saw little need to elaborate greatly upon its provisions.[136] This aspect of Sir Gerald Hurst's decision would not have been remarkable to contemporary lawyers. Lastly, Sir Gerald Hurst dismissed Butcher's counterclaim for rescission on the basis that the mutual mistake was whether or not the property was within the Rent Restriction Acts and that this was a mistake of law and not one of fact. Sir Gerald Hurst expressed great sympathy for Butcher's case[137] and preferred his evidence over Solle's,[138] but upheld the application of the Rent Acts. Butcher brought an appeal from this decision.

F. THE COURT OF APPEAL

It is important to recognise that the Court of Appeal was faced with an unmeritorious plaintiff. The Lords Justices were forceful in their opinions as to the plaintiff's behaviour and the injustice of his position. The cause of the injustice was that the plaintiff was a professional, knowledgeable about the nature of rent restrictions, and he had known when he contracted that the flat had been previously let and that that rent would therefore be the standard rent.[139] He had, however, advised the defendant that he could charge £250 and that there was no previous control.[140] It may have been that Solle had led Butcher into the very purchase of the head lease of Maywood House as Solle had advised Butcher as to the economic feasibility of the flats and assisted in arranging the purchase. Bucknill LJ clearly found it unpalatable that Solle unashamedly admitted that he was 'taking advantage of our mistake to get the flat at 140l for seven years'.[141] Solle also admitted that he did not care when he rented the flat what the controlled rent was, he meant to pay to £250 for seven years.[142] In these circumstances, it was unfair that Solle should be able to benefit from the mistake.[143] Jenkins

---

[136] See RE Megarry, *The Rent Acts* (4th edn, London, Stevens & Sons, 1949) 139–40, (6th edn, London, Stevens & Sons, 1951) 296–9.
[137] [1950] 1 KB 671, 699.
[138] *Ibid*, 676.
[139] *Ibid*, 683 (Bucknill LJ).
[140] *Ibid*.
[141] *Ibid*. See also the comments of Denning LJ at 694.
[142] *Ibid*, 698.
[143] *Ibid*, 690 (Denning LJ).

LJ, while compelled to find for Solle on the law, described his case as being 'as completely devoid of merit as any case could well be'.[144] The potential harm to Butcher was great. If Solle succeeded, not only would Butcher be compelled to rent the flat to him at an uneconomic rate when the parties had freely agreed to a higher amount, but there remained the four other flats in Maywood House. They all had tenants in 1939[145] and would also be subject to rent restrictions under the 1939 legislation. If the other tenants were so minded, they too could have sought a lower rent.[146] Had this occurred, their suits would undoubtedly have been successful[147] and the resultant lowering of the rental income of all of the flats would have stripped Butcher of any profit his legitimate and essential undertaking had generated. The difficulty for the court was how to remedy the injustice which would follow from a strict application of the Rent Acts without generally upsetting the protection necessary for tenants in post-war, housing deprived Britain. In other words, the court sought to help Butcher, but in such a way as to cause the least interference with the Rent Acts. To interfere with the Rent Acts generally would, apart from the legal consequences, have undesirable social consequences for all tenants—undesirable consequences that Parliament had expressly sought to avoid. Butcher's counsel suggested four possible options: first, that the county court judge had erred in his decision that the flat had not undergone a change of identity; secondly, that Solle was estopped from relying on his legal rights under the Rent Acts; thirdly, that the contract should be rescinded because Butcher had contracted with Solle on the basis of an innocent misrepresentation; and fourthly, that the contract should be rescinded because of the common mistake of the parties.

The Court of Appeal was quick to dismiss the argument that the county court judge had erred in his finding that the flat had not undergone a change of identity. There are indications that they believed that the trial judge had not fully understood the nature of the repairs undertaken, but that these repairs were not sufficient to change the identity of the flat. There

---

[144] *Ibid*, 699.

[145] See *Kelly's Directory of Beckenham Penge and Neighbourhood* (44th edn, London, 1939) 144, and the Register of Electors 1939–40, Beckenham North Electoral Division Polling District U Copers Cope Ward, 6.

[146] There is no suggestion in the judgment that they did. It is recorded that the plaintiff advised the defendant as to the rent at which all the flats could be let and that he let the other flats on long lets: [1950] 1 KB 671, 694–5. Of the other four flats, the relevant Registers of Electors records that the tenants in flat 5 left after four years, the tenants in flats 2 and 3 remained for five years, and the tenant in flat 4 remained until the demolition of Maywood House.

[147] It would appear that their suits would have been successful even where Solle's failed. The mistake in relation to the other five flats would have been a unilateral mistake of Butcher's alone and, unless this mistake was known to these other tenants, rescission would not lie.

are likely two reasons why this ground was so quickly dismissed. The first is that the issue was one of fact and appellate courts are reluctant to over-turn such findings absent an egregious error. Secondly, it would have been dangerous to find that these repairs did change the identity of the flat. Parliament had found it necessary in these unusual circumstances to protect tenants from both rent rises and dispossession. Virtually all privately rent-ed properties were within the ambit of this protection: substantial numbers of these London properties had been damaged by enemy action. To find, at the appellate level, that such repairs and refurbishments amounted to a change of identity was to remove these damaged properties from the pro-tection conferred by Parliament. For these reasons, the Court of Appeal spent little time on the issue.[148]

Two options appeared as possible solutions to the dilemma: estoppel or rescission. Rescission could be based on either misrepresentation or mis-take. Misrepresentation was quickly discarded by two of the Lords Justices for two reasons. The most signficant reason was that the lease had been executed under seal. Absent fraud (which was not alleged here), an execut-ed lease could not be rescinded for an innocent misrepresentation after completion.[149] While Denning LJ doubted the authority that propounded this position, the other Lords Justices would not have rescinded the lease for misrepresentation.[150] The second reason for refusing rescission was on the basis that there was no misrepresentation. This had the advantage of avoid-ing the legal problem concerning the rescission of a lease executed under seal. Bucknill LJ preferred this ground and held that absent a specific find-ing of fact by the trial judge, there had been no misrepresentation by Solle.[151] Jenkins LJ also agreed that there had not been a misrepresentation in this case because the entire issue was one of law and 'the expression of an opinion bona fide held on a question of law is not misrepresentation'.[152] Denning LJ alone would have found that there had been an actionable mis-representation.[153]

This left mistake and estoppel. Policy reasons favoured rescission for mis-take because it could allow justice in Butcher's case and simultaneously pre-serve the general protection of the Rent Acts in other cases. Estoppel was

---

[148] Bucknill LJ informed counsel for the plaintiff that there was little need to hear him fur-ther on the issue of change of identity: [1950] 1 KB 671, 679.

[149] *Ibid*, 702 (Jenkins LJ). The major authority was *Angel v Jay* [1911] 1 KB 666.

[150] *Ibid*, 695.

[151] *Ibid*, 687.

[152] *Ibid*, 703. Since the House of Lords' decision in *Kleinwort Benson Ltd v Lincoln CC* (n 8), it has been recognised that a misrepresentation of law can be actionable: *Pankhania v Hackney LBC* [2002] EWHC 2441, approved in *Brennan v Bolt Burdon* [2004] EWCA Civ 1017, [2005] QB 303 [10] (Maurice Kay LJ) and [25] (Bodey J).

[153] *Ibid*, 695.

not attractive because to find that Solle had been estopped from relying on his strict legal rights would be to create a rule of general application to other cases. It is no surprise that the Lords Justices rejected this possibility.[154] Their reason was that section 1 of the 1920 Act expressly provided that the parties to a lease could not expressly exclude the provisions of the Act by their own contractual terms. If an express promise by a tenant to preclude the operation of the Acts was prohibited, then so too should a similar promise implied by reason of the tenant's words or conduct be prohibited. The Court of Appeal was also bound by the recent decision in *Welch v Nagy*,[155] a similar case in which there was an unequivocal finding that the jurisdiction of the Rent Acts could not be ousted by estoppel. The basis for this decision was that the court could not, by finding an estoppel, provide itself with a jurisdiction which Parliament had denied to it.[156]

In contrast, finding a mistake in equity preserved the jurisdiction of the Rent Acts and allowed a just result for Butcher. The Lords Justices were divided in their judgments on the issue of mistake. Jenkins LJ, dissenting, maintained that the mistake in this case was not of a character which allowed rescission. While accepting *Cooper v Phibbs*[157] as good law, he distinguished it from the case before him. *Cooper v Phibbs* had concerned the question of a private right affecting the basis of a contract: this case was concerned with the effect of public statutes upon the contract made and such a mistake was one of law. Furthermore, if rescission were available because of misapprehension or ignorance, it would allow parties to entirely frustrate the operation of the Rent Acts. The provisions of section 1 of the Rent Act 1920 were imperative and the necessary implication of the section was that the tenant, regardless of ignorance or misapprehension, could not be obliged to pay more than the standard rent and could hold his tenancy on the permitted rent. There was the real possibility of injustice to tenants if a lease could be rescinded. Finally, the influence of *Bell v Lever Brothers*[158] is apparent in the opinion that regardless of the effect of the Rent Acts, the contract was 'in all respects precisely the contract the parties intended to make'.[159]

Denning and Bucknill LJJ, in the majority, found that as a result of the mistake the lease could be rescinded on terms. They appear sympathetic to the nature of the mistake made. Substantial moneys had been expended upon the alteration and restoration. The work was undertaken (as it necessarily would

---

[154] *Ibid*, 687–9 (Bucknill LJ), 690 (Denning LJ) and 707 (Jenkins LJ).
[155] [1950] 1 KB 455. The case had been decided three weeks earlier.
[156] *Ibid*, 464 (Asquith LJ).
[157] (1867) LR 2 HL 149.
[158] [1932] AC 161.
[159] [1950] 1 KB 671, 705.

have to be if Britons were to be housed) before the law had definitively decided the interaction between damage by enemy action and a change of identity under the Rent Acts.[160] Bucknill LJ found that the parties had considered the application of the Rent Acts and mistakenly concluded that the flat was outside their jurisdiction. This left the issue of whether the mistake was one of fact (for which rescission would be available) or law (for which it would not). On this issue Bucknill LJ found that it was 'a question of fact, and the principle applies to this case which was laid down by Lord Westbury in his speech in *Cooper v Phibbs*'.[161] Denning LJ gave what has been regarded as the leading, and the most controversial, judgment. His summary of the relevant facts[162] indicates that he was attempting to prevent an injustice whereby the plaintiff received a benefit at the expense of the defendant. Denning LJ was concerned to point out that the tenant, Solle, had acquired a long let of seven years of the flat. He had agreed a fair and economic rent for this flat, a rent which could lawfully have been obtained under the Rent Acts had proper procedures been followed. By unashamedly relying upon the mutual mistake, he sought to obtain a benefit: a rent below market value and below what the parties had agreed. The benefit would be obtained at Butcher's expense; had Butcher been aware of the application of the Rent Acts to the flat, he could have implemented the proper procedures under the Acts to charge this market rent to Solle or another tenant. The injustice that would be created by an automatic application of the Rent Acts could be prevented by rescinding the contract. Denning LJ noted, on the basis of *Cooper v Phibbs* and *Erlanger v New Sombrero Phosphate Co*,[163] that rescission operates only where the parties can be restored to their original positions and it was thus necessary to impose terms in this case. Without terms, rescission would mean that a tenant could

---

[160] The pages of the *Estates Gazette Digest* in the late 1940s are replete with such cases in a section headed 'War Damage'. The cases were by no means consistent, though they seemed to indicate that substantial damage by enemy action was required: see eg the later comments of Lord Radcliffe in *Langford Property Co v Batten* (n 122) 240. Thus structural alterations, improvements, the addition of extra rooms and a larger garden did not change the identity of the dwelling house in *Hemns v Wheeler* (n 127), but where half a flat was destroyed by a direct hit from a bomb, the remainder (with a garage) had assumed a new identity in *Langford Property Co v Sommerfield* (n 98). In cases where a dwelling house had been rebuilt after its entire destruction by enemy action, courts had given the tenant dispossessed through destruction an order for possession of the rebuilt premises in *Simper v Coombes* [1948] 1 All ER 306 and *Denman v Brise* [1949] 1 KB 22, but denied it to the tenant in *Ellis & Sons v Sisman* [1948] 1 KB 653.

[161] [1950] 1 KB 671, 685. Bucknill LJ's reasoning as to why the issue was one of fact rather than law was unusual in that it was directed more to whether or not the issue was one of fact or law for the purposes of whether or not an appeal would lie, rather than the nature of the mistake made.

[162] *Ibid*, 694–5.

[163] (1878) 3 App Cas 1218.

be evicted by his landlord. Following two nineteenth century cases,[164] Denning LJ imposed terms which allowed Solle to remain in the flat as a licensee and while Butcher was thus in possession of the flat he could serve the requisite notice under the 1938 Act[165] which would allow him lawfully to increase the rent to the amount originally agreed. Solle was not to be forced into the new lease for he would be free to vacate the flat. If he vacated the flat, he would not be able to recover the amounts paid.

Denning LJ reached his conclusions about mistake on grounds that were immediately open to criticism.[166] He recognised the authority of *Bell v Lever Brothers* and held that a contract could, in certain circumstances, be found to be void. He also stated that the House of Lords had been concerned with the position at law and not equity. Courts of equity had long had the power to set aside a contract entered into under a mistake and, where appropriate, could set aside the contract on terms. He relied upon *Cooper v Phibbs* as authority for this position as well as the (even earlier) cases of *Lansdown v Lansdown*[167] and *Bingham v Bingham*.[168] He stated:[169]

> a contract is also liable in equity to be set aside if the parties were under a misapprehension either as to facts or as to their relative and respective rights, provided that the misapprehension was fundamental and that the party seeking to set it aside was not himself at fault.

In this way, Denning LJ sought to restate or clarify the law on the following lines: common law courts might find a contract void for mistake, but, in circumstances where the contract was valid at law, a court of equity

---

[164] *Garrard v Frankel* (1862) 30 Beav 445, 54 ER 961, and *Paget v Marshall* (1884) 28 Ch D 255. Both were cases involving mistaken leases. Neither was free from doubt.

[165] Pursuant to s 7(4).

[166] Professor Goodhart was generally critical of the decision and particularly of *Cooper v Phibbs* as providing a court with the equitable power to rescind a valid lease where the court found it unconscientious for the leasee to enforce it: 'ALG', 'Rescission of Lease on the Ground of Mistake' (1950) 66 *LQR* 169, 170. Grunfeld, although generally supportive of the possible effect of the decision, was not without doubts about Denning LJ's explanation of the interface of law and equity: C Grunfeld, 'Common Law and Equity' (1952) 15 *MLR* 297, 307–9. Later authors have been divided over the merits of *Solle v Butcher*: CJ Slade, 'The Myth of Mistake in the English Law of Contract' (1954) 70 *LQR* 385; KO Shatwell, 'The Supposed Doctrine of Mistake in Contract: A Comedy of Errors' (1955) 33 *Can Bar Rev* 164; LB McTurnan, 'An Introduction to Common Mistake in English Law' (1963) 41 *Can Bar Rev* 1; S Stoljar, 'A New Approach to Mistake in Contract' (1965) 28 *MLR* 265; J Cartwright, '*Solle v Butcher* and the Doctrine of Mistake in Contract Law' (1987) 103 *LQR* 594; JC Smith, 'Contracts—Mistake, Frustration and Implied Terms' (1994) 110 *LQR* 400; A Phang, 'Common Mistake in English Law: The Proposed Merger of Common Law and Equity' (1989) 9 *LS* 291. Ultimately, in *The Great Peace* (n 3), it was held to be unsustainable.

[167] (1730) Mos 364, 25 ER 441; 2 Jac & W 205, 37 ER 605.

[168] (1748) 1 Ves Sen 126, 27 ER 934; Belt's Supplement 79.

[169] [1950] 1 KB 671, 693.

might find that the contract was nevertheless voidable for a fundamental mistake. Denning LJ's statement of this principle has been criticised and, in *The Great Peace*,[170] was found not to represent the law.

Two questions arise. Why did he make this statement, and was there a basis for this equitable jurisdiction? It is beyond the scope of this chapter to attempt a satisfactory answer to the second question. It can be noted that there is merit in Denning LJ's view that the House of Lords was not concerned there with the effect of equity upon the contract.[171] Prior to *Cooper v Phibbs* there was a remedy given by courts of equity to rescind a contract for mistake.[172] Such a jurisdiction appears to have been somewhat out of place and overlooked following the 'fusion' of law and equity effected by the Judicature Acts. In short, there is more strength to Denning LJ's view than has since been recognised.

The practical answer to the first question of why he made this restatement of the law is that it was the only method available to reach a just resolution of the case. The case could not be factually distinguished from *Bell v Lever Brothers*. Indeed, Lord Atkin in *Bell v Lever Brothers* recognised an operative mistake as to mistaken attributes with such a narrow ambit that it is difficult to envisage many cases falling within it.[173] Following the decision, few cases succeeded in this area of law. It was highly unlikely that the lease in *Solle v Butcher* would thus be found to be void at common law. It is important to remember that prior to 1966, the House of Lords itself would have been unable to overturn *Bell v Lever Brothers*.[174] In this light, Denning LJ's resort to equity can be seen as a way of solving some of the intractable difficulties involved in the applicability, or rather the practical inapplicability, of *Bell v Lever Brothers*. The usual concern, expressed by Lord Atkin in *Bell v Lever Brothers*, in finding that a contract has been

---

[170] *Great Peace* (n 3).

[171] It does not seem to have been specifically raised, neither were distinctions drawn to the House of Lords. See C MacMillan, 'How Temptation Led to Mistake: An Explanation of *Bell v Lever Bros Ltd*' (2003) 119 *LQR* 625 in which I have presented the unsatisfactory nature of the result in this case. See also the comments by Steyn J in *Associated Japanese Bank v Crédit du Nord* [1989] 1 WLR 255, 266.

[172] See eg H Ballow [?], *A Treatise of Equity, with the Addition of Marginal References and Notes, by John Fonblanque* (Dublin, 1793) 106; E Fry, *A Treatise on the Specific Performance of Contracts* (London, 1858) 221; J Story, *Commentaries on Equity Jurisprudence, as Administered in England and America* (2nd edn, London, 1839) vol II, 125. Authority can be found in the early case law: *Gee v Spencer* (1681) 1 Vern 32, 23 ER 286; *Broderick v Broderick* (1713) 1 P Wms 239, 24 ER 369; *Lansdown* (n 167); *Martin v Savage* (1740) Barn C 190, 27 ER 608; *Bingham* (n 167); *Calverley v Williams* (1790) 1 Ves Jun 210, 30 ER 306; *Hitchcock v Giddings* (1817) 4 Price 134, 146 ER 418; *Colyer v Clay* (1843) 7 Beavan 188, 49 ER 1036.

[173] Some recognition of this dilemma can be seen in Steyn J's judgment in *Associated Japanese Bank* (n 170) 267–8.

[174] *Practice Statement* [1966] 3 All ER 77.

formed under a fundamental and mistaken assumption was not present in *Solle v Butcher* because the Court of Appeal was not upsetting the sanctity of contract and intervening to destroy an apparent bargain. The reverse was true: the intervention of the court was to prevent an injustice by allowing the parties to proceed with the bargain that they had struck by allowing the bargain to be reformed in accordance with the requirements of the (interfering) statute. In this sense, the court protected the reasonable expectations of the parties; expectations that would have been destroyed by the unimpaired operation of the Rent Acts. Denning LJ, writing extrajudicially on the subject of landlord and tenant, described the 1939 Act as an instance where 'Parliament intervened drastically with freedom of contract'.[175]

An additional reason why the Court of Appeal was at pains not to find the lease void is that it is likely that many other parties were in much the same position, in a post-war Britain drastically short of houses. Prices were rising and landlords faced increased repair costs. Landlords would also have sought to let their accommodation at rents beyond the set standard rent. The temptation to displace tenants on the grounds that a misapprehension had rendered the contract void for mistake would have been great. By finding the contract voidable in equity, this temptation was diminished. Denning LJ also sought to revive the earlier jurisdiction of the courts of equity because it provided a necessary and practical doctrine in the modern world. Writing about the decision extrajudicially, he commented that the infusion of equity removed the awkward dilemma that had faced common law courts of finding the contract either entirely bad or entirely good.[176] *Bell v Lever Brothers* is an unreliable decision upon which to found a doctrine of common mistake.[177] The practical effect of that decision is to limit mistake to a very narrow range of cases. The result of a mistake successfully established provides a harsh remedy: the contract is void. Denning LJ sought not only to recognise a broader jurisdiction of equitable mistake but also to provide a flexible remedy, which could provide as much justice as the circumstances of the case would allow. The flexible remedy of rescission on terms is a desirable one not only for the parties to a contract, but also for those outside the contract.

G. IMPLICATIONS OF THE DECISION

It was noted at the outset that mistake stands at the border between contract and restitution. The case has implications for both areas of law. Some of these will now be considered.

---

[175] Sir Alfred Denning, *The Changing Law* (London, Stevens & Sons, 1953) 46.
[176] *Ibid*, 60.
[177] MacMillan (n 171).

1. Contract

The most detailed discussions of the case have occurred in relation to contract law and it was in contract law that the Court of Appeal was to disapprove of the equitable jurisdiction relied upon by Denning LJ. *Solle v Butcher* is best seen as a decision from which later courts could further develop the law, in the way that the principle in *High Trees*[178] was further developed. It was not; the cases that applied it were few and far between. This likely contributed to the uncertainty inherent in the decision. Academics and lawyers alike were puzzled by how to distinguish the tests in law and in equity. Developments in other areas of contract and tort law soon overtook the need for relief provided in *Solle v Butcher*. In particular, the House of Lords expanded the ambit of misrepresentation in *Hedley Byrne & Co Ltd v Heller & Partners Ltd*,[179] and this was further expanded shortly thereafter by Parliament with the enactment of the Misrepresentation Act 1967. The establishment of negligent misrepresentation and the enactment of the far-reaching Misrepresentation Act 1967 has meant that English law can afford a wide number of claimants relief for misrepresentation. Mistakes are rare. In comparison to misrepresentation under the 1967 Act, mistakes are hard to establish and damages are unavailable. The older mistake cases contain factual situations which would now fall within misrepresentation. English law has developed a broad doctrine of misrepresentation at the expense of mistake. English law has been suspicious of the uncertainty introduced by finding an apparent contract void for mistake. This suspicion is particularly pronounced in the cases involving commercial parties who dislike the uncertainty of a contract voidable for mistake. It is smaller, generally non-commercial parties, to whom the remedy of rescission and rescission on terms is appealing because of the remedial flexibility. It is also likely that their arrangements are comparatively simple; the more complex the arrangements, the less likely rescission on terms is either possible or desirable.

The lasting effect of *The Great Peace* is yet to be determined.[180] The immediate effect is unlikely to be one which encourages further litigants into this uncertain arena. This is unfortunate, for the development of the

---

[178] *High Trees* (n 4).

[179] [1964] AC 465.

[180] *Great Peace* (n 3). A range of commentators have expressed differing opinions as to the merits of this case: A Chandler, J Devenney and J Poole, 'Common Mistake: Theoretical Justification and Remedial Inflexibility' [2004] *JBL* 34; FMB Reynolds, 'Reconsider the Contract Textbooks' (2003) 119 *LQR* 177; SB Midwinter, '*The Great Peace* and Precedent' (2003) 119 *LQR* 180; A Phang, 'Controversy in Common Mistake' [2003] *Conv* 247; C Hare, 'Inequitable Mistake' (2003) 62 *CLJ* 29; G Jones (ed), *Goff and Jones: The Law of Restitution* (6th edn, London, Sweet & Maxwell, 2002) 281 (written prior to the judgment in the Court of Appeal).

doctrine of mistake has depended upon these hardy individuals. The area is one which needs greater consideration.

2. Restitution

In discussing the relationship between contract and restitution, it was suggested by Professor Beatson that to allow restitutionary claims where there is a subsisting contract is to allow the possibility that the parties' own allocation of risk and determination of value will be subverted.[181] In some exceptional cases, however, it may be that a restitutionary claim can exist in circumstances where it would not be inconsistent with or nullify a contractual obligation.[182] Professor Birks employed this argument to state that in circumstances where there is a valid contract which contains an unlawful obligation, courts have sometimes found that there can be no restitutionary claim to recover amounts paid pursuant to this unlawful obligation because 'the validity of the contract is conclusive'.[183] In other cases, however, courts have found that while the contract was valid, a restitutionary claim would be allowed to recover amounts paid pursuant to this invalid obligation. In these rare cases, there is a total failure of basis for the particular obligation within an otherwise valid contract and 'when the obligation goes, the basis of the enrichment which it purported to explain fails totally'.[184] These cases 'appear to put the orthodox doctrine under pressure'.[185] Sir Gerald Hurst's decision in *Solle v Butcher* is one of the two principal English authorities[186] put forward to support this interpretation of the law, because he allowed the lease to stand while ordering a repayment of the rent paid in excess of the standard rent. It is unfortunate that a copy of Sir Gerald Hurst's decision is unavailable for it appears, with respect, to have led Professor Birks into an erroneous conclusion about the decision. In *Solle v Butcher*, the amount was ordered to be repaid because the relevant legislation compelled it to be repaid. The twin pillars of the Rent Acts were: first, to set a standard rent for housing which could not be circumvented by

---

[181] J Beatson, 'Concurrence of Restitutionary and Contractual Claims' in W Swadling and G Jones (eds), *The Search for Principle, Essays in Honour of Lord Goff of Chieveley* (Oxford, OUP, 1999) 142, 152–3.

[182] *Ibid*, 154.

[183] Birks (n 7) 122.

[184] *Ibid*, 123.

[185] *Ibid*.

[186] The other is *Queen of the River Steamship Co v Conservators of the River Thames* (1899) 15 TLR 474. Professor Birks also cites the Australian case of *Roxborough v Rothmans of Pall Mall Australia Ltd* [2001] HCA 68, (2002) 187 CLR 465 as further support for this exceptional circumstance. In this case, recovery was allowed where a distinct and severable obligation failed: there is no reference to *Solle v Butcher*.

the parties; and second, to provide tenants with security of tenure. A provision for repayment was necessary to support the first pillar: if landlords could retain overpayments, it provided an unattractive means of circumventing the legislation through compulsion exerted upon those needing accommodation in times of housing shortages (the very evil at which the Rent Acts were addressed). The second pillar, security of tenure, meant that the lease—the contract—had to be found valid once the necessary conditions were met. Understood in this context, Sir Gerald Hurst's decision in no way places the orthodox doctrine under pressure.

In the two English cases provided by Professor Birks to support the orthodox doctrine that restitution will not be allowed where the contract remains valid, *Orphanos v Queen Mary College*[187] and *Green v Portsmouth Stadium*,[188] the relevant statue which prescribed the invalidity was silent as to the subject of repayments. The earlier case of *Green* reaffirms why a protected tenant could receive his overpayment while the court simultaneously reaffirmed the validity of his contract. Green, a bookmaker, was charged more than was permitted by law when he entered the defendant's stadium. The Court of Appeal refused to allow him to recover the overpayments. Interestingly, Lord Denning (a judge familiar with the operation of the Rent Acts) refused to allow Green to recover the overpayments. Green had contracted with the stadium knowing of the overcharge: he was thus barred from claiming the excess which had arisen as a result of this contract. Lord Denning raised the procedure of the Rent Acts with Green's counsel.[189] In giving his judgment, Lord Denning stated that recovery would not be allowed in Green's case because he was forced to rely upon the statute to establish the overcharging and the statute did not provide a restitutionary right, as the Rent Acts did. In Lord Denning's words:[190]

> It is most significant that the Act does not say that the overcharge shall be recoverable. In modern statutes, such as the Rent Restriction Acts, dealing with such matters as premiums, one finds that if it is intended that an overcharge shall be recoverable the Act says so. This Act does not.

---

[187] [1985] AC 761.

[188] [1953] 2 QB 190.

[189] *Ibid*, 194. Green's counsel had attempted to argue that Green had a common law right to recover the payments which arose independently of the statute, based on Lord Mansfield's exception in *Browning v Morris* 2 Cowp 790, 792; 98 ER 1364, 1364–5. When Lord Denning raised the point that the Rent Acts specifically provided that recovery was available to tenants, counsel was forced to concede that the statute had an importance 'not previously realized and rather force the plaintiff to rely on the Act'. The statute in question, the Betting and Lotteries Act 1934, prescribed penal consequences, rather than restitutionary rights, in the event of overcharging.

[190] *Ibid*, 195.

Viewed in this light, it is difficult to assert that the county court decision in *Solle v Butcher* establishes a broad exception allowing restitutionary rights for the failure of a particular obligation within the context of a valid contract. Support for such a position must be found elsewhere.

H. EPILOGUE

The most intriguing question to be answered is what Solle did next. While leave to appeal to the House of Lords was granted,[191] it was not made. Solle, with his wife Frances, stayed in the flat until some time in 1953. They left before the expiration of the original seven years, but some time after the Court of Appeal's order. Some arrangement between the parties obviously followed the case. The accommodation must have been desirable. Solle appears to have remained in Beckenham; when he died in 1987 he was resident in a block of flats very close to where Maywood House had stood. Maywood House itself changed hands twice more. It was sold by auction in May 1957[192] and again, with vacant possession, in March 1960.[193] Not long after, the building was pulled down and five detached houses built in its place. The tennis courts damaged by the landmine in 1940 have largely recovered and play has long since resumed.

---

[191] 66 TLR (Pt 1) 448, 468.
[192] The advertisement appeared in *The Times*, 30 April.
[193] The advertisement appeared in *The Times*, 9 February.

Index

Abinger, Baron, 107

Actio de in rem verso
  frustrated contracts, 262

Actio personalis moritur cum persona
  (personal action dies with person),
  167, 170–5
  contracts under seal, 173
  debt claims, 171–2
  exceptions to, 173, 176–7
  Hambly v Trott decision, 168
  origins, 170
  Phillips v Homfray decision, 181
  tort actions, 173, 176–7
  trespass to land, non-waiver of, 178
Actions *in rem*, 176
Addison, Charles, 30
Adkins (Bow St officer), 49–51
Administrators
  personal actions brought against,
  168
Aerial bombardments, 329, 331, 346
Agency
  problem of, Erlanger v New
  Sombrero Phosphate Company
  decision, 136–43
  promotors as agents, at time of origi-
  nal purchase, 158
Agnosticism, 191
Agreement to pay
  and performance of service, 1–2
Aiscough, Alan, 9, 15
American Law Institute
  *Restatement of the Law of
  Restitution*, 275
Ames, James Barr, 35, 180–1
Ancient Law (H Maine), 32

Anderson, Sir James, 124
Anglican Church, 192–3
  see also Sisterhoods, Anglican
Anson, Sir William Reynell, 31, 33–4
Anticipatory breach, doctrine, 88–9
Apostolic Succession, doctrine, 197
Aquinas, Thomas, 22
Arden, Sir Pepper, 137
Aristophanes, 72
Arnold JL, 288
Arrest, immunity from, 50
Assent, and contracts, 31
Association of British Chamber of
  Commerce, 278–9
Assumpsits
  claims in, 1, 4, 16–17
  consideration, pleading of, 1, 4, 17
  contractual, 32
  debts, 16, 171–2
  implied, 28, 30
  indebitatus *see* Indebitatus assumpsits
  Lamplugh v Brathwaite decision, 1–2,
  16–17
  non-contractual
    money had and received, action for,
    20–22, 27, 32
  special *see* Special assumpsits
Aston J, 177
Athaenaeum (periodical), 67–8, 70
Atheism, 191
Atkin LJ, 252, 272, 275, 277, 355–6
Atkins, George, 77, 81–2, 113
Atkinson, Lord, 220
Atwright, Henry, 46–7
Australia, implied contract analysis, 37
Authorship, profession of, 67, 94